D0710334

# WILLS AND ADMINISTRATIONS

## OF

## ISLE OF WIGHT COUNTY, VIRGINIA,

### 1647-1800

By

BLANCHE ADAMS CHAPMAN

Reprinted in an Improved Format

With a Consolidated Index
By

JESSICA BUDICK
and
ANITA COMTOIS

GENEALOGICAL PUBLISHING CO., INC.
BALTIMORE     1975

Originally Published
Smithfield, Virginia
1938


Reprinted
Three Volumes in One
In an Improved Format
With a Consolidated Index
Genealogical Publishing Co., Inc.
Baltimore, 1975

Library of Congress Cataloging in Publication Data
Chapman, Blanche Adams, 1895-
　　Wills and administrations of Isle of Wight County, Virginia.
　　Reprint of the 1938 ed. published in Smithfield, Va.
　　1. Wills—Isle of Wight Co., Va. 2. Isle of Wight Co., Va.—Genealogy.
I. Title.
F232.I8C6 1975　　　　　　　929'.3755'54　　　　　　74-18117
ISBN 0-8063-0647-5

Made in the United States of America

## FOREWORD

Any abstract is at best but a skeleton of the original record, and, in a work of the scope of this one,
through necessity, it can contain little more than a
list of the names to be found during the period
covered.  All of the "clues" in these human documents—
in many instances the only written evidence that such
a person ever lived, loved and died—have to be omitted.
From the original often may be discerned the taste,
education, manner of living, measure of success, and
even the vocation of the testator.  It is hoped that
these abstracts may serve as an index for people of
Isle of Wight descent, if a real study of ancestry
is desired beyond the knowledge of mere political
and military preferment.

Blanche Adams Chapman
Smithfield, Virginia

# CONTENTS

## VOLUME I

## VOLUME II

## VOLUME III

*VOLUME I*

FERN, Timothy: Legatees, eldest son; youngest son and daughter. Land at
Rappahannock to be divided between my three children. Wife Extx.
Daniel Boucher and John Munger, Overseers. January, 1651.
    Wit: George Gillie, Thomas Dickson.          Page 1

BAGNALL, Roger: Leg. wife Rebecca; to each of my children; son James.
October 19, 1647.
    Wit: Joseph Weeks, Charles Stewart.         Page 12

DEATH, Richard: Leg. to the child unborn of my daughter Elizabeth Dodman,
wife of John Dodman of Mulberry Island; John Dodman Jr. and Richard
Dodman sons of John Dodman Sen; son William Death, citizen and merchant
tailer of London; to Christopher Neale son of Daniel Neale of Isle of
Wight.
    Wit: William Westuray.              Page 17

WILMOTH, Edward: Leg. wife Annis; daughter Frances; sons John and Robert.
Overseers, John Jackson and George Colecroft. February 15, 1647.
    Wit: John Jackson, John Carter.          Page 19

JONES, Anthony: Leg. brother William if he comes to live in this country,
the plantation where Thomas Parker lives, if he desires to return home
3,000 pounds of tobacco; to daughter-in-law Ann Smith; sister Catherine
Jones; God-son Anthony Binford; Thomas and John Smith 2,000 acres on
Blackwater; wife Ann. August 16, 1649.
    Wit: Robert Watson, Edward Chetwood, Thomas Brasee.    Page 25

JEWRY, William: Leg. Elizabeth Penny daughter of Richard Penny; Robert
Ruffin, son of William Ruffin; John Arram, son of John Arram. Ex.
friend John Arram. January 1, 1651.
    Wit: Richard Penny, William Ruffin, William Westray.    Page 26

WATSON, Robert, Nuncupative: Leg. brother James Watson's child 200 A. on
Pagan Creek, bounding on Samuel Matthews; brother John Watson. November
6, 1651.
    Proved by Mr. Robert Dunster, Minister and Mr. Richard Lockyer,
    Merchant. Mrs. Ann Watson, Relict of said Robert Watson acknowl-
    edgeth that he gave the wife of Toby Hurst a cow and desired her
    to remember the youngest daughter of Thomas Fleuellen.    Page 29

VASSER, John: Leg. eldest son John Vasser; Mildred Vasser; Peter Vasser;
Ann Vasser; eldest daughter Elizabeth; wife Elizabeth. Overseers,
Mr. James Pyland and Thomas Walton. January 14, 1650.
    Wit: John Lewis, Richard Ames, Thomas Walton.

VALENTINE, John: Leg. eldest son James; eldest daughter Ann; second daughter
Elizabeth; youngest daughter Margaret; wife Elizabeth. Overseers, John

Marshall and William Lewis.
      Wit: Will Westray, Nicholas Nethercoat. May 8, 1652.    Page 30

STILES, John: Leg. son John; God-son John Murry; God-daughter Elizabeth
Johnson; God-daughter Joane Madden; wife Elizabeth; friend Humphrey
Clark. October 26, 1652.
      Wit: Thomas Johnson, James Pyland.    Page 37

UPTON, John: Leg. eldest son John Upton, tract in tenure of John King,
James Bagnall and Nicholas Morris, if he dies before he becomes 21, to
William, Elizabeth, Sarah and Margaret Underwood; land at Rappahannock
to daughters-in-law, Elizabeth, Sarah and Margaret Underwood. Extx.
wife Margaret Upton. Overseers, Major George Fawdon, William Underwood
and James Taylor, Clerk. Ann Williamson, wife of James Williamson to
be an equal sharer in my land at Rappahannock. January, 16--
      Wit: John Gatlin, James Taylor.
      Proved December 16, 1652 by William Underwood and Edward Skinner.
    Page 38

COBB, Joseph, aged 60 years: Leg. wife Elizabeth 300 A. called Goose Hill
land; son Benjamin; son Pharoah; daughter Elizabeth. March 1, 1653/4.
      Wit: Joseph Dunn, John Childs.    Page 44

REYNOLDS, Christopher, Planter: Leg. son Christopher land that Richard
Jordan liveth on; son John; son Richard; daughter Abbasha; daughter
Elizabeth; daughter Jane; George Rivers; unborn child; wife Elizabeth.
May 1, 1654.
      Wit: Sylvester Bullen, Anthony Matthews.    Page 46

TABERER, Joshua: Leg. brother Thomas Taberer; brother William Taberer of
the County of Derby; brother Thomas' only daughter and heir Ruth Taberer
my estate in England. Mentions last will and testament of his father
William Taberer of the County of Derby. November 24, 1656.
      Wit: William Lewer, Francis Higgins.    Page 48

CLARK, Humphrey: Leg. son John; wife Jane; daughter-in-law Jane Brunt (?);
I acknowledge tobacco due from John Shery doth belong to Jane Brunt;
kinswomen Jane How and Mary Clark, whereas Mary Clark is a covenant
servant for seven years, I do give her three years of her time; benefit
of one-half of the labor of my servants shall be made use of for the
maintenance of my son John Clark at school; to Thomas Holmes; to
William Godwin and John Williams, Welchman and my servant, each of them
one cow. Extx. wife Jane. Overseer, Robert Bird. March 3, 1655.
      Wit: Thomas Holmes, William Bracey, Alice Bostock.    Page 70

DUNSTER, Robert: Leg. wife; brother Leonard Dunster; to his son. May 17,
1656.
      Wit: William Travers, William Jux, Elizabeth Webb, Thomas Wright.
    Page 74

OLIVER, John bound for England: Leg. son John; two daughters land at
Blackwater; wife Ellen. Extx. wife. Overseers, friends James Pyland
and Robert Bird. Dated April 19, 1652. Recorded June 16, 1655.
      Wit: James Pyland, John Burton, John Reining.    Page 79

MOONE, Captain John, born at Berry near Gosport in ye Parish of Stoak in
Hampshire in England; Leg. wife Prudence; daughter Sarah my now dwelling
house named Bethlehem, with all ye land from Pagan Creek, joining upon
Henry Watts; second daughter Susanna land that Samuel Nichols liveth
upon on the easterly side of Bethlehem Creek, now named Bethsaida; daughter
Mary land that lyeth at Red Point called Bethany, where Dennis Syllivant
liveth. My Brew House at Jamestown to be sold. To Joan Garland my wife's

daughter or her child if living the year after my decease; William Wilson, my wife's son; Peter Garland my wife's son-in-law. Provision for disposal of land in England, mortgaged to Mr. Owen Jennings of Portsmouth and cattle left to destitute people of the Lower Parish of Isle of Wight. August 12, 1655.                                                        Page 81

BARECROFT, Charles: Leg. wife Magdalin; son William.
      Wit: Richard Williams, George Moore.   March 12, 1654.   Page 90

CHETWINE, Edward: Leg. to James House and Thomas Atwill one year of their time; to former what is mine at Mr. Aldreds; Christopher Holmes; John Young; Mr. Robert Watson; Henry Pitt; John Inglish; Nicholas Aldred; Mrs. Ann Jones and all her children; to my brother all my lands etc. with thanks that he hath supplied me, notwithstanding he hither sent me for a sacrifice. Exs., Mr. Robert Watson and Henry Pitt. September 27, 1649.
      Wit: William Ruffin, Thomas Brock.                          Page 113

COOPER, Justinian: Leg. all my God-children; my brother Richard Cossey the land that he and John Snellock live on by the river side; Edward Pyland the son of James Pyland tobacco to be paid in 1651. Wife Ann Extx. Overseer, Captain William Barnard.   March 26, 1650.
      Wit: James Pyland, John Britt.                               Page 114

---

WILL AND DEED BOOK #1

GREENWOOD, Thomas: Leg. kinsman Valentine Chitty, 50 A. where James Wilson (?) lives, at expiration of his time to go to my grandson Edward Greenwood; son Edward; wife Elizabeth Extx.  D. March 19, 1656.  R. April 9, 1658.
      Wit: James Pyland, James Willson.                            Page 571

Sale of land Patented by Thomas Greenwood shows the widow married James Pyland and that in 1674 she was the wife of Thomas Edwards.
      Witnesses to conveyance, Timothy Fenn, John Davis, William Lewer. Those witnessing the delivery, Joseph Bridger, William Cole, John George, Nicholas Hill, Thomas Woodward, James Powell, Nicholas Smith. April 9, 1675.                                                   Page 572

BIRD, Robert: Leg. wife Susan; two servants John Daniels and Jane Williams their time; daughter Susannah my plantation bounding on Mr. Seaward and Mr. Winn, also cattle formerly given her by Captain Luck; Mr. Edward Saunders, Surgeon; daughter Elizabeth; God-son John Davis the son of John Davis; to every one of my servants a cow and calf at freedom, only Proctor excepted; Ann West.  Overseers, beloved friends, Mr. William Yarrett, Mr. William Bressey, Mr. John Hardy and Samuel Haswell. November 22, 1656.
      Cod., to John Gaine the son of Thomas Gaine.  Dec. 27, 1658.
      Wit: John George, Edward Saunders, Thomas Gordon.
      Jurantur coram nobis, James Pyland, John Bond, Francis Hobbs, Nicholas Hill, J. Bazeley, Daniel Boucher.                         Page 574

HARDY, George: Leg. Kinsman George Hardy, Jr. and Christian Willson to divide movable estate between them after the decease of my wife; my mill to said kinsman and his heirs, for lack of such heirs to Thomas Hardy and Christian Willson; seal ring to George Hardy, Jr.; the land I bought of Mr. John Stevens to Christian Willson; the land which I bought of Mr. Stamp to belong to the mill; I desire my wife to look after Thomas Hardy as my kinsman; I give one thousand pounds of tobacco towards the

3

building of the church in this parish in case it be built of brick; to
Christian Willson the land now in suit between me and the successors of
Justinian Cooper.  D.  March 16, 1654.  April 14, 1655.
    Wit:  Karby Kigan, John Jennings, George Woodward.    Page 576

BENN, Christopher:  Leg. son James the plantation which I bought of Thomas
Harris on Pagon Creek; eldest daughter Ann; daughter Margaret; daughter
Elizabeth; wife Mary.  D.  April 11, 1659.  R.  September 26, 1659.
    Wit:  William Travers, Henry Tandey.    Page 577

KIGAN, Karbry:  Leg. wife Catherine; unborn child, in the event the said
child does not live the land to Robert Cowfield the son of Capt. William
Cowfield; to Elizabeth Cowfield; to Katherine the daughter of John Tew;
to John King; to John Norton's child; to my countryman John Rogers of
the Middle Plantation.  Exs., friend Capt. William Cowfield and his
wife Katherine.  D.  January 12, 1657.  R.  February 9, 1657.
    Wit:  John Twy, William Almand.    Page 585

TOOK, James:  Leg. son Thomas the tract on which I live being a patent of 800
acres, also a patent called "White Marsh" and my seal signet ring; to
daughter Dorothy, the wife of John Harvey, who are now at the "South-
ward"; son William.  Ex., son Thomas.  D.  February 1, 1659.  R.  February
2, 1662.
    Wit:  Thomas Carter, Thomas Gwaltney.    Page 590

## DEED BOOK #I

WADE, Christopher:  Account Estate, signed Susanna Wade, Extx.  Debts paid
to Thomas Giles, Joseph Woory, William West, William Johnston, Col. John
Pitt, Capt. Thomas Godwin, Major Arthur Allen, Dr. Johnson, Timothy
Walker, Col. James Powell, James Bonn.  October 9, 1691.
    Examined by Thomas Moore and Will Bradshaw.    Page 127

RICHARDSON, John:  Estate account delivered by John Sherrer.  9th of 8ber
1694.  Above particulars delivered to the custody of John Sherrer and
Ri'd Loyd.  August 13, 1694.    Page 128

EDWARDS, Robert:  Estate presented by Owen Griffin.  December 10, 1694.
    Page 131

GRIFFIN, John:  Leg. sister Ann Tallogh; sister Sarah Tallogh the tobacco
my father Thomas Griffin gave my brother Thomas Griffin.  Ex. father
James Tallogh.  D.  December 4, 1694.  R.  December 10, 1694.
    Wit:  James Benn, Arthur Smith, Jr., Edward Goodson.    Page 133

BEST, Peter:  Leg. eldest son William; son Peter; son Christopher land at
Kingsale; youngest son Thomas; wife Mary.  D.  October 20, 1695.
R.  ----------
    Wit:  Thomas Hawkins, James Macfaddon, Christopher Best.  Page 147

BEST, Martha, wife of John Best then deceased.  Nuncupative will.  Leg. Mr.
Luke Haveild and his heirs.  Proved by her mother, Mrs. Silvestra Hill,
widow, John Jennings and wife Mary who relinquishes her right to Dr. Luke
Haveild of Chuckatuck.  October 20, 1695.
    Wit:  John Goodrich, Charles Chapman.    Page 149

PYLAND, Richard:  Leg. wife and five children.  Extx. wife Elinor.  D.  February
2, 1692/3.  R.  ----------
    Wit:  Thomas Moore, Henry White.    Page 161

PENNY, William: Leg. daughter Elizabeth; daughter Mary; John Volentine; James Vollentine; sister Francis; sister Elizabeth. Extx. daughter Elizabeth. D. May 23, 1695. R. ----------
        Wit: Anthony Holladay, Robert Marshall.                    Page 174

JOYNER, Thomas: Appraisers of estate, Arthur Pursell, Will Godwin, Alek Mathews, Will Bradshaw. October 6, 1695.                    Page 176

WHITLEY, John: Account of his estate returned by his widow Mary Whitley Adm. Among items tobacco which was given my daughter Olive Mackdowell by her father James Mackdowell. 1695.                    Page 178

PARTRIDGE, James: Nuncupative will proved by Susannah Garner and Elizabeth Noyall. Leg. wife and daughters; his daughter-in-law had been provided for already. 1695.                    Page 182

WATKINS, John Sen.: Nuncupative will, proved by William Crumpler and William Daws (?). Leg. wife Mary; son John land that Thomas English lives on; grand-son John Watkins; grand-son George English. January 7, 1694.
                                                                   Page 183

DENSON, Will: Appraisers of estate John Coggan Sen. and John Moore. September 9, 1695.                    Page 184

POWELL, William: Leg. wife Elizabeth; son John; son Nathaniel; son Jacob; son William and son Thomas land on Bowsarrow Swamp; daughter Elizabeth wife of John Poopes (?). December 11, 1695.
        Wit: Thomas Powell, Thomas Gale, Richard Hutchins.    Page 192

ALLEN, Henry: Appraisal presented by Thomas Bullock. Appraisers, Jacob Durden, Simon Everett, Will Murfrea. June 9, 1695.                    Page 193

SMITH, Nicholas: Leg. wife Ann one-half of my estate; other one-half to my grand-daughter, the daughter of Thomas Powell now living in the Province of Maryland and her two children; Nicholas Miller. Extx. wife and grand-daughter. November 19, 1695.
        Wit: Arthur Allen, John Davis, Will Webb, Edward Miller.
                                                                   Page 195

COLLINS, John Jr.: Appraisal presented by George Moore, and appraised at the home of John Collins Sen. by John Carrell, Thomas Thropp. February 10, 1695. R. 1696.                    Page 200

ELMES, Thomas: Appraisal ordered February 1695, signed by George Moore. Appraisers, John Carrell, Thomas Thropp. April 4, 1696.    Page 200

JENNINGS, John: Leg. sister Sarah Luckes, brother Will Thomas; son George. Exs. my mother Silvestra Hill and Will Thomas. D. December 31, 1695. R. ----------
        Wit: Francis ------, Martha Thropp, Thomas Heathfield, Will Thomas.                    Page 201

---

## WILL and DEED BOOK #2

ROYL, James: Leg. Daniel Long whole estate. D. April 29, 1666. R. June 20, 1666.
        Wit: William Ridwell, Thomas Grosse, Joan ------.    Page 43

ROYALL, James: Appraisal ordered June 20, 1666. Appraisers John Askew,
    John ------, John Watson, John Fendry. R. August 9, 1666. Page 44

JEFFRIES, Richard: Appraisal ordered August 11, 1666. Appraisers, John
    Snellock, Morgan Lewis, John Newman, Thomas Ward. Signed by Alice
    Councilling (?) the relict. September 10, 1666. Page 45

WILSON, William: Appraisal taken November 16, 1665. Mr. Peter Garland Adm.
    Appraisers, Francis Ayres, Richard Williamson, Thomas Griffin, George
    Surbe. R. August 9, 1666. Page 46

LUKE, Paul: Leg. wife Sarah; son Richard; daughter Katherine; said daughter
    a heiffer given her by Mr. James Took. D. October 14, 1666. R. December
    10, 1666.
        Wit: Edm. Pryme, James Bragg, Owen Griffin. Page 47

WESTON, John: Appraisal ordered December 10, 1666. Appraisers, Francis Skyner,
    Francis Ayres, Peter Garland. Signed by John Marshall and John Pitt and
    presented by the relict. March 11, 1666. Page 48

TANNER, Thomas: Appraisal ordered December 10, 1666. Signed Garrett Altman
    and John Council. January 15, 1666. Thomas Parker was sworn before the
    worshipful Nicholas Smith that the above is the whole estate. Teste
    John Burnett. R. March 11, 1666. Page 48

ELDRIDGE, Samuel: Account of his estate presented by Thomas More who married
    his relict. August 22, 1667. Page 49

GLANE, Robert: Leg. wife Mary; daughter Elizabeth; unborn child. D. September
    24, 1667. R. November 9, 1667.
        Wit: Robert King, Mathew Shaw. Page 50

GLANE, Robert: Appraisal taken November 16, 1667 by William Smith, Robert King,
    John Triprony and Garrett Altman. R. December 9, 1667. Page 50

BRASWELL, Robert: Leg. daughter Jane Stoikes and her children; daughter
    Rebecca West; son Robert; son Richard; servant Elizabeth Hall, daughter
    Ann Bagnall. Mr. Richard Izard and George Guillen (?) to be guardian of
    my children; daughter Ann Bagnall. D. February 15, 1667. R. May 1,
    1668.
        Wit: George Guillen, Richard Izard. Page 52

BOUCHER, Daniel: Leg. to my kinsman Robert Boucher; daughter Elizabeth; to
    Hodges Councill the younger; to William the son of William Huntt; to my
    son-in-law George Williams; to Mary the daughter of William Huntt; to
    Elizabeth Munger the daughter of John Munger; to Elizabeth Davis the
    daughter of John Davis, decd.; if my daughter Elizabeth dies without
    issue estate to my kinsman Robert Boucher; remainder to the grandchildren
    of my deceased wife Elizabeth. Friends John Hardy and Thomas Taberer
    overseers. December 4, 1667. R. May 1, 1668.
        Wit: Hodges Councill, William Bacon. Page 53
        Underwritten as followeth:
        In lieu of the horse and furniture given to Peter Vasser, Mr.
    Boucher gives him the second colt etc.- in the presence of Mr. Flake,
    Alexander Matthews, Thomas Taberer. Under his hand on the will is written:
    Memo. - there is a hogshead of tobacco in my house belonging to Mrs.
    Elinor Moseley, widow in Bristol. R. May 1, 1668. Page 53

BRASWELL, Robert: Appraisal of his estate May 11, 1668. Cattle at Mr. Robert
    Stoarkes (?); at William West etc. Appraisers: Giles Driver, Benjamin
    Beall, Robert Coleman, Francis Ayres. R. June 9, 1668. Page 55

BOUCHER, Daniel: Inventory of the estate taken in his lifetime by his direction the 11th day of March, 1667. This inventory was taken the day Mr. Daniel Boucher died in the presence of Mr. Robert Flake and Alexander Matthews. R. Aug. 10, 1668.                                        Page 57

LUKE, Paul: Inventory of his estate taken Oct. 20, 1666. Presented by Sarah Watson, relict of Paul Luke. R. Aug. 10, 1668.                Page 58

WEST, Nicholas: Inventory and appraisal of his estate taken Jan. 20, 1667. Appraisers: John Hardy, Arthur Smith, Richard Sharpe, George Smith. Presented by Sarah Watson, late the relict of said West. R. May 1, 1668.                                                            Page 59

KING, Henry: Leg. my daughters Susanna and Elizabeth 900 acres given me by my deceased father and confirmed by my mother Elizabeth King since deceased; to my wife Ruth 100 acres adjacent to Mr. England; to this Parish where I now live-------- for the maintenance of a free school; to John Russell now my servant; my two daughters to be brought up to learning. D. March 2, 1668. R. May 3, 1669.
    Wit: Edward Poynter, John Holly.                          Page 61

REYNOLDS, John: Leg. my brother George Rivers; brother Richard; sister Jane; sister Elizabeth Rivers; to Robert Driver; to Elizabeth River's daughter Mary; to my sister Elizabeth Jordan a bill of Robert Clothier's, at her decease to her son Richard Jordan. D. March 11, 1668. R. May 3, 1669.
    Wit: Anselm Baylie, William Bradshaw.                    Page 62

BOND, John- Gent.: Leg. son William; son John; daughter Francis; wife Dorothy; Capt. ffrancis England; Lt. Arthur Smith; Mr. Richard Sharpe. D. Jan. 16, 1668. R. May 3, 1669.
    Wit: John Bennett, Thomas Offe (?), William Cooke.      Page 63

FFENERYEAR, John: Leg. to brother Edmund the crop made in year 1670; to sister Ann; to Richard Smookum one year of his time; to Mary Pope the daughter of Thomas Pope; to William Frizzell son of William Frizzell; to wife Ann. Wife extx. D. March 17, 1668. R. May 3, 1669.
    Wit: John Burnell, Frances Elliott.
    Before sealing my will ---- that my well beloved father-in-law, Mr. Richard Izard be my overseer.                             Page 64

STRATFORD, William: Nuncupative will: I appoint my well beloved friend Mr. Francis Mason executor of my whole estate both here and in England. I desire him to sell my lands in Northampton, money to be divided among my sisters and brothers. R. Aug. 9, 1669.
    Wit: John Crafte, Will Wells, Alice Harris.             Page 64

POOLE, Joseph: Leg. wife Elizabeth, to her only son Edward Champion; to Thomas Blake's daughter, to Elias Fort Jr.; to daughter of John Storie; to Christopher Johnson. John Britt and Elias Fort to see my will performed. D. January 8, 1668. R. May 3, 1669.
    Wit: Thomas Barlow, Robert Poole.                        Page 65

    Appraisal estate of Joseph Poole ordered May 3, 1669. Appraisers: Thomas Barlow, Edward Brantley, Charles Williams, Elias Fort. R. May 13, 1669. Presented by Elizabeth Poole.                    Page 66

WILLIAMS, Morgan: Inventory and appraisal of his estate ordered May 3, 1669. Appraisers: Thomas Barlow, John Bressie, Edward Brantley, Elias Fort. R. May 8, 1669. Presented by Dorothy Williams.                Page 66

GIBBS, Edward: Appraisal of his estate ordered May 3, 1669. Appraisers: Giles Driver, Arthur Smith, Richard Sharpe, George Williams. Presented by Elizabeth Gibbs.  R.  May 10, 1669.

BREWER, John:  Nuncupative will.  Margarett Skynor aged forty-six or there-
about, sworn saith; that Mr. John Brewer the deponent's brother did say
that his estate was to be divided between his wife and sons John and
Thomas.  James Valentine, aged twenty-four, sworn - the same testimony.
R.  June 9, 1669.  Page 68

IZARD, Richard:  Leg. daughters Mary and Martha; wife Rebecca; to James
Bagnall the son of James Bagnall.  Overseer son-in-law James Bagnall.
D.  May 22, 1669.  R.  June 9, 1669.
Wit:  John Burnell, Richard Anglea.  Page 69

BOND, Major John:  Inventory and appraisal of his estate.  Presented by Mrs.
Dorothy Bond.  Appraisal ordered June 16, 1669.  Appraisers:  Nicholas
Cobb, Pharoah Cobb, John Watson, Edmund Prime.  Page 70

BAKER, Francis:  Leg. wife Hannah, to my children, John, ffrances and Elizabeth, to unborn child.  Robert Kea to see my will performed and to look
after my children in case of the mortality of my wife.  D.  June 19, 1669.
R.  August 9, 1669.
Wit:  Phillip Burrows, Margarie Kea, Robert Kea.  Page 72

YALDEN, Mr. Edward:  Inventory of his estate taken before Capt. Fulgham,
Mr. John Hardy and Mr. Thomas Taberer.  R.  September 6, 1669.
Page 73
Appraisal estate of Edward Yalden, Sept. 7, 1669.  Appraisers:
John Munger, John Walton, John Carrell, Richard Parker.  R.  Sept. 11,
1669.  Page 74

BAKER, Lt. Francis:  Appraisal of his estate ordered Aug. 9, 1669.  Appraisers:
John Munger, John Walton, John Carrell, Richard Parker.  R.  Aug. 16,
1669.  Page 75

YALDEN, Edward:  Nuncupative will.  Estate to his father and mother in Hampshire.  William Yarret to take care of his estate.  Proved by the oaths
of Richard Gross aged twenty-six and Elizabeth Walton, aged fifty-seven.
D.  Sept. 9, 1669.  R.  Oct. 9, 1669.  Page 76

GODBEHERE, John:  Appraisal of his estate ordered Aug. 9, 1669.  Appraisers:
John Gutridge, ffrancis Rayner, Edward Poynter, Nicholas Jones.
R.  Oct. 9, 1669.  Page 76

PERRY, Phillip:  Aged seventy-years.  Leg. eldest son Phillip (under twenty-
one); youngest son John; wife Grace.  Friend Ralph Channell overseer.
D.  Nov. 20, 1667.  R.  Oct. 9, 1669.
Wit:  James Bagnall, Anselme Baylie.  Page 77

BROWN, Edward:  Leg. son Edward; daughter Elizabeth; wife Ellinor.  Friends
Robert Flake and Richard Bennett overseers.  D.  Nov. 18, 1669.  R.  Dec.
9, 1669.
Wit:  John Clark, Phillip Hamiser (?), Martin Luther.  Page 79

BRASWELL, Mr. Robert:  Account of his estate in the hands of Richard Izard.
Presented by Rebecca Izard.  R.  Jan. 10, 1669.  Page 80

INGRUM, Roger:  Inventory of his estate presented by John Munger.  R.  Jan.
10, 1669.  Page 82

NORSWORTHY, Mr. John:  Inventory and appraisal of his estate.  Appraisers:
Thomas Parker, Robert King, William Smith, John Abott.  Presented by
Mrs. ffrancis Norsworthy.  R.  August 9, 1670.

OGBORN, Symond: Leg. son Nicholas; daughter Mary; son Symond; wife Lucie; servant Thomas Davis; to my loving wife and my children by her viz. Symond, Elinor, Elizabeth and Katherine. D. March 24, 1668. R. Feb. 9, 1669.
    Wit: Thomas Taberer, Elizabeth Merritt.          Page 83

MOSS, Thomas-tailor: Leg. to John the son of John Whitley; Thomas Richards; Thomas Ward Jr. John Whitley Jr. Ex. D. Dec. 14, 1669. R. Feb. 9, 1669.
    Wit: John Richards, John Iles.          Page 84

GRIFFEN, Thomas: Leg. son Thomas the land I bought of Capt. Fulgham and my brother William Godwin to give him assurance of same at court; to Thomas Bush; to God-daughter Ann Wilkinson; wife Ann and unborn child. D. Nov. 8, 1669. R. April 9, 1670.
    Wit: William Godwin, John Iles, John Pitt.          Page 84

WILLIAMSON, Robert, Doctor in Physic: to be buried as near as maybe to my late deceased father-in-law, Mr. Arthur Allen. Leg. wife Jone, son Robert (under eighteen) land at Blackwater; sons George Arthur and ffrancis. Friends Major Nicholas Hill and Capt. John Grove executors in trust. Son Robert Ex. D. Feb. 16, 1669. R. May 2, 1670.
    Wit: John Hardy, William Sherwood.
Mr. Robert Burnett as marrying the relict of Robert Williamson gave Bond for estate Nov. 2, 1672. Security, Mr. Driver and Mr. Arthur Allen.          Page 85

WILLIAMSON, Robert: Inventory of his estate presented by the relict Jone Williamson, June 9, 1670.          Page 87

BARNETT, Robert: Leg. Garrett Altman; wife if she comes to Virginia. Garrett Altman Ex. D. Feb. 8, 1669. R. Aug. 9, 1670.
    Wit: George Manne, Richard Jackson.          Page 88

BRAGG, James: Leg. my three children, James, Elizabeth and Anne; James Barnes son of Thomas Barnes; wife Elizabeth. D. April 29, 1670. R. Sept. 9, 1670.
    Wit: William Lugg, Thomas Gaymie (?).          Page 88

BARNETT, Robert: Appraisal of his estate by Robert King, Thomas Parker, Thomas Empson, John Triprong. Presented by Garrett Altman. R. Sept. 9, 1670.          Page 89

LEWIS, Thomas: Appraisal of his estate ordered July 2, 1670. Appraisers, George Hardy, John Snellocke, Thomas Ward, John Allen. Presented by Mrs. Rebecca Lewis. R. Sept. 9, 1670.          Page 89

COLIER, Robert: Inventory of his estate presented by Mr. Thomas Harris. R. Sept. 9, 1670.          Page 90

STANTLIN, Darby: Leg. wife Gulian, sick at present time, if she should die, my friend Mathew Waikley to remain on my plantation until Henry King becomes of age; in case of wife's death and of her son Henry King my plantation to Mathew Waikley. Friends Nicholas Cobb and Richard Sharpe to see my will performed. D. April 25, 1670. R. Oct. 25, 1670.
    Wit: Nicholas Cobb, William Cole, Richard Sharpe.
    Bequests to son Henry King acknowledged in open court by Gulian Stantlin and confirmed by Mathew Waikley her now husband. R. Oct. 25, 1670.          Page 90

DIXSON, Thomas: Appraisal of his estate taken by Thomas Barloe, Edward Brantley, Robert Roe, Elias Fort. Presented by Henry Martin who married the relict of Thomas Dixson. R. Oct. 25, 1670. Page 91

OGBURNE, Symon: Inventory of his estate presented by his relict Lucie
Ogburne. R. Nov. 9, 1670. Page 93

VIVIAN, Thomas: Inventory of his estate presented by Elizabeth Vivian.
D. July 25, 1670. R. Nov. 9, 1670. Page 94

COLIER, Robert: Appraisal of his estate made Dec. 15, 1670, by Henry
Plumpton, James Collins, John Porter. Presented by Richard Sharpe
and John Watson. R. Jan. 9, 1670. Page 94

WOTTEN, Thomas: Leg. wife Sarah; only son Richard; at son's death if without
heirs to next kin of name in Northamptonshire at a town called Caster
near Peterborough. Friends, James Sampson and Richard Briggs, overseers.
D. March 15, 1669. R. Dec. 9, 1670.
Wit: Elizabeth Sampson. Page 94

MUNGER, John: Leg. eldest son John; second son Robert my land at Blackwater;
daughter Mary; rest of estate between my wife and all my children.
Supervisors of my will my "lo. sonne" Timothy Fenn, and friends Thomas
Taberer, John Carrell, Thomas Carter. D. Jan. 2, 1670. R. Feb. 9,
1670.
Wit: John Carrell, Mary Monger, Mary Whitten. Page 95

LUPO, Phillip Sen.: leaving for London to look after certain lands and goods
as heir to Phillip Lupo, Goldsmith my father, or to my brother James
Lupo, or to my sister Katherine Mosecroft lately deceased. Leg. estate
in Virginia to be divided between my wife Marie; oldest son Phillip;
son James; daughter Mary Ryall. Overseers, William Webb and Robert
Kea. D. March 8, 1668. R. Feb. 9, 1670.
Wit: William Axum, Thomas Abbott. Page 96

Inventory of the estate taken March 8, 1668. Signed Phillip
Lupo. R. February 9, 1671.
Wit: Robert Kea, William Webb. Page 96

RIDLEY, William: Leg. daughter-in-law Jane Tuke, wife of William Tuke of
Surry County; her mother's possessions to her four children; to Mary the
daughter of Edmond Prime; to Elizabeth the daughter of Edmond Prime; to
Edmond Prime's five children; to Mary the daughter of John Crew; to
John the son of Edmond Prime; to Mr. Barham's two daughters Elizabeth
and Pearlie; to William Tuke of Surry, my wife's son-in-law. I desire
that Henry Gray the father of my servant John Gray may have him until
his term be expired. Mr. Charles Barham Ex. Thomas Harris and Thomas
Tuke overseers. D. May 1, 1671. R. Oct. 19, 1671.
Wit: George Bell, Robert Jones. Page 98

LEWIS, Arthur: Appraisal of his estate, presented by Tobias Keeble who
married the relict of said Lewis. Appraisers: William Ernest, John
Dun, John ffrizell, John Goodwin. D. April 12, 1671. R. Oct. 19, 1671.
Page 99

COLE, William: Appraisal of his estate, taken Nov. 24, 1670. Appraisers:
Anthony Mathews, Owen Griffin, John Portis. Presented by James Pedden
to Mr. John Hardy and William Oldis. R. Oct. 19, 1671. Page 99

BREWER, John: Appraisal of his estate, taken June 14, 1662, by Richard
Penny, Thomas Parker, Thomas Clark. Presented by Mrs. Ann Holladay,
relict and admtx. of said Brewer. R. Oct. 19, 1671. Page 100

CLARK, James: Inventory of his estate presented by Judith Clark his relict.
D. Oct. 3, 1672. R. Oct. 9, 1672. Page 102

MUNGER, John: Appraisal of his estate, ordered Sept. 7, 1671. Appraisers:
Robert Kae, Edmond Vickens (?), William Will, Thomas Edwards. Presented
by Mrs. Mary Munger. R. Dec. 11, 1671. Page 103

WHITLEY, John: Leg. son John; wife Ann; son Thomas 200 acres I purchased of
Capt. Anthony Fulgham, adjoining the land of William Godwin; son William
200 acres adjoining Mr. William Bressie; daughter Elizabeth; to my son-
in-law John Williams; to Ann the daughter of John Williams. Wife Extx.
D. Feb. 21, 1670. R. Feb. 9, 1671.
Wit: John Burnell, William Robson. Page 105

MORRIS, William: Leg. son Morgan 100 acres on Blackwater that I bought of
Christopher Holleman; son John; son William; daughter Elizabeth; wife
Elizabeth. Wife extx. D. ---------- R. April 9, 1672.
Wit: William Oldis, Robert Ruffin, Andro -- (?). Page 106

THOROGOOD, John: Appraisal of his estate, taken Feb. 22, 1671. Appraisers:
Richard Penny, Robert King, Daniel Miles, John Ross. Presented by Capt.
Joseph Bridger. R. April 9, 1672. Page 107

BRIM (or BRUIN), Thomas: Appraisal and the division of his estate requested
by Elizabeth the relict and Ann Madison, grandmother to the orphans of
said Bruin. - of the household goods 1/3 was retained by the widow and
Ann Madison received 3/5 of the remainder in the behalf of three of her
grandchildren which she hath with her; Thomas Bruin 1/5 and Elizabeth
Bruin widow 1/5 in behalf of a female born after the marriage of said
Bruin with the said Elizabeth. Appraisers: Thomas Norsworthy, George
Lucke, Peter Hayes. R. May 1, 1672. Page 109

HARRIS, Thomas: Leg. son Thomas; son John; land in Corotoman in Lancaster
County to son Thomas; Wife Alice; daughter Mary. Major Nicholas Hill
and John Jennings overseers. D. March 30, 1672. R. June 10, 1672.
Wit: Francis Hobbs, Lewis Rogers. Page 111

HERRING, John: Leg. son Anthony; wife Margerie; to John Whitfield.
D. ---------- R. June 10, 1672.
Wit: John Vickars, Ambrose Bennett, Thomas Grosse, Edward
Lassetter, Jr. Page 112

WATSON, Sarah: Leg. daughter Katherine Luke to be placed in the custody of
William Yarret and his wife; if said daughter dies without heirs her
estate to William Yarret, Jr. and my brother in England - in Solembareth
in Gloucestershire. Thomas Taberer and Edward Jones, overseers.
Feb. 22, 1671. R. Aug. 9, 1672.
Wit: Mathew ----------, John Clemains. Page 112

HIGGINS, Roger: Leg. mother Mary Lupo; at the death of mother my cattle at
Edward Millers and Thomas Wombwells to be divided between my brother
James Higgins and my Godson Roger Hodges; to my brother Robert Hodge's
eldest son; to his second son Elias; to his third son Roger; to James
Lupo; to Ann the wife of Nicholas Ogburne. Brother Robert Hodges Ex.
D. April 16, 1672. R. Aug. 10, 1672.
Wit: Edmond Prime, Nicholas Ogburne. Page 113

WILLIAMS, George, tailor: Leg. son William to Mr. Pharoah Cobb; son George
to Mr. Henry Applewhaite; daughter Elizabeth to Mr. William Bressie and
his wife Susanna, if it shall please God to send them back to Virginia.
Mr. Arthur Smith, Pharoah Cobb and Henry Applewhaite, overseers.
D. Feb. 12, 1671. R. Oct. 9, 1672.
Wit. Giles Limscott, Richard Lewis. Page 114

11

DUTHAIS, Charles: Leg. wife Dinah; Goddaughter Joyce Wollard. D. April 18, 1672. R. October 9, 1672.
Wit: Martin Coulbron, Joseph fford.                         Page 114

WARREN, William: Leg. William Hutchins; Roger Ingram; Joseph Thorpe; Henry Kae; Capt. John Jennings. Ex. friend Robert Kae the elder. August 24, 1672. R. October 24, 1672.
Wit: Timothy ffenn, William Lewis.                         Page 115

WILLIAMSON, Robert: Appraisal of his estate, taken November 25th, at the house of Mr. Robert Burnett. Divided between the relict and four orphans, by Robert Kae, Arthur Smith, Richard Sharpe, Robert fflake. R. December 9, 1672.                         Page 116

WOODHOUSE, John: Account of his estate, presented by Mr. Giles Driver. January 9, 1672.                         Page 117

PROCTOR, Ambrose, Jr.: Leg. son Ambrose; son John; son William; Godson Charles Beckett; wife Elizabeth. D. March 27, 1672. R. January 9, 1672.
Wit: George Bell, John Crofts, John Davis.
Elizabeth the relict of Ambrose Proctor Jr. acknowledges a gift of a heifer to her daughter Elizabeth.                         Page 118

NICHOLSON, Richard: Inventory of said Richard Nicholson, who has been deceased about three years, now given by his wife to the best of her remembrance. Signed Marriable Pullen als Nicholson and now the widow of Abraham Pullen. R. Sept. 9, 1673.                         Page 118

CARTER, Thomas: Inventory of his estate. Signed Elinor Groves. R. Sept. 9, 1673.                         Page 120

WATSON, John: Inventory of his estate, taken October 14, 1673. Administrators: Capt. Arthur Smith and Mr. Richard Sharpe. R. December 9, 1673.
                         Page 121

DAVIS, Richard: Appraisal of the estate of Richard Davis, decd. attached by the sheriff in ye behalf of Joseph fford, by Phillip Pardoe and Thomas Ward. R. Feb. 9, 1673/4.                         Page 123

ROE, Robert: Appraisal of his estate, presented December 9, 1674 by William Powell; taken by Francis Hutchins, William Smelly, John More. R. April 9, 1675.                         Page 123

BENN, Mary: Inventory of her estate, presented by James Benn. The said estate to be used for the benefit of his deceased sister's child. R. October 9, 1674.                         Page 126

TRIPONNEY, John: Appraisal of his estate, taken February 20, 1674 by John Giles, Thomas Parker, Robert King and John Powell.                         Page 127

CROSBY, John: according to my late deceased wife Elizabeth's request on her death bed to Mrs. Jane Oldis, my said wife's daughter Margaret Davis my estate. D. January 9, 1674.
Wit: Robert Ruffin, Will Lane.                         Page 127

PITT, Robert: Leg. daughter Martha; son John; grandson John Pitt; grandson William Pitt; grandson Robert Pitt; daughter Mary Brassiuer; daughter Hester Bridger; daughter Elizabeth Norsworthy; grandson Robert Pitt, son of Robert Pitt decd.; my house and land to be for the relief of poor women as a gift from my deceased wife Martha. Ex. son John. D. June 6, 1672. R. January 9, 1674.
Wit: Richard Jones, Thomas Hill.                         Page 128

12

CLARKE, Thomas: Appraisal of his estate, taken April 29, 1675 by John
Marshall, Anthony Holladay, John Asson, James House. Signed Elizabeth
Clarke. R. May 1, 1675. Page 129

WILDS, Thomas: Appraisal of his estate, by Richard Penny, William Frizzell,
Peter Best and Neale Mason. May 1, 1675. Signed Ann Wilds. Page 129

SCULLEY, Cornelius: Nuncupative and proved by Elizabeth Lassells and Daniel
Long. Leg. sons John and Cornelius; daughter Elizabeth; at death of
wife two sons to Daniel Long and daughter to Elizabeth Lassells.
R. May 1, 1675. Page 130

GOODWYN, John: Inventory of his estate, presented by Ann the relict of said
Goodwyn. R. June 9, 1675. Page 131

SCULLY, Cornelius: Appraisal of his estate taken June 25, 1675 by Edward
Lassells, Ambrose Bennett and Daniel Long. R. August 9, 1675.
Page 131

LEWIS, Benedict: Appraisal of his estate, presented by the widow and taken
by John Vicars, Mickaell Fulgham and Toby Keeble. R. August 9, 1675.
Page 132

BRESSIE, John: Appraisal of his estate, taken October 26, 1675 by Thomas
Moore, Thomas Edwards and John Collins. R. October 26, 1675.
Page 132

GROSS, Richard: Appraisal of his estate, taken August 23, 1675 by Peter
Banton, John Walton, William Hittchens, William Lewis. Page 132

HILL, Nicholas: Leg. wife Silvestra; son Richard; son Ralph; daughter Agnes
(a mantle that was her Mother's and her wedding ring); daughter Martha;
son George; daughter Mary; son Nicholas; daughter Anna; daughter Eliza-
beth; my wife and her six children to have the legacy given her by Major
General Bennett; my three children by a former wife. Overseers, Major
James Powell, Mr. Thomas Taberer, Mr. William Bressie and John Jennings.
D. April 19, 1675. R. October 20, 1675.
Wit: John Grayham, John Newman, Mary Davis. Page 133

IZARD, Rebeccah: Leg. daughter Rebecca Bagnall; daughter Martha; Mary Bennett;
James Bagnall the son of James Bagnall; Nehemiah Hunt the son of Godfrey
Hunt; Elizabeth Rieves the daughter of Henry Rieves. Overseers, my sons
James Bagnall, Henry Rieves and Ambrose ---------. October 15, 1675.
Wit: John Burnell, William Westar. Page 135

CLAY, John: Leg. son William the plantation purchased of Mr. Anthony
Spiltimber; eldest son Thomas; Elizabeth Clay the daughter of William
Clay; Goddaughter Mary Hardy; son John fifty acres of land purchased
of Andrew Robison, given to his wife by her father Dunston. Extx. wife
Mary. D. April 7, 1675. R. October 20, 1675.
Wit: Roger Delke, John Sowers, Robert Kae. Page 135

ROE, Robert: Leg. son Robert; daughter Margaret. Extx. wife and overseers,
Elias Fort and Thomas Moore. D. December 28, 1675. R. January 7, 1675.
Wit: Thomas Moore, William Groves. Page 137

MIDDLETON, Robert: Appraisal of his estate presented by Anselm Bailey,
February 17, 1675 and taken by William Oldis, Richard Jordan Sr.,
Tristram Knowles and William Bradshaw. R. February 17, 1675.
Page 137

CLAY, William: Leg. cousin Thomas, son of my brother Thomas Clay; Mary the

youngest daughter of Henry Reynolds; brother John Clay and his daughter Elizabeth; my daughter Elizabeth. Extx. wife Judith. January 10, 1675.
Wit: George Hardy Sr., Thomas Baker. Page 137

GROSS, Thomas: Leg. eldest son William; youngest son Francis; son Thomas; eldest daughter Susanna; youngest daughter Mary. Extx. wife Susanna. D. February 27, 1675. R. February 27, 1675.
Wit: Daniel Miles, James Benn. Page 138

AYRES, Francis: Leg. wife Jane; Humphry Clark the son of John Clark; reversion to Robert Clark, brother of said Humphry. Humphry Clark is to live with his grandmother my beloved wife Jane. Wife Extx. Overseers, Robert Flake and John Clark. D. January 13, 1675. R. April 10, 1676.
Wit: John Burnell, Jere Martin, James Tullagh. Page 139

WEBB, James: Appraisal of his estate taken February 17, 1675, by Anthony Holladay, Thomas Green, Richard Penny and John Vicars. March 1, 1675/6.
Page 140

MASON, William: Division of his estate, ordered April 10, 1676, between his wife Joane and daughter Elizabeth, made by John Wakefield and Charles Williams. April 12, 1676. Page 141

WALTON, Elizabeth: Leg. Thomas Moore. D. December 23, 1675. R. August 9, 1676.
Wit: George Moore, Margaret Williams, Priscilla Champion.
Page 141

KANEDY, Morgan: Appraisal of his estate, ordered May 11, 1676, taken by John Snellock and Richard Coresey. Henry Goad who married Kanedy's widow gave bond for the estate of his children with Morgan Lewis his security. R. May 12, 1676. Page 142

DENSON, William: Leg. wife Francis; son William; son James; daughters Francis and Katherine. Wife Extx. D. November 15, 1675. R. April 9, 1677.
Wit: Nathaniel Raven, William Scott, Jr., William Smelly.
Page 142

HARRIS, Martha: Appraisal of the estate of Martha Harris, widow and late wife of Edward Harris, presented by George Hardy and Phillip Pardoe. May --, 1677. Page 143

VALENTINE, James, of the Lower Parish: Leg. wife Mary; son John; son James; my children. Wife Extx. D. Oct. 25, 1676. R. June 9, 1677.
Wit: John Hathaway, Margaret Miles, Margaret Long. Page 144

ENGLAND, Francis, of Blackwater in Isle of Wight: Leg. daughter Ann Branch, wife of George Branch and her sons, George, Francis and John Branch. Wife Joyce, Extx. Overseers, John Gutridge and John Pearson. D. May 13, 1677. R. June 9, 1677.
Wit: Nicholas Davis, George Cripps, Richard Bennett. Page 144

WARE, Thomas: Leg. two daughters; land in Surry to three sons; wife. Overseers, Robert Kay and Edward Bechinoe. D. April 8, 1675. R. June 9, 1677.
Wit: Edward Bechinoe, Richard Briggs, Richard Piland. Page 145

DUNNIN, John: Leg. Roger Ingrum; Mr. Giles Driver's wife and his daughter Hardy Driver. Giles Driver Ex. D. December 28, 1676. R. July 9, 1677.
Wit: Richard Ainsley, William Bradshaw. Page 145

14

HARDY, John: Leg. daughter Olive Driver, wife of Giles Driver; daughter
Lucy Councill, wife of Hodges Councill; daughter Debora Hardy; daughter
Olive Driver's two children; daughter Lucy Councill's three children;
my wife's grandchild John Johnson; son-in-law Robert Burnett; William
Mayo. Wife Alice Extx. D. October 7, 1675. R. Une 9, 1677.
Wit: Richard Rennalds, Will Jenkins. • • • Page 146

DRIVER, Giles: Leg. son Robert; son Charles; son Giles; son John; daughter
Hardy. Wife Extx. D. December 12, 1676. R. December 29, 1676.
Wit: Will Bradshaw, Richard Reynolds. Page 147

ALLEN, John, of Warwick Creek Bay: Leg. Godson John Harebottle, son of
John Harebottle decd.; Ann Wilson daughter of Jane Wilson. Wife
Margaret Extx. D. March 20, 1676. R. June 9, 1677.
Wit: Philip Pardoe, Thomas Lee, Winifret Luger. Page 147

LEWIS, Morgan: Leg. wife Sarah; daughter Sarah; my three daughters; John
Ingram. D. January 26, 1676/7. R. June 9, 1677.
Wit: George Hardy Sr., Philip Pardoe.
Appraisers of estate, June 7, 1677: George Hardy Sr., Richard Hansford
and Phillip Pardoe. Presented by Mrs. Sarah Lewis. R. June 9, 1677.
Page 148

HARRIS, Edward: Appraisers, Edward Bechinoe, Richard Corsey, John Williams
and Richard Hansford. Presented by Mr. George Hardy. R. June 9, 1677.
Page 149

SKINNER, Lt. Richard: Appraisers, Edward Bechinoe, Richard Briggs, Herman
Hill. D. April 17, 1677. R. June 9, 1677. Page 149

HOUSE, James: Appraisers, John Powell, Thomas Emson, Robert King. Presented
by Mrs. Mary House. D. April 15, 1677. R. June 9, 1677. Page 150

DRIVER, Giles: Appraisers, Robert Coleman, Thomas Green, Richard Jordan, Sr.,
Thomas Giles, Daniel Long. D. June 9, 1677. R. June 9, 1677.
Page 150

DUNNING, John: Inventory of his estate presented by Mrs. Olive Driver.
R. June 9, 1677. Page 151

EARNEST, William: Appraisal by Robert Worgar, John Marshall, Michael Fulgham.
Presented by his widow. R. June 9, 1677. Page 151

VALENTINE, James: Appraisal by Richard Penny, John Vicars, Michael Fulgham,
John Frizzell, Jr. D. June 20, 1677. R. August 9, 1677. Page 151

SMITH, Virgus: Nuncupative, proven by John Newman, age 35 years and Thomas
Wombwell. Leg. wife and children; son John and unborn child. R. September 10, 1677. Page 152

SKINNER, Richard: Leg. Skinner Rawlins; if without heirs to the next heir
of my daughter's body; wife and my two daughters. D. July 10, 1677.
R. October 9, 1677.
Wit: Edward Bechinoe. Page 152

PETTIS, Roger: Inventory presented by the widow. D. October 8, 1677.
R. October 8, 1677. R. October 9, 1677. Page 153

WOODWARD, Thomas: Leg. wife; son Thomas all land at Blackwater; land adjoining John Fulgham to daughter Katherine; daughter Elizabeth; daughter
Mary; daughter Rachell; provision for son John's children if any in
England. Exs. son Thomas and daughter Philerita. D. October 5, 1677.

R.   October 9, 1677.
      Wit: Anthony Fulgham and John Wingate.              Page 153

TAYLOR, William, of London:  Merchant.  Nuncupative, proven by George Hardy,
    Elizabeth Smith and Ralph Hill, at a court held at the house of Major
    James Powell.  He requested Mr. Kearnie to attend to all of his business.
    R.   October 24, 1677.                              Page 153
    Appraisal by Edward Bechinoe, George Hardy, James Sampson, Richard Briggs.
    Presented by Barnabie Kearnie.  D.  October 25, 1677.  R.  November 20,
    1677.                                               Page 154

MADISON, Richard:  Leg. daughter Elizabeth Waugh the wife of John Waugh;
    wife Anne.  D.  October 16, 1676.  R.  January 9, 1677.
      Wit:  John Burnett, John ----------.              Page 155

FRANCIS, John:  Nuncupative, proven by Elizabeth Gandy (?) and Elizabeth
    Roberts.  Leg. son John and wife Jone.  R.  February 11, 1677.
                                                        Page 155

WALE, John:  Appraisal by Richard Penny, William Frissell, John Frissel,
    Clement Creswell.  D.  October 20, 1677.            Page 155

COMBES, Henry, of the Upper Parish:  Leg. wife Mary.  17th day of Xber, 1677.
    R.  April 9, 1678.
      Wit:  George Hardy, Sr., John Coker, George Williams.   Page 156

PARDOE, Phillip:  Inventory presented by Rebecca Pardoe.  D.  April 6, 1678.
    R.  April 9, 1678.                                  Page 157

VICARS, John:  Planter, Leg. eldest son John; son Ralph; Goddaughter Mary
    Knight.  Wife Jane Extx.  D.  September 13, 1677.  R.  May --, 1678.
      Wit:  Joseph Bridger, Toby Keeble.                Page 158

PETTIS, Roger:  Inventory of Roger Pettis the son of Roger Pettis decd.
    R.  May --, 1678.                                   Page 160

SMITH, Virgus:  Division of his estate among John, Virgus and Sarah Smith.
    R.  May 1, 1678.                                    Page 160

BRUCE, Robert:  Inventory presented by the relict Elinor Nocton(?).
    R.  June 11, 1678.                                  Page 161

VICARS, John:  Appraisal by John Dunn, James Hunter, John Lewis, Thomas Poole.
    Presented by the widow.  R.  June 8, 1678.          Page 161

CROSBY, John:  Inventory presented by Ansell Bayley.  R.  June 10, 1678.
                                                        Page 162

EMSON, Thomas:  Appraisal by Thomas Parker, Robert King, William Smith,
    John Weston.  D.  June 10, 1678.  R.  June 21, 1678.   Page 162

PARDOE, Phillip:  Appraisal by George Hardy, Edward Bechinoe, Richard Briggs,
    Richard Corsey.  Presented by Major James Powell, administrator.
    D.  April 18, 1678.  R.  August 9, 1678.            Page 162

HILL, Lt. Col. Nicholas:  Inventory presented by Mrs. Silvestra Hill.
    August 9, 1678.                                     Page 163

WALKER, Daniel:  Leg. wife Abigail; children Mary and Sarah; reversion to
    Robert and Elizabeth Bressie, the children of Robert Bressie.
    D.  January 21, 1676.  R.  August 9, 1678.
      Wit:  George Hardy, Sr., Martha Banister.         Page 164

SMITH, Robert: Leg. son Robert; wife Extx. D. June 29, 1678. R. August 9, 1678.
Wit: John Daniell, Richard Sharpe. Page 164

WOODWARD, Thomas: Inventory presented by Katherine the relict, daughter Philarita and son Thomas Woodward. R. August 9, 1678. Page 165

ENGLISH, John: Leg. daughter Francis Iles; daughter Elizabeth Church; son-in-law John Watts; grandson John Iles; grandson John Watts; daughter Alice Watts; my three daughters, Mary, Sarah and Martha English. Overseers: daughter Francis Iles and son-in-law John Watts. D. August 13, 1678. R. October 9, 1678. Page 166

WALKER, Daniel: Inventory presented by Abigail Walker, the relict. R. October 9, 1678. Page 167

DEW, John: Leg. wife Elizabeth; son John (under 18); Wife Extx. Overseers: my father, friend Alexander Webster; my well beloved brother John Sherrow Jr. and friend George Bell Jr. D. January 31, 1677. R. October 17, 1678. Wit: Francis Floid, Thomas Williamson. Page 167

FULGHAM, Anthony: Leg. brother Nicholas; reversion to brother Michael; reversion to John the son of Anthony Fulgham; reversion to female children of Nicholas Fulgham; kinswoman Martha, daughter of my brother Michael Fulgham, 100 A. adjoining land of William Sellers; my Mother, the time I have in Richard Smoakham; brother John's children. D. October 14, 1678. R. December 9, 1670.
Wit: John Pitt, Richard Smoakham. Page 168

DEW, John: Inventory presented by Elizabeth Dew the widow. R. October 17, 1678. Page 168

EMSON, Thomas: Division of his estate between the widow and children, George, Elizabeth, Sarah, Jane, Thomas, Martha and Ann; made by Richard Penny, Thomas Parker, John Marshall and Robert King. Ordered October 17, 1678. Page 169

GEORGE, John: Leg. son Isack; grandson John George (under 6 years); daughters Rebecca and Sarah; grandchildren John and Joyce Lewis; children of Phillip Pardoe; children of my daughter Sarah Peddington, which she had by my son Morgan Lewis; kinswoman Mary Baugh; wife Ann. Wife Extx. Overseers: Major James Powell and Thomas Taberer. D. August 2, 1678. R. January 9, 1678.
Wit: Robert Parker, Thomas Taberer, Edward Bechinoe, George Branch. Page 170

REDDING, Richard: Nuncupative. Proven by Roger Wildes and Edward Rylie. On November the 12th they were sent for by said Redding, who was sick at the house of Richard Silvester. Leg. John Watts and Richard Silvester. R. January 9, 1678. Page 171

LONG, John: Leg. wife Margaret; son John. Friend Daniel Miles, overseer. D. October 19, 1678(?). R. February 10, 1678.
Wit: John Marshall, Sr., Daniel Miles. Page 171

GROVES, William: Appraisal by John Harris, Edward Brantley, Elias Fort, Edward Grantham. Presented by Mrs. Elinor Groves. Ordered 21st of 9 mo. 1677. R. February 9, 1678. Page 172

POWELL, Nathaniel: Appraisal by John Moore, Francis Hutchins, Jeremiah Exum, William Smelley. Presented by Lucretia the relict and now wife of John Corbit. R. March 10, 1678. Page 172

JENNINGS, John: Leg. son John; daughter Martha; daughter Mary my land on Lyon's Creek; daughter Sarah the land bought of Valentine Chitty; son-in-law William Seward; George Seward; wife Mary. (children under 17). Overseers: Capt. Edmund Wickens, Lt. George Moore, Thomas Moore, William Seward. D. October 19, 1678. Wit: George Lewer, Mathew Wood.
    Codicil: my overseers to pay to the orphans of Mr. William Seward three servants, for which I am indebted to them. D. 10th day of 9ber, 1678. R. March 10, 1678/9.
    Wit: Nicholas Smith, Thomas Taberer, Martha Fones.     Page 173

HAYES, Peter: Leg. Mother; sister Ann Cornes; reversion to my cousin Thomas Bythessa (?). D. May 7, 1678. R. March 10, 1678.
    Wit: Anthony Fulgham, Hugh Humphrey.     Page 175

WILLIAMS, Rowland: Nuncupative. Proven by Roger Wildes and Charles Cartwright. Leg. son George, who is to live with Michael Rogers and daughter Mary, who is to live with Thomas Parker. R. March 10, 1678.
     Page 175

COCKINS, William: Appraisal by Edward Brantley, John Britt, William Baldwin, Edward Champion. Presented by the widow. Ordered March 10, 1678. R. April 9, 1679.     Page 176

AYRES, Francis: Inventory presented by Jane Clarke, formerly the wife of said Ayres. R. March 10, 1678/9.     Page 187

LONG, John: Appraisal by John Marshall, Anthony Holladay, Humphry Marshall. D. February 20, 1678/9. R. April 9, 1679.     Page 188

FORT, Elias: Appraisal by Edward Brantley, John Britt, William Baldwin, Edward Champion. D. March 10, 1678. R. April 9, 1679.     Page 188

BARLOW, Thomas: Planted in ye Upper Parish. Leg. son George; wife Elizabeth. Overseers: George Moore and Thomas Moore. D. January 13, 1678. R. April 9, 1679.
    Wit: Henry Goldham, John Story.     Page 189

MORRIS, Richard: Appraisal by Richard Wilkinson, James Tullaugh, Anthony Fulgham, George Allen, (among items, - "one hundred and ninety-five books, which we cannot value the worth of them."). Ordered November 20, 1677. No recording date given.     Page 189

AYRES, Francis: Appraisal by Michael Fulgham, Daniel Long, James Tullaugh, Edward Lassells. D. March 10, 1678/9. R. April 9, 1679.
    Division of estate between the relict and Humphry Clarke, son of John Clarke. Jane formerly the wife of said Ayres now the wife of Henry Clarke; made by Edward Lassells, Daniel Long, James Benn. D. April 14, 1679. R. May --, 1679.     Page 191

SNELLOCK, John: Leg. the two children of Henry King, late of Blackwater, decd.; John Newman's four children; John Williams and his two sons John and Richard; John Corsie, son of Richard Corsie; Richard Piland; John Story; Margaret Dayway; Robert Beedles; James Powell; Jane Dobbs the money which George Moore oweth me. D. April 29, 1679. R. May 1, 1679.     Page 193

CORSEY, Francis: Leg. son John to be left in the care of Mr. Thomas Groves of London. D. ---------- R. May 1, 1679.
    Wit: John Bellew, George Moore.     Page 193

CORSEY, Richard: Leg. son John; Wife Francis; cousin Richard Williams; Edward Phillips; Goddaughter Franis Canedy. Wife Extx. Overseers: George

Moore and Thomas Moore.  D.  April 16, 1679.  R.  May 1, 1679.
  Wit:  Richard Powell, Elinor Powell and Thomas Moore.  Page 194

BARTLETT, Robert:  Nuncupative, proven by Thomas Lamb, age 44 years and
  Elizabeth Davis age 35 years.  Leg. a daughter, who was left in the
  tuition of Tobias Kebble.  R.  May 1, 1679.  Page 194

BRIGGS, Richard:  Leg. four sons to whom he leaves 500 A. in Surry near the
  Richneck, Alexander, where John Frillipse lives; John, where Lewis
  Williams lives; Robert where John Hodges lives; Francis over the swamp
  joining upon Mr. Edwards; to James and Edmund Briggs the land whereon
  I now live, adjoining the land of Edward Bechinoe and Major Hill; I
  dispossess my wife Margaret of any interest or possession of my land;
  son Edmund to be placed with Mr. John Spiers, doctor in Nansemond; son
  James with Major James Powell, his Godfather; James Largie, his wife
  and children.  Overseers:  Capt. Samuel Swann of Surry and Thomas Moore.
  D.  March 30, 1678.  R.  June 9, 1679.
    Wit:  James Largie, Isabel Largie.  Page 195

BECHINOE, Edward:  Leg. wife Mary; son George; Richard Walton (?).  D.  April
  15, 1679.  R.  June 9, 1679.
    Wit:  William Best, Joseph Ford.  Page 196

CORSEY, Richard:  Appraisal by George Branch, Thomas Culley, John Gutridge, Jr.,
  John Collins.  Ordered May 16, 1679.  R.  May --, 1679.  Page 197

REIDINGS, Richard:  Appraisal by Humphry Marshall, Roger Wildes, John Weston,
  Edward Reyley.  Presented by John Watts and Richard Silvester.
  R.  January 14, 1678.  Page 198

BARTLETT, Robert:  Inventory presented by Tobias Kibble.  June 9, 1679.
  Page 198

JENNINGS, John:  Inventory presented by Mary Alley, late wife to said Jennings.
  D.  June 3, 1679.  R.  June 9, 1679.  Page 199

BARLOW, Thomas:  Appraisal by Richard Piland, John Britt, John Williams,
  Edward Grantham.  Presented by Mrs. Elizabeth Baldwin.  D.  May 3, 1679.
  R.  June 9, 1679.  Page 200

WICKINS, Capt. Edmund:  Appraisal by George Bechinoe, Richard Piland, Richard
  Wotten, William Baldwin.  D.  May 8, 1679.  R.  June 9, 1679. Page 201

CRIPPS, Joyce:  Leg. husband George Cripps the lands and tenements given me
  by my former husband, Francis England; to the son of Francis England's
  brother, if he comes to Virginia and makes claim to the said land within
  seven years; my sister Skinner; Nicholas Davis the plantation on which
  he lives; Sarah Lupo; Mr. George Branch's three children, Francis, John
  and Ann; orphan boy that liveth with me, named Anthony Lewis; Margaret
  wife of Peter Vasser; Susan Braswell, my sister's daughter; my three
  Goddaughters, Elizabeth Hayes, Joyce Butler and Joyce Womble; my three
  Godsons, James Bennett, Nicholas Davis and William Phillips; my mother
  Flake.  My husband Ex.  D.  April 18, 1679.  R.  June 9, 1679.
    Wit:  John Gutridge, Rebecca Davis, Will Evans.  Page 202

DANIELL, John:  Planter.  Leg. wife Elizabeth, son Thomas; son William.
  Wife Extx.  D.  March 30, 1679.  R.  July 17, 1679.
    Wit:  Phillip Thomas, Richard Reynolds.  Page 203

CORSEY, Richard:  Estate settled by Thomas Alley, John Gutridge, and John
  Collins; paid Capt. Applewhaite, attorney of Capt. Thomas Groves;
  paid Major James Powell, to be accountable to the orphan when he becomes

of age. Court held at the home of Mrs. Bromfield. R. September 19, 1679. Page 204

BURNETT, Robert: Leg. daughter Ann, 100 A. in Lower Parish, adjoining Pharoah Cobb, the said land being now in the possession of my Mother; also the plantation that my brother William Mayo lives on. Wife Extx. Overseers: my brothers, Mr. Arthur Allen and Mr. John Bromfield. D. ----------- R. July 17, 1679.
    Wit: William Mayo, Roger Jones. Page 206

LINSEY, Ann: Leg. daughter Mary a heiffer to be purchased of Mathew ffones; Henry Wheeler's son John; son John; daughter Mary to be placed in the care of Elizabeth Baker of Surry; daughter Ann in care of Mrs. Mary Hardy; my four children. George Hardy, Sr. Ex. D. April 22, 1679. R. November 10, 1679.
    Wit: William Smith, Henry Wheeler. Page 207

DAVIS, Nicholas: Appraisal by George Branch, Jr., Frances Poiner (?), Edward Poynter. Ordered April 9, 1680. R. June 9, 1680. Page 209

FLY, William: Appraisal by Boaz Gynn, Roger Davis, Ralph ----------. D. January --, 1679. Page 209

ALLEN, George: Appraisal by Richard Wilkinson, John Whitley, John Turner. Presented by Prudence Allen the widow. D. February 6, 1679. R. April 9, 1680. Page 210

DANIELL, John: Division of his estate made by Richard Sharpe, Pharoah Cobb, Owen Griffin. D. May 15, 1680. Page 211

HOWELL, John: Appraisal taken by John Newitt and John Warner. D. July 22, 1680. Page 211

ELLMS, Thomas: Leg. son Thomas; son John, land adjoining William Lewer and John Jennings; daughter Sarah; wife. Overseers: friends Charles Edwards and Capt. John Gutrich. D. Sept. 1, 1680. R. October 9, 1680.
    Wit: Edward Miller, Thomas Ryall, Nicholas Ogbourne. Page 213

NEWMAN, William: Nuncupative, proven by James Riddick, age 50 years and John Dunford, age 34 years. Leg. debts to be paid to Mr. Timothy Walker and Doctor Taylor, a mare he owned at Mr. Thomas Taberers to be given Mr. Henry Baker to whom he was indebted. R. October 9, 1680. Page 213

MACOANE, Neall: Leg. wife Ann and my children; Godson Thomas Armer, son of William Armer; daughter Mary Hawkins. Friends, William Frissell and Clement Craswell to divide estate. D. ---------- R. December 9, 1680.
    Wit: William Frissell, Thomas Hawkins. Page 214

BENNETT, Ambrose: Leg. Wife Elizabeth; unborn child; reversion to Mary Beale, daughter of Benjamin Beale; Alice Blackit; Martha Rutter, daughter of Walter Rutter; Isacke Williams. Wife Extx. Overseers: Col. Arthur Smith and Richard Reynolds, Sr. D. August 30, 1680. R. December 9, 1680.
    Wit: Walter Rutter, Christopher Wade. Page 214

MATTLAND (indexed Macland), Daniel: Leg. son Daniel; daughter Mary; daughter Anne; wife Elizabeth. Overseers: cousin John Mattland and friend Joseph Ford. D. June --, 1680. R. February 9, 1680.
    Wit: Margaret Briggs, Richard Gray. Page 215

BRIGGS, Richard: Appraisal by George Moore, Robert Kae Sr., William Evans. Presented by Samuel Swann and Thomas Moore. R. March 9, 1680.
Page 216

WAIKLEY, Mathew: Nuncupative, proven by Owen Griffin and Alexander Mathews. Leg. Henry King's son; John Davis, son of Roger Davis. Estate to be divided between Henry King and his son. R. March 9, 1680. Page 217

EDWARDS, Robert: Inventory presented by Mary Edwards. May 2, 1681.
Page 217

PHILLIPS, William, of Blackwater: Inventory presented by Mary Phillips. R. June 9, 1681. Page 217

RENNOLLS, Henry: Leg. wife Joyce; children Henry and Sarah. Debts to Robert Kae to be paid. D. April 6, 1679. R. June 9, 1681.
Wit: Mathew Foanes, Henry Wheeler, Robert Kae. Page 218

MACKELAND, Daniell: Account presented by Joseph Ford for the use of Mary Mackeland. R. August 9, 1681. Page 218

BETTELL, Robert: Leg. wife and children. Overseers: John Collins and John Story. D. January 12, 1679. R. October 10, 1681.
Wit: Edmund Barker, John Story. Page 219

PHILLIPS, William: Appraisal by Edward Poynter, John Gutridge, Jr., George Cripps, Thomas Smith. D. July 1, 1681. Page 219

RENNELS, Henry: Appraisal by George Hardy, Roger Archer, Robert Kae, Sr. Presented by Joyce Page alias Rennells. D. June 9, 1681. Page 219

BATEMAN, William: Nuncupative, proven by Elizabeth Goldwin, age 31 years, sayeth said Bateman being at the house of the deponent's sister, declared his brother and sister were unhuman to him ---- whole estate to him or her at whose house he should decease etc. Further proof by Thomas Hutchins, age 24 years; that said Bateman was at the house of Mr. Thomas Giles etc. Deposition of Richard Read, age 27 years and of John Brown, age 44 years.
    Probate is therefore granted Mr. Thomas Gyles on the said William Bateman's estate. R. October 11, 1681. Page 220

BITTLE, Robert: Inventory presented by Sissely Toule of her former husband's estate. D. April 29, 1681. Page 221

RUTT, Abraham: Appraisal by William Baldwin, Edward Grantham, John Duck. Ordered November 9, 1681. Page 221

BITTLE, Robert: Account of the part of his estate which belongs to his son John, presented by John Rosser. R. December 9, 1681. Page 221

WOODWARD, Thomas: Additional inventory of his estate, presented by John Giles and Philarita his wife. R. December 9, 1681. Page 222

JACOBS, John: Inventory presented by Thomas Wood. R. January 9, 1681/2.
Page 222

STORY, John: Of Upper Parish. Leg. son John in care of Richard Piland; son Thomas to William Hichens; son William to my wife Judith. Overseers: my neighbor Will Evans and Richard Piland. D. December 3, 1681.
R. January 9, 1681/2.
    Wit: Thomas Edwards, John Collins, George Moore. Page 222

MATHEWS, Anthony: Leg. John Moore, the eldest son of Ann Mathews, my now
wife the land adjoining Edward Hale; James Bacon the plantation whereon
I live after the death of his mother, my new wife. Wife Extx. D. May 6,
1681. R. January 9, 1681/2.
    Wit: William Dodd, Robert Kae, Sr., Elizabeth Voater (?).
                                                        Page 224

STORY, John: Appraisal by Thomas Moore, John Williams, John Gutridge, Jr.
    D. January 9, 1681. R. January 21, 1681/2.            Page 224

BROMFIELD, John: Appraisal by Robert Coleman, Thomas Giles, Ambrose Bennett,
    Richard Reynolds. No dates.                           Page 225

WOODWARD, Thomas, Sr.: Division of his estate by Thomas Green, James Tullaugh,
    Daniel Long and Richard Wilkinson. Mrs. Katherine Woodward's part; the
    children's part; Mrs. Philarita Giles' part and Thomas Woodward's.
    D. December 9, 1681. R. December 15, 1681.            Page 226

HILL, Lt. Col. Nicholas: Appraisal by William Webb, William Hutchins, John
    Davis, John Munger. D. October 9, 1679. R. May 1, 1682.    Page 227

EDWARDS, Peter: Leg. daughter Jeane my cattle, after Mr. Richard Lovegrove
    hath his share; John Coggan. I desire that my daughter may live with
    Mr. John Moore of Scotland in the western branch of the Nansemond.
    Daughter now six years old. At decease of John Moore and his wife,
    my child to return to John Coggan and his wife. Overseers: Richard
    Lovegrove and John Coggan. D. ---------- R. May 1, 1682.
    Wit: John Moore, Thomas Underwood.                     Page 227

POOLE, Thomas: Age about 60 years. Leg. grandchild Poole Hawle; 100 A. where
    John Hawle lives to my grandchild John Hawle; daughter Christain Hawle.
    Wife Christain Extx. September 12, 1681. R. June 9, 1682.
        Mary Jeruise, age 40 years, declared this to be the will of Thomas
    Poole. Susanna Calloway, age 40 years, sayeth the same; - that Thomas
    Poole requested John Frizzell to bring the will which he made three or
    more years ago. He took it and made another, which is the same will
    now presented in Court. R. June 9, 1682.              Page 229

YARRETT, William: Leg. grandchild Henry Wiggs the younger; daughter Elizabeth
    Murry; daughter Margaret the land adjoining William Bressie; daughter
    Elizabeth the land adjoining John Murry's land. Thomas Taberer Ex.
    Trustees, Thomas Cooke and Francis Renn. D. March 9, 1679. R. August 9,
    1682.
        Inserted at the bottom of the will: - It was further declared by
    my deceased father that my brother John Murry should have certain things
    to which I agree; also a bequest to William the son of John Richards.
    R. July 8, 1682.
        Wit: Edmund Prime, Francis Wrenn.                  Page 229

EDWARDS, Peter: Appraisal by William Scott, Robert Couger, Robert Lawrence,
    Francis Hutchins. D. July 27, 1682.                   Page 230

GOLBURNE, Martin: Estate sold at outcry. Signed by Will Evans. D. July 6,
    1682.                                                  Page 231

BRIGGS, Margaret: Of Upper Parish, widow. Leg. granddaughter Ruth Browne,
    to be paid my son-in-law William Browne her father; son Josias Wood;
    daughter Margaret Wood. Friend Joseph Ford Ex. D. November 16, 1682.
    R. December 9, 1682.
        Wit: William Browne, Robert Caufield.
    Appraisal of estate by John Shelton, Richard Piland, Thomas Wood, Richard
    Wootten. Signed Joseph Ford. D. 14th day of 10th mo. 1682. R. May 1,
    1683.                                                  Page 232

BARNES, Thomas:  Leg. son John; son James; daughter Ann; wife Diana.
   D. ---------  R.  June 9, 1683.
      Wit:  John Jones, Ambrose Hadley.                    Page 233

BODDIE, William:  Leg. daughter Mary Browne the plantation upon which she
   now lives, between the land of Edmund Windum and John Champion; Mary
   Browne's four children.  D. 8th day of 7th mo. 1683.  R.  August 9, 1683.
      Wit:  William Graves (?), James Bragg, Elizabeth Roberts.
                                                          Page 234

ASKEW, John:  Appraisal by John Nevill, Christopher Ward, Hopkins Howell.
   August 23, 1683.  September 10, 1683.                  Page 234

CRESWELL, Clement:  Leg. son John Whitfield, legacy which Margery Herring
   left him; son John, I do give to William Armor until he is 21 years old,
   if said Armor does not use him kindly, Thomas Hawkins shall keep him.
   Said John was seventeen years old in April 1683; son Clement to live
   with Thomas Hawkins, he now being 15 years old in April 1683; daughter
   Jennet Macon.  Wife Ann Extx.  D.  March 12, 1682.  R.  November 9, 1683.
      Wit:  Thomas Hawkins, John Frizzell.                Page 235

GARDNER, John:  Appraisal by Thomas Giles, Richard Lewis, William Godwin,
   John Nevill.  D.  February 21, 1683/4.  R.  March 14, 1683.  Page 236

WILSON, James:  Appraisal by John Clay and Roger Archer.  Presented by John
   Wilson.  D.  March 3, 1683/4.  R.  March 9, 1683/4.     Page 236

ROGERS, Edward:  Leg. Anne Mathews; John Moore and James Bacon to whom I
   give 900 A. in Stafford County at the head of Potomake Creek, on which
   Joseph Henson lives, also all property in Isle of Wight County.
   D.  September 13, 1683.  R.  March 9, 1683/4.
      Wit:  John Jones, Thomas Mason.                     Page 237

LOE, Thomas:  Leg. Mary Long; Lydia Silvester; Adam Murry, Olive and Prudence
   Pitt.  Lt. Col. John Pitt Ex.  D.  January 19, 1683.  R.  March 10, 1683.
      Wit:  Lawrence Story, James Carver, John Pitt.      Page 237

CLAY, William:  Appraisal by John Guteridge, Thomas Moore, Will Evans.
   R.  March 10, 1683/4.
      Account of the estate of William Clay of Lawnes Creek.  D. 1675.
   Given by William Clay's will and delivered by his widow. ---------Given
   by Mr. John Clay's will to Elizabeth the daughter of said William.  I
   certify that the above particulars were the proper estate of the aforenamed
   William Clay at his death in the year 1675, part whereof being in his
   possession and the residue delivered at his death to Judith the relict
   of said William Clay, by the subscriber as relict and Extx. of the last
   will and testament of his father, Mr. John Clay.  Signed, Mary Archer.
   D.  February 9, 1683/4.                                Page 238

RICHARDS, Ann:  Leg. husband, to my daughter my land; reversion to grandson
   Robert Bevan; reversion to Maddison Street; tobacco which Robert Bevan's father
   left him to be put into the custody of John Street.  Personal estate to be
   divided between John Strre, William Lowder and Robert Bevan.  D.  November 25,
   1683.  R.  April 9, 1684.
      Wit:  Adam Murrey, Richard Turner.                  Page 238

LOCKHART, John:  Leg. Ellinor Lewis.  Exs. friends, James Tullaugh and Robert
   Scott.  D.  March 7, 1681.  R.  March 10, 1683.
      Wit:  James Hunter.                                 Page 239
   Daniel Griggs, age 43 years claimed said Lockhart was indebted to him,
   etc.  R.  April 9, 1684.

WOODWARD, Katherine: Leg. children, Katherine, Elizabeth, Mary, John and
Rachell; daughter Philarita Giles and her son, which is not yet
christened. D. April 17, 1684. R. June 9, 1684.
Wit: John Giles, Nicholas Fulgham. Page 239

ROGERS, Edward: Estate appraised by Owen Griffin, Ambrose Hadlie and Alex.
Mathews. September 9, 1684. Page 239(?)

BOND, Dorothy: son John; grandson William Watson to live with Richard Sharpe;
son William. Friends, Richard Sharpe and George Bell, trustees.
D. July 10, 1684. R. October 9, 1684.
Wit: William Blunt, Nicholas Cobb. Page 239

LOCKHART, John: Appraisal by Thomas Pitt and Joseph Woory of his estate at
the house of Col. Joseph Bridger and at the house of John Frizzell.
D. September 12, 1684. Page 242

BRIDGER, Joseph: recording his disinheritance of his son Joseph; land in
Maryland and Virginia to his sons Samuel and William. R. April 9, 1685.
Page 242

WARD (?), Jane: Of Lower Parish. Leg. son-in-law Thomas Ward. D. March 26,
1681. R. April 9, 1685.
Wit: John Pitt, Nicholas Fulgham. Page 243

BOND, Dorothy: Division of estate made by Mr. Owen Griffin, Nicholas Cobb
and John Portis. Page 244

LEWIS, William: Leg. eldest daughter Mary; second daughter Sarah; wife
Martha. Ex., Robert Thomas. Children's guardians, Robert Thomas and
William Evans. D. --- 10, 1684. R. May 1, 1685.
Wit: Robert Brock, Mary Bamber. Page 245

WRENN, Francis: Appraisal by John Carroll, Timothy Fenn, William Hutchins,
John Lewis. D. February 14, 1684. R. May 16, 1685. Page 245

EDWARDS, Robert: Appraisal by John Portis, Alexander Mathews, Thomas Parnell.
R. July 9, 1685. Page 245

CLAY, John: Appraisal by George Hardy, Sr., Thomas Wood, Richard Hansford,
John Greenwood. D. May 16, 1685. R. August 10, 1685. Page 246

HUTCHINGS, William: Leg. Judith Roberson; wife Elizabeth. Wife Extx.
D. March 20, 1684. R. December 9, 1685.
Wit: John Gutridge, John Lewis. Page 247

BURNELL, John: Leg. son John; Eles Shepley, the wife of Jonathan Shepley,
money in the hands of Mr. Couley; daughter Susanna Couley. Giles
Limscott to be paid 200 pounds of tobacco for my funeral. Exs., Mr.
Joseph Woory, Col. Arthur Smith, James Tullaugh. D. October 20, 1685.
R. December 9, 1685.
Wit: Ann Tullaugh, Richard Reynolds, Isabell Williams. Page 247

PARKER, Thomas: Age 56. Leg. eldest son John, land on Hugh's Island; son
Thomas; son Francis; son George; daughter Elizabeth; daughter Mary;
daughter Ann. Wife Extx. D. November 16, 1685. R. February 9, 1685.
Wit: Robert King, Sr., Robert King, Jr., Garrett Altman.
Page 247

RICHARDSON, William: Of Upper Parish. Leg. Katherine my now wife one-half
of my land; other half to Mary Wisse to educate her daughter Elizabeth;
reversion to my brother John Richardson. Exs., Thomas Atkinson, Peter
Hayes. D. October 21, 1680. R. February 9, 1685.
Wit: Henry Goldham, George Cripps, P. Wall. Page 248

24

COBB, Nicholas: Nuncupative, proven by William Blunt, age 60 years and
Richard Bell and his wife Sarah Bell. Leg. son Nicholas; son Edward;
daughter Mary; daughter Sarah. R. May 8, 1686.                    Page 249

BRIDGER, Joseph: Leg. wife Hester; son Samuel land bought of John and William
Gatlin, whereon John Cooke now lives, also one-half of plantation at
Curawoak; son William land granted me by escheat of 850 A. formerly
belonging to Nathan Floyd, except what is disposed of by me to Francis
Hobbs, Mrs. Dorothy Bond and William Blunt, also two tracts taken up by
Col. Pitt, Mr. William Burgh and myself containing 3000 A., except 600
A. sold to Lt. Col. John Pitt, part of this tract leased by me to
Thomas Mandue, Richard Parker, William Worrell, Richard Jones, Thomas
Reeves, Robert Sturdy and others, also tract leased to Christopher
Wade; to my wife the land on which I now dwell of 850 A. formerly
belonging to Capt. Upton and 300 A. formerly belonging to Mr. Seward
on which Mr. Izard, Ould Phillips and William Lewis lived, reversion
to son Joseph with half of the tract at Curawoak and a tract at Monokin;
Daughters, Martha Godwin, Mary, Elizabeth and Hester; my mother, Mrs.
Mary Bridger. Wife Extx., with the assistance of Lt. Col. John Pitt,
Thomas Pitt and Col. Arthur Smith. D. August 3, 1683.
        Revocation of all bequests to son Joseph. October 18, 1683.
        Wit: James Bennett, Robert Pitt, Samuel Luck, Richard Glover.
R. April 9, 1685.                                                Page 250

GREEN, Thomas: Leg. son Thomas the plantation at Red Point; wife Mary; son
George 250 A. commonly called Poplar Neck, now in the occupation of
William Sackworth; son John; son William; aforesaid sons 300 A. now in
the possession of John Bunkley, adjoining land of Thomas Poole and James
Bagnall; the mill I purchased of Col. Bacon to my wife; daughter Mary
Davis. Personal estate to be divided between William, Prudence, Sarah,
Bridgett, Elizabeth, John Green and wife Mary. Exs., wife and son George.
D. October 22, 1685. R. June 9, 1686.
        Wit: John Pitt, Nicholas Fulgham, Thomas Bevan.          Page 252

        Appraisal of estate, presented by Mrs. Mary Green, by Richard Wilkinson,
James Tullaugh, Daniell Long, Thomas Ward. R. June 19, 1686.
                                                                 Page 253

CLARKE, Margaret: Leg. son William land given me by my father William Yarrett.
D. August 9, 1686.
        Wit: Thomas Moore, Robert Scott. Acknowledged in court by
        Margaret Clarke, August 9, 1686.                        Page 253

MacQUINAY, Michael: Of Western Branch, Planter. Leg. Wife Elizabeth;
youngest son Barnabie; eldest son John. Wife Extx. D. April 15, 1686.
R. August 9, 1686.
        Wit: Robert Cooper, Mary Daniel, Jeremiah Exum, John Moore.
                                                                 Page 254

Received of Mrs. Hester Bridger, Extx. of Col. Joseph Bridger, legacy left
my wife Martha. Signed Thomas Godwin.
        Wit: John Pitt, Arthur Smith. July 16, 1686.
Same acknowledgment to wife Mary. Signed Richard Tibbott.
        Wit: John Pitt, Arthur Smith. July 16, 1686.
Same acknowledgment to wife Elizabeth. Signed Thomas Lear.
        Wit: Arthur Smith, Thomas Godwin. August 4, 1686.       Page 254

BRIDGER, Col. Joseph: Appraisal by James Powell, Arthur Smith, Henry Applewhaite, Henry Baker. June 28, 1686.                              Page 255

WATSON, John: Division of estate between his orphans, John, Mary and
William Watson. R. Sept. 27, 1686.                              Page 262

PERKINS, Edward: Leg. William Murphy, Sr., reversion to his son William, if he pay John Lawrence and John Jordan; James Tynes the son of Nicholas Tynes; Margaret Murphy, daughter of William Murphy. Ex., William Murphy, Sr. D. August 22, 1686. R. December 9, 1686.
    Wit: Thomas Davis, Thomas Oglethorphe, John Wilkinson.   Page 264

TOMLIN, Mathew: Leg. John Turner; Mary Turner, my grandchild; son Mathew the plantation whereon Richard Braswell lives; grandson Mathew Tomlin land adjoining John Fulgham. Ex., son Mathew. D. March 7, 1684. R. December 9, 1686.
    Wit: Richard Sharpe, Jenkins Dorman.           Page 264

WOOTEN, Richard: Leg. son Richard; son Thomas the plantation on which Francis Floid lives; wife and three children. Overseer: Henry Baker. D. September 28, 1686. R. March 9, 1686/7.
    Wit: Thomas Wood, George Groves.         Page 265

RATCLIFFE, Richard: Leg. son Richard; son Cornelius; son John; daughters, Elizabeth, Sarah, Mary and Rebecca Ratcliffe. Wife Elizabeth Extx. Overseers: John Copeland, Daniel Sandburne, William Oudeland, Edmond Belson. D. September 6, 1686. R. March 9, 1686/7.
    Acknowledged by Richard Ratcliffe, himself in open Court.
                                          Page 265

WOOTEN, Richard: Appraisal by George Bechinoe, Richard Piland. R. May 2, 1687.                                    Page 266

MADDIN, Henry: Inventory presented by John Whitley. D. March 30, 1687. R. May 2, 1687.                            Page 266

WILLIAMS, John: Leg. son Thomas; daughter Elizabeth; son John; daughter Anne; daughter Sarah; Charles Durham. Wife Extx. D. February 7, 1686. R. May 2, 1687.
    Wit: Will Bradshaw, Charles Durham.         Page 267

HOWELL, Hopkins: Leg. wife Mary; son Hopkins the land formerly belonging to my brother Thomas Howell; daughter Mary; reversion to my brother's eldest son Thomas Howell; John Hale, Jr.; John Howell. D. March 9, 1686. R. May 2, 1687.
    Wit: Edmond Godwin, Robert Merser, Elizabeth Merser, Bridget Askque.                         Page 267

ELMS, Thomas: Appraisal by John Davis, Will Webb, Richard Beighton, John Mecar (?). D. February 9, 1680. R. June 17, 1687.    Page 267

SHEWGAR, Margaret: Inventory presented by John Grisswood. D. June 9, 1687. R. June 17, 1687.                        Page 268

ASKEW, William: Inventory presented by Anthony Power. D. June 9, 1687.
                                        Page 268

BLUNT, William: Inventory presented by Edward Cobb, who married his relict. R. July 9, 1687.                          Page '269

HOWELL, Hopkins: Inventory presented by Mary Howell. D. July 23, 1687. R. August 13, 1687.                      Page 269

MATHEWS, Ralph: Nuncupative, proven by Boaz Gwin and Robert Brock. Leg. wife and three children. Overseer: Col. Smith or his son Arthur. R. August 13, 1687.                         Page 269

WILLIAMS, John: Appraisal by John Dun, John Frissell, Tobias Keeble. D. August 20, 1687.                        Page 270

BECHINOE, George: Leg. wife Mary; Mary, Susanna and Edward Bechinoe; unborn child; my son. D. June 10, 1687. R. October 10, 1687.
Wit: Ralph Shurley, Robert Kae. Page 270

WILLIAMS, David: Leg. eldest son John; son David; daughter Hester, heiffer given her by George May; wife Sarah. William Frizzell, Sr. and Thomas Hawkins to look after the boys' schooling. D. September 28, 1686. R. October 10, 1687.
Wit: Thomas Hawkins, Henry Best. Page 270

BATHE, Katherine: Nuncupative, proven by Arthur Smith, age 49 years, Henry Clarke and John Watson. Leg. son-in-law Stephen Horsefield, his wife and children; son Arthur Whitehead, whom she declared was unnatural to her. R. October 11, 1687. Page 271

COLLINS, William: Appraisal presented by Nicholas Smith, by William Smith, Robert King, John Weston. D. October 21, 1687. R. -----------, 1687.
Page 271

HODGES, Robert: Appraisal by John Goodrich, Timothy Fenn, William Webb. D. November 9, 1687. Page 272

MACKDOWELL, James: Leg. daughter Olive, cattle at George Norsworthy's to be used for her schooling; wife Mary. Wife, Extx. Lt. Col. Pitt and Tristram Norsworthy, trustees. D. January 27, 1686. R. December 10, 1687.
Wit: John Pitt, Thomas Norsworthy. Page 272

POWELL, Thomas: Leg. Thomas, Nathaniel, William and John Powell; son William; daughter-in-law Elizabeth Powell; daughter-in-law Lucretia Corbett; Lucretia, John, Roberta and Elizabeth Powell. Son William Ex. D. July 12, 1683. R. February 9, 1687/8.
Wit: Thomas Griffen, Francis Hutchins. Page 272

WADE, Christopher: Inventory presented by Arthur Whitehead. R. February 9, 1687/8. Page 273

BOND, John: Leg. William Manyard; William Watson; son John; Joyce Farnum to live with my two children; reversion of bequest to son John to afore-mentioned Manyard and Watson. Ex., John Bell my wife's brother. D. February 15, 1687. R. April 9, 1688.
Wit: Edmond Prime, John Portis, Rueben Gladhill, Thomas Dorrell.
Page 274

THORNTON, John: Leg. son William; daughter Ellinor; wife Willmuth, at her decease to her two sons, Richard and Robert Sims (?). D. April 3, 1687. R. May 1, 1688.
Wit: John Cogan, Jr., Thomas Gale. Page 274

BECHINOE, Edward: Inventory presented by Mary Bechinoe, widow. Later items, signed Mary Grove. D. February 9, 1687/8. R. May 1, 1688. Page 275

WOMBWELL, Thomas: Leg. son Thomas (not 17); son John; daughter Joyce; daughter Margaret; wife Elizabeth. Overseers: friends Thomas Taberer and John Murry. D. March 3, 1687. R. May 1, 1688.
Wit: Richard Beighton, John Person. Page 275

SHEEPHARD, John: Leg. wife Alice; son William; daughter Susannah; reversion to my brother Edward Holloway and his children; cousin Fortune Maget; at decease of wife son William to Robert Lacie of the Lower Parish of Surry County; daughter to Elizabeth Gainer of the Upper Parish of Isle of Wight. Overseers: Robert Lacie and John Barnes of the Lower Parish

of Surry, John Murry and Joseph Copeland of Upper Parish of Isle of Wight and Henry Wiggs of the Lower Parish of Isle of Wight. D. April 2, 1686. R. May 1, 1688.
    Wit: Thomas Proud, John Mory, John Grove, Nathaniel Eglome.
Page 275

HUNTER, James: Leg. wife Ann and her children. Capt. Thomas Goodwin, Marcy Lewis and John Lewis to be assistants to my wife. D. ----------
R. May 1, 1688.
    Wit: James Browne, Martin Luther.
Inventory presented by Ann Hunter. D. April 27, 1688.     Page 276

GRISSWOOD, John: Appraisal by George Hardy, Sr., Mathew Foanes. R. May 1, 1688.     Page 277

PARNELL, Thomas: Cooper. Leg. son Thomas the plantation bought of Mr. Francis Ayres and 150 A. of a patent adjoining John Richardson and Peter Hayes; son Joseph land bought of Edmond Palmer, adjoining upon Henry West, Anthony Mathews and Col. Smith, also tract at Curawaugh bought of Col. Arthur Smith; daughter Susannah; wife and three daughters; John Drake; sister Mary Williams; sister Jemima Drake; Joane Johnson; cousin John Williams; cousin Sarah Williams; Boaz Gwin; my man Thomas Williams his freedom. Overseers: John Fulgham, John Williams and Thomas Williams. D. October 10, 1687. R. June 9, 1688.
    Wit: Boaz Gwin, Thomas Williams, Robert Littleboy.     Page 278

MILES, Daniel: Leg. son John; son Edward; youngest son Daniel; Elizabeth Ebson. Wife Extx. D. March 1, 1687/8. R. June 9, 1688.
    Wit: Ralph Channell, William Frissell.     Page 278

MARSHALL, John: Leg. son Humphrey; youngest son; wife; daughter Mary. Overseers: brother Humphrey Marshall and Peter Best. D. October 4, 1687. R. June 9, 1688.
    Wit: Nicholas Casey and Edward Miles.     Page 279

MOORE, John: Of Lower Parish. Leg. wife Elizabeth; eldest son John; son William; son Thomas; daughters Ann and Elizabeth the land adjoining Thomas Parnell. Wife, Extx. D. March 18, 1686/7. R. June 9, 1688.
    Wit: John Sellers, Jenkins Dorman.     Page 279

HOBBS, Francis: Leg. Alice Davis; cousin John Davis; cousin Margaret Harris the daughter of John Harris. Ex., brother John Harris. D. March 4, 1687. R. June 9, 1688.
    Wit: John Davis, George Bell, Jr., Thomas Harris.     Page 280

WATSON, William: Nuncupative, proven by John Prime, age 22 years and John Portis age 29 years. Whole estate to brother John, since his sister was unnatural to him. R. June 9, 1688.     Page 280

HUNTER, James: Appraisal by William Pitt, John Lewis, Tobias Keeble.
R. June 6, 1688.     Page 280

HOLMES, Christopher: Appraisal by Robert King, Sr., Thomas Munsford, Peter Best. R. June 23, 1688.     Page 281

ATKINSON, Thomas: Leg. son William; son Peter; son Samuel; wife Susan; daughter Sarah; daughter Katherine; four sons. Wife Extx. D. January 19, 1687/8. R. June 9, 1688.
    Wit: Richard Holleman, John Atkinson, William Gwaltney, Mary Parnell.     Page 281

CRIPPS, George: Leg. servant man Henry Luter, land adjoining George Hardy

and Francis Rayner; Edward the son of George Bechinoe and his wife Mary; Elizabeth Gutridge the daughter of Capt. John Guteridge and Anne his wife, reversion to her two sisters, Honor and Constance. Wife Mary Extx. Suit to dropped against Mr. George Moore. Overseers: Capt. John Gutheridge and William Evans. D. August 31, 1687. R. October 10, 1687.
    Wit: Francis Taylor, Edmond Palmer, James Y-----, Anne Miles, Anne Palmer, Will Evans.         Page 281

DOLES, Thomas: Appraisal by John Sherrer, Anthony Crocker, John Britt. Presented by Mrs. Mary Doles. Ordered June 4, 1688.     Page 282

PITT, Thomas: Leg. wife Mary; son Thomas; son Henry; daughters, Martha, Mary, Elizabeth, Anne and Patience. Wife Extx. Codicil: to Thomas and Francis Gross, 130 A. where they now live, part of Spark's patent; to Michael Fulgham, 50 A. part of same patent. D. April 21, 1687. R. February 21, 1687/8.
    Wit: Luke Havield, Anthony Holladay.     Page 283

LARAMORE, Roger: Inventory presented by Walter and Alice Walters. D. April 2, 1687.     Page 284

PARNELL, Thomas: Inventory presented February 26, 1688.     Page 284

BRANCH, George: Appraisal taken in the presence of George Branch, James Lupo, Francis Branch, John Branch and Ann Branch. D. May 18, 1688.
    Page 285

HARRIS, Thomas: Leg. son Edward; son John; son Thomas; son Robert; daughter Jane Jones; daughter Ann; son Robert to live with John Fulgham; son George with John Turner; son Martin with his brother; son William with Bridgman Joyner; daughter Ann with Mrs. Ann Sharpe; three grandchildren. Exs., son Edward, John Fulgham and John Turner. D. March 14, 1687/8. R. October 9, 1688.
    Wit: John Sherrer, John Coggan.     Page 286

PARNELL, Thomas: Appraisal by Peter Vasser, John Sherrer, John Sojernor. August 17, 1688.     Page 287

CALLAWAY, Richard: Appraisal by James Benn and Daniel Long. August 8, 1688.
    Page 287

WILLIAMSON, Robert: Inventory presented by his brother George Williamson. (no dates given)     Page 287

SHAW, Mathew: Estate sold at outcry. March 1, 1687/8.     Page 288

HOLE, John: Appraisal by Richard Sharpe, Owen Griffen, Boaz Gwin. D. November 26, 1688. R. December 10, 1688.     Page 288

KAE, Robert: the elder of Upper Parish. Leg. my four grandchildren, the daughters of Timothy Fenn and his wife Elizabeth. Son Robert, Ex. D. November 17, 1688. R. December 10, 1688.
    Wit: Sarah Griswood, Will Evans.     Page 289

BRANTLEY, Edward Sr.: Leg. son Edward and his son James 165 A. of land; son Phillip and his son Edward; son John and his son John; daughter Mary; to my sons' eldest sons. Daughter Mary Extx. D. March 30, 1688. R. January 9, 1688/9.
    Wit: John Whetstone, Anne White, Will Evans.     Page 289

SAMPSON, James: Leg. daughter Margaret, the wife of Nicholas Wilson; Mr. George Moore and his wife; son James; daughter Clarke; John Browne.

William Evans, Ex.
Codicil:  deceased wife requested me to take notice that she did leave her two daughters Margaret and Elizabeth 300 A. apiece.
D.  February 4, 1688/9.  R.  April 9, 1689.
Wit:  John Whetstone, Henry White.                    Page 291

OGLETHORPE, Thomas:  Leg. daughters, Katherine, Sarah and Margaret; reversion to Richard Thomas and his eldest son.  Overseers: Simon and John Everett.  Exs., my two youngest daughters.  D.  March 31, 1687.  R.  February 9, 1687/8.
Wit:  Richard Thomas, Godfrey Hunt, Ralph Pee.       Page 292

LINNSCOTT, Giles:  Nuncupative, proven by John Goodrich, age 37 years, by Thomas Elmes, age 20 years; by Roger Ingram, age 32 years.  Leg. Robert Fenn; his brother to have nothing.  D.  February 18, 1688.  R.  April 9, 1689.                                                     Page 292

BLUNT, Richard:  Estate sold at outcry by order of the Court.  R.  June 4, 1688.                                                     Page 293

FENN, Timothy:  Appraisal by John Goodrich, John Davis, Thomas Thropp, Charles Edwards.  D.  10th of Xber, 1688.  R.  May 7, 1689.  Page 293

EVANS, William:  Leg. son Thomas all my land at Kingsale; son Robert; wife and children.  Wife Extx.  Her father, Mr. Robert Flake my overseer.
D.  July 12, 1689.  R.  August 9, 1689.
Wit:  Henry Baker, Thomas Moore, Robert Flake.       Page 294

LUGGE, Peter:  Nuncupative, proven by Thomas Boulger, Francis Smith.  Leg. two daughters, son Peter.  R.  August 9, 1689.           Page 294

OGLETHORPE, Thomas:  Inventory presented by John Askew.  R.  October 9, 1688.
                                                     Page 295

EVANS, William:  Appraisal by Thomas Moore, John Goodrich, Edward Champion, William Baldwin.                                         Page 295

PITT, Thomas:  Appraisal by Henry Applewhaite, Anthony Holladay, Thomas Giles, Richard Wilkinson.  D.  July 22, 1689.               Page 296

POOLE, Richard:  Of Upper Parish.  Leg. daughter Elizabeth; daughter Ellianor; daughter-in-law Jane Grosse.  Wife Jane, Extx.  Overseers:  Col. James Powell and Will Evans.  D.  June 17, 1689.  R.  October 9, 1689.
Wit:  Edward Mathews, Will Evans.                    Page 297

CULLEN, Thomas:  Appraisal taken by William Mayo, William Smealy, William Murphy, Francis Bridle.  Robert Lawrence and Jeremiah Exum presented the account of the estate.  R.  October 23, 1689.       Page 298

WHITAKER, John:  Nuncupative, proven by Mary Collins, age 50 years, by James Briggs, age 21 years, by John Riggs.  Leg. the child of Peter Fiveash, to whom he was Godfather, one-half of his estate; the other half to be divided between the people who looked after him.  R.  January 9, 1689.
                                                     Page 300

WEBSTER, Alexander:  Nuncupative, proven by George Bell Sr., John Crue, age 30 years, and John Shearer.  Leg. George Bell, Jr.; John Harris; Hannah Brown the daughter of John Brown.  R.  November 1, 1688.  Page 300

WESTON, John:  Leg. wife Anne and my children.  D.  December 25, 1684.
R.  April 9, 1690.
Wit:  Robert King, Sr., William Collins.             Page 300

RICHARDSON, John: Leg. wife Phillis; son William; son John; eldest daughter
    Phillis; Richard Loyd. Wife Extx. Overseers: Peter Vasser, Peter
    Hayes. D. ---------- R. April 9, 1690.
        Wit: Richard Loyd, Peter Hayes, Peter Vasser, Mary Branch.
                                                            Page 300

WILLIAMS, John: Leg. son John; son Richard; John Corsey to be maintained out
    of my estate for my proportion of the time William Exum and I were
    obliged to keep him; James Piland, my Godson; two sons the bequest made
    them by Mr. Snellock. Two sons, Exs. Overseers: Thomas Moore, Richard
    Piland and James Powell. D. March 1, 1689. R. April 9, 1690.
        Wit: Richard Piland, Margaret Lewis, John Jennings.    Page 301

SHEEPHARD, John: Appraisal by William Browne, William Baldwin, William
    Bamer. D. April 13, 1689.                                 Page 302

CHESTNUTT, Alexander: Appraisal by William West, John Nevill, William Godwin.
    R. May 20, 1690.                                          Page 302

MANNING, James: Account of estate, ---- among items, to Francis Floyd for
    looking after the man, his wife and children; estate to be divided
    into two parts. 1689.                                     Page 303

LINNSCOTT, Giles: Nuncupative, proven by Charles Edwards, age 49 years and
    Jane Edwards, age 49 years. Leg. his estate to his brother in England;
    brother Richard Pope not to inherit any of it. R. June 9, 1690.
                                                            Page 303

HORSEFIELD, Stephen: Appraisal by Edward Goodson, Robert Brock, Boaz Gwin.
    Ordered November 4, 1689.                                 Page 304

LEWIS, John: Leg. wife Ann; my wife's three children, William Macon,
    Mary Hawkins and Ann Surbe. D. August 8, 1690. Acknowledged in
    Court by John Lewis, August 9, 1690.                      Page 304

POOLE, Richard: Appraisal by William Clarke, John Carrell. Not dated.
                                                            Page 305

WILLIAMS, John: Inventory presented by John and Richard Williams. D. March 22,
    1689/90.                                                  Page 305

GORING, Ezekiel: Inventory of his estate and that of an orphan boy he kept
    named William Story. Signed Elianor Lucy. Not dated.      Page 306

CULLY, John: Appraisal by James Benn, Walter Rutter, Daniel Long.
    D. December 8, 1690. R. December 9, 1690.                 Page 306

WORGAR, Robert: Inventory presented by John Watkins. R. February 9, 1690/1.
                                                            Page 306

MANN, Thomas: Appraisal by William Duck, John Watkins, Robert Johnson.
    Not dated.                                                Page 307

FULGHAM, Michael: Leg. son Anthony; son Michael the plantation on which
    William Baldwin lives; wife Ann; daughter Sarah; daughter Marth;
    daughter Mary; daughter Ann; daughter Susanna; daughter Ruth. Wife
    Extx. Overseers: brothers Nicholas and John Fulgham. D. February 17,
    1690/1. R. March 9, 1690/1.
        Wit: William Baldwin, James Benn, Nicholas Fulgham.   Page 307

MAY, George: Nuncupative, proven by Anthony Power, age 34 years and William
    Jones, age 22 years. Leg. to Mary and Cuthbert ------; to William

Williams' youngest son; to one of Mallack's children.  R.  April 9,
1691.                                                        Page 307

GRAVE, John:  Leg. the obligation of Arthur Allen's to John Murry and Thomas
     Proud; money to repair our Meeting House on Levy Neck field; Elizabeth
     Murry; Susan Bressie; Samuel Newton; John Harris; Peter Grimes; John
     Lux; William Richards; John Murry's three sons, John, William and
     George; Sarah Miller; my sister's son Walter Potter; nephew Peter
     Grave; John Lewis.  A copy of my will to be sent to England.
     D.  10 day of 10 mo. 1689.  R.  June 9, 1691.
          Wit:  Thomas Taberer, John Carrell, Edward Miller, William Wilson,
                Thomas Proud.                                 Page 308

POPE, Thomas:  Leg. sons Robert and William land adjoining William Boddie;
     daughter Joyce; daughter Mary; son John; son Thomas; wife Joyce;
     George Goodwin.  Son Thomas Ex.  D.  September 27, 1684.  R.  August 10,
     1691.
          Wit:  Thomas Hawkins, John Powell.                  Page 308

FULGHAM, Michael:  Appraisal by John Clarke, James Tullaugh, Daniel Long.
     D.  July 26, 1691.                                       Page 309

HALLIMAN, Christopher:  Leg. son Thomas; son William; son Christopher; son
     Richard; daughter Anne Atkisson; daughter Mary Atkisson; wife Mary.
     Wife Extx.  D.  April 24, 1691.  R.  August 10, 1691.
          Wit:  John Tharpe, Thomas Ward, Charles Dennis.     Page 309

ILES, Frances:  Of Lower Parish.  Leg. daughter Judith Norsworthy what is
     due her from her deceased father's estate; son John Isles; son Tristram
     Norsworthy; daughter Frances Hodges and her eldest daughter, Frances
     Housden (?); daughter Elizabeth Bridger.  Son Tristram Norsworthy Ex.
     D.  May 15, 1691.  R.  August 10, 1691.
          Wit:  Thomas Hawkins, John Iles.                    Page 310

CHERRIEHOLME, Marmaduke:  Late of Virginia, now resident of Charles Towne in
     ye County of Middlesex in New England, Chirurgeon.  Leg. friend
     Bartholomew Greene of Charles Towne, mariner; my father Thomas
     Cherrieholme, late of Wakefield in the Kingdom of England, Apothecary.
     Ex., Bartholomew Greene.  D.  November 19, 1690.  R.  November 26, 1690.
          Wit:  Thomas Fosdick, Richard Young, Jacob Stevens, Mary Leman.
                                                              Page 311

PITT, Thomas:  Additional appraisal by Henry Applewhaite, Thomas Giles,
     Anthony Holladay, Richard Wilkinson.                     Page 311

BALDWIN, William:  Appraisal by John Clarke, James Benn, Daniel Long, James
     Tullaugh.  Not dated.                                    Page 312

BREAD, Richard:  Age 60 years.  Leg. whole estate to wife Ann and her heirs.
     D.  July 4, 1691.  R.  December 15, 1691.
          Wit:  James Riddick, Henry Baker.                   Page 313
     Appraisal of estate by John Goodrich, Sr. and William Browne.
                                                              Page 313

WHITAKER, John:  Inventory presented by J. Powell.  R. February 27, 1691/2.
                                                              Page 313

LEWIS, Richard:  Of the Lower Parish.  Leg. wife Sarah; son Richard the
     plantation on which William Duck lives, said Duck to take in tuition
     my son  Richard; son Thomas the land I have rented James Cullie, Mr.
     Thomas Giles to take my said son, if Mr. Giles should die then he may be
     free; daughter Ann, to be placed in the care of Mr. Bressie; daughter

32

Elizabeth in the care of Richard Reynolds and his wife Elizabeth; unborn
child. Overseers: Thomas Joyner, Jr. and Richard Reynolds, Jr.
D. December 13, 1691. R. March 26, 1692.
    Wit: Joshua Turner, Alexander Mathews, Hugh Bressie, Luke Kent.
                            Page 314

MOORE, John: Appraisal by Phillip Raiford and George Pierce. D. March 6,
1692.                                                    Page 315

SMELLY, William: Leg. son William my plantation at Curawaugh; son Robert;
son Lewis; son John; wife Ellianor. Wife Extx. D. August 5, 1689.
R. August 9, 1692.
    Wit: James Doughtie, John Brian, Robert Horning, Francis Bridle.
                            Page 316

ARMER, William: Leg. youngest son Robert; daughter Ann; son William; son
Thomas; daughter Mary; wife Mary. D. November 21, 1691. R. August 9,
1692.
    Wit: Thomas Hawkins, James Mackfaden.            Page 317

WILLIAMS, John Sr.: Leg. wife Anne; eldest son John land in Isle of Wight
unless he had rather stay in Surry County, where he is now seated;
son Theophilus; son William land in Newport Parish; son Thomas land
in Surry; son Nicholas land in Surry; son Richard land in Surry;
daughter Mary; daughter Jane; granddaughters, Anne, Bridget and Mary
Browne; my boy William Hickman; Daniel Long, Jr. Reference to cattle
at Thomas Wrights. Wife Extx. D. March 9, 1691/2. R. August 9, 1692.
    Wit: Boaz Gwin, Thomas Gaynie, Alexander Mathews.     Page 318

PITT, William: Appraisal by John Frissell, James Garner, John Dun.
D. May 13, 1692.                                Page 319

OGBOURN, Nicholas: Appraisal taken at the house of Ann Ogbourn by William
Webb, Thomas Thropp. D. October 15, 1692.          Page 319

LEWIS, John: Leg. Phillip Brantley and his five children; sister Joyce
Brantley; Phillip Pardoe; Elizabeth Pardoe; Sarah Dadway; my mother
Rebecca Pardoe. Mother, Extx. D. 1st of Xber 1692. R. December 9,
1692.
    Wit: Thomas Ranckhorne, Richard Piland, John Shelton.   Page 320

TETHER (?), George: Inventory recorded Xber 26, 1692.     Page 320

BECHINOE, George: Estate divided by George Moore and Henry Baker between
the orphans and George Groves. R. September 29, 1692.     Page 321

POWELL, James: Leg. sister Mary Heath; Nicholas Wilson; Margaret the wife
of Nicholas Wilson; Ann the daughter of Nicholas Wilson; James Wilson;
Godson James Baker; Ambrose Griswood; Capt. Richard Tibbott; Henry
Tooker; Henry Baker; Richard Stone. Wife Anne Extx. D. January 5,
1692/3. R. February 9, 1692.
    Wit: Richard Stone, John Bell.                   Page 322

TOWLE, Richard: Leg. my three youngest children of Susanna Braswell, Richard
William and Elizabeth Braswell. Ex., John Riggs. D. 5th of 9ber 1692.
R. February 9, 1692.
    Wit: Thomas Moore, Robert Horner, Sarah Wakefield.     Page 323

PROCTOR, Ambrose: Leg. son John; son Reuben; daughter Anne; son Jeremiah;
wife Mary. D. May 28, 1689. R. February 9, 1692.
    Wit: Gilbert Adams, John Davis.                  Page 325

FRIZELL, John: Of the Upper Parish. Leg. son William land adjoining Col.
Smith and Richard Reynolds; daughter Susanna; daughter Mary; daughter
Elizabeth; wife Susanna. Wife Extx. D. August 19, 1692. R. April 10,
1693.
        Wit: John Portis, Sr., Edward Griffen, John Davis.     Page 326

CROCKER, Anthony: Nuncupative, proven by John Newman, Nicholas Filberd (?),
John Geruise. Leg. son Robert; son William; son Edward; daughter Mary;
wife Mary. D. May --, 1693. R. August 9, 1693.     Page 327

WILLIAMS, Thomas, Sr.: Leg. son John the land bought of George Perrie; son
Richard; son Thomas the right to the land I was to have of Will Bracey;
son Arthur; daughter Mary; daughter Ann; wife. D. January 28, 1691.
R. August 9, 1693.
        Wit: John Jones, Thomas Williams, Martin Luther.
Inventory presented by Mary Williams. R. October 9, 1693.     Page 328

EDWARDS, Thomas: Inventory, presented by Elizabeth Edwards. 8th of Xber
1693.     Page 329

CROCKER, Anthony: Inventory, presented by Mary Crocker. R. December 9,
1693.     Page 329

SMITH, Arthur: Of Warrisqueake. Leg. sons Arthur and Richard, the land
called the Freshett; Godson Arthur Long; son George, the land known as
John Roe's Neck; daughter Jane, land adjoining Christopher Reynolds;
son Thomas; Godson Arthur Virgin, son of Robert Virgin; Godson Arthur
Taylor, son of John Taylor. To be buried by my late beloved wife.
Son Thomas Ex. Overseers: Peter Hull, Peter Knight, and George Hardy.
D. October 1, 1645. R. February 9, 1693.
        Wit: Benjamin Buckley, James Rochz, Robert West.     Page 330

FENN, Robert: Of Upper Parish. Leg. cousin Elizabeth Fenn, the land ad-
joining Peter Benton; cousin Kae Fenn; cousin Mary Fenn; cousin Martha
Fenn; Goddaughter Elizabeth Gray, daughter of Richard Gray. Exs.,
John Carrell, Sr. and his son William Carrell. D. January 20, 1694.
R. March 9, 1693.
        Wit: George Frizell, Richard Pell, Thomas Carrell, Thomas
          Robinson.     Page 332

WARD, Thomas: Appraisal by John Giles, Nicholas Fulgham, Thomas Norsworthy,
Thomas Whitley. Presented by Mary Ward. R. February 9, 1693.
    Page 333

MACODINE, Phillip: Appraisal by John Giles, James Tullagh, Daniel Long.
D. January 9, 1693. R. January 29, 1693.     Page 334

ALLEN, George: Inventory presented by Rebekah Allen. R. May 1, 1694.
    Page 335

WOORY, Joseph: Appraisal by Arthur Smith, Thomas Giles, James Benn, Henry
Applewhaite. Presented by Samuel Bridger and Elizabeth his wife,
relict and admtx. D. February 15, 1693. R. June 9, 1694.     Page 336

WILSON, John: Inventory, presented by Katherine Wilson. R. June 9, 1694.
    Page 343

PENNY, Richard: Leg. eldest daughter, Frances Partridge, daughter Elizabeth
Noyall; granddaughter Elizabeth Clarke; grandson Thomas Clarke; son
John; grandson Richard Penny; granddaughter Mary, the daughter of John
Penny; granddaughter Mary, daughter of Will Penny; Elizabeth Penny, the
daughter of Will Penny; son Will; daughter Mary the wife of Robert

Marshall; grandson Richard Gray. Son-in-law Robert Marshall Ex.
D. April 14, 1693. R. June 9, 1694.
    Wit: Peter Best, Will Williams, Thomas Hawkins.        Page 344

HAWKINS, Thomas: Appraisal by Humphrey Marshall, Thomas Smith, Will Williams,
Will Penny. Presented by Mary Hawkins, Admtx. D. June 20, 1694.
R. August 9, 1694.                                  Page 346

PEDDON, James: Of the Lower Parish. Leg. wife Jane. Wife Extx.
D. October 16, 1693. R. August 9, 1694.
    Wit: Richard Reynolds, Will Arrington.           Page 347

WILSON, John: Appraisal by Robert Kae, John Brantley, Will Thomas. Presented
by Katherine Wilson, the relict. D. July 27, 1694. R. August 9, 1694.
                                                        Page 348

ALTMAN, John: Inventory presented by Ann Altman. R. August 9, 1694.
                                                        Page 348

FENN, Robert: Appraisal by John Carrell, Thomas Thropp, Richard Gray,
William Webb. Ordered March 9, 1694. R. August 9, 1694.    Page 349

TABOROR, Thomas: Leg. grandson Joseph Copeland, my land called Basses
Choice; grandson Thomas the son of John Newman; daughter Ruth Newman;
grandson Thomas the son of William Webb; daughter Mary Webb the land
I bought of Charles Edwards, on which John Bidgood now lives; daughter
Newman's children; daughter Christian's children; daughter Elizabeth
Copeland's children; granddaughter Christian Jordan; Elizabeth Wombwell's
children; Thomas Wombwell. Grandson Joseph Copeland Ex. D. January 24,
1692. R. February 9, 1694.
    Wit: John Davis, Nicholas Miller. Administration granted Mr.
John Newman during the minority of Joseph Copeland.
    Codicil: to grandchildren, Joseph Copeland, Thomas and Isabella
Newman. R. February 9, 1694.
    Wit: Susanna Blunt, Charles Chapman.        Page 350

DUN, John: Nuncupative, proven by Will Morgan, age 48 years, Thomas Davis
and John Davis. Leg. old Arthur Smith and James Benn Sr. Not dated.
                                                      Page 358

POYELLS, William: Inventory presented by Elizabeth Poyells. Not dated.
                                                    Page 357

SMITH, Nicholas: Inventory presented by Humphrey Marshall. June 5, 1696.
                                                    Page 358
    Appraisal by Thomas Giles, Anthony Holladay, James Benn. July 23, 1696.
                                                  Page 361

CROCKER, Anthony: Inventory presented by Ann Crocker. Not dated. Page 365

JENNINGS, John: Inventory presented by Silvestra Hill. D. January 10,
1695/6. R. June --, 1696.                           Page 365

CROCKER, Anthony: Appraisal by Arthur Jones, Robert Munger, Edward Jones.
D. May 5, 1696.                                      Page 366

LUX, Will: Appraisal by Thomas Thropp, William Browne, John Carrell.
Ordered August 10, 1696. R. September 18, 1696.        Page 367

NEWMAN, John: Leg. wife Ruth; son Thomas land called Cookes Quarter, adjoining John Screws; daughter Isabella; William Holden, when he becomes
free. Wife Extx. D. December 11, 1695. R. ----------
    Wit: James Day, Thomas Hebby (?), Ann Brassell.    Page 368

GOODRICH, Capt. John: Leg. son George land adjoining Thomas Proud and Thomas Thropp; son John the land on which Thomas Drew now lives; land bought of Gilbert Adams to my two aforesaid sons; daughters, Honour, Constancy and Mary; daughter Elizabeth the land given her by her grandfather-in-law, George Cripps. Wife Extx. Overseers: my brother Robert Kae and Mr. James Day. D. January 13, 1695. R. June 9, 1696.
    Wit: Robert Thomas, Martha Thropp, Edward Farnesfield, Thomas
        Proud.                                                      Page 369

DAVIS, Thomas: Appraisal taken at the house of William Webb Jr., by John Carrell, Thomas Thropp, William Webb. Ordered August 10, 1696.
                                                                    Page 370

MOORE, Thomas: Leg. Edward Champion, Jr. the land I bought of Edward Cobb; Orlando Champion the land on the west side of the Blackwater Swamp, part of a patent between John Clarke and John Atkins; Edward Champion, Sr., the father of Orlando; Alice Champion the daughter of Edward Champion; Benjamin Champion the son of Edward; brother George Moore and Charles Chapman, tobacco in trust for the benefit of my niece Magdalen Carter; the same amount for Priscilla Champion. Wife and brother Exs. Overseers: Charles Chapman and Mr. Carrell.
D. September 28, 1696. R. 9th of 10 mo. 1696.
    Wit: John Carrell, Richard Lewis, Charles Chapman.    Page 371

JENNINGS, John: Appraisal by John Carrell, William Webb, William Browne. Signed, Silvestra Hill. Ordered January 10, 1696. R. June 9, 1696.
                                                                    Page 372

WILSON, Nicholas: Appraisal by John Skelton and Thomas Wood. December 9, 1696.                                                               Page 373

HARDY, George: Leg. son Richard land in Isle of Wight and Surry; youngest son Thomas land in Surry; grandchildren Richard and George Jarrett; daughters, Mary and Sarah. D. March 5, 1693/4. R. June 9, 1696.
    Wit: Richard Stone, Mathew Fones.                       Page 374

BALDWIN, William: Appraisal by John Whetstone and John Williams.
D. February 2, 1696. R. June 9, 1696.                       Page 375

GAINOR, Samuel: Appraisal by John Carrell and Samuel Eldridge. R. June 9, 1696.                                                              Page 375

FRANCIS, John: Account of estate, among items --- clothing for Ann Francis' when she was married to Anthony Crocker. Presented by George Rivers. Not dated.                                                            Page 377

SMITH, Arthur: Of Lower Parish. Leg. son Thomas; John Hole land bought of Richard Hutchins, reversion to his mother Mary Pitt; son George land adjoining William Thomas and Mrs. Burnett, Mr. Sharpe and Henry Wiggs; if my son Arthur departs this life and comes no more to this country, reversion of his land to my grandson Arthur Benn; Jeremy Fly 200 A.; daughters, Jane Benn, Sarah Monro and Mary Pitt; if without heirs my land for a free school in Newport Parish; wife. Exs., Arthur and George Smith. Overseer: Capt. James Benn. D. December 2, 1696.
R. June 10, 1697.
    Wit: Henry Applewhaite, Boaz Gwin, Robert Brocke.       Page 377

DAVIS, Hugh: Leg. Capt. William Randolph; estate in England to my father, Hugh Davis, Sr. Capt. Randolph Ex. D. May 18, 1683. R. November 9, 1697.                                                              Page 381

BENN, James: Leg. son James; son Arthur; son George land purchased with

William Evans on Beaver Dam Swamp, from Mathew Strickland; daughters, Mary, Sarah, Jeane and Anne; wife Jane; Mary Knight. Wife Extx. Overseers: John Giles, George Smyth and James Tallagh. D. February 6, 1696. R. April 9, 1697.
    Wit: James Tallagh, Henry Butts, Mary Knight, John Giles, Nicholas Fulgham. Page 381
Appraisal by Nicholas Fulgham, Thomas Pitt, John Clark, John Watts. D. May 5, 1697. Page 382

BRADDY, Patrick: Nuncupative, proven by John Skelton and his wife Susanna. Leg. wife Elizabeth and children. R. June 9, 1697. Page 383
Appraisal by John Skelton and Thomas Wood. D. August 4, 1697. Page 384

BAMPTON, William: Appraisal by John Watts, Kingsmell Minard, John Wilson. Ordered April 9, 1697. Page 384

JONES, John: Leg. son Abraham land in the Upper Parish on Blackwater; daughter Ann the wife of John Barnes, 150 A. on Blackwater adjoining land of William Chambers; daughter's son John Barnes; son John; wife Ann 200 A. in the Lower Parish. Wife Extx. D. July 6, 1697. R. ------
    Wit: Joshua Turner, Sr., Joshua Turner, Jr., John Blake.
Page 385

WATTS, John: Leg. son John; daughter Sarah Pope; my three youngest children. Exs., son John and son-in-law Henry Pope. D. January 20, 1697/8. R. February 9, 1697/8.
    Wit: James Tullagh, Jane Benn, Henry Butts. Page 386

WILSON, Margaret: Nuncupative, proven by Nicholas Renalls, age 18 years and William Deloach, age 20 years. Leg. son James; that Mr. Moore and James Sampson should have nothing to do with her estate. Exs., Thomas Clarke and John Browne. Not dated. Page 386

MARSHALL, Robert: Leg. son Robert; son John; son Humphrey the land which my father Richard Penny gave me; son Joseph; son James; daughter Mary; daughter Elizabeth; wife Mary. Wife Extx. D. July 18, 1698. R. August 2, 1698.
    Wit: Anthony Holladay, Humphrey Marshall, John Penny. Page 387
Appraisal by Thomas Brewer, John Mackmiall, Thomas Gross. Presented by Mary Marshall. R. September 2, 1698. Page 388

GOODRICH, John, Sr.: of Upper Parish. Leg. son Charles; wife Rebecca; John Goodrich the son of my wife Rebecca, reversion to my grandson John Goodrich the son of Captain John Goodrich. Wife Extx. D. August 20, 1695. R. June 9, 1698.
    Wit: Robert Kae, Robert Riddick, George Riddick, Joseph Ford.
Page 389

TULLAUGH, James: Leg. son James; daughter Sarah, daughter Anne; brother Robert Tullagh in Ireland; brother John Tullagh; legacy left my two daughters by their brother John Griffen. Two daughters Extx. Trustee, John Giles. D. March 26, 1698. R. May 2, 1698.
    Wit: Richard Reynolds, John Street, Ann Street. Page 390

MILES, William: Leg. wife Anne; John Baker, son of Henry Baker, 400 A. on Blackwater adjoining John Oliver; reversion to James Baker the brother of John. Wife Extx. D. March 14, 1695/6. R. August 9, 1698.
    Wit: Henry Baker, William Browne. Page 392

PROUD, Thomas: Leg. John Goodrich; Robert Kae. D. July 15, 1698. R. August 9, 1698.

Wit: Edward Farnsfield, Bridgett Lewis, Richard Pope. Page 393
Appraisal by Thomas Thropp, William Browne, Richard Gray. R. August 20, 1698. Page 394

GWIN, Boaz: Inventory presented by Sarah Gwin. Not dated. Page 396

BLAKE, John: Inventory recorded February 9, 1697. Page 397

GRIFFETH, Owen: Leg. daughter Ann; daughter Sarah; son Edward; son Owen; son John; grandson John Griffeth; granddaughter Patience Griffeth; Margaret Edwards; Judy Edwards; wife Mary; son-in-law William Johnson and my daughter. Wife Extx. D. July 15, 1698. R. September 9, 1698.
Wit: Henry Applewhaite, Jane Bragg. Page 397

SHEWMAKE, Arnell: Leg. son Moses; daughter Alice; granddaughter Dorothy Davis; daughter Jane; daughter Sarah; daughter Margery; daughter Frances; beloved wife. D. December 9, 1697. R. February 9, 1698.
Wit: Boaz Gwin, Thomas Gaynie. Page 399

RUTTER, Walter: Appraisal by William West, Charles Durham, Richard Reynolds. D. September 7, 1698. Page 400

WILSON, Margaret: Appraisal by Thomas Woodley and John Brantley. R. November 16, 1697. Page 401

TULLAUGH, James: Appraisal by Robert Coleman, William West, Charles Durham. Signed, Sarah and Ann Tullagh. R. November 29, 1698. Page 402

LEWIS, Daniel: Leg. son Daniel; daughter Sarah; wife Sarah. D. July 23, 1697. R. April 9, 1698.
Wit: Francis Lee, Henry Dixon, John Skelton, Sr. Page 406

COOKE, Henry: Of the Upper Parish. Leg. wife and unborn child. Wife Extx. Overseers: my father William Cooke and brother Reuben Cooke. D. May 13, 1696. R. August 9, 1698.
Wit: John Carrell, Thomas Carter, Jr., Reuben Cooke, Peter Heyle (?). Page 406

COOK, William, Sr.: Leg. son John; son William; son Reuben; son Thomas; loving wife. D. May 17, 1698. R. ----------
Wit: Peter Vasser, Peter Hayes, James Atkisson. Page 407

JENNINGS, John: Leg. sister Sarah Lucks; brother William Thomas; son George. Mother Silvestra Hill Extx. Brother William Thomas to be her assistant. D. 31st of 10 mo. 1695. R. June 9, 1698.
Wit: Francis Taylor, Martha Thropp, Thomas Heathfield, William Thomas. Page 408

COUNCIL, Hodges: Leg. eldest son Hodges land on Blackwater, at his death to his son Hodges; son John the land I bought of Robert Lawrence and George Peirce; son Hardy; son Robert; daughter Christian the wife of Edward Bryan; daughter Lucy. D. April 10, 1699. Recorded in open court by Hodges Council, April 10, 1699.
Wit: Joseph Bridger, John Keaton, Jr. Page 409

POPE, Robert: Leg. wife Elizabeth. D. June 5, 1698. R. April 10, 1699.
Wit: Thomas Bevan, John Luck. Page 410

BEST, Peter: Leg. eldest son William; son Peter; son Christopher land at Kingsale; youngest son Thomas; wife Mary. Wife Extx. D. October 20, 1693. R. June 9, 1698.
Wit: Thomas Hawkins, James Mackfadden, Christopher Best.
Page 410

JOYNER, William: Leg. son William; son Abraham; son Israel; youngest son
Joseph; wife Mary; three daughters. Wife Extx. D. May 21, 1698.
R. December 9, 1698.
Wit: William Body, Theophilus Joyner.                    Page 411
Appraisal by Arthur Pursell and Henry Turner. R. December 14, 1698.
Page 412

DAVIS, Thomas: Leg. eldest son Thomas land adjoining the land of John Smith
in Upper Norfolk County; daughter Mary; daughter Sarah; son Daniel;
wife Grace. Wife Extx. D. July 30, 1698. R. October 10, 1698.
Wit: Daniel Miles, William Whitfield.                    Page 413

LONG, Daniel: Leg. son Daniel; son Robert; son Edward; son John; daughter
Elizabeth. Friends Stephen Smith and Thomas Right to divide my estate
between my wife and children. D. January 5, 1696. R. December 9, 1698.
Wit: John Clarke, Thomas Right, Robert Brock.          Page 413

BRADSHAW, William: Appraisal by William Body, Thomas Joyner, Giles Driver,
Henry Turner. December 15, 1698.                         Page 414

GARDNER, James: Appraisal by John Barton, John Cotten, John Parnell.
January 26, 1698/9.                                     Page 415

WATTS, John: Appraisal by Thomas Pitt, Kingsmell Minard, Thomas Gross,
Robert Pope. April 9, 1698.                             Page 416

GOODRICH, Capt. John: Appraisal by John Carrell, Thomas Thropp, William
Browne, Richard Gray. August 9, 1698.                   Page 417

ATKINSON, Susanna. Inventory presented by Thomas Atkinson. Not dated.
Page 418

DRIVER, Robert: Appraisal by John Council, Charles Durham, William West, Jr.,
John Parmentoe. Signed Elizabeth Driver. May 19, 1699.   Page 419

COUNCIL, Hodges: Leg. eldest son Hodges; grandson Hodges Council; son John;
son Robert; daughter Christian the wife of Edward Briand; daughter Lucy.
Son Hardy Ex. D. August 9, 1699. R. August 9, 1699.
Wit: Arthur Smith, Thomas Smith, Mary Smith.           Page 419

CURRER, Sarah: Daughter and heir of John Currer of N. C., decd. Leg.
cousin Robert Cooper, orphan of Robert Cooper; cousin Thomas Cooper
the son of Robert Cooper, cattle at Nicholas Tynes and estate in the
hands of Thomas Laton in N. C. Exs., cousins Robert and Thomas Cooper
with the assistance of my aunt Sarah Williams their mother. D. July 28,
1698. R. August 9, 1699.
Wit: Jacob Ricks, Henry Sanders, Thomas Haile.         Page 421

COLLINS, Alice: Inventory presented by Will English. February 3, 1699/1700.
Page 422

SHARPE, Richard: Leg. Anne Harris in case she recovers from this present
sickness; cousin Richard the son of my cousin Richard Reynolds the
full term of my lease from Col. Arthur Smith; Cristopher and Sharpe
Reynolds the sons of my cousin Richard Reynolds. Ex., Richard Reynolds.
D. January 15, 1699/1700. R. April 9, 1700.
Wit: Henry Applewhaite, John Hood, John Watson.         Page 422

GARLAND, Peter: Leg. wife Grace; son Samuel; son John; daughters Sarah and
Debora to have their share of my land where their husbands, William
Macone and William Daniel now live; daughter Anna. Exs., wife and son
Samuel. D. September 6, 1694. R. ----------
Wit: John Giles, John Surby, John Acon (?).            Page 423

BELL, Richard: Inventory presented by Sarah Bell. R. April 9, 1700.
Page 424

NEWMAN, Mrs. Ruth: Inventory presented by Thomas Newman. R. April 9, 1700.
Page 424

MURRY, Alexander: Appraisal by Will Parker, Francis Parker, John Parker.
D. September 19, 1698. R. ------- 1700. Page 425

HYDES, Ann: Inventory presented by John Turner. Not dated. Page 426

WEBB, William, Jr.: Leg. my youngest cousin Mary Ricketts a mare at Capt.
John Davis; wife Mary. Wife Extx. D. September 19, 1699. R. June 10,
1700.
Wit: Caleb Taylor, Richard Gray. Page 426

DRIVER, Capt. Charles: Appraisal by Thomas Bevan, Adam Murray, Nicholas
Fulgham, Richard Wilkinson. D. April 9, 1700. R. June 3, 1700.
Page 427

CORSY, John: Appraisal by Thomas Thropp, Peter Deberry, William Browne,
John Whitson. May 21, 1700. Page 428

DAY, James: Leg. son James; son Thomas; son William; daughter Elizabeth;
wife Mary; aunt Mrs. Silvestra Hill; my brother and sister Chapman;
my brother and sister Swann; Mrs. Isabella Havield; Mr. John Havield;
Major Henry Baker; Major Henry Tooker; Major Arthur Allen. Wife and
Luke Havield Exs. Friends, Mr. Micajah Perry, Mr. Thomas Lane and
Mr. Richard Perry to dispose of my property in ye Parish of St. Peters
ye Poor in London. D. August 10, 1700.
Wit: Thomas Rieves, George Bechinoe, Barnaby Mackinnie.
Codicil: to ever honored mother, Mrs. Mary Cropley. D. August 10,
1700. R. January 9, 1700/1.
Wit: Barnaby Mackinnie, Thomas Rieves. Page 428

WILMOTT, William: Appraisal by John Skelton, William Thomas, Thomas Hardy.
Not dated. Page 431

BRASIE, William: Of Levy Neck. Leg. John Harrison my kinsman, son of John
and Milboran Harrison lately deceased, land bounding on John Murrey
and John Carroll; to his brother William Harrison the rest of the land
purchased of John Seward; Samuel Newton of Lawnes Creek Parish in
Surry Co.; Thomas Page, taylor of Nansemond Co.; the three children of
James Tullagh's of ye Lower Parish; Hugh Brasie; William Brasie; wife
Susanna. Trustees, Daniel Sanborne of the Lower Parish of Isle of
Wight; Henry Wiggs, carpenter; Isack Reeks, Clerke of ye Yearly Meeting;
John Jordan son of Thomas Jordan lately deceased and Robert Lacie of
Lawnes Creek in Surry. Wife Extx. D. January 22, 1699. R. June 9,
1701.
Wit: Martha Thropp, William Wilson, Samuel Eldridge, Elizabeth
Gainer, John Crabham. Page 431

WRIGHT, Thomas: Leg. son John; son James; son Thomas; son Joseph; daughter
Mary; wife Elizabeth. Wife Extx. D. October 23, 1700. R. September 9,
1701.
Wit: Richard Wilkinson, Jr., George Wright, Violet Wright.
Page 433

MURRAY, Ann: Age 49. Nuncupative, proven by Francis Parker and Robert King.
Leg. son John Collins; daughter Ann Collins; daughter Martha Murray;
daughter Mary Murray; last two named daughters to live with their uncle
Robert King. R. February 10, 1700/1. Page 434

MURRAY, Ann: Appraisal by Tristram Norsworthy, Francis Parker, William
Smith, James Bagnall. D. June 9, 1701. Page 435

EXUM, William: Of the Upper Parish. Leg. daughter Deborah Jones; wife
Jane; son William land on the Blackwater; son Francis land on Black-
water. Wife Extx. D. December 3, 1700. R. February 10, 1700/1.
Wit: Nathaniel Whitby, George Gurney. Page 436

PARKER, John: Appraisal by Tristram Norsworthy, Will Smith, Ralph Frizzell,
William Smith, Jr. Presented by Mary Parker. Signed William Smith, Jr.
February 18, 1700/1. Page 437

KING, Mrs. Sarah: Appraisal by Tristram Norsworthy, William Smith, William
Smith, Jr., Ralph Frizzell. Presented by Robert King. February 10,
1700/1. Page 437

LEWIS, John: Age 37 years. Leg. brother John Kingsmichael; daughter Mary;
daughter Sarah; aforesaid girls to live with their uncle John Kingsmichael; son Arthur to live with my cousin John Mainard. D. January 13,
1700. R. February 10, 1700.
Wit: James Brown, Elizabeth Brown, Ann Farmer. Page 439

COBB, Pharoah: Appraisal by James Bragg, Nathaniel Berry, Henry Applewhaite,
Jr. Estate divided into three parts. May 31, 1701. Page 440

LEWIS, William: Appraisal by James Browne, Thomas Grosse, James Hunter,
John Watts. Not dated. Page 441

CORSY, John: Appraisal by Thomas Thropp, Peter Deberry, William Browne,
John Whitstone. May 21, 1700. Page 442

COLLINS, Alice: Estate divided by George Moore and Robert Kae. April 8,
1700. Page 442

WILKTON, John: Appraisal by Will Williams, Thomas Clarke, John Penny,
Thomas Grosse. August 9, 1701. Page 442

DRIVER, Capt. Charles: Appraisal by Thomas Bevan, Adam Murray, Nicholas
Fulgham, Richard Wilkinson. D. April 9, 1700. R. June 3, 1700.
Page 443

TULLAGH, James: Estate divided by Will West, Jacob Darden, Charles Durham.
Not dated. Page 443

PAGE, John: Leg. wife Ann; son John; daughter Elizabeth. D. March 22,
1700. R. ---------
Wit: Thomas Clarke, John Crane, Margery Crane. Page 444

STURDY, John: Leg. Jane Jones for her care in looking after me in ye time
of my affliction; Robert Glover; Goddaughter Sarah Jones; Elizabeth
Simons, daughter of John Simons; Francis Gross. Ex., friend Thomas
Gross. D. April 14, 1702. R. ----------
Wit: John Barrett, William Harris, Mildred Harris. Page 444

UNDERWOOD, Thomas: Leg. son Thomas; son John; son William; unmarried
daughters; wife. D. August 3, 1702. R. August 9, 1702.
Wit: James Doughty, James Ross, John Byrd. Page 445

DAY, James: Inventory presented by Luke Haveild. D. March 9, 1701/2.
R. June 9, 1702. Page 446

FIVEASH, Peter: Appraisal made by William Thomas, John Brantley and Richard
Hardy. April 28, 1702. Page 449

BAGNALL, James:  Appraisal made by William Williams, John Mackmiall and James
House.  April 9, 1702.                                       Page 450

BAGNALL, James:  Nuncupative will.  Leg. daughter Rebeccak; daughter Sarah;
sister Martha Rutter; daughter Mary; son Nathan; son Robert; son
Joseph; wife.  D. ----------  R.  April 9, 1702.            Page 451

PARKER, Francis:  Deposition -- I have no other objections against this
within mentioned will.  April 9, 1702.                      Page 453

BATHY, John:  Deposition -- that Robert Bagnall said he would make his
father's will null and void.  April 9, 1702.                Page 453

BAGNALL, Sarah:  Deposition -- I heard Robert Bagnall say if he had ye will
he would burn it.  April 9, 1702.                           Page 453

PITT, John of ye City of Bristol:  Leg. father Colonel Robert Pitt; son John
land at Chuckatuck, whereon he now lives; son James; son Henry; grandson Robert Pitt; daughter Sarah Norsworthy; daughter Martha Norsworthy;
daughter Prudence Driver; daughter Mary Drury; daughter-in-law Ann
Bromfield her father John Bromfield's estate.  Ex., son John.
D.  Nov. 28, 1702.  R.  Jan. 9, 1702/3.
    Wit:  Daniel Carver, George Allen, Richard Grammell.    Page 454

BELL, George:  Leg. wife Joyce; son George; daughter Elizabeth.  Wife Extx.
D.  June 22, 1702.  R.  9th day of 7 month 1702.
    Wit:  John Davis and Francis Floyd.                     Page 456

THOMAS, Phillip:  Leg. daughter Mary Goodson the wife of Edward Goodson;
son William; son John.  Ex., son John.  D.  November 13, 1702.
R.  February 9, 1702/3.
    Wit:  Margaret Edwards, Judey Edwards.                  Page 456

PITT, Col. John:  Appraisal by Anthony Holladay, Thomas Norsworthy, Humphrey
Marshall, Nicholas Fulgham.  March 9, 1702/3.               Page 457

SHERRER, John, Jr.:  Appraisal by William Exum, John Williams, Francis Exum.
April 9, 1703.                                              Page 458

BATTEN, Daniel:  aged 64.  Leg. daughter Anne; son John; granddaughter
Martha Welch; daughter Sarah Welch; grandson Robert Smith.  Ex., son
Daniel.  D.  February 18, 1702.  R.  June 9, 1703.
    Wit:  Francis Parker, Edward Long, William Daniell.     Page 459

HAMPTON, Thomas:  Leg. son Francis; son Thomas land at Kingsale; son John;
daughter Mary; daughter Elizabeth; daughter Sarah.  Wife Elizabeth Extx.
June 28, 1703.  R.  December 9, 1703.
    Wit:  John Denson, James Denson, Francis Bridle.        Page 459

JACKSON, Richard:  Leg. son Richard; son John; daughter Mary; daughter Anne;
daughter Sarah; wife Priscilla and her daughter Ann Clerke.  Wife Extx.
D.  April 4, 1703.  R.  December 9, 1703.
    Wit:  John Wrenn, John Crabham, Ann ------.             Page 460

KAE, Robert:  Leg. son Robert; son John; son Henry; son Charles; son Stephen;
daughter Sarah.  Wife Ann Extx.  D.  October 12, 1703.  R. ----------
    Wit:  Robert Thomas, John Wrenn, Honor Goodrich.        Page 460

SHELTON, John:  Leg. wife and children.  Wife Extx.  D.  Oct. 24, 1701.
R.  April 10, 1704.
    Wit:  Thomas Sharpe, Henry Baker.                       Page 461

APPLEWHAITE, Henry: Leg. son Henry the land I bought of Edmond Palmer; son
Thomas one-half of my tract on Blackwater, where John Davis lives; son
William the other part of same tract; son John the land I bought of
Roger Davis; daughter Anne; grandson Henry Applewhaite. Wife Extx.
D. August 26, 1703. R. May 9, 1704.
    Wit: John Street, Maddison Street, John Hood.          Page 462

WRIGHT, George: Appraisal by William Hunter, Robert Clark, John Street,
Edward Browne. October 6, 1702.                         Page 463

WELCH, William: Leg. daughter Anne; daughter Martha; daughter Sarah; wife
Sarah. D. January 2, 1703. R. June 9, 1704.
    Wit: John Smith, Jeremiah Wormington, Henry Best.     Page 464

KAE, Capt. Robert: Appraisal by John Brantley, George Barlow, William
Thomas, Richard Hardy. April 10, 1704.                  Page 464

SHELTON, John: Appraisal by William Thomas, William Browne, John George.
April 10, 1704.                                        Page 464

COOKE, John: Appraisal by George Pierce, William Johnson, John Bardin,
Arthur Whitehead.                                      Page 464

PORTIS, John Jr.: Carpenter. Leg. wife Deborah. Wife Extx. Codicil -
"I do desire my wife Deborah may not be anyways hindered or delayed
---- after debts are paid in her departing ------ expedition of this
country to Pensilvania." D. October 19, 1704. R. December 9, 1704.
    Wit.                                                Page 465

FRANKLYN, Peter: Leg. daughter Susan; daughter Mary; wife. D. August 11,
1704. R. February 9, 1704/5.
    Wit: Thomas Hill, Thomas Boulger.                   Page 466

PIERCE, George: Appraisal by Arthur Whitehead, William Johnson, Henry Pope.
April 9, 1705.                                         Page 466

NOLLIBOY, Daniel: Nuncupative. Leg. daughter Mary; daughter Sarah; son
James. Proven by Richard Mathews and John Corbett. April 9, 1704.
                                                        Page 467
    Inventory of estate returned by Daniel Nolliboy. November 9, 1704.
                                                        Page 467

HAREBOTTLE, Thomas: Of the Upper Parish. Leg. wife Rebecca reversion to
her son John Goodrich. D. June 5, 1704. R. June 9, 1705.
    Wit: George Gurney, John Raynor.                    Page 467

FONES, Mathew: Leg. wife Abigail; son Robert; son John; son Thomas; to
Thomas Fones the son of John Fones; daughter Mary; Ann Bennett, daughter
of William Bennett. Wife Extx. Capt. Arthur Smith to make an equal
division of estate. D. Oct. 11, 1703. R. August 9, 1704.
    Wit: Thomas Wood, George Wood, Phillip Pardoe.      Page 468

TURNER, John: Nuncupative, as told to us by ye widow Tomlyn: Leg. son
John plantation at Chuckatuck; sons James and John the plantation
where John Coffer did live; son William the plantation on which Thomas
Phillips lives; sons Joseph and Simon land on Boddie's Branch, adjoining
Mr. Hardy and Edward Harris; granddaughter Anne Everett. Son William
Ex. Overseers: Edward Harris and Thomas Harris. D. March 25, 1705.
R. June 9, 1705. Signed by Edward Harris, John Johnson, Jr.,
Jenkins Dorman, William Westray and Mary Tomlyn.       Page 468

MOORE, John: Of the Lower Parish: Leg. wife Margaret; at her death to my
five grandchildren, ye three sons and two daughters of John Coggan, the

eldest not now in this country. Wife Extx. Thomas Gale and John
Sellaway appointed Exs. at decease of wife. D. April 18, 1702.
R. October 9, 1704.
    Wit: Jenkins Dorman, Henry Pope, John Pope, Francis Cooke.
Page 469

SMITH, William: Leg. wife Mary; son William the land he and John Batten
live on, adjoining Thomas Altman and the widow Weston; son Nathaniel
the plantatation called Jones', where John Altman lives; son Nicholas
the plantation on which Thomas Bulger lives, also all the land between
it and Major Burwell. Bagnall and Parker; son Joseph the plantation
on which the Widow Franklyn lives; daughter Ann Weston; Elizabeth
Parker; Sarah Bulger; granddaughter Ann Barnes. Wife Extx.
D. January 5, 1704. R. 10th day of 7 month 1705.     Page 470

WRIGHT, George: Inventory presented by John and Violet Driver. September 7,
1702.     Page 471

WALTON, John: Leg. Judith Williams; Elizabeth Watts; son Thomas; wife Mary.
Reversion of legacy to son to cousin John Hill of Sherfford in
Lincoln-shire. Mr. Henry Baker to assist my Extx. D. August 16,
1705. R. November 9, 1705.
    Wit: Will Wilsom, William Clarke, Jr., William Clarke, Sr.,
        Susanna Jordan, Mary Clarke.     Page 471

BRADSHAW, John: Leg. son John; son George; son Nicholas; daughter Ann;
son Vincent; daughter Sarah; daughter Mary; wife Sarah. August 29,
1705. R. May 5, 1706.
    Wit: John Bidgood, Edward Miller.     Page 472

BURNE, Owen: Nuncupative, proven by Henry Flowers and Thomas Mandew.
Leg. son John; son William; daughter Ann; wife Hannah. D. May 21,
1705. R. October 9, 1705.     Page 472

MACLAND, John: Leg. daughter Alice Bryant; grandchildren Nicholas, John
and Elizabeth Perry; grandchildren Woodham, William, John, Mary and
Alice Bryant; wife Elizabeth Extx. D. June 1, 1705. R. November 9,
1705.
    Wit: Arthur Smith, Mary Smith, Elizabeth West.     Page 473

TURNER, John: Appraisal by John Fulgham, Francis Williamson, Phillip
Raiford and Edward Boykin. 1705.     Page 474

GREEN, George: Leg. wife Anne; brother John Green the Red Point plantation
on which Sarah Bradshaw now lives; to wife Anne my plantation at Poplar
Neck, part of which I have sold Richard Wilkinson; brother William;
brother-in-law Jeremy Proctor and his wife Bridget; sister Elizabeth;
sister Mary; sister Elizabeth Murray; to brother John the debt John
Pilkington owes me. Father Jeremiah Exum and brother Richard Exum,
Overseers. Wife Extx. D. October 8, 1705. R. January 9, 1706/7.
    Wit: Robert Lawrence, Sr., Robert Lawrence, Jr., Thomas
        Browne.     Page 475

HILL, Silvestra: Leg. friend Mary the wife of Henry Baker the land I now
dwell on, that is the plantations on which live Andrew Griffin, Sarah
Guilford, John Bidgood, William Thomas and Benjamin Folder (?); Goddaughter Mary the daughter of Henry and Mary Baker; the plantations
on which Richard and Francis Wrenn live to be sold for the benefit of
the poor of the Upper Parish; Elizabeth the wife of Nathaniel Ridley;
James, Thomas and William Day; Anne Chapman the wife of Charles
Chapman and her three sons; Henry Baker. Ex. Henry Baker. D. October 7,
1706. R. January 9, 1706/7.
    Wit: William Browne, Francis Lee, James Wilson, Sarah Guilford.
Page 475

BOULGER, Thomas: Of the Lower Parish. Leg. wife Sarah; daughter Sarah.
D. March 14, 1705/6. R. August 9, 1706.
Wit: Jacob Barnes, Stephen Wesson, Joseph Wesson.          Page 476

JONES, Ann: Leg. son John the 300 A. purchased of Edmond Palmer, John
Portis, Sr. and Henry Martin; son Abraham; son John's three children,
Joseph, John and Ann; daughter Ann Barnes. Capt. Arthur Smith and
Henry Applewhaite, Overseers. D. April 15, 1704. R. January 9,
1706/7.
Wit: John Watts, John Duke, Henry Applewhaite.          Page 477

SEWARD, John: Trustees, Stephen Warren, Thomas Walter and Richard Kelson
my servant. Leg. eldest son John the tract called "Levy Neck"; son
James land on Blackwater; wife Sarah; Sarah the wife of John Graves;
servant Richard Seward's term of three years to be at the disposing
of Stephen Warren. D. February 9, 1650. R. April 9, 1706/7.
Wit: Godfrey Price, Henry Moore, Edward Gibbs.          Page 478

FRIZZELL, William: Planter. Leg. daughter Isabella and her husband Thomas
Sawyer; grandson William the son of John Frizzell decd., 100 A. near
the Courthouse; grandson John Sawyer; granddaughter Mary Sawyer;
granddaughter Sarah Sawyer; granddaughter Susan Pope; granddaughters
Mary and Elizabeth Frizzell. Exs., daughter Isabella and Thomas Sawyer.
D. October 25, 1706. R. March 10, 1706/7.
Wit: Jacob Barnes, Mathew Whitfield, John Lawrence.          Page 479

RIVERS, George: Leg. wife Mary and her daughter Mary; daughter Sarah.
Wife Extx. Arthur Jones, trustee. D. March 16, 1706/7. R. April 9,
1707.
Wit: Arthur Jones, Charles Jordan, Richard Jordan.          Page 479

SHERRER, John: Leg. Elizabeth Sherrer, the widow of John Sherrer, Jr., the
plantation which she now lives on to fall to John Sherrer my grandson;
son Thomas; Robert Sherrer 100 A. beginning on John Britt's corner.
Ex., my son Alexander. D. January 23, 1705. R. March 10, 1706/7.
Wit: John Williams, John Stevenson.          Page 480

WEATHERALL, John, Jr.: Appraisal by James Brown, John Bunkley, Joseph
Burke and John Williams. August 17, 1706.          Page 480

MATHEWS, Richard: Inventory presented by Alexander Mathews. D. February 7,
1706/7. R. February 10, 1706/7.          Page 481

MILLER, Nicholas: Appraisal by John Davis, John Johnson, John Bidgood,
James Lupo. D. February 10, 1706/7.          Page 481

HARDY, John: Inventory of his estate presented by John Johnson. Not dated.
Page 481

MURRAY, Adam: Appraisal by Richard Wilkinson, Jr., John Surby, Robert
Richards and John Turner. D. January 1, 1706/7.          Page 481

SKELTON, John: Account of estate presented by Susanna Skelton. Not dated.
Page 482

BULLS, Henry: Appraisal by Giles Driver, John Jordan and Thomas Williams.
Estate in the hands of Jeremy ffly. Not dated.          Page 482

BEST, Henry: Appraisal by Humphry Marshall, William Willimas, Edward
Miles and John Penny. Not dated.          Page 483

RICKS, Jacob: Appraisal by Jacob Darden, Henry Pope and Thomas Gale.
D. October 9, 1704.          Page 483

POPE, Richard: Inventory presented by Thomas Wren. D. February 1, 1704/5.
Page 483

JOHNSON, John: Leg. daughter Martha; son John my goods at Blackwater, aforesaid son and daughter one shilling of my last wife's estate; daughter Patience; daughter Mary; wife Mary. D. January 7, 1703. R. August 9, 1707.
    Wit: James Lupo, Sarah Lupo, Susanna Braswell.    Page 484

PORTIS, John: Leg. son John; son Thomas; daughter Susanna; son George, wife Jane. D. April 7, 1703. R. October 9, 1707.
    Wit: William Copeland, Sarah Jordan, Richard Reynolds, Ambrose Hadley.    Page 485

NORSEWORTHY, William: Leg. cousin Juliana Norseworthy; cousin Peter Blake; cousin Thomas Norseworthy, the son of my brother George decd.; cousin Martha Norseworthy the daughter of aforesaid brother; sister Martha Boyd; all of brother George's children; cousin George Norseworthy, the son of Tristram Norseworthy; cousin Martha Norseworthy the daughter of sister Martha Boyd; cousin John Norseworthy; cousin George Norseworthy, who is now in England. Ex., my cousin John Norseworthy. D. August 10, 1707. R. December 9, 1707.
    Wit: John Pitt, Martha Boyd, Martha Norseworthy, John Norseworthy.    Page 485

WILLIAMS, John: Leg. son John; daughter Sarah. Extx., eldest daughter Alexandra. Overseers: James Sampson and George Piland. D. March 15, 1707/8. R. May 1, 1708.
    Wit: George Piland, James Piland, ffrancis Lee.    Page 486

JOYNER, Thomas, Sr.: Leg. wife Elizabeth; son Thomas; eldest daughter Christian; son Benjamin; Henry Turner; son James the old plantation on which William Kinchen lived; youngest daughter Martha; son John; son Nehemiah; grandson Thomas Joyner; cousin Lucy Joyner; daughter Elizabeth; daughter Deborah. Extx., wife Elizabeth. D. April 21, 1708. R. October 9, 1708.
    Wit: William West, Jenkins Dorman, James Barnes.    Page 486

BALDWIN, Benjamin: Leg. loving wife; son William; daughter Jane; daughter Mary; daughter Sarah; daughter Prudence. Wife Extx. D. February 22, 1707/8. R. May 1, 1708.
    Wit: Robert Brock, Thomas Minn (?), Abraham Jones.    Page 488

TYNES, Nicholas: Leg. son Nicholas the plantation on which Robert Thomas lives; daughter Margaret Packett (?); daughter Mary; daughter Eleanor; daughter Sarah; son-in-law Edward Packett. Ex., son Nicholas. D. September 28, 1708. R. February 9, 1708/9.
    Wit: James Johnson, Francis Corbett, Francis Seagrave. Page 489

WEST, William of Newport Parish: Leg. son William; son Richard all my land between William Green and Robert Bagnall; son Robert; daughter Mary Green; daughter Rebeckah. Extx., my wife. D. October 20, 1708. R. February 9, 1708/9.
    Wit: Thomas Allen, John Butler, John Giles.    Page 490

SIKES, Thomas: Leg. son Thomas; daughter Elizabeth; son John; wife Elizabeth, property which belonged to her first husband Thomas Hampton; daughter Mary. Exs., Thomas Sikes and Elizabeth Sikes. D. April 29, 1708. R. August 9, 1708.
    Wit: Richard Exum, Robert Lawrence, Robert Cooper.    Page 491

BROWNE, William: Appraisal by John Williams, Arthur Jones and William Exum. Not dated.    Page 492

CLARKE, William: Appraisal by Thomas Thropp, John Monger and Roger Hodges.
June 9, 1708.                                                    Page 493

NORSWORTHY, Capt. William: Appraisal by Francis Parker, Robert King and
Nicholas Casey. December 15, 1707.                              Page 493

HAREBOTTLE, Rebecca: Leg. daughter Elizabeth; daughter Jane; son John.
D. Feb. 22, 1705. R. August 9, 1706.                           Page 493

REYNOLDS, Richard: Appraisal by Giles Driver, Thomas Allen, John Wright
and John Parmento. June 24, 1707.                               Page 494

----------: Appraisal by John Davis, John Bidgood and James Lupo. June 9,
1708.                                                           Page 495

MACKLAND, Bryan: Appraisal by John Rogers, Hodges Council and John Dun.
August 24, 1708.                                                Page 495

DENSON, Francis: Leg. son James; son John; daughter Sarah Meredith the wife
of Joseph Meredith; granddaughter Frances Denson the daughter of my son
John; grandsons John and William the sons of my son John; grandson
John Kensy, son of my daughter Katherine Kensy; to grandchildren Joseph,
William and Sarah Meredith, children of Joseph Meredith. Exs., sons
James and John. D. February 3, 1708/9. May 2, 1709.
    Wit: Woodham (Needham?) Bryan, Alice Bryan, Isack Ricks, Sr.,
         Richard Hutchins.                                      Page 496

VASSER, Peter: Leg. son John land adjoining John Clark; son Peter; son
William; son Samuel; daughter Elizabeth Carroll; son Daniel; daughter
Mary; son Joseph. Extx., wife Margaret. D. January 22, 1708.
R. July 9, 1709.                                                Page 497

BROWNE, William: Account of estate. Received from Patrick Braddy as a
legacy to his daughter Mary from Margaret Wood; tobacco received from
Joseph Ford, Ex., of the will of Margaret Briggs as a legacy to Ruth
Browne decd., sister of Mary Blunt; to legacy given by Josias Wood to
Mary Browne als Blunt. Presented by Richard Blunt. Aug. 1, 1709. We
have adjusted the claims of Richard Blunt the administrator of William
Browne, late of this County. Proven by the evidence of Ann Davis and
Thomas Thropp, who married Mary the Extx. of Joseph Ford. Signed Henry
Baker and Nathaniel Ridley.                                     Page 498

ROGERS, Michael of Newport Parish: Leg. grandson John Thomas; granddaughters
Mary and Elizabeth Thomas. Ex., grandson Richard Thomas. D. April 5,
1710. R. August 9, 1710.
    Wit: Francis Parker, Nathan Bagnall, Daniel Batten.         Page 499

CARTER, Thomas: Leg. daughter Martha; son Alexander. Ex., my loving wife.
D. February 6, 1709. R. April 10, 1710.
    Wit: Thomas Ward, William Little, John Whetstone.           Page 499

ELDRIDGE, Samuel: Leg. son William; son Samuel; daughter Elizabeth; daughter
Martha; son William to my loving friend Murfrey; son Samuel to my
brother-in-law William Hook; daughter Martha to Elizabeth Gayner, if
she should die before said daughter is 16, to her daughter Mary Gainer.
Exs., friends William Hook and Roger Tarlton. D. April 9, 1709.
R. May 2, 1709.
    Wit: Francis Seagrave, Roger Tarlton, John Tarlton.         Page 500

BLAKE, Thomas: Leg. grandson Thomas Blake; son William; wife Alice; daughter
Isoddemias Christian Burgess; daughter Judith W. Smith; daughter Elizabeth.
Extx., wife Alice. D. January 30, 1707/8. R. December 20, 1709.
    Wit: James Bacon, John Hylliard, John Prime, Richard Blunt.
                                                                Page 501

PROCTOR, John: Leg. wife Elizabeth; among my children; Edward Cockerell. Brother Robert Little to be an assistant to my wife. D. ---------- R. August 9, 1710.
    Wit: Thomas Moore, Thomas Manes (?), Edward Cockerell.   Page 501

RYALL, Thomas: Leg. son Thomas; grandson Lawrence Brown; wife Isabel; my four children, George, Charles, John and Isabel. Extx., wife. D. May 26, 1709. R. ------------ 1709.
    Wit: John Carroll, Elizabeth Carroll, William Clark.   Page 502

WILLIAMS, John: Appraisal by Peter Deberry, John Weston, Richard Lewis and James Piland. February 9, 1708/9.   Page 502

WEST, William, Jr.: Appraisal at the house of Martha West by John Wright, Edward Long, John Butler and Thomas Wootten. 1709.   Page 503

WILLIAMS, Richard: Appraisal by John Weatherall, James House and James Brown. 1710.   Page 504

DANIEL, Thomas: Appraisal by Robert Brock, John Browne, John Frizzell and Thomas Calcote. Signed by Elizabeth Daniel. Not dated.   Page 504

BOYD, Thomas: Leg. God daughter Priscilla Scutchins, the daughter of Thomas Scutchins; God daughter Elizabeth White the daughter of John White; Thomas Boyd the son of my brother John Boyd and my kinswoman Henrietta Carroll the daughter of my sister Elizabeth Carroll in ye Kingdom of Ireland; father-in-law Mr. Francis Oberthorne; wife Martha my watch at her death to James Day; friend Thomas Jordan. Exs., wife and friend John Lear. D. July 12, 1710. R. October 9, 1710.
    Wit: Thomas Jordan, James Pitt, Thomas Cutchins.   Page 506

SMITH, Jane, widow: Leg. John Bythessa; young Robert Bythessa; Mary Corns; son William; son John; daughter Sarah; sister Elizabeth Deberry my two youngest children; sister Mary Bethessa my eldest son William. Exs., Peter Deberry and Robert Bythessa. D. November 5, 1710. R. November 9, 1710.
    Wit: James Piland, Elizabeth Wood.   Page 508

POPE, Richard: Estate sold. February 28, 1704.   Page 508

KAE, Capt. Robert: Account of estate. Tobacco due Alice Riddick, late the wife of said Kae. Paid the orphans of Capt. John Goodrich decd. Paid John Fiveash in full for his wife's part of her father Timothy Fenn's estate. Paid Martha Fenn in full. Paid William Smith for Eleanor Manning. Signed George Riddick. Audited by Henry Baker and Nathaniel Ridley. February 21, 1709/10.   Page 509

BOYD, Thomas: Appraisal by Thomas Applewhaite, Thomas Brewer, Francis Parker, Stephen Smith and Tristram Norsworthy. January 24, 1710.   Page 510

STORY, Lawrence: Leg. wife Susanna; my five children, John, Elizabeth, Thomas, Joseph and Mary. Exs., wife and son Thomas. Overseers to will: friends Joseph Bridger and Mr. Thomas Norsworthy. D. July 22, 1710. R. February 2, 1710.
    Wit: Robert Richards, Jr., Thomas Richards, Joseph Bridger. Susanna Story signed a bond with William Williams and John Wright her security. February 26, 1710.   Page 512

LUCK, John: Bond of Martha Luck to administer on his estate signed by Nicholas Fulgham and Charles Fulgham. February 26, 1710.
    Wit: H. Lightfoot.   Page 514

BENNET, Richard: Leg. Mary Throp, the daughter of Daniel Lewis; John
Mangum; James Coffield; sons Richard and James; Susanna Lewis; Martha
Lewis; wife Sarah, land on Blackwater with reversion to James Bennet
the son of Richard Bennet. Estate to be divided by Thomas Thropp,
Peter Deberry, Robert Bsviary and George Barlow. Extx., wife Sarah.
D. December 4, 1709. R. February 26, 1710.
   Wit: Thomas Thropp, William George, Mary Cornes, John Mangum.
   Col. Henry Baker was the security on the bond of Sarah Bennet.
                                                        Page 515

CHAPMAN, Charles: Leg. son John; grandson Charles; friend Arthur Smith;
son Joseph. Ex., son Joseph. D. December 20, 1710. R. February 26,
1710.
   Wit: Arthur Smith, Robert Brock.                    Page 516

CANNADAY, Samuel, Sr.: John Brewer and his wife Joanna sign a bond to administer his estate, with Benjamin and Robert Ricks their security.
March 26, 1711.                                         Page 517

LUCK, John: Appraisal by Thomas Bevan, William Green, John Chapman and
John Garland. Signed Martha Luck. March 26, 1711.      Page 517

STORY, Lawrence. Appraisal by Richard Wilkinson, Robert Richards, Jr.,
Samuel Garland and Thomas Whitley. March 26, 1711.     Page 518

HART, Thomas: Hopkins Howell's bond to administer estate, signed by Thomas
Howell and Benjamin Ricks. The bond of Robert Hart, William Goodman
and Robert Sherrer for the estate of Thomas Hart the orphan of Thomas
Hart, decd. March 26, 1711.                            Page 519

PITT, Thomas: Thomas Pitt to administer the estate, with Arthur Smith and
Henry Applewhite on his bond. March 26, 1711.          Page 520

CANNADAY, Samuel: Leg. wife Joannah; son Samuel. D. July 16, 1710.
R. March 26, 1711.
   Wit: William Page, Edward Cobb, Sr., Samuel Cannaday, Jr.
                                                        Page 521

PITT, Mrs. Mary: Appraisal by George Norsworthy, Thomas Brewer, Francis
Norsworthy, Tristram Norsworthy and Steven Smith. Presented by
Thomas Pitt. April 23, 1711.                           Page 522

ALLEN, Thomas: Leg. son Roger; son Thomas the elder; son Nicholas; son
Thomas the younger; William Rutter; wife Martha; daughter Anne.
Wife Extx. D. February 20, 1710/11. R. May 25, 1711.
   Wit: John Butler, William Butler, Thomas Wootten.   Page 522

STREET, John: Leg. daughter Ann Street; son George; daughter Sarah Turner;
daughter Mary Whitley; son Madison; son-in-law John Turner. Ex.,
loving wife. D. November 11, 1710. R. May 25, 1711.
   Wit: Thomas Bevan, John Joliff, Sarah Joliff.       Page 523

RICHARDS, William, Sr.: Leg. Mary Driver the daughter of Sary Driver, wife
of Giles Driver, Jr.; if without issue to the rest of the children of
my cousin Sarah Driver. Ex., Giles Driver, Jr. D. March 31, 1711.
R. June 25, 1711.
   Wit: Joseph Bridger, Mathew Shaw, Thomas Richards.  Page 524

WAILES, Nicholas: Appraisal by Stephen Smith, Robert Long; Anthony Fulgham.
Signed Mary Wale. April 23, 1711.                      Page 525

CHAPMAN, Charles: Appraisal by George Bell, John Bell, Thomas Harris,

                              49

Jeremy Proctor. Signed Joseph Chapman. June 25, 1711. Page 526

GEORGE, John: Appraisal by John Brantley, Thomas Hardy, George Riddick, and George Barlow. Page 527

WHITEHEAD, Arthur: Leg. son William; wife Mary Ex. D. January 11, 1710/11. R. ----------
    Wit: Philip Rayford, Philip Pierce, Thomas Boone. Page 528

BULLOCK, Thomas of the Lower Parish: Leg. son Thomas; son James; son William; son Joseph; son John; wife Mary. Exs., brothers William and John Bullock. D. January 25, 1709/10. R. ---------
    Wit: William Kerle, Samuel Boazman, James Bullock. Page 529

SCOTT, Robert: Leg. son Robert; cousin Catherine Scott the daughter of Richard Scott; wife Jane. Exs., wife, William Scott the son of William Scott and my brother-in-law John Roberts. D. April 21, 1711. 24th of 7 mo. 1711.
    Wit: John Denson, Thomas Gale, Alice Gale. Page 530

MORRIS, John: Leg. daughter Mary; son John; wife Jane. Wife Extx. D. March 18, 1710/11. R. ----------
    Wit: Thomas Hollyman, Christopher Hollyman. Page 530

THORPP, Thomas: Leg. wife Mary; William George and his wife Sarah; Stratfield Thorpp; son John, if he will not be ruled by my wife to care of Mathew Jordan; daughter Martha; daughter Ann; provision for unborn child. Wife Extx. D. August 4, 1711. R. January 28, 1711.
    Wit: Thomas Rosser, Francis Lee, William Dixson. Page 531

RICHARDS, William: Appraisal by William Hunter, Thomas Wooten, John Butler, John Wright, Giles Driver, Jr. June 25, 1711. Page 532

MARSHALL, Humphrey: Leg. grandson Humphrey Scutchins, land adjoining John Marshall; grandson Joseph Scutchins; land on which Thomas Hill lives to my daughter Mary Hill; grandson Thomas Applewhite; daughter Anne Applewhite; daughter Sarah Scutchins; John Thomas the son of Elizabeth Thomas; wife. Exs., son-in-law Henry Applewhite and Col. Samuel Bridger. D. December 18, 1711. R. ----------
    Wit: Anthony Holliday, William Williams, John Briggs. Page 533

FULGHAM, John: Leg. son John; son Anthony; son Michael; wife Anne; son Edmond. Wife Extx. D. June 7, 1701. R. ----------
    Wit: George Williamson, Francis Williamson, Barnabe Mackine, William West. Page 535

REYNOLDS, Richard of the Parish of Newport: Leg. wife Elizabeth; son Richard; son Sharpe; son Christopher; the land on which Edward Griffeth lives to Richard Jackson; grandson ---- Reynolds; what is due Elizabeth Lewis one of the daughters of Richard Lewis to be paid. Exs., my wife and sons. D. July 27, 1711. R. May 26, 1712.
    Wit: A. Smith, Giles Driver, Jane Benn. Page 536

JORDAN, John: Leg. wife Margaret; son John; four youngest daughters, Mourning, Elizabeth, Mary and Susanna; daughter Martha. Wife Extx. My three brothers, James, Richard and Benjamin Jordan overseers. D. February 12, 1710. R. May 6, 1712.
    Wit: John Watts, Poole Hall, John Howell. Page 538

BAKER, Henry: aged 67. Leg. wife Mary; son Henry; son James; son Lawrence; son William; daughter Mary; daughter Sarah; daughter Catherine; daughter Elizabeth. Wife Extx. D. June 10, 1709. R. July 28, 1712.
    Wit: Thomas Sharpe, John Hawkins, John Cary. Page 539

BRIDELL, Francis: Leg. daughter Mary Denson, wife to John Denson; grandson Francis Hampton, land adjoining Wm. Murfrey and Thomas Gale; daughter-in-law Elizabeth Sikes; grandchildren, John, William, Francis, James, Mary, Sarah Eleanor and Anne Denson; my granddaughter-in-law Elizabeth Hampton; wife Mary. Wife Extx. D. May 5, 1712. R. ----------
    Wit: Wiliam Kerle, Roger Tarlton, Sr., Roger Tarlton, Jr.
                                          Page 541

LUPPO, James: Leg. son Philip; daughter Sarah Lilbourne; daughter Ann Bidgood; daughter Mary; Elizabeth Bidgood; son John; wife Sarah. Wife Extx. D. April 26, 1712. R. October 27, 1713.
    Wit: James Day, John Bidgood, Thomas Wrenn.        Page 542

WEST, Robert: Leg. son Henry; wife Isabella; son Arthur; son Robert; son William; Thomas Green. Wife Extx. D. June 7, 1712. R. ----------
    Wit: William Green, Richard West, Mary Green.     Page 542

GLEDHILL, Mary: Leg. son James Day; only surviving Ex. of my decd. husbands, James Day and John Johnson; money in hands of Micajah Pery and Co., Merchants in London, also a large sum in the possession of John Lear and his wife Elizabeth of Nansemond, the Exs. of Mrs. Isabella Haveild, Extx. of Capt. Luke Haveild of Nansemond and one of the Exs. of said James Day; - sons James Day and Nathaniel Ridley to settle said estates. D. November 30, 1712. R. January 26, 1712.
    Wit: Francis Wrenn, Thomas Wrenn, John Ogbourne.    Page 543

PITT, Robert: Leg. brother John Monro; sisters, Sarah, Henrietta and Mary Monro; uncle James Pitt the plantation on which he lives and the one on which John George lives; uncle Henry Pitt; my father-in-law and mother; brother John Monro the land adjoining Cole Bridger; uncle John Pitt the land on which Susanna Moscrop and Mathew Shaw live; town land for a Gleab; Mary Pitt the daughter of Mr. Thomas Pitt; Elizabeth Bridger the daughter of Capt. Jos. Bridger; Mary Moscrop the daughter of Thomas Moscrop; Sarah Watts the daughter of John Watts; Martha Norsworthy the daughter of Mr. John Norsworthy; Jane Smith the daughter of Col. Arthur Smith. Exs., father-in-law Andrew Monro and uncle Henry Pitt. D. July 10, 1711. R. January 26, 1712.
    Wit: Arthur Smith, Mary Smith, John Driver.     Page 544

MACKCONE, William: Leg. daughter Sarah; son William; son Neall; son Peter; son John; daughter Mary Whitley; daughter Jennett; son Joseph; wife Sarah. Exs., wife and son Neall. D. November 10, 1711. R. January 26, 1712.
    Wit: William Green, Thomas Owen.         Page 545

HUGGINS, William: Appraisal by Thomas Newsum, Owen Merrick, Lawrence Hunt. December 10, 1712.                    Page 546

SANBOURNE, Daniel: Leg. my --- Elizabeth Jordan all the land which I bought of Thomas Munford, Edward Griffen, Giles Lawrence, Abraham Bruce and Christopher Holmes; her husband Joshua Jordan; grandson Woodson Sanbourne Woodson; granddaughter Sarah the daughter of Joshua Jordan; wife Elizabeth. Wife Extx. D. 16th of 12 mo. 1711. R. November 24, 1712.
    Wit: William Best, Richard Ratcliff, Elizabeth Ratcliff, Humphrey Marshall, Benjamin Callaway.           Page 546

WIGGS, Henry: Leg. son George; son William; son Luke; daughter Catherine, daughter Sarah; granddaughter Catherine -----; daughter Elizabeth; son Henry; rest of estate between my 4 sons and 4 daughters. Wife Extx. Overseers: Mathew Jordan, Blackaby Terrall, John Scott. D. June 18, 1711. R. ----------

Wit:   John Hillyard, Richard Reynolds, Jr., Thomas Calcote,
       James Bragg, Ezekial Fuller.                        Page 547

PITT, Robert:  Appraisal by Thomas Moscrop, William Williams, Nicholas
    Fulgham and Thomas Bevan.  Signed by Andrew Monro, Clarke.  June 26,
    1712/13.                                               Page 548

SURBEY, John:  Appraisal by William Williams, Richard Pilkmien (?), Thomas
    Whitley, Thomas Turner.  February 23, 1712.            Page 549

LEWIS, John:  Appraisal by John Davis, John Munger, John Bidgood and John
    Harrison.  February 16, 1712/13.  Ann Lewis the widow signed. Page 550,
                                                                     551

ALTMAN, Thomas:  Leg. Godson Thomas Altman; cousin John Altman, the son of
    Garrett Altman; wife Elizabeth; Garrett Altman; cousin John Altman son
    of John Altman.  Wife Extx.  D.  May 12, 1712.  R.  January 26, 1712.
       Wit:  Thomas Applewhite, Bartholemew Larner.        Page 551

CALLOWAY, Benjamin:  Appraisal by John Penny, Henry Pitt, Humphrey Marshall.
    Signed Sarah Calloway.  January 26, 1713.              Page 552

MACKHONE, William:  Appraisal by Thomas Bevan, Thomas Moscrop and Robert
    Richards.  Signed Sarah Maccone.                       Page 553

DEBERRY, Peter:  Leg. daughter Priscilla, wife of Zacharias Maddera; son
    John land adjoining William Thomas; daughter Sarah the wife of John
    Warren, part of Piland's patent; son John the bed on which I now lie
    at the house of James Sampson; wife Elizabeth.  Exs., wife and brother
    John Brantley.  D.  December 30, 1712.  R.  March 28, 1712.
       Wit:  Nathaniel Ridley, James Sampson, James Madera, Mary
             Sampson.                                      Page 554

HADLEY, Ambrose:  Leg. son Robert land I bought of William Boddie; son
    Ambrose; son Henry; now wife Margaret; son-in-law Richard Gent; daughter
    Elizabeth Edwards.  Wife Extx.  D.  March 5, 1703/4.  R.  April 27, 1713.
       Wit:  William Boddie, Martin Luther, Deborah Portis, John Boddie,
             Henry Goldham, Abraham Jones.                 Page 555

HARRIS, Thomas:  Appraisal by R. Proctor, John Harrison, Philip Wheadon,
    James Wilson.  Signed Judith Harris.  March 23, 1712/12.  Page 556

DEBERRY, Peter:  Appraisal by Mathew Jones, John Davis, Robert Lancaster,
    Richard Gray.  Signed Elizabeth Deberry.  April 27, 1713.  Page 557

BEEL, Benjamin:  Leg. wife Martha; son Benjamin; daughter Mary; daughter
    Patience; daughter Florence; daughter Martha.  Exs., wife and son
    Benjamin.  D.  February 12, 1712/13.  R.  April 27, 1713.
       Wit:  Thomas Dixon, Rich. Beele, Sol. Horner, John Nevill.
                                                           Page 558

HARRIS, John of the Upper Parish:  Leg. daughter Alice; daughter Elizabeth;
    daughter Isabel; land given me by Hugh Campbell of Cureweak (?);
    Lawrence Brown, when he is free; wife Mary; daughter Susanna; daughter
    Anne, daughter Mary; daughter Martha.  Wife Extx.  Overseers: Mathew
    Jordan and John Scott.  D.  February 12, 1712.  R.  May 25, 1713.
       Wit:  Judith Harris, William Story, Mathew Jordan.  Page 559

BALEY, John:  Leg. son William; wife; my six daughters; daughter Anne.
    Wife Extx.  D.  18th of 7 mo. 1712.  R.  May 25, 1713.
       Wit:  William Clary, Robert Bayley, Samuel Cornwell.
       Presented by his widow, Elizabeth Bayley.           Page 560

ASQUE, John of Warwick County: Leg. beloved friend Mathew Jones, Jr. D. March 5, 1713. R. May 25, 1713.
  Wit: A. Orbos, Hester Brown.      Page 561

BEELE, Benjamin: Appraisal by Jacob Darden, William Murfey, John Watts and Robert Smelly. Signed Martha and Benjamin Beele. April 27, 1713.
                   Page 563

BRIDGER, Samuel: Leg. James Webb; wife Elizabeth. Wife Extx. D. April 22, 1704. R. May 25, 1713.
  Wit: Thomas Godwin, Sr., Thomas Pitt.    Page 564

JONES, Susanna: Leg. husband Arthur Jones; my father Henry King; daughter Elizabeth; daughter Mary. D. December 19, 1691. R. May 26, 1713.
  Wit: John Person, Richard Bennett, Jr., John Person, Jr.,
     Richard Jones, Thomas Proud.    Page 565

ASQUE, John: Inventory presented by Mathew Jones. June 14, 1713. Page 565

CASEY, Nicholas of the Lower Parish: Leg. son Nicholas; son Thomas; three youngest daughters by my last wife; son Richard; daughter Ann; daughter Mary; daughter Sarah; wife Jane; five youngest children, Martha, Jane, Ruth, Nicholas and Thomas. Exs., wife and son Richard. D. April 17, 1713. R. June 27, 1713.
  Wit: Stephen Smith, John Wheal (?); Daniel Degan, Joshua
     Jordan.            Page 566

ROBERTS, Jane: Leg. son Robert Eley, part of a patent granted John Roberts and Jane his wife; grandson Robert Scott; daughter Mary Parker and her husband William Parker, decd.; granddaughter Martha Sanders; to Thomas Jones the land he bought of my brother Richard Braswell; my -------- Rebeckah Brinkley; daughter Jane Scott; son John Roberts; son Thomas Roberts. D. June 26, 1711. R. August 24, 1713.
  Wit: William Scott, Jr., Robert Scott, John Sellaway. Page 567

HARRIS, John: Appraisal by Rueben Proctor, William Balmer, Elias Hodges and Roger Hodges. Signed Elizabeth Harris. August 8, 1713. Page 568

CASEY, Nicholas: Appraisal by Francis Parker, Tristram Norsworthy, Thomas Grosse and Thomas Applewhaite. August 21, 1713.  Page 569

BAYLEY, John: Appraisal by William West, William Kinchin, Thomas Williams and John Joyner.           Page 570

BULLARD, Thomas of the Lower Parish: Leg. wife Hannah my mill in Nansemond County; daughters, Hannah, Elizabeth and Mary. D. April 26, 1713. R. 28th of 10 mo. 1713.
  Wit: John Howell, Henry Bullard, Nicholas Askew. Page 571

WEST, Robert: Appraisal by Henry Pope, Thomas Powers, Bridgeman Joyner, and William Bridger. July 29, 1713.     Page 572

BRIDGER, Joseph: Leg. son Joseph; son Robert; son William; son John; son James; daughter Hester; daughter Elizabeth; to sons, Robert, William and John the land I bought of Walter Rutter, formerly granted old Mr. Izard; wife Elizabeth. Wife Extx. Trustees, brother Samuel and William Brider and Tristram Norsworthy. D. March 14, 1712/13. R. January 25, 1713.
    Wit: William Bridger, Sarah Terrell, Elizabeth Watts,
     William Dixon.         Page 574

WEBB, William of the Upper Parish: Leg. son Richard land bought of John

Briand; youngest son William; wife Mary; to Thomas, William, Susannah and Joseph Webb; - Mathew, Richard and Elizabeth have already had their part. Exs., wife and Thomas Webb. D. June 6, 1708. R. January 25, 1713.

    Wit: John Ogbourne, John Munger, Henry Kae.     Page 575

BRIDGER, Capt. Joseph: Appraisal by William Williams, Richard Wilkinson, Thomas Moscrop and Robert Richard, Jr. Signed by Elizabeth Bridger.
    Page 576

LEGGE, John: Appraisal by Robert Brock, Timothy Tynes; Mathew Lowry. January 25, 1713.     Page 578

EDWARDS, Charles: Leg. wife Mary, the money due me from James Day and Christopher Dickinson; James Briggs, Jr. the son of James Briggs; Edmond Briggs; daughter Elizabeth; daughter Sarah Briggs; grandson William Skelton; grandson James Skelton; granddaughter Sarah Skelton; grandson Thomas Skelton; grandson Charles Stevens; wife Mary. Wife Extx. D. December 10, 1713. R. March 23, 1713.
    Wit: John Hillyard, James Briggs, Thomas Skelton.     Page 578

BEVAN, Thomas: Leg. son Thomas; wife Mary; son Peter; daughters Mary and Elizabeth; for want of heirs my estate to the right heirs of Thomas Hayes of Northumberland County. Wife Extx. D. September 6, 1710. R. June 28, 1711.
    Wit: Nathaniel Ridley, Richard Wilkinson, John Chapman. Page 579

DAVIS, John of the Upper Parish: Leg. wife Mary; son Samuel; son Thomas land in Surry, which was bought of Edward Grantham; son John; daughter Sarah; daughter Elizabeth; daughter Prudence; son William the land on which Thomas Robertson lived; daughter Mary the wife of William Murray; granddaughter Elizabeth Murray, the daughter of said William; brother William Green, friends Nathaniel Ridley and James Day to make the division of my estate. Wife Extx. D. December 31, 1712. R. June 28, 1714.
    Wit: Nathaniel Ridley, Richard Webb, Thomas Webb, Mary Maccoding.     Page 581

CARRELL, John: Leg. son William; son John; wife Elizabeth; children, Thomas, Joseph, Benjamin, Samuel and Elizabeth. Wife Extx. D. May 14, 1710. R. August 23, 1714.
    Wit: John Whetstone, Thomas Carrell, Mary Carrell.     Page 585

COOPER, Robert: Inventory, September 10, 1714.     Page 585

HAIL, John: Nuncupative, proven by Mary Burnett and Elizabeth Howell. That he authorized Richard Mathews to be his Ex. and gave him his little daughter and two youngest sons, Samuel and Thomas. Signed by aforesaid and Benjamin Jordan. Statement April 23, 1714.
R. November 22, 1714.     Page 585

MOORE, George, age 78 years: Leg. wife Jennie; granddaughter Jane White. Wife Extx. D. November 30, 1710.
    Wit: Elizabeth Browne, Henry Baker, Lawrence Baker.
Codicil: grandson George Carter; grandson John White; grandson Moore Thomas White; grandson William White; grandson Henry White, land adjoining Thomas Carter; grandson Samuel Williams, reversion to his brother John Williams; grandson George Piland; grandson Thomas Piland. R. January 24, 1714. Will presented by Magdaline Carter.
    Wit: William Baldwin, James Sampson, Henry White.     Page 586

HAIL, John: Appraisal by Jacob Darden, John Watts and Thomas Dixon. November 22, 1714.     Page 587

BEAL, Benjamin: Additional appraisal presented by Martha Beal and Benjamin Beal. Page 587

CARROLL, John: Appraisal by Elias Hodges, Roger Hodges and Thomas Wrenn. February 26, 1714/15. Page 588

ASQUE, John: Appraisal by Thomas Gale, John Neavil, Michael Murfrey and Richard Mathews. Signed Catherine Asque. January 24, 1714. Page 589

BRIDGER, Joseph: Additional appraisal. Signed Elizabeth Bridger. March 28, 1715. Page 589

MAYO, William, Sr. of the Lower Parish: Leg. son William, with reversion of bequest to James Mayo; son John; son Peter; wife Isabel; youngest daughter Mary; daughter Margaret; daughter Patience. Exs., wife and my brother Bridgeman Joyner. D. July 14, 1713. R. April 25, 1715.
　　Wit: Joseph Joyner, Joshua Joyner, William Page. Page 590

GLADHILL, Rueben: Leg. sister Mary Atkinson; Mary Edwards; Ann Chapman; brother William Gladhill and Joseph Chapman to divide my estate between themselves. D. February 19, 1714/15. R. April 25, 1715.
　　Wit: William Thomas, Richard Webb. Page 591

BEVAN, Thomas: Inventory presented by Mary Bevan. May 23, 1715. Page 592

BRIDGER, Col. Samuel: Inventory presented by Madam Elizabeth Bridger. May 23, 1715. Page 593

MURPHERY, William, Jr.: Appraisal by Thomas Gale, John Pope, John Sellaway and John Mackmiall. April 28, 1715. Signed Mary Murphery. Page 594

LUCK, John: Account of estate. Cash from Bermuda. Due Nicholas Fulgham and Charles Fulgham. Signed Robert Richards, Jr. June 27, 1715. Page 595

MAYO, William: Inventory, presented by Isabel Mayo. July 5, 1715. Page 595

PARMENTO, John: Appraisal taken at the house of John Murray, by John Long, Thomas Wootten, Richard Casey, John Butler and John Watts. Signed by John and Mary Murray. June 27, 1715. Page 597
Mary Murray, late the wife of John Parmento.

GOODMAN, William: Inventory presented by Rebeccak Goodman. June 20, 1715. Page 597

GILES, Thomas: Leg. Newport Parish 400 A. for a Gleab, adjoining land of John Pernel; John and Thomas Smelly the sons of Robert Smelly; Robert, ths son of Robert Smelly; Giles Smelly; Lewis Smelly; wife Ellenor; Eleanor Smelly. Wife Extx. D. April 2, 1715. R. September 26, 1715.
　　Wit: Arthur Smith, Thomas Nickson, John Carner, John Pernel. Page 597

HALL, John: Appraisal by John Long, John Watts and Thomas Uzzell. October 24, 1716. Page 599

MAYO, William: Appraisal by Robert Lawrence, Richard Wooten, James Tullaugh. Signed Isabel Mayo and Bridgeman Joyner. July 25, 1715. Page 600

GOODMAN, William: Appraisal by John Williams, Thomas William, Thomas Holliman, John Wombwell. November 25, 1715. Page 601

BONICKE, Edward: Leg. Alexander Forbes all my estate in Virginia; my daughter in England; to Hon. Col. Pollock all my estate in N. C. D. February --, 1714. R. 28th of 9ber, 1715.
Wit: Edward Chitty, James Booth, Mathew Booth.     Page 602

DRIVER, Giles: Appraisal by John Watts, Mathew Lowry, John Butler. January 9, 1715.     Page 602

SMITH, Mary: Leg. daughter Ann Wesson; daughter Sarah Bulger; daughter Elizabeth Parker; son William; granddaughter Anna Barnes; son Nicholas; son Joseph; grandson Will Smith; grandson Peter Lugg; grandson Nathaniel Parker; daughter Anne Smith; daughter Martha Smith. Son Joseph Ex. Friends Will Green, John Pitt and Henry Pitt to divide my estate. D. October 12, 1715. R. January 23, 1715.     Page 605

GILES, Thomas: Inventory presented by Eleanor Giles. November 23, 1715.
Page 606

DEBERRY, Peter: Account of estate, examined by Mathew Jones and Joseph Copeland. Signed Elizabeth Deberry. October 24, 1715.     Page 606

COLEMAN, Robert: Leg. Eleanor Giles; brother Stephen's sons; Richard Batten; Benjamin Beale; Elizabeth Murrey; George Martin; John Watts; Christopher Reynolds and his wife Ann. Exs., Christopher Reynolds and his wife. D. March 8, 1715. R. ------------
Wit: John Butler, Rodger Murrey.     Page 607

GILES, John: Leg. wife Philirita; all my children. D. March 1, 1703. R. ----------
Wit: Anthony Holliday, Frances Greenfield, Nicholas Fulgham, Adam Murrey.     Page 607

HOLLIDAY, Samuel: Appraisal by Robert King, Thomas Gross, John Penny and Francis Parker. Signed Mary Holliday. April 19, 1716.     Page 608

WORRELL, Richard of the Lower Parish: Leg. son William; son Richard; wife Dorcas; my three daughters. Ex., my father-in-law Henry Runnalds. D. March 22, 1715/16. R. -----------
Wit: William Wesura (?), John Wesura.     Page 609

BROWN, John: Appraisal by Robert Brock, John Frissell, Thomas Summerell and Thomas Calcote. January 23, 1715.     Page 610

WOOD, Thomas of the Upper Parish: Leg. son George; my grandson -------; William Drew of the Lower Parish of Surry County, land sold him. Wife Elizabeth Extx. D. November 25, 1715. R. ----------
Wit: James Piland, Catherine Piland, Mary Bennett.     Page 611

WORRELL, Richard: Appraisal by Philip Rayford, Philip Pierce and John Barden. Signed Henry Runnalds.     Page 611

PARNELL, John: Leg. son Thomas; son James land adjoining James Jolley; son Benjamin, son Joseph; son-in-law John Chestnutt. Wife Extx. D. January 17, 1715/16. R. ----------
Wit: Jacob Darden, John Gardner, John Joyner.     Page 612

LEE, Francis: Leg. son Francis; among all my children. Son Francis Ex. D. October 5, 1716. R. ----------
Wit: Nicholas Derring, Henry White, Mary Roberson.     Page 613

GLADHILL, Reuben: Appraisal by George Goodrich, Philip Wheadon, Roger Hodges and Thomas Wrenn. June 10, 1716. Signed by Joseph Chapman and William Gladhill.     Page 614

WHITLEY, Thomas of the Lower Parish: Leg. daughter Elizabeth; daughter
Martha; daughter Priscilla; wife Mary; son Thomas; son William; son
George; son John; son Maddison.    Son Thomas Ex.  D.  December 5, 1715.
R. ----------
  Wit: Maddison Street, John Garland, Mary Garland.  Page 615

WHITLEY, Thomas: Appraisal by John Wright, Arthur Benn, John Garland,
Robert Richards, Jr.  April 22, 1717.      Page 616

LEE, Francis: Appraisal by George Goodrich, Elias Hodges, Roger Hodges.
                 Page 616

CARRELL, Thomas: Leg. son James; son Thomas; son John; son Robert; son
William; wife Mary.  Wife Extx.  D.  October 1, 1716.  R. ----------
  Wit: John Brantley, Clay Brantley, Thomas Holleman.  Page 616

PENNY, John of the Lower Parish: Leg. son John; son Ralf; son William;
daughter Sarah; daughter Margaret Williams; grandson John Williams;
daughter Elizabeth Right; wife Lucy.  Wife Extx.  D.  May 17, 1715.
R. ----------
  Wit: Thomas Copeland; Humphrey Marshall, Joseph Marshall.
                 Page 617

GILES, John:  Inventory. 1717.        Page 619

BRIDGER, Elizabeth: Leg. granddaughter Elizabeth Norsworthy; granddaughter
Martha'Norsworthy; daughter Patience Milner; daughter Elizabeth Wilkinson; cousin Joseph Godwin's son Samuel; granddaughter Patience Milner;
cousin Joseph Godwin's daughter Elizabeth.  D.  April 5, 1717.  R. ------
  Wit: Elizabeth Price, Joseph Godwin.    Page 619

UNDERWOOD, Thomas: Leg. son William; wife Dianah; daughter Mary; son Thomas;
daughter Jane Flowers; daughter Grace Cane; daughter Elizabeth Williams;
daughter Ann Pope; son John; Elizabeth Carver an orphan who lives with
me.  Ex., son William.  D.  August 4, 1714.  R. ----------
  Wit: John Allen, Elizabeth Allen, William Havett (?),
    John Sellaway, Joseph Godwin.    Page 620

HARDIE, Thomas: Leg. wife Mary; daughter Sarah; son George; son Thomas,
the land in Surry on which John Shelly lives; son Richard the land on
which John Ingram and John Skelton live.' Wife Extx.  D.  January 7,
1711.  R. ----------
  Wit: Richard Gray, Thomas Parke, Nathaniel Munger.  Page 622

BRIDGER, Madam Elizabeth: Appraisal taken at the house of Mr. William
Wilkinson, Jr., by John Chapman, Thomas Moscrop, Henry Pitt. Page 623

HARDY, Thomas: Appraisal by Will Drew, John Brantley, and Will Ruffin.
Signed by Charles Jarrett and Mary his wife, Extx. of Thomas Hardy.
September 13, 1717.        Page 625

WILKINSON, Richard: Leg. daughter Rachel; son Richard; son-in-law Henry
Turner; Elizabeth Turner; daughters, Ann, Mary and Elizabeth.  Exs.,
son Richard and daughter Rachel.  D.  May 27, 1715.  R. ----------
  Wit: Humphrey Wigginson, Elizabeth Turner.  Page 625

JORDAN, Benjamin: Leg. wife Sarah; son Benjamin; daughter Margaret;
daughter Sarah.  Wife Extx.  Overseers: James, Robert and Richard.
Money due me from Robert Wise to heirs.  D.  February 8, 1715.
R. ----------
  Wit: Alexander Campbell, John Bradley, Mary Hurst.  Page 627

PARKER, Francis: Leg. wife Elizabeth; daughter Martha; son Nicholas land
    bought of Daniel Batten; son Nathaniel property in Hampton. My land
    to be divided by Tristram Norsworthy, Sr. Ex., son Nathaniel.
    D. October 1, 1717. R. -----------
        Wit: Tristram Norsworthy, George Norsworthy, Joshua Jordan.
                                                            Page 628

OGBOURN, Nicholas: Appraisal at the house of Thomas Richards, by Anthony
    Fulgham, Thomas Gross, Samuel Garland, John Garland. February 22, 1713.
                                                            Page 629

RICKES, John: Leg. William Watkins the son of John Watkins, who lives with
    me; brothers, Robert, James, Isaac, and Abraham Rickes; sister Jane
    Rickes. Exs., brothers, Abraham and Robert. D. September 8, 1711.
    R. ----------
        Wit: John Pool, Sarah Watkins, John Watkins.        Page 629

WEST, Francis: Leg. cousin Francis West, the son of John West; to the rest
    of the children of John West; Judith Perry; Thomas Perry; cousin John
    Guillam, the son of Capt. Hinchie Guillam. D. October 8, 1715.
    R. ----------
        Wit: George Washington, John Washington, Hincha Gilliam.
                                                            Page 631

CLEMENTS, Francis: Leg. son Francis; son Benjamin; son Thomas; friend
    Capt. Nathaniel Ridley and his wife Elizabeth; friend James Stanton;
    daughter Mary; daughter Elizabeth. Wife Lydia Extx. D. November 22,
    1717. R. ----------
        Wit: James Stanton, James Stanton, Jr., Richard Jones,
        John Allen.                                         Page 632

BODIE, William: Leg. grandsons, William and Thomas Brown and their sisters;
    daughter Elizabeth Mathews; son John; my now wife Mary. Ex., son John.
    D. December 17, 1712. R. February 25, 1717.
        Wit: John Jones, Joseph Chapman, H. Lightfoot.      Page 633

PARKER, Francis: Appraisal presented by Nathaniel. June 19, 1718.
                                                            Page 633

SCOTT, William: Leg. wife Elizabeth; son William; son Robert; son John;
    daughter Elizabeth Holloway; grandsons, John, Thomas and William
    Holloway; daughter Catherine; daughter Sarah. Exs., son Robert and
    daughter Sarah. D. September 8, 1716. R. ----------
        Wit: John Denson, John Allen, Richard Selloway, Thomas Sikes.
                                                            Page 635

JORDAN, Joshua: Leg. mother-in-law Sarah Sanborne; wife Elizabeth; daughters,
    Sarah, Rachel, Mary, Elizabeth, Margaret and Susanna; son Mathew; son
    Joshua; provision for unborn child. Exs., wife and brothers, Robert
    and Mathew. D. February 28, 1717. R. ----------
        Wit: Thomas Copeland, Cornelius Ratcliff, Henry Davis. Page 637

RATCLIFF, Richard: Leg. son Richard; wife Elizabeth; son Cornelius; son
    John; daughter Mary and her husband Thomas Newman; daughter Rebeccah
    and her husband Richard Jordan; the children of my two deceased daughters,
    Elizabeth and Sarah. Exs., wife and son Richard. D. October 27, 1718.
    R. October 27, 1718.
        Wit: William Best, Humphrey Marshall, Thomas Copeland. Page 638

SMITH, Stephen: Leg. daughter Martha; daughter Sarah's seven children;
    wife Mary; Mary Ratcliff. Cousin Joseph Smith and Mr. Henry Pitt and
    William Green to divide my estate. D. May 5, 1718. R. ----------
        Wit: William Weston, Joseph Weston, Smith Collins.  Page 639

WILES, Zacharias: Leg. wife Dorothy; son Joseph; daughter Mary; daughter Sarah; son Moses; daughter Ann. Joseph Smith, William Weston and Joseph Weston to divide my estate. Exs., wife and son Joseph. D. May 14, 1718. R. ----------
Wit: Ralph Frissell, Joseph Weston. Page 640

WHETSTONE, John: Appraisal by John Macon, William Drew, and Richard Gray. Not dated. Page 641

RATCLIFF, Richard: Appraisal by Thomas Applewhaite, Humphrey Marshall, Henry Pitt and William Best. October 27, 1718. Page 640

JORDAN, Joshua: Inventory presented by Elizabeth Jordan. Page 641

FIELDS, John: Appraisal by John Hyllyard, Thomas Harrison and William Smith. November 24, 1718. Page 642

GREEN, John: Appraisal by Robert Lancaster, Roger Hodges, Philip Wheadon, Edward Miller. December 30, 1718. Page 643

HOLLADAY, Anthony: Leg. son Jonas; daughter Sarah Murphrey; son-in-law Jonas Knott and Mary his now wife; granddaughter Elizabeth Holladay; grandson Joseph Holladay, part of the land I bought of brother Marshall; grandson Anthony Covington Holladay, son of Lemuel; granddaughter Catherine Murphery; children of son Lemuel decd.; children of son Joseph decd.; children of daughter Sarah Murphery; daughter Mary Knott; grandson William Knott. Exs., son Jonas and grandson Anthony Covington Holladay. D. January 3, 1718. R. ----------
Wit: John Yeates, James Knott, Jr., Thomas Burrage. Page 644

GROSS, Thomas: Leg. wife Elizabeth; son Francis; son Thomas; son Joshua; daughter Hannah; daughter Mary Frissel; daughter Elizabeth Hines; daughter Susanna Long. Exs., wife and son Joshua. D. November 29, 1715. R. April 27, 1719.
Wit: Thomas Pitt, Mary Pitt, Jane Benn. Page 645

HARDY, Thomas: Account current of his estate, returned by Charles and Mary Jarrett. April 27, 1719. Page 647

CARRELL, Mary: Appraisal by George Riddick, James Briggs and Richard Gray. April 27, 1719. Page 647

BAGNALL, Robert: Leg. wife Rebecca the land on which John Wright now lives; sister Charity Davis; daughter-in-law Sarah Marshall. John Watts, James Jordan, John Butler and John Long to divide my estate between my wife and my daughter-in-law. Wife Extx. D. February 27, 1718. R. April 27, 1719.
Wit: John Long, Thomas Green, William West. Page 648

LONG, Edward: Leg. son Robert; son Edward; son James. Wife Extx. D. February 10, 1718. R. April 27, 1719.
Wit: John Long, John Watts. Page 648

WHITE, John: Leg. son Joseph; daughter Sarah; daughter Mary; son William; daughter Rachell; son Thomas; son John; daughter Elizabeth Scott; my young daughter Elizabeth White. Ex., son-in-law William Scott. D. March 4, 1718. R. April 27, 1719.
Wit: Thomas Copeland, Humphrey Marshall. Page 649

MURRE, John: Leg. wife Priscilla; John and James Hall; Peter Hall; cousin Roger Murre; brother Roger Murre; sister Ann; sons-in-law John and James Parmentoe; wife Mary. Ex., Robert Driver. D. March 13, 1718.

R. April 27, 1719.
    Wit: Robert Driver, Roger Murre, Richard Jordan.          Page 650

MURRE, John: Appraisal by Benjamin Beal, John Watts, Thomas Wooten and John
    Chestnutt. R. April 27, 1719.                              Page 651

WHITE, John: Appraisal by Thomas Copeland, Henry Pitt, Humphrey Marshall
    and William Best (?). R. April 29, 1719.                   Page 651

DARDEN, Jacob: Leg. son Stephen land in Wainoke Neck; son John; son
    Benjamin; son Jacob; son Samuel; son Henry; the daughter of Thomas
    Giles, my daughter's child; son Joseph. Exs., wife Ann and son Jacob.
    D. April 14, 1717. R. June 22, 1719.
    Wit: William Murfrey, Sarah Murfrey, Charles Roberts.      Page 654

WILSON, John: Leg. son John; servant William. Wife Extx. D. March 18,
    1718/19. R. June 22, 1719.
    Wit: Thomas Murry, Thomas Davis.                           Page 655

ALLEN, Martha: Leg. daughter Martha Long; daughter Patience Keally; Nicholas
    Allen; Thomas Allen, Jr.; Thomas Allen ye elder; Roger Allen; son William
    Rutter; daughter Ann Allen. Ex., son William Rutter. D. November 5,
    1718. R. June 22, 1719.
    Wit: William Green, Thomas Wooten, Rebecca Gray.           Page 656

LONG, Edward: Appraisal by William Wilkinson, William Price and Thomas
    Uzzell. April 27, 1719.                                    Page 658

WEATHERELL, William: Appraisal by John Watts, Thomas Wootten, William Price
    and Thomas Uzzell. April 27, 1719.                         Page 659

LONG, Robert: Appraisal taken at the house of Susan Long by Arthur Benn,
    Anthony Fulgham and Henry Pitt. April 27, 1719.            Page 660

BARLOW, George: Leg. son John; daughter Elizabeth; son George; daughter
    Sarah; daughter Mary; son Thomas. Wife Extx. with the assistance of
    John Brantley. D. December 10, 1718. R. ----------
    Wit: John Brantley, Hester Brantley.                       Page 661

PARSON, John: Leg. wife Francis, son John. Wife Extx. D. October 20, 1707.
    R. ----------
    Wit: Henry Baker, John Whetstone, Thomas Ward, John Mangum.
                                                               Page 662

KEIGHLEY, John: Leg. John Scritor (?) and his son John; William Barden; Richard
    Pierce; John Teasley; William Page; Virgus Smith; Thomas Aultman. Ex.,
    Mr. John Hurst of Nansemond County. I am the executor of ye former will
    of Ann Pierce decd., ye March 14, 1718/19. D. March 30, 1719.
    Wit: William Page, John Barden, William Barden.
    Codicil: I make Thomas Jones, John Teasley and Richard Pierce my execu-
    tors, since my friend John Hurst is not willing to accept the executor-
    ship. D. March 31, 1719. R. ----------                     Page 662

-----

ADMINISTRATIONS AND PROBATES

-----

BARECROFT, Charles: Administration requested by George Moore, son-in-law of
    the said Barecroft in behalf of Maudlin Barecroft, relict and William
    Barecroft her son. D. September 23, 1661. R. October 24, 1661.

Security, Mr. ffrancis England, Mr. Flake.                    Page 1

BROWN, John: Dying intestate, Edward Gibbs requested administration.
   Oct. 14, 1661.
          Security, Mr. ffulgham and Mr. Driver.                Page 1

HOLLAGHANE, Water (Walter): Dying intestate, Mr. Thomas Culmer requested
   administration. Oct. 14, 1661.
          Security, Mr. George Moore.                           Page 1

HASWELL, Samuel: Dying intestate, John Hardy requested administration in
   behalf of the said Haswell's brother in England. May 1, 1662.
          Security, Mr. Richard Sharpe, Mr. Arthur Smith.       Page 2

CORESEY, Richard: Estate left to his wife Useley for the use of his
   children. Wife qualified. D. Feb. 20, 1661. R. Aug. 22, 1662.
          Security, John Brigg, George Mansfield.               Page 2

COOZ, William: Dying intestate, administration requested by Nicholas Cobb
   for his creditors. Oct. 9, 1662.                             Page 2

WEBB, John: By will left all of his estate to John Portis and Joseph
   Carrell. Proven by John Hardy and Richard Jordan. Administration
   granted legatees. D. Dec. 9, 1662. R. Dec. 24, 1662.        Page 3

BAZELEY, Job: Dying intestate, the relict Amy Bazeley requested administration. D. Dec. 22, 1662. R. Jan. 5, 1662.                    Page 3

THOMAS, Griffeth: Appointed by will, John Pitt his executor, who requests
   the probation of the will. D. Feb. 9 last past. R. March 23, 1662.
          Security, Captain Bridger, Thomas Greene.             Page 3

LEWIS, William: Late of this Colony, appointed John Lewis his Executor.
   Probate requested. Feb. 9, last past. R. March 23, 1662.
          Security, Mr. Andrews, Mr. Izard.                     Page 4

BANISTER, Elizabeth, widow: Francis Baker requests administration on behalf
   of her children. D. May 1, last. R. May 21, 1663.
          Security, Mr. Kae, Mr. Daniel Mackland.               Page 4

WATSON, John: Dying intestate, relict Hannah Watson requests administration.
   D. June 9,        R. June 9, 1663.
          Security, Richard Penny, Thomas Empson.               Page 4

BRAE, Edward: Appointed by will, Helenor Brae, his relict, Extx. Probate
   requested. Sept. 19, 1663.
          Security, Henry Joyce, Roger Ingram.                  Page 4

BLITH, William: Appointed by will Richard Sharpe overseer for Sarah his
   relict and Christopher and William Blith his sons. Nov. 24, 1663.
          Security, William Oldis, Thomas Pope.                 Page 5

GRAY, Mary: Appointed Anthony Mathews administrator on her estate for the
   use of her son Walter Gray in ye County of Dorset, England. Dec. 9,
   R. Dec. 28, 1663.
          Security, William Morris, Christopher Holleman.       Page 5

ADAMS, Captain Thomas: Ordered estate sold and put in the charge of Mr.
   Edward Bushell for term of four years. D. Dec. 9,      R. Dec. 28,
   1663.
          Security, Col. Swann, Lt. Col. Jordan, Mr. Kae.       Page 5

ROBESON, Frances: Relict of Thomas Robeson, late of this county, requested administration on his estate. Feb. 9,       R. Feb. 29, 1663.
Security, Mr. Taberer, John Snellock.       Page 6

PARKER, Thomas: By will ordained that his wife Frances should have one-third of his estate, other two-thirds to his children. Relict requests probation. Feb. 9,       R. Feb. 29, 1663.
Security, Mr. Nicholas Smith, Thomas Parker.       Page 6

PILAND, James: Appointed his wife Elizabeth, Extx. Probation requested. Feb. 9,       R. Feb. 29, 1663.
Security, Mr. Kae, Mr. John Snellock.       Page 6

VAUGHAN, John: Dying intestate, administration requested by his relict Ellinor Vaughan. Feb. 9,       R. Feb. 29, 1663.
Security, John Britt, John Collins.       Page 6

DAVIS, John: Dying intestate, Mary Davis, relict requests administration. Feb. 18, 1663. R. March 25, 1664.
Security, Mr. England, Mr. Flake.       Page 7

AYRES, Richard: Dying intestate, Francis Ayres, brother to the said Richard requested administration. Feb. 18, 1663. R. March 23, 1664.
Security, George Empson, Walter Richards.       Page 7

WRIGHT, Thomas: By will appointed Elizabeth Wright, his relict Extx. Probate requested. Feb. 18, 1663. R. March 25, 1664.
Security, George Empson, John Asque.       Page 7

MOONE, Prudence: Dying intestate, William Wilson, the son of the said Prudence requests administrations. March 9, 1663. R. March 25, 1664.
Security, Peter Garland, Anthony Mathews.       Page 7

BEDFORD, Peter: Dying intestate, Mary Bedford the relict requests administration. June 9, 1664. R. Aug. 19, 1664.
Security, George Moore, John Britt.       Page 8

COLE, Mary: Orphan dying intestate, administration requested by Thomas Barlow, her guardian. June 9, 1664. R. Aug. 19, 1664.
Security, George Moore, John Snellock.       Page 8

LEWER, William: By will appointed Mary Lewer, his relict his Extx. June 9, 1664. R. April 19, 1664.       Page 8

WESTURAY, William: By will appointed Elizabeth Westuray, his relict his Extx. Aug. 9, 1664. R. Aug. 19, 1664.
Security, Thomas Green, John Vicars.       Page 8

POWELL, Edward: Dying intestate, administration requested by George Bell. Oct. 11, 1664. R. Oct. 11, 1664.
Security, Thomas Ware (Ward), John Wakefield.       Page 9

BRADDY (BRADIE), Patrick: Appointed Elizabeth Braddy, his relict, Extx. April 10, 1665. R. June 21, 1665.
Security, Mr. Taberer, George Moore.       Page 9

ELDRIDGE, Samuel: Dying intestate, administration requested by Thomas Moore, who married his relict. April 10, 1665. R. June 21, 1665.
Security, George Moore, ----- Brantlie.       Page 10

BAYLIE, Peter: Appointed his wife Wilthim Baylie, Extx. May 1, 1665. R. June 21, 1665.
Security, Thomas Edwards, James Marlowe.       Page 10

EMPSON, George:  Dying intestate, Thomas Empson his brother requested
   administration.  May 1, 1665.
         Security, Mr. Driver, William Goering.          Page 10

WILSON, William:  Dying intestate, Peter Garland, requests administration
   in the right of Mary, Prudence, and Abigail, daughters of his late
   wife, Joan Garland, the sister of the said William Wilson.  Nov. 10,
   1665.  R.  Jan. 19, 1665.
         Security, John Pitt, Richard Penny.          Page 10

MIDLANE, George:  Left his estate to his two daughters, Mary and Sarah Mid-
   land, with Jeremiah Martin, overseer.  Dec. 9, 1665.  R.  Jan. 19, 1665.
         Security, Mr. Marshall, Benjamin Beal.          Page 11

WILSON, James:  By nuncupative will left entire estate to George Bell.
   Dec. 14,        R.  Jan. 19, 1665.
         Security, John Wakefield, John Collins.          Page 11

TROTMAN, Stephen:  Dying intestate, administration requested by Edward
   Miller.  Dec. 14,        R.  Jan. 19, 1665.
         Security, Thomas Edwards, George Bell.          Page 11

BROWN, John:  Dying intestate, administration requested by Bridgett Brown,
   his relict.  Feb. 9, 1665.  R.  March 26, 1666.
         Security, Mr. Arthur Smith, Edward Gibbs.          Page 11

GODWIN, Thomas:  Dying intestate, administration requested by Ann, his
   relict.  Feb. 9, 1665.  R.  March 26, 1666.
         Security, Mr. Taberer, Mr. Kae.          Page 12

GRIFFIN, Samuel:  Appointed Mary Davis his Extx.  Feb. 9, 1665.  R.  March 26,
   1666.
         Security, Thomas Harris, John Monger.          Page 12

JONES, Ralph:  Entire estate by will to John Hardy.  March 9, 1665.
   R.  March 26, 1666.
         Security, Thomas Barlow.          Page 12

WARREN, David:  Dying intestate, administration requested by George Walker
   in the right of Margaret Walker, the relict.  April 9, 1666.  R.  June 7,
   1666.
         Security, Mr. Taberer, William Huntt.          Page 12

BRUCE, John:  Dying intestate, administration requested by John Davis, in
   right of Mary the relict.  April 9, 1666.  R.  June 7, 1666.
         Security, George Moore, George Bell.          Page 13

ROYALL, James:  By will appointed Daniel Long, Executor.  June 20, 1666.
   R.  Oct. 25, 1666.
         Security, John Vicars, Thomas Grosse.          Page 13

JEFFRIES, Richard:  Dying intestate, administration requested by John
   Councilling, who married the relict of the said Jeffries.  Aug. 9,
   1666.  R.  Oct. 25, 1666.
         Security, Mr. England, George Branch.          Page 13

PITT, Captain Henry:  Dying intestate, Thomas Pitt his son requests administration.  10 of 7ber 1666.  R.  Oct. 25, 1666.          Page 13

WESTON, John:  Dying intestate, Elizabeth his relict requests administration.
   Dec. 10, 1666.  R.  Jan. 21, 1666.
         Security, James House, John Ross.          Page 14

LUKE, Paul: By will appointed Sarah his relict, Extx.   Dec. 10, 1666.
   R.   Jan. 21, 1666.
            Security, Mr. George Moore, John Littford.                    Page 14

JAMES, John: Dying intestate, administration requested by Diana his relict.
   Jan. 9, 1666.  R.  Jan. 21, 1666.
            Security, Thomas Barlow, John Davis.                          Page 14

WEST, Nicholas:  Administration requested by John Watson in right of his
   wife Sarah, who was the relict of the said West.  Nov. 9, 1667.
   R.  Feb. 18, 1667.
            Security, John Portis, John Davis.                            Page 15

GLANE, Robert:  Appointed by will, Mary his relict, Extx.  Nov. 9, 1667.
   R.  Feb. 18, 1667.
            Security, John Tripcony, John Ross.                           Page 15

HUNTT, William:  Dying intestate, administration requested by Richard
   Parker, who married Judith the relict of the said Huntt.  May 1, 1668.
   R.  Aug. 20, 1668.
            Security, Francis Baker, Thomas Edwards.                      Page 15

BRASWELL, Richard:  Appointed his sons Richard and Robert his executors,
   Mr. George Gwillian and Mr. Richard Izard his overseers, qualified
   during their minority.  May 1,      R.  Aug. 20, 1668.
            Security, Mr. Thomas Green, Richard Penny.                    Page 16

BOUCHER, Daniel:  Appointed by will, Mr. John Hardy and Mr. Thomas Tabarer,
   who qualified in behalf of his daughter, Elizabeth Boucher.  Aug. 20,
   1668.                                                                  Page 16

CURTIS, William:  Dying intestate, administration requested by his relict
   Alexandre.  Jan. 9, 1668.  R.  April 28, 1669.
            Security, George Moore, Thomas Barlow.                        Page 17

WILLIAMS, Morgan:  Dying intestate, administration requested by his relict,
   Dorothy.  May 3, 1669.  R.  23 of 7ber 1669.
            Security, Thomas Moore, John Britt.                           Page 17

GIBBS, Edward:  Dying intestate, administration requested by his relict,
   Elizabeth.  May 3,      R.  23 of 7ber 1669.
            Security, William Bressie, John Vicars.                       Page 17

BOND, Major John:  Named in will wife, Dorothy, Extx.  May 3,
   R.  23 of 7ber 1669.
            Security, Francis England, Arthur Smith.                      Page 18

SMITH, George:  Dying intestate, Ann the relict requests administrations.
   May 3,      R.  23 of 7ber, 1669.
            Security, Arthur Smith, Richard Sharpe.                       Page 18

CARTER, Thomas:  Dying intestate, administration requested by the relict
   Elinor.  May 3,      R.  23 of 7ber, 1669.                             Page 18

REYNOLDS, John:  By will appointed his brother Richard Reynolds his executor.  May 3,      R.  23 of 7ber, 1669.
            Security, Benjamin Beale, Ambrose Bennett.                    Page 19

POOLE, Joseph:  By will appointed Elizabeth his relict Extx.  May 3,
   R.  23 of 7ber 1669.
            Security, John Britt, Thomas Blake.                           Page 19

FFENERYEARE, John: By will appointed Ann his relict Extx. May 3,
R. 23 of 7ber 1669.
Security, Mr. Izard, Mr. Thomas Green.                    Page 19

KING, Henry: By will appointed Ruth his relict, Extx. May 3,    R. 23 of
7ber 1669.
Security, John Newman, John Gutheridge.                   Page 20

IZARD, Richard: By will appointed Rebecca his relict Extx. May 3,
R. 23 of 7ber 1669.
Security, Mr. Marshall, Lt. Smith, Mr. Sharpe.            Page 20

BREWER, John: By nuncupative will appointed Ann his relict Extx. June 9,
R. 23 of 7ber 1669.
Security, Mr. Marshall, Mr. Ayres, Mr. Vicars.            Page 20

BAKER, Lt. Francis: By will appointed Hannah his relict, Extx. Aug. 9,
1669. R. 23 of 7ber 1669.
Security, Lt. Symon Ogborne, William Webb.               Page 21

GODBEHERE, John: By nuncupative will appointed George Cripps his executor.
Aug. 9, 1669. R. 23 of 7ber 1669.
Security, Captain Francis England, Thomas Moore.          Page 21

NOWLEY, Edward: By nuncupative will appointed William Yarrett, Extx.
Sept. 9,      R. 23 7ber 1669.
Security, William Bressie, Thomas Harris.     .           Page 21

PERRY, Philip: Ralph Channell in the right of Grace his wife and the relict
of the said Perry requested probation. Oct. 9, 1669. R. Oct. 28, 1669.
Security, Richard Penny, James Bagnall.                   Page 22

NICHOLSON, Richard: Dying intestate, administration requested by the relict,
Mariable. Feb. 9, 1669. R. March 2, 1669.
Security, Thomas H-----, John Richards.                   Page 22

RICHARDS, Walter: Dying intestate, administration requested by the relict,
Elizabeth. Feb. 9, 1669. R. March 2, 1669.
Security, John Pitt, George Lucke.                        Page 22

MOSS, Thomas: By will appointed John Whitley, Sr. his executor and Thomas
Whitley, Sr., overseer. Feb. 9, 1669. R. March 2, 1669.
Security, George Lucke, John Richards.                    Page 23

BROWNE, Edward: By will appointed Ellinor his relict executrix and Robert
Flake and Richard Bennett, overseers. Overseers qualified. R. March 2,
1669.
Security, Thomas Atkinson, John Clark.                    Page 23

OGBORNE, Symon: By will appointed Lucie his relict, Extx. Feb. 9, 1669.
R. March 2, 1669.
Security, Thomas Harris, John Newman.                     Page 23

NORSWORHTY, John: Dying intestate, administration requested by Frances
his relict. April 9, 1670. R. April 20, 1670.
Security, John Pitt, Mr. William Oldis.                   Page 24

GRIFFEN, Thomas: By will appointed Ann his relict, Extx. April 9, 1670.
R. April 20, 1670.
Security, Robert Smith, William Godin (Godwin).           Page 24

DIXSON, Thomas: Dying intestate, administration requested by Henry Martin, who married Mary the relict of the said Dixson. May 2, 1670. R. June 24, 1670.
        Security, Mr. Thomas Moore, Mr. Robert Roe.        Page 24

PILAND, Edward: Dying intestate, administration requested by his brother Richard Piland. May 2, 1670. R. June 24, 1670.
        Security, Thomas Edwards, John Guteridge.        Page 25

FULGHAM, Captain Anthony: Dying intestate, administration requested by his relict, Martha. May 2, 1670. R. June 24, 1670.
        Security, John Fulgham, Michael Fulgham.        Page 25

LEWIS, Thomas: Dying intestate, administration requested by his relict, Rebecca. Aug. 9, 1670. R. Oct. 20, 1670.
        Security, Lt. Col. John George, Morgan Lewis.        Page 25

BRAGG, James: Dying intestate, administration requested by the relict, Elizabeth. Sept. 9, 1670. R. Oct. 20, 1670.
        Security, Thomas Harris, John Portis.        Page 26

GRANTLIN, Darby: By will appointed his wife Gulian, Extx. Probation requested by Mathew Waikley her now husband. Oct. 25, 1670. R. Dec. 2, 1670.
        Security, Mr. Applewhaite, James Pedden.        Page 26

BARNETT, Robert: By will appointed Garrett Altman, Ex. Oct. 25, 1670. R. Dec. 2, 1670.
        Security, John Abbott, William Rogers.        Page 26

VIVIAN, Thomas: Dying intestate, administration requested by the relict, Elizabeth. Nov. 9, 1670. R. Dec. 2, 1670.
        Security, William Earnest, Thomas Hipkins.        Page 27

COLE, William: By a nuncupative will, bequeathed his whole estate to James Pedden. Nov. 9, 1670. R. Dec. 2, 1670.
        Security, John Portis, Roger Pitt (?).        Page 27

COLLIER, Robert: Dying intestate, administration requested by William Earnest in the right of his wife Katherine, whom the decedent acknowledged as his kinswoman. Dec. 9, 1670. R. April 6, 1671.
        Security, John Vicars, John Ross.        Page 27

WOOTTEN, Thomas: By will appointed his son Richard his executor. Dec. 9, 1670. R. April 6, 1671.
        Security, Mr. James Sampson, John Collins.        Page 27

LEWIS, Arthur: Dying intestate, administration requested by Tobias Keeble, who married his relict. Aug. 9, 1ast. R. Sept. 27, 1671.    Page 28

MUNGER, John: By will appointed Thomas Taberer, overseer. Feb. 9, 1670. R. April 6, 1671.
        Security, Mr. Kae, William Webb.        Page 28

RIDLEY, William: By will appointed Mr. Charles Barham his Ex. Oct. 19, 1671.
        Security, Mr. Robert Kae, John Jennings.        Page 28

WHITLEY, John: By will appointed Ann, his relict, Extx. Feb. 9, 1671. R. May 8, 1672.
        Security, Mr. John Pitt, Thomas Poole.        Page 29

MORRIS, William: By will appointed his relict, Elizabeth his Extx.
April 9, 1672. R. May 8, 1672.
Security, Richard Jordan, Sr., Henry Joyce.                    Page 29

HARRIS, Thomas: By will appointed his relict Alice his Extx.  June 10,
1672. R. Nov. 13, 1672.
Security, John Newman, Edward Brantley.                    Page 29

HERRING, John: By will appointed his relict, Margerie his Extx.  June 10,
1672. R. Nov. -- 1672.
Security, Thomas Poole, Thomas Grosse.                    Page 30

CLARK, James: Dying intestate, administration requested the relict, Judith.
Aug. 9, 1672. R. Nov. 13, 1672.
Security, William Warren, William Hitchens.                    Page 30

KNIGHT, William: Dying intestate, administration requested by Frances Knight.
Aug. 10, 1672. R. Nov. 13, 1672.
Security, Captain Arthur Smith, Mr. George Moore.                    Page 31

HIGGENS, Roger: By will appointed Robert Hodges, his executor.  Aug. 10,
1672. R. Nov. 13, 1672.
Security, John Harris, Nicholas Ogbourne.                    Page 31

HUGGENS, Mathew: Dying intestate, administration requested by James Pedden,
who married his relict. Oct. 9, 1672. R. Oct. 13, 1672.
Security, Anthony Mathews, George Moore.                    Page 31

DURFACE, Charles: By will appointed his relict, Diana, his Extx.  Oct. 9,
1672. R. Oct. 13, 1672.
Security, John Davis, Joseph Ford.                    Page 32

WILLIAMS, George: By will appointed his friends, Mr. Arthur Smith, Mr.
Pharo Cobb and Mr. Henry Applewhaite his overseers. Oct. 9, 1672.
R. Oct. 13, 1672.
Security, Richard Sharpe, Francis Ayres.                    Page 32

WARREN, William: By will appointed Mr. Robert Kae, his executor.  Oct. 24,
1672. R. Nov. 13, 1672.
Security, Timothy Fenn, William Lewis.                    Page 32

LEWIS, Thomas: Dying intestate, administration requested by his relict,
Martha. Dec. 9, 1672. R. Feb. 4, 1672/3.
Security, John Britt, Sergeant John Davis.                    Page 32

BETHESEA, Robert: Dying intestate, administration requested by Daniel
Water, who married his relict. Jan. 10, 1672. R. Feb. 4, 1672/3.
Security, Edmond Wickens, Thomas Barloe.                    Page 33

PROCTOR, Ambrose: Appointed by will his relict Elizabeth his Extx.  Jan. 9,
1672. R. Feb. 4, 1672/3.                    Page 33

LATIMORE, Hugh: Dying intestate, administration requested by his relict,
Jane. Feb. 9, 1674. R. March 22, 1674.
Security, John Sherrer, Alexander Webster.                    Page 33

WATSON, John: Dying intestate, administration requested by Mr. Richard
Sharpe and Captain Arthur Smith in right of the heirs. Oct. 9, 1673.
R. Oct. 31, 1673.
Security, Mr. Applewhaite, Mr. Ayres.                    Page 34

YOUNG, John: Dying intestate, administration requested by John Perry, who
married Elizabeth, ye daughter and heir of the decedent. Aug. 10, 1674.
R. Sept. 30, 1674.

Security, John Marshall, Francis Ayres.          Page 34

RUFFIN, William: Dying intestate, administration requested by Robert Ruffin,
     his son and heir.  Jan. 9, 1674.  R.  March 22, 1674.
          Security, Captain William Oldis, Mr. William Body.     Page 34

PITT, Colonel Robert: By will appointed his son, Capt. John Pitt Ex.
     Jan. 9, 1674.  R.  March 22, 1674/5.
          Security, Richard Wilkinison, Thomas Green.          Page 34

WILDES, Thomas: Dying intestate, administration requested by William
     Collins, who married Ann his relict.  April 9, 1675.  R.  June 15, 1675.
          Security, Thomas Parker, Thomas Poole.          Page 35

GODWYN, John: Dying intestate, administration requested by his relict, Ann.
     April 9,          R.  June 15, 1675.
          Security, Thomas Pope, Daniel Long.          Page 35

CLARK, Thomas: Dying intestate, administration requested by his relict,
     Elizabeth.  April 9, 1675.  R.  June 15, 1675.
          Security, Richard Penny, Humphrey Marshall.          Page 35

SCULLEY, Thomas: Dying intestate, administration requested by his relict,
     Elizabeth.  May 1, 1675.  R.  June 15, 1675.
          Security, Thomas Pope, Daniel Long.          Page 35

WALTON, Richard: Dying intestate, administration requested by his relict,
     Elizabeth.  June 9, 1675.  R.  June 15, 1675.
          Security, --------- (?), Thomas Moore.          Page 36

LEWIS, Benedict: Dying intestate administration requested by his relict,
     Hannah.  June 9, 1675.  R.  June 15, 1675.
          Security, Richard Silvester, John Perry, Sr.          Page 36  .

LUCKE, George: By nuncupative will appointed his relict Elizabeth his
     Extx.  Aug. 9,          R.  Sept. 4, 1675.
          Security, Richard Wilkinson, John Vicars.          Page 36

ROE, Robert: Dying intestate, administration requested by William Powell,
     his greatest creditor.  Aug. 9, 1675.  R.  4th of 7ber 1675.
          Security, Thomas Powell, John Moore.          Page 36

BRESSIE, John: Dying intestate, administration requested by his relict,
     Sarah.  Aug. 9, 1675.  R.  Sept. 4, 1675.
          Security, Colonel George Moore (?), John Britt.          Page 37

GROSSE, Richard: Dying intestate, administration requested by his relict,
     Jane.  Aug. 9, 1675.  R.  4th of 7ber 1675.
          Security, Timothy Fenn, John Davis.          Page 37

IZARD, Rebecca (widow): By will appointed James Bagnall, Henry Reeves and
     Ambrose Bennett, overseers.  Oct. 20, 1675.  R.  Nov. 15, 1675.
                                                            Page 37

CLAY, John: By will appointed his relict, Mary, Extx.  Oct. 20, 1675.
     R.  Nov. 15, 1675.
          Security, Thomas Barloe, Daniel Macland.          Page 37

HILL, Nicholas: By will appointed his relict, Silvestra his Extx.  Oct. 21,
     1675.  R.  Nov. 15, 1675.
          Security, Mr. Robert Flake, Mr. Robert Kae.          Page 38

ROE, Robert: By will appointed Jane his relict, Extx. Jan. 10, 1675.
R. Feb. 12, 1675.
Security, Thomas Moore, Elias Fort. Page 38

MIDDLETON, Robert: Dying intestate, administration requested by Anselm
Bailey, his greatest creditor. Jan. 10, 1675. R. Feb. 12, 1675.
Security, Andrew Shield, William Bradshaw. Page 38

CLAY, William: By will appointed his relict, Judith, Extx. Feb. 17, 1675.
R. March 15, 1675/6.
Security, George Hardy, Sr., John Clay. Page 38

GROSSE, Thomas, Sr.: By will appointed his relict, Susanna, his Extx.
Susanna Grosse dying before the probation of the will, Thomas Grosse
the eldest son qualified. Feb. 17, 1675. R. March 15, 1675.
Security, Michael Fulgham, Clement Creswell. Page 39

HERRIN (HERRING), Margerie (widow): By nuncupative will, bequeathed her
estate to John Whitfield, orphan. Clement Creswell his father-in-law
qualified. Feb. 17, 1675. R. March 15, 1675/6.
Security, Thomas Munford, Daniel Long. Page 39

WEBB, James: By will appointed his relict Elizabeth, his Extx. Elizabeth
Webb ordained her father, Colonel Thomas Godwin her lawful attorney,
who qualified. Feb. 17, 1675. R. March 15, 1675/6.
Security, Col. Thomas Godwin, Jeremiah Exum. Page 39

MASON, William: Dying intestate, administration requested by the relict,
Joane. April 10, 1676. R. June 16, 1676.
Security, Sergeant John Davis, John Lewis. Page 40

PITT, Roger: Dying intestate, administration requested by Susanna, his
relict. April 10, 1676. R. June 16, 1676.
Security, John Newman, John Harris. Page 40

AYRES, Francis: By will appointed his relict, Jane, his Extx. April 10,
1676. R. June 16, 1676.
Security, Mr. William Bressie, Mr. Peter Banton. Page 40

DRIVER, Giles: By will appointed his relict, Olive his Extx. June 9, last.
R. Aug. 11, 1677.
Security, Mr. Robert Burnett, Mr. Richard Reynolds. Page 41

VALENTINE, James: By will appointed his relict, Mary, his Extx. June 9,
R. Aug. 11, 1677.
Security, Humphrey Marshall, James Benn. Page 41

HOUSE, James: Dying intestate, administration requested by his relict, Mary.
June 9, 1677. R. Aug. 11, 1677.
Security, Roger Wiles, Neale Mackone. Page 42

SKINNER, Richard: Dying intestate, administration requested by his relict,
Mary. April 9, 1677. R. Aug. 11, 1677.
Security, Mr. Robert Flake, Mr. George Moore. Page 42

OLIVER, John: Dying intestate, administration requested by Jane Roe.
Aug. 11, 1677.
Security, Mr. George Moore, Edward Grantham. Page 42

HARRIS, Edward. Dying intestate, administration requested by George Hardy
in behalf of the orphans. May 1, 1677. R. Aug. 11, 1677.
Security, Mr. Philip Pardoe, Henry Combes. Page 42

LEWIS, Morgan: By will appointed his relict Sarah, Extx. June 9, 1677.
R. Aug. 11, 1677.
Security, Mr. George Hardy, Philip Pardoe.          Page 43

DUNNIN, John: By will appointed Mr. Giles Driver, who is now deceased,
Olive Driver his relict qualified. June 9, 1677. R. Aug. 11, 1677.
Security, John Bromfield, Mr. Robert Burnett.          Page 43

HARDY, John: By will appointed his relict, Alice, Extx. June 9, 1677.
R. Aug. 11, 1677.
Security, Mr. Robert Burnett, Mr. William Mayo.          Page 43

WARE, Thomas: By will appointed his relict, Ann, Extx. June 9, 1677.
R. Aug. 11, 1677.
Security, Richard Piland, John Williams.          Page 44

ALLEN, John: By will appointed his relict, Mary, Extx. June 9, 1677.
R. Aug. 11, 1677.          Page 44

DIXON, William: By will appointed his relict, Frances, Extx. April 9, 1677.
R. Aug. 11, 1677.
Security, William Yearett (Yarrett), Edward Jones.          Page 44

COCKINS, William: Dying intestate, administration requested by Edward
Grantham in right of his wife, the relict of the said Cockins. March 10,
1678. R. April 9, 1679.
Security, Mr. George Moore, Mr. Thomas Moore.          Page 45

JENNINGS, Captain John: By will appointed his relict, Mary, his Extx.
Probation requested by Mr. Thomas Alley, who married the relict of the
said Jennings. March 10, 1678. R. April 9, 1679.
Security, Mr. Robert Flake, Lt. George Moore.          Page 45

WILLIAMS, Rowland: Dying intestate, administration requested by Thomas
Parker and Michael Rogers in behalf of the orphans. March 10, 1678.
R. April 9, 1679.
Security, Thomas Parker, Michael Rogers.          Page 46

FFOARTE (FORT), Elias: Dying intestate, administration requested by his
relict, Phillis. March 10, 1678. R. April 9, 1679.
Security, Mr. Thomas Moore, Mr. John Newman.          Page 46

BARLOW, Thomas: By will appointed his relict, Elizabeth, Extx. April 9,
1679. R. April 9, 1679.
Security, Mr. Thomas Moore, Mr. George Moore.          Page 46

SNELLOCK, John: By will appointed Major James Powell his Ex. April 19, 1679.
Page 47

BECHINOE, Edward: By will appointed his relict, Mary, Extx. June 9, 1679.
R. Feb. 27, 1679.
Security, Richard Bennett, Mr. Richard Sharpe.          Page 47

BARTLETT, Robert: By nuncupative will left his daughter to Tobias Kibble,
who requested administration. June 9, 1679. R. Feb. 27, 1679.
Security, John Watts, John Wesson.          Page 48

BRIGGS, Richard: By will appointed Major Samuel Swann and Mr. Thomas Moore
Exs. Request probation in behalf of James and Edward Briggs his
children. June 9, 1679. R. Feb. 27, 1679.
Security, Captain Henry Applewhaite, John Bromfield.          Page 48

CORSEY, Frances: By will appointed Mr. Thomas Groves Executor of one half of her estate to educate her son John the orphan of Richard Corsey. Thomas Groves qualified by his attorney, Capt. H. Applewhaite. Aug. 11, 1679. R. Feb. 27, 1679.
    Security, ------ Williams, William Evans.        Page 48

DAYWAY, Isaac: By will appointed his relict, Margaret, Extx. July 17, 1679. Feb. 27, 1679.        Page 49

DANIELL, John: By will appointed his relict, Elizabeth, Extx. Probation requested by Thomas Goldham, who married the relict of the said Daniell. Aug. 9,    R. Feb. 27, 1679.        Page 49

LONG, John: By will appointed his relict, Margaret, his Extx. Feb. 10, 1678. R. Feb. 27, 1679.
    Security, John Gardner, John Marshall.        Page 49

FLY, William: By nuncupative will appointed his relict, Mary, Extx. Dec. 9, 1679. R. Feb. 27, 1679.
    Security, Roger Davis, John Burnell.        Page 50

ALLEN, George: Dying intestate, administration requested by his relict, Prudence. Feb. 9, 1679. R. Feb. 27, 1679.
    Security, John Combes, John Turner.        Page 50

BROMFIELD, John: Dying intestate, administration requested by his relict, Oliffe in behalf of his orphans. Feb. 9, 1679. R. Feb. 9, 1679.
    Security, Col. Pitt, Mr. Thomas Giles.        Page 50

MACONE, Neale: By will appointed his relict, Anne, Extx. Dec. 9, 1680. R. Jan. 14, 1680.
    Security, John Nevill, Richard Reynolds.        Page 51

WOODWARD, Thomas, Jr.: Dying intestate, administration requested by Katherine Woodward in behalf of her son John Woodward, next brother to the said Thomas. Feb. 9, 1680.
    Security, Nicholas Fulgham, John Whitley.        Page 51

WAIKLEY, Mathew: By nuncupative will, whole estate to Henry King. March 9,    R. March 18, 1680.        Page 51

PHILLIPS, William: Dying intestate, administration requested by his relict, Ann. June 9,    R. June 18, 1681.
    Security, George Bell, Thomas Blake.        Page 52

EDWARDS, Robert: Dying intestate, administration requested by his relict, Mary. May 2, 1681. R. June 18, 1681.
    Security, Henry King, Owen Griffen.        Page 52

REYNOLDS, Henry: By will appointed his relict, Joyce Extx. June 9, 1681. R. June 18, 1681.
    Security, Thomas Ward, Henry Clark.        Page 52

BITTLE, Robert: By will appointed his wife, Urseley, Extx. May 2, 1682. R. June 18, 1681.        Page 53

RUTT, Abraham, (blacksmith): Dying intestate, administration requested by John Britt in behalf of the daughter Ann Rutt. Sept. 9, 1681. Dec. 9, 1681.
    Security, William Evans, John Sherrer.        Page 53

BATEMAN, William: By nuncupative will appointed Mr. Thomas Gyles his Ex. Oct. 11, 1681. R. Feb. 9, 1681/2.        Page 53

JACOBS, John: Dying intestate, administration requested by Thomas Wood.
Oct. 11, 1681. R. Feb. 9, 1681/2.
    Security, John Clay, Ralph Hill.                              Page 54

MATHEWS, Anthony: By will appointed his relict, Ann, Extx.  Jan. 9, 1681/2.
R. Feb. 9, 1681/2.
    Security, John Moore, James Bacon.                           Page 54

EDWARDS, Peter: By will appointed John Coggan his Ex.  June 9, 1682.
R. Oct. 24, 1682.
    Security, John Moore, Richard Hutchins.                      Page 54

POOLE, Thomas: By will appointed his wife, Christian, Extx.  June 9, 1682.
R. April 9, 1683.
    Security, William Evans, Richard Poole.                      Page 55

BRIGGS, Margaret: By will appointed John Ford, Ex.  Dec. 9, 1682.
R. June 9, 1683.
    Security, George Moore, George Cripps.                       Page 55

BARNES, Thomas: By will appointed his widow, Diana, Extx.  June 9, 1683.
R. 9th of Xber 1683.
    Security, John Jackson, Thomas Williams.                     Page 55

ASKEW, John: Dying intestate, administration requested by his relict,
Bridgett.
    Security, John Nevill, William Murfrey.                      Page 56

CRESWELL, Clement: By will appointed his relict, Ann, Extx.  Nov. 9, 1683.
June 9, 1684.
    Security, Thomas Hawkins, William Mecone.                    Page 56

GARDNER, John: Dying intestate, administration requested by his relict,
Mary.
    Security, Thomas Joyner, James Gardner.                      Page 56

ROGERS, Edward: By will appointed Ann Mathews, his Ex.  March 10, 1683.
R. June 9, 1684.
    Security, Thomas Gany (?), James Pedden.                     Page 57

LOCKHART, John: Dying intestate, administration requested by James
Tullaough.  Sept. 9,     R. Sept. 12, 1684.
    Security, Robert Coleman, Richard Reynolds, Sr.              Page 57

CLAY, John: Dying intestate, administration requested by John Brantley in
behalf of his wife and her sister Sarah Clay.  May 1, 1685.
R. Dec. 9, 1685.
    Security, William Evans, William Baldwin.                    Page 57

WRENN, Francis: Dying intestate, administration requested by his relict,
Elizabeth.  Feb. 9, 1684.  R. Dec. 9, 1685.
    Security, Giles Limscott, John Shephard.                     Page 58

LEWER, William: By will appointed Robert Thomas, Ex.  He refused to
qualify, probation requested by Thomas Thorpe, who married the relict
of the said Lewer.  Dec. 9, 1685.  R. Feb. 27, 1685.            Page 58

HITCHINGS, William: By will appointed his relict, Elizabeth, Extx.
Dec. 9, 1685.  R. April 9, 1686.
    Security, John Goodrich, William Clay.                       Page 58

PARKER, Thomas: By will appointed his relict, Frances, Extx.  Feb. 9, 1685.

R.  May 1, 1686.
    Security, William Smith, James Tullaugh.          Page 58

COBB, Nicholas:  By nuncupative will, his estate to his son Edward and
    daughter Mary.  May 8, 1686.  R.  Oct. 24, 1686.      Page 59

RICHARDSON, William:  By will appointed Thomas Atkinson and Peter Hayes,
    Exs.  May 8,     R.  Oct. 24, 1686.        Page 59

GREEN, Thomas:  By will appointed his relict, Mary and his son George
    Green, Exs.  June 9,     R.  Oct. 24, 1686.      Page 59

MacQUINNEY, Michael:  By will appointed his relict, Elizabeth, Extx.
    Aug. 9,     R.  Oct. 24, 1686.         Page 59

PERKINS, Edward:  By will appointed William Murfrey, Ex.  Dec. 9, 1686.
    R.  Oct. 21, 1687.          Page 60

WALTON, Richard:  By will appointed his relict, Joyce, Extx.  March 9, 1686/7.
    Oct. 21, 1687.          Page 60

WILLIAMS, John:  By will appointed Ann his relict, Extx.  May 2, 1687.
    R.  Oct. 21, 1687.          Page 60

HOWELL, Hopkins:  By will appointed his relict, Mary, Extx.  May 2, 1687.
    R.  Oct. 21, 1687.          Page 60

MADDIN, Henry:  Dying intestate administration requested by John Wheatley
    as marrying the sister of the said Maddin.  May 2, 1687.  R.  Oct. 21,
    1687.          Page 61

JOLLY, John:  Dying intestate, administration requested by William Jolly.
    June 9,     R.  Oct. 21, 1687.        Page 61

WILLIAMS, John:  Dying intestate, administration requested by his son
    John Williams.  Aug. 13, 1687.  R.  Oct. 21, 1687.     Page 61

MATHEWS, Ralph:  By will appointed his relict, Alice, Extx.  Aug. 13, 1687.
    R.  Oct. 21, 1687.          Page 61

CRIPPS, George:  By will appointed his relict, Mary, Extx.  Oct. 10, 1687.
    R.  Oct. 21, 1687.          Page 62

JORDAN, John:  Dying intestate, administration requested by his relict,
    Jane.  Oct. 10,     R.  Oct. 21, 1687.      Page 62

COLLINS, William:  Dying intestate, administration requested by Alexander
    Murre, who married Anne, the relict of the said Collins.  Oct. 10,
    R.  Oct. 21, 1687.          Page 62

WOOD, Mathew:  Dying intestate, administration requested by his relict,
    Jane.  Oct. 10,     R.  Oct. 21, 1688.      Page 62

BATHE, Katherine:  By will appointed Stephen Horsefield, Ex.  Oct. 11, 1687.
    R.  April 23, 1688.         Page 63

HODGES, Robert:  Dying intestate, administration requested by John Downes.
    Nov. 9, 1687.  R.  April 23, 1688.        Page 63

WILLIAMS, David:  By will appointed his relict, Sarah, Extx.  Oct. 10,
    R.  Oct. 20, 1688.          Page 63

73

WADE, Christopher: Dying intestate, administration requested by his relict, Susanna. Dec. 9, 1687. R. Sept. 23, 1688. Page 64

LARAMORE, Roger: Dying intestate, administration requested by Walter Walters, who married the relict of the said Laramore. Dec. 9, 1687. R. Oct. 20, 1688. Page 64

BOND, John: By will appointed John Bell, Ex. April 9, 1688. R. April 23, 1688. Page 65

WOMBWELL, Thomas: By will appointed his relict, Elizabeth, Extx. Oct. 20, 1688. Page 65

HUNTER, James: By will appointed his relict, Ann, Extx. May 1, 1688. Page 65

GRISSWOOD, John: Dying intestate, administration requested by his relict, Sarah. May 1, 1688. R. Oct. 20, 1688. Page 65

BECHINOE, George: By will appointed his relict, Mary, Extx. May 1, 1688. R. Oct. 20, 1688. Page 66

BRANCH, George: Dying intestate, administration requested by James Lupo. June 9, 1688. R. Oct. 20, 1688. Page 66

PARNELL, Thomas: By will appointed his relict, Susanna, Extx. June 9, 1688. R. Oct. 20, 1688. Page 66

MARSHALL, John: By will appointed his relict, Susanna, Extx. June 9, 1688. R. Oct. 20, 1688. Page 67

MILES, Daniel: By will appointed his relict, Margaret, Extx. June 9, R. Oct. 20, 1688. Page 67

MOORE, John: By will appointed his relict, Elizabeth, Extx. June 9, R. Oct. 20, 1688. Page 67

HOBBS, Francis: By will appointed John Harris, Ex. June 9, R. Oct. 20, 1688. Page 67

CALLAWAY, Richard: Dying intestate, administration requested by his relict, Susanna. June 9, R. Oct. 20, 1688. Page 68

DOLES, Thomas: Dying intestate, administration requested by his relict, Mary. June 9, R. Oct. 20, 1688. Page 68

FONES, Christopher: Dying intestate, administration requested by Joseph Bridger. June 9, R. Oct. 20, 1688. Page 69

POWELL, Thomas: By will appointed William Powell, Ex. Feb. 9, 1687/8. R. April 23, 1688. Page 69

WILLIAMSON, Robert: Dying intestate, administration requested by George Williamson. Aug. 9, 1688. R. Oct. 20, 1688. Page 69

HOLE, John: Dying intestate, administration requested by his relict, Mary. Aug. 9, R. Oct. 20, 1688. Page 70

KAE, Robert: By will appointed Robert Kae, Ex. Dec. 10, 1688. R. April 20, 1689. Page 70

FENN, Timothy: Dying intestate, administration requested by Robert Kae in behalf of the orphans. Dec. 10, 1688. R. April 20, 1689. Page 70

BRANTLEY, Edward: By will appointed Mary Brantley, his daughter Extx. Jan. 9, 1688. R. April 20, 1689. Page 71

WILLIAMS, Rowland: Dying intestate, administration requested by Charles Baker as marrying the only daughter of the said Williams. Jan. 9, 1688. R. April 20, 1689. Page 71

LINNSCOTT, Giles: By nuncupative will appointed Robert Fenn, Ex. April 9, R. April 20, 1689. Page 71

HARRIS, Thomas: By will appointed Edward Harris, Ex. April 9, R. April 20, 1689. Page 72

SHEPHERD, John: Dying intestate, administration requested by James Riddick, who married the relict of the said Shepherd. April 9, R. April 20, 1689. Page 72

WATSON, William: By will appointed John Watson, his brother, Ex. June 9, 1688. R. April 20, 1689. Page 72

PITT, Thomas: By will appointed his relict, Mary, Extx. Aug. 9, 1688. R. Oct. 20, 1689. Page 73

CULLEN, Thomas: Dying intestate, administration requested by Thomas Sykes, Robert Lawrence and Robert Cooper. July 9, R. Oct. 20, 1689. Page 73

EVANS, William: By will appointed his relict, Katherine, Extx. Aug 9, R. Oct. 20, 1689. Page 73

CULLEY, John: Dying intestate, administration requested by Edward Brown as marrying the relict of the said Culley. Oct. 9, 1690. R. April 28, 1691. Page 74

FULGHAM, Michael: By will appointed his relict, Ann, Extx. March 9, 1690/1. R. April 28, 1691. Page 74

RICHARDSON, John: By will appointed his relict, Phillis, Extx. April 9, R. Oct. 22, 1690. Page 74

WESTON, John: Dying intestate, administration requested by his relict, Ann. May 1, 1690. R. Oct. 22, 1690. Page 75

CHESTNUTT, Alexander: Dying intestate, administration requested by John Parnell, who married the relict of the said Chestnutt. May 1, R. Oct. 22, 1690. Page 75

POPE, Thomas: By will appointed Thomas Pope, Ex. Aug. 10, 1691. R. Oct. 29, 1691. Page 75

ISLES (GILES?), Frances: By will appointed Tristram Norsworthy, Ex. Aug. 10, R. Oct. 29, 1691. Page 76

FULGHAM, Michael: Administration requested by John and Nicholas Fulgham. July 9, R. Oct. 29, 1691. Page 76

GRAVE, John: By will appointed John Murry, Ex. June 9, R. Oct. 29, 1691. Page 76

BALDWIN, William: Dying intestate, administration requested by Benjamin
Baldwin. June 9,      R. Oct. 29, 1691.                    Page 77

BREAD, Richard: By will appointed his relict, Anne, Extx. Dec. 15, 1691.
R. April 29, 1692.                                         Page 77

MARSHALL, Robert: By will appointed his relict, Mary, Extx. Aug. 9,
R. Oct. 10, 1698.                                          Page 78

PROUD, Thomas: By will appointed Captain Robert Kae, Ex. Aug 9,
R. Oct. 10, 1698.                                          Page 78

TULLAUGH, James: By will appointed Sarah and Ann Tullaugh, Exs.
May 1,      R. June 9, 1698.                               Page 78

MILES, Ann: Dying intestate, administration requested by Mr. Henry Baker.
Oct. 10,      R. Dec. 9, 1698.                             Page 79

BENN, Captain James: By will appointed his relict, Jane, Extx.    Page 79

POPE, Robert: By will appointed his relict, Elizabeth, Extx. April 10,
R. Aug. 9, 1699.                                           Page 79

CORSY, Richard: Dying intestate, administration requested by John and
Richard Williams. Aug. 9,      R. Dec. 18, 1700.           Page 81

CORSY, John: Dying intestate, administration requested by his relict,
Elizabeth. Feb. 9,      R. Dec. 18, 1700.                  Page 81

SHARPE, Richard: By will appointed Richard Reynolds, Jr. Ex. April 9,
R. Dec. 18, 1700.                                          Page 81

DRIVER, Charles: Dying intestate, administration requested by his relict,
Prudence. April 9,      R. Dec. 18, 1700.                  Page 82

NEWMAN, Ruth: Dying intestate, administration requested by her son, Thomas
Newman.                                                    Page 82

WILMOTT, William: Dying intestate, administration requested by Elizabeth
Clark, widow. 9th of Xber. R. April 25, 1701.             Page 85

DAY, James: By will appointed Captain Luke Haveild, Ex. R. April 25,
1701.

*VOLUME II*

---

## BOOK II

THE GREAT BOOK

PIERCE, Ann: Of the Lower Parish. Leg. John Keighly, the plantation on which I live for seven years, at expiration of time, I give it to John Teasley's son John; to Patience Carver; my movable estate to John Keighly. D. March 14, 1718/19. R. June 22, 1719.
      Wit: John Teasley, Thomas Altman, Peter Davis.     Page 1

WEST, Francis: Inventory signed by John Gilliam. D. January 10, 1718.
      Page 1

RIDLEY, Nathaniel: Leg. beloved wife Elizabeth; son Nathaniel; daughter Mary; son Thomas land adjoining Anthony Quant; daughter Elizabeth; daughter Lydia; God-son, Robert Hodges. Wife, Extx. D. March 10, 1718/19. R. July 27, 1719.
      Wit: James Day, Julia Day, Roger Hodges.     Page 2

WEST, William: Leg. son Thomas; daughter Sarah, if she marries Samuel Williams; daughter Elizabeth; daughter Mary; daughter Ann. D. May 4, 1719. R. July 28, 1719.
      Wit: Richard Price, Joseph Goden (Godwin).     Page 3

HOWELL, Thomas: Leg. son Thomas, the tract of land lying upon Blunt's Creek which I bought of Samuel Godwin, Jr.; son William; daughter Sarah; wife Rebecak. Wife, Extx. D. March 16, 1718/19. R. August 24, 1719.
      Wit: John Dawson, Joseph Bradshaw, John Lucas.     Page 4

BEVAN, Mary: Of Newport Parish. Leg. son Thomas; son Peter; daughter Mary; daughter Elizabeth. Ex., son Thomas. D. March 2, 1718/19. R. August 24, 1719.
      Wit: William Taylor, Jeremiah Proctor.     Page 4

DARDEN, Jacob: Inventory, signed by Ann Darden and Jacob Darden. 28th of 7ber 1719.     Page 5

HOLLADAY, Anthony: Appraised by Henry Pitt, George House, Thomas Copeland. R. September 28, 1719.     Page 6

JOHNSON, William: Leg. wife Sarah; son John; son William; son Thomas; son Benjamin; friend Hardy Council. Ex., son John Johnson. D. April 10, ----. R. September 28, 1719.
      Wit: Hardy Council, Robert Council, James Council.     Page 9

RAYNER, Francis: Of the Upper Parish. Leg. wife Joanna; my two daughters, Joanna, the wife of Thomas Ward and Frances, the wife of William Little; grandson Samuel Rayner, the son of my deceased son John Rayner; to Joseph the son of Thomas Ward until Samuel Rayner is seventeen; reversion of bequests to the said Joseph Ward. Aforesaid sons-in-law my Exs. D. September 29, 1716. R. September 28, 1719.
      Wit: Charles Goodrich, Sr., Charles Goodrich, Jr., Lawrence Baker.     Page 9

PITT, Henry: Leg. my children, John, Joseph and Mary; to son John the gold seal ring, which my father gave me. Wife, Extx. D. February 6, 1718.

R. October 28, 1719.
> Wit: Arthur Smith, John Turner, Mary Smith.     Page 10

WRENN, Francis: Of the Upper Parish. Leg. wife Elizabeth; to my children.
Friends, George Goodrich and Thomas Wrenn to see my will performed.
D. January 29, 1718. R. September 28, 1719.
> Wit: William Gainor, Richard Jordan, William Allen.     Page 10

WILLIAMS, John: Appraised by Philip Rayford, John Mackmial, Jacob Darden.
Signed Mary Williams. October 26, 1719.     Page 11

JOHNSON, William, Sr.: Inventory presented by John Johnston. October 26,
1719.

RIDLEY, Nathaniel: Appraised by (pages transposed) September 24, 1719.

PITT, Henry: Appraised by John Chapman, Richard Wilkinson, Thomas Moscrop.
Signed Mary Pitt. Ordered October 26, 1719. R. 28 of Xber 1719.
> Page 17

SIKES, John: Of the Lower Parish. Leg. son Joshua; wife Sarah. Exs. wife
and son Joshua. D. August 5, 1719. R. February 22, 1719/20.
> Wit: Thomas Moore, Rebecak Howell, John Davis.     Page 18

MURPHERY, William: Account estate, to the widow's third, to be paid the
four orphans. Signed by Barnabie and Mary Mackinnie. February 22,
1719/20.     Page 19

MONRO, Mr. Andrew: Appraised by Thomas Moscrop, William Wilkinson, William
Price. Ordered January 25, 1719. Signed Sarah Monro. R. February 22,
1719.     Page 20

EXUM, Jeremiah: Leg. daughter Elizabeth; daughter Mourning; daughter
Christian, the land I bought of James Collins; granddaughter Catherine
Scott; my cousin Jane Exum; daughter Sarah; daughter Mary; daughter
Jane; wife. D. September 3, 1712. R. March 28, 1720.
> Wit: John Gibbs, Thomas Godwin, Jr., Mary Godwin.     Page 21

WEBB, James: Leg. William Wilkinson and his wife, 250 acres, at their decease to be equally divided between Giles and Richard Webb. Exs.
William Wilkinson and his wife. D. January 19, 1719. R. March 28,
1720.
> Wit: John Watts, James Snowden, William Leune (?).     Page 22

WADE, Edward: Appraised by William Spivey, John Teasley, John Powell. No
date.     Page 22

EVANS, William: Appraised by John Chapman, Robert Richards, Thomas Bevan.
Ordered, January 25, 1719. R. March 28, 1720.     Page 23

JOYNER, Bridgman: Appraised by Thomas Mandew, Giles Driver, Andrew Griffin.
Ordered in October last past. R. December 4, 1719. Signed Ann Joyner.
> Page 23

BEVAN, Mary: Appraised by John Wright, Daniel Riggins, Charles Fulgham.
R. December 21, 1719.     Page 24

HUNT, Lawrence: Appraised by Edward Simmons, Edward Brantley, Richard Smith,
John Person, Jr. D. November 7, 1719. R. April 20, 1720.     Page 25

WATKINS, George: Leg. friend Joseph Bracher (?). D. August 15, 1719.
R. April 25, 1720.

Wit: Elizabeth Luter, John Bowen. Page 25

STRICKLIN, Samuel: Leg. son Stephen; son Samuel; son Joseph; daughter
Rachell. Ex., wife Abigail. D. May 27, 1718. R. April 25, 1720.
Wit: Mathew Stricklin, Joseph Stricklin. Page 26

HOWELL, Mathew: Leg. son Thomas; son Joseph; unborn child; to wife due me
from John Gent, also money due me from Richard Braswell, John Edwards
and Henry Flowers. Exs., my father,Joseph Lane, Sr., Joseph Lane, Jr.
and my wife Mary. D. January 11, 1719. R. April 25, 1720.
Wit: Thomas Jarrett, Arnale Pew. Page 26

BODDIE, John: Leg. son William; son John; wife Elizabeth. Wife, Extx.
D. March 10, 1719/20. R. April 25, 1720.
Wit: Mary Applewhite, Robert Hadley, Richard Gent. Page 27

RODWELL, John: Leg. sister Elizabeth Atkins, wife of Christopher Atkins;
to Lucy Atkins, daughter of aforesaid; to their third child, Christopher
Atkins. D. January 20, 1719. R. April 25, 1720.
Wit: John Simpson, Frances Cocke. Page 28

LANQUISHEAR, Robert: Of the Upper Parish. Leg. wife; granddaughter Unity
Lanquisher; grandson Samuel Lanquisher; grandson William Lanquisher
my plantation on the Blackwater at the death of my wife; granddaughter
Lettis Pitman; granddaughter Ann Pitman; grandson Samuel Pitman; son
Samuel Lanquisher; son-in-law Thomas Pitman; daughter Elizabeth Pitman;
son Robert Lanquisher; to son Robert's eldest daughter. Exs., wife
and son Robert Lanquisher. D. April 28, 1720. R. May 23, 1720.
Wit: James Piland, Benjamin Hoddg (Hodges), Roger Ingram.
Page 28

TILLER, John: Appraised by Edward Symonds, Edward Brantley, Richard Smith.
R. May 23, 1720. Page 29

LARNER, Bartholomew: Leg. kinswoman Mary Laughle; Thomas Copeland and his
heirs; Joseph Weston. D. March 8, 1719/20. R. May 23, 1720.
Wit: Thomas Applewhaite, John Gray. Page 30

LANCASTER, Robert: Appraised by John Brantley, Richard Gray, Benjamin
Hodges. Ordered May 23, 1719. R. June 27, 1720. Signed Robert
Lancaster. Page 30

GARELL, Jone: Leg. son Thomas Cooke; Elizabeth Weaver; Joannah Burah (?);
son William Cooke; John Carrell; son Reuben Cooke. D. March 31, 1720.
R. June 27, 1720.
Wit: Edward Chitty, Abraham Baggett. Page 32

WILSON, John: Appraised by George Goodrich, Thomas Wrenn, Joshua Copeland.
Ordered June 21, 1719. R. June 27, 1720. Signed by Frances Wilson.
Page 33

LEGG, Ann: Inventory, signed by William Warr (?). D. May 19, 1720. R.
June 27, 1720. Page 34

SHELLY, John: Of the Upper Parish. Leg. to brother Thomas Shelly; to
Elizabeth Ogburne, the dishes at John Harris'; to my son John Phillips
Shelly. Ex., brother Thomas Shelly. D. June 23, 1718. R. June 27,
1720.
Wit: George Riddick, John Brantley. Page 35

MATTHEWS, Alexander: Of ye Lower Parish. Leg. daughter Sarah Fulgham;
to my three grandchildren, Thomas, A------ and Catherine Joyner; son

81

Alexander Matthews; wife Catherine. Exs., wife and son Alexander. D. May 23, 1713. R. June 27, 1720.
    Wit: John Jones, Joshua Turner, Joseph Chapman.          Page 36

HUNTER, William: Leg. wife Elizabeth; daughter Mary; daughter Ann; daughter Martha. My brother James Hunter, Thomas Moscrop and William Green to divide my estate. Wife, Extx. D. April 29, 1720. R. July 25, 1720.
    Wit: William Green, Robert Smith.                        Page 36

SMITH, Mary: Leg. daughter Mary Kelly; grandson Nicholas Ogburne; daughter Martha Smith; daughter Mary Smith; my grandchildren, Simon, Elizabeth and Mary Ogburne. Joseph Smith, William Weston and Joseph Weston to divide my estate. Exs., daughter Martha Smith and Joseph Weston. D. August 12, 1719. R. July 25, 1720.
    Wit: Joseph Smith, John Daniel.                          Page 37

SHELLY, John: Appraised by Lawrence Baker, James Briggs, James Sampson. R. July 25, 1720.                                          Page 38

HARRISON, William: Appraised by ------- Miller, ------- White, ------- Lee. R. July 25, 1720.                                          Page 39

HILL, Thomas: Leg. wife Mary; son Joseph; son Thomas; daughter Mary, the land bought of Mr. Alexander Forbes, which formerly belonged to Mrs. Silvestra Hill; daughter Ann. Exs., wife and son Thomas Hill. D. May 3, 1719. R. July 25, 1720.
    Wit: (torn)                                              Page 39

WATKINS, James: Appraised by Thomas English, Philip Pierce, Nicholas Tynes. R. July 25, 1720. Signed Martha Watkins.                  Page 40

BENNETT, Richard: Of ye Upper Parish. Leg. son Richard; son ----- land to be taken our of Mr. John Coffer's patent of 1450 acres; to Jane Coffer and her sons, Robert and John Coffer, the land where I now live which I bought of Mr. William Miller; to Richard Coffer; to Magdalen Coffer; to my granddaughter Frances Manggum; daughter Silvestra. Exs., Jane Coffer and William Allen. Friends, John Carter and James Carter to see that my will is performed. D. March 30, 1720. R. May 23, 1720.
    Wit: John Carter, James Carter, William Allen, Sr.       Page 41

WOODLEY, Andrew: Leg. son Thomas; ------ ye two brothers, Thomas and John Woodley; grandson John Copeland; granddaughter Elizabeth Copeland; to my daughter Copeland. Ex., son John Woodley. D. September 25, 1718. R. August 22, 1720.
    Wit: A. Forbes, George Bell, Thomas Wilson.              Page 42

HODGES, Roger: Appraised by George Goodrich, Thomas Wrenn, Edward Miller. R. May 8, 1720.                                            Page 43

BRANCH, Francis: Leg. son Francis; my wife; son George; son Benjamin; daughter Elizabeth; daughter Mary; daughter Sarah; daughter Liddia; daughter Jane; daughter Hannah; daughter Martha; daughter Ann; to my cousin Catherine Branch. Exs., son Francis, wife and daughter Mary. D. April 22, 1717. R. August 22, 1720.
    Wit: John Joyner, Elizabeth Doiel, Elizabeth Benson.     Page 44

BENNETT, Richard: Appraised by Arthur Jones, Thomas Ward, William Bell. Signed Jane Coffer. R. August 22, 1720.                      Page 45

HARRIS, George: Leg. son George; son Robert; daughter Elizabeth; daughter Sarah; son Joseph; son William. Wife Martha Harris, Extx. D. December 15, 1719. R. August 22, 1720.

Wit: Martin Harris, Daniel Doyle, John Bowen.                    Page 47

LARNER, Bartholomew: Appraised by Charles Norsworthy, William Best,
    Humphry Marshall. R. August 22, 1720.                       Page 47

SMITH, Martha: Appraised by Tristram Norsworthy, Robert Richards, Henry
    Pitt. Ordered July 26, 1720. R. August 15, 1720. Recorded as the
    estate of Mary Smith. Ralph Frissell an Appraiser. Signed by Joseph
    Weston.                                                     Page 49

WATTS, John: Appraised by William Wilkinson, Thomas Uzzell, William Price.
    Ordered May 24, 1720. R. August 22, 1720.                   Page 49

EXUM, William: Leg. son John; son William; son Joseph; son Robert; daughter
    Anne; daughter Sarah; wife Susan. D. April 25, 1720. R. August 25,
    1720.
        Wit: Thomas Atkinson, Francis Exum, William Crocker.    Page 51

GODWIN, William: Leg. son William; son John; son Joseph; daughter Sarah
    G------; daughter ------ Bridger; daughter Mary Whitehead; daughter
    Martha Cotton; daughter Jane. Wife Elizabeth, Extx. D. November 21,
    1710. R. September 26, 1720.
        Wit: William Pope, John Whitley, James Edwards.         Page 52

DUKES, John: Of the Lower Parish. Leg. son ------; son John; son James;
    son Robert; estate between my wife and children, sons to be of age
    at 21 and daughters at marriage. D. March 16, ----. R. August 3, 1720.
        Wit: (torn)                                             Page 53

HILL, Thomas: Appraised by ------ Wrenn, John Goodrich. R. September 26,
    1720.                                                       Page 54

BARNES, James: Leg. son Thomas; son Edward, ye gun I bought of Philip
    Thomas; wife Sarah. D. March 2, 1719/20. R. October --, 1720.
        Wit: William Thomas, Susannah Gregory, John Dunkley.    Page 55

DOYLE, Samuel: Leg. son Daniel; son Edward; daughter Elizabeth; daughter
    Mary. Wife Jane, Extx. D. March 1, 1719/20. R. October 24, 1720.
        Wit: Richard Batman (?), Joseph Bradshaw.               Page 55

MATTHEWS, Richard: Leg. daughter Mary Howell; granddaughter Mary Howell;
    granddaughter Mary Matthews; son Richard ------. D. (torn). R. No-
    vember --, 1720.
        Wit: Jacob Darden, Thomas E------, Edward ------.       Page 56

BODDIE, John: Appraised by Arthur Pursell, Thomas Woodley, James Bragg.
    R. November 28, 1720.                                       Page 57

KIRLE, William: Leg. eldest son William Kirle, the son of Margaret Cobb,
    daughter of Robert and Elizabeth Cobb; to my son Robert Kirle, the
    son of Margaret Cobb, daughter of Robert and Elizabeth Cobb; wife
    Ellinor; -- my ------ to wit., George, William and Joseph the sons
    of ------, when their mother Elianor marries again; my son William
    Kirle, the son of Elioner Kirle. Wife, Extx. D. December 24, 1719.
    R. November 28, 1720.
        Wit: Michael M------, John Murphrey, Sarah ------.      Page 58

COLWELL, John: Of ye Lower Parish. Leg. Elizabeth Harris; Edward Green;
    to Benjamin Crocker, the son of Robert Crocker; to Arthur Crocker,
    land adjoining John Rochell; to William Crocker; Joseph Crocker; Eliza-
    beth Crocker; Mary Crocker; Sarah Crocker; all the children of Robert
    Crocker. Ex., Robert Crocker. D. August 10, 1720. R. January 23,

1720.
Wit: Needham Bryan, Nathaniel Powell.                    Page 59

LAWRENCE, Robert: Leg. to my ------ during her natural life; to my ------ to him and his heirs forever; son Robert; after decease of my wife, certain bequests to my son-in-law Henry Gay. Ex., son-in-law John Gay. D. April 20, 1720. R. January 23, 1720.
Wit: Ambrose Sanders, Jane Gay.                    Page 59

PAGE, Thomas: Leg. wife Alice; son Thomas; daughter Rebecka; daughter M------; daughter Alice; granddaughter ------ Gay. Ex., son John Page. D. February 20, 1719. R. ------, 1720.
Wit: Mary Ricks, Abraham Ricks, William ------.                    Page 60

GREEN, John: Leg. daughter Mary, the wife of Peter Williams; son Peter; daughter Sarah, the wife of Robert Coggens; son Edward; son Thomas; wife Ann. Wife, Extx. D. March 21, 1719. R. January 23, 1720.
Wit: Arthur Smith, Patrick Sweeney, Mary Bryan.                    Page 61

DAVIS, Mary: Leg. daughter Prudence; grandson William Da------; son Samuel and all my children. Daughter Prudence Davis, Extx. I request Captain James Day and my brother William Green to assist her. D. September 20, 1720. R. January 23, 1720.
Wit: William Green, Sarah Murry, Thomas Davis.                    Page 61

TERRELL, Joane: Appraised by Reuben Cooke; Thomas Holliman; John Stevenson, Christopher Holliman. R. January 23, 1720.                    Page 62

HAYES, Peter: Of ye Upper Parish. Leg. son Robert; to my ------ John and Peter Stevens; to ------ther Hayes. Wife Elizabeth, Extx. D. November 10, 1720. R. February 27, 1720.
Wit: Arthur Jones, William Crocker, Robert Hayes.                    Page 63

WILSON, James: Leg. son William; son George; son John; son James; son Gutridge; son Joseph; son Samuel; son Benjamin. Extx., loving wife. D. March 28, 1720. R. February 27, 1720.
Wit: George Goodrich, John Goodrich.                    Page 64

FRISSELL, John: Leg. sister Mary Frissell; to the widow of my brother George Frissell; Cousin Ann Frissell; cousin, Violet Frissell; cousin, Mary Frissell; cousin, John Driver; to Thomas Smith. Sister Mary, Extx. D. August 24, 1720. R. February 27, 1720.
Wit: Arthur Smith, Bridgett Ducke.                    Page 64

LAWRENCE, Robert: Appraised by Thomas Gale, Jacob Darden, Thomas Sikes, John Pope. R. February 27, 1720.                    Page 65

MEECUM, John: Appraised by John Crews, John Brantley, Richard Gray. Signed by Susanna Meecum. February 6, 1720/1.                    Page 67

DUCKES (DUKES), John: Appraised by Ambrose Adley (Hadley), Timothy Tynes, Jeremiah Fly. Signed by Bridgett Duckes. Ordered November 8, 1720. R. February 27, 1720.                    Page 67

DAVIS, John: Appraised by John Screws, Jr., Richard Blunt, Edward Crocker, Arthur Davis. Signed Susanna Davis. Ordered January 23, 1720/21. R. February 27, 1720.                    Page 68

MURRE, John: Appraised by Philip Wheadon, John Miller, Ellis (Elias) Hodges. R. February 27, 1720/21.                    Page 69

LAWRENCE, Robert: Additional Appraisal. Signed by John Gay.                    Page 70

PARDUE, Phillip: Appraised by John Brantley, John Fiveash, Richard Gray. Ordered March 11, 1720/21. R. March 27, 1721. Page 71

BULGER, Sarah: Leg. brother William Smith; sister Parker; brother Nicholas Smith; to Mary Loathlin; sister Martha Smith; brother Joseph Smith; to Anna Barnes; cousin William Smith; sister Weston, at her decease to Joseph Weston; remainder of my estate to be divided between Nicholas, Joseph, Anna and Martha Smith. Ex., brother Joseph Smith. D. January 4, 1720/21. R. March 27, 1721.
    Wit: James Benn, William Hawkins. Page 71

BARNES, Jacob: Appraised by Thomas Copeland, Henry Pitt, Humphry Marshall. Ordered October 22, 1720. R. March 27, 1721. Page 72

LOGAN, Elizabeth: Appraised by Edward Driver, Giles Driver. Ordered February 27, 1720/21. R. March 27, 1721. Page 74

WOOD, Elizabeth: Of ye Upper Parish. Leg. James Pyland, my whole estate. Ex., James Pyland. D. November 22, 1720. R. March 27, 1721.
Page 75

HOUSE, George: Leg. brother James House; my wife Elizabeth. Wife, Extx. D. April 16, 1714. R. April 24, 1721.
    Wit: Anthony Holliday, Brian Dogan, Ann Cuningham (?), Robert Lawrence. Page 76

WILLIAMS, Thomas: Appraised at the plantation of Mary Williams, by Nathaniel Parker, William Hawkins, Thomas Parker, William Weston. Ordered March 27, 1720. R. April 24, 1721. Page 77

DRIVER, Mary: Leg. son Giles; son Charles; daughter Hardy Goodson; daughter Mary House; daughter Susanna Bulls (?); granddaughter Sarah Driver; son Thomas. Exs., sons Thomas and William Driver. D. August 24, 1719. R. April 24, 1721.
    Wit: Christopher Reynolds, John Butler. Page 79

BENBRIGG, George: Leg. whole estate to John Butler, Sr. D. December 28, 1720. R. April 24, 1721.
    Wit: Edward Driver, Thomas Driver, John Driver. Page 80

DENSON, James: Leg. son James; daughter Frances; daughter Sarah; son Joseph my plantation in Nansemond County, also my land in Charles City County, in Parish of Weyanoke; wife Sarah; cousin James Denson, the son of John Denson; to unborn child. Wife, Extx. D. July 15, 1720. R. April 24, 1721.
    Wit: Richard Hutchins. Page 80

LUCK, John: Appraised by Philip Wheadon, William Baker, John Miller, Thomas Renn. Ordered March 16, 1720/21. R. May 22, 1721. Page 82

MATHEWS, Richard: Inventory, signed by Richard Mathews. May 22, 1721.
Page 83

DRIVER, Charles: Appraised by Richard Casey, John Butler, Christopher Reynolds. Ordered May 12, 1721. R. May 22, 1721. Signed Giles Driver. Page 84

JONES, Richard: Of ye Upper Parish. Leg. daughter Ann Bell, the land on which she and her husband William Bell live; son Samuel; son Richard; daughter Elizabeth; daughter Christian; daughter Sarah; daughter Mary; daughter Martha Davis; wife Elizabeth; son Joseph; son Benjamin. Wife Extx. Friends William Bell and Thomas Harris to see my will

performed. R. May 22, 1721.
    Wit: William Gainor, Arthur Davis, William Allen.          Page 84

AMOS, William: Of the Lower Parish. Leg. my friend Elizabeth Whitaker,
    the daughter of Elizabeth Whitaker of Denby (Denbeigh), Warwick County;
    friend, Col. John Allen; friend James Pyland all my books on Physick,
    Surgery and all my instruments. Elizabeth Whitaker, Extx. D. May
    10, 1720. R. June 26, 1721.
        Wit: William Drew, Mathew Jones, Lawrence Baker.      Page 86

INGRUM, John: Of the Upper Parish. Leg. son Roger; son John; daughter
    Elizabeth; son William. Ex., son John Ingrum. D. December 21, 1720.
    R. June 26, 1721.
        Wit: James Pyland.                                    Page 87

MURPHRY, William: Leg. son Micaell, the land I purchased of Robert Hooks
    and of Jacob Darden; son John; wife Sarah; son William; daughter
    Catherine; daughter Margaret Lawrence; daughter Elizabeth Farrow (?);
    daughter Elinor Kirle; daughter Sarah; daughter Ann. Exs., sons
    Michael and John Murphry. D. November 14, 1717. R. June 26, 1721.
        Wit: Roger Tarleton, Jr., Joseph Tarleton, William Tarleton.
                                                              Page 88

SEWARD, William: Leg. son Benjamin; daughter Sarah; daughter Elizabeth;
    daughter Mary; son Samuel; wife Elizabeth. R. July 24, 1721.
        Wit: Joseph Holt, John Dortch.                        Page 90

BRANTLEY, Edward: Aged 72 years. Leg. son Edward; grandson John Balmer.
    Exs., wife Ann and Dave Evans. D. ------, 1720. R. July 24, 1721.
        Wit: John Brantley, James Madree (?).                 Page 90

BROWNE, John: Leg. son James, my land on Timothy Walker's road in Surry
    County; son Thomas land on the same road; daughter Elizabeth; daughter
    Mary; daughter Ann Camerine; daughter Bridgett Wresbury. Exs., sons
    James and Thomas Browne. D. January --, 1720/21. R. July 24, 1721.
        Wit: Thomas Nickson, George Goodson, Peter Green.     Page 90

MURPHRY, William: Appraised by Jacob Darden, John Pope, Richard Pope,
    Thomas Gale. Signed by Michael and John Murphry. R. July 24, 1721.
                                                              Page 91

HALL, Pool: Leg. my second son Joseph; if he pays my debt to Capt. William
    Wilkinson; third son John Hall; first son Thomas Poole Hall; between
    my wife and all my children. D. November 20, 1720. R. August 28, 1721.
        Wit: William Price and Thomas Uzzell.                 Page 95

AMOS, William: Appraised by James Wilson, George Riddick, John Brantley,
    Richard Gray. Signed Elizabeth Whitaker. R. August 28, 1721.
                                                              Page 96

WORMINGTON, Jeremiah: Estate sold by order of Court. Signed, Joseph God-
    win, Sheriff. R. August 28, 1721.                         Page 98

MARTIN, George: Estate sold by order of Court. Signed Joseph Godwin,
    Sheriff. R. August 28, 1721.                              Page 98

RIDLEY, Nathaniel: Account of the stock, returned by Joseph Copeland and
    Ellis (Elias) Hodges. R. August 28, 1721.                 Page 100

GIBBINS, John: Leg. Mr. William Kinchen; Henry Harris; Mathew Harris;
    Mary Adkins, the daughter of James Adkins; John Jackson; Thomas Harris,
    the son of Edward Harris; Robert Harris. Ex., Mr. William Kinchen.

D. August 20, 1721. R. September 25, 1721.
Wit: Edward Chitty, Edward Harris. Page 101

DOWLES, Thomas: Leg. son Thomas; son Joseph; daughter Ann; daughter Elizabeth; daughter Martha; daughter Christian; daughter Easter; daughter
Rebecca; daughter Rachell. Wife Catherine, Extx. D. February 19,
1720/21. R. September 25, 1721.
Wit: Edward Chitty, Thomas Stevenson. Page 102

HOWELL, Mathew: Appraised by Thomas Jarrell, John Edwards, Robert Newsum.
Ordered April 21, 1720. Signed by Joseph Lane. R. September 25, 1721.
Page 103

HALL, Pool: Appraised by John Long, John Wright, William Price. R.
September 25, 1721. Page 105

GOODRICH, George: Leg. daughter Elizabeth; at the death of my wife, I
desire that William Seward to take care of her. D. March 15, 1720/
21. R. September 25, 1721.
Wit: Alexander Forbes, John Goodrich. Page 106

COLES, Sarah: Appraised by John Miller, Henry White, George Bradshaw.
R. October 23, 1721. Page 107

PARMENTER, Na: Estate sold by order of Court. Signed by Joseph Godwin,
Sheriff. October 23, 1721. Page 107

THROPP, John: Leg. sister Sarah Batt; sister Stratfield Pierce; after the
decease of my mother-in-law Mary Bell, to my sister Sarah Batt's two
sons, she had by William George, Elias and William George; to Mathew
Jordan ten pounds with which to repair the Meeting House at "Levy
Neck"; friend Susanna Jordan; my cousin Thomas Pearce. Ex., friend
William Batt. D. January 20, 1720/21. R. November 27, 1721.
Wit: John Miller, Abraham Cole, John Bradshaw. Page 108

BRACEY, Francis: Inventory. R. February 26, 1721. Page 109

GOODRICH, George: Appraised by Joseph Copeland, Thomas Wrenn, Elias Hodges.
Presented by Thomas Walton, Sheriff. R. February 27, 1721. Page 110

RIGINS, Daniel: Appraised at the house of Ann Rigins by Charles Fulgham,
Robert Richards, Jr., Christopher Dickinson. R. March 26, 1721.
Page 111

BELL, John: Leg. son John; son George; son Benjamin; son Edward; daughter
Alice Miller; daughter Olive Bell; wife Sarah and her three daughters
and son. Exs., wife and friend John Miller. D. April 21, 1721.
R. March 26, 1722.
Wit: William Dixson, Thomas Roberts, Thomas Goodson. Page 113

DAVIS, Thomas: Of ye Upper Parish. Leg. son Thomas and William the tract
of land, which I bought of the widow Blake, on which my son John
lived; daughter Frances Williamson; son George Williamson; wife
Elizabeth, the plantation bought of William Exum; son Benjamin;
grandson Thomas Davis; son Edward. Wife, Extx. D. March 4, 1721.
R. April 23, 1722.
Wit: William Bridger, Thomas Ryall, William Story. Page 114

KEA, Robert: Appraised by James Wilson, James Pyland, George Riddick.
R. April 23, 1722. Page 116

DRIVER, John: Appraised by Timothy Tynes, William Brock, John Butler.

Ordered March 26, 1722. Presented by Elizabeth Driver, his widow. R. April 23, 1722.
Page 117

WILLIAMSON, George: Leg. son George; son Robert; grandson Jacob Darden; to son John and son Robert my tract of land on the Blackwater; son Thomas; daughter Hester, the plantation on which Mr. Rueben Proctor lives, being land escheated by Col. Joseph Bridger and so made over to my mother and my brother Robert Williamson by the said Col. Bridger; daughter Mary; daughter Patience; daughter Elizabeth; daughter Juliana. Son Robert, Ex. D. April 26, 1721. R. May 28, 1722.
    Wit: Francis Williamson, William Vasser, Joseph Price. Page 118

WILLIAMSON, George: Appraised by William Crocker, William Vasser, William Moore, Edward Chitty. Signed by Robert Williamson. Page 120

BELL, John: Appraised by John Woodley, Reuben Proctor, Thomas Goodson. Signed Sarah Bell. R. June 25, 1722. Page 121

LOWERY, Arthur: Appraised by Joseph Parnell, John Dowles. Signed by Jane Lowery. R. September 24, 1722. Page 123

MORSE, Richard: Appraised by William Arrington, Owen Myrick, John Sorjiner (?). Signed by Mary Chapman. R. July 23, 1722. Page 122

LARNER, Bartholomew: Additional Inventory. Signed by Thomas Copeland. 24 of 7ber 1722. Page 123

CLARKE, John: Leg. loving wife; to Thomas Davison, the son of William Davison; to William Phillips, the son of John Phillips, the tract on which my son James Clarke lived until he died; to Jane Hunnifort; son William; to Mary Davison and Mary Phillips. Ex., William Davison. D. March 17, 1721/22. R. November 26, 1722.
    Wit: Edward Chitty, Joseph Parnell. Page 124

LANCASTER, Sarah: Leg. granddaughter Ann Craft; granddaughter Sarah Meacor; granddaughter Ann Kea; to Mary Mangum, the daughter of John Mangum; to Bridgett Bennett, the daughter of James Bennett; to Sarah Bennett, the daughter of James Bennett; granddaughter Elizabeth Meacor; granddaughter Martha Meacor; granddaughter Susan Meacor; to Mary Ussery; to my sister Elizabeth Hood; to Mary Sowdell; daughter Susanna Meacor; grandson Lewis Meacor; to Mary Jonas; to Benjamin Bell; to Samuel (?); remainder of my estate to my daughter Mary Bell. Mary Bell, Extx. D. October 31, 1722. R. January 29, 1722.
    Wit: Thomas Roser, William Hood. Page 125

GRAY, Richard: Of ye Upper Parish. Leg. son John; daughter Elizabeth; daughter Mary; daughter Martha; grandson Benjamin Gray, if Mary, the wife of James Maddera will allow my Executors to keep him; to my grandchildren, John, Rodgers and Elizabeth Delk; daughter Patience. Estate to be divided by Mathew Wills, Thomas Moreland and Lawrence Baker. Exs., son John and daughter Mary Gray. D. October 21, 1722. R. February 25, 1722.
    Wit: Mathew Wills, Francis Wills, Lawrence Baker. Page 126

GOODSON, Edward: Leg. daughter Joan Floyd; daughter Martha. Joan Floyd, Extx. D. December 3, 1722. R. February 25, 1722.
    Wit: Nicholas Tines, Jr., William Couldson. Page 127

WATTS, John: Appraised at the request of Joseph Wright, by John Hurst, Thomas Uzzell, John Wright. R. February 25, 1722. Page 128

UNDERWOOD, William: Appraised by Thomas Gale, Giles Driver, John Sellaway.

December 24, 1722.                                                    Page 129

GOODSON, Edward:  Appraised by Thomas Uzzell, John Dawson, Theophilus
    Joyner.  Signed by Joane Floyd.  R. March 25, 1723.          Page 129

EVANS, William:  Additional Inventory.  Signed by Charles Fulgham.  R.
    March 26, 1723.                                              Page 131

DEES, Manll:  Appraised by Benjamin Chapman Donaldson, James Turner, Ed-
    ward Simmons.  Ordered November last.  R. April 22, 1723.    Page 132

----------:  Appraised by Henry Pitt, Thomas Muscrop, Thomas Copeland.
                                                                 Page 133

FULLER, Ezekiell:  Leg. son Ezekiell; son Solomon; daughter Ann; daughter
    Mary; son Benjamin; son John; son Joseph; son Arthur; son Timothy;
    son Henry; daughter Martha Whitley; daughter Onner Allen; wife De-
    borah.  D. November 19, 1722.  R. June 24, 1723.
        Wit:  Arthur Smith, Mathew Lowry, William Ward.          Page 133

CLARKE, John:  Appraised by Thomas Williams, Thomas Ward, George Carter,
    William Davison.  R. August 26, 1723.                        Page 134

MATTHEWS, Alexander:  Appraised by Arthur Smith, John Dawson, Thomas Wood-
    ley, Ambrose Hadley.  R. July 22, 1723.                      Page 135

PRICE, Thomas:  Appraised by Christopher Reynolds, Thomas Pinner, Benjamin
    Beale.  Signed by Abraham Cornall (?).  R. September 23, 1723.
                                                                 Page 137

AMOS, Dr. William:  Estate settled by James Day and Mathew Jones.  R.
    September 24, 1723.                                          Page 140

WEST, William:  Estate settled by Arthur Whitehead.  R. October 29, 1723.
                                                                 Page 140

NORSWORTHY, Thomas:  Leg. cousin Elizabeth, the daughter of my brother
    John Norsworthy; cousin Leah Norsworthy, cousin Julian, the daughter
    of my brother John Norsworthy, to John Marshall the son of Humphry
    Marshall; to Martha Baker, the daughter of my sister Martha Baker.
    Ex., brother Charles Norsworthy.  D. July 31, 1723.  R. October 29,
    1723.
        Wit:  James Benn, Thomas Goodman.                        Page 141

GILES, Thomas:  Appraised by Robert Richards, Jr., Thomas Green.  Ordered
    September 5, 1723.  R. October 24, 1723.  Arthur Benn also an
    appraiser.                                                   Page 141

MEACOME, Thomas:  Appraised by James Wilson, James Briggs, Thomas Skelton.
    Ordered September 20, 1723.  R. October 28, 1723.            Page 143

ATKINSON, John:  Of ye Upper Parish.  Leg. wife Ann; son Christopher; son
    John; daughter Ruth; daughter Hannah Cooke; daughter Ann Garrell;
    daughter Mary Richardson; daughter Olive Bruce; daughter Elizabeth
    White.  Wife, Extx.  D. April 18, 1717.  R. October 28, 1723.
        Wit:  William Atkinson, Joseph Chapman, Hugh Hunniford.  Page 144

ATKINSON, James:  Leg. daughter Mary; son James; wife Mary.  Exs., wife
    and daughter Mary Atkinson.  D. July 28, 1723.  R. December 23, 1723.
        Wit:  Thomas Atkinson, John Stevenson.                   Page 146

MOSCROP, Thomas:  Leg. wife Susanna; daughter Mary; daughter Jean, re-

                                    89

version of bequests to brother Mathew's son Thomas, if living, if not to his son John and James Middleton the son of Jane Middleton. Exs., daughter Mary, Robert Murry and Christopher Dickinson. D. ———, 1723. R. January 27, 1723.
    Wit: Elizabeth Shaw, Robert King, Robert Murry.     Page 146

EVERITT, Thomas: Leg. son Thomas; son John; son Samuel; loving wife. Exs., brother Samuel Everitt and Thomas Dixson. D. October 9, 1723. R. January 27, 1723.
    Wit: Samuel Everitt, Thomas Dixon, Jennet Jenkins.     Page 148

MOSCROP, Thomas: Appraised by Robert Richards, John Butler, John Hurst. R. February 24, 1723.     Page 149

DAY, Thomas: Of ye Upper Parish. Leg. aunt Elizabeth Lear; cousin Thomas Day, all the land that I bought of John Thomas, with reversion of the bequest to my cousin James Ridley; to sister Jones; brother James Day; to brother-in-law Mathew Jones; to brother-in-law William Bridger; to the three daughters of Nathaniel Ridley and the daughter of Mathew Jones. Ex., Mathew Jones. D. January 19, 1723. R. February 24, 1723.
    Wit: Joseph Seward, William Bamer, Elizabeth Hodges.     Page 151

EDWARDS, James, Sr.: Leg. son Robert; son Joshua; son James; daughter Sarah Poope (Pope). Wife Ann, Extx. D. July 16, 1723. R. February 24, 1723.
    Wit: John Whitley, John Williams, Joshua Turner.     Page 151

ENGLISH, William: Appraised by James Piland, James Wilson, Benjamin Hodges. Signed Anne English. Ordered February 14, 1723/4. R. February 24, 1723.     Page 152

LUNDY, James, Sr.: Leg. son James; daughter Burchel; son Edward; son Robert; daughter Elizabeth; son Thomas a tract of land after the decease of John Tiller and Susanna his wife; wife Elizabeth. Wife, Extx. D. February 20, 1717. R. March 23, 1723.
    Wit: Thomas Harris, Thomas Addison, Catherine Harris. Presented in Court by Elizabeth Perry, formerly Elizabeth Lundy.     Page 153

WESTON, Stephen: Of Newport Parish. Leg. loving mother; brother Joseph; sister Anne; sister Mary; brother William; brother Benjamin. Ex., brother Joseph. D. February 20, 1723. R. March 23, 1723.
    Wit: Peter Lugg, Nathaniel Parker.     Page 154

DAY, Thomas: Appraised by Joseph Copeland, James Wilson, Thomas Wrenn. Signed Mathew Jones. R. March 23, 1723.     Page 155

RICKS, Isaac: Leg. son Isaac; son Abraham; son Robert, the plantation on which my son John formerly lived; son James; daughter Jean; two grandchildren, Isaac and Martha, the children of my deceased son Jacob. Exs., son James and daughter Jean Ricks. D. September 26, 1721. R. April 27, 1724.
    Wit: John Sellaway, Thomas Sikes, John Page, William Denson, William Wilkinson.     Page 157

SELLAWAY, John, Sr.: Leg. wife Margaret; son Richard; son John; daughter Margaret, now the wife of Henry Sanders; grandson John Sanders; son-in-law John Allen and my daughter Elizabeth, his wife; grandson John Allen; daughter Martha; daughter Mary; daughter Katherine. Wife, Extx. D. January 24, 1712. R. April 28, 1724.
    Wit: William Havett (?), Robert Cogen, William Cogen. Page 158

VASSER, William: Of ye Upper Parish. Leg. daughter Mary; son Joseph; son Benjamin; daughter Ann; son William; daughter Olive; son Jacob; son Jonathan; daughter Rebecca; son Peter. Wife Ann, Extx. D. June 25, 1723. R. May 25, 1724.
    Wit: John Williams, Francis Williamson, George Williamson, William Moore.     Page 160

KEA, Robert: Account of estate returned by Ralph and Alexandera Murry. R. June 22, 1724.     Page 161

JORDAN, Richard: Leg. wife Rebecca; son Richard; son Joseph; son Benjamin; son Mathew; daughter Elizabeth; daughter Mary; daughter Patience. Exs., wife and brother James Jordan. D. December 26, 1723. R. October 26, 1724.
    Wit: John Howell, Edward Haile, Robert Tyler.     Page 161

ENNIS, Walter: Appraised by Joseph Parker, Francis Myrick, Joseph Turner. Signed by Winifred Ennis. Ordered October 30, 1724. R. November 23, 1724.     Page 163

LONG, John: Leg. son John; daughter Martha; reversion of bequest to son John to Henry and Samson West. Wife, Extx. D. March 16, 1720/21. R. December 28, 1724.
    Wit: John Long, William West, John Wright.     Page 163

RAYFORD, Phillip: Leg. son Robert; daughter Mary; daughter Anne; daughter Patience; to son Robert all the cattle at John Person's; daughter Sarah; son William; son Mathew; son Phillip; wife. Son Robert, Ex. Brother-in-law William Kinchen and brother-in-law William Crumpler, trustees. D. July 23, 1724. R. December 28, 1724.
    Wit: John Crumpler, William Crumpler, Jr.     Page 164

DRIVER, Joseph: Appraised by William Green, John Wright, Richard Wilkinson, Epaproditus Williams. Ordered February 24, 1724. R. February 23, 1725. Signed by Edward Driver.     Page 165

MURRY, John: Leg. son George; son William; daughter Elizabeth Woodson; grandson Thomas Murry, the son of my deceased son John Murry; grandson William Murry, the son of my son William; grandson George Murry, the son of my son George; son Thomas; grandson James Woodson. D. October 1, 1724. R. March 22, 1724.
    Wit: Richard Hurst, Edward Miller, John Miller.
    Codicil changing bequests.
    Wit: Thomas Wrenn, Elias Hodges.     Page 166

NORSWORTHY, Tristram: Of Newport Parish. Leg. youngest son George, the plantation on which Mycell Rogers lived (not 18); second son John; Eldest son Tristram; wife Sarah; daughter Sarah; daughter Elizabeth; daughter Frances; daughter Martha. Son Tristram, Ex. Friends, John and George Norsworthy, overseers. D. March 5, 1709/10.
    Wit: Joseph Bridger, Thomas Walton, William Williams, George Norsworthy.     Page 167

Note, that the above and subsequent wills were left in the office unrecorded by Mr. Henry Lightfoot, late Clerk, my predecessor, wherefore, I have committed them to record, lest the County, sustain damage. Signed, James Ingles.     Page 167

ARRINGTON, William: Leg. son Arthur; son William; son John; grandson William Arrington; son Benjamin; daughter Mary Sykes; daughter Elizabeth Crumpler; daughter Sarah Riggan; granddaughter Ann Riggan; wife Elizabeth. Exs., sons John and Benjamin Arrington and wife. D.

May 4, 1725.  R.-------------.
Wit:  James Cooper, John Dunkley.                      Page 169

FULGHAM, Nicholas:  Leg. son Nicholas; the land I purchased of my cousin
John Fulgham to my son Charles; to grandson John Lucks, land on the
Blackwater; daughter Martha, the wife of Robert Richards; daughter
Susannah, the wife of Thomas Whitley; grandchildren, Susannah, Robert
and Mary Richards.  Exs., Nicholas and Charles Fulgham.  D. January
6, 1719/20.  R.----------------.
Wit:  Mathew Lowrey, Arthur Smith, Arthur Smith, Jr.    Page 170

BEST, Mary:  Leg. daughter Ann; son William; son Thomas; grandson Daniel
Batten; son John.  Exs., son John and John Hawkings.  D. January 8,
1724.  R.-----------.
Wit:  James Montgomery, Grace Minton.                   Page 171

MONRO, Sarah:  Of Newport Parish.  Leg. son Robert Pitt; daughter Henri-
etta Monro; daughter Sarah Monro; daughter Mary Monro.  Ex., son
John Monro.  D. May 31, 1725.  R.-----------.
Wit:  John House, Edward Weatherly.                     Page 172

DAY, James:  Leg. son James; son Thomas.  Exs., wife and son James Day.
D. September 26, 1725.  R.-----------.
Wit:  W. Bridger, Jr., Melchizadick Webb, John Proctor. Page 172

NORSWORTHY, George:  Leg. wife Christian; son George; daughter Elizabeth,
a negro at Capt. William Wilkinson's, in lieu of what her grandmother
Elizabeth Bridger left her; to daughter Martha, what her grandmother
Elizabeth Bridger left her; daughter Christian.  Exs., wife and
brother-in-law William Scott.  D. December 4, 1724.  R.-----------.
Wit:  Tristram Norsworthy, Peter Lugg, William Denson.  Page 173

SMELLY, Lewis:  Leg. son Giles; daughter Elizabeth Joyner; daughter Ann;
daughter Mary; wife Elizabeth.  Exs., wife and son Giles Smelly.
D. October 20, 1724.  R.-----------.
Wit:  John Dunkley.                                     Page 174

BRASWELL, Richard:  Leg. son Richard; son Robert; son Valentine; son Jacob; son John; daughter Martha Murfrey; daughter Ann Strickland;
daughter Jane Williams; granddaughter Susannah Braswell.  Ex., wife
Sarah.  D. July 28, 1724/25.  R.-----------.
Wit:  Edward Powers, Sr., Edward Powers.                Page 174

WALSTEN, Mary:  Of ye Lower Parish.  Leg. daughter Mary Baldwin; daughter
Sarah Baldwin; daughter Prudence Baldwin; son William Baldwin.  Exs.,
grandsons, Mathew and Arthur Lowry.  D. June 14, 1725.  R.-----------.
Wit:  John Dawson, Theophilus Joiner.                   Page 175

WHITLEY, Arthur:  Appraised at the house of Thomas Allings, by William
Noyall, Richard Casey, John Butler.  D. April 23, 1725.  Page 175

BROWN, Edward:  Appraised at the house of Gyles Driver, by Christopher
Reynolds, John Butler, William Noyall.  November 23, 1725.  Page 176

NORSWORTHY, George:  Appraised by Henry Pitt, Arthur Benn, Thomas Copeland.
March 12, 1724.                                         Page 176

KING, Robert, Sr.:  Leg. son Robert; son Henry; son Samuel; son Arthur;
daughter Sarah Weston.  Ex., son Robert.  Thomas Moscrop, to divide
estate.  D.-----------.  R.-----------.
Wit:  Thomas Moscrop, Robert Murry, Sarah Pilkington.  Page 178

BRANTLEY, John: Appraised by James Pyland, Arthur Wills (?), James Wilson.
April 26, 1725.                                                          Page 180

FORBES, Alexander: Appraised by Elias Hodges, Samuel Davis, Thomas Mu----.
April 21, 1726.                                                          Page 180

BRIDGER, Col. Samuel: Account estate. To William Wilkinson and Elizabeth
his wife one-third of her father William Webb's estate. We the subscribers, Thomas Walton and Mathew Jones have settled the accounts
of Col. Bridger and Madam Elizabeth Bridger.                             Page 182

DRIVER, Gyles: Appraised by John Council, John Dawtrey (Daughtrey),
Richard Wootten. 1725.                                                   Page 183

WATTS, John: Account estate, settled by Joseph Godwin, William Wilkinson.
                                                                        Page 184

NORSWORTHY, Tristram: Appraised by Nathaniel Parker, Joseph Smith, William
Weston, Thomas Parker. March 22, 1725.                                   Page 186

KING, Robert: Appraised by Joseph Smith, William Smith, Tristram Norsworthy, William Weston. November 17, 1725.                               Page 188

FULGHAM, Nicholas: Appraised by Hugh Giles, Richard Wilkinson, Christopher
Dickinson.                                                               Page 189

WILKINSON, Richard: Leg. daughter Rachel; son Richard; son-in-law Henry
Turner; to Elizabeth Turner, who now lives with me; daughter Elizabeth; daughter Mary; daughter Ann; if my daughter Elizabeth should
die before her husband her part to return to my children. Exs.,
son Richard and daughter Rachel. D. May 27, 1715. R.-----------.
Wit: Humphry Higginson, Elizabeth Turner.                               Page 192

FULGHAM, John: Leg. son John; son Anthony ------. Not completed ------ to
be found in Book A.                                                      Page 193

WOODLEY, John: Leg. son John; daughter Frances; wife Frances. If my son
and daughter die without heirs, bequests to Elizabeth Copeland the
daughter of Joseph Copeland. Wife, Extx. D. December 9, 1724.
R.-----------.
Wit: Daniel Elbank, Alexander Forbes, Thomas Woodley.    Page 194

FIVEASH, Thomas: Of the Upper Parish. Leg. cousin Martha, the daughter of
John Fiveash; cousin Francis, the son of John Fiveash; cousin Mary,
daughter of Thomas Fiveash; brother Peter Fiveash; sister-in-law
Martha Harris, the clothes, which belonged to my wife. Brother Peter
Fiveash, Ex. D. January 4, 1725/6. R.-----------.
Wit: James Pyland, Elizabeth Sparkman.                   Page 194

THOMAS, John: Leg. wife Hannah, 100 acres; son Richard 100 acres adjoining
John Clark, John Sherrard, West and Portis; son Samuel; son Jacob
384 acres. Ex., Joseph Weston. Son Jacob in the care of Joseph
Weston. D. December 31, 1725. R.-----------.
Wit: John Williams, John Johnson.                        Page 195

HARRISON, John: Appraised by Henry White, Thomas Wrenn. June 24, 1725.
                                                                        Page 196

DRIVER, Giles: Leg. daughter Mary; daughter Sarah; daughter Prudence;
daughter Patience; son William the plantation on which my brother
Thomas Driver now lives; son Giles; daughter Mary to be satisfied
with the bequest left her by her uncle, William Richards. Exs., wife

and brother-in-law Robert Richards. D. January 9, 1724. Robert Richards, John Lawrence, Christopher Reynolds, Jr., Giles Driver, Thomas Driver or any three of them to divide my estate.
Wit: Thomas Loyde, John Lawrence, Thomas Driver.          Page 199

GOODMAN, Rebeccah: Leg. son William; daughter Mary Evans; daughter Ann Bell. Son William, Ex. D. October 24, 1727. R.-----------.
Wit: Charles Binns, Elizabeth Atkinson.          Page 199

UNDERWOOD, Thomas: Leg. wife Mary; son William; son John; daughter Sarah; daughter Mary; daughter Ann; daughter Elizabeth; son Thomas. Exs., wife and son William Underwood. D. September 29, 1729. R.-----------.
Wit: William Crumpler, John Crumpler.          Page 200

---

## WILL BOOK III

GREEN, Thomas: Appraised by Richard Wilkinson, Arthur Benn, Robert Richards, Jr. Signed Mary Green. Ordered May 23, 1726. R. June 27, 1726.          Page 1

DAY, Captain James: Appraised by Henry Applewhaite, Joseph Godwin, Thomas Applewhaite. Signed Ann Day. Ordered April 13, 1726. R. July 25, 1726.          Page 2

RICHARDS, Thomas: Leg. son Thomas; daughter Ann; daughter Prudence. Ex., brother Robert Richards, Jr. D. February 23, 1725/26. R. July 25, 1726.
Wit: Robert Richards, Jr., Edward Driver.          Page 6

THOMAS, John: Appraised by Francis Williamson, John Johnson, Joseph Price. Signed Joseph Weston. Ordered June 8, 1726. R. July 25, 1726.
Page 6

COPELAND, Joseph: Leg. wife Mary; son John; daughter Elizabeth; son Thomas. Wife, Extx. D. February 28, 1725/26. R.-----------.
Wit: Richard Webb, John Lupo, Melchizideck Inslie (?). Page 8

BIDGOOD, John, Jr.: Leg. wife Ann; daughter Mary; son William; son John; son James; son Josiah; (all under eighteen). Wife, Extx. D. March 18, 1715. R. August 22, 1726.
Wit: Joseph Copeland, Thomas Wrenn.          Page 9

COPELAND, Joseph: Appraised by Samuel Davis, Thomas Murry, Benjamin Hodges. R. August 22, 1726.          Page 10

GRIFING (GRIFFIN), Robert: Appraised by John Hodges, Philip Wheadon, Benjamin Hodges, Henry White. R. June 26, 1727.          Page 11

GRIFIN (GRIFFIN), Andrew: Leg. son Ephenetus, 300 acres upon the Black Creek; son Mathew 300 acres on the Blackwater. Wife Mary, Extx. D. June 20, 1726. R. September 26, 1726.
Wit: Thomas Joyner, William Jones.          Page 11

BIDGOOD, John: Appraised by Elias Hodges, John Miller, Peter Woodward, Thomas Murry. R. October 24, 1726. Signed Ann Bidgood.          Page 12

WILLIAMS, Richard: Appraised at the house of Joseph Hall by John Hurst, Joseph Wright, John Wright, Michael Fulgham. Ordered September 27, 1726. R. October 24, 1726. Page 12

PRIME, John: Leg. wife Martha, reversion of bequest at her death to my nephew Thomas Wright; to nephew Robert Ruffin. Wife, Extx. D. March 4, 1717/18. R. November 28, 1726.
    Wit: Joseph Chapman, John Screws, Edward Crocker. Page 12

DAY, Ann: Leg. brother Joseph Allen; brother Arthur Allen; sister Elizabeth Allen; cousin Mary Bridger; cousin James Bridger; Ann Burnett; Mary Bridger; Katherine Allen; James Allen; sister Elizabeth Bridger; brother William Bridger, my diamond ring that was Thomas Day's; Helena Worden (?); brother John Allen; John Worden, Jr. Exs., brothers Arthur and Joseph Allen. D. December 2, 1726. R. January 23, 1726.
    Wit: Roger Delk, John Bruce, Mourning Thomas. Page 14

COUNCIL, Hodges: Leg. wife Rebecca; son John; son Hodges; son James; daughter Sarah. Wife, Extx. D. October 8, 1720. R. January 23, 1726.
    Wit: William Daughtry, John Daughtry, Robert Wilkins. Page 15

STEVENSON, John: Leg. son John; son Abraham; son Thomas; son Charles; son George; daughter Mary; son William. Wife Elizabeth, Extx. D. November 23, 1727. R. February 27, 1727.
    Wit: Thomas Flowers, Abraham Baggett. Page 16

EVERITT, Simon: Of the Lower Parish. Leg. son Thomas 225 acres adjoining the land of Richard Mathews; grandson Simon Everitt, son of my son John; son Samuel, land on Poplar Swamp; son Simon land on Mill Dam Swamp; son Joseph; son Thomas; daughter Jannett. D. September 14, 1726. R. February 27, 1726.
    Wit: Jacob Darden, William Thomson, Thomas Dixon. Page 17

EXUM, Ann: Leg. daughter Elizabeth; granddaughter Katoren Godwin; grandson Jeremiah Lawrence; grandson Exum Scott; granddaughter Ann Murfry; grandson Richard Exum Outland; daughter Mary Mackquinny; daughter Jane Outland; daughter Mourning Scott and her children; daughter Christian Norsworthy; my deceased daughter Sarah's children. Ex., son-in-law William Scott. D. February 3, 1726/27. R. March 27, 1727.
    Wit: Thomas Sikes, James Denson, Henry Sanders. Page 19

BRESEY, Hugh: Leg. son William; grandson Francis, the land on which his father lived at sixteen; son Hugh; son Campion; daughter Elizabeth Elsberry; son Michael; daughter Susannah Britt; to son Thomas' son Hugh. D. December 30, 1721. R. March 27, 1727.
    Wit: Owen Griffin, John Turner, Joshua Turner. Page 20

GODWIN, Elizabeth: Leg. son John; son William; my five daughters. Ex., son John Godwin. D. February 4, 1726/27. R. March 27, 1727.
    Wit: John Chestnutt, Thomas Whitley, John Whitley. Page 21

BROCK, Susannah: Of the Lower Parish. Leg. daughter Elizabeth Reynolds; grandson John Reynolds; son Thomas Calcote. Ex., son Thomas Calcote. D. March 7, 1723/24. R. March 27, 1727.
    Wit: Arthur Smith, Jr. Page 22

GRAY, Richard: Leg. wife Rebecca; daughter Ann; daughter Rebecca; daughter Mourning; son John; daughter Martha Brown her mother's chest; my wife and the children I had by her, viz: James, Ann, Rebecca and Mourning. Exs., wife and son James. D. November 11, 1724. R. March

27, 1727.
 Wit: Thomas Applewhaite, Joseph Wiles. Page 22

EXUM, Ann: Appraised by Thomas Glae, Thomas Sikes, Robert Eley. R. April
 24, 1727. Page 24

GODWIN, Elizabeth: Appraised by Benjamin Beale, John Chestnutt, John
 Whitley. R. May 22, 1727. Page 26

HODGHES, Elias: Leg. daughter Sarah Davis; wife Sarah; daughter Mary.
 Wife, Extx. D. April 2, 1727. R. Mary 22, 1727.
 Wit: John Goodrich, John Hodghes. Page 27

RIDDICK, George: Leg. Catherine Moreland to be paid what is due her from
 her father's estate; to my cousins, Charles, Samuel and George Goodrich; I desire that Edward Wood shall be at liberty from all persons,
 whatsoever; my land to be divided between my sons-in-law, Thomas
 Moreland and John Goodrich. D. April 7, 1727. R. May 22, 1727.
 Wit: Peter Fiveash, John Carroll. Page 29

GARLAND, John: Of the Lower Parish. Leg. sons, John Samuel and Joseph
 my land in Carolina; son John the plantation bought of John Page;
 son Peter; daughter Sarah; to my wife; daughter Mary Daughtrey; to
 my five youngest children, viz: Joseph, Ann, Prudence, Patience and
 Samuel. Ex., son John Garland. D. March 9, 1726/27. R. May 22, 1727
 Wit: Hugh Giles, Anthony Fulgham, George Clarke. Page 30

WILKINSON, Richard, Jr.: Appraised at the house of Joseph Smith, by
 Tristram Norsworthy, William Hawkins, George Norsworthy. R. May 23,
 1727. Page 31

KEA, Stephen: Appraised by James Pyland, John Brantley, Peter Fiveash.
 R. June 26, 1727. Page 32

WEBB, William: Appraised by Samuel Davis, Henry White, Thomas Murry.
 Ordered May 22, 1727. R. June 26, 1727. Page 32

BRIGGS, Mary: Leg. daughter Elizabeth Throp, the money in the hands of
 Col. Bridger; son Benjamin Bell; daughter Ann Crafts. Ex., Samuel
 Crafts. D. March 21, 1726. R. June 26, 1727.
 Wit: James Bell, William Cogin, John Grisard. Page 33

CRAFTS, Thomas: Of the Upper Parish. Leg. wife Mary; son Thomas; son
 John; son Samuel; daughter Mary; daughter Martha Brantley; daughter
 Elizabeth Tewell. D. October 29, 1722. R. July 24, 1727.
 Wit: Thomas Hylliard, Michael Harris, Hugh Edwards. Page 34

MAKER, Susanna: Leg. daughter Mary Maker; daughter Ann; daughter Susannah;
 to unborn child; to my four eldest children. My children in the care
 of Roger Ingram. Exs., Roger Ingram and William Dixon. D. June 12,
 1727. R. August 28, 1727.
 Wit: Susannah Maker, Elizabeth Welch. Page 35

WILLIAMS, Thomas: Appraised by John Mangum, Thomas Ward, William Bell.
 R. August 28, 1727. Page 36

WILLIAMS, Thomas: Of the Upper Parish, Planter. Leg. wife Susannah, if
 she should marry the reversion of the bequests left her to sons John
 and Thomas; daughter Joyce; son Joseph; I desire that my wife's son
 Thomas Davis, may be paid, what his father, John Davis left him.
 Wife, Extx. D. March 5, 1726/27. R. May 22, 1727.
 Wit: Michael Deloach, Joseph Quantock. Page 37

DELOACH, Michael: Planter. Leg. wife Mary; son Thomas; son Michael.
Wife, Extx. D. April 20, 1727. R. August 28, 1727.
Wit: John Williams, Joseph Quantock. Page 38

RICHARDS, Thomas: Appraised by Thomas Copeland, John Penny, Thomas Gross.
R. October 24, 1726. Page 39

LINSEY, John: Of the Upper Parish. Leg. wife Ann; son Roger; son William.
D. August 25, 1726. R. August 28, 1727.
Wit: John Miller, Mary Miller. Page 40

KEA, Henry: Of the Upper Parish. Leg. wife Elizabeth; son William; son
Robert; son Thomas; daughter Mary. Wife, Extx. D. April 19, 1727.
R. August 28, 1727.
Wit: James Pyland, John Welch. Page 40

CLOTHIER, John: Appraised by Thomas Mandew, Thomas Underwood, Abraham
Joyner. R. September 25, 1727. Page 41

SCREWS, John: Leg. son William; son Robert; son Edward; daughter Mary;
daughter Elizabeth; son Joseph; to beloved wife; to my youngest daughter; son John. D. August 27, 1720. R. September 25, 1727.
Wit: George Pyland, Benjamin Hodges. Page 42

BOULTON, John: Leg. son Richard; to Ann Hyde; to Henry Bradley. I desire
that Ann Hyde may not be molested until my son becomes of age. Ex.,
William Simmons. D. November 26, 1726. R. September 25, 1727.
Wit: William Watkins, Sarah Watkins, Ann Hyde. Page 42

JONES, Joseph: Leg. wife Elizabeth; son William; to Francis Ward the land
on which he lives, if he pays the balance due to my son William;
daughter Mary. Exs., wife Elizabeth; friends Francis Williamson and
John Dunkley and brother-in-law William Kinchen, Jr. D. December 5,
1726. R. September 25, 1727.
Wit: John Exum, John Dunkley, William Jones (?). Page 43

SUGARS, John: Leg. daughter Elizabeth Bynum; daughter Abigail Jones, the
land upon which Edward Jones lives; daughter Priscilla; grandson
Sugars Jones. Wife Elizabeth, Extx. D. December 1, 1726. R. September 25, 1727.
Wit: Francis Arrington, George Bruton, Mary Walker. Page 45

GARLAND, John: Appraised by Charles Fulgham, Richard Wilkinson, William
Green, Epaproditus Williams. R. November 26, 1727. Page 47

HODGES, Elias: Appraised by Thomas Hall, John Goodrich, Thomas Murry.
R. November 22, 1727. Page 48

MAKER, Susanna: Appraised by James Pyland, Peter Fiveash, James Wilson.
R. November 26, 1727. Page 49

SCREWS, John: Inventory returned by Mary Screws. R. November 26, 1727.
Page 50

NORSWORTHY, Christian: Leg. son George; daughter Christian; daughter-in-
law Elizabeth; daughter-in-law Martha to her uncle Charles Norsworthy;
cousin Christian Outland; cousin Elizabeth Scott; to friend James
Turner; if my children die in their minority, bequests to be equally
divided between the children of brothers-in-law William Scott and
William Outland. D. November 6, 1727. R. November 26, 1727.
Wit: Edward Mason, George Lawrence. Page 50

JOLLEFFE, James: Of the Lower Parish. Leg. wife Mary; son John; daughter
Elizabeth land which adjoins, John Butler and Christopher Reynolds;
son James. Wife, Extx. D. February 28, 1726. R. November 26, 1727.
Wit: John Roberts, Christopher Reynolds, John Smelly.     Page 51

BRIGGS, James: Appraised by James Wilson, Thomas Skelton, Thomas Shelly.
Ordered August 2, 1727. R. January 22, 1727.                Page 52

BRIDGER, Elizabeth: Leg. son Joseph; son John; son Robert; daughter Hester;
daughter Elizabeth. Exs., sons Robert and John Bridger. D. December
14, 1727. R. January 22, 1727.
Wit: Mary Whitley, Edward Driver.                        Page 54

TILLER, Susannah: Leg. son Major; daughter Judith Smith; daughter Mary
Rives; daughter Elizabeth Reid; daughter Ann Adams. Ex., son John
Reid. D. January 5, 1724/25. R. January 22, 1727.
Wit: John Edwards, Robert Hicks, Jr.                     Page 55

SEGRAVES, Francis: Leg. daughter Frances the wife of Jonathan Sanderson;
daughter Lucretia, the wife of Thomas Turner; son William; daughter
Elizabeth; son Francis; daughter Ann; daughter Susanna; daughter
Sarah; wife Lucretia. Exs., wife and son William Segraves. D. Octo-
ber 9, 1725. R. January 22, 1727.
Wit: Richard Hutchins, Abraham Ricks.                    Page 56

DOGAN, Bryan: Appraised by Richard Wilkinson, Robert Richards, Joseph
Norsworthy, Edward Driver. R. January 22, 1727.          Page 57

BUNKLEY, Robert: Appraised at the house of Thomas Newman, by Henry Pitt,
Joseph Wright, Thomas Gross. February 26, 1727.          Page 57

HURST, John: Leg. wife Mary, the plantation bought of William Price; son
James; son William; son John; sons Philip and Walter to be bound  out
at 14 to learn a trade; daughter Alice; daughter Mary; son John a
ring given him by Dorothye Hurst. Wife, Extx. D. January 1, 1727.
R. February 26, 1727.
Wit: Joseph Wright, Robert Brown, John Anthonyrue.      Page 58

FULGHAM, Michael: Leg. son John; grandson Henry West, the son of Henry
West; brother Anthony Fulgham; Hardy Council to have the upbringing
of my son John, who is to be of age at 18. Wife, Extx. D. January 12,
1727. R. February 26, 1727.
Wit: James Benn, John Wright.                            Page 59

STORY, Thomas: Leg. sister Elizabeth Smith; sister Mary Story; brother
John Story; sister Elizabeth's four children, to one of them named
Mary Smith; to Goddaughter Mary Driver. Exs., my two sisters. D.
December 29, 1727. R. February 26, 1727.
Wit: John Giles, Richard Scammell.                      Page 60

JOLLEY, James: Of the Lower Parish. Inventory presented by his Executrix.
February 26, 1727.                                      Page 61

COPELAND, Joseph: His estate which was in the possession of Thomas Copeland, decd., appraised by Samuel Davis, Henry White, Thomas Murry,
Benjamin Hodges. March 25, 1728.                        Page 62

ANDREWS, John: Appraised by Thomas Godwin, Jr., John Saunders, Robert
Coging. March 25, 1728.                                 Page 63

COOKE, Isack: Of Newport Parish. Leg. brother John Cooke; sister Bridgett
Rogers; sister Mary Stringer; to Roger Nevill. Ex., Roger Nevill.

D. March 6, 1727/28. R. March 25, 1728.
    Wit: Jacob Darden, John Murfrey, John Sikes.                Page 63

MACKMIAL, Thomas: Appraised by James Johnson, John Darden, William Daniel.
    Signed by Thomas Gale, Jr. March 25, 1728.                  Page 64

HURST, John: Appraised by William Noyall, John Wright, Joseph Wright.
    March 25, 1728.                                             Page 64

JONES, Mathew: Leg. son Scervant my tract in Warwick County, devised me
    by my father; my sister Margaret Jones and cousin Mathew Jones to
    raise the aforesaid son; daughter Ann the plantation bought of Thomas
    Briant at Nottoway Swamp; daughter Margaret the land adjoining Dr.
    Browne's line; daughter Agathy, the tract which was a survey of
    Henry Sumerlings on the Notoway River, reversion of bequest to son
    Albridgeton; son Britton, 144 acres in Warwick County, which I bought
    of Edward Kippen and the rest of my land on the Nottoway; my land
    and stock to be sold in Brunswick County; to loving wife. Extx.,
    Elizabeth Jones. D. January 28, 1727/28. R. March 25, 1728.
        Wit: Mary Wrenn, Ann Bidgood.                           Page 66

KEA, Henry: Appraised by James Pyland, James Wilson, Thomas Moreland.
    March 25, 1728.                                             Page 66

SURGINOR, John: Leg. son Robert, with reversion of the bequest to my son
    John, the younger; son Benjamin; daughter Mary; daughter Ann; son
    John the elder. Ex., son Robert Surginor. D. October 3, 1727. R.
    March 25, 1728.
        Wit: Edward Chitty, John Stevenson.                     Page 68

BRIDGER, Joseph John: Leg. brother James; uncle Joseph Allen; to my loving
    father, 350 acres at Round Hill. Exs., father and uncle Joseph Allen.
    D. December 3, 1727. R. March 25, 1728.
        Wit: Reuben Proctor, Elizabeth Brantley, Ann Burnett.
        Will presented by William Bridger and Joseph Allen.     Page 68

GENT, John: Leg. eldest son Thomas; youngest son John; to loving wife.
    Exs., Oliver Woodward, Thomas Allen. D. December 3, 1727. R. March
    28, 1728.
        Wit: Oliver Woodward, Christopher Reynolds, John Gurley.
                                                                Page 68
JONES, Jacob: Leg. brother William Jones. Ex., brother Nathan Jones.
    D. November 21, 1727. R. March 25, 1728.
        Wit: John Bowen, Mathew Griffin, Elinor English.        Page 69

STORY, Thomas: Appraised by Robert Richards, Joseph Norsworthy, Richard
    Scammell. March 25, 1728.                                   Page 71

SAMPSON, James: Leg. son Barcroft; daughter Margaret 100 acres adjoining
    Isaac Jarrett and Nicholas Derring; daughter Elizabeth 100 acres on
    which the widow Madera now lives, adjoining the land of Edward Brant-
    ley and Burwell's line; daughter Ann Derring, the plantation on which
    her husband Nicholas Derring now lives. Trustees, Samuel Croft and
    John Floyd. D. November 30, 1727. R. March 25, 1728.
        Wit: James Ingles, Charles Goodrich, Thomas Jones.      Page 71

WHITLEY, Mary: Appraised by Robert Wright, James Wright, Christopher
    Dickinson. April 22, 1728.                                  Page 73

GLOVER, George: Appraised by Mathew Wills, Roger Ingram, William Bidgood.
    April 22, 1728.                                             Page 73

DAY, Capt. James: Account estate. Errors accepted by Joseph Allen, the
Ex. of Ann Day, decd. Examined by Thomas Walton, James Benn. March
25, 1728.                                                    Page 74

SURGINOR, John: Appraised by Thomas Holliman, Joseph Parnall, William
Crocker. April 22, 1728.                                     Page 75

THOMAS, William: Appraised by John Davis, Thomas Davis, Richard Webb.
April 22, 1728.                                              Page 75

MILLER, John: Appraised by William Harrison, Benjamin Hodges, William
Bamer, Philip Wheadon. April 22, 1728.                       Page 76

GRESHION, James: Leg. wife Margaret, the rent due me from Charles Ryall.
D. September 20, 1727. R. April 22, 1728.
        Wit: Nicholas Pyland, John Cortis, Jan Bates Cortis. Administra-
tion granted Buller Herbert, his greatest creditor.         Page 76

HIDEN, Ephraim: Leg. daughter Elizabeth; daughter Sarah. Exs., Captain
Wilkinson and my wife Elizabeth. D. January 25, 1727/28. R. April
22, 1728.
        Wit: William Morgin (?), Daniel Gray.                Page 77

PEARCE, Philip: Leg. wife Sarah; son Nathan; son Arthur; son Simon; son
Richard; son Thomas. Exs., wife Sarah and son Richard Pearce. D.
March 20, 1727/28. R. April 22, 1728.
        Wit: Richard Teasley, Peter Mackone, George Teasley. Page 78

PYLAND, James: Leg. wife Elizabeth; son James, my box of doctor's instruments; daughter Ann; son Thomas; son William; daughter Katherine; son
Edward. D. March 20, 1727/28. R. April 22, 1728.
        Wit: Robert Butler, Ann Fones.                       Page 78

WATTS, Thomas: Of the Lower Parish. Nuncupative will·presented by Rachel
Smith, Ar. Smith and Arthur Smith. Leg. Arthur Smith; Rachel Smith
and her brother Arthur Smith; to kinsman William Lane. D. March 15,
1727/28. R. April 22, 1728.                                  Page 80

DRIVER, Thomas: Appraised by William Noyall, Arthur Benn, Timothy Tines.
Signed John Butler, Adm. Ordered February 26, 1727. R. May 27, 1728.
                                                             Page 79

WRENCH, John: Leg. wife Elizabeth; son Samuel Farmer Wrench; son John
Wrench, the plantation on which Thomas Hail lived; two sons of age at
18. D. February 8, 1727. R. April 22, 1728.
        Wit: John Hail, Joyce Cambell, John Heard.           Page 80

BRAGG, James: Of Newport Parish. Leg. Thomas Story, who married my daughter Elizabeth; daughter Sarah Driver; daughter Mary Norsworthy. Extx.,
wife Mary Bragg. D. April 29, 1727. R. April 22, 1728.
        Wit: James Giles, Hugh Giles.                        Page 82

BRADSHAW, Nicholas: Leg. daughter Elizabeth, whom I leave in the care of
my sister, Mary Bradshaw; daughter Ann; daughter Mary; my two youngest
children to be in the care of John and Mary Corbill. Exs., brothers,
John and George Bradshaw. D. January --, 1727. R. April 22, 1728.
        Wit: Joseph Godwin.                                  Page 82

WATTS, Thomas: Appraised by William Brock, Thomas Brown. Adm., Rachel
Smith. May 27, 1728.                                         Page 83

COPELAND, Thomas: Appraised by James Giles, Charles Norsworthy, William
Best, Humphrey Marshall. Ordered April 22, 1728. R. May 27, 1728.
                                                             Page 84

WARD, Thomas: Planter. Leg. wife Jane; daughter Hannah, if without heirs

to son John; daughter Mary; son Benjamin; daughter Olive; son Francis. Exs., wife and son Benjamin Ward. D. April 15, 1727. R. May 27, 1728.
Wit: John Williams, Joseph Quantock, Sus. Williams.    Page 87

MURREY, William: Appraised by William Harrison, John Goodrich, Benjamin Hodges. May 27, 1728.    Page 89

PEARCE, Philip: Appraised by John Teasley, Ralph Vickers, William Page. May 27, 1728.    Page 89

BOWIN, Richard: Leg. wife Elizabeth; daughter Millicent; daughter Mary; daughter Elizabeth; daughter Rebecca; between all my children. Extx., wife. D. September 9, 1727. R. May 27, 1728.
Wit: P. Mackone, Richard Pierce, Richard Teasley.    Page 90

PENNY, Ralph: Leg. wife and unborn child, the land on which Francis Floyd now lives, reversion of bequest to my brothers, William and John Penny. Exs., wife and Christopher Dickinson. D. February 5, 1727/28. R. May 27, 1728.
Wit: William Hawkins, Joseph Smith, Joseph Williams.    Page 91

WRENCH, John: Appraised by Joseph Wright, Benjamin Beale, John Wilkinson. Ordered April 22, 1728. R. May 27, 1728.    Page 93

LILBURN, Sarah: Appraised by John Davis, Thomas Davis, Richard Webb. Signed John Lupo, Adm. Ordered April 8, 1728. R. May 27, 1728.
    Page 94

FARECLOTH, William: Leg. son Benjamin; son Moses; daughter Hannah; daughter Elizabeth Mercer; daughter Sarah Revell; son William; granddaughter Martha, the daughter of Samuel Farecloth; to Sarah Pope, the wife of Henry Pope. Exs., daughter Hannah and sons Moses and Benjamin Farecloth. D. January 9, 1727. R. May 27, 1728.
Wit: Joseph Cobb, Robert Scott.
Codicil: In which Robert Scott is made trustee.
Wit: John Revell, Joseph Cobb.    Page 96

JOYNER, Thomas: Leg. brother Jonathan; brother Mathew; sister Cherry; sister Patience; sister Elizabeth; brother Alexander; brother-in-law John Dunkley. Exs., brother Alexander and John Dunkley. D. April 8, 1728. R. May 27, 1728.
Wit: Richard Lewis, Edward Boykin.    Page 97

BOYKIN, Edward: Leg. son John; wife Ann, among all my children. Exs., wife and son John. D. January 4, 1725/26. R. May 27, 1728.
Wit: James Atkinson, Mary Atkinson, John Dunkley.    Page 98

SAMPSON, James: Appraised by Lawrence Baker, Robert Ffoues, Roger Ingram. Signed Nicholas Derring. R. May 27, 1728.    Page 98

BRADSHAW, Richard: Appraised by James Hunter, William Williams, Robert Browne. Signed George Bradshaw. R. May 27, 1728.    Page 100

DENSON, James: Account Estate. Received by Francis Denson, orphan of James Denson; received by me, Thomas Gale, Jr., guardian of Joseph, the orphan of James Denson. Presented by Thomas Walton, Gent., late Sheriff of· this County. R. November 26, 1728.    Page 101

COOKE, Isaac: Appraised by John Garner, John Marshall, Michael Murfree. Signed Roger Nevill. R. June 24, 1728.    Page 102

FULGHAM, Anthony: Appraised by Francis Gross, John Rodway, William Rutter, William West. Ordered May 27, 1728. R. June 24, 1728.     Page 103

ASKEW, Nicholas: Appraised by John Wilkinson, John Garner, Benjamin Beal. Ordered May 27, 1728. R. June 24, 1728.     Page 104

HALL, Poole: Appraised by John Wright, Joseph Wright, Richard Casey. R. June 24, 1728.     Page 104

FLOWERS, Henry: Appraised by George Washington, Oliver Woodward, Benjamin Johnston. Signed Mary Flowers. Ordered April 22, 1727/28. R. June 24, 1728.     Page 106

RICHARDS, Robert: Leg. loving wife; son William; granddaughter Prudence Driver; granddaughter Prudence Richards; son Robert; son Thomas. Exs., wife and son Robert Richards. D. August 11, 1724. R. June 24, 1728.
    Wit: Edward Driver, Joseph Driver.     Page 107

GRAY, John: Leg. wife Ann; son Richard; son Aaron; daughter Ann West; daughter Mary; daughter Sarah; daughter Elizabeth. Exs., sons Richard and Aaron Gray. D. March 29, 1728. R. June 24, 1728.
    Wit: Henry Applewhaite, John Hawkins.     Page 108

PENNY, Ralph: Appraised by Nathaniel Parker, Joseph Smith, John Williams, Joseph West, at the house of Mary Penny. R. June 24, 1728.     Page 109

RICHARDS, Robert: Inventory presented by Elizabeth Richards. R. August 26, 1728.     Page 109

BOWIN, Richard: Appraised by John Teasley, Ralph Vickers, William Page. R. August 26, 1728.     Page 111

HIDEN, Ephraim: Appraised by Joseph Wright, George Crudup, John Monro. R. August 26, 1728.     Page 111

NORSWORTHY, Christian: Appraised by Joseph Smith, Henry Pitt, Robert Bridger. Signed William Scott. R. October 26, 1728.     Page 112

MARSHALL, Joseph: Appraised by Francis Gross, Thomas Gross, William Richards. Ordered June 24, 1728. R. August 26, 1728.     Page 114

RIGIN, Ann: Nuncupative will, proven by Mary Smith and Elizabeth Richards. William Noyall to have the care of her two children, Daniel and Patience Rigin; bequest to Martha Noyall. (Recorded as Ann Riggin). D. June 19, 1728. R. October 26, 1728.     Page 115

JORDAN, Margaret: Appraised by Charles Reynolds, Joseph Wright, Robert Driver. Signed John Jordan. Ordered May 27, 1728. R. August 26, 1728.     Page 115

HOWELL, John: Leg. wife Mary; son John; son William; son Samuel; son James, land adjoining Benjamin Beal; my three daughters. Exs., wife and son John. D. January 1, 1727. R. August 26, 1728.
    Wit: John Heard, John Hale, Edward Hale.     Page 116

JONES, Mathew: Appraised by Lawrence Baker, Thomas Murry, Samuel Davis. R. August 26, 1728.     Page 117

WRENN, Thomas: Leg. wife Elizabeth, the plantation called the "Freshet"; son Thomas; son John; son James; daughter Mary; my estate to be divided among all my children by Samuel and John Davis. Exs., wife

and son John. D. February 14, 1725/26. R. August 26, 1728.
    Wit: Samuel Davis, Benjamin Bidgood, Jer. Proctor.    Page 118

WOODLEY, John: Account estate. Signed Frances Woodley. Examined by W.
    Bridger and Thomas Walton. R. August 27, 1728.    Page 119

WILSON, John: 1720. Account estate. Signed Frances Woodley. Examined
    by W. Bridger and Thomas Walton. R. August 27, 1728.    Page 121

WILLIAMS, Epaphroditus: Leg. sister Juliana Wright; sister Mary Hale;
    to Mary, the daughter of Nathan Bagnall and his wife Ann; to Rachele,
    the daughter of Thomas Parker and his wife Rachele; my wife Rachele,
    at her death to Susanna and Priscilla Marshall, the daughters of
    Humphrey Marshall; to Sarah Pilkington, Jr. Wife, Extx. D. July
    14, 1728. R. September 23, 1728.
    Wit: Thomas Bevan, Hugh Giles.    Page 123

LONG, John: Appraised by William Noyall, John Wright, Christopher Reynolds.
    Ordered August 26, 1728. R. September 23, 1728.    Page 125

WILLIAMS, Epaphroditus: Appraised by Hugh Giles, William Green, Charles
    Dickinson. R. October 28, 1728.    Page 125

JOYNER, Abraham: Leg. son Abraham; son William; daughter Elizabeth;
    daughter Sarah; to all my children. D. July 9, 1727/28. R. October
    28, 1728.
    Wit: William Joyner, Joseph Joyner, John Joyner.    Page 126

POPE, Henry: Leg. son William; son Henry; son Richard; son Jacob; son
    John; daughter Mary Williams; daughter Jane Braswell; son Joseph a
    tract of land on Blackwater Creek; daughter Mourning a tract on the
    Meherrin River; son Thomas a tract on the Murrachock River; son
    Samuel; to Mary Clothier at her freedom from my wife; to cousins,
    Edward and John Pope. Exs., wife Sarah and son John Pope. D. May
    28, 1728. R. October 28, 1728.
    Wit: Epenetus Griffin, John Denson, Jr., Martin Cleuse (?).
        Page 127

DUCK, William: Leg. wife Margery; son Timothy; son Robert, land adjoining
    John Carr; my two eldest sons, William and John; son Jacob; daughter
    Bridget; daughter Dorothy; daughter Isabel. Wife, Extx. D. August
    4, 1727. R. October 28, 1728.
    Wit: Hardy Council, John Johnson, John Duck.    Page 128

HOWELL, John: Appraised by B. Beal, John Garner, Robert Driver. R.
    October 28, 1728.    Page 129

HOUSE, James: Leg. son James; son Thomas; to my daughter-in-law, Mary
    House, the wife of son Thomas; son John; daughter Ester; to Ann
    House Wetherall; granddaughter Cleary House; daughter Hester. William
    Hawkins and my son John to divide my estate. Ex., son John House.
    D. March 23, 1727/28. R. October 28, 1728.
    Wit: William Hawkins, John Anthony Rue.    Page 129

INGRUM, Roger: Appraised by William Harrison, Benjamin Hodges. Signed
    Elizabeth Ingram. Ordered August 26, 1728. R. November 11, 1728.
        Page 130

WARD, Thomas: Appraised by Arthur Jones, John Mangum, William Bell. R.
    November 25, 1728.    Page 133

PRICE, Joseph: Leg. cousin William Price, Jr.; wife Martha. Exs., loving

father, Francis Williamson and wife Martha. D. March 7, 1725/26.
R. November 25, 1728.
      Wit: Abraham Bagget, Francis Harris.            Page 133

RIGGAN, Ann: Appraised by Robert Richards, Joshua Whitney, Christopher
    Reynolds. Signed William Noyall. R. November 25, 1728.    Page 134

DANIEL, John: Leg. wife Elizabeth and my two children. Wife, Extx. D.
    January 24, 1727/28. R. November 25, 1728.
        Wit: Joseph Norsworthy, Thomas Norsworthy.      Page 134

LOWRY, Mathew: Appraised by John Dawson, Timothy Tines, Thomas Uzzell.
    Ordered October 25, 1728. R. November 25, 1728.       Page 135

GENT, John: Appraised by George Washington, Benjamin Johnston, John Barnes,
    Sr. Signed by Thomas Allen and Oliver Woodward. R. March 25, 1728.
                                                  Page 136

BENN, Arthur: Leg. son James (not 21); son Arthur, land on the Nottoway
    River; daughter Mary; son Christopher land on the Nottoway; wife Frances.
    Wife, Extx. D. May 8, 1728. R. December 23, 1728.
        Wit: Arthur Smith, John Lowe, James Benn.       Page 137

RIDDICK, George: Appraised by Peter Fiveash, James Piland, John Bunkley.
    R. December 23, 1728.                        Page 139

COGGAN, William: Appraised by Richard Price, William Pope, John Teasely.
    Ordered November 25, 1728. R. January 27, 1728.       Page 140

JOYNER, Abraham: Appraised by Epenetus Griffin, Hodges Council, Robert
    Johnson. R. January 27, 1728.                 Page 140

BUTLER, John: Appraised by Timothy Tynes, Arthur Benn, Christopher Rey-
    nolds. Signed Ann Butler. Ordered February 26, 1727. R. January 1,
    1728.                                      Page 141

KERLL, Eleanor: Appraised by Benjamin Beal, John Wilkinson, John Garner,
    Thomas Gale, Jr. Ordered December 23, 1728. R. January 27, 1728.
                                                  Page 142

YOUNG, Alexander: Leg. friend, John Exum, my whole estate. D. December
    25, 1726. R. January 27, 1728.
        Wit: John Dunkley.                      Page 143

FULLGAM, Michell: Of the Upper Parish. Leg. to my cousin John Fulgham;
    to cousin John Williamson; sister Mary Fulgham; brother John Fulgham.
    Ex., brother Edman. D. November 26, 1728. R. January 27, 1728.
        Wit: John Johnson, Anthony Fulgham, Mary Johnson.    Page 144

RUTTER, William: Nuncupative will, proven by Arthur Brown and Joshua
    Hunter. Signed by Mary Rutter. He desired that William Wootten
    should have what was his, and that the remainder of his estate should
    belong to his wife. R. January 27, 1728.          Page 145

TURNER, Joshua: Appraised by Theophilus Joyner, John Garner, William God-
    win. Signed by Christopher Dickinson. Ordered November 26, 1728.
    R. January 27, 1728.                          Page 145

TOWNSAND, Henry: Appraised by Thomas Pursell, Hugh Mathis, William Blake.
    Ordered January 25, 1728/29. R. January 27, 1728.      Page 145

BENN, Arthur: Appraised by Robert Richards, John Chapman, Christopher

Dickinson. R. January 27, 1728. Page 146

COUNCILL, James: Appraised by William Daughtry, John Lawrence, William
Fowler. R. February 24, 1728. Page 148

DANIEL, John: Appraised at the house of Elizabeth Daniel by Christopher
Dickinson, Joseph Norsworthy, John Chapman. R. February 24, 1728.
Page 149

POPE, Henry: Appraised by Robert Johnson, Epenetus Griffin, John Bowin.
(Estate in N. C. mentioned.) R. February 24, 1728. Page 149

SHELLY, John: Account of estate, examined by James Baker and Joseph
Bridger. R. February 24, 1728. Page 150

PITT, Thomas: Appraised at the house of Henry Pitt by William Weston,
Francis Gross, Robert Murray. Ordered October 24, 1726. R. February 24, 1728. Page 151

SCOTT, John: Appraised by Joseph Parke, William Blake, Francis Sharpe.
Signed by Francis Scott. Ordered February 8, 1728/29. R. February
24, 1728. Page 151

SCOTT, Robert: Appraised by George Washington, Henry Applewhite, Benjamin
Johnston. Signed Elizabeth Scott. R. March 24, 1728. Page 152

JOHNSON, John: Appraised by Thomas Williams, Thomas Turner, Virgus Smith.
R. March 24, 1728. Page 153

BURNETT, Ann: Of the Upper Parish. Leg. cousin Joseph Williamson. Ex.,
brother Francis Williamson. D. April 8, 1729. R. April 28, 1729.
Wit: William Dixon, Elizabeth Brantley. Page 154

RUNELS, Henry: Leg. son John; daughter Patience; daughter Darkes Bowin;
daughter Elizabeth Johnson; wife Elizabeth; son-in-law John Weaid;
son-in-law John Bowin, my Ex. D. February 11, 1725/26. R. April
28, 1729.
Wit: Joseph Bradshaw, John Denson, Jr. Page 155

PIERCE, Jeremiah: Appraised by Thomas Murray, Thomas Hill, Benjamin
Hodges. R. April 28, 1729. Page 156

LOWRY, Martha: Of the Lower Parish. Leg. daughter Ann; son Henry; daugh-
ter Mary; grandchildren, James and Martha Lowry. Daughter Ann, Extx.
D. January 21, 1729. R. April 28, 1729.
Wit: William Wiggs, John Garner, John Bunkley. Page 156

PROCTOR, Reuben: Of the Upper Parish. Leg. cousin Reuben Proctor, the
son of George Proctor; to cousin George Proctor's children; to brother Jeremiah Proctor's children. Ex., brother Jeremiah Proctor.
D. April 11, 1729. R. April 28, 1729.
Wit: William Dixon, Samuel Davis, Joseph Williamson. Page 157

FULGHAM, Micael: Inventory, returned by Mary Fulgham. R. May 26, 1729.
Page 158

JOYNER, Thomas, Jr.: Inventory presented by John Dunkley. R. May 26, 1729.
Page 158

FULGHAM, John: Leg. my estate to all my children. Ex., son Anthony Fulgham. D. December 14, 1728. R. May 26, 1729.
Wit: John Westray, Martha Norsworthy, John Johnson. Page 159

POWELL, Nathaniel: Leg. wife Mary; son Jacob; son Arthur; son Nathaniel; (sons under 18) daughter Mary; daughter Rachel. D. October 23, 1728. R. May 26, 1729.
    Wit: Robert Berryman, James Brown. Page 159

TARLETON, Roger: Leg. son Roger; grandson James, the son of Thomas Tarleton; granddaughter Ann, the daughter of Roger Tarleton; daughter Sarah Nolleboy; to granddaughter Sarah, the daughter of Daniel Nolleboy; son William; son Thomas; daughter Elizabeth Nash; daughter Mary Jolliff; son Joseph; wife Margaret. Ex., son Joseph Tarleton. D. December 12, 1726. R. April 28, 1729.
    Wit: Abraham Ricks. Page 161

POWERS, Edward, Sr.: Leg. son William; to Charles Powers; wife Elizabeth; to Elizabeth Darden, the wife of John Darden; son Edward; residue of my estate to be divided among my four sons and three daughters. D. April 7, 1729. R. May 26, 1729.
    Wit: Davie Hooper, Joseph West, Jacob Johnson. Page 162

PURCELL, Arthur: Leg. son Arthur land on the Blackwater; son Thomas the land I bought of Thomas Joyner; daughter Isabella, the wife of Arthur Whitehead; loving wife. Exs., sons Arthur and Thomas Purcell. D. April 21, 1717. R. May 27, 1729.
    Wit: Arthur Smith, Joshua Turner, Mathew Lowry.
    Presented by Mary Purcell, widow. Page 163

GOODSON, Thomas: Appraised by Thomas Calcote, Thomas Summerell, Thomas Uzzell. Ordered November 25, 1728. R. May 5, 1729. Page 164

RUNNELLS, Henry: Appraised by Hodges Council, Epenetus Griffin, Joseph Bracher. R. June 23, 1729. Page 166

KINDRED, Samuel: Leg. son John land on Reedy Branch, and Blunt's Swamp; wife Mary; son Samuel, land adjoining Charles Porter and James Braswell; the plantation on which John Williams lives to be sold; to daughters, Sarah and Faithe, the land in Surry County on which Mathew Delk lives; daughter Jane; daughter Mary; daughter Catherine; daughter Elizabeth. Ex., -----------. D. January 25, 1728/29. R. June 23, 1729.
    Wit: Samuel Adkins, James Braswell. Page 166

Deposition of Robert Berryman, proving that he wished his wife to have everything he had not given his children. R. June 23, 1729.
Page 168

FULGHAM, John: Appraised by Arthur Pursell, John Johnson, John Batten. R. June 23, 1729. Page 169

PROCTOR, Rueben: Appraised by Samuel Davis, John Davis, Thomas Murry. R. July 28, 1729. Page 169

SCOTT, John: Leg. wife Joan; refers to negroes left his children by their uncle, James Tooke; daughter Mary; daughter Sarah; daughter Elizabeth; to James Tooke Scott; to Thomas Scott; to my cousin William Hollowell, 200 acres upon Kingsale Swamp, which was given me by my deceased father William Scott. Exs., wife Joan and son James Tooke Scott. D. March 12, 1728/29. R. July 28, 1729.
    Wit: William Wilson, William Dixon, Thomas Harris, George Bell.
Page 171

TARLETON, Roger: Appraised by Thomas Gale, Jr., Jacob Darden, Michael Murphrey. R. July 28, 1729. Page 172

POWERS, Edward, Sr.: Appraised by Samuel Brown, John Vasser, Arthur Whitehead. R. July 28, 1729. Page 173

BENN, Arthur: Appraised by Samuel Browne, John Vasser, James Garner, William Hickman. Ordered November 28, 1728. R. August 25, 1729. Page 174

BARLOW, Sarah: Leg. daughter Mary; son Thomas; granddaughter Sarah Carrell. Ex., son Thomas Barlow. D. March 19, 1728/29. R. August 25, 1729.
Wit: William Dixon, John Brantley, Clay Brantley. Page 175

MURRY, John: Account of estate. To clothing and bringing up the child. Examined by Thomas Walton and James Baker. R. August 9, 1729. Page 175

VASSER, Peter: Appraised by Robert Mounger, William Jones, Richard Atkinson. Ordered May 26, 1729. R. June 14, 1729. Page 176

PURSELL, Arthur: Appraised by John Johnson, John Turner, Daniel Herring. R. August 25, 1729. Page 177

WILLIAMS, Peter: Appraised by John Chapman, John Monro, Thomas Gross. Signed Mary Williams. Ordered August 25, 1729. R. 22d. of 7ber 1729. Page 178

POWELL, Nathan(iel): Appraised by William Pope, Robert Crocker, Simon Everett. Signed by Robert and Mary Berryman. R. September 22, 1729. Page 179

CROCKER, William: Leg. son Joseph; daughter Patience; daughter Mary. Wife Mary, Extx. D.-----------. R. October 27, 1729.
Wit: Robert Crocker, Joseph Crocker. Page 179

RICHARDS, Robert: Appraised at the homes of Robert Richards, Mrs. Elizabeth Richards and William Richards, by John Chapman, Charles Dickinson, John Clark. R. October 27, 1729. Page 180

GREEN, William: Leg. son Bartholomew, the land on which Christopher Dickinson now lives, also my mill in the Upper Parish now in the occupation of Henry White, for Capt. Joseph Bridger's life; son George my land at the "Freshet," now in the tenure of William Davis; wife Mary; daughter Sarah Bevan; to Martha Montgomery; to Mary, Elizabeth and Green Green, the daughters of Mary Green, widow; daughter Prudence; daughter Rebecca. My estate to be divided by Samuel Davis, John Davis, Arthur Smith and Christopher Dickinson. Exs., wife Mary and Samuel Davis. D. January 27, 1727/28. R. October 27, 1729.
Proved by depositions of Richard West and William Pilkington, aged 30 years. Page 183

WIGGS, Katherine: Leg. son William; refers to deceased husband, Henry Wiggs; son George; son Luke; daughter Sarah, jugs bought of Benjamin Chapman; daughter Catherine Stevenson; daughter Mary Britt; daughter Elizabeth Bressey. Ex., son George. D. June 4, 1729. R. November 24, 1729.
Wit: William Brock, Thomas Calcote, George Goodson. Page 184

WEBB, William: Account estate. To burying John Webb, to the said Webb's wife's part; due to Samuel Webb, orphan. Examined by Thomas Walton and James Baker. R. November 24, 1729. Page 186

LONG, Daniel: Appraised by Hugh Giles, Robert Richards, Robert Murray.

Ordered November 24, 1729. R. December 22, 1729. Page 186

KINDRED, Samuel: Appraised by Martin Middleton, John Rochel, Samuel Atkinson. R. December 22, 1729. Page 187

RUTTER, William: Appraised by William Noyall, John Wright, Joseph Wright. Ordered January 27, 1728. R. December 22, 1729. Page 188

BUNKLEY, John: Leg. son Robert; daughter Ann; daughter Sarah; son John; daughter Mary Morgan; to my two sons named John. Ex., wife Bridget. D. June 10, 1725. R. December 22, 1729.
    Wit: William Green, James Brown, Ann Hail, Sarah Bunkley.
Page 188

CHAPMAN, Joseph: Leg. wife Alice; son Charles, the land I bought of John Butler and of John Rodaway; to son-in-law John Applewhite; daughters, Mary, Martha, Elizabeth and Alice. D.----------. R. December 22, 1729.
    Wit: Thomas Uzzell. Page 189

MORELAND, Edward: Appraised by William Holliman, William Richardson, Christopher Holliman. Signed Unity Moreland. R. December 22, 1729.
Page 191

WHITE, William: Leg. my mother; to John Lee; to Francis Lee; to Mary White; to John White; brother John White; brother Thomas White; to Mary Bell; brother Henry White; sister Jane Lee. D. October 13, 1722. R. February 23, 1729.
    Wit: Thomas Rosser, Samuel Williams. Page 191

LONG, Daniel: Additional appraisal by Hugh Giles, Robert Richards. R. February 23, 1729. Page 193

BOYKIN, John: Appraised by Francis Williamson, John Dunkley, Edward Harris. R. February 23, 1729. Page 194

BUNKLEY, John: Appraised by W. Bridger, Jr., Robert Brown, George Mynard. Ordered January 17, 1729/30. R. February 23, 1729. Page 194

BOLTON, John: Appraised by Benjamin Clements, John Arrington, Thomas Macey. Signed by William Simmons. R. March 23, 1729. Page 195

FULGHAM, Anthony: Additional appraisal by Francis Gross, John Rodway, William West. R. March 23, 1729. Page 195

CROCKER, William: Appraised by John Pope, Simon Everett, John Cain. Signed Mary Crocker. Ordered March 14, 1729. R. March 23, 1729.
Page 196

JOLLEY, James: Appraised by William Noyall, Robert Driver, Christopher Reynolds, William West. R. March 23, 1729. Page 197

TIDMASH, Giles: Leg. son Giles; wife Sarah. Wife, Extx. D. July 30, 1728. R. March 23, 1729.
    Wit: Sarah Lee, John Lett. Page 198

PILKINGTON, William: Appraised by Wm. Bridger, Jr., John Monro, Robert Browne. Ordered February 28, 1729. R. March 23, 1729. Page 198

WHITE, John: Leg. son Valentine; wife Elizabeth; to John Carpenter; daughter Millicent; daughter Jane; daughter Mary; son William; son Jonathan. Exs., wife and son Valentine White. D. January 23, 1726/27.

R. March 23, 1729.
    Wit: James Ramsey, John Carpenter, Elizabeth Redish.    Page 198

HARRIS, Thomas: Leg. son Joshua; daughter Mary; to my unborn child. Exs.,
    wife Hannah and brother Henry Harris. D. December 25, 1729. R. March
    23, 1729.
    Wit: Thomas Harris, Thomas Atkinson.    Page 199

BREWER, Thomas: Leg. daughter Mary; daughter Ann, the plantation I bought
    of John Hall on which the widow, Mary Williams now lives; son John,
    the tract I bought of Wm. Thompson on Gray's Creek in Surry County;
    son Thomas the tract I bought of Col. Wm. Cole and the one I bought
    of Mr. Thomas Swann, called "Quin-Quan"; son John the money in the
    hands of Mr. Perry. Ex., son Thomas. D. March 4, 1729. R. March
    23, 1729.
    Wit: Humphrey Marshall, Robert Marshall, Elizabeth Marshall.
                                                                Page 200

CHAPMAN, Joseph: Appraised by William Wilson, Ambrose Hadley, Edward
    Crocker. R. April 27, 1730.    Page 201

GARLAND, John: Settled by William Wilkinson and John Chapman. 1727.
    R. April 27, 1930.    Page 204

HILYARD, Thomas: To be buried by my deceased wife. Leg. son Edward;
    son John; daughter Mary. Ex., friend Samuel Alexander. D. March 20,
    1729. R. May 25, 1730.
    Wit: John Jones, Samuel Alexander, Ann Spann (?).    Page 205

MACKMAILL, John: Leg. loving wife; son John; son Philip, 100 acres at
    Corrawock, the plantation on which David Williams lived, also the
    land on the road from Pursell's mill to the chapel; land called
    Clark's Posen to be sold and the money divided among my daughters
    by this present wife; to my five married daughters; to my wife and
    her seven children. Ex., son John Mackmaill. Overseers, Jacob
    Darden and Richard Pope. D. December 22, 1728. R. May 25, 1730.
    Wit: Jacob Darden, John Mackmaill.    Page 205

BREWER, Thomas: Appraised by John Monro, W. Bridger, Jr., Francis Gross.
    R. May 25, 1730.    Page 206

MACKMAILL, John: Appraised by John Johnson, William Wesuray, John Tomlin,
    Mathew Tomlin. R. July 27, 1730.    Page 209

JONES, Edward: Leg. eldest son Edward; son William; son Joseph land on
    the Blackwater; daughter Jane; daughter Sarah; daughter Deborah;
    daughter Mary; wife Deborah. Exs., wife and sons Joseph and William
    Jones. D. January 15, 1722. R. July 27, 1730.
    Wit: Thomas Lane, John Brown, Peter Vasser.    Page 210

RICKES, James: Leg. brother Isaac Rickes; brother Abraham Rickes, Mary
    his wife and their daughter Martha; brother Robert Rickes and his
    son Robert; sister Jane Sellaway and her son John Sellaway; to Jacob
    Rickes; to John Rickes, the son of Isaac Rickes; to William, the
    son of Jacob Rickes. Exs., Abraham and Robert Rickes. D. April 7,
    1730. R. July 27, 1730.
    Wit: William Denson, John Roberts.    Page 211

NEVILL, John: Leg. daughter Penelope; daughter Elizabeth; daughter Mar-
    tha; daughter Elenora; daughter Florence; daughter Mary; daughter
    Patience; daughter Sarah; daughter Ann. Exs., wife and son John
    Nevill. D. September 30, 1726. R. July 27, 1730.

HILLIARD, Thomas: Appraised by William Brock, Thomas Calcote, Edward
     Davis. Ordered May 25, 1730.                              Page 214

RICKES, James: Inventory presented by Abraham and Robert Rickes. August
     24, 1730.                                                 Page 215

HOGGARD, Patrick: Appraised by Thomas Calcote, William Brock, George
     Whitley. Ordered January 17, 1729. R. September 28, 1730.  Page 215

RICKES, James: Appraised by Thomas Gale, Jr., Robert Coggan, William
     Powell. R. September 28, 1730.                            Page 216

SAULS, Abraham: Leg. William Broom; son John; son Abraham; daughter
     Elizabeth; daughter Sarah, a bequest left her by her grandmother.
     Extx., loving wife. D. April 3, 1730. R. September 28, 1730.
          Wit: Thomas Lumbly, Thomas Brown, Thomas Wood.       Page 218

TIDMASH, Gyles: Inventory signed by William Bidgood and presented by
     Sarah Tidmash. R. September 28, 1730.                     Page 218

PITMAN, Thomas: Leg. son Thomas; son Samuel; son Robert; son Ambrose;
     son John; son Arthur; son Samson; son Joseph; to daughters, Ann,
     Olive, Pratta, Elizabeth, Lucy and Faith. Trustees, Robert Lancaster,
     John Dunkley and Robert Monger, Jr. D.-----------. R. September 28,
     1730.
          Wit: Joseph Strickling, Thomas Pitman, Edward Hood.
          Robert Lancaster's deposition in reference to the location
          of his land.                                         Page 220

GOODSON, Thomas: Settlement of Estate. To funeral charges for said
     Goodson and his wife. Settled by Henry Applewhaite and Thomas Wal-
     ton. R. September 28, 1730.                               Page 220

BOYKIN, Edward: Appraised by Francis Williamson, John Dunkley, Mathew
     Kinchin. Ordered February 24, 1728. R. September 28, 1730. Page 221

JONES, Joseph: Inventory presented by William Kinchen, Jr. R. Septem-
     ber 28, 1730.                                             Page 223

STRICKLAND, Mathew: Leg. son John, 100 acres on the Green Pond; son
     William; son Sampson; son Mathew; son Jacob; daughter Sarah; daughter
     Ann; daughter Elizabeth; daughter Jane; son Joseph. Exs., wife Ann
     and son Joseph. D. July 14, 1730. R. October 25, 1730.
          Wit: Arthur Taylor, Joseph Strickland, Mathew Cooper.  Page 224

GRAY, Richard: Leg. mother Ann Gray; sister Ann West; sister Mary Wil-
     lett; sister Elizabeth; sister Sarah. Ex., brother Aaron Gray.
     D. October 20, 1729. R. October 25, 1730.
          Wit: Ann Gray, Sarah Gray.                           Page 225

PARKER, Nathaniel: Of Newport Parish. Leg. eldest son Nicholas; son
     Nathaniel, one-half of my lots in the town of Hampton; wife Ann;
     daughter Martha; daughter Mary. Ex., brother Nicholas Parker. D.
     June 29, 1730. R. November 23, 1730.
          Wit: Thomas Applewhite, Joseph Bridger, Thomas Parker. Page 226

HAMPTON, Thomas: Appraised by Jacob Darden, Robert Smelly, John Marshall.
     Ordered October 26, 1730. R. November 23, 1730.           Page 229

BRIDGER, William: Leg. son William; to grandson Joseph Bridger; to William

Dixon; to Mr. Thomas Bray, the cane, which was his father's; son
James the plantation on which Jonathan Jones now lives, the land
which belonged to his deceased brother Joseph Bridger at Round Hill,
I have sold to Major Benjamin Edwards for 25₤, my said son to be
under the guardianship of Arthur Smith, Jr. and his wife Elizabeth,
until he is eighteen; to Elizabeth Smith. Ex., Arthur Smith, Jr.
D. September 27, 1730. R. November 23, 1730.
    Wit: William Crumpler, William Crumpler, Jr.        Page 230

BROWN, Edward: Appraised by Benjamin Wilson, Edward Harris, Abraham Ste-
    venson. R. November 23, 1730.                       Page 231

BRIDGER, Col. William: Appraised by Henry Applewhite, Thomas Applewhite,
    Thomas Walton. R. December 28, 1730.                Page 232

PITMAN, Thomas: Appraised by Robert Lancaster, John Dunkley, Robert
    Monger, Jr. R. January 25, 1730/31.                 Page 238

SALMON, James: Leg. daughter Phillips; to William Salmon; son James; to
    Mary Salmon; to Thomas Salmon; to John Salmon; to Sarah Salmon; to
    John Bass. Ex., son James Salmon. D. November 18, 1730. R. March
    22, 1730.
        Wit: John Bass, John Dortish (?).               Page 240

GRAY, Richard: Appraised by William Best, Humphrey Marshall, John Penny.
    R. January 25, 1730.                                Page 241

FULGHAM, Anthony: Appraised by Francis Williamson, John Little, Joshua
    Turner. Ordered June 24, 1729. R. January 25, 1730/31.    Page 242

PARKER, Nathaniel: Appraised by Hugh Gyles, John Norsworthy, Tristram
    Norsworthy. R. January 25, 1730/31.                 Page 243

RUTTER, William: Appraised at the house of Mary Rutter, by Joseph Wright,
    William Noyall, John Wright. R. February 22, 1730/31.    Page 244

HARRIS, Thomas: Appraised by Edward Brantley, John Tharp, Thomas Purcell.
    R. February 22, 1730/31.                            Page 245

EVERETT, Samuel: Appraised by Michael Murphrey, Jacob Darden, Thomas
    Gale, Jr., Benjamin Beal. Ordered January 25, 1730. R. February
    22, 1730/31.                                        Page 246

PILKINGTON, William: Appraised by W. Bridger, John Monro, Robert Brown.
    R. February 22, 1730/31.                            Page 247

BRANTLEY, John: Leg. to granddaughters, Elizabeth, Martha and Mary Loo-
    pers (Lupo); to grandson John, the son of my son Clay Brantley; to
    grandson Thomas Brantley, the son of my son Clay; to friend Thomas
    Walton. Ex., son Clay Brantley. D. February 1, 1730/31. R. March
    22, 1730/31.
        Wit: Thomas Walton, Elizabeth Walton.           Page 248

SKELTON, Thomas: Leg. grandson William, the son of John Tuke and Eliza-
    beth his wife; to daughter Ann; daughter Mary, the land on which
    William Gladhill, formerly lived; to friends, James Baker, Thomas
    Shelly, James Wilson and Lawrence Baker. Extx., daughter Ann Skelton.
    D. January 26, 1730. R. March 22, 1730/31.
        Wit: Priscilla Fones, Lawrence Baker.           Page 249

WHITE, John: Appraised by Thomas Cook, Henry Harris, William Lee. R.
    March 22, 1730.                                     Page 251

COBB, Edward: Leg. son Henry; daughter Susan Rede (Read ?); to loving wife; my sons have had their share. Ex., son Henry Cobb. D. November 26, 1729. R. March 22, 1730/31.
Wit: Edward Cobb, Richard Williams, John Johnson. Page 251

LUNDY, James: Account of estate returned by Joseph Perry. R. March 22, 1730/31. Page 253

SIKES, Thomas: Leg. son Thomas; son Joseph; son William; daughter Elizabeth; daughter Jane. Extx., wife Elizabeth Sikes. D. January 19, 1730. R. March 22, 1730/31.
Wit: Thomas Gale, Jr., Francis Denson, John Denson. Page 254

BOYKIN, Edward: Account of estate, returned by Edward Boykin, Jr. Examined by Francis Williamson and John Dunkley. R. March 22, 1730/31.
Page 255

SCREWS, John: Leg. son John; son William; son Joseph; son Arthur; daughter Elizabeth; to loving wife. D. November 9, 1729. R. April 26, 1731.
Wit: John Britt, Charles Jordan.
Presented by Elizabeth Screws, relict. Page 256

POWELL, John: Of the Lower Parish. Leg. son John; son Jacob; daughter Sarah Hutchings; granddaughter Mirikia Hutchins; son Moses; son Henry; daughter Patience; son Arthur. Extx., wife Deborah Powell. D. February 18, 1730. R. April 26, 1731.
Wit: Thomas Gale, Jr., Thomas Bullock, Thomas Gale. Page 257

SALMON, James: Appraised by Owen Mirick, Timothy Thorp, John Thorp. R. April 26, 1731. Page 258

DICKINSON, Christopher: Appraised by Robert Richards, John Wright, John Chapman. Ordered March 22, 1730. R. April 26, 1731. Page 261

SYKES, Thomas: Appraised by Jacob Darden, Mick'l Murfee, Robert Eley. Signed Elizabeth Sykes. Ordered March 22, 1730. R. April 26, 1731.
Page 264

SCREWS, John: Appraised by Richard Blunt, Ambrose Hadley, Edward Crocker. R. May 24, 1731. Page 268

POWELL, John: Appraised by Jacob Darden, John Marshall, Mick'l Murphry. R. April 24, 1731. Page 269

WILLIAMS, Epaphroditus: Account of estate. Examined by John Chapman, Christopher Reynolds, William Noyall. R. May 24, 1731. Page 270

WOODLEY, John: Appraised by Thomas Murry, John Davis, Joseph Chapman. Signed Mrs. Frances Woodley. Ordered September 18, 1726. R. September 26, 1726. (Note by Clerk, omitted in proper place). Page 273

PROCTOR, Rueben: Settlement of estate, to money in the hands of Thomas Davis and William Dixon. Audited by Thomas Walton and James Ingles. R. June 28, 1731. Page 278

NORSWORTHY, Thomas: Settlement. Errors accepted by Thomas Walton, audited by James Ingles, Samuel Davis and Lawrence Baker. R. July 26, 1731.
Page 278

STRICKLAND, Mathew: Appraised by Robert Crocker, John Cain, Robert Berryman. Ordered October 26, 1730. R. July 26, 1731. Page 280

GUTTERIDGE, John: Appraised by William Sellers, Oliver Woodward, Thomas
    Carter. R. July 26, 1731.                                    Page 282

DOWLES, John: Of the Upper Parish. Leg. daughter Alice Dukes, after the
    death of her mother; daughter Ann; daughter Mary; daughter Ruth;
    daughter Susan. Exs., daughters, Ruth and Susannah Dowles. D.
    August 23, 1731. R. August 23, 1731. Acknowledged in court by the
    said John Dowles.                                            Page 283

HOLLYMAN, Christopher: Leg. son James; son John. Extx., wife Susannah
    Hollyman. D. August 2, 1729. R. October 25, 1731.
        Wit: Thomas Hollyman, Sr., Josiah John Hollyman, Thomas Holly-
    man, Jr.                                                     Page 284

NORWOOD, Richard: Appraised by Thomas Cook, Joseph Parks, Edward Brant-
    ley. R. October 25, 1731.                                    Page 285

MEACUM, John: Estate, audited by James Ingles, Lawrence Baker. R. No-
    vember 23, 1731.                                             Page 287

MEACUM, Susanna: Account estate, signed by Roger Ingram, William Dixon.
    Audited by Thomas Walton and James Ingles. R. November 23, 1731.
                                                                 Page 288

SANDERS, Robert: Of the Lower Parish. Leg. to cousin Robert Sanders, the
    son of Thomas Sanders, decd., land on the Queen's Grave Swamp; cousin
    Francis Sanders, the son of Francis Sanders; to cousin Elizabeth
    Sanders, daughter of Thomas Sanders, decd.; to her brother Thomas;
    to cousin Richard Sanders, the son of Thomas Sanders, decd., the land
    I bought of Elizabeth Thomas; to John Sanders, the son of Francis
    Sanders; to Thomas, the son of Thomas Sanders, Decd., land called
    "Half Moon"; to my cousin Phebe Winborn. Exs., John Winborn and
    Robert Sanders. D. July 12, 1731. R. December 27, 1731.
        Wit: Richard Thomas, Lawrence Wolferston, John Thomas. Page 289

HOLLYMAN, Christopher: Inventory, presented by James Hollyman. R. De-
    cember 27, 1731.                                             Page 291

HARRIS, Thomas: Inventory, supplemented by Henry Harris. R. March 27, 1732.
                                                                 Page 292

PETERSON, John: Leg. to Burrell Brown, 400 acres, if no issue to return
    to my son Batt Peterson; to Jeremiah Brown, 200 acres, being the
    plantation on which Joseph Perry lived, if without heirs, to return
    to my son John; to John Smith 100 acres on the Fox Branch; to Mathew
    Parham of Isle of Wight County, 100 acres on the same Branch; to
    grandson John Eppes, 100 acres on which Jonathan Carter lived, also
    100 acres on which Robert Ellis lived and 400 acres out of the tract
    I bought of Edmond Mecarty, on Meherrin River and Jenitoe Creek; to
    son Batt; to son John; daughter Mary Spain; daughter Judith Thweatt;
    daughter Ann Thweatt. Exs., sons Batt and John Peterson. D. March
    1, 1731. R. January 24, 1731.
        Wit: William Thweatt, Miles Thweatt, John Sturdivant.   Page 292

COGGAN, William: Appraised by Thomas Gale, Jr., Robert Eley, Jr., Jacob
    Darden. R. March 27, 1732.                                   Page 295

WALTERS, Walter: Of the Lower Parish. Leg. granddaughter Martha Brown,
    the plantation on which Robert Owen lived; to granddaughter Alice
    Powell, land adjoining John Powell and William Watkins at Currawoak;
    to grandsons Benjamin and Walter Morrell, land on Blackwater, ad-
    joining Bridgeman Joyner; to George Morrell and Mary his wife, land

adjoining Richard Beal; granddaughter Mary Morrell; wife Alice. D.
November 26, 1730. R. January 23, 1731/32.
    Wit: Jacob Darden, Sarah Darden, John Chapman.
    Revocation of certain bequests. R. March 27, 1732.
    Wit: Jacob Darden, Stephen Darden, John Powell.     Page 297

BODY, Mary: Widow and late wife of William Body. Leg. son-in-law Thomas
Drake; daughter Mary Bragg; daughter Judith Clark; daughter Sarah
Joiner. Ex., Thomas Drake. D. January 17, 1727. R. April 24,
1732.
    Wit: George Washington, Richard Drake, Francis Jones.   Page 299

BATEN, Richard: Leg. son Edward, land between Kingsale Swamp and Blackwater; to my daughter; to my wife. Ex., son Richard Baten. D.
January 28, 1731/32. R. April 24, 1732.
    Wit: John Williams, Thomas Gawker, Richard Williams.   Page 300

THORNTON, Thomas: Appraised by Thomas Hill and John Goodrich. Ordered
February 28, 1731. R. April 24, 1732.     Page 301

SAUNDERS, Robert: Appraised by John Daughtry, William Daughtry, Robert
Carr, Jr., John Council. Signed by John Winborn, Ex. R. May 22,
1732.     Page 302

HOWEL, John: Leg. loving wife; daughter Penelope; brother William Howell;
rest of my estate to be divided between my wife and James Howell,
Samuel Howell and Martha Howell and my daughter Penelope. D. March
20, 1731/32. R. June 26, 1732.
    Wit: Thomas Pinner, Joseph Bullock, Thomas Dixson.
    Presented by Elizabeth Howell.     Page 304

BRASWELL, Susannah: Leg. son Richard; son William; granddaughter Elizabeth
Braswell; daughter Ann; grandson John Riggs; son James. Trustees,
Richard Jones and Richard Jordan. D. October 22, 1714. R. June 26,
1732.
    Wit: William Allen, Richard Jones, Richard Jordan.   Page 304

FULGHAM, Edmond: Appraised by Arthur Purcell, John Little, Mathew Tomlin.
Ordered March 27, 1732. R. July 24, 1732.     Page 306

JOYNER, Alexander: Appraised by William West, Robert Monger, Jr., Thomas
Warren. R. July 24, 1732.     Page 307

HOWEL, John: Appraisal by Robert Driver, Benjamin Beal, John Garner.
R. July 24, 1732.     Page 308

BRIDGER, William: Of the Lower Parish. Leg. brother James Bridger, land
on Blackwater Swamp; to son Joseph, 15₺ paid yearly to my trusty
friend Arthur Smith until he is 18, I desire that he should live
with his grandfather and grandmother, if his grandmother should die,
I wish him to live with Arthur Smith and his wife Elizabeth. Ex.,
Arthur Smith. D. April 2, 1732. R. July 24, 1732.
    Wit: William Smith, John Bruce, W. Simmons.     Page 309

BRIDGER, William: Appraised by John Monro, Henry Pitt, Francis Gross.
R. August 28, 1732.     Page 311

RICHARDS, William: Nuncupative will, proven by John Rodway, Gyles Driver,
Olive Driver. Of Newport Parish. He desired that his wife Frances
should have the estate of her deceased husband, Arthur Benn, and for
what was his own he desired that she should have one third of what he
had and his two children, viz: William and Jane should have the rest;

his deceased wife's clothes to his said daughter. D. July 3, 1732.
R. August 28, 1732.                                          Page 314

FULGHAM, Michael: Appraised by William Noyall, John Wright, Christopher
    Reynolds. Ordered February 26, 1727. R. August 28, 1732.    Page 315

HARRISON, John: Settlement of estate by Lawrence Baker, Thomas Hill and
    James Ingles. To Nicholas Casey and Thomas White, who married two
    of the daughters of the said John Harrison and Benjamin Hodges, who
    married his widow and relict. R. August 25, 1732.           Page 318

HALL, Poole: Additional inventory, presented by William Todd. R. August
    28, 1732.                                                   Page 319

FULGHAM, Anthony: Account current, signed by Hugh Gyles and John Chapman.
    R. September 25, 1732.                                      Page 319

BOYKIN, William: Leg. wife Margaret, the plantation I bought of Thomas
    Boykin; son Simon; son William land at Roanoke bought of James Spears;
    son John, land bought of my brother Thomas Boykin; son Thomas land
    on Tucker's Swamp, on which John Phillips lived; daughter Martha;
    my four sons my land at Fishing Creek in North Carolina. D. June 19,
    1731. R. September 25, 1732.
        Wit: William Carrell, Thomas Moore, Jr., M. Kinchin.    Page 321

WIGGS, Sarah: Leg. my three sisters, Catherine Stevenson, Mary Britt and
    Elizabeth Brassey; brother Luke Wiggs; friend Henry Applewhite. Ex.,
    brother George Wiggs. D. July 26, 1732. R. September 25, 1732.
        Wit: Gwin Summerell, Violet Frissell.                   Page 324

DICKINSON, Christopher: Estate settled by Hugh Gyles, John Chapman. R.
    September 25, 1732.                                         Page 324

BRASSEE, William: Of the Upper Parish. Leg. son William; son Thomas;
    wife Jane. Ex., son William Brassee. D. May 22, 1732. R. January
    22, 1732.
        Wit: Robert Edwards, William Edwards, Henry Edwards.    Page 325

RICHARDS, William: Appraised by John Chapman, Hugh Gyles, Robert Driver.
    R. October 24, 1732.                                       Page 326

INGRAM, Roger: Account current, signed by William English. Examined
    by Thomas Hill, John Goodrich.                             Page 328

JORDAN, James: Leg. son John, if without heirs to grandson James Jordan;
    daughter Elizabeth Scott; land bought of Joseph Bridger to my grand-
    son James Jordan Scott; son James' children. D. October 8, 1732.
    R. January 22, 1732.
        Wit: Mathew Jordan, Mary Jordan, Thomas Parr.           Page 328

APPLEWHITE, Thomas: Leg. wife Martha; son Thomas; son Henry; son John;
    daughter Holland Copeland; daughter Martha Weston; daughter Mary
    Benn; daughter Ann. Exs., wife and son Henry Applewhite. D. June
    15, 1728. R. January 22, 1732.
        Wit: Everett West, John Hokins (?).                     Page 329

JORDAN, James: Appraised by B. Beal, Joseph Wright, Robert Driver. Signed
    by John Jordan.                                            Page 331

GALE, Thomas: Leg. wife Alice; daughter Sarah; daughter Elizabeth Sykes;
    daughter Mary Bryant; daughter Alice Eley; son Thomas. Extx., wife
    Alice. D. November 15, 1732. R. February 26, 1732.

Wit: William Scott, Thomas Bullock, John Hampton.    Page 331

OSBOURNE, Edward: Appraised by Thomas Shelly, John Barlow, John Floide.
R. February 26, 1732.    Page 333

BRASSEE, William: Appraised by John Turner, John Whitley, William Brassee. R. February 26, 1732.    Page 333

STREET, Maddison: Of the Lower Parish. Leg. cousin George Whitley; cousin
Maddison Whitley; cousin Mary, the daughter of brother George Street,
the plantation on which Thomas Daniels lives; cousin John Whitley;
cousin Thomas Whitley; to Goddaughter Martha Whitley; to Egbell Sawyer Jones; sister Sarah Turner; cousin Henry Turner; sister Ann Smith;
cousin Sarah Smith, the daughter of John Smith; Mary the daughter
of Thomas Bevan. Ex., cousin George Whitley. D. November 19, 1732.
R. February 26, 1732.
      Wit: Mary Smith, Charles Fulgham, William Lane.    Page 334

STREET, Maddison: Appraised by Hugh Gyles, John Wright, George Clark.
    Page 338

HOLYDAY, Samuel: Settlement of the estate in the hands of Anthony Covington Holyday, by William Wilkinson, Benjamin Willett. R. March 26,
1733.    Page 338

FULGHAM, Anthony: Of the Upper Parish. Leg. John Oin (?) son Anthony;
wife Sarah. D. December 18, 1728. R. January 25, 1730.
      Wit: John Johnson, Joshua Turner, Jr., Joshua Turner, Sr.
    Page 349

BENN, James: Leg. wife Mary; son James (not 21); son George, land I
bought of John Calloway, also the land formerly belonging to Josiah
Harrison; to unborn child; daughter Mary. Extx., wife Mary. D.
August 30, 1732. R. April 23, 1733.
      Wit: George Benn, Elizabeth Copeland, Jane Casey.    Page 340

SHERRER, Sarah: Appraised by Charles Chapman; Richard Blunt, William
Clarke. Signed Edward Crocker. Ordered March 26, 1733. R. April
23, 1733.    Page 343

WHITE, Henry: Leg. wife Sarah; silver which I have sent for by Captain
Turner, to son Baker; daughter Mary. Friends, Mr. Mathew Wills and
William Baker to divide my estate. D. February 17, 1733. R. May
28, 1733.
      Wit: William Glover, John White, Lawrence Baker.    Page 344

JOHNSON, Robert: Leg. son Robert; son James; son John; son Abraham; son
Isaac, land adjoining Thomas Swann; son Jacob; wife Ann; daughter
Catherine Council; daughter Priscilla Council; daughter Ann Griffin;
daughter Mary; daughter Sarah. Wife, Extx. D. September 24, 1732.
R. May 28, 1733.
      Wit: Thomas Drake, Jr., Richard Worrell, John Dawson, Jr.
    Page 345

CLEMENTS, Francis: Estate, signed by Joseph Lane and Lydia Clements, Extx.
Ordered December 2, 1718. R. May 28, 1733.    Page 347

SANDERS, Henry: Inventory, presented by John Sanders. R. June 25, 1733.
    Page 349

DANIEL, John: Estate settled by Hugh Gyles and George Clarke. R. June 25,
1733.    Page 349

116

EDWARDS, Hugh: Appraised by John Chapman, George Clark, John Wright. Signed Mary Edwards. Ordered April 23, 1733. R. June 25, 1733.

Page 350

BOYKIN, William: Appraised by John Dunkley, Francis Williamson, M. Kinchin. R. June 25, 1733.

Page 351

BENN, Captain James: Appraised by Hugh Giles, George Clark, William Noyall. R. June 25, 1733.

Page 354

PENNY, Ralph: Settlement, by John Chapman, Benn Willett. R. July 23, 1733.

Page 356

RICHARDS, William: Appraised by Francis Gross, Benn Willett, Robert Driver. R. July 23, 1733.

Page 356

WESTBROOK, John: Leg. daughter Ann; son John; son Thomas; daughter Sarah; son William; son James; sister Elizabeth; beloved wife. D. February 13, 1719. R. July 23, 1733.
    Wit: Edward Simmons, Thomas Perry, Walker Enniss.

Page 357

MILLER, Edward: Leg. son Edward; son John; son William; daughter Sarah; wife Martha. Friends, Mathew Jordan, Thomas Murry, John Davis and William Harrison to divide my estate. D. February 12, 1727. R. August 27, 1733.
    Wit: John Hodges, Benjamin Hodges.

Page 358

TERALL, Blackabee: Leg. grandson James Jordan; grandson Joseph Jordan; granddaughter Ann Jordan; son-in-law James Jordan. D. September 7, 1726. R. August 27, 1733.
    Wit: Thomas Goodson, Edward Davis.
    Presented by Patience Jordan, the widow of James Jordan.

Page 360

JORDAN, James: Appraised by William Bidgood, William Wilson, Joseph Hill. Ordered January 22, 1732. R. September 24, 1733.

Page 362

BUTLER, Ann: Appraised by Timothy Tines, Joseph Wright, Richard Kersey. Ordered May 28, 1733. R. October 22, 1733.

Page 369

ROW, John: Appriased by John Johnson, William Pope, Richard Williams. R. October 22, 1733.

Page 370

GENT, John: Appraised by Nicholas Williams, Robert Rickes; Francis Jones. Signed by Oliver Woodward and Thomas Allen. R. October 22, 1733.

Page 370

REYNOLDS, Christopher: Appraised by Hugh Giles, Richard Williams, Joseph Wright. Ordered March 27, 1733. R. October 22, 1733.

Page 372

GARLAND, John: Appraised by John Chapman, John Wright, Charles Fulgham, Edward Driver. Ordered April 23, 1733. R. October 22, 1733. Signed Martha Garland.

Page 375

RICHARDS, Robert: Leg. daughter Prudence Driver; to Peter Green; daughter Sarah Croom; to Martha, the daughter of Patience and Peter Green; daughter Susannah; son Robert; daughter Sarah; granddaughter Martha Green. August 6, 1733. R. November 26, 1733.
    Wit: Edward Driver, Edward Croom.

Page 377

POPE, Richard: Leg. son Henry; son Richard; wife Sarah; daughter Jane; daughter Sarah; daughter Charity Pope. Exs., wife and son Henry Pope.

D. September 24, 1733. R. November 26, 1733.
    Wit: Thomas Gale, John Williams, Jr., Jacob Powell.    Page 378

BATEN, Richard: Appraised by John Johnston, Richard Williams, William
    Daughtrey. R. November 26, 1733.                      Page 380

HOWELL, John: Settlement of estate by Abraham Rickes and Benjamin Beal.
    R. November 26, 1733.                                 Page 381

SAMPSON, James: Estate settled by Lawrence Baker, Thomas Murry, and John
    Goodrich. R. January 28, 1733.                        Page 382

RICHARDS, Robert: Appraised by Richard Wilkinson, Joseph Wright, John
    Clark, John Chapman. R. January 28, 1733.             Page 383

GULLEDGE, Edward: Appraised by Edward Lundy, Harmon Read, William Lee.
    R. January 28, 1733.                                  Page 386

NORWOOD, Elizabeth: Appraised by Thomas Cook, Henry Harris, Thomas Smith.
    Ordered August 7, 1733. R. January 28, 1733.          Page 386

SPECIAL, Samuel: Appraised by Timothy Tynes, Sharp Reynolds. Ordered
    November 6, 1733. R. January 28, 1733.                Page 388

THORNTON, William: Account current, signed by Abraham Rickes, Benjamin
    Beale. R. February 25, 1733.                          Page 388

GOODRICH, George: Settlement of estate, to balance due to the widow, to
    Mary Goodrich, orphan; to Joseph Clinch in the right of his wife
    Elizabeth. Signed Hugh Giles and Thomas Hill. R. February 25, 1733.
    The receipt of Joseph Clinch was witnessed by William Seward.
                                                          Page 389

PARKER, Nicholas: Account current, to Nicholas Parker, orphan, his estate.
    Signed Ann Parker. R. February 25, 1733.              Page 390

HARRIS, Edward: Of the Upper Parish. Leg. son Edward, land adjoining
    John Johnson and John Turner, being land which was granted to my
    father, Thomas Harris; son Jacob, land on the Flatt Swamp of the
    Meherrin River; sons Nathan and West Harris, the land granted me on
    the north side of Warwick Branch; son Daniel; daughter Ann; daughter
    Martha Williamson; son James; wife Mary. Ex., son Nathan Harris.
    D. April 27, 1733. R. March 25, 1734.
    Wit: Thomas Atkinson, John Harris.                    Page 391

WILLIAMS, John: Leg. son Richard; son John; son David. Extx., wife Mar-
    garet Williams. D. December 17, 1733. R. March 25, 1734.
    Wit: Thomas Parker, Joseph Weston.                    Page 393

MARSHALL, Joseph: Account estate, signed by William Wilkinson, Charles
    Fulgham. R. March 25, 1734.                           Page 394

HOLLYMAN, Thomas: Of the Upper Parish. Leg. grandson Joseph Hollyman
    land on Blackwater Swamp; grandson Arthur Hollyman; to Robert Carrell;
    wife Elizabeth; to William Hollyman. D. December 31, 1732. R. March
    25, 1734.
    Wit: Thomas Atkinson, John Hollyman, Jr.              Page 395

CARRELL, Joseph: Leg. my two brothers, Benjamin and Samuel Carrell;
    cousin Benjamin, son of Benjamin Carrell; cousin Thomas, son of
    Samuel Carrell; to Sarah White. Ex., brother Benjamin Carrell. D.
    March 1, 1733. R. March 25, 1734.

## WILL BOOK FOUR

COX, Francis: Appraised by Thomas Jarrell, William Pope, John Thomas.
Ordered February 25, 1733. R. April 22, 1734.                    Page 1

BATEMAN, Richard, Sr.: Settlement ordered November 26, 1733. Signed
Hardy Council, Francis Jones. R. April 22, 1734.                 Page 1

PITT, Henry: Appraised by Benn Willett, Humphrey Marshall, James Hunter.
R. April 22, 1734.                                               Page 2

LUCUS, Mary: Leg. son John; son William. Ex., son William Lucus. D.
December 31, 1729. R. May 27, 1734.
Wit: John Dunkley, Abigail Waynfield, William Reynolds.
Page 3

PITT, Thomas: Account estate, examined by Joseph Godwin, William Wilkinson, John Monro. R. May 28, 1734.                             Page 4

FRIZZEL, Ralph: Leg. wife Mary; daughter Ann Holyday; daughter Mary Rey-
nolds; son Ralph; six children now with me, viz: James, John, Joshua,
Elizabeth, Lucy and Sarah. Exs., wife and son James Frizzell. D.
January 19, 1733. R. May 27, 1734.
Wit: Joseph Wiles, Joseph Weston.                           Page 6

GLOVER, Sarah: Appraised by Thomas Moreland, James Carrell, Thomas Shelly.
Ordered February 25, 1733. R. May 27, 1734.                      Page 8

MERCER, James: Leg. wife Mary; daughter Mary; son John; daughter Ann;
daughter Martha; son Robert; son James; son Thomas; to my unnamed
son; daughter Elizabeth; daughter Patience; daughter Sarah; son-in-
law Robert Williamson. Wife Mary, Extx. D. December 11, 1720. R.
June 24, 1734.
Wit: William Kinchin, Arthur Purcell.                       Page 11

HAWKINS, William: Appraised by Joseph Smith, Thomas Parker, Tristram
Norsworthy. Ordered July 12, 1734. R. July 22, 1734.        Page 14

INGRAM, Roger: Leg. wife Elizabeth; son John; son Roger; daughter Sarah;
daughter Elizabeth; son Richard; son William. Exs., Thomas Shelley
and Benjamin Hodges. D. March 12, 1733/34. R. September 23, 1734.
Wit: William Dixon, Thomas Stark, William Atkinson.
Exs., refused and wife Elizabeth qualified.                 Page 18

CARR, John: Yeoman. Leg. daughter Mary; daughter Elizabeth; daughter
Sarah; son William; son Abraham; son Hardy; daughter Grace; son John;
son Robert; daughter Eleanor Duck; to my wife and my three young sons.
Ex., son Robert Carr. D. May 19, 1734. R. September 23, 1734.
Wit: John Darden, John Duck, John Carr.                     Page 21

BAKER, Mary: Widow of Henry Baker, Gent. Leg. son William land in Nansemond County, called "Wickums"; son Lawrence; son James; son Henry;
daughter Mary; daughter Sarah; daughter Katherine. Ex., son Lawrence
Baker. D. March 5, 1732. R. September 23, 1734.
Wit: Nicholas Derring, James Briggs, Robert Davis.          Page 22

DAVIS, Thomas: Leg. to William, the son of William Davis, deceased; to Elizabeth Gray; to John Davis, the son of Samuel Davis; to my daughter Elizabeth at 18, if she should die without heirs, my estate to the sons of my three brothers and my sister Prudence Wrenn. Exs., brother Samuel Davis and friend James Day. D. August 15, 1734. R. September 23, 1734.
    Wit: Samuel Davis, Elizabeth Gray.        Page 23

STARK, Thomas: Appraised by Thomas Moreland, James Carrell, Thomas Shelley. Ordered May 27, 1734. R. October 28, 1734.        Page 24

WESTBROOK, John: Appraised by Nathaniel Ridley, Edward Brantley, Thomas Cook. Signed by John Person. R. October 28, 1734.        Page 25

ROW, John: Appraised by Richard Williams, William Pope, John Johnson. R. October 28, 1734.        Page 26

WILLIAMS, Mary: Leg. son George; son-in-law Mathew Jones; daughter Sarah Brown; daughter Mary Williams; son Peter. Exs., my brother Peter Green and my son Peter Williams. D. October 27, 1734. R. November 25, 1734.
    Wit: Thomas Gross, Anthony Covington Hollyday.        Page 28

BAKER, Mary: Appraised by Samuel Davis, Thomas Murry, John Goodrich. R. November 25, 1734.        Page 28

GILES, Eleanor: Leg. son Robert Smelly; grandson John Smelly; to my son Robert Smelly's wife; to Grandsons Robert and Thomas, the sons of Robert Smelly; to Elizabeth Smelly, the wife of my son Lewis Smelly; to Joshua Whitney, Jr., the son of my granddaughter; to Lewis, the son of William Joyner. Ex., my grandson John Smelly. D. February 17, 1732. R. November 25, 1734.
    Wit: Thomas Uzzell, H. Lightfoot.        Page 29

WILLIAMS, Mary: Appraised by Francis Gross, Thomas Gross, Thomas Applewhite, Anthony Covington Holyday. R. December 23, 1734.    Page 31

WARREN, William: Appraised by Joseph Gray, John Hodges, John Dunkley. Ordered December 21, 1734. R. January 27, 1734.        Page 32

SMELLEY, Robert: Leg. son John; son Thomas; son Robert. Exs., sons Robert and Thomas Smelley. D. August 2, 1734. R. January 27, 1734.
    Wit: Thomas Gale, John Mackmial.        Page 34

MACKMIALL, John: Aged 25 years. Leg. wife Elizabeth; to my unborn child. Wife, Extx. D. October 18, 1734. R. January 27, 1734.
    Wit: Mathew Westray, John Batten.        Page 35

CARR, John: Appraised by James Johnson, Jr., John Darden, John Duck. R. January 27, 1734.        Page 36

MURRY, George: Appraised by John Miller, Benjamin Hodges, Peter Woodward. Ordered March 7, 1725. R. January 27, 1734.        Page 37

MINYARD, William: Appraised by Joseph Wiles, George Parker, Robert King. R. January 27, 1734.        Page 38

DAVIS, Thomas: Appraised by Thomas Hill, John Goodrich, Melchizedeck Deshey. R. January 27, 1734.        Page 39

PARKER, George: Leg. daughter Mary; son John; to John Gray; to Sarah Weston; to William Smith, Jr.; son Francis; daughter Elizabeth. Money

for the last two children to be placed in the hands of Mr. Nathaniel Bagnall, William Smith, Jr. and Henry King, whom I appoint my Exs. D. January 27, 1734. R. February 24, 1734.
Wit: Robert King, John Gray. Page 41

UNDERWOOD, Thomas: Inventory presented by William Underwood. R. February 24, 1734. Page 42

PITT, John: Leg. daughter Martha, the land on which Captain Joseph Bridger now lives; grandson Joseph Bridger, the land on which John Turner now lives; daughter Rachel, the land on which Ann Smith now lives, also the land on which Elizabeth Shaw lives; daughter Esther; daughter Prudence, the land on which Edward Driver and Robert Smith live; daughter Ann Godwin, the land on which William Godwin and Samuel Croom live; grandson William Bridger. Ex., William Godwin. D. December 19, 1729. R. February 24, 1734.
Wit: Edward Driver, Richard Pilkington. Page 43

BOYKIN, William: Account estate, to Thomas Vaughan, who married the Extx. Examined by John Dunkley and Mathew Kinchin. R. February 24, 1734.
Page 44

POWELL, William: Leg. son William; son Joseph, land at Corrowaugh, adjoining Robert Carr; son Benjamin; son-in-law Samuel Redlehusk; daughter Martha; daughter Rebecca Wilkinson; daughter Mary Holland; daughter Rachel; daughter Alice; daughter Lydia; wife Mary. Ex., son William. D. October 3, 1734. R. March 24, 1734.
Wit: John Darden, Thomas Powell, Daniel Day. Page 46

PITT, Captain John: Appraised by Hugh Giles, Thomas Whitfield, George Clark. R. March 24, 1734. Page 47

PARKER, George: Appraised by Mathew Jones, Francis Gross, Giles Driver. R. March 24, 1734. Page 49

NORWOOD, Richard: Appraised by Nathaniel Ridley, John Person, J. Edwards. Ordered June 24, 1734. R. March 24, 1734. Page 48

BROWN, Joseph: Appraised by John Pitt, Richard Snowden, Anthony Covington Holyday, John Penny. Ordered February 24, 1734. R. March 24, 1734.
Page 50

MACKMIALL, John: Estate authorized to be sold by Jacob Darden. R. March 24, 1734. Page 51

JORDAN, Richard: Appraised by Arthur Jones, Joseph Ward, John Davis. Ordered April 12, 1735. R. April 28, 1735. Page 52

FULGHAM, Anthony: Account estate, examined by William Wilkinson, Benn Willett. R. April 28, 1735. Page 54

POWELL, William: Appraised by George English, James Johnson, Thomas Powell. R. April 28, 1735. Page 55

INGRAM, Roger: Appraised by Thomas Hill, Thomas Moreland, Thomas Murry, Samuel Davis. R. May 26, 1735. Page 57

CARR, Robert: Leg. wife Mary; son Robert; daughter Elizabeth Darden. Exs., wife and son Robert Carr. D. May 10, 1734. R. May 26, 1735.
Wit: Hardy Council, Michael Council, Charles Council. Page 59

BRIGGS, Henry: Appraised by Richard Kirby, Thomas Macey, Arthur Arrington.

R. May 26, 1735.

BUNKLEY, John: Appraised by John Pitt, Richard Snowden, Robert Brown.
    Ordered March 24, 1734/35. R. May 26, 1735.                    Page 62

TAYLOR, Edward: Leg. son Joseph; son Edward; son George; daughter Eliza-
    beth. Wife, Extx. D. June 29, 1734. R. May 26, 1735.
         Wit: Robert Eley, Jr., Ambrose Saunders, Sarah Ogbourne.
                                                                   Page 63

WARREN, William: Appraised by Mathew Kinchin, John Dunkley, Joseph Gray.
    Ordered April 28, 1735. R. May 26, 1735.                       Page 64

BRASWELL, Sarah: Leg. grandson John Braswell, Jr.; daughter Jane; grand-
    son Benjamin Braswell; to the other children of my son John, viz.:
    Mary, William and Sampson. Exs., son John Braswell and grandson John
    Braswell. D. March 20, 1733/34. R. May 26, 1735.
         Wit: Richard Blow, Jr., Samuel Smith, Samuel Willis.      Page 65

KEA, Henry: Account estate, funeral charges for his daughter Mary Kea.
    Signed Richard Webb and William Bidgood. Examined by Thomas Moreland
    and James Carrell.                                             Page 65

BRIGGS, Henry, Jr.: Account estate, signed William Barton. Examined by
    Joseph Gray and M. Kinchin. R. May 26, 1735.                  Page 66

WOOD, George: Appraised by William Killebrew, Martin Middleton, Peter
    Durdinow. Ordered January 27, 1734. R. June 23, 1735.         Page 68

DRIVER, Thomas: Appraised by Hugh Giles, Joseph Wright, Timothy Tynes.
    Funeral expenses for the said Driver and his wife and for his son
    Thomas Driver. R. June 23, 1735.                              Page 69

NORSWORTHY, Charles: Leg. wife Ann; eldest son Charles; second son Thomas;
    son George; daughter Ann; to my unborn child. Wife, Extx. D. Novem-
    ber 17, 1734. R. June 23, 1735.
         Wit: Benn Willett, Peter Best.                           Page 69

DICKINSON, Christopher: Settlement of estate, to a third part paid to
    John Bridger, who married the widow; to the three orphans. Examined
    by Lawrence Baker, Thomas Moreland, Joseph Hill. R. June 23, 1735.
                                                                   Page 71

KINCHEN, William: Leg. son Mathew; daughter Elizabeth Exum; grandson
    William Jones; daughter Martha Jarrell; daughter Patience Taylor and
    her husband Etheldred Taylor; daughter Sarah Godwin; granddaughter
    Martha Godwin; son William; wife Elizabeth; grandson William Kinchen;
    granddaughter Mary Jones. Ex., son Mathew Kinchen. D. August 13,
    1734. R. July 28, 1735.
         Wit: Arthur Purcell, John Dunkley, Henry Flowers.        Page 72

NORSWORTHY, Charles: Appraised by Benn Willett, Thomas Applewhite, Hum-
    phrey Marshall. R. July 28, 1735.                             Page 75

BEVAN, Thomas: Leg. son Thomas (not 21); son George; son Robert; son
    Joseph; daughter Mary; wife Mary. Exs., wife and son Thomas Bevan.
    D. March 22, 1734. R. August 25, 1735.
         Wit: Hugh Giles, Rachel Davis.                           Page 76

WILLIAMS, Garret: Leg. wife Elizabeth; son Daniel. Extx., wife Elizabeth
    Williams. D. May 10, 1735. R. August 25, 1735.
         Wit: William Watkins, William Jelks, Isaac Winingam.     Page 80

PORTER, Charles: Appraised by John Rochel, William Turner, Martin Middleton. R. October 27, 1735. Page 81

RIGIN, Ann: Account estate, signed by William Noyall. Examined by John Chapman, Hugh Giles. R. October 27, 1735. Page 82

LILBURN, Sarah: Account estate, signed by W. Bidgood. Examined by Jesse Brown and Henry West. R. October 27, 1735. Page 83

WILLIAMS, Mary: Account of estate in the hands of Peter Green. Examined by Thomas Woodley, Thomas Summerell, Thomas Calcote. R. November 24, 1735. Page 85

LOWRY, Mathew: Joannah Lowry's account against her husband's estate. Examined by William Brock and Timothy Tynes. R. November 24, 1735. Page 86

JONES, Richard: Inventory, presented by Elizabeth Jones. R. November 24, 1735. Page 87

WHEADON, Philip: Leg. son James; son Joseph. Ex., son Joseph Wheadon. Friends, Lawrence Baker, John Hodges and John Goodrich to divide estate. D. November 27, 1735. R. January 26, 1735.
Wit: John Goodrich, Rachel Miller. Page 88

VICK, Robert: Of Nottoway Parish. Leg. son Robert; son Joseph; son Benjamin; son Nathan; wife Sarah; daughter Mary. Exs., wife and son Robert Vick. D. October 25, 1735. R. January 26, 1735.
Wit: J. Turner, Richard Vick, Jacob Vick. Page 88

PENNY, John: Leg. wife Mary; son John; youngest son William. Wife, Extx. D. July 20, 1735. R. January 26, 1735.
Wit: Anthony Covington Holladay, Benn Willett. Page 90

BRADSHAW, Nicholas: Account estate, to Ralph Frizzell for Mary Bradshaw, to Elizabeth Bradshaw; to John and George Bradshaw. R. January 26, 1735. Page 91

MOXSON, Robert: Inventory. R. January 26, 1735. Page 92

WHEADON, Philip: Appraised by Thomas Murry, William Harrison, Benjamin Hodges. R. February 23, 1735. Page 92

APPLEWHAITE, John: Leg. wife Sarah; to my unborn child; sister Ann; to the heirs of Mary Benn, given them by my deceased father; brother Thomas; sister Holland Copeland; sister Martha Weston; friend Thomas Copeland. Exs., wife and friend Henry West. D. December 20, 1735. R. February 23, 1735.
Wit: Peter Best, Thomas Copeland. Page 94

HAMPTON, John: Of the Lower Parish. Leg. brother Francis Hampton; to John, the son of Francis Hampton; to Martha Hampton; to Mary Hampton; to John, the son of Michael Murphry; to Rachel, the daughter of Thomas Hampton; to Sarah Simmons, my sister; to John Hole; my wife Ann and at her death to go to Benjamin Hampton, if without heirs, reversion to John Hampton. D. February 19, 1735. R. March 22, 1735.
Wit: Thomas Gale, Thomas Bullock, Jacob Powell. Page 95

GOODMAN, William. Appraised by Arthur Jones, William Crocker, W. Pitman. R. March 22, 1735. Page 96

JORDAN, Richard: Account of estate examined by Robert Cannon and Joseph

WRENN, John:  Appraised by John Goodrich, William Harrison.  R. April 26,
1736.                                                        Page 100

PARKER, Thomas:  Leg. eldest son William; son Elias; daughter Ann; son
Thomas; son Wilkinson; daughter Sabre; daughter Priscilla; grandson
Elisha Parker; daughter Rachel.  Wife, Extx.  D. January 30, 1735.
R. April 26, 1736.
        Wit: Robert King, George Norsworthy, James Bagnall.    Page 101

BAGNALL, Nathan:  Leg. wife Ann; son Joseph; son James; daughter Mary;
daughter Easter; daughter Ann; son Nathan; son Richard; son Joshua;
son William; son Samuel.  Exs., wife Ann and son James Bagnall.  D.
February 30, 1735.  R. April 26, 1736.
        Wit: William Smith, Joseph Weston, William Smith, Jr.  Page 102

NORWOOD, William:  Leg. to William, the son of Henry Harrison; to John,
the son of Thomas Clark; sister Rebecca; sister Elizabeth; sister
Mary; sister Hannah; to Elizabeth Vaughan; my clothes between Henry
Harrison and Thomas Clarke.  Exs., brothers Henry Harrison and Thomas
Clarke.  D. February 8, 1735.  R. April 26, 1736.
        Wit: Benjamin Chapman Donaldson, Charles Travers, John Gladish.
                                                             Page 103

WHITNEY, Joshua:  Leg. wife Mathon; son David; son Jeremiah; son Samuel;
daughter Kolzing; son Joseph; daughter Ruth; son Francis; daughter
Ketring.  Exs., sons, David and Jeremiah Whitney.  D. December 26,
1735.  R. April 26, 1736.
        Wit: John Bentley, Jeremiah Bentley, James Blair.
        (Will also proven in North Carolina)                 Page 104

BALDWIN, William:  Appraised by Richard West, John Wright, John Clark.
R. May 24, 1736.                                             Page 106

BULLS, Martha:  Appraised by Robert Driver, B. Beal, John Garner, Joseph
Garner.  Ordered April 26, 1736.  R. May 2, 1736.            Page 107

BEVAN, Peter:  Appraised by Charles Fulgham, John Gibbs, George Whitley.
Signed Bartholomew Green.  R. May 24, 1736.                  Page 108

DRIVER, Robert:  Appraised by Francis Gross, John Rodway, Humphrey Marshall.
Ordered April 26, 1736.  R. May 24, 1736.                    Page 108

PENNY, John:  Appraised by Edmond Godwin, Thomas Applewhaite, Benn Willett.
R. May 24, 1736.                                             Page 109

RICHARDS, Robert:  Estate in the hands of Charles Fulgham.  Examined by
Joseph Godwin, Thomas Walton, Thomas Pierce.                 Page 110

BRADGG, Mary:  Leg. granddaughter Sarah Driver; granddaughter Hester Driver;
grandson Charles, the son of Edward Driver; grandson Joseph Norsthey
(Norsworthy ?); granddaughter Martha Norsthey; granddaughter Mary
Norsthey; grandson Charles Norsthey; son-in-law Edward Driver and
son-in-law Joseph Norsthey; granddaughter Mary Driver.  Exs., son-
in-law Edward Driver, friend Thomas Whitfield, Jr.  D. July 31, 1735.
R. May 24, 1736.
        Wit: Henry Applewhaite, William Frizzell.            Page 111

KINCHEN, Mathew:  Leg. mother Elizabeth; brother William; my wife Elizabeth; to unborn child, with reversion of bequest to William, the son
of Etheldred Taylor and to William Jones, the son of Elizabeth Exum;

to William Jarrell, if he performs an agreement, which I had with Gilbert Mackinnie; to William, the son of my brother William Kinchen; my uncle Thomas; friend John Dunkley; sister Elizabeth; sister Martha; sister Patience; to James Godwin's children, James, Martha and Mathew Godwin. Exs., brothers-in-law, Thomas Jarrell and Etheldred Taylor. D. March 4, 1735/36. R. May 24, 1736.
Wit: John Dunkley, Thomas Joyner, Edward Buxton.            Page 113

WARREN, Thomas: Leg. wife Sarah; son Thomas; daughter Mary; daughter Jane; daughter Martha; daughter Patience. Wife, Extx. D. September 9, 1735. R. May 24, 1736.
Wit: John Dunkley, John Warren.            Page 115

DUCK, John: Leg. daughter West; wife Priscilla. Wife, Extx. D. March 20, 1735. R. May 24, 1736.
Wit: William Noyall, John Long, John Parmentoe.            Page 116

FERRELL, Silvester: Leg. wife and children. D. April 10, 1736. R. May 24, 1736.
Wit: Robert Murry, Patrick Sweney.            Page 117

NORSWORTHY, Tristram: Appraised by Samuel Whitfield, Giles Driver, Joseph Wheston, Robert King. Ordered June 11, 1736. R. June 28, 1736.
Page 117

CARTER, George: Inventory presented by Sarah Carter. R. June 29, 1736.
Page 118

INGRAM, Roger: Settlement of estate. To widow's part, to John Ingram, to Roger Ingram, to Richard Ingram, to William Ingram, to Sarah Ingram, to Elizabeth Ingram. Examined by Samuel Davis, Thomas Murry. R. June 28, 1736.            Page 119

NORWOOD, Elizabeth. An error in appraising negroes which were her dower in my father's estate. Signed Thomas Clarke, Ex. of William Norwood, who was the Adm. of Elizabeth Norwood. R. June 29, 1736.            Page 121

JONES, Mathew: Account estate, examined by Hardy Council and James Baker. R. June 29, 1736.            Page 121

CARTER, Thomas: Of the Lower Parish. Leg. sons James and Benjamin, a tract on the south side of the Nottoway River, adjoining George Gurley and George Carter and William Edwards; son Samuel; son William; wife Elizabeth; daughter Elizabeth; daughter Ann. Wife, Extx. D. November 10, 1732. R. July 26, 1736.
Wit: George Gurley, Augustine Hixson.            Page 122

BROWN, Samuel: Appraised by John Chesnutt, John Gibbs, George Whitley. R. July 26, 1736.            Page 123

APPLEWHITE, John: Appraised by Joseph Weston, Humphrey Marshall, Thomas Applewhite, Edmond Godwin. Ordered March 24, 1735. R. July 26, 1736.            Page 124

DAVIS, Robert: Leg. son Thomas, land on the Blackwater; son Arthur Davis; between my wife and all my children. Exs., wife and son Thomas Davis. D. June 22, 1736. R. July 26, 1736.
Wit: John Davis, William Murry, John Wills.            Page 125

KINCHEN, Mathew, Gent.: Appraised by Francis Williamson, Thomas Joyner, John Dunkley. R. August 23, 1736.            Page 126

WILLIAMS, Peter and Mary:  Division of their estates, to the four
    eldest children, to the youngest son George Williams, by Samuel Davis
    and Thomas Woodley.  R. August 23, 1736.                     Page 131

VASSER, John, Jr.:  Appraised by Arthur Whitehead, John Pope, Jr., Thomas
    Davis.  Signed Sarah Vasser.  Ordered August 13, 1736.  R. August
    23, 1736.                                                    Page 132

DUCKE, John:  Appraised by John Darden, John Eley, William Fowler.  Ordered
    May 24, 1736.  R. August 23, 1736.                           Page 132

CANNON, Robert:  Appraised by Joseph Ward, John Davis, Thomas Shurly.
    Ordered July 29, 1736.  R. August 23, 1736.                  Page 134

WHITNEY, Joshua:  Appraised by Richard West, Thomas Summerell, Timothy
    Tynes.  R. August 23, 1736.                                  Page 134

MORELAND, Catherine:  Appraised by Richard Hardy, John Gray, Benjamin
    Carrell.  R. August 23, 1736.                                Page 135

LITTLE, Robert:  Of the Upper Parish.  Leg. sons John and Jacob, land which
    is to be divided between them by John Person and John Inman; to my
    sons and three daughters now living with me; to Lewis Dupree, the
    son of John Dupree; to Sarah Oaks, the daughter of Joseph Oaks;
    daughter Elizabeth Oaks; daughter Lucy Dupree.  Exs., son John and
    daughter Sarah Little.  John Person, overseer.  D. March 29, 1736.
    R. August 23, 1736.
        Wit: John Inman, Lewis Dupra, Charles Travers.           Page 136

VASSER, John:  Leg. son after his mother's death; to daughter Sarah; daugh-
    ter Elizabeth; granddaughter Sarah Vasser; wife Margaret.  My estate
    to be divided into three parts, one part to my wife; one to Simon
    Everett, and the third to my son Nathan Vasser.  Exs., wife Margaret
    and Simon Everett.  D.----------.  R. August 23, 1736.
        Wit: John Drake, Thomas Williams, John Marshall.         Page 137

NOWSOM, William:  Appraised by Arthur Whitehead, John Pope, Jr., Thomas
    Grangshaw (?).  Ordered January 26, 1735.  R. September 28, 1736.
                                                                 Page 137

EVANS, David:  Appraised by Francis Williamson, Thomas Moore, John Dunkley.
    Signed Elizabeth Evans.  Ordered July 8, 1736.  R. September 13, 1736.
                                                                 Page 138

TURNER, James:  Leg. Martha Pugh; daughter Kizzia; wife Mary.  Exs.,
    Joseph West and Thomas Crinshaw.  D. November 7, 1735.  R. September
    28, 1736.
        Wit: Samuel Willis, Joseph West.                         Page 139

SCABOTH, William:  Leg. son William; son John; son Thomas; son Edward;
    son David; son Samuel; daughter Jane; daughter Sarah; wife Sarah.
    Exs., wife and son William.  D. November 9, 1735.  R. September 28,
    1736.
        Wit: Robert Ricks, William Wood, Richard Bryant, John Wood.
                                                                 Page 140

FOSTER, John:  Leg. eldest son Christopher; son John, land adjoining
    Charles Barham and Thomas Phillips; son Arthur; wife Mary; daughter
    Elizabeth; daughter Faith; daughter Mary; daughter Lucy; daughter
    Sarah.  Exs., wife and my brother Christopher Foster.  D. February
    23, 1735.  R. September 28, 1736.
        Wit: Richard Griffith, Christopher Foster, Faith Emry, Fortune

FULGHAM, Nicholas: Leg. son Nicholas; son Joseph; son Joshua; daughter Elizabeth; daughter Susanna; daughter Martha. Exs., wife Isabella and son Nicholas Fulgham. D. July 7, 1736. R. September 28, 1736.
Wit: Charles Fulgham, Mary Bevan, Elizabeth Smith. Page 142

VASSER, John: Appraised by John Pope, Samuel Browne, Richard Price. R. October 25, 1736. Page 143

WARREN, Thomas: Inventory presented by Sarah Warren. R. October 25, 1736.
Page 145

NORWOOD, James: Inventory presented by Thomas Smith. R. October 25, 1736.
Page 145

DAVIS, Robert: Appraised by Samuel Carrell, Thomas Shelley, James Briggs. Ordered July 26, 1736. Page 146

DAVIS, John: Appraised by John Pope, Richard Vick. Signed Elizabeth Davis. Ordered October 7, 1936. R. October 25, 1736. Page 147

JOLLEY, James: Account of estate, paid John, the son of the said James Jolly, decd. Examined by John Monro and Jacob Darden. R. November 22, 1736. Page 148

WORRELL, William: Leg. son William; son John; to my honored father; wife Ann. Ex., friend John Dew, Jr. D. September 21, 1736. R. November 22, 1736.
Wit: H. Edwards, Augustine Nickson. Page 148

COOK, Thomas, Sr.: Leg. son Thomas; son Jones; daughter Sarah; daughter Susannah; son Benjamin; son John; daughter Rebecca; son Arthur. Exs., sons Thomas and Jones Cook. D. January 21, 1735/36. R. November 22, 1736.
Wit: John Brantley, Valentine White. Page 149

MORELAND, Catherine: Account of estate, returned by Thomas Moreland. R. November 22, 1736. Page 150

WRIGHT, John: Leg. son James; son John; daughter Sarah Browne. Exs., wife Martha and son John Wright. D. August 15, 1736. R. November 22, 1736.
Wit: William Noyall, John Long, Priscilla Hall. Page 150

FLY, Jeremiah: Leg. son-in-law William Bulls; son John; daughter Rachel; daughter Charity; wife Mary; daughter Mary. Wife, Extx. D. November 19, 1733. R. December 27, 1736.
Wit: Arthur Smith, Rachel Smith. Page 151

FOSTER, John: Appraised by Thomas Hoult, Charles Barham, Thomas Phillips. R. December 27, 1736. Page 152

LUGG, Peter: Appraised by Robert King, William Smith, Aaron Gray. Ordered September 27, 1736. R. December 27, 1736. Page 153

VICK, Robert: Appraised by Arthur Whitehead, Robert Newsom, Henry Thomas. R. February 28, 1736. Page 154

CARTER, Thomas: Appraised by Richard Blow, Jr., Henry Thomas, Robert Newsom. Ordered January 15, 1736. R. February 28, 1736. Page 155

GAY, Henry: Leg. son Henry; son John; son Thomas; son William; son Joshua; daughter Sarah Babb. Ex., son Thomas Gay. D. February 3, 1735/36. R. April 25, 1737.
        Wit: James Denson, Joseph Denson.        Page 156

BRANTLEY, Edward: Of Nottoway Parish. Leg. wife Elizabeth; son James; son Lewis; son Joseph; son John. Exs., sons Lewis and James Brantley. D. January 26, 1736. R. April 25, 1737.
        Wit: Joseph Claud, James Bass, William Spence, Charles Bass.
        Page 157

MOXSON, Robert: Account of estate returned by John Pitt, the Adm. R. April 26, 1737.        Page 158

BOYKIN, Edward: Appraised by James Turner, John Inman, John Jones. Ordered March 21, 1736/37. R. April 26, 1737.        Page 159

COPELAND, John: Appraised by Thomas Murry, John Hodges, William Glover, Mel'k Deshey. Ordered November 22, 1736. R. April 25, 1737.
        Page 159

WRENN, Elizabeth: Appraised by James Day, John Hodges, William Glover. R. May 23, 1737.        Page 160

CROCKER, William: Leg. son Anthony; son Peter; son Arthur; son William; daughter Elizabeth. Wife Katherine, Extx. D. December 4, 1735. R. May 23, 1737.
        Wit: John Wombwell, Joseph Wombwell, Joseph Grotten (?).
        Page 160

RYALL, Thomas: Account estate, among items, paid to Thomas Ryall, the son of Thomas Ryall, decd. Examined by James Baker and Hardy Council. R. May 23, 1737.        Page 162

STEVENSON, John: Leg. son John; son Peter; son William, the land I bought of Edward Boykin; son Solomon; son George; daughter Mary; daughter Elizabeth. Wife Katherine, Extx. D. February 24, 1728/29. R. May 23, 1737.
        Wit: Francis Exum, Joseph Ward.        Page 162

BOYKIN, William: Settlement of estate made by John Dunkley, Thomas Gale. R. May 23, 1737.        Page 163

TURNER, John: Appraised by Hugh Giles, Charles Fulgham, Joseph Wright. Ordered November 22, 1736. R. May 23, 1737.        Page 164

GAY, Henry: Appraised by Robert Eley, Jr., Eley Eley, Jonathan Weaver. R. May 23, 1737.        Page 165

STEVENSON, William: Appraised by Richard Blunt, John Williams, William Clark. Signed Giles Kelly. R. May 23, 1737.        Page 166

BARNES, John: Leg. son John, land adjoining Nicholas Williams and Richard Washington; son Thomas; daughter Elizabeth Flowers; grandson Henry Flowers; son William; daughter Juda Davis; daughter Best; son Jacob, land adjoining on Arthur Washington and Edward Flowers; son Joshua; daughter Sarah Summerell land adjoining Robert Lawrence; to Thomas Crafford; to loving wife. Exs., sons Jacob and Joshua Barnes. D. March 27, 1736. R. May 23, 1737.
        Wit: William Williams, Thomas Allen, Benjamin Flowers. Page 167

BALDWIN, William: Account of estate, examined by Benn Willett and John

Chapman.  R. June 27, 1737.                                    Page 169

BULLS, Martha:  Account of estate returned by John Chesnutt.  R. June 27,
    1737.                                                      Page 170

WILLIAMSON, Francis:  Nuncupative will, proven by Francis Williamson, Arthur
    Williamson and Thomas Williamson.  Leg. son Francis; son James; son
    Benjamin; son Joseph; daughter Martha; daughter Sarah; daughter Mourn-
    ing; son Hardy; to my wife.  D. March 14, 1736.  R. June 27, 1737.
                                                               Page 170

ROBERSON, Jonathan:  Leg. wife Elizabeth, reversion at her death, to her
    daughter Mary Whitfield; to my cousin James Roberson, if he serves out
    his indenture.  D. March 22, 1736/37.  R. June 27, 1737.
        Wit:  William Murfee, James Davis.                     Page 170

JORDAN, Elizabeth:  Account of estate, returned by Mathew Jordan.  D.
    December 1, 1733.  R. July 25, 1737.                       Page 171

WORRELL, William:  Appraised by John Pope, Arthur Whitehead, Richard Vick.
    R. July 25, 1737.                                          Page 172

WAINWRIGHT, William:  Appraised by Timothy Tynes, Thomas Brock, Thomas
    Browne.  Ordered June 27, 1737.  R. July 25, 1737.         Page 172

BAYTON, Richard, Jr.:  Appraised by John Williams, William Pope, John
    Johnston.  R. July 25, 1737.                               Page 173

BRADDY, Elias:  Leg. daughter Elizabeth, my land in North Carolina; daugh-
    ter Mary; son Elias; wife Margaret.  Exs., son Elias and son-in-law
    Henry Crafford.  D. March 2, 1735.  R. July 25, 1737.
        Wit:  John Joyner, James Joyner.                       Page 173

SUMMERELL, Thomas:  Appraised by Joseph Hill, Ambrose Hadley, W. Bidgood.
    R. July 25, 1737.                                          Page 175

BRANTLEY, Edward:  Appraised by Simon Turner, Henry Harris, Thomas Barrow.
    Signed Lewis and James Brantley.  R. July 25, 1737.        Page 176

BRAGG, Mary:  Account estate, returned by Thomas Whitfield, Jr. and Edward
    Driver.  R. August 22, 1737.                               Page 177

VASSER, John:  Additional appraisal by John Pope and Richard Price.  R.
    September 26, 1737.                                        Page 178

WILLIAMSON, Francis, Jr.:  Appraised by John Dunkley, James Atkinson, John
    Holleman.  Ordered September 21, 1737.  R. September 26, 1737.
                                                               Page 178

APPLEWHAITE, John:  Appraised by Joseph Hill, Ambrose Hadley, Edward
    Crocker.  Ordered May 6, 1737.  R. September 26, 1737.     Page 179

BOACH, William:  Leg. Edward Guleg; Ann Guleg; William Guleg, the land in
    the hands of Henry Adams; to Lucy Guleg.  Exs., Harmon Read, Henry
    Adams.  D. September 7, 1737.  R. October 24, 1737.
        Wit:  Francis Stainback, William Lee, Edward Guleg.    Page 181

INGRAHAM, Jeremiah:  Leg. my honourable father; my sister Wardwell, all my
    wife Elizabeth's clothes; to my brother John's son Jeremiah; brother
    Edward; brother John; brother Joshua and brother Isaac; Captain Samuel
    Little in New England, my trustee for my friends, and he is to send
    whomever he thinks fitting with a power of attorney to receive my

                                129

estate, by the first opportunity after my executors have made up an
account here in Virginia. Exs., James Carrell and Richard Hardy. D.
September 10, 1737. R. October 24, 1737.
  Wit: William Hurdle, Roger Delk, John Welch, Peter Hardin.
                                                          Page 181

PARNAL, Joseph: Of the Lower Parish. Leg. eldest son Thomas; son William;
    daughter Elizabeth; son Joseph; my youngest son John; wife Elizabeth.
    Ex., son Thomas Parnal. D. March 10, 1736. R. November 28, 1737.
      Wit: Arthur Moore, William Vasser, Jacob Moore.       Page 182

CHAPMAN, John: Of the Lower Parish. Leg. daughter Patience Wiles; son
    John my "Bath Seal"; son Charles; daughter Mary; son Joseph; sons
    William and Thomas to live with their mother until they are 14; wife
    Mary; daughter Elizabeth. Exs., wife Mary and son Charles Chapman.
    D. September 10, 1736. R. November 28, 1737.
      Wit: Charles Fulgham, Jr., Mary Bevan.                Page 183

WESTRAY, Robert: Appraised by John Bowin, John Lawrence, Virgus Smith.
    Signed Mary Westray. R. November 28, 1737.              Page 185

BRADDY, Elias: Appraised by John Joyner, James Turner, Chaplin Williams.
    Ordered August 22, 1737. R. November 28, 1737.          Page 185

CHAPMAN, John: Appraised by Hugh Giles, John Applewhaite, Thomas Whitfield.
    R. November 28, 1737.                                   Page 186

DUGAN, Bryan: Estate settled by Hugh Giles and Charles Fulgham. R. Novem-
    ber 28, 1737.                                           Page 187

INGRAHAM, Jeremiah: Appraised by James Carrell, John Gray, Thomas Moreland.
    R. November 28, 1737.                                   Page 187

MANGUM, John: Appraised by John Davis, Edward Brantley, Joseph Ward. Signed
    Frances Mangum. Ordered September 26, 1737. R. November 28, 1737.
                                                            Page 189

CALECLOUGH, Thomas: Appraised by Robert Driver, Thomas Uzzell, John Smelly.
    Ordered November 28, 1737. R. January 23, 1737.         Page 190

SHARRO, Elizabeth: Of the Lower Parish. Leg. son John; daughter Elizabeth
    Thomas; daughter Eleanor Thomas; grandson William Screws. Ex., Joseph
    Parnal. D. January 8, 1736. R. January 23, 1737.
      Wit: Luke Wiggs, Joseph Parnal.                       Page 192

WILLIAMS, Richard: Leg. son John, land on which Arthur Edwards now lives;
    son Solomon, land on which John Row did live; son Mathew; daughter
    Mary; wife Sarah; son Elisha my land in Nansemond County, adjoining
    William West; son George land in Nansemond; son Joshua land in Nanse-
    mond; son Daniel land in Nansemond; friend William Wiggins; to my
    young children. Ex., son Daniel Williams. D. November 8, 1737. R.
    February 27, 1737.
      Wit: John Johnston, James Garner, Elisha Williams.    Page 193

WILLIAMS, John: Leg. wife Sarah; son Richard, when he is 18; daughter
    Elizabeth. Ex., brother Elisha. D. November 21, 1737. R. February
    27, 1737.
      Wit: John Johnston, Nathan Godwin, George Williams.   Page 195

CHAPMAN, Joseph: Settlement of estate by Joseph Hall and William Ponsonby.
    R. February 27, 1737.                                   Page 196

MARRINER, John: Appraised by John Goodrich, William Harrison, John Hodges, Benjamin Hodges. February 27, 1737. Page 196

GREEN, Mary: Of the Parish of Newport. Leg. children of my daughter Mary Bevan; son Bartholomew; children of my son Thomas; children of my daughter Montgomery; daughter Martha; son George; daughter Prudence; daughter Rachel; daughter Martha Applewhaite. Daughter Prudence Green, Extx. D. November 19, 1737. R. February 27, 1737.
    Wit: John Long, Bartholomew Lightfoot. Page 197

COOK, Thomas: Appraised by Simon Turner, Henry Harris, Jacob Harris. R. February 27, 1737. Page 198

APPLEWHAITE, Thomas: Settlement of estate and an account current of the estate of Henry Applewhaite was presented by Joseph Weston and Samuel Whitfield. R. February 27, 1737. Page 200

GRAY, John: Leg. son William; son Richard; son John; son Mathew; son Henry; daughter Margaret; daughter Patience; wife Elizabeth. Wife, Extx. D. December 13, 1737. R. March 27, 1738.
    Wit: Richard Hardy, Elias Wills. Page 200

BROWN, Joseph: Account estate examined by Joseph Godwin and John Monro. R. April 24, 1738. Page 201

CALECLOUGH, Thomas: Account estate examined by John Monro and Jacob Darden. R. April 24, 1738. Page 202

STEPHENS, William: Additional appraisal by William Clark, Richard Blunt, John Williams. R. April 24, 1738. Page 202

SHARRO, Elizabeth: Inventory returned by Richard Thomas. R. April 24, 1738. Page 203

LOWRY, Joanna: Of the Lower Parish. Widow. Leg. son James Lowry; son Mathew Lowry; rest of my estate to be divided among Francis, Thomas, George and Joseph Floid. Ex., my son George Floid. D. March 30, 1736. R. May 22, 1738.
    Wit: Robert Tynes, Elizabeth Driver. Page 203

WILLIAMS, John: Appraised by Anthony Lewis, William Pope, James Edwards. R. May 22, 1738. Page 204

SMITH, Thomas: Appraised by James Turner, Simon Turner, Henry Harris. Signed Samuel Smith. R. May 22, 1738. Page 205

GRAY, John: Appraised by James Carrell, Thomas Barlow, Samuel Carrell. Signed Elizabeth Gray. R. May 22, 1738. Page 206

LEE, Peter: Appraised by Jacob Harris, Valentine White, Robert Lundy. Signed William Lee. R. June 26, 1738. Page 208

LOWRY, Joanna: Appraised by Timothy Tynes, William Best, Edward Davis. R. June 26, 1738. Page 208

PEARCE, Philip: Account estate, signed by Sarah Pearce and examined by Richard Hardy and Etheldred Taylor. R. July 24, 1738. Page 209

TURNER, John: Account estate, among items, paid John Dugan, the orphan of Bryan Dugan. Examined by Hugh Giles, Joseph Godwin, William Wilkinson. R. July 24, 1738. Page 209

MEACUM, Lewis: Appraised by Thomas Murry, William Harrison, Benjamin
Hodges. R. July 24, 1738.                                      Page 210

HOLLYMAN, Elizabeth: Leg. grandson Arthur Hollyman; grandson Joseph Hollyman; to Sarah Watson; to Susannah Hollyman; to Thomas Hollyman, Jr.,
the son of William Hollyman; to Mary Proctor. Ex., kinsman William
Hollyman. D. March 17, 1736/37. R. August 28, 1738.
        Wit: Thomas Atkinson, John Hollyman.                  Page 211

NIXON, Augustine: Appraised by Thomas Taylor, Robert Pitman, Arthur Taylor.
Ordered January 23, 1737. Account of his estate examined by Thomas
Jarrell, Jr. and Richard Blow, Jr. R. September 25, 1738.    Page 212

COPELAND, John: Estate account, paid Thomas Copeland his part of his
father's. Examined by Samuel Davis and James Baker. R. October 24,
1738.                                                         Page 213

MORELAND, Thomas: Appraised by James Carrell, Samuel Carrell, Thomas Barlow. Signed John Moreland. Ordered March 29, 1738. R. October 23,
1738.                                                         Page 214

LEWIS, Zebulon: Leg. son Benjamin; son Nathan; son Zebulon; daughter Patience; loving wife. D. August 6, 1738. R. October 23, 1738.
        Wit: Christopher Kilbee, John Harris, Benjamin Cooper. Page 215

INGRAHAM, Jeremiah: Estate settled by Lawrence Baker and Nicholas Bourden.
R. October 23, 1738.                                          Page 216

TEASLY, John: Appraised by William Page, Ralph Vickers, Richard Pierce.
Signed Richard Teasly. Ordered June 26, 1738. R. November 27, 1738.
                                                              Page 217

COGGAN, Robert: Of the Lower Parish. Leg. son John; son Robert; daughter
Elizabeth Stevens; daughter Ann Stevens; daughter Sarah. Exs., wife
Sarah and son John Coggan. D. January 30, 1737. R. November 27, 1738.
        Wit: William Denson, Thomas Gale, John Badgett.       Page 218

BARNES, Jacob: Appraised by Robert King, Humphrey Marshall, William Smith.
Signed Francis Floyd. R. November 27, 1738.                   Page 219

FULGHAM, Nicholas: Appraised by Hugh Giles, Thomas Whitfield, Joseph Norsworthy. R. February 26, 1738.                                 Page 219

BEVAN, Thomas: Appraised by Hugh Giles, Charles Fulgham, Thomas Whitfield.
Ordered November 24, 1738. R. February 26, 1738.             Page 220

NORSWORTHY, Christian: Account current, paid John Norsworthy, guardian of
Martha Norsworthy, the things given her in the will of her father,
George Norsworthy; paid John Monro, the things given his wife in her
father's will. Signed William Scott. R. February 26, 1738/39.
                                                              Page 221

NORSWORTHY, Tristram: Account estate, examined by Joseph Godwin, Joseph
Weston, Samuel Whitfield. R. March 26, 1739.                  Page 222

BRADDY, William: Appraised by William Clark, Thomas Coffer, Joseph Atkinson. Signed Olive Braddy. Ordered January 22, 1738. R. March 26,
1739.                                                         Page 223

HOLLYMAN, Elizabeth: Appraised by Samuel Crafts, Arthur Crocker, Josiah
John Holliman. R. March 26, 1739.                             Page 224

COGGAN, Robert: Appraised by John Sellaway, William Bullock, Richard Sellaway. R. March 26, 1739. Page 225

LAWRENCE, John: Of the Parish of Newport. Leg. son John, land on the
Blackwater on which William Freeman lives; son William; daughter
Margaret; daughter Priscilla; son-in-law Robert Carr to be paid his
wife's part of my estate; daughter Sarah Moore; daughter Elizabeth.
Exs., wife and son William Lawrence. D. January 27, 1738. R. April
23, 1739.
Wit: Robert Lawrence, Charles Council, Thomas Brewer. Page 226

EXUM, Robert: Appraised by John Dunkley, Francis Williamson, Joseph Exum,
Thomas Joyner. Ordered February 26, 1738. R. April 23, 1739.
Page 227

LEWIS, Zebulon: Appraised by John Brassell, John Fort, Christopher Foster.
Signed Jane Lewis. R. April 23, 1739. Page 229

BRANTLEY, Edward: Account estate, examined by James Ridley and Nathaniel
Ridley. Signed James and Lewis Brantley. R. May 28, 1739. Page 230

DICKINSON, Christopher: Account estate, paid John Bridger in right of
his wife, examined by William Wilkinson, Hugh Giles, Charles Fulgham.
R. June 25, 1739. Page 231

MOORE, Tristram: Nuncupative will. May 11, 1739. Deposition of Mr. James
Ransom, aged about 35: that he had intended disinheriting his son
Thomas, but if he lived he would buy land on this side of the river
for his son; and that he designed his land in Gloucester County, for
his son James. Deposition of Joyce Carrell, aged about 30 years:
heard him say that his land in Gloucester was to go to his son James,
whom he desired his father to bring up. Deposition of Roger Stanley,
aged about 45 years: that he heard him say, that his son Thomas was
to have twenty pounds to buy land etc. R. July 23, 1739. Page 232

REVELL, Randall: Leg. son Joseph John; son Mathew, 130 acres that I bought
of William Thomas; son Holladay. Ex., son Joseph John Revell. D.
December 30, 1733. R. July 23, 1739.
Wit: John Dunkley, Thomas Warren, John Exum. Page 232

ELEY, Robert, Sr.: Leg. son Robert, land on Long Branch, adjoining John
Roberts, Henry Sanders and Mr. John Lear; son James; son Edward; son
John; son Michael; daughter Christian; daughter Mourning; son William;
to Martha, the daughter of my son James; son Eley; daughter Martha
Williams; daughter Rebecca Williams. Exs., sons, Robert and Michael
Eley. D. April 5, 1738. R. July 23, 1739.
Wit: Joseph White, William Denson, George Armstrong. Page 233

HUNTER, James: Of the Parish of Newport. Leg. granddaughter Mary Allen;
granddaughter Elizabeth Allen; daughter Sarah; daughter Mary Allen;
son Joshua. Ex., son Joshua Hunter. D. August 23, 1735. R. July 23,
1739.
Wit: John Monro, ------- Snowden. Page 235

LEWIS, Anthony: Leg. sons Thomas and Anthony my land on the Blackwater;
wife Elizabeth. Exs., my wife and two sons. D. September 30, 1717.
R. July 23, 1739.
Wit: Elias Ballard, William Butler, Mary Butler, John Butler.
Page 236

MATHEWS, John: Appraised by Thomas Pursell, Newitt Drew, William B-------.
Signed by Martha Mathews. R. August 27, 1739. Page 237

SMITH, Thomas: Account estate, presented by Elizabeth Parnall. Examined by Nathaniel Ridley, Howell Edmunds. R. August 27, 1739. Page 237

LEWIS, Anthony: Appraised by Samuel Browne, Richard Price, Lewis Bryan. R. September 24, 1739. Page 240

ATKINSON, James: Leg. son Thomas; son Timothy; daughter Mary; daughter Drusilla; daughter Sarah Ingram; son James; wife. Exs., sons Timothy and Thomas Atkinson. D. September 20, 1737. R. September 24, 1739.
Wit: William Ingram, Elizabeth Evans, Thomas Atkinson. Page 241

GOOLD, Mary: Of Nottoway Parish. Leg. daughter Elizabeth; daughter Mary; son Thomas. Ex., son Thomas Goold. D. February 22, 1738/39. R. September 24, 1739.
Wit: William Smith, George Smith. Page 242

BENSON, William: Leg. son Samuel; son Bryant; son Benjamin; daughter Bersheba; daughter Brambly; friend John Phillips. Ex., son Bryant Benson. D. August 9, 1739. R. September 24, 1739.
Wit: John Phillips, J. Gray. Page 243

JORDAN, James: Account estate, examined by James Baker, Nicholas Bourden. R. November 26, 1739. Page 244

STEVENSON, William: Account estate, examined by William Hodsden, James Ridley. Signed Giles Kelly. R. November 26, 1739. Page 248

MOORE, Tristram: Appraised by Richard Hardy, James Carrell, Thomas Barlow. R. November 26, 1739. Page 249

LAWRENCE, John: Inventory presented by Margaret and William Lawrence. R. January 28, 1739. Page 250

DAVIS, Samuel: Leg. wife Amy; son John; son Samuel, land at Meherrin; daughter Mary; daughter Sarah; daughter Amy; daughter Marcella. Wife, Extx. Brother John Davis and brother-in-law Nicholas Bourden to collect all debts. D. November 16, 1738. R. January 28, 1739.
Wit: John Davis, John Gemmill, N. Bourden, Thomas Murry.
Page 250

BRADSHAW, William: Of Newport Parish. Leg. brother Richard Bradshaw; daughter Emey; daughter Mary; my cousin Richard Bradshaw. Ex., brother Richard Bradshaw. D. October 25, 1739. R. January 28, 1739.
Wit: John Britten, Lewis Bryan, Mary Murelle. Page 252

WESTON, Benjamin: Leg. wife Isabella, the estate which belonged to her, when I married her; my own estate to be equally divided between my wife and my children, Joseph, Mary and Samuel Weston. Wife, Extx. D. September 27, 1739. R. January 28, 1739.
Wit: Charles Fulgham, Joseph Weston. Page 253

SUMMERELL, Thomas: Leg. son Gwin; daughter Sarah Wilson; son John; granddaughter Mary Wainwright; granddaughter Sarah Wainwright; granddaughter Martha Wilson; my daughter Mary Wainwright's children; granddaughter Jane Summerell. Ex., son John Summerell. D.----------. R. February 25, 1739.
Wit: William Brock, William Wainwright. Page 254

JOYNER, Theophilus: Leg. son Joseph; son Theophilus; son John; son Henry; son Lazarus; daughter Sarah Dawson; daughter Mary Garland; daughter Mary; daughter Prudence; wife Henrietta. Exs., wife and son John Joyner. D. January 15, 1724/25. R. February 25, 1739.

Wit: Robert Johnson, James Johnson. Page 255

WHITFIELD, Mary: Leg. to Benjamin, the son of Benjamin Beel (Beal); to
Richard Beel, the son of Richard Beel; to William, the son of my cousin
William Bradsha; to Richard Casey, Jr., to Martha Casey, the daughter
of Richard Casey. Extx., Martha Casey. D. November 21, 1737. R.
February 25, 1739.
Wit: William Noyall, Martha Noyall. Page 256

APPLEWHAITE, Martha: Of Newport Parish. Leg. son Thomas, and to his son
John; daughter Holland Copeland; daughter Martha Weston; granddaughter
Mary Benn; granddaughter Holland Applewhaite; grandson Thomas Cope-
land; grandson James Benn; grandson Henry Applewhaite; daughter Ann
Parker. Ex., son-in-law William Parker. D. July 30, 1739. R. Feb-
ruary 25, 1739.
Wit: Thomas Copeland. Page 257

WRIGHT, Martha: Leg. daughter Sarah Browne; son James; daughter-in-law
Mary Wright. Ex., son John Wright. D. January 4, 1738/39. R. Feb-
ruary 25, 1739.
Wit: William Noyall, Elizabeth West. Page 258

MARSHALL, Mary: Leg. son Robert; son John; daughter Elizabeth Robertson;
son Joseph; daughter Mary Penny; son James; grandson Joseph, son of
Humphrey Marshall, land called "Pines", which is mentioned in my hus-
band's will. Ex., son Humphrey Marshall. D. September 30, 1732. R.
February 25, 1739.
Wit: Robert Driver, John Penny, Anthony Covington Holladay.
Page 259

DRIVER, Edward: Leg. son Charles; daughter Mary; daughter Sarah. Exs.,
friends Robert Driver and Thomas Whitfield. D. Novmeber 25, 1739.
R. February 25, 1739.
Wit: Joseph Bridger, Joseph Wright. Page 260

RICHARDS, William: Account, examined by John Monro and Joseph Weston.
R. February 20, 1739. Page 261

MONTGOMERY, Benjamin: Account estate, among items, paid for the orphans;
examined by Hugh Giles and Thomas Applewhaite. R. February 1739.
Page 262

BRADSHAW, William: Appraised by John Bowin, John Lawrence, William ffouller
(Fowler). R. February 25, 1739. Page 263

WESTON, Benjamin: Appraised by Hugh Giles, Jacob Dickinson, Joseph Norsworthy. R. February 25, 1739. Page 263

DAY, James: Leg. daughter Mary; daughter Martha; to unborn child; loving
wife. Exs., wife and William Hodsden. D. October 6, 1739. R.
March 24, 1739.
Wit: Thomas Day, Thomas Smith, Elizabeth Jones. Page 264

MACY, Thomas: Leg. wife Jane, Ester Williams and Ambrus Williams, the
plantation on which I live, at the death of my wife the said plantation to return to Richard Kirby and Macy Mary his wife and the plantation they now live to return to Ester Williams and Ambrus Williams.
Exs., Richard Kirby and Ambrus Williams. D. March 12, 1739. R. March
24, 1739.
Wit: Ambrus Williams, Moddy Kirby. Page 265

HARRIS, Robert: Leg. daughter Ann; son Charles; son Michael; son Joseph;

son James; son Mathew. Ex., son Michael Harris. D. March 22, 1739. R. April 28, 1740.
    Wit: John Dunkley, Josiah John Holleman.                Page 266

JOYNER, Thomas: Leg. daughter Cherry Harris; son Jonathan, the land on which William Thomas did live and on which Arthur Smith now lives; son Mathew; daughter Patience; daughter Elizabeth; son Thomas; daughter Catherine Dunkley; granddaughter Catherine Joyner; wife Patience. Exs., son Mathew and son-in-law John Dunkley. D. April 13, 1740. R. April 28, 1740.
    Wit: Thomas Williams, Virgus Smith.                Page 267

PILAND, James: Inventory, presented by Elizabeth Piland. R. April 28, 1740.
                                                              Page 270

REVELL, Randall: Appraised by Thomas Williams, John Washington, William Bailey. R. April 28, 1740.                                Page 272

BROWNE, Samuel: Leg. son John; grandson Josias, son of Walter Browne; son Jesse Browne, all my books, instruments and Medecines; daughter Mary, the wife of John Drake; grandson Jesse Drake, land on the Nottoway River; daughter Sarah, wife of John Battel; grandson William Battel; grandson Jesse Battel; grandson Samuel, the son of John Browne; granddaughter Sarah, the daughter of Walter Browne; grandson Samuel, the son of Henry King and his wife Martha; grandson Samuel Nicholas Drake; granddaughter Penelope, the daughter of William Lawrence and his wife Penelope; son Jesse Browne, land on Indian Branch in North Carolina. Ex., son Jesse Browne. D. October 7, 1739. R. June 23, 1740.
    Wit: Hardy Council, John Gemmill, John Dunkley, John Eley.
                                                              Page 274

FORBES, James: Appraised by Thomas Day, William Harrison, Benjamin Hodges, George Wilson. Signed James Baker. Ordered February 25, 1739/40. R. July 28, 1740.                                Page 278

BROCK, William: Appraised by Timothy Tynes, Thomas Browne, Peter Green. Ordered June 23, 1740. R. July 28, 1740.                Page 280

HARRIS, Robert: Appraised by Thomas Williamson, Arthur Williamson, Josiah John Holleman. R. July 28, 1740.                Page 282

HAWKINS, William: Account estate, examined by William Wilkinson, Hugh Giles. R. July 28, 1740.                                Page 283

PILAND, James: Account estate; among items, paid to James Wilson, for Esther Brantley; to funeral charges for his son. Signed Elizabeth Briggs. Examined by James Baker, Lawrence Baker, N. Bourden. R. July 28, 1740.                                Page 284

KAE, Robert Fenn: Leg. brother Thomas; brother William Kae; to Thomas Casse (Casey); rest of estate to be equally divided between William Brantley, Thomas Rosser and Joseph Floyd. Ex., Thomas Casse. D. February 10, 1739/40. R. July 28, 1740.
    Wit: Nicholas Casey, William Richards.                Page 285

RICHARDS, Thomas: Leg. brother Simon Ogburn; brother John Ogburn; sister Elizabeth Ogburn; sister Mary Ogburn; sister Prudence Richards; sister Ann Richards; rest of estate to Nicholas Casey. Ex., Nicholas Casey. D. March 9, 1740. R. July 28, 1740.
    Wit: Robert Fenn Kae, Thomas Casey.                Page 286

WOMBWELL, Thomas: Of Blackwater, Planter. Leg. son John, the plantation of my father, Thomas Wombwell's; son Joseph; wife Sarah; son Thomas, the land which lies below that of my brother John Wombwell's; daughter Sarah Goodrich; daughter Mary Crocker. Wife, Extx. D. December 7, 1731. R. April 25, 1740.
  Wit: Francis Ward, William Allen.     Page 287

CARRELL, Samuel: Leg. son Thomas; wife Joice; son John. Wife, Extx. D. September 28, 1737. R. August 25, 1740.
  Wit: Richard Hardy, James Piland.     Page 288

APPLEWHAITE, Henry: Appraised by William Pope, Edward Cobb, James Edwards, John Johnson. Signed Mary Applewhaite. Ordered March 1739. R. August 25, 1740.     Page 290

BEST, William: Appraised by John Rodway, Samuel Whitfield, Thomas Gross. Signed Jane Best. D. August 19, 1740. R. August 25, 1740. Page 292

HARRIS, Edward: Leg. son Edward, land on the Blackwater; son Lewis, land on the Three Creeks, which I bought of John Dortch; son Joel; son Amos; son Hardy; daughter Mary; daughter Ann; wife Ann. Timothy Thorpe and Owen Mirick to divide the land between sons Joel and Amos. Exs., wife and son Edward Harris. D. August 26, 1739. R. September 22, 1740.
  Wit: Nathaniel Ridley, Timothy Thorpe.    Page 293

NEWMAN, Thomas: Leg. wife Mary; son John; my wife to pay to her son Joseph out of her part of my estate; John Newman to pay Joseph Bunkley, out of his part of my estate. Ex., son John Newman. D. March 9, 1739. R. September 22, 1740.
  Wit: Richard Jordan, James Jones, Thomas Parr.   Page 295

PIERCE, Thomas: Leg. daughter Mary, my house in Hampton; daughter Martha; son Thomas; wife Judith. Exs., wife and friend Alexander Hamilton. D. March 19, 1739/40. R. October 27, 1740.
  Wit: John Summerell, Nicholas Curle.    Page 296

DAUGHTRY, Joseph: Leg. loving mother; brother John Daughtry's son Richard; to cousin William, the son of John Daughtry; to John, the son of my brother John Daughtry; sister Mary Holland; sister Elizabeth Haslep. Ex., brother John Daughtry. D. September 23, 1740. R. October 27, 1740.
  Wit: Robert Carr, James Robertson, William Daughtry. Page 298

DRIVER, Edward: Appraised by Joseph Wright, Joseph Bridger, John Applewhaite. Signed Robert Driver. R. October 27, 1740.   Page 299

MILLER, John: Appraised by John Hodges, William Harrison, Benjamin Hodges. Signed Nicholas Miller, R. November 24, 1740.  Page 300

SMITH, Nicholas: Appraised by Joseph Wright, Robert King, Anthony Fulgham. Signed Joseph Smith. Ordered February 25, 1739. R. November 24, 1740.
               Page 301

KILLEBREW, William: Appraised by Nathaniel Ridley, Howell Edmonds, James Ridley. Ordered April 15, 1740. R. November 24, 1740. Page 302

EXUM, Robert: Additional Inventory, returned by Patience Exum. R. November 24, 1740.          Page 304

MATTHEWS, Zeakell: Leg. son Zeakell; son Edward; to James Bennett; daughter Martha Hunnicutt; daughter Priscilla Morgan; daughter Elizabeth; to my wife and seven children, viz.: Elizabeth, Sarah, Mary, Unity, Edmond,

Moses and Enos. Wife, Extx. D. March 21, 1738/39. R. December 22, 1740.
Wit: Nathaniel Ridley.                                                    Page 305

KILLEBREW, William: Appraised by Thomas Barrow, John Barrow, Martin
Middleton. R. December 22, 1740.                                          Page 306

HARRIS, William: Appraised by John Bowin, John Dawson, Nicholas Williams.
Signed Rebecca Harris. Ordered October 30, 1740. R. January 26, 1740.
                                                                         Page 308

PIERCE, Thomas: Appraised by Joseph Hill, John Summerell, William Ponsonby.
R. February 23, 1740. Signed Judith Pierce.                              Page 309

JONES, James: Appraised by George Parker, John Newman, William Howell.
Ordered January 26, 1740/41. R. February 23, 1740.                       Page 313

MURRY, Thomas: Leg. daughter Mary, the wife of Benjamin Davis; wife Sarah;
daughter Sarah; daughter Easter; daughter Elizabeth, the wife of John
Lee. Wife, Extx. D. August 27, 1740. R. February 23, 1740.
Wit: Thomas Stevens, Benjamin Brantley, Charles Fulgham.
                                                                         Page 315

NEAVILLE, John: Leg. son John; son Thomas; son Joseph; daughter Penellipen.
Ex., John Marshall, Jr. D. January 1, 1740. R. February 23, 1740.
Wit: Thomas Gale, B. Beale, Thomas Bullock.                              Page 317

WARD, John: Leg. daughter Mary; wife Sarah. Exs., wife Sarah and Hugh
Norvell. D. January 20, 1739. R. March 23, 1740.
Wit: Hugh Norvell, William Spence, William Broom.                        Page 318

NEAVILLE, John: Appraised by Robert Driver, Joseph Meredith, John Chestnutt.
Ex., John Marshall. R. March 23, 1740.                                   Page 320

PIERCE, Jeremiah: Account estate, examined by John Davis, William Hodsden,
N. Bourden. Signed Honour Pierce. R. March 23, 1740.                     Page 323

BRIDGER, Col. William: Account estate, examined by William Hodsden, James
Ridley. R. April 27, 1741.                                               Page 324

BOYKIN, Edward: Account estate, examined by John Person, Howell Edmunds,
Benjamin Blunt. R. April 27, 1741.                                       Page 327

ELEY, Ely: Appraised by John Bowin, John Denson, Jr., Joshua Joyner.
Ordered August 25, 1740. R. April 27, 1741.                              Page 328

APPLEWHAITE, Henry: Leg. son John, the land I bought of Robert King; son
Arthur; daughter Sarah, the land on Nottoway River, on which the widow
Mary Applewhaite now lives; son Thomas; granddaughter Ann, the daughter
of Thomas Applewhaite; daughter Amy Davis; daughter Priscilla Ridley;
daughter Ann Godwin; to grandson Henry Applewhaite; wife Ann. Wife,
Extx. D.----------. R. April 27, 1741.
Wit: William Ponsonby, Elizabeth Daniel.                                 Page 329

DARDEN, Jacob: Leg. son Jacob; son Charles, all my land in Nansemond, the
said son to remain with Samuel Lawrence until he is 19. Exs., brother-
in-law Samuel Lawrence and son Jacob Darden. D. March 25, 1739. R.
April 27, 1741.
Wit: George Lawrence, John Marshall.                                     Page 332

ALLEN, Thomas: Leg. eldest son Arthur; son Thomas; daughter Ann; daughter
Honour, her mother's clothes. Exs., Roger Allen and George Bell.

138

D. April 12, 1741. R. April 27, 1741.
   Wit: George Whitley, Roger Woodward, Richard Braswell.   Page 333

SMITH, Thomas: Of Nottoway Parish. Leg. son William, the land I bought of
   Richard Lundy; son George, land at the Three Creeks' Bridge; son Thomas;
   daughter Rachel; son Joseph; daughter Mary Lundy. Exs., wife and son
   Joseph Smith. D. November 28, 1740. R. April 27, 1741.
      Wit: James Ridley, James Sammons.
      Presented by Elizabeth and Joseph Smith.               Page 334

WILKINSON, William: Leg. son William, land in Nansemond County; son Willis,
   land in Isle of Wight County, on which Robert Smith and William Lain.
   Overseers, John Wills, John Summerell, Thomas Swann, John Wilkinson.
   Exs., sons William and Willis Wilkinson. D. March 6, 1740. R. May
   25, 1741.
      Wit: Jacob Spicer, Richard Smith, John Pitt.           Page 335

LOYD, Thomas: Leg. son Thomas; son Joseph; son William; son Moses; daughter
   Charity; wife Charity; to Mary Conner. Exs., wife and son Thomas
   Loyd. D. February 23, 1740. R. May 25, 1741.
      Wit: John Darden, Mary Conner, Susanna Gwinn.          Page 337

WOODWARD, Oliver: Leg. eldest son Roger; son Oliver; son Samuel; son
   Richard; son John; son Joseph; daughter Patience; daughter Mary. Ex.,
   son Samuel Woodward. D. February 23, 1740. R. May 25, 1741.
      Wit: George Washington, Thomas Alling, Jacob Flowers.  Page 338

ALLEN, Thomas: Appraised by George Washington, Benjamin Johnston, Jr.,
   Thomas Drake, Sr. R. May 25, 1741.                        Page 340

DARDEN, Jacob: Appraised by John Darden, Thomas Bullock; Theophilus Joyner. Signed Jacob Darden. R. May 25, 1741.                Page 342

BRANTLEY, James: Appraised by Thomas Harris, John Miller, Edward Miller,
   Richard Jordan. Signed Martha Brantley. Ordered February 23, 1740/
   41. R. May 25, 1741.                                      Page 347

HOW, Morris: Appraised by John Goodrich, Melchizedeck Deshey, John Wrenn.
   Signed Richard Jordan. Ordered April 27, 1741. R. May 25, 1741.
                                                             Page 348

FLOYD, Francis: Appraised by John Rodway, Robert King, Humphrey Marshall,
   Samuel Whitfield. Ordered March 23, 1741. R. May 25, 1741.  Page 349

NORSWORTHY, George: Inventory of estate, presented by James Tooke Scott.
   Ordered December 8, 1739. R. June 22, 1741.               Page 351

BATTEN, Daniel: Leg. son John; son Daniel; daughter Esther; wife Sarah;
   daughter Jean; daughter Patience; daughter Priscilla. Wife, Extx.
   D. January 7, 1740. R. June 22, 1741.
      Wit: William Eley, Mathew Westray, Thomas Bracey.      Page 352

JACKSON, Richard: Of Nottoway Parish. Leg. wife Sarah; daughter Mary;
   daughter Sarah; daughter Katherine; granddaughter Ann Stuart. Wife,
   Extx. D. October 14, 1740. R. June 22, 1741.
      Wit: Benjamin Jenkins, John Jackson, Timothy Atkinson. Page 354

VAUGHAN, John: Leg. wife Elliner; to Vaughan Kilburne, all my land at the
   death of my wife; to John Simmons, the minor son of John Simons, Jr.
   of Surry County; reversion of the bequest made to John Kilburn also
   to him. John Simmons, Sr. to care for the bequest made to his grandson. Ex., Vaughan Kilburne. D. February 9, 1736. R. July 27, 1741.

THOMAS, William: Leg. wife Mary; son Richard, land on the Meherrin River, adjoining Samuel Smith; son Samuel, the plantation on which I live. Wife, Extx. D. May 18, 1741. R. July 27, 1741.
Wit: Lewis Brantley, Nathaniel Morrell, Ann Gray.          Page 356

HARRIS, Edward: Inventory presented by Mary Harris. R. July 27, 1741.
Page 356

JORDAN, James: Appraised by Peter Woodward, Joseph Hill, Arthur Jones. Signed Richard Jordan. Ordered May 25, 1741. R. July 27, 1741.
Page 360

LOYD, Thomas: Appraised by John Darden, William Lawrence, Jeremiah Lawrence. Signed Charity Loyd. R. July 27, 1741.          Page 361

BATTEN, Daniel: Appraised by Daniel Herring, John Tomlin, Mathew Tomlin, William Eley. R. July 27, 1741.          Page 363

NORWOOD, William: Account estate, examined by John Person, James Ridley, Benjamin Blunt. R. July 27, 1741.          Page 364

STEPHENS, Edward: Account estate, presented by Hardy Council. Examined by James Baker. R. July 27, 1741.          Page 366

APPLEWHAITE, Henry: Appraised by William Pope, John Johnson, Edward Cobb, James Edwards. R. August 24, 1741.          Page 367

FIVEASH, Alice and Peter: Their estates appraised by N. Bourden and Thomas Murrey. Signed by John Davis. D. October 18, 1739. R. August 24, 1741.          Page 369

WOODWARD, Oliver: Appraised by Richard Blow, Jr., Henry Thomas, George Gurley. Signed Samuel Woodward. Ordered May 25, 1741. R. August 24, 1741.          Page 371

APPLEWHAITE, Henry: Inventory returned by Ann Applewhaite. R. August 24, 1741.          Page 374

NORSWORTHY, George: Account estate; to Major O'Sheal for discovering and establishing old Col. Norsworthy's will; to William Scott's trouble in attending the suit against Martha Norsworthy. The estate was paid in equal shares to John Monro, the widow Beshier and James Tooke Scott. Examined by James Baker and N. Bourden. R. August 24, 1741. Page 375

FULGHAM, Edmund: Account estate, returned by Benjamin Turner. R.---------.
Page 376

BRIDGER, Captain William: Account estate returned by Arthur Smith, Jr. Examined by Edmond Godwin and Jesse Browne. R. October 26, 1741.
Page 377

BRANTLEY, James: Account estate, returned by Martha Brantley. Examined by Charles Travers and William Washington. R. November 23, 1741.
Page 378

DAVIS, Robert: Account estate, returned by Elizabeth Davis. R. November 23, 1741.          Page 379

BRADDY, Elias: Leg. mother Margaret Braddy, all my land in Virginia and North Carolina. Mother, Extx. D. June 16, 1738. R. November 23,

1741.
Wit: Samuel Taylor, Henry Crafford.                    Page 380

WILES, Joseph: Of Newport Parish. Leg. wife Lucy; daughter Martha; son
    Joseph; daughter Mary; to John Frizzell. Ex., John Frizzell, who is
    to have the care of my son Joseph Wiles. D. August 17, 1741. R.
    December 28, 1741.
        Wit: John Driver, John Ballard.                Page 381

WILLIAMS, Margaret: Leg. son David; grandson John, son of David Williams;
    granddaughter Mary, the daughter of Richard Williams; to Mary Altman.
    Ex., son John. D. September 10, 1740. R. December 28, 1741.
        Wit: William Penny, Mary Altman.                Page 382

MARSHALL, Humphrey: Estate appraised by John Rodway, Thomas Grosse and
    Thomas Whitfield. Signed Ann Marshall. Ordered October 26, 1741.
    R. December 28, 1741.                               Page 383

WILKINSON, Col. William: Appraised by Hugh Giles, John Monro, Robert King.
    Signed Charles Fulgham, Jr. Ordered July 27, 1741. R. December 28,
    1741.                                               Page 385

GRAY, John: Estate appraised by Samuel Whitfield, William Parker, Aaron
    Gray. Signed Hannah Gray. Ordered August 24, 1741. R. December 28,
    1741.                                               Page 387

HILL, Thomas: Account estate, returned by George Wilson, examined by
    William Hodsden, Thomas Smith and N. Bourden. The above account
    examined and allowed by me as guardian to the heir-at-law, signed
    John Newsum. R. December 28, 1741.                  Page 388

WILES, Joseph: Estate appraised by John Rodway, Thomas Whitfield, Anthony
    Fulgham. Signed John Frizzell. R. January 25, 1741. Page 389

DERRING, Nicholas: Leg. son James; son Miles; daughter Susannah; wife Mary.
    Exs., sons James and Miles. D. July 2, 1741. R. January 25, 1741.
        Wit: Richard Jordan, Jennings Ingraham, Sarah Meacom. Page 390

JARRELL, Thomas, Sr.: Leg. grandson Thomas Turner; daughter Ann Turner;
    daughter Sarah Parker; to grandson Thomas Parker, two negroes in the
    possession of Richard Parker; son Thomas; grandson Thomas Jarrell.
    Ex., son Thomas. D. April 20, 1741. R. February 22, 1741.
        Wit: Richard Blow, Jr., Micajah Edwards, Benjamin Flowers.
                                                     Page 391

WILLIAMS, John: Leg. Robert Jones; to my housekeeper, Mary Davis; son
    Jonas. Ex., son Jonas Williams. D. March 12, 1740/41. R. February
    22, 1741.
        Wit: Arthur Jones, Thomas Parnall.              Page 393

DERRING, Nicholas: Estate appraised by Thomas Day, John Goodrich, Edward
    Brantley. Signed James Derring. R. February 22, 1741. Page 394

REYNOLDS, Christopher: Account estate, which was divided between the
    widow and orphans. Examined by Hardy Council, Thomas Gale, John
    Dunkley. R. February 22, 1741.                      Page 396

JORDAN, James: Account estate, examined by N. Bourden and Jordan Thomas.
    R. February 22, 1741.                               Page 397

LEWIS, Zebulon: Account estate, signed by John and Jane Brassell. Examined
    by J. Simmons, Timothy Thorpe, James Ridley. R. February 22, 1741.
                                                     Page 398

COGAN, Robert: Account estate, returned by Sarah Cogan. Examined by Abram Ricks, Thomas Gale, William Denson. R. February 22, 1741. Page 399

BRADSHAW, William: Account estate returned by Richard Bradshaw. Examined by J. Gray, Ethd. Taylor. R. March 22, 1741. Page 399

MURFREE, Sarah: Leg. son William; daughter Ann; daughter Catherine Bryan. Ex., son William Murfree. D. December 26, 1740. R. April 26, 1742. Wit: John Daughtry, William Daughtry. Page 400

WHITE, Ann: Leg. son John; grandson Thomas White; granddaughter Mary White, with the reversion of the bequest to William and Thomas White, the sons of John and Thomas White. Ex., son George Thomas White. D. September 18, 1739. R. May 24, 1742. Wit: John Goodrich, Edward Brantley. Page 401

COPELAND, Thomas: Leg. sister Mary Whitfield; sister Martha Summerell; sister Sarah; sister Ann; to Samuel Copeland; mother Holland Copeland. Ex., brother Joseph. D. November 22, 1741. R. May 24, 1742. Wit: Henry Pitt, Jr., James Bagnall. Page 402

GOODWIN (GODWIN ?), Samuel: Estate appraised by John Applewhaite, Richard Reynolds, Joseph Wright. Signed by Jacob Dickinson. Ordered March 22, 1741. R. May 24, 1742. Page 403

BENN, Captain James: Account estate returned by Joseph Wright. Examined by Joseph Weston, Joseph Smith, Hugh Giles. R. May 25, 1742.
Page 405

FRIZZELL, Ralph: Estate appraised by John Rodway, Robert King, Anthony Fulgham, Giles Driver. Signed by John Frizzell. Page 406

WHITLEY, Mary: Estate appraised by Abraham Nicholas, George Minard, Thomas Applewhaite. Signed Samuel Holladay. D. 1741. R. May 24, 1742.
Page 407

WILSON, Goodrich: Leg. mother Honour Pierce, with reversion of bequests to Mary Wilson, the daughter of my brother George Wilson; if she dies under age, to George Wilson; to Sarah White; to Jeremiah Price; to Baker White; to Brother Samuel Wilson. Ex., George Wilson. D. April 5, 1742. R. June 28, 1742. Wit: Edward Goodrich, James Calcote. Page 408

WHITE, Ann and Thomas: Estates appraised by Edward Goodrich, N. Bourden, Thomas Day, Edward Brantley. Ordered March 22, 1741. R. July 26, 1742. Page 409

WILSON, Goodrich: Estate appraised by Thomas Day, John Goodrich, William Miller. R. July 26, 1742. Page 410

VAUGHAN, John: Inventory returned by Vaughan Kilburn. R. July 26, 1742.
Page 411

WALTON, Colonel Thomas: Estate appraised by John Goodrich, N. Bourden, John Davis. Signed by Charles Portlock. Ordered May 24, 1742. R. August 23, 1742. Page 411

DANIEL, Thomas: Estate appraised by Richard West, George Green, Thomas Wills. Ordered May 24, 1742. R. August 23, 1742. Page 413

MURFREE, Sarah: Inventory returned by William Murfree. R. August 23, 1742.
Page 414

DRIVER, Edward: Account estate, signed by Robert Driver. Examined by Thomas Gale, John Jordan. R. August 23, 1742.     Page 415

WARREN, Thomas: Account estate, presented by Thomas Williams, Jr. Examined by John Davis and Edmond Godwin. R. August 24, 1742.     Page 416

BRADDY, Elias: Inventory returned by Margaret Braddy. R. August 23, 1742.
     Page 417

WILKINSON, Richard: Of Newport Parish. Leg. granddaughter Mary Holladay, with reversion to granddaughter Easther Holladay; grandson James Peden; grandson Wilkinson Parker; granddaughter Ann Peden; granddaughter Mary Holladay; granddaughter Charity Holladay; daughter Mary Peden, the wife of the Rev. Mr. James Peden; daughter Ann Bagnall; refers to Nathan Bagnall, my said daughter's deceased husband; grandson William Bagnall; daughter Rachel Norsworthy; refers to Thomas Parker, my said daughter Rachel's deceased husband; to granddaughter Elizabeth Godwin the wife of Thomas Godwin; grandson William Parker; grandson Nathan Bagnall; to Ann Giles; grandson Richard Bagnall. Ex., son-in-law Anthony Holladay. D. April 13, 1741. R. September 27, 1742.
     Wit: John Applewhaite, George Reynolds, Lemuel Godwin. Page 418

WILLIAMS, Rachel: Of Newport Parish. Leg. to Ann the daughter of the Rev. James Peden and Mary his wife; to Mary the daughter of Anthony Holladay and Easter his wife; to Easter Holladay, the daughter of aforesaid; to Charity Holladay, the daughter of aforesaid; to Sabra Parker; to Mary Scutchins, the wife of Samuel Scutchins; to Mary Scutchins, the daughter of aforesaid; to William Parker; to Thomas Parker; to John Wright, the son of John Wright and Juliana his wife; to Elizabeth Pilkington; to Ann Chapman, the wife of Charles Chapman; to Ann Bagnall, relict of Nathan Bagnall; to my kinswoman, the eldest daughter of Joseph Turner by his first wife; to Mary Chapman, the relict of John Chapman; to the Rev. John Gemmell; to Hugh Giles; to Anthony Holladay, who married my kinswoman, Easter Wilkinson. Ex., Anthony Holladay. D. August 4, 1741. R. September 27, 1742.
     Wit: Hugh Giles, Thomas Norsworthy, Ann Marshall.     Page 422

SMITH, Arthur: Gentleman. Leg. wife Mary; son Arthur, my seal ring; son Thomas, the tract of land which my father gave to my brother Thomas Smith, where John Summerell and William Wainwright now live; also land on the Blackwater, being part of the tract, which I sold to Henry and Robert Edwards; daughter Mary to be maintained by my two sons at their discretion, so long as she remains in the condition, she is now in; daughter Jane Ridley; daughter Olive Hodsden; daughter Martha Day; grandson Joseph Bridger; to Sarah Stringer. Wife, Extx. D. August 31, 1741. R. September 27, 1742.
     Wit: John Summerell, John Smith, George Williams.     Page 424

GROSS, Thomas: Leg. daughter Elizabeth; son Francis; daughter Mary Covington Hunter; Joshua Hunter to be paid what I owe him; daughter Angelina. Ex., Christopher Haines. D. August 27, 1742. R. September 27, 1742.
     Wit: John Driver, Rebecca Haines.     Page 426

CLARK, William: Of the Parish of Newport. Leg. wife Ruth; son Joseph; son Benjamin; daughter Elizabeth; daughter Sarah; daughter Ann. Wife, Extx. D. January 17, 1737/38. R. September 27, 1742.
     Wit: Thomas Atkinson, Robert Exum, Hugh Hunniford.     Page 427

COBB, Edward: Leg. son James; son Edward; son-in-law Thomas Summerell; daughter Elinor. Exs., sons James and Edward Cobb. D. August 22, 1742. R. September 27, 1742.
     Wit: Benjamin Johnson, James Edwards, Jr., James Edwards, Sr.
     Page 428

LITTLE, John: Of Newport Parish. Leg. son John; daughter Rebecca Hynes; son Barnaby; daughter Martha; son John. Wife, Extx. D. October 29, 1739. R. September 27, 1742.
        Wit: Robert Johnson, Jr., William Page.        Page 430

INGLISH, William: Estate appraised by Benjamin Hodges, Thomas Day, William Harrison, Edward Goodrich. Ordered May 24, 1742. Account of his estate examined by John Davis, William Hodsden and Edward Goodrich. R. September 27, 1742.        Page 432

SCREWS, Mary: Appraisal estate by Benjamin Hodges, William Harrison, Thomas Day. R. September 27, 1742.        Page 433

SCREWS, William: Account estate, to bringing up four small children. Examined by William Hodsden, John Davis and Edward Goodrich. R. September 27, 1742.        Page 434

BUNKLEY, George: Nuncupative will, proven by Peter Kelly, John Watts and Sarah Alderson, in which he left his whole estate to his sister Sarah Bunkley. D. August 20, 1742. R. September 27, 1742.        Page 434

WILKINSON, Richard: Estate appraised by Hugh Giles, Joseph Wright, Joseph Weston, Richard Reynolds. Signed by Anthony Holladay. R. October 25, 1742.        Page 435

FIVEASH, Alice and Peter: Estates examined by N. Bourden, Thomas Murry. Signed John Davis. R. October 25, 1742.        Page 438

CLARK, William: Estate appraised by Joseph Atkinson, Richard Thomas, Edward Haile. Signed Joseph Clark. R. October 25, 1742.        Page 439

GROSS, Thomas: Estate appraised by John Rodway, John Clark, Anthony Fulgham. Signed Christopher Haines. R. October 25, 1742.        Page 440

FIVEASH, Peter: Account estate, examined by Thomas Smith, William Hodsden, Charles Portlock. R. October 25, 1742.        Page 441

WAINWRIGHT, William: Account estate, to expense of bringing up Benjamin Wainwright. Examined by John Wills, William Ponsonby, Joseph Baker. R. October 25, 1742.        Page 443

SUMMERELL, Thomas, Jr.: Estate examined at the house of John Summerell, by John Wills, Joseph Baker, William Ponsonby. R. October 25, 1742.
        Page 444

BASDEN, Joseph: Inventory presented by James Basden. R. October 25, 1742.
        Page 444

HODGES, Elias: On the motion of William Harrison, a clause in his will to be explained in reference to the gift of a slave and her increase to his daughter Mary. The depositions of John Goodrich and John Hodges, filed. R. October 25, 1742.        Page 445

WILLIAMS, Rachel: Inventory presented by Anthony Holladay. R. November 22, 1742.        Page 446

BRIDGER, William: Account of his estate which belongs to his orphan Joseph Bridger. Signed by Arthur Smith. R. November 22, 1742.
        Page 447

HOLLEMAN, Elizabeth: Account estate, by sale for Arthur and Joseph Holleman, legacies left them by their grandfather Thomas Holleman. Signed

Thomas Atkinson. R. November 22, 1742. Page 449

BASDEN, Joseph: Account estate. R. November 22, 1742. Page 450

SMITH, Thomas: Inventory returned by Elizabeth and Joseph Smith. R. November 22, 1742. Page 451

NORSWORTHY, Charles: Account estate, examined by Hugh Giles and Robert King. R. November 22, 1742. Page 432

WILKINSON, Colonel William: Account estate, expenses for William and Willis Wilkinson; to Charles Fulgham in part toward his wife's claims. Signed Thomas Swann. R. December 27, 1742. Page 452

ALLEN, Thomas: Account estate, examined by George Washington, J. Jarrell, Richard Blow, Jr. Signed George Bell and Roger Allen. R. January 24, 1742. Page 453

LITTLE, John: Inventory presented by the Extx. R. January 24, 1742.
Page 454

WESTON, Benjamin: Account estate, examined by Hugh Giles, Thomas Applewhaite, John Applewhaite. R. February 28, 1742. Page 455

PIERCE, Thomas: Leg. Jeremiah Pierce and Honour Pierce. D. November 25, 1742. R. February 28, 1742.
Wit: John Miller, Joseph Jones. Page 456

JORDAN, Mathew: Leg. son Mathew; daughter Dorothy; daughter Elizabeth; daughter Martha; unborn child; wife Patience. Exs., wife, Abraham Ricks, Samuel Cornwell. D. November 19, 1742. R. March 20, 1743.
Wit: Thomas Deloach, Sampson Flake, Mary Delk. Page 456

COBB, Edward: Inventory presented by Edward and James Cobb. R. March 28, 1743. Page 458

KINCHEN, Mathew: Inventory presented by Thomas Jarrell and Etl'd. Taylor, Exs. R. March 28, 1743. Page 459

MORELAND, John: Estate appraised by Thomas Day, Thomas Shelly, Thomas Barlow. Signed Edward Goodrich. Ordered October 25, 1742. R. April 25, 1743. Page 459

JORDAN, Mathew: Estate appraised by John Garner, Francis Ward, Thomas Cofer. Signed Patience Jordan. R. May 23, 1743. Page 461

EDWARDS, James: Leg. friend William Pope; friend Nathan Godwin; son David; son James; son John; son William; son Jonas; son Nathan; son Albridgeton. Wife, Extx. D. April 5, 1743. R. May 23, 1743.
Wit: Benjamin Johnston, William Pope. Page 464

GOODWIN, Joshua: Estate appraised by Robert King, Anthony Fulgham, Giles Driver. Signed Thomas Goodwin. R. May 23, 1743. Page 465

MORELAND, John: Account estate, examined by Thomas Smith, N. Bourden, John Mallory. R. May 23, 1743. Page 467

WALTON, Colonel Thomas: Account estate, examined by N. Bourden, John Davis and Edward Goodrich. Signed by Charles Portlock. R. May 23, 1743.
Page 468

JORDAN, Joshua: Estate appraised by Joseph Weston, Robert King, John Rodway.

Signed Sarah Jordan. Ordered June 3, 1743. R. June 27, 1743.

Page 469

MILLER, John: Account estate, to his daughter Mourning's funeral expenses. Examined by N. Bourden, John Davis, Edward Goodrich. R. June 27, 1743.

Page 470

RICKS, Robert: Leg. wife Elizabeth; son Robert, the land on which William Wood formerly lived; daughter Mary; daughter Elizabeth; neighbor Nicholas Williams; son Richard. Exs., wife and son Robert Ricks. D. March 25, 1741. R. July 25, 1743.
      Wit: William Scott, Jr., John Dendon, Jr., Joseph West, Jere'h Lawrence, Jacob Johnson. Page 471

EDWARDS, James: Inventory presented by Allinor Edwards. R. July 25, 1743.

Page 474

WILLIAMSON, Francis: Leg. wife Ann; son Arthur; son Joseph; son Benjamin; granddaughter Mourning Williamson; daughter Martha Atkinson; grandson Francis Williamson; granddaughter Elizabeth ------; grandson Jesse Williamson; grandson Arthur Williamson; granddaughter Martha Williamson; grandsons, Burwell, Joseph, Hardy, Absolom, Benjamin and James Williamson. Exs., sons Arthur and Benjamin Williamson. D. May 14, 1743. R. August 22, 1743.
      Wit: James Simmons, Thomas Williamson. Page 476

RATCLIFF, John: Inventory presented by Richard Jordan. R. August 23, 1743.

Page 478

HOW, Morrice: Account estate, paid for schooling his children. Signed Richard Jordan. Examined by N. Bourden and Jordan Thomas. R. September 20, 1743. Page 479

JORDAN, James: Account estate, examined by Jordan Thomas and N. Bourden. Signed Richard Jordan. Page 479

SCOTT, Robert: Leg. sister Katherine Watkins; cousin James Tooke Scott; cousin Thomas Scott; cousin Elizabeth Bacon, the daughter of John Hollowell; to Elizabeth Denson, the daughter of John Scott; cousin Joseph Hollowell; cousin Sarah Hollowell; cousin William Scott, son of my brother William Scott. Ex., brother William. D. May 24, 1743. R. October 24, 1743.
      Wit: Joseph White, William Denson, Henry Saunders. Page 480

SCOTT, Robert: Inventory returned by William Scott, Jr. R. October 24, 1743. Page 482

KINCHEN, Mathew: Account estate, signed by Thomas Jarrell and Eth'd Taylor. Examined by J. Gray and John Ruffin. R. November 29, 1743. Page 482

INGRAM, Roger: Leg. brother John Ingram; sister Elizabeth; Goddaughter Ann Shelly; brother John is to maintain my mother. Ex., brother John Ingram. D. November 3, 1743. R. February 27, 1743.
      Wit: Benjamin Chapman Donaldson, Giles Bowers. Page 486

BRITT, William: Leg. son Alexander; daughter Mary; to the rest of my children. Wife Elizabeth, Extx. D. August 5, 1743. R. March 26, 1744.
      Wit: George Goodrich, John Britt. Page 487

MOORE, Thomas: Of Nottoway Parish. Leg. son Thomas; son William; son Abraham. Ex., son Abraham Moore. D. August 12, 1743. R. March 26, 1744.
      Wit: Jonathan Joyner, Timothy Atkinson. Page 487

DRIVER, Giles: Leg. daughter-in-law Mary Driver; grandson Robert Driver; granddaughter Sarah Driver; daughter Ann Garland; son Giles; to my mother; grandson Dempsey Driver; son John; son Charles; son Joseph; wife Olive. Ex., son John Driver. D. September 23, 1743. R. March 26, 1744.
    Wit: James Frizzell, John Frizzell.             Page 490

PARKER, William: Leg. wife Ann; daughter Rachel; daughter Bathsheba. D. May 23, 1743. R. April 23, 1744.
    Wit: Nathan Bagnall, Thomas Parker.         Page 490

DAVIS, Thomas: Account estate, examined by Richard Hardy and Thomas Smith. R. June 25, 1744.                                       Page 491

WHITE, George Thomas and Ann: Account of their estate, examined by Richard Hardy, N. Bourden. Widow and orphans referred to. Signed John Mecum. R. June 25, 1744.                                   Page 493

TALLAUGH, James: Estate appraised by John Johnson, William Fowler, John Lawrence. Ordered February 27, 1743. R. June 25, 1744.     Page 493

JONES, William: Leg. son Joseph; son Jess; daughter Olive; daughter Honour; daughter Mary; granddaughter Lucy Jones; wife Elizabeth. Exs., sons Joseph and Jesse. D. December 29, 1742. R. June 25, 1744.
    Wit: Arthur Sherrod, Nathan Godley, Elizabeth Sherrod.   Page 495

BASDEN, Joseph: Division of his estate; to Robert Basden; to Martha Basden; to Lilburn Low; to representatives of Ledbetter Low, decd.
                                            Page 496

RIGGIN, Daniel: Leg. cousin Rachel Noyall, my plantation on which William Wainwright lives; sister Patience Shivers; to Jonas Shivers; to my uncle William Noyall; to Henry Shivers. Ex., William Noyall. D. March 3, 1743/44. R. July 23, 1744.
    Wit: Joshua Hunter, John Harrison, William Richards.   Page 497

POPE, William: Estate appraised by Henry Thomas, Arthur Vick, Richard Blow, Jr. June 27, 1743. Signed Patience Pope. R. April 15, 1744.
                                            Page 499

DAVIS, Elizabeth: Estate appraised by John Hodges, George Wilson, William Glover. R. July 23, 1744.                             Page 499

DAY, James: Estate appraised by Benjamin Hodges, Melchiz'd Dushee, Thomas Day. Signed Martha Day and William Hodsden. R. August 27, 1744.
                                            Page 502

PARKER, William: Estate appraised by Joseph Wright, Joseph Weston, Thomas Whitfield, Samuel Whitfield. Signed Ann Parker. R. August 27, 1744.
                                          Page 504

ENGLISH, William: Account estate, Examined by James Ridley and Arthur Applewhaite. Signed William Hodsden. R. August 27, 1744.   Page 505

BEVAN, Thomas: Account estate settled at the house of Joseph Baker, by John Summerell, Joseph Wright and Joseph Baker. (First item dated 1735.) R. August 28, 1744.                       Page 506

WILLIAMSON, Francis, Sr.: Inventory presented by Arthur and Benjamin Williamson. R. September 24, 1744.              Page 508

WILKINSON, Richard: Account estate, errors accepted and contents received by agreement the 6th of July, by John Parker, Nathan Bagnall, George Norsworthy, Rachel Norsworthy, Ann Bagnall, James Peden, Mary Peden and Anthony Holladay. R. September 24, 1744.                    Page 509

BEAL, Benjamin: Leg. wife Sarah; daughter Sarah Godwin; son Benjamin; daughter Mary; daughter Rachel Dixson; daughter Wilkinson; wife Sarah Beal. Ex., son Benjamin Beal. D. August 7, 1744. R. September 24, 1744.
    Wit: Thomas Gale, John Chestnutt, John Garner.            Page 511

WRENN, Olive: Nuncupative will, proven by N. Bourden, William Williams and William Murrey. That she desired that her child should have everything, which belonged to her. D. August 1, 1744. R. October 22, 1744.
                                            Page 515

CLEMENTS, John: Inventory of estate, returned by George Ellsey (?). R. October 22, 1744.                                            Page 515

COLSON, William: Account estate, dated 1741, returned by John Person, Gent., Sheriff. R. October 22, 1744.                              Page 516

WILLIAMS, John: Leg. daughter Elizabeth Williams. Ex., friend Benjamin Hodges. D. October 4, 1744.
    Wit: N. Bourden, Philip Fones, Lewis Thomas.
    Codicil: If my daughter dies without heirs, my estate to be equally divided between James Pyland, Jr., the son of James Pyland and John Carrell, the son of Samuel Carrell. D. November 2, 1744. R. November 26, 1744.
    Wit: N. Bourden, Thomas Rosser, Prudence Bourden.        Page 517

PROCTOR, Jeremiah: Estate appraised by John Wrenn, William Glover, Melchizadeck Dushee. Signed Susanna Proctor. Ordered July 21, 1744. R. November 26, 1744.                                        Page 519

HARRISON, William: Estate appraised by William Harrison, Benjamin Hodges, Nicholas Casey. Signed Temperance Harrison. Ordered October 6, 1744. R. November 26, 1744.                                        Page 520

WRENN, Olive: Account sales, signed, Francis Wrenn. R. November 26, 1744.
                                            Page 521

LAWRENCE, Robert: Of Newport Parish. Leg. son Hardy; son Robert; son George; son Charles; daughter Sarah; daughter Priscilla; wife Ann; brother John Lawrence; son Charles to be placed in the care of his grandfather Hardy Counil. Wife Ann, Extx. D. November 1, 1743. R. January 28, 1744.
    Wit: William Lawrence, John Lawrence, Hardy Council.    Page 522

MARSHALL, Humphrey: Of Newport Parish. Leg. brother Robert; brother John; sister Elizabeth Roberson; to John Marshall the son of my brother Joseph; sister Mary Penny; brother James Marshall; to John Penny, the plantation on which I live, Mary Sikes to have half of the said plantation during her widowhood; if John Penny should die without issue the bequest to my brother James Marshall; to William Penny the son of John. Exs., James Marshall and John Penny. D. January 3, 1744. R. Janaury 28, 1744.
    Wit: John Driver, Charles Driver.                      Page 524

ATKINSON, Thomas: Estate appraised by Robert Tynes, James Simmons and Richard Thomas. Signed Joseph Atkinson. Ordered October 22, 1744. R. January 28, 1744.                                          Page 525

JORDAN, Mathew: Account estate, to cash due Mary Jordan the orphan of James Jordan. Signed Lawrence Baker and Jordan Thomas. R. January 28, 1744. Page 527

WHEADON, Joseph: Leg. John Carrell; to Thomas Carrell; wife Joice; brother James Wheadon; nephew Joseph Wheadon. Extx., wife Joice Wheadon. D. December 1, 174-. R. February 25, 1744.
      Wit: Wil. Salter, Thomas Mean (?), William Balmer, Jr. Page 52-

WILLIAMS, George: Leg. son George; son Thomas; son Roland; grandson Thomas Clark land on Nottoway Swamp; wife Elizabeth and at her death to be divided among all my children. Exs., wife and son Roland. D. August 26, 1737. R. February 25, 1744.
      Wit: Robert Ricks, William May. Page 529

LONG, Edward: Estate appraised by William Wainwright, John Wright, Joshua Hunter. Signed by Ann Daniel. Ordered Janaury 28, 1744. R. February 25, 1744. Page 531

FULGHAM, John: Estate appraised by Thomas Whitfield, Robert King, Nathan Bagnall. Signed Mich'l Fulgham. Ordered January 28, 1744. R. February 25, 1744. Page 531

WILES, Joseph: Estate appraised by John Summerell, John Wills, Thomas Applewhaite. R. February 25, 1744. Page 532

GROSS, Thomas: Account estate, settled at the house of Christopher Haynes, by John Summerell,. John Wills and Thomas Applewhaite. R. February 25, 1744. Page 533

MARSHALL, Humphrey: Estate appraised by John Rodway, Anthony Fulgham, Thomas Whitfield. Signed by James Marshall and John Penny. R. March 25, 1745. Page 533

JOYNER, John: Of the Lower Parish. Leg. cousin Theophilus Joyner, my whole estate. Ex., Theophilus Joyner. D. January 3, 1741. R. April 22, 1745.
      Wit: John Whitley, William Whitley, Thomas Uzzell. Page 535

WILLIAMS, John: Inventory of estate returned by Benjamin Hodges. R. June 24, 1745. Page 535

WILSON, John: Appraisal of estate by Nelchizadeck Deshey, William Glover, John Wrenn. Ordered April 22, 1745. R. June 24, 1745. Page 536

GEMMILL, Rev. Mr. John: Estate appraised by John Davis, Thomas Day, Benjamin Hodges, William Hodsden. Signed by Robert Burwell. R. July 22, 1745. Page 538

BRASWELL, Richard: Leg. son William and son Joseph, my Exs.; daughter Elizabeth; son John; loving wife. D. April 21, 1744. R. August 26, 1745.
      Wit: Benjamin Johnson, Jr., Joseph Woodward, Arthur Edwards.
Page 541

RICHARDS, Thomas: Account estate, examined by John Summerell, John Applewhaite, Hugh Giles. R. August 26, 1745. Page 541

GARDNER, William: Estate appraised by Robert Driver, John Garnes (Garner), Thomas Joiner. Signed John Gardner. Ordered January 28, 1744. R. August 26, 1745. Page 542

NEAVILLE, John: Division of estate to sons, John, Thomas and Joseph and
    daughter Penelope. Examined by Hardy Council, Abram Ricks and William
    Denson. Signed by John Marshall. R. August 26, 1745.        Page 544

    Further accounts of the orphans of John Neaville, the share of Thomas
    Neaville to be divided among the three surviving children. R. August
    26, 1745.                                                    Page 545

APPLEWHAITE, Henry, Jr.: Account estate returned by Philip and Mary Brantley.
    Examined by Thomas Gray and Peter Butts. R. September 23, 1745.
                                                                 Page 547

--------------------

## WILL BOOK FIVE

--------------------

LAWRENCE, Robert: Inventory of his estate returned by Ann Lawrence. R.
    October 28, 1745.                                            Page 1

JOYNER, John: Inventory of his estate returned by Theophilus Joyner. R.
    October 28, 1745.                                            Page 1

MEACOM, Lewis: Account estate, to the expense of bringing up two small
    children. Signed John and Ann Potter. Examined by Thomas Smith and
    Thomas Day. R. October 28, 1745.                             Page 2

WINDHAM, Reuben: Inventory presented by Edward Windham. R. January 27,
    1745.                                                        Page 3

PURSELL, Arthur: Leg. son Arthur; son Philip; daughter Sarah Johnson;
    daughter Mary Fulgham; daughter Patience Exum; daughter Elizabeth
    Turner; daughter Ann; daughter Jean; daughter Martha. My estate to
    be divided by Thomas Williamson and Josiah John Holleman. Exs., wife
    Sarah and son Arthur Pursell. D. July 10, 1745. R. January 27, 1745.
            Wit: Thomas Williamson, Michael Harris.              Page 3

NEWSUM, Thomas: Leg. son Nathan; son Benjamin; son Jacob; son David; my
    son Thomas Barham; daughter Sarah Barham; wife Elizabeth. Exs., wife
    and son Jacob Newsum. D. October 14, 1745. R. January 27, 1745.
            Wit: Nathaniel Ridley, Jesse Browne.
    (Refers to land left his children by their brother.)         Page 5

BRADSHAW, John: Leg. cousin Sarah Bradshaw, the daughter of my brother
    George; cousin Martha Davis, the wife of Edward Davis. Exs., cousin
    Edward Davis and Charles Fulgham. D. August 27, 1737. R. January 27,
    1745.
            Wit: Charles Fulgham, Ann Harris.                    Page 7

JOHNSON, William: Estate appraised by Harris Taylor, Thomas Davis, Simon
    Everitt. Signed Peter Johnson. R. January 27, 1745.          Page 7

BRASWELL, Richard: Inventory of his estate returned by William and Joseph
    Braswell. R. January 27, 1745.                               Page 9

BRADSHAW, John: Estate appraised by Benjamin Hodges, Arthur Applewhaite,
    Nicholas Miller. Signed by Edward Davis. R. February 24, 1745.
                                                                 Page 9

WEATHERALL, Aquilla: Estate appraised by Richard Snowden, Joseph Bridger,
    John Pitt. Signed Charity Weatherall. Ordered June 24, 1745.

MORGAN, Walter: Estate appraised by John Hodges, William Miller, Benjamin
    Hodges, William Harrison. Signed W. Bidgood. R. March 24, 1745.
                                                           Page 12

NEWSUM, Thomas: Inventory presented by Elizabeth and Jacob Newsum. R.
    March 24, 1745.                                        Page 13

MOSCROP, Susanna: Leg. grandsons, Adam and Thomas Murry, the sons of
    Robert Murry, decd.; daughter Mary Godwin; granddaughter Jane Apple-
    whaite; granddaughter Mary Frizzell; sister Elizabeth Driver; to
    Joseph Weston; to my five grandchildren, Mary Frizzell, Elizabeth
    Godwin, Thomas Godwin, William Godwin and James Godwin. Ex., Joseph
    Weston. D. October 18, 1745. R. March 24, 1745.
        Wit: David Williams, Jacob Thomas.                 Page 14

MORGAN, Walter: Account estate, examined by N. Bourden, James Ridley, A.
    Jones. R. March 24, 1745.                              Page 15

READ, William: Leg. daughter Ann; son Samuel; son John; wife Elizabeth.
    D. April 21, 1739. R. April 28, 1746.
        Wit: John Person, Robert Deane.                    Page 16

JOHNSON, Thomas: Leg. son Joseph; son Moses; loving wife. D. April 25,
    1744. R. May 8, 1746.
        Wit: Thomas Pate, Joseph Johnson.                  Page 17

MOSCROP, Susanna: Estate appraised by Charles Fulgham, Jr., Joseph Bridger,
    Jr., Thomas Wills. Signed Joseph Weston.               Page 17

GARDNER, William: Account estate, examined by Thomas Gray and David Hunter.
    R. May 9, 1746.                                        Page 19

PITT, Thomas: Estate appraised by Anthony Fulgham, Giles Driver, Christopher
    Haines. Signed Martha Pitt. Ordered April 28, 1746. R. June 12, 1746.
                                                           Page 20

MINARD, George: Estate appraised by James Godwin, John Pitt, Joseph Bri-
    dger, Jr. Signed Ann Minard. Ordered April 28, 1746. R. June 12,
    1746.                                                  Page 21

SNOWDEN, Richard: Estate appraised by John Monro, John Pitt, Edmond Godwin.
    Signed Margaret Snowden. Ordered May 8, 1746. R. June 12, 1746.
                                                           Page 22

READ, William: Estate appraised by Thomas Clarke, Simon Harris, John Jones.
    Signed Elizabeth Read. R. June 12, 1746.               Page 23

PITMAN, Edward: Estate appraised by Jordan Thomas, Thomas Cole, Arthur
    Crocker. Signed Martha Pitman. R. June 12, 1746.       Page 24

WRIGHT, Joseph: Estate appraised by Joseph Weston, Joseph Norsworthy,
    Richard Reynolds. Signed Martha Wright. Ordered November 25, 1745.
    R. June 12, 1746.                                      Page 24

MCKENNY, Gilbert: Estate appraised by Timothy Thorpe, Henry Rose, James
    Jones. Signed Sarah McKenny. R. July 10, 1746.         Page 26

RICKS, Abraham: Leg. daughter Mary Jordan of North Carolina; daughter
    Elizabeth Pritchard; daughter Lydia Beal; daughter Martha Lawrence,
    land adjoining that of John Lawrence and Thomas Smelley; daughter

Patience Jordan; daughter Ann Marshall; daughter Mourning Jordan. Josiah Jordan and John Lawrence to collect my debts. William Denson, Exum Scott, Joseph White and William Scott to assist in settling my estate. Exs., son-in-law Josiah Jordan and daughter Mourning Jordan. D. June 24, 1746. R. July 10, 1746.
    Wit: James Jordan Scott, John Outland, Jacob Powell.    Page 26

SUMMERELL, John: Leg. wife Lydia; daughter Sarah; daughter Jean. Wife, Extx. D. February 14, 1745. R. August 24, 1746.
    Wit: Hugh Giles, Edmond Godwin, James Fulgham.    Page 28

GIBBS, Ralph: Estate appraised by John Rodway, Christopher Haines, Stephen Smith. Signed Sarah Gibbs. Ordered April 28, 1746. R. August 14, 1746.    Page 29

ATKINSON, Thomas: Account estate, to a negro delivered to Richard Atkinson. Examined by John Ruffin and N. Bourden. Signed Joseph Atkinson. R. October 9, 1746.    Page 31

RICKS, Abraham: Estate appraised by Robert Eley, Joseph Meredith, Michael Eley. To legacies delivered to Josiah Jordan, to Patience Jordan, to John Lawrence, to John Marshall, to Joseph Jordan, to Thomas Pritchard. R. October 9, 1746.    Page 32

BLOW, Richard: Estate appraised by Joseph Cobb, Thomas Crainshaw, George Gurley. Appraisal at "Contentney," Craven County, North Carolina. Signed by Henry and Ann Vaughan. R. October 9, 1746.    Page 37

WOMBWELL, Joseph: Of Nottoway Parish. Leg. daughter Elizabeth; daughter Patience; daughter Sarah; son Jesse; son Mathew. Wife Ann, Extx. D. August 19, 1746. R. November 13, 1746.
    Wit: Benjamin Bayley, Arthur Holleman, John Smith.    Page 38

WOMBWELL, Joseph: Estate appraised by Joseph Phillips, Charles Calthorpe, Thomas Brown. Signed Ann Wombwell. R. January 8, 1746.    Page 39

MILLER, William: Leg. son James; son William; if sons should die without heirs, Martha Casey is to inherit James estate and my brother John Miller's children to inherit William's estate. Exs., wife Margaret, friend George Wilson and friend Edward Goodrich. D. July 3, 1746. R. January 8, 1746.
    Wit: Ann Briggs, Susanna Derring, William Williams.    Page 40

NOYALL, William: Of Newport Parish. Leg. daughter Martha Norsworthy; daughter Ann Harrison; daughter Jane; daughter Mary Richards; daughter Elizabeth Pitt; wife Martha; daughter Sarah; daughter Priscilla; daughter Rachel. Exs., wife and daughter Rachel Noyall. D. March 28, 1746. R. January 8, 1746.
    Wit: William Brock, James Godwin, John Pitt.    Page 41

ADKINS, Samuel: Leg. son Moses; son Samuel; son Michael; son Thomas; wife Elizabeth. Exs., wife and son Samuel Adkins. D. May 22, 1746. R. February 12, 1746.
    Wit: John Rotchell, John Turner, Howell Edmunds.    Page 43

JOHNSON, William: Account estate, examined by William Hodsden and Thomas Gray. Signed Peter Johnson. R. February 12, 1746.    Page 44

WILLIFORD, John: Appraised by Lawrence Lancaster, Joseph Lancaster, John Stephenson. Signed Elizabeth Williford. R. February 12, 1746.
   Page 45

JOYNER, Lazarus: Leg. brother Henry; brother Arthur; rest of my estate to be divided among Henry Joyner, Arthur Joyner, Prudence Long; sister Mary Tynes; sister Martha Joyner. Exs., brothers John and Henry Joyner. D. December 30, 1746. R. March 12, 1746.
    Wit: Richard Norsworthy, Tristram Norsworthy, Nathaniel Norsworthy. Page 46

BLAKE, William: Of Nottoway Parish. Leg. wife Mary; son Sessums; son Benjamin; son Thomas; son Joseph; among all my children. Exs., wife Mary, son Joshua Claud and son Thomas Blake. D. November 1, 1742. R. March 12, 1746.
    Wit: John Barrow, Samuel Smith. Page 47

PAGE, William: Of Nottoway Parish. Leg. granddaughter Mary Page; wife Ann and at her decease to Betty Fort, if she should die without heirs to Joshua Fort. Exs., John and Rebecca Fort. D. October 16, 1746. R. March 12, 1746.
    Wit: John Land, Robert Land. Page 49

EVERITT, Simon: Leg. son Joseph; son Simon; grandson Amos Williams; to Catherine Due (Dew ?); daughter Patience Turner; daughter Sarah Turner. Exs., sons Joseph and Simon Turner. D. November 5, 1743. R. March 12, 1746.
    Wit: William Bynum, Elizabeth Bynum, Faith Taylor. Page 49

DAWSON, Martin: Leg. son Henry; daughter Elinor Jones; daughter Sarah Inman; son Joshua; daughter Martha Dinkin (?); to my housekeeper, Mary Cocks; daughter Margaret Warren. Exs., sons-in-law, John Jones and Robert Warren. D. September 16, 1745. R. March 12, 1746.
    Wit: Henry Crafford, John Pierce, Henry Dawson. Page 51

Oct. 9, 1746. Henry Dawson entered caveat against the said will, for a revocation thereof. Rebecca Dawson, widow and relict refused to accept the provisions made for her, etc. Page 51

JORDAN, Charles, Sr.: Estate appraised at the house of Mary Jordan, by William Rand and Joseph Baker. Ordered March 24, 1746/47. R. April 9, 1747. Page 53

MILLER, William: Estate appraised by John Mallory, John Hodges, Benjamin Hodges. Signed by Edward Goodrich and George Wilson. R. April 9, 1747. Page 54

NOYALL, William: Estate appraised by Joseph Bridger, John Monro, John Pitt. Signed Martha Noyall. R. May 14, 1747. Page 56

JOHNSON, Thomas: Estate appraised by Timothy Thorpe, John Myrick, John Thorpe. Signed Mary Johnson. Ordered May 8, 1746. R. May 14, 1747. Page 58

GEMMILL, Rev. Mr. John: Estate examined by Lawrence Baker, R. Hardy and T. Day. Signed Robert Burwell. R. May 14, 1747. Page 58

COCKSEY, William: Leg. wife Judith; son John. Ex., son John Cocksey. D. February 21, 1745/46. R. May 14, 1747.
    Wit: Absalom Atkinson, Peter Vasser, John Nanny. Page 60

MURPHRY, Michael: Leg. son John; daughter Elizabeth Dixon; daughter Mary; daughter Sarah; daughter Elender; grandson Michael Murphry. Ex., son John Murphry. D. July 2, 1743. R. May 14, 1747.
    Wit: John Garner, B. Beal. Page 61

WRENN, Mary:  Leg. daughter Ann Potter; daughter Martha Cary; daughter
    Patience Bell; my grandchildren, Mary Meacom, Lewis Meacom, William
    Cary, Joseph Cary, Charity Cary, Richard Bell, Benjamin Bell and Mary
    Bell.  Ex., Mr. John Wrenn.  D. January 27, 1746.  R. May 14, 1747.
        Wit:  Wil. Salter, Benjamin Bell, William Cary.          Page 62

SUMMERELL, John:  Estate appraised by Edmond Godwin, Thomas Wills, Charles
    Fulgham, Jr.  Signed Hugh Giles.  R. June 11, 1747.          Page 63

DAY, Captain James:  Account estate, examined by Edward Goodrich and Charles
    Portlock.  Signed William Hodsden and John Mallory.  R. June 11, 1747.
                                                                 Page 65

JOHNSON, James:  Leg. grandson John Corbett; daughter Mary Corbett; son
    James; daughter Martha Mayo; daughter Eleanor Ricks; granddaughter
    Patience Johnson, daughter of son John; son Samuel; son Richard;
    daughter Catherine Burn; son Robert; daughter Grace Powell; wife Mary;
    son Benjamin; granddaughter Mary Johnson.  Ex., son Benjamin Johnson.
    D. January 30, 1745/46.  R. June 11, 1747.
        Wit:  John Darden, John Gwinn, Johnson Corbett.          Page 67

DAWSON, Martin:  Estate appraised by Henry Crafford, James Turner, Benjamin
    Blunt.  Account of things carried away by Rebecca Dawson into Caro-
    lina.  R. July 9, 1747.                                      Page 70

WEST, Richard:  Of Newport Parish.  Leg. son Everitt; son Giles; daughter
    Rebecca Smelley; son Jacamy; son Robert, land adjoining on Merchant
    Perry; son James; daughter Ann; wife Ann.  Ex., Hugh Giles.  D. July
    3, 1746.  R. July 9, 1747.
        Wit:  Charles Fulgham, Benn Willett, John Wills.         Page 71

DAWSON, Martin:  Account estate, to paid the following legacies, to John
    Inman, to John Jones, to Robert Warren, to Henry Dawson, to Joshua
    Dawson, to Martin Dickins.  Signed John Jones.  R. July 9, 1747.
                                                                 Page 73

WOODWARD, Oliver:  Account estate, paid Richard Woodward, paid Joseph
    Woodward in part of his share.  Signed Samuel Woodward.  Examined by
    Thomas Gray and James Holt.  R. July 9, 1747.                Page 74

PARKER, George:  Leg. wife Martha; daughter Mourning; son James; daughter
    Ann; daughter Sarah; eldest daughter Isabell and her first child.
    Exs., wife and friend Thomas Parker.  D. May 15, 1747.  R. August
    13, 1747.
        Wit:  James Jordan, John Wrench.                         Page 76

DARDEN, Jacob:  Account estate, among items to cash my father received
    as a legacy to me from my grandfather George Williamson.  Signed
    Jacob Darden.  Examined by William Hodsden and James Ridley.  R.
    August 13, 1747.                                             Page 77

WIGGS, George:  Leg. sister Elizabeth Brassey; brother Luke Wiggs; cousin
    Elizabeth Brassey.  Sister Elizabeth Brassey, Extx.  D. July 30, 1747.
    R. October 8, 1747.
        Wit:  Robert Tynes, Arthur Applewhaite.                  Page 78

NEAVILLE, Elizabeth:  Leg. daughter-in-law Mary Sikes; granddaughter Mary
    Sikes; daughter-in-law Rachel Wainwright; to Amy and Ann Wainwright;
    to daughter-in-law Mary Neaville; to granddaughter Elizabeth Neaville;
    granddaughter Rachel Nolleboy; granddaughter Elizabeth Garner; grand-
    daughter Sarah Murphry; granddaughter Elinor Everett; daughter Sarah
    Carter; son Francis Hampton; daughter Mary Marshall; son-in-law James

Marshall. Ex., son-in-law James Marshall. D. September 21, 1747. R. October 8, 1747.
    Wit: John Marshall, Jacob Darden, John Everitt.     Page 79

PARKER, George: Estate appraised by Samuel Godwin, Edmund Godwin, Robert Driver. Signed Martha Parker. R. November 12, 1747.     Page 81

PITT, Thomas: Account estate examined by Hugh Giles and John Applewhaite. R. November 12, 1747.     Page 84

POWELL, William: Leg. to William Speight, son of John Speight, with reversion of the bequest to his brother John; to my brother Nathaniel's son Nathaniel; to James Davis; to Elizabeth Speight, the daughter of John and Elizabeth Speight; to Ann, the daughter of James Davis. Exs., John and William Speight. D. September 13, 1747. R. November 12, 1747.
    Wit: Thomas Gale, Mary Gale, Thomas Outland.     Page 85

CARTER, Katherine: Leg. daughter Kezia; daughter Elizabeth Perry. D. May 28, 1746. R. December 10, 1747.
    Wit: Thomas Clifton, John Calthorpe.     Page 87

GRIMMER, Robert: Estate appraised by Benjamin Johnston, Sr., Benjamin Johnston, Jr., Nathan Vasser. Signed by Sarah Grimmer and William Grimmer. Ordered August 13, 1747. R. December 10, 1747.     Page 88

VICKERS, Ralph: Leg. grandsons, Thomas and Simon Boykin, the land which I bought of Benjamin Boykin; granddaughter Martha Boykin; daughter Margaret Vaughan, the wife of Thomas Vaughan. Ex., brother Abraham Carnall. D. February 10, 1741. R. January 14, 1747.
    Wit: Joseph Powell, Hardy Council, Thomas English.
Abraham Carnall refused executorship and Simon Boykin qualified.
     Page 89

BLOW, Richard, Jr.: Account estate, examined by Edmond Godwin and Thomas Wills. Signed Henry Vaughan. R. January 14, 1747.     Page 92

GOODRICH, Benjamin: Estate appraised by Samuel Jones, Richard Jones and John Jordan. Ordered October 8, 1747. Signed William Goodrich. R. March 10, 1747.     Page 93

SMITH, William: Leg. wife Mary; son William; son Stephen; son Nathaniel; granddaughter Elizabeth, the daughter of William Smith; granddaughter Mary, the daughter of Stephen Smith; daughter Elizabeth Rodes. Ex., son Stephen Smith. D. February 20, 1746. R. March 10, 1747.
    Wit: Peter Ballard, Joseph Weston.     Page 96

APPLEWHAITE, Ann: Widow. Leg. son Thomas; granddaughter Ann Applewhaite the daughter of my son Thomas; daughter Ann Godwin; daughter Priscilla Ridley; daughter Amy Jones; son John; grandson Henry, the son of Henry Applewhaite, decd.; granddaughter Amy Applewhaite the daughter of my son Henry; granddaughter Ann Ridley; granddaughter Sarah Davis; grandson Henry Applewhaite, son of my son Arthur; grandson John Lawrence, son of my daughter Sarah Lawrence. Ex., son Arthur Applewhaite. D. July 26, 1746. R. March 10, 1747.
    Wit: William Ponsonby, Ann Ponsonby, Ann Hunt, Elizabeth Daniel.
     Page 97

PRICE, Richard: Estate appraised by Francis Wills, Benjamin Johnston, William Hickman. Ordered November 25, 1745. Sarah Grimmer and William Grimmer returned the estate of Robert Grimmer, who was the administrator of the estate of said Richard Price. R. March 10, 1747. Page 99

BUTLER, Christopher: Estate appraised by James Godwin, John Smelley, Christopher Reynolds. Signed John Butler. Ordered March 10, 1747. R. April 14, 1748.                                                    Page 100

HOLLOWELL, Sarah: Leg. sister Judith; to Mourning, the daughter of my brother Joseph Hollowell; brother William. Ex., brother William Hollowell. D. February 16, 1745. R. April 14, 1748.
    Wit: John Murry, Sarah Murry, Benjamin Hodges, Benjamin Davis.
                                            Page 102

DRIVER, Robert: Leg. daughter Prudence Jordan; daughter Juliana; daughter Elizabeth; daughter Mary; daughter Patience; grandson William Jordan; son Robert at nineteen. Ex., Giles Driver. D. March 1, 1747. R. May 12, 1748.
    Wit: John Chestnutt, Joshua Chestnutt, Thomas Pledger.   Page 103

CARRELL, James: Estate appraised by John Hodges, William Harrison, James Piland. Signed Mary Carrell. R. May 12, 1748.                      Page 105

RICHARDS, Robert: Estate appraised by Richard Reynolds, Joseph Norsworthy, John Scammell. Signed Mary Richards. Ordered March 10, 1747. R. May 12, 1748.                                                      Page 107

HOLLOWELL, Sarah: Inventory of her estate presented by William Hollowell. R. June 9, 1748.                                                    Page 108

SMITH, Lawrence: Leg. daughter Faithy Harris; son Joseph; son Absalom; son Flood; daughter Jane; daughter Hannah; daughter Sarah; wife Jane; son Lawrence. Wife, Extx. D. June 10, 1746. R. June 9, 1748.
    Wit: Richard Holleman, James Turner, Jr., Jacob Little.
                                            Page 110

CASEY, Richard: Leg. wife Jane; daughter Ann; daughter Sarah; daughter Patience; daughter Martha; son Richard; grandson John S. Wills; daughter Ann Applewhaite; friend John Wills; daughter Martha Wills; daughter Sarah Smelley. Ex., friend John Wills. D. March 8, 1745/46. R. June 9, 1748.
    Wit: Barth'w Lightfoot, William Wills.                    Page 112

DESHEY, John: Leg. loving mother; cousin John Wrenn; cousin Mary Brantley; cousin James Wrenn; cousin Joseph Wrenn; cousin William Wrenn; cousin Elizabeth Brantley; cousin Martha Bidgood's children; cousin Francis Wrenn, in case he should not return the legacy to be given John Wrenn; cousin Joseph Webb. Mother Mary Deshey, Extx. D. October 24, 1747. R. June 9, 1748.
    Wit: Thomas Smith, William Glover, Elizabeth Smith.     Page 114

REW, John Anthony: Of Newport Parish. Leg. Jane Brown, the daughter of Samuel Brown, decd.; to Elizabeth Brown, the daughter of aforesaid; to Martha Pitt; to Sarah Pitt, the wife of Joseph Pitt; to Mary Brown, the daughter of Joseph Brown; to John Brown, the son of William Brown. D. March 21, 1746/47. R. June 9, 1748.
    Wit: William Brown, Jane Brown, Elizabeth Brown, Joseph Bridger, Jr.                                                        Page 115

DELOACH, Thomas: Leg. son Samuel; son Thomas; son Solomon; grandson Richard Deloach. Exs., sons William and Solomon Deloach. D. October 26, 1747. R. June 9, 1748.
    Wit: Robert Booth, J. Gray.                             Page 117

PAGE, William: Estate appraised by Charles Barham, Thomas Holt, Peter Butts. Signed John Fort. R. June 9, 1748.                             Page 118

EDWARDS, John: Leg. son John; daughter Ann, the cattle bought at the widow Hart's and widow Culpeper's sale; daughter Mary; wife Ann. Exs., son John and Henry Harris. Brother Nathaniel Edwards, trustee. D. April 27, 1748. R. August 11, 1748.
Wit: Chaplain Williams, Thomas Taylor, Harris Taylor.     Page 121

BIDGOOD, William, Sr.: Leg. wife Hester; son William; daughter Ann Miller; son Josiah; son John; son Richard; daughter Elizabeth. Exs., friends, Nicholas Miller, Sr. and Edward Davis, Sr. D. May 14, 1748.
Wit: John Bidgood, John Miller, Benjamin Davis.
Codicil: son Josiah to be bound to Samuel Person; son John to Robert Williams; son Richard to James Derring; and the church-wardens to place Elizabeth, where she will not suffer too much. D. August 11, 1748.
Wit: Joseph Hill, Blake Baker, Mathew Jones.     Page 123

SMITH, William: Appraised by Joseph Weston, Robert King, Robert Brown. R. August 11, 1748.     Page 127

REW, John Anthony: Estate appraised by John Pitt, Samuel Godwin, James Godwin. Signed William Brown. R. August 11, 1748.     Page 129

DAVIS, William: Estate appraised by Benjamin Clements, William Andrews, John Brown. Ordered July 6, 1745. R. August 11, 1748.     Page 130

FULGHAM, Charles: Estate appraised by Charles Chapman, John Godwin, Jonathan Godwin. Signed Charles Fulgham. R. August 11, 1748.     Page 131

DRIVER, Robert: Estate appraised by John Marshall, Jr., Joseph Bridger, Jr., John Smelley. Signed Giles Driver. R. August 11, 1748.
Page 133

PITT, Henry: Leg. son William; son Joseph Major Pitt; son Thomas; daughter Elizabeth Bagnall; daughter Ann Driver; granddaughter Lydia Benn; son Henry; daughter Patience Fulgham. Exs., son Henry Pitt and daughter Patience Fulgham. D. December 9, 1747. R. August 12, 1748.
Wit: David Williams, William Bagnall, Richard Bagnall. Page 135

JORDAN, Mathew: Leg. wife Dorothy; son Josiah; son Matthias, the land which I bought of my cousin Mathew Jordan; daughter Charity; daughter Comfort. Friends, William Harrison, George Wilson and William Hodsden to divide my estate. Wife, Extx. D. September 27, 1747. R. October 13, 1748.
Wit: William Hodsden, William Harrison, George Wilson. Page 137.

SIMMONS, James: Estate appraised by Robert Johnson, William Davis, Augustine King. Ordered August 11, 1748. R. October 13, 1748.     Page 139

DIXON, Thomas: Leg. son William, the land which I bought of Godfrey Hunt, it being the land on which my son Thomas lived; son Nicholas; daughter Martha, now the wife of Thomas Pearse; grandson Thomas Dixon; wife Penelope; daughter Penelope, the wife of Joseph Bullock; daughter Mourning, wife of Joshua Crudup; daughter Patience, wife of Jonas Shivers. Exs., wife and son Nicholas. D. April 26, 1746. R. January 12, 1748.
Wit: Joseph Meredith, Robert Walker, Henry Bullard, Florence Bullard, Mary Simmonds.     Page 141

LEE, John: Planter. Leg. son Thomas; daughter Jane. To be buried in the Bay Church Yard. Exs., Peter Fiveash, Henry Harrison. D. January 9, 1748. R. January 12, 1748.
Wit: William Harrison, Wil. Salter, Thomas Rosser.     Page 143

GARNER, James: Leg. son John; son Jesse; son Joseph; son James; daughter Sarah; daughter Olive; daughter Patience Crooms; cousin Benjamin

Garner. Exs., brother Joseph Garner and son Joseph Garner. D. July 22, 1748. R. January 12, 1748.
  Wit: John Smelley, Joseph Garner, William Godwin.  Page 144

SMITH, Hannah: Leg. brother Joseph Smith; cousin William Smith; cousin Nicholas Smith; to John Weston; to Joseph Wiles; cousin Nathaniel Parker; cousin Martha Smith; the estate of my deceased sister Martha Smith is to be divided between Nathaniel Parker and Martha Smith. Ex., Nicholas Parker. D. December 9, 1748. R. January 12, 1748.
  Wit: Joseph Weston, Edward Ballard.  Page 146

SMITH, Lawrence: Estate appraised by John Jones, John Harris, Simon Harris. Signed Jane Smith and Absalom Smith. R. January 12, 1748. Page 147

BALLARD, Peter: Estate appraised by Samuel Whitfield, Robert King, Nicholas Parker, Joseph Weston. Signed Edward Ballard. Ordered August 12, 1748. R. January 12, 1748.  Page 148

POWELL, John: Leg. son Joshua; son John; son William; son Joseph; daughter Patience Norsworthy; daughter Ann Pierce; daughter Elizabeth Johnson; wife Sarah. Exs., wife and John Darden. D. September 3, 1748. R. January 12, 1748.
  Wit: John Darden, William Watkins, William Watkins, Jr.

                    Page 149

WEBB, Richard: Of Newport Parish. Leg. wife Mary; to my children, who now live with me; refers to daughter Martha. Exs., wife and Joseph Webb. D. February 6, 1745/46. R. February 9, 1748.
  Wit: John Carey, William Glover, Samuel Webb.
  Will presented by Mary Pollard, late widow and relict of the decedent.  Page 152

BIDGOOD, William: Estate appraised by John Smith, John Chapman, Charles Chapman. Signed Nicholas Miller. R. February 9, 1748. Page 153

PITT, Henry: Estate appraised by Charles Fulgham, Thomas Whitfield, Sr., Robert King, Samuel Whitfield. Signed Henry Pitt. R. February 9, 1748.  Page 156

POWELL, John: Estate appraised by William Watkins, William Spivey, Thomas English. Signed John Darden. R. March 9, 1748. Page 158

GARNER, James: Estate appraised by Theophilus Joyner, John Garner, John Chesnutt. Signed Sarah Garner. R. March 9, 1748. Page 159

DESHEY, Mary: Leg. cousin James Wrenn; James Wrenn to pay a bequest to the two daughters of Ann Bracy, the wife of Francis Bracy; also to pay John, Joseph and William Wrenn, Mary and Elizabeth Brantley and Martha Bidgood's children; cousins, James and Joseph Jordan. Exs., cousins, James and Joseph Jordan. D. October 20, 1748. R. March 9, 1748.
  Wit: Thomas Smith, William Glover, John Chesnutt. Page 162

JOYNER, John: Of Nottoway Parish. Leg. son Solomon; daughter Elizabeth Lott (?); daughter Martha Clark; daughter Esther Beal. Ex., son Absalom. D. September 2, 1748. R. March 9, 1748.
  Wit: Chaplain Williams, Henry Crafford, William Grizard.

                    Page 163

PITT, John: Leg. son John; son Edmond; daughter Elizabeth; daughter Mary; daughter Lidia; son Joseph. Exs., brother Joseph Pitt and brother-in-law Thomas Godwin. D. November 17, 1748. R. March 9, 1748.
  Wit: Charles Fulgham, Joseph Bridger, Jr., John House. Page 164

ADAMS, David: Estate appraised by Harmon Read, William Lee, William Wommack. Signed Robert Adams. Ordered May 19, 1748. R. March 9, 1748.

Page 166

PITT, Thomas: Estate appraised by Anthony Fulgham, Giles Driver, Christopher Haines. R. March 9, 1748.

Page 167

BROCK, Robert: Estate appraised by Thomas Davis, Samuel Blow, Nathaniel Davis. Signed Lucy Brock. Ordered February 9, 1748. R. March 9, 1748.

Page 168

SMITH, Hannah: Estate appraised by Samuel Whitfield, Robert King, Joseph Copeland. Signed Nicholas Parker. Ordered January 12, 1748. R. April 18, 1749.

Page 169

WESTBROOK, James: Leg. wife Elizabeth; son Benjamin; son Jesse; brother Thomas Westbrook; friend Joshua Claud; brother-in-law, William Vaughan; to Helica, daughter of Thomas Westbrook; son Dempsey. Exs., brother John Westbrook and brother-in-law William Vaughan. D. February 24, 1748/49. R. April 13, 1749.
Wit: James Ramsey, Thomas Westbrook, Helica Westbrook. Page 170

WHITEHEAD, Arthur, Jr.: Of Nottoway Parish. Leg. son Arthur, land on Blunt's Swamp; brother Lewis Whitehead; son Lazarus; son William; son Jesse; daughter Edith; daughter Seallah; wife Patience. Exs., wife and brother Lewis Whitehead. D. January 6, 1748. R. April 13, 1749.
Wit: Arthur Whitehead, Sr., Joseph Cobb, Jr., Mary Whitehead.

Page 172

DESHEY, John: Estate appraised by Edward Goodrich, George Wilson, William Harrison, John Hodges. Signed John Wrenn. Ordered June 9, 1748. R. April 13, 1749.

Page 174

ROCHESTER, William: Of Nottoway Parish. Leg. son Joshua; daughter Ann; daughter Charity; wife Catherine. Ex., Nicholas Gurley. D. January 1, 1748/49. R. April 13, 1749.
Wit: George Gurley, James Carter, George Gurley, Jr. Page 176

POPE, Joseph: Leg. son Hardy; son John; son Joseph; son Samuel; wife Sarah and my five children. Exs., wife and Henry Crafford. D. January 27, 1748/49. R. April 13, 1749.
Wit: John Bowen, William Harris, Joseph Braches (?), Henry Pope. Page 177

WRENN, James: Estate appraised by Edward Goodrich, George Wilson, William Harrison. Signed John Wrenn. Ordered March 9, 1748. R. April 13, 1749.

Page 178

HOUSE, James: Estate appraised by Joseph Bridger, Robert Bridger, James Godwin. Ordered April 13, 1749. R. May 11, 1749.

Page 178

SMITH, Martha: Estate appraised by Joseph Copeland, Samuel Whitfield, Robert King. Signed Joseph Smith. Ordered January 12, 1748. R. May 11, 1749.

Page 179

HAWKINS, Mary: Estate appraised by Joseph Weston, Thomas Whitfield, Robert King. Signed William Hawkins. Ordered April 13, 1749. R. May 11, 1749.

Page 180

POPE, Joseph: Estate appraised by Joseph Bowen, M. Griffin, William Bulls. Signed Henry Crafford. R. May 11, 1749.

Page 182

JONES, Elizabeth: Estate appraised by Edward Goodrich, William Harrison, John Hodges. Signed Nathaniel Ridley. R. May 11, 1749.  Page 184

BROCK, Richard: Leg. daughter Mary; loving wife. D. January 17, 1748/49. R. May 11, 1749.
        Wit: Thomas Atkinson, Benjamin Britt, Richard Willis.  Page 186

JOYNER, John: Estate appraised by Henry Dawson, Joshua Dawson, James Turner. Signed Absalom Joyner. R. June 1, 1749.  Page 187

WEBB, Richard: Estate appraised by John Mallory, John Wrenn, William Glover. Ordered February 9, 1748. R. June 1, 1749.  Page 188

HARRISON, John: Estate appraised by Joseph Bridger, James Godwin, Edmond Godwin. Signed Ann Harrison. Ordered July 8, 1748. R. June 1, 1749.
        Page 189

GOODRICH, John: Leg. son Edward; son John; son George; daughter Mary Davis; to Samuel, the son of John Davis; daughter Ann Gray; daughter Honour; son George, the money in the hands of William Harrison; to wife. Exs., sons, Edward and John Goodrich. Friends, William Harrison and Samuel Wilson, overseers. D. February 6, 1746/47. R. June 1, 1749.
        Wit: George Wilson, Thomas Morgan.  Page 191

DELOACH, Thomas: Inventory returned by William and Solomon Deloach. R. July 6, 1749.  Page 193

HAINES, Edward: Estate appraised by Philip Moody, Daniel Batten, John Batten. Ordered March 9, 1748. R. July 6, 1749.  Page 194

SCOTT, Thomas: Of Newport Parish. Leg. my mother, reversion at her death to Thomas, the son of my brother James Tooke Scott; to Ann, the daughter of James Tooke Scott; to sister-in-law Christian Scott; to George Norsworthy Scott, the son of my brother, James Tooke Scott. Exs., mother Jean Scott and brother James Tooke Scott. D. January 7, 1748. R. August 3, 1749.
        Wit: James Baker, William Hollowell.  Page 195

BARLOW, Thomas: Leg. nephew William Carrell; wife Martha; daughter Ann; son Jesse; daughter Mary. Exs., wife and nephew William Carrell. D. December 3, 1748. R. August 3, 1749.
        Wit: R. Hardy, Peter Fiveash, James Piland.  Page 196

PEDIN, James: My body to be buried in or at the "Brick Church" of Isle of Wight County. Leg. wife Mary, during her good behaviour; daughter Ann, which was given to her by her aunt, Mrs. Williams; son James; daughter Mary. Extx., wife Mary, if she fails to conduct herself wisely, my children to be placed in the care of the Rev. Mr. John Reid, Minister in Newport Parish. To brother John Pedin, Merchant in Mauchtine (?). D. April 15, 1746. R. August 3, 1749.
        Wit: John Applewhaite, William Hawkins.  Page 198

MILLER, John: Estate appraised by Benjamin Hodges, John Gibbs, John Murry. R. August 3, 1749.  Page 200

PITT, John: Estate appraised by James Godwin, Samuel Godwin, Charles Fulgham. Signed Joseph Pitt. R. August 3, 1749.  Page 200

LEE, John: Estate appraised by William Hodsden, George Wilson, Robert Hodges. Signed Peter Fiveash and Henry Harrison. Ordered January 12, 1748. R. August 3, 1749.  Page 202

DESHEY, Mary: Estate appraised by John Mallory, John Davis, Joseph Jones. Signed James Jordan. R. August 3, 1749. Page 204

FOWLER, William: Of the Parish of Newport. Leg. grandson William Fowler; son Samuel; son Joseph; daughter Ann Bryant; son James; granddaughter Ann Fowler, daughter of Arthur Fowler; son Edmond; wife Rebeccah. Ex., son Arthur Fowler. D. December 31, 1748. R. August 3, 1749.
Wit: John Darden, Hardy Darden, James Holland. Page 205

FOWLER, William: Estate appraised by John Lawrence, William Lawrence, William Edmonds. Signed Arthur Fowler. R. September 9, 1749.
Page 206

ROBINSON, James: Inventory of estate, returned by Jonathan Robinson. R. September 7, 1749. Page 208

DAVIS, Samuel, Gent.: Estate appraised by John Goodrich, J. Day, Peter Woodward. Signed Henry Harrison, Lawrence Smith, John Inman. Ordered February 28, 1739. R. September 7, 1749. Page 209

DAVIS, Samuel: Account estate, paid legacy to Samuel Davis, to cash, being the property of Amy Jones, raised out of the stock, for the payment of a legacy to John Davis. Signed Joseph and Amy Jones. Examined by Robert Burwell and William Hodsden. R. September 7, 1749. Page 211

DAUGHTRY, John: Leg. wife Margaret; to my lawful heir. Extx., wife Margaret Daughtry. D. April 28, 1742. R. October 5, 1749.
Wit: Jesse Browne, William Moore, William Lawrence. Page 213

LUCKS, John: Estate appraised by Charles Portlock, Nicholas Casey, Robert Hodges. Signed John Hodges. Ordered June 9, 1748. R. October 5, 1749. Page 214

BREWER, William, Sr.: Of Newport Parish. Leg. wife Catherine; son George; daughter Mary; daughter Sarah; daughter Elizabeth; daughter Christian; son Michael; son William; son John. Exs., wife and son George Brewer. D. February 24, 1748/49. R. October 5, 1749.
Wit: Robert Whitfield, Johnson Corbett, Samuel Corbett.
Page 216

GIBBS, Ralph: Account estate, examined by Hugh Giles and Richard Reynolds. R. December 7, 1749. Page 217

GILES, Hugh, Sr.: Estate appraised by Richard Reynolds, Joseph Norsworthy, Lemuel Godwin. Ordered August 3, 1749. Signed Mary Pedin. R. December 7, 1749. Page 218

BREWER, William: Estate appraised by William Lawrence, John Lawrence, William Edmonds. Signed George Brewer. Ordered October 5, 1749. R. December 7, 1749. Page 220

DRIVER, Robert: Account estate, examined by Richard Reynolds and Richard Jordan. R. December 7, 1749. Page 221

HARRISON, William: Account estate, examined by Nicholas Parker and Robert King. R. December 7, 1749. Page 222

BIDGOOD, William: Account estate. Nicholas Miller and Edward Davis, Exs. To paid Reuben Proctor, the balance of his uncle's estate in Bidgood's possession; paid John Bidgood, the balance of Ann Proctor; to Ambrose Proctor; to the orphans of Walter Morgan. R. January 4, 1749.
Page 223

JOHNSON, James: Estate appraised by Hardy Council, John Darden, Hardy
   Darden. Signed Rebecca Johnson. R. January 4, 1749.          Page 224

WILLIFORD, John, Jr.: Account estate, signed by Elizabeth Williford. R.
   January 4, 1749.                                             Page 227

BARLOW, Thomas: Estate appraised by William Harrison, Henry Harrison,
   George Wilson. Signed by Martha Barlow. R. January 4, 1749.
                                                                Page 227

GARNER, James: Account estate, examined by Thomas Gale, Bartholomew Lightfoot, John Marshall. R. January 4, 1749.                     Page 229

JORDAN, Mathew, Jr.: Account estate, examined by James Baker, Lawrence
   Baker, Jordan Thomas. R. February 1, 1749.                   Page 231

CARRELL, James: Account estate, examined by Lawrence Baker and R. Hardy.
   R. February 1, 1749.                                         Page 231

WRENN, John: Account estate, examined by James Baker. Signed by N. Bourden
   and Prudence, his wife. R. March 1, 1749.                    Page 233

MILLER, Nicholas: Estate appraised by Joseph Hill, Charles Chapman, John
   Gibbs. Ordered January 4, 1749. Signed Alice Miller. R. March 1,
   1749.                                                        Page 234

CHAPMAN, Charles: Leg. daughter Rachel; daughter Ann; daughter Reodia.
   Ex., Thomas Parker. D. August 10, 1749. R. March 1, 1749.
      Wit: Timothy Low, West Gross.
   Thomas Parker refused to be executor, Joseph Chapman qualified.
                                                                Page 235

CARRELL, Mary: Leg. son Thomas; my children, Mary, James and Richard to
   live with their brother Thomas Carrell. Lawrence Baker and Richard
   Hardy, trustees. D. November 6, 1749. R. March 1, 1749.
      Wit: Richard Carter, Martha Barlow, Elizabeth Gray.       Page 236

DAUGHTRY, John: Inventory, returned by Margaret Daughtry. R. March 1, 1749.
                                                                Page 237

JONES, Thomas: Of the Parish of Newport. Leg. son Thomas; son William;
   daughter Mary Inglish; daughter Ann Johnson, the estate, which I have
   brought to my son-in-law, Abraham Johnson; daughter Catherine Griffin;
   daughter Sarah Johnson; daughter Martha Johnson; son Philip. Ex.,
   son Philip Jones. D. November 15, 1748. R. March 1, 1749.
      Wit: John Darden, James Johnson, Jr., Henry Hedgepath. Page 238

JORDAN, Joshua: Account estate, examined by Edmond Godwin and John Monro.
   R. March 1, 1749.                                            Page 239

JOHNSON, James: Thomas Gale, John Eley and James Bridger were appointed to
   set apart the dower of Rebecca Johnson in the estate of her husband.
   R. March 1, 1749.                                            Page 240

MACY, Thomas: Estate appraised by Benjamin Clements, John Brown, Henry
   Simmons. Ordered April 28, 1740. R. April 5, 1750.           Page 240

BROWN, Charles: Estate appraised by Charles Simmons, William Andrews,
   John Brown. Signed Richard Kirby, Jr. Ordered February 12, 1746.
   R. April 5, 1750.                                            Page 242

WHITFIELD, William: Nuncupative will, proven by Holland Copeland. That he left his whole estate to his eldest son, Isham Whitfield.  R. April 5, 1750.                                                                      Page 244

CARRELL, Mary: Estate appraised by James Piland, Henry Harrison, Samuel Wilson.  Signed T. Carrell.  R. April 4, 1750.                      Page 245

MUNDELL, Frances: Of Nottoway Parish.  Leg. son John Scott; son William Scott; son John Mundell, the negro left me by my brother.  Ex., son William Scott.  D. May 20, 1747.  R. April 5, 1750.
          Wit: Charles Travers, Amos Garris, William Carrell.    Page 246

CHAPMAN, Charles: Estate appraised by Richard Reynolds, John Godwin, Jonathan Godwin.  Signed Joseph Chapman.  R. June 7, 1750.    Page 247

GREGORY, Robert: Estate appraised by John Gibbs, Edward Davis, Joseph Hill. Signed Charles Chapman.  Ordered December 7, 1749.  R. June 7, 1750.
                                                                   Page 248

ELEY, Eley: Account estate, signed by William and Ann Joiner.  Examined by William Hodsden and R. Hardy.  R. June 7, 1750.               Page 249

JONES, Thomas: Estate appraised by John Darden, Robert Eley, John Roberts. Signed Philip Jones.  R. July 5, 1750.                            Page 250

WAINWRIGHT, William: Estate appraised by Richard Reynolds, Thomas Wills, Joseph Norsworthy.  Signed Elizabeth Wainwright.  Ordered October 5, 1749.  R. July 5, 1750.                                          Page 252

WILLIAMS, William: Estate appraised by Benjamin Beal, Needham Nolley, Samuel Mathews.  Signed John Mariner.  Ordered June 7, 1750.  R. July 5, 1750.                                                         Page 252

SIMMONS, James: Account estate, examined by Thomas Gale, John Eley, James Bridger.  Signed Philip Moody.  R. July 5, 1750.             Page 253

APPLEWHAITE, Henry, Jr.: Account estate, returned by Philip and Mary Brantley.  R. July 5, 1750.                                          Page 255

JORDAN, Mathew, Jr.: James Baker and Jordan Thomas were appointed to set apart the dower of Patience Jordan, the widow of said Mathew Jordan, Jr.  R. July 5, 1750.                                          Page 255

PITT, Henry: Account estate, examined by Edmond Godwin, Charles Fulgham, Thomas Whitfield.  R. July 5, 1750.                             Page 256

WHITFIELD, William: Estate appraised by George Norsworthy, Nicholas Parker, Robert King.  R. July 5, 1750.                                Page 257

WESTBROOK, James: Account estate, examined by Joshua Claud, Thomas Clifton, John Person, Jr.  Signed by John Westbrook and William Vaughan.  R. July 5, 1750.                                                       Page 258

WESTON, Joseph: Leg. daughter Mary; daughter Tabitha; wife Mary; daughter Ann Smith.  Wife, Extx.  D. September 24, 1748.  R. September 6, 1750.
          Wit: Charles Fulgham, Moses Wiles.                       Page 259

DAVIS, John: Leg. son Samuel; nephew William Goodrich.  Ex., John Goodrich. D. July 2, 1750.  R. September 6, 1750.
          Wit: Edward Goodrich, John Davis, William Davis.        Page 260

HARDING, Sarah: Leg. son Benjamin; grandson John Harding, son of Benjamin Harding; grandson Abraham Harding, son of James Harding; daughter

Martha Jordan, the wife of John Jordan; daughter Sarah Gray, the wife of Henry Gray. Ex., son Solomon Harding. D. January 6, 1747. R. September 6, 1750.
    Wit: Arthur Crocker, Thomas Cole, William Cofer.     Page 261

JOLLY, John: Estate appraised by John Smelly, Thomas Norsworthy, Christopher Reynolds. Signed Ann Jolly. Ordered June 7, 1750. R. September 6, 1750.    Page 262

DARDEN, Jacob: Estate appraised by John Baldwin, Christopher Reynolds, John Butler. Signed Elizabeth Darden. Ordered July 5, 1750. R. September 6, 1750.    Page 264

DAVIS, William: Account estate, examined by Edmond Godwin, Jordan Thomas. Signed J. Simmons. R. September 6, 1750.    Page 267

CHESNUTT, John: Estate appraised by Christopher Reynolds, John Powell, Bartholomew Lightfoot. Signed Martha Chesnutt. Ordered July 5, 1750. R. September 6, 1750.    Page 268

DICKINSON, Jacob: Leg. wife Mary; son Christopher; daughter Chasity; daughter Celia, provision for unborn child. D. February 7, 1749/50. R. September 6, 1750.
    Wit: Thomas Willis, John Godwin, Robert Bevan.    Page 269

DERING, Nicholas: Account estate, to James Samson's orphans, their legacies, paid to William Miller; to Ann Diamond for schooling my sister; legacies paid to son James, son Miles and daughter Susanna. Signed James Dering. Examined by James Baker and Lawrence Baker. R. October 4, 1750.    Page 272

MILLER, Nicholas: William Hodsden, Robert Tynes and William Hollowell, appointed to set aside the dower of Alice Miller, widow of said Nicholas Miller. R. October 4, 1750.    Page 274

SIMMONS, James: John Eley, James Bridger and John Marshall, appointed to set aside the dower of Ann Simmons, the widow of James Simmons. R. October 4, 1750.    Page 274

DENSON, William: Leg. daughter Elizabeth Eley; son Edmond; son William, negroes, whom I leave in the care of my friend William Eley; granddaughter Amy Eley; friend Hannah Best; son John; grandson Benjamin Eley; wife Ann. Friend Exum Scott to have the care of my son William. Wife Ann, Extx. D. July 2, 1750. R. October 4, 1750.
    Wit: William Eley, James Arthur, Miles Wills.    Page 274

DAY, Daniel: Leg. wife Mary. Exs., wife and George Taylor. D. May 19, 1750. R. November 1, 1750.
    Wit: Robert Eley, George Taylor, Edward Taylor, Joseph Taylor.
    Page 275

ELEY, Robert, Sr.: Leg. son Gale, the land I bought of Mary Parker; son Robert; wife Allis; daughter Amy; daughter Martha; daughter Rebecca; daughter Allis Darden. Exs., wife and son Gale Eley. D. March 29, 1750. R. November 1, 1750.
    Wit: John Roberts, Thomas Roberts, Henry Saunders.    Page 276

WESTON Joseph: Inventory, presented by Mary Weston. R. November 1, 1750.
    Page 278

GODWIN, Sarah: Leg. loving aunt Mary Dickinson; to Chastity Dickinson; to Sally Dickinson. Ex., aunt Mary Dickinson. D. August 23, 1750.

R. November 1, 1750.
Wit: Richard Reynolds, John Godwin, Wilkinson Parker.     Page 279

WILLIAMS, Richard:  Estate appraised by Joseph Cobb, Thomas Cranshaw,
Nathan Vasser. R. December 6, 1750.  Account estate of Richard
Williams, which is divided into eight parts, "due to each child,"
examined by J. Baker and Isaac Fleming. R. December 6, 1750.
Page 281

GAY, Thomas:  Leg. son Thomas; son John; son Charles; daughter Mary; son
William; son Edmond; son Jonathan. The "Monthly Meeting" to settle
my children. Ex., William Eley. D. October 26, 1750. R. December 6,
1750.
Wit: John Williams, Richard Pope, Mary Coggan.     Page 282

DAVIS, John:  Estate appraised by John Mallory, William Glover, George Wilson.
Signed John Goodrich. Ordered September 6, 1750. R. December 6, 1750.
Page 284

DELOACH, Thomas:  Estate appraised by Francis Ward, Benjamin Ward, Thomas
Copher. Ordered September 6, 1750. R. February 7, 1750. Account
estate, to searching for the said Thomas Deloach in Blackwater Swamp.
To paid John Bryant for dividing for him. Signed John Deloach. R.
February 7, 1750.     Page 285

WHITEHEAD, Arthur, Jr.:  Estate appraised by Joseph Cobb, Jr., John Pope,
Thomas Crenshaw. Signed by Lewis Whitehead, Patience Jones, T. Jones.
Estate account in North Carolina, Signed Lewis Whitehead, Patience
Jones and Thomas Jones. R. February 7, 1750.     Page 288

DENSON, William:  Estate appraised by Henry Saunders, Josiah Jordan, James
Hough. Signed Ann Denson. R. February 7, 1750.     Page 291

WESTRAY, Elizabeth:  Widow. Leg. son William the plantation devised to me
by the will of John Mackmial; daughter Eunice; daughter Martha; son
Robert; son Benjamin, to be placed with John Westray, Jr.; son William
with Thomas Harris; daughter Eunice with my mother, Elizabeth Nelms;
daughter Martha, with my sister Mary Corbett. Ex., John Westray, Jr.
D. November 28, 1750. R. February 7, 1750.
Wit: William Eley, John Westray, Patience Westray.     Page 293

POPE, William:  Estate appraised by Ratclif Boon, Jr., John Wheeler, William
Segrave. Signed John Pope. Ordered December 6, 1750. R. February 7,
1750.     Page 295

LAWRENCE, Margaret:  Leg. son John; son William; granddaughter Penelope
Lawrence; daughter Priscilla; daughter Elizabeth; grandson Robert
Carr; daughter Margaret Daughtry; daughter Sarah Moore; son William.
Ex., son John Lawrence. D. September 26, 1746. R. February 7, 1750.
Wit: William Driver, John Loyd, Giles Smelly.     Page 296

CROCKER, Arthur:  Estate appraised by Peter Woodward, Thomas Copher, William
Copher. Ordered December 6, 1750. R. February 7, 1750.     Page 298

GODWIN, James:  Leg. son Joseph; son James; daughter Martha. Exs., wife
Elizabeth and brother Samuel Godwin. D. October 1, 1750. R. February
7, 1750.
Wit: Thomas Willis, James Pitt.     Page 300

DICKINSON, Jacob:  Estate appraised by Jonathan Godwin, John Godwin, Joseph
Norsworthy. Signed Mary Dickinson. R. February 7, 1750.     Page 301

CHAPMAN, Charles: Account estate, examined by Richard Reynolds and Joseph Norsworthy. Signed Joseph Chapman. R. February 7, 1750. Page 302

WHITEHEAD, Arthur, Jr.: Account estate, examined by Thomas Jarrell, Jesse Browne and A. Jones. R. March 7, 1750. Page 303

EDWARDS, John: Estate appraised by Arthur Whitehead, Chaplain Williams, John Edwards. Signed John Edwards and Henry Harris. Inventory of estate in North Carolina filed. Ordered August 11, 1748. R. March 7, 1750. Page 304

CROOM, Edward: Estate appraised by Thomas Norsworthy, John Smelly, John Newman. Signed Patience Croom. Ordered January 7, 1750. R. March 7, 1750. Page 306

CROCKER, Katherine: Estate appraised by Peter Woodward, Thomas Copher, Francis Ward. Signed Anthony Crocker. Ordered February 7, 1750. R. March 7, 1750. Page 308

ELEY, Robert: Estate appraised by James Hough, Robert Cogan, John Cogan. Signed Alice Eley. R. March 7, 1750. Page 309

MILLER, Alice: Leg. son George; daughter Martha; son Thomas. Ex., son George Miller. D. January 16, 1750. R. March 7, 1750.
    Wit: William Hollowell, James Tooke Scott, John Gibbs. Page 312

DAY, Daniel: Estate appraised by Abraham Johnson, James Johnson, John Roberts. Signed Mary Day and George Taylor. R. March 7, 1750.
Page 313

DANIEL, William: Leg. son Peter; son William; son John; daughter Mary Rite; daughter Sarah Barrett; daughter Deberry Lucas; daughter Ann; daughter Garland; son James. Wife, Deborah, Extx. D. September 10, 1738. R. March 7, 1750.
    Wit: John Darden, Mary Darden. Page 315

INGLISH, John: Leg. daughter Ann; daughter Mary; daughter Charity. Wife Mary, Extx. D. November 13, 1750. R. March 7, 1750.
    Wit: William Watkins, Jr., Jesse Watkins, Jacob Spivey.
Page 318

COUNCIL, Hardy: Of Newport Parish. Leg. wife Susannah; daughter Mary; daughter Ann; daughter Martha; daughter Lucy; son Hardy, 100 acres on which John Sherard, Jr., now lives; son Charles; son Michael, land in North Carolina; daughter Susannah; daughter Christian; son Joshua. Exs., wife Susannah and son Charles Council. D. February 22, 1748/49. R. March 7, 1750.
    Wit: Jacob Dickinson, Robert Johnson, Hardy Lawrence. Page 319

JONES, Mathew: Settlement of estate; to James Ridley, his part of his father's estate; to Dr. Browne, for his wife's share; to Mr. Portlock for his wife's share; to Francis Jones for his wife's share. R. March 7, 1750. Page 322

JARRELL, Thomas: Inventory presented by Thomas Jarrell. R. April 4, 1751.
Page 322

BROWN, Charles: Account estate, examined by Benjamin Simmons and Charles Simmons. Signed Richard Kirby, Jr. R. April 4, 1751. Page 323

GAY, Thomas: Estate appraised by Robert Coggan, John Coggan, Richard Sellaway. Signed William Eley. R. April 4, 1751. Page 324

WILLS, Thomas: Of Newport Parish. Leg. son Miles; son John; son Josiah; wife Martha. Extx., wife. D. October 18, 1750. R. April 4, 1751.
Wit: John Wills, Miles Milner, Mary Milner.                    Page 326

DICKINSON, Jacob: Account estate, examined by Thomas Gale, Charles Fulgham and Richard Reynolds. R. April 4, 1751.                    Page 328

INGLISH, John: Estate appraised by William Watkins, Hardy Darden, Jesse Watkins. Signed Mary Inglish. R. April 4, 1751.                    Page 330

MILLER, Alice: Estate appraised by William Harrison, Benjamin Hodges, John Gibbs. Signed George Miller. R. April 4, 1751.                    Page 332

MINARD, George: Account estate, examined by Charles Fulgham. Signed Ann Minard. R. April 4, 1751.                    Page 333

REW, John Anthony: Account estate, examined by John Rodway, Charles Fulgham. Signed William Brown. R. May 2, 1751.                    Page 335

SHELLEY, Thomas: Leg. wife Jane; daughter Elizabeth; son James; daughter Martha; daughter Ann; son Thomas, the plantation on which James Briggs formerly lived. Exs., wife and son James Shelley. D. March 8, 1750. R. May 2, 1751.
Wit: Lawrence Baker, Joseph Figg, Katherine Baker, Ann Baker.
Page 336

GAY, Thomas: Account estate, examined by Thomas Gale and John Marshall. Signed William Eley. R. May 2, 1751.                    Page 337

RICHARDS, Robert: Account estate, examined by Richard Reynolds and John Applewhaite. R. May 2, 1751.                    Page 339

MILLER, George: Leg. brother Thomas; sister Martha. Ex., brother Thomas Miller. D. April 14, 1751. R. May 2, 1751.
Wit: William Brown, Reuben Proctor, Mary Pate.                    Page 340

HOLLEMAN, John: Leg. son Jesse; son Jeddia; son Christopher; daughter Mary. Wife Elizabeth, Extx. D. October 12, 1750. R. June 6, 1751.
Wit: William Gwaltney, Thomas Gwaltney.                    Page 341

SHELLEY, Thomas: Estate appraised by James Dering, Arthur Davis, Thomas Carrell. R. June 6, 1751.                    Page 342

UZZELL, Thomas: Of Newport Parish. Leg. daughter Martha; son James; son Thomas; wife Sarah; daughter Elizabeth Newman; daughter Mary Lowry. Exs., wife and sons, Thomas and James Uzzell. D. April 14, 1748. R. June 6, 1751.
Wit: John Smelly, Theophilus Joiner, Bartholomew Lightfoot.
Page 345

LANE, William: Estate appraised by Samson West, George Smith, George Whitley. R. June 6, 1751.                    Page 346

DAVIS, Samuel: Leg. my mother Amey Jones, my plantation at Meherrin; sister Mary White; cousin Ann White; cousin Mary White; sister Sarah; sister Amey; sister Marcella. Ex., my father-in-law. D. November 28, 1750. R. June 6, 1751.
Wit: John Davis, Sarah Davis, Amy Davis.                    Page 348

WILLIAMS, Mathew: Estate appraised by Thomas Parker, Joseph Copeland, Giles Driver. Signed Nicholas Parker. Ordered March 7, 1750. R. June 6, 1751.                    Page 349

KING, Robert: Estate appraised by Nicholas Parker, Samuel Whitfield, Thomas Parker. Signed Elizabeth King. Ordered April 4, 1751. R. June 6, 1751.                                                                      Page 350

HOLLEMAN, John: Estate appraised by Peter Woodward, Thomas Copher, Thomas Cole. Signed Elizabeth Holleman. R. August 1, 1751.        Page 352

UZZELL, Thomas: Estate appraised by Bartholomew Lightfoot, Christopher Reynolds, John Joyner. Signed James Uzzell and Thomas Uzzell. R. August 1, 1751.                                                               Page 354

COOK, Reuben: Leg. son John; son Benjamin; son Joel; son Nathan; daughter Ann Whitehead; daughter Hannah; daughter Thamer; wife Hannah; son William. Ex., son Joel Cook. D. November 19, 1750. R. August 1, 1751.
          Wit: Lawrence Lancaster, Thomas Betts.                 Page 355

GOODWIN, Lemuel: Estate appraised by Nicholas Parker, Joseph Copeland, Anthony Fulgham, Charles Fulgham. Ordered April 4, 1751. R. August 1, 1751. Signed Mary Goodwin.                                   Page 357

WESTRAY, Elizabeth: Estate appraised by Arthur Turner, Daniel Batten, John Batten. Signed John Westray, Jr. R. September 5, 1751.
                                                                 Page 359

SUMMERELL, John: Account estate, examined by William Hodsden, John Applewhaite, Charles Fulgham. Signed Catherine Giles, administrator of Hugh Giles, who was the executor of the said John Summerell. R. September 5, 1751.                                               Page 361

DAY, Thomas: Leg. wife Mary; son Thomas; son John. Exs., wife, Mr. William Hodsden and Major Benjamin Cocke. D. July 24, 1750. R. October 3, 1751.
          Wit: William Harrison, James Wheadon.                 Page 363

GROSS, Francis: Of Newport Parish. Leg. daughter Patience; son Joshua; daughter Hannah; son Thomas Davis Gross; son Jonathan; daughter Sarah Bevan, the wife of Robert Bevan. Exs., son Joshua Gross and daughter Patience Gross. D. September 18, 1750. R. October 3, 1751.
          Wit: Hugh Giles, West Gross.                          Page 365

WILLS, Thomas: Estate appraised by Arthur Applewhaite, Richard Reynolds, John Smelly. Signed Martha Wills. R. October 3, 1751.       Page 367

WEST, Richard: Estate appraised by Richard Reynolds, John Clark, Augustine King. Signed Robert West. Ordered September 5, 1751. R. October 3, 1751.                                                             Page 369

MILLER, Nicholas: Account estate, examined by James Tooke Scott, William Hodsden, William Hollowell. R. October 3, 1751.             Page 371

ROCHESTER, William: Estate appraised by Micajah Edwards, Henry Thomas, Arthur Williams. Signed Nicholas Gurley. R. October 3, 1751.
                                                                 Page 372

BRIDGER, Joseph: Leg. grandson John Davis Bridger; son James; brother Robert Bridger; son William; granddaughter Mary, the daughter of my son Joseph Bridger; granddaughter Keziah Bridger; granddaughter Sarah Bridger; granddaughter Ann Bridger; granddaughter Hester Bridger; daughter Martha Jones; daughter Margaret Goodrich; daughter Mary; daughter Agatha; daughter Katherine. Exs., sons-in-law, John Goodrich and Joseph Jones. D. September 5, 1751. R. October 4, 1751.

Wit: George Reynolds, Hester Whitfield, Ann Giles.    Page 373

MACKOY, Caleb: Estate appraised by Richard Reynolds, Samson West, John
Clark. Signed Martha Mackoy. Ordered August 1, 1751. R. October 4,
1751.                                                      Page 374

BULLOCK, Joseph: Leg. wife Penelope; son Willis; son Thomas. Wife, Extx.
D. March 10, 1750/51. R. November 7, 1751.
        Wit: William Howell, John Newman.                 Page 377

COOK, Reuben: Estate appraised by Peter Woodward, Thomas Coffer, Anthony
Crocker. R. November 7, 1751.                             Page 377

GROSS, Francis: Estate appraised by Richard Reynolds, Jonathan Godwin,
John Godwin. Signed Joshua Gross. R. November 7, 1751.   Page 380

GILES, Captain Hugh: Estate appraised by Jonathan Godwin, John Godwin,
Samson West. Signed by Katherine Giles. Ordered April 4, 1751. R.
November 7, 1751.                                         Page 381

HAINES, Edward: Account estate, to cash received in Gloucester County.
Signed Sarah Haines.                                      Page 383

WHITLEY, Thomas: Estate appraised by John Clark, John Goodrich, Joseph
Norsworthy. Ordered April 4, 1751. R. November 7, 1751.  Page 383

GRAY, Aaron: Estate appraised by Nicholas Parker, Joseph Hawkins, Henry
King. Signed Sarah Gray. R. November 7, 1751.            Page 384

WOMBWELL, Joseph: Account estate, examined by R. Kello, Samuel Blow,
Etel'd Taylor. R. November 7, 1751.                       Page 387

MILLER, George: Estate appraised by Benjamin Hodges, John Gibbs, Charles
Chapman. R. November 7, 1751.                             Page 388

CARRELL, Mary: Account estate, examined by Richard Hardy and Henry Harrison.
Among items, the amount of Mr. James Carrell's personal estate. Signed
Thomas Carrell. R. December 4, 1751.                      Page 389

BULLOCK, Joseph: Estate appraised by William Bullock, Benjamin Beal,
Thomas Pledger. Signed Penelope Bullock. R. December 5, 1751.
                            .                             Page 390

ALLEN, Joseph: Estate appraised by Benjamin Crocker, Henry Vaughan, John
Jones. Signed Mary Booth, late Allen, and William Bynum, who was
security for due administration on the estate. Account estate, among
items, to James Allen to Thomas Tabour, to Judy Tabour, late Allen.
R. December 5, 1751.                                      Page 392

TURNER, Thomas: Estate appraised by Daniel Herring, Henry Johnson, Robert
Johnson. Signed Martha Turner. Ordered September 5, 1751. R. February 6, 1752.                                            Page 393

NORSWORTHY, George: Leg. wife Rachel; reversion of bequest to nephew
William Norsworthy, the son of my brother Tristram Norsworthy. Ex.,
my son-in-law Thomas Parker. D. October 14, 1751. R. February 6,
1751.
        Wit: Mary Norsworthy, Nicholas Parker.            Page 397

SELLAWAY, John: Leg. granddaughter Martha Sellaway. Ex., son John Sellaway.
D. December 10, 1751. R. February 6, 1752.
        Wit: Jesse Watkins, William Eley, Edmund Westray.  Page 398

TOMLIN, John, Sr.: Leg. son John; son Joseph; my mother. Exs., wife
Martha and son James Tomlin. D. August 6, 1750. R. February 6, 1752.
    Wit: Daniel Herring, John Harris, Martha Tomlin.     Page 399

PEDIN, Mary: Of Newport Parish. Leg. daughter Ann; son James; daughter
Mary. Friend Anthony Holladay of Nansemond County to have the care
of my children and to be my executor. D. October 24, 1751. R. February 6, 1752.
    Wit: Sarah Bridger, Samson West, Ann Giles.     Page 401

POWELL, Thomas: Leg. son Godfrey; wife Sarah; daughter Ann Cogan. Ex.,
son Godfrey Powell. D. February 28, 1750. R. February 6, 1752.
    Wit: John Marshall, Ann Marshall, Martha Howell.     Page 402

WEST, Ann: Leg. daughter Ann; son James; son Robert. Ex., son Robert West.
D. December 19, 1750. R. February 6, 1752.
    Wit: John Wills, Jr., Priscilla Hall.     Page 403

WESTRAY, Elizabeth: Account estate, examined by Philip Moody, William Eley,
John Marshall. Among items, paid Patience Westray. Signed John Westray, Jr. R. February 16, 1752.     Page 404

APPLEWHAITE, John: Account estate, examined by William Ponsonby and Arthur
Applewhaite. To paid Edward Cruise and Thomas Pope for schooling.
R. February 6, 1752.     Page 405

WEST, Robert: Leg. son Richard, land adjoining Merchant Perry; son Ralph;
sister Ann West; brother James West. Ex., brother Giles West. D.
September 19, 1751. R. February 6, 1752.
    Wit: Joshua Hunter, Jacemy West, Sarah Gibbs.     Page 405

DAY, Thomas: Estate appraised by George Wilson, William Harrison, Joseph
Jones. R. February 6, 1752.     Page 407

WHITLEY, Thomas: Account estate, examined by Richard Reynolds and Joseph
Norsworthy. R. February 6, 1752.     Page 409

POWELL, Thomas: Estate appraised by Benjamin Beale, John Garner, John
Burt. Signed Godfrey Powell. R. February 6, 1752.     Page 410

SELLAWAY, John: Estate appraised by Daniel Herring, John Saunders, Henry
Saunders. R. March 5, 1752.    ·     Page 413

WEST, Everett: Estate appraised by Joshua Hunter, William Brown, Bartholomew
Lightfoot. Ordered August 1, 1751. R. March 5, 1752.     Page 416

WARD, Benjamin: Estate appraised by Peter Woodward, Thomas Coffer, Richard
Jones. Signed Sarah Ward. Ordered February 6, 1752. R. March 5,
1752.     Page 417

PLEDGER, Thomas: Leg. son Thomas; wife Mary; daughter Martha; daughter Ann;
daughter Mourning. Exs., wife and son Thomas Pledger. D. January 26,
1752. R. March 5, 1752.
    Wit: Charles Chesnutt, Thomas Norsworthy, Benjamin Hampton.
     Page 418

MCKOY, Caleb: Account estate, examined by Richard Reynolds, John Clark,
Thomas Miller. R. March 5, 1752.     Page 419

SMITH, Thomas: Leg. wife Elizabeth; son Thomas; daughter Sarah; son Arthur,
land including that on which John Summerell and William Wainwright
formerly lived. Exs., wife and brother Arthur Smith. D. March 31,

1748. R. March 5, 1752.
    Wit: William Hodsden, John Wrenn, Jeremiah Proctor.    Page 422

KING, Captain Robert: Estate examined by Samuel Whitfield, Nicholas Parker.
R. March 5, 1752.    Page 423

BRASSIE, William: Of the Parish of Newport. Leg. son John; son William;
son Nathan; son Jesse; wife Susannah. D. December 14, 1751. R. June
4, 1752.
    Wit: William Edwards, Robert Edwards.    Page 424

PURSELL, Phillip: Leg. brother-in-law John Fulgham; to his son John Fulgham;
sister Mary Fulgham; to her daughter Patience Fulgham; sister Sarah
Johnson; sister Patience Exum; sister Elizabeth Turner; sister Ann;
sister Joan; sister Martha. Ex., brother Arthur Pursell. D. January
3, 1752. R. June 4, 1752.
    Wit: John Fulgham, Anthony Fulgham.    Page 425

RODWAY, John: Leg. daughter Patience Brown; wife Susannah; daughter Mary;
daughter Susannah. Wife, Extx. D. March 11, 1750/51. R. June 4,
1752.
    Wit: Charles Fulgham, Nathaniel Hunt, Richard House.    Page 427

WEST, Robert: Estate appraised by Augustine King, Richard Reynolds, George
Whitley. Signed Giles West. Ordered February 6, 1752. R. June 4,
1752.    Page 428

DRIVER, Edward: Additional account estate, examined by Richard Reynolds
and Joseph Norsworthy. D. June 4, 1752.    Page 430

WILLIS, Thomas: Leg. brother Robert Willis; brother John Willis in Scotland;
wife Martha; to George, the son of Robert Willis, attorney at law. Exs.,
friends, John Woodrop, James Arthur, William Hodsden. D. December 6,
1750. R. June 4, 1752.
    Wit: Samuel Wentworth, Joseph Baker, P. Billings, Edward Archer.
    Page 430

SMITH, Thomas: Estate appraised by Edward Goodrich, William Harrison,
William Glover. R. June 4, 1752.    Page 432

BENN, Captain James: Estate account, examined by Thomas Applewhaite and
Charles Fulgham. R. June 4, 1752.    Page 435

DAUGHTRY, William, Sr.: Leg. son John; with reversion of bequest to his
son Moses, if without heirs to his brother Benjamin; daughter Priscilla
Hedgepeth; daughter Mary Holland; grandson William Holland; daughter
Elizabeth Parker; grandson John Daughtry, Jr. Ex., grandson John
Daughtry, Jr. D. December 24, 1751. R. July 2, 1752.
    Wit: Robert Whitfield, Charles Darden, Richard Daughtry.
    Page 436

PORTLOCK, Charles: Leg. son Nathaniel; son Charles; loving wife. D.
February 15, 1750. R. July 2, 1752.
    Wit:---------------------.    Page 439

PIERCE, John: Of Newport Parish. Leg. daughter Elizabeth; daughter
Mourning; John Segraves, the son of Susanna Seagraves; wife Esther.
Exs., friends, William Pierce and Charles Norsworthy. D. December 19,
1751. R. July 2, 1752.
    Wit: James Bridger, Robert Coggan, Amy Pierce.    Page 440

HOUSE, James: Estate appraised by Samuel Holladay, Joseph Wail, William

CROCKER, Edward: Leg. son William; daughter Martha Hadley; grandson Joseph Crocker. Ex., son Thomas Crocker. D. September 24, 1751. R. July 2, 1752.
      Wit: Henry Mitchel, Charles Chapman. Page 442

POPE, Joseph: Account estate, examined by R. Kello and Jordan Thomas. Among items, expense for Samuel and John Pope. Signed Henry Crafford. R. July 2, 1752. Page 443

TYNES, Timothy: Leg. son Robert; grandson Timothy, the son of Robert Tynes; wife Elizabeth. Exs., wife and son Thomas Tynes. D. August 26, 1747. R. August 6, 1752.
      Wit: William Ponsonby, Joseph Hill, Robert Tynes. Page 446

WILLIS, Doctor Thomas: Estate appraised by Nicholas Parker, Anthony Fulgham, Charles Fulgham. Signed Martha Willis. R. August 6, 1752. Page 447

BRIDGER, Joseph, Jr.: Estate appraised by Richard Reynolds, Thomas Miller, Joseph Norsworthy. Ordered June 4, 1752. R. August 6, 1752.
Page 449

EXUM, Mary: Leg. son Francis; daughter Elizabeth Smith; daughter Olive Williamson; daughter Ann Williamson. Daughter Mary Exum, Extx. D. June 1, 1749. R. August 6, 1752.
      Wit: James Sampson Clark, Samuel Cornwell, Jordan Thomas.
Page 451

GROSS, Francis: Account estate, examined by Richard Reynolds, Jonathan Godwin, John Godwin. R. August 6, 1752. Page 453

DAUGHTRY, William: Estate appraised by James Bryant, Jacob Butler, John Lawrence. R. August 6, 1752. Page 455

BRASEY, Elizabeth: Leg. cousin Henry Wiggs; cousin John Wiggs; cousin Mary Everitt; grandson Richard Jordan; grandson Mathew Jordan; granddaughter Hannah Jordan; daughter Mary Jordan; son Francis; granddaughter Mary Outland, my estate in the hands of John Outland; daughter Elizabeth Outland. Exs., Mathew Jordan and Francis Bracey D. July 23, 1751. R. August 6, 1752.
      Wit: Thomas Gale, Charles Chesnutt, Godfrey Powell. Page 456

WARD, Benjamin: Account estate, examined by Jordan Thomas and Charles Fulgham. Signed Sarah Ward. R. August 6, 1752. Page 458

---

## WILL BOOK SIX

WEBB, Richard: Account estate, examined by Edward Goodrich and William Harrison. R. September 14, 1752. Page 1

BURT, John: Estate appraised by Benjamin Beal, John Garner, Godfrey Powell. Signed Sarah Burt. Ordered August 6, 1752. R. September 14, 1752.
Page 2

POPE, John, Sr.: Leg. son John; grandson Joseph, the plantation on which his father William Pope lived; daughter Mary Beal. Extx., daughter Priscilla Pope. D. March 1, 1750. R. September 14, 1752.

ALLEN, Joseph: Account estate, examined by Joseph Gray, Thomas Jarrell, Howell Edmunds. Signed Mary Buthe. Among items, a negro in the possession of William Bynum, guardian to the heir at law. R. May 15, 1752.     Page 5

POPE, John: Estate appraised by Ratcliff Boone, Jr., Henry Johnson, John Stephens. Signed Priscilla Pope. R. October 5, 1752.     Page 6

WEST, Richard: Account estate, examined by Thomas Gale, Charles Fulgham, Richard Reynolds. R. October 5, 1752.     Page 7

DRIVER, Edward: Estate appraised by David Williams, James Frizzell, Nicholas Parker. Signed Ann Driver. Ordered June 4, 1752. R. October 5, 1752.     Page 8

BRACEY, Elizabeth: Estate appraised by John Baldwin, John Murfrey, John Garner. Signed Mathew Jordan. R. October 5, 1752.     Page 10

DAY, Thomas: Codicil to his will presented by Benjamin Cocke, with a survey of his land. Bequest to his wife to be used for the schooling of his sons, John and Thomas Day. R. October 5, 1752.     Page 12

MILLER, William: Lawrence Baker, John Hodges and William Harrison, appointed to allot the dower of Margaret Wilson, late widow of William Miller. R. November 2, 1752.     Page 13

PIERCE, John: Estate appraised by Thomas Inglish, William Segrave, William Gay. Signed Hester Pierce. R. November 2, 1752.     Page 14

WEST, Robert: Account estate, examined by Richard Reynolds, Augustine King, John Goodrich. R. December 7, 1752.     Page 17

FRIZZELL, John: Leg. wife Mary; son Ralph; daughter Mary. Exs., wife and James Frizzell. D. March 27, 1752. R. December 7, 1752.
    Wit: Robert Lawrence, Joseph Driver.     Page 18

WHEADON, Joyce: Leg. Susannah Hardiman; Sarah Wheadon; son-in-law John Carrell; Thomas Hardiman; Mary Wheadon; son-in-law Thomas Carrell; Patience Wheadon; Martha Wheadon, daughter of James Wheadon; John Jennings Wheadon; Martha Fiveash; John Tann (?). Ex., Thomas Carrell. D. October 28, 1752. R. December 8, 1752.
    Wit: Peter Fiveash, John Fiveash.     Page 19

WRENN, John: Of Newport Parish. Leg. son John; daughter Elizabeth; daughter Sally; daughter Martha; wife Mary. Exs., son John Wrenn and his uncle Joseph Wrenn. D. April 14, 1752. R. December 8, 1752.
    Wit: Arthur Pollard, William Glover, John Cary.     Page 21

WOODWARD, John: Estate appraised by Edmund Westray, John Westray, John Sellaway. Signed Daniel Herring. Ordered December 7, 1752. R. January 4, 1753.     Page 22

BRASSIE, William: Estate appraised by George Hall, Thomas Woodley, William Davis. R. January 4, 1753.     Page 24

FULGHAM, Jesse: Estate appraised by Henry Pitt, Samuel Garland, Anthony Fulgham. Ordered June 4, 1752. Signed William Hodsden. R. January 4, 1753.     Page 26

MOSCROP, Susanna: Account estate, examined by William Hodsden, Charles

Fulgham. Among items, to cash paid Arthur Applewhite by decree of Isle of Wight County Court, being the moiety of a balance due to Thomas Moscrop's estate. R. January 4, 1753. Page 26

EXUM, Mary: Inventory of estate, signed by William and Mary Jordan. R. January 4, 1753. Page 27

SHAW, Elizabeth: Of the Parish of Newport. Leg. grandson Hansford Whitley; Samuel Jones; sons-in-law, John Smith and Timothy Lane; Joseph Whitley and Mary his wife. Exs., Joseph Whitley and Mary his wife. D. February 12, 1752. R. January 4, 1753.
    Wit: Richard Reynolds, Joshua Gross. Page 28

WHEADON, Joyce: Estate appraised by James Piland, John Bennett, William Cary. R. February 1, 1753. Page 29

WILLIAMSON, Ann: Leg. sister Sarah Exum; Moses Exum; brother John Exum; brother William Exum; brother Joseph Exum; cousin Ann Westray; cousin Susannah Atkinson; sister Sarah Exum; to Eliza Exum. Exs., friend Thomas Williamson and brother John Exum. D. March 14, 1752. R. February 1, 1753.
    Wit: Charles Binns, Jacob Williamson, Daniel Mackey. Page 32

JOINER, Theophilus: Estate appraised in Carolina by Benjamin Williams, John Tine, Joseph Boon. Appraised in Isle of Wight by James Uzzell, Bartholomew Lightfoot, John Smelly. Signed John Joiner. Ordered March 5, 1752. R. February 1, 1753. Page 33

CROOM, Edward: Estate account, examined by John Marshall and John Smelly. Among items, coffin for his son Joseph Croom. Signed Patience Croom. R. February 1, 1753. Page 36

LANE, William: Account estate, examined by Richard Reynolds and Charles Fulgham. R. February 1, 1753. Page 38

TOMLIN, Joseph: Estate appraised by Daniel Herring, Jr., John Westray, Edward Westray. Signed Lucretia Tomlin. Ordered November 2, 1752. R. March 1, 1753. Page 39

GRAY, Elizabeth: Estate appraised by Richard H------, William -------, Henry ------- (torn). R. March 1, 1753. Page 40

BROCK, Robert: Account estate, examined by Dolphin Drew. Signed Lucy Brock. R. March 1, 1753. Page 41

CROCKER, Katherine: Account estate, examined by Jordan Thomas. Signed Anthony Crocker. R. March 1, 1753. Page 43

CROCKER, Arthur: Account estate, examined by Jordan Thomas. R. March 1, 1753. Page 43

WILSON, John: Account estate, examined by Edward Goodrich, John Mallory, George Wilson. Signed William Carrell. R. March 1, 1753. Page 44

DRIVER, Giles: Inventory of estate, presented by John Driver. R. April 5, 1753. Page 45

HODGES, Benjamin: Leg. daughter Hartwell Davis; cousins, Elizabeth, Ann and John Hodges, the children of John Hodges. Ex., cousin John Hodges. D. February 28, 1752. R. April 5, 1753.
    Wit: James Tooke Scott, Nicholas Miller, ------ Jordan.
Page 47

HAINES, Edward: Estate account, examined by John Eley and John Marshall. Signed Sarah Haines. Four children mentioned. R. April 5, 1753.
Page 49

PORTLOCK, Charles: Estate appraised by Edward Goodrich, Nicholas Casey, Thomas Casey. R. April 5, 1753.
Page 50

DRIVER, Giles: Account estate, examined by Robert Barry and James Arthur. To paid Giles Driver a legacy paid Charles Driver, a legacy, paid Joseph Driver, a legacy. Signed John Driver. R. April 6, 1753.
Page 52

DRIVER, Olive: Inventory of estate, presented by John Driver. R. April 6, 1753.
Page 54

CALCOTE, Thomas: Leg. son Joseph; son James; daughter Mary Wentworth; grandson Henry Calcote; granddaughter Ann Bevan, her mother has had her full part of my estate. Exs., sons, James and Joseph Calcote. D.-----------. R. April 6, 1753.
    Wit: -------------------------.
Page 55

GOODRICH, Samuel: Estate appraised by Richard Jones, John Jordan, Francis Wrenn. Ordered August 6, 1752. R. April 6, 1753.
Page 56

BRADDY, Olive: Estate appraised by Francis Ward, Thomas Copher, Mason Braddy. Signed James Sampson Clark. Ordered March 1, 1753. R. May 3, 1753.
Page 56

GRAY, John: Account estate, examined by James Baker, Lawrence Baker and Richard Hardy. Among items, expense for maintaining six children. R. May 3, 1753.
Page 58

PEDIN, Mary: Estate appraised by Richard Reynolds, Joseph Norsworthy, Sampson West. Signed Anthony Holladay. Account estate examined by John Hyndman and James Sheddon. Expense listed for three children. R. May 3, 1753.
Page 59

DRIVER, Olive: Account estate, examined by James Arthur and Robert Barry. Signed John Driver. R. July 5, 1753.
Page 63

GOODRICH, Samuel: Account estate, examined by Jordan Thomas and Richard Jones. R. July 5, 1753.
Page 64

FORBES, James: Account estate, examined by Jordan Thomas and Richard Jones. R. July 5, 1753.
Page 65

HOUSE, John: Estate appraised by John Monro, Samuel Godwin and Joseph Wail. Signed Jonathan Godwin. Ordered June 7, 1753. R. July 5, 1753.
Page 66

DAVIS, John: Account estate, examined by John Wills, Thomas Applewhaite, Charles Fulgham. R. July 5, 1753.
Page 67

SHELLY, Thomas: Account estate, examined by William Hodsden and Lawrence Baker. R. August 2, 1753.
Page 69

GRAY, Mrs. Elizabeth: Account estate, examined by Lawrence Baker, Richard Hardy and James Baker. R. September 6, 1753.
Page 69

SMITH, William: Leg. daughter-in-law Mary Williams; daughter Patience; son Joseph; daughter Elizabeth; wife Elizabeth. D. December 28, 1752. R. September 6, 1753.

Wit: William Hawkins, Stephen Smith.           Page 71

WILLIAMSON, Ann: Inventory presented by John Exum. R. November --, 1753.
Page 71

DELK, John: Leg. sister Elizabeth Screws; to Lucy Owen, the daughter of
Elizabeth Screws; Elizabeth Delk; Scelton Delk; wife Mary, with reversion of bequest to all my brothers and sisters. D. September 29,
1753. R. November 1, 1753.
Wit: R. Hardy, William Burt, William Cary.           Page 72

WOODWARD, John: Account estate, examined by John Eley, James Bridger and
John Westray. Signed Daniel Herring, Jr. Ordered November 1, 1753.
R. January 3, 1754.           Page 74

FRIZZELL, John: Estate appraised by Giles Driver, Samuel Whitfield, Henry
Pitt. Signed James Frizzell. Ordered December 7, 1752. R. January
3, 1754.           Page 75

TURNER, Thomas, Sr.: Account estate, examined by James Bridger, John Eley,
Daniel Herring, Jr. Signed Martha Turner. R. January 3, 1754.
Page 76

BRADDY, Olive: Account estate, examined by Jordan Thomas and Dolphin Drew.
Signed James Sampson Clark. R. January 3, 1754.           Page 77

DICKINSON, Jacob: Account estate, examined by John Applewhite and Richard
Reynolds. R. January 4, 1754.           Page 78

HOUSE, John: Account estate, examined by John Monro, Willis Wilkinson.
R. February 7, 1754.           Page 80

BROWNE, John: Leg. sister Mary. Ex., father Thomas Browne. D. January
10, 1754. R. February 7, 1754.
Wit: Philip Moody, Edward Haile, William Turner.           Page 81

DELK, John: Estate appraised by James Piland, R. Hardy, Jeremiah Pierce.
R. February 7, 1754.           Page 82

DENSON, John: Leg. son John; son-in-law, Thomas Dreaper; son Francis; son
William; daughter Ann; son James; daughter Sarah; daughter Ellenor;
daughter Patience. Ex., daughter Ann Denson. D. July 1, 1748. R.
February 7, 1754.
Wit: William Scott, Samuel Sebrell, Jr., Alse Page, Thomas Gay.
Page 83

GREGORY, Robert: Account estate, examined by Joseph Hill, Robert Tynes.
Signed Charles Chapman. R. March 7, 1753.           Page 85

HOWELL, James: Estate appraised by John Rampson, Joseph Bullard, Benjamin
Beale. Signed Jonas Shivers. Ordered February 7, 1754. R. March
7, 1754. Account estate, examined by William Hodsden and Joseph Hill.
R. March 7, 1754.           Page 85

GAY, Thomas: Leg. son Jethro; daughter Mary; son Thomas; son William;
daughter Foreby; son John. Ex., William Gay. D. March 18, 1754.
R. April 4, 1754.
Wit: John Outland, Thomas Outland, Jesse Hutchins.           Page 86

DAY, Thomas: Account estate, examined by Joseph Bridger and William Harrison. Signed John Mallory. R. April 4, 1754.           Page 87

WHITE, John: Leg. son William; daughter Mary, whom I place in the care of Francis Wrenn and his wife Mary. Exs., John Murry and Francis Wrenn. D. December 7, 1753. R. May 2, 1754.
    Wit: James Baker, James Baker, Jr.                    Page 88

BRACY, Michael: Leg. cousin Sarah, the daughter of brother Hugh Bracy; cousin William Bracy; to brother Hugh's daughters, Martha and Emma Bracy; rest of estate among the children of my brothers and sisters. D. January 17, 1748/49. R. May 2, 1754.
    Wit: Casper Mintz, William Crocker, William Blunt.    Page 90

WILLIAMS, David: Leg. daughter Rebecca Driver; wife Ann; son James; son John; son David; son Richard. Exs., wife and son James Williams. D. October 20, 1753. R. May 2, 1754.
    Wit: Richard Jordan, Anthony Fulgham, John Williams.  Page 91

GILES, Hugh: Account estate, examined by John Applewhite and Charles Fulgham. R. May 2, 1754.                              Page 92

BRIDGER, Major Joseph: Account estate, examined by William Hodsden and Joseph Bridger. Signed Joseph Jones and John Goodrich. R. May 2, 1754.
                                                         Page 94
BRANTLEY, Edward: Inventory presented by William Harrison. R. May 2, 1754.
                                                         Page 95

WHITE, John: Estate appraised by Samuel Wilson, John Barlow, Jr., James Dering. R. June 6, 1754.                         Page 96

GAY, Thomas: Estate appraised by Henry Saunders, James Hough, John Coggan. Signed William Gay. R. June 6, 1754.              Page 98

LIGHTFOOT, Henry: Estate appraised by William Hodsden, William Rand, Arthur Applewhite. Ordered May 29, 1754. R. June 6, 1754.   Page 99

WILLS, Thomas: Account estate, examined by John Applewhite, Giles Driver. Signed William Richards. R. June 6, 1754.         Page 101

WEATHERALL, Aquilla: Account estate, examined by John Pitt, Samuel Godwin, Willis Wilkinson. Signed Charity Weatherall. R. July 4, 1754.
                                                         Page 102

DELK, John: Account estate, examined by R. Hardy, William Carrell, Dolphin Drew. R. July 4, 1754.                         Page 102

LIGHTFOOT, Henry: Estate appraised by Robert Tynes, Arthur Applewhaite and James Calcote. R. July 4, 1754.               Page 104

WALTON, Thomas: Estate appraised by John Hyndman, Jordan Thomas, George Wilson. R. July 4, 1754.                          Page 105

CALCOTE, Joseph: Estate appraised by Arthur Applewhite, Bartholomew Lightfoot, Benjamin -------. R. July 5, 1754.         Page 105

SCOTT, Thomas: Appraised August 3, 1749 by John Gibbs and Joseph Hill. R. August 1, 1754.                                Page 107

    Account estate, examined by James Baker.              Page 109

SMITH, Arthur: Appraisal estate by James Calcote, Christopher Reynolds, Benjamin Brock. Ordered June 6, 1754. R. August 1, 1754.   Page 108

WILLIAMS, David: Estate appraised by Henry King, Anthony Fulgham, Samuel

Whitfield. R. August 1, 1754.

SIMMONS, James: Additional appraisal by Robert Johnston and Augustine
King. Signed Philip Moody. R. August 1, 1754. Page 111

WESTON, William: Estate appraised by John Monro, Samuel Godwin, Joseph
Pitt. R. August 1, 1754. Page 112

CALCOTE, Thomas: Estate account, examined by John Hyndman, James Shedden,
Andrew Mackie. Signed Elizabeth Calcote. R. September 5, 1754.
Page 114

REYNOLDS, Sharpe: Leg. cousin Richard Reynolds; cousin George Reynolds;
Sarah Wootten; cousin Christopher, the son of Christopher Reynolds,
decd. Ex., cousin Christopher Reynolds. D. July 8, 1754. R. Septem-
ber 5, 1754.
Wit: Bartholomew Lightfoot, John Green, Richard Casey, Ralph
Carter, Arthur Goodson. Page 115

MINIARD, Ann: Estate appraised by John Monro, Anthony Fulgham, Samuel
Godwin. R. September 5, 1754. Page 116

GODWIN, James: Estate appraised by Robert Bridger, Joseph Pitt, Nicholas
Wale (Wail). Ordered February 7, 1750. R. September 5, 1754.
Page 117

MILLER, William: Account estate, examined by Andrew Mackie and William
Davis. R. September 5, 1754. Page 118

JONES, Mrs. Elizabeth: Account estate, examined by John Hyndman, James
Shedden. R. September 5, 1754. Page 120

REYNOLDS, Sharpe: Estate appraised by Thomas Norsworthy, James Calcote,
Robert Tynes. R. October 3, 1754. Page 121

LIGHTFOOT, Henry, Sr.: Account estate, examined by John Wills and Charles
Fulgham. To paid the widow to Bartholomew Lightfoot, to Henry Light-
foot, Jr., to Thomas Lightfoot, to Mary Reynolds, to Patience Reynolds.
R. October 3, 1754. Page 122

PERSON, Samuel: Leg. cousin Samuel, son of Francis Person; cousin Jesse,
son of Francis Person; cousin George, son of John Glover; cousin Ben-
jamin, son of Jesse Hargrave; Samuel Pretlow; John Pretlow; cousin
Joseph, son of Francis Person; cousin John, son of Henry Person; cousin
Samuel, son of Lemuel Hargrave; sister Mary Glover; cousin Mary,
daughter of Francis Person; cousin Henry, son of Francis Person; cousins,
William, James and Jacob, the sons of Francis Person; to my cousin
Absalom Holowell's daughter; cousins, Elizabeth and Sarah Glover;
cousin Sarah Person, cousin John, the son of Francis Person. Exs.,
Jordan Thomas and Thomas Pretlow. D. February 17, 1753. R. October
3, 1754.
Wit: Joseph Mangum, Henry Mangum, Samuel Person, Constant
Mangum. Page 123

WOODLEY, Thomas. Of Newport Parish. Leg. son John; son Thomas; daughter
Martha; grandson Willis Wilson; grandson John Wilson; granddaughter
Mary Milner; grandson Samuel Milner. Ex., son John Woodley. D. April
24, 1754. R. October 3, 1754.
Wit: Ambrose Hadley, Joseph Hill, Mathew Jones, Arthur Davis,
Jordan Thomas. Page 125

WOODLEY, Henry: Of Newport Parish. Leg. brother Thomas; brother John;

sister Martha. Ex., brother John. D. April 11, 1754. R. October 4, 1754.
    Wit: Ambrose Hadley, Mathew Jones, John Fiveash.     Page 127

BARLOW, John: Leg. son Benjamin; son John; son James; son Thomas; son William; grandson John, son of John Barlow; grandson Nathaniel Barlow. Exs., wife and son Thomas. D. November 15, 1752. R. November 7, 1754.
    Wit: Jordan Thomas, John DeLoach, John Wombwell.     Page 128

BRACY, Michael: Estate appraised by William Davis, John Morris, George Hall. R. November 7, 1754.     Page 129

BAGNALL, Ann: Leg. daughter Ann; daughter Easter Norsworthy; son Richard; son James; son Nathan; son William; son Samuel; daughter Mary Pitt. Ex., son William Bagnall. D. March 30, 1754. R. November 7, 1754.
    Wit: Nicholas Parker, Nathaniel Parker.     Page 130

WILLIAMS, John: Leg. son Joseph; daughter Ann Pope; son-in-law Nathan Pope; son-in-law Joseph Hollowell; son-in-law Richard Pope; son John Williams. Exs., son John and son-in-law Richard Pope. D. September 22, 1754. R. November 7, 1754.
    Wit: William Scott, John Pinner, Thomas Gay.     Page 131

HARRIS, Thomas: Estate appraised by Edward Haile, William Turner, Arthur Turner. Signed John Harris. R. January 2, 1755.     Page 132

MINARD, Ann: Estate accout, examined by Charles Fulgham. Signed Joseph Minard. R. January 2, 1755.     Page 134

WILLIAMS, John: Thomas Gale, James Hough, John Marshall, Jr. in the presence of William Eley, William Pass and John Baldwin, assigned the dower of Rebecca, the widow of John Williams. R. January 2, 1755.
     Page 135

WILLIAMS, John: Estate appraised by Thomas Gale, John Marshall, Jr., William Pass. R. January 2, 1755.     Page 137

BARLOW, John: Estate appraised by Richard Jones, Seth Hunter, Francis Wrenn. R. January 2, 1755.     Page 140

BRIGGS, Edmund: Estate appraised by Richard Jones, Thomas Copher, Francis Ward. Signed Hannah Briggs.     Page 142

SMITH, Arthur: Estate appraised in Surry County be Wil. Seward, John Ruffin, William Seward, Jr. Appraised in Isle of Wight County by Samuel Wentworth, Bartholomew Lightfoot, Arthur Applewhaite, James Easson. R. February 6, 1755.     Page 152

HOWELL, William: Leg. daughter Elizabeth Rodes; son Thomas; wife; daughter Mary; daughter Sarah; daughter Rachel; daughter Mourning; daughter Martha; son John. D. November 24, 1754. R. February 6, 1755.
    Wit: James Jordan, Thomas Jones.     Page 154

TOMLIN, Joseph: Account estate, examined by John Eley, Daniel Herring, Edmund Westray. Signed Lucretia Tomlin. R. February 6, 1755.
     Page 155

REYNOLDS, Rebecca: Leg. daughter Tabitha; son Richard; son George; son Christopher; grandson Richard, the son of Richard Reynolds. Exs., son Richard and daughter Tabitha Reynolds. D. May 4, 1745. R. March 6, 1755.

Wit: Robert Tynes, Peter Green, Ann Green. Page 156

GRAY, Aaron: Account estate, examined by Charles Fulgham and Richard Reynolds. R. April 4, 1755. Page 157

HOWELL, William: Estate appraised by Thomas Bullock, William Bullock, John Newman. Signed Elizabeth Howell. R. April 4, 1755. Page 158

THOMAS, John: Account estate, examined by Joseph Gray and Richard Kello. Among items, to my wife's distributive slaves of the balance. (Not signed.) D. February 3, 1735. R. April 3, 1755. Page 160

GODWIN, James: Account estate, examined by John Monro and Willis Wilkinson. To Henry Best and Elizabeth his wife, Extx. R. April 2, 1755.
Page 161
Account of his estate in the hands of Samuel Godwin, examined by John Monro and Willis Wilkinson. Page 162

BARLOW, John: Account estate, examined by James Baker and Richard Baker. Signed Thomas Barlow. R. April 3, 1755. Page 163

REYNOLDS, Rebecca: Estate appraised by Bartholomew Lightfoot, William McConnell, Robert Tynes. Page 164

MACCLAREN, James: The son of Alexander MacClaren of McChristown in the Parish of Kilmadock, Pertheshire, North Britain. Leg. wife Martha, all my portion of the Laird ship, of the aforesaid place. Extx., wife Martha. D. September 8, 1754. R. April 4, 1755.
Wit: John Reid, James Benn. Page 167

SMITH, Thomas: Account estate, examined by John Hyndman, Andrew Mackie, James Sheddon. Signed Elizabeth Smith. R. April 4, 1755. Page 168

MATHEWS, Richard: Leg. daughter Mary Pope; granddaughter Mary Meriday; son Richard; son John; son Abraham; granddaughter Martha Bayley; son Joshua; daughter Susannah Hail. Exs., sons Samuel and Joseph Mathews. D. December 21, 1754. R. May 1, 1755.
Wit: William Pope, Samuel Everitt, John Everitt. Page 173

GAY, Thomas: Estate appraised by John Eley, John Darden, Robert Coggan. R. February 6, 1755. Page 174

BELL, Benjamin: Estate appraised by James Dering, Samuel Wilson, John Bennett. Ordered April 26, 1755. R. May 1, 1755. Page 175

DAUGHTRY, John: Estate appraised by John Darden, William Lawrence, John Lawrence. Signed Elizabeth Daughtry. Ordered October 3, 1754. R. June 5, 1755. Page 176

BRANTLEY, Clay: Leg. son John; granddaughter Elizabeth, daughter of Thomas Brantley; grandsons, James and Thomas, the sons of my son Thomas Brantley; daughter-in-law Lucy Brantley; to John, Benjamin and Thomas, the sons of Benjamin Brantley. Ex., son Thomas Brantley. D. March 25, 1753. R. June 5, 1755.
Wit: Roger Delk, Jacob Bruce. Page 178

CARRELL, Thomas: Estate appraised by Edward Goodrich, John Miller, John Hodges. Ordered June 4, 1752. R. June 5, 1755. Page 180

WALKER, John: Estate appraised by James Easton, William Rand, William Hodsden. Ordered May 1, 1755. R. June 5, 1755. Page 182

MATHEWS, Richard: Estate appraised by Benjamin Beal, Jonas Shivers, John
Garner. Signed Samuel and Joseph Mathews. R. July 3, 1755. Page 183

WHEADON, Joice: Account estate, examined by Richard Hardy and Dolphin Drew.
To a legacy paid to James Wheadon for John Jennings Wheadon; to Peter
Fiveash for Martha Fiveash, to John Carrell for Mary his wife, to
John Carrell; to Thomas Hardyman. R. July 3, 1755.           Page 184

HOLLEMAN, Susannah: Leg. brother James Holleman; sister Mary; sister
Sarah; sister Rachel; to Susanna Holleman; to Deudatus Boykib; to
Jesse, the son of John Holleman; to Joddia and Christopher, the sons
of John Holleman; Mary the daughter of John Holleman; Susanna Vasser;
to brother John Holleman's children and Joseph John, Elijah, Susanna
and Mary, the children of brother Joseph Vasser. Ex., brother Joseph
Vasser. D. June 3, 1755. R. July 3, 1755.
        Wit: William Crocker, Joseph Crocker, Thomas Gwaltney. Page 186

HOW, Benjamin: Estate appraised by William Bidgood, Edward Dews, William
Carrell. Ordered December 5, 1754. R. August 7, 1755.      Page 188

PERSON, Samuel: Estate appraised by Samuel Jones, Joseph Mangum, Richard
Jones. R. September 4, 1755.                                Page 190

GARLAND, Samuel: Estate appraised by Nicholas Parker, Thomas Parker, Henry
King. Signed Ann Garland. Ordered August 7, 1755. R. September 4,
1755.                                                       Page 195

HOW, Banjamin: Account estate examined by Edward Goodrich and John Mallory.
R. October 2, 1758 [sic].                                   Page 196

GRAY, Aaron: Charles Fulgham and Richard Reynolds, appointed to assign
the dower of Sarah, the widow of Aaron Gray; paid to Bignall Tuel as
dower in the right of his wife Sarah, the widow of Aaron Gray. R.
October 2, 1758 [sic].                                      Page 197

SANDERS, Solomon: Account estate, examined by Charles Fulgham and Richard
Reynolds. R. November 7, 1755.                              Page 204

WESTRAY, John: Leg. son John; son Edmund; son Benjamin; daughter Martha;
daughter Mary; wife Ann; daughter Ann Pierce. Exs., sons, John and
Edmund. D. December 23, 1755. R. January 1, 1756.           Page 205

GOODWIN, Samuel: Account estate, examined by Jesse Browne, William Haynes,
James Jordan Scott. Paid, their share of estate: Thomas, William,
Lemuel and Joshua Goodwin, paid to Albridgeton Jones the share of
Jacob Dickinson. R. January 1, 1756.                        Page 207

MURRY, Sarah: Estate appraised by John Hodges, George Wilson, Edward Goodrich and William Harrison. R. January 1, 1756.             Page 208

DRIVER, Robert: Estate appraised by Richard Reynolds, George Whitley,
Giles West. Ordered December 4, 1755. R. February 5, 1756. Page 209

SANDERS, Solomon: Additional estate, appraised by Richard Reynolds, Jonathan Godwin, George Whitley. Signed Thomas Lile. R. February 5, 1756.
                                                            Page 211

DELOACH, Mary: Estate appraised by Francis Ward, John Stallings, Thomas
Copher. Signed Michael Deloach. Ordered January 1, 1756. R. March
4, 1756.                                                    Page 212

HARDY, Richard: Leg. son Richard; daughter Sarah; wife Mary. Exs., wife

and son Richard Hardy. D. December 6, 1755. R. March 4, 1756.
Wit: Hugh Vance, James Piland, Patience Gray. Page 213

CALCOTE, Joseph: Account estate examined by Bartholomew Lightfoot and
William Rand. Paid the widow and two orphans. R. March 4, 1756.
Page 214

PILAND, James: Estate appraised by Peter Fiveash, John Bennett, John
Carrell. Signed Elizabeth Piland. R. June 3, 1756. Page 216

HARDY, Richard: Estate appraised by Peter Fiveash, Jeremiah Pierce, John
Bennett. Signed Mary Hardy. R. June 3, 1756. Page 218

WALTON, Thomas: Account estate, signed by William Hodsden. By balance
in the hands of Jesse Browne and Albridgeton Jones, administrators
of the estate of Charles Portlock, who was the administrator of Thomas
Walton. Paid the widow her share and the heir-at-law. R. June 3,
1756. Page 221

WILLIAMS, Joseph: Leg. son John; daughter Rebecca; wife Mary. Exs.,
wife and Jethro Gale. D. January 26, 1756. R. June 3, 1756.
Wit: Thomas Gale, John Richards, John Gay. Page 222

WHEADON, Joyce: Account estate, examined by Peter Fiveash and Richard
Hardy. Signed Thomas Carrell. R. June 3, 1756. Page 224

BRANTLEY, James: Estate appraised by Francis Exum, Simon Turner, Thomas
Clark. Signed Ruth Brantley. Ordered April 1, 1742. R. July 1, 1756.
Page 224

VANCE, Hugh: Leg. wife Lydia; son James; Charles Portlock; Nathaniel
Portlock. Power of attorney given Captain Samuel Wentworth to recover
a negro in Jamaica. Exs., wife and friend James Easson. D. April
2, 1756. R. July 1, 1756.
Wit: William Hodsden, Nicholas Casey. Page 226

HAILE, Edward: Of Newport Parish. Leg. son William; son Thomas; wife
Elizabeth; daughter Hannah; daughter Mary; daughter Sarah; son John;
son Edward. Ex., son Edward Haile. D. May 29, 1755. R. August 5,
1756.
Wit: Benjamin Pynes, William Pynes, Jane Pynes, Richard
Johnson. Page 227

WESTRAY, John: Estate appraised by Robert Johnson, Arthur Turner, Daniel
Batten. R. August 5, 1756. Page 229

BENN, Captain James: Additional account estate, examined by John Wills
and Charles Fulgham. R. August 5, 1756. Page 231

SCOTT, Joannah: Leg. granddaughter Ann Scott; to Ann Coffield; to Sarah
Coffield; to Christian Coffield; to Courtney Coffield; to George
Norsworthy Scott; son James Tooke Scott. D. July 17, 1756. R.
September 2, 1756.
Wit: Edward Goodson, Mary Harris. Page 232

TOMLIN, Mathew: Leg. son Mathew; son Nathan; son Robert; daughter Martha.
Ex., son Robert Tomlin. D. December 1, 1751. R. September 2, 1756.
Wit: James Bridger, Daniel Herring, Edmund Fulgham. Page 233

LEE, John: Account estate, examined by Dolphin Drew and Richard Hardy.
R. September 2, 1756. Page 234

SMITH, Arthur: Account estate, examined by John Hyndman, James Easson, James Sheddon. Signed Elizabeth Smith. R. September 2, 1756.
Page 235

SMITH, Thomas: Additional accout with the estate of Arthur Smith. Signed Elizabeth Smith. Examined by James Easson, James Sheddon and John Hyndman. R. September 2, 1756.
Page 241

CARY, William: Estate appraised by John Welch, John Carrell, Richard Hardy. R. November 4, 1756. Signed William Cary.
Page 243

BRANTLEY, James: Account estate, examined by H. Edmonds, John Person and David Edmonds. Among items, to Lewis Brantley, judgement recovered by Francis Myrick against them as surviving executors of Edward Brantley, decd. R. December 2, 1756.
Page 244

LAWRENCE, Jeremiah: Leg. to George and Charles, the sons of my brother Robert Lawrence, land in Southampton County; to Sarah Lawrence, if she pays a bequest to her brothers, Hardy, Robert, George and Charles Lawrence; to Charles, the son of Jacob Darden; to brother Samuel; to sister Ann Joiner and her husband, William Joiner and her children; brother John; to Samuel, the son of brother John Lawrence. Ex., brother John Lawrence. D. November 30, 1755. R. December 2, 1756.
Wit: Josiah Jordan, Joseph Scott, Joseph Meredith.
Page 246

GODWIN, Joshua: Account estate, examined by Joseph Bridger and Dolphin Drew. Estate paid to William Godwin; to Jacob Dickinson in right of his wife, one of the sisters of Lemuel Godwin and Thomas Godwin. D. April 27, 1743. R. December 2, 1756.
Page 247

WHITE, John: Account estate, examined by Richard Baker and Dolphin Drew. Signed Francis Wrenn and John Murry. R. December 6, 1756.
Page 249

BAKER, James: Leg. to Henry, the son of my brother Henry Baker, decd., of North Carolina; to my kinswoman, Mary, the wife of James Calcote; to John Glover, the son of William Glover; to Katherine, Richard, Ann and James Baker, the children of my brother Lawrence Baker. Exs., brother Lawrence and Richard Baker. D. September 14, 1754. R. December 2, 1756.
Wit: R. Kello, William Goodrich, William Marlow.
Page 250

GARLAND, Samuel: Estate appraised by Thomas Parker, Nicholas Parker, Henry King. Ordered August 7, 1755. Signed Ann Garland. R. September 4, 1755.
Page 251

GOODWIN, Lemuel: Account estate, examined by John Applewhaite and Richard Reynolds. R. January 6, 1757.
Page 252

HAILE, Edward: Estate appraised by William Jordan, Anthony Crocker, Andrew Sikes. R. January 6, 1757.
Page 253

SCOTT, Joanna: Estate appraised by Thomas Whitfield, John Gibbs, John Murry, Nicholas Miller. R. February 3, 1757.
Page 256

BEST, Thomas: Estate appraised by Richard Bagnall, Samuel Whitfield, Joseph Copeland. Signed Nicholas Parker. Ordered October 7, 1756. R. February 3, 1757.
Page 258

WRENN, Joseph: Estate appraised by John Mallory, John Cary, William Glover. Ordered January 6, 1757. R. February 3, 1757.
Page 259

GOODRICH, Benjamin: Account estate, examined by Dolphin Drew, James Dering,

Richard Jones. Signed William Goodrich. R. February 3, 1757.

Page 260

DRIVER, Robert: Account estate, examined by Thomas Miller and Richard Reynolds. R. February 3, 1757.                                                   Page 262

HOLLEMAN, Susanna: Account estate, examined by Joseph Gray and Richard Kello. R. March 3, 1757.                                                       Page 263

SCOTT, William: Leg. wife Elizabeth; son William, land in Southampton County; son Robert; daughter Mary; daughter Elizabeth; unborn child. Exs., wife, Thomas Pretlow and Joseph Scott. D. November 13, 1756. R. March 3, 1757.
      Wit: Mary Pretlow, William Maycock, James Tyrie.          Page 264

VANCE, Hugh: Estate appraised by William Hodsden, William Harrison, Joseph Jones. R. March 3, 1757.                                                   Page 265

BRIGGS, James: Leg. daughter Katherine; son Robert; friend Richard Baker to be guardian for son Robert; wife Elizabeth; son William; daughter Priscilla Clayton; daughter Catherine. Ex., friend Richard Baker. D. November 30, 1756. R. June 2, 1757.
      Wit: Benjamin Baker, Mary Clayton.                       Page 268

LAWRENCE, William: Leg. daughter Penelope; son John; wife Sarah; son John land in Southampton County; daughter Molly; daughter Ann; daughter Sally; son Miles. Exs., wife and brother-in-law Arthur Applewhaite. D. September 8, 1756. R. June 2, 1757.
      Wit: John Darden, Jesse Watkins, Joshua Council.       Page 269

BABB, Mary: Leg. son William; daughter Mary Driver; to Thomas Pinner; daughter Patience Pinner; daughter Sarah Gay; grandson John a legacy in the possession of his father Joshua Gay; granddaughter Martha Gay; son Robert. Ex., son Robert Babb. D. September 23, 1754. R. July 7, 1757.
      Wit: John Driver, Sarah Driver.                        Page 273

PITT, John: Account estate, debtor to the estate of Joseph Pitt, decd. Examined by Willis Wilkinson, Nicholas Parker. R. July 7, 1757.
Page 274

PERSON, Samuel: Account estate, examined by Richard Baker and Dolphin Drew. Signed Thomas Pretlow and Jordan Thomas. R. July 7, 1757.
Page 276

GUTRE, Daniel: Leg. son Benony; son Reuben; wife Jane to maintain my younger children. D. February 2, 1757. R. July 7, 1757.
      Wit: John Bowden, Jacob Thomas.                        Page 278

MARSHALL, Robert: Of Nansemond County. Leg. son Robert the land adjoining that of my brother John Marshall; daughter Mary Cashwell; daughter Priscilla Collifer; daughter Elizabeth; to Rachell Marshall; to Jesse Godwin Marshall. Ex., daughter Rachell Marshall. D. February 29, 1756. R. July 7, 1757.
      Wit: Thomas Applewhaite, Jesse Marshall, Mary Frizzell.
Page 280

BRIGGS, James: Estate appraised by William Harrison, Benjamin Harrison, Michael Smelly (?). R. July 7, 1757.                                         Page 281

PITT, Henry: Leg. son Henry; rest of estate to be divided among all of my children. Exs., wife Mary and Nicholas Parker. D. June 14, 1757.

R. August 4, 1757.
   Wit: James Channel, Joseph Whitley, Samuel Bagnall.     Page 282

BARLOW, Thomas: Account estate, examined by Richard Hardy and Edward
   Goodrich. R. August 4, 1757.                           Page 285

POPE, William: Account estate, examined by Robert Holland and William
   Segraves. Among items, funeral expenses for William Pope, Garlent
   Pope and his son William Pope. R. August 4, 1757.      Page 286

PITT, Henry: Estate appraised by Joseph Copeland, Tristram Norsworthy
   and Thomas Parker. Signed Nicholas Parker and Mary Pitt. R. October
   6, 1757.                                                Page 287

HAIL, Elizabeth: Leg. daughter Mary; son Thomas; grandson Joseph Hail;
   daughter-in-law Hannah Hail; daughter Sarah; son Joseph; son John;
   daughter Elizabeth Turner. Ex., son John Hail. D. October 16, 1756.
   R. October 6, 1757.
   Wit: Benjamin Pynes, Tabitha Haile, Martha Bell.       Page 289

EVERITT, Joseph: Leg. daughter Elizabeth; wife; to Joshua House; son Joseph.
   Ex., son Joseph Everitt. D. June 27, 1756. R. October 6, 1757.
   Wit: Joseph Meredith, Alexander Young, Joseph Darden, John
   Darden.                                                Page 290

HAIL, Edward: Leg. son Benjamin; son Edward; son Joshua; son Joel; son
   James; son Reuben; son Jesse; daughter Rebecca; daughter Naomi. Extx.,
   wife Elizabeth. D. September 19, 1757. R. October 6, 1757.
   Wit: Benjamin Pynes, John Cook, Thomas Hail.           Page 291

COUNCIL, Susannah: Leg. daughter Susannah; daughter Christian Daughtry;
   daughter Mary Brantley; son Joshua; daughter Martha Fowler; daughter
   Lucy Johnson; daughter Ann Lawrence; son Charles; son Michael; granddaughter Selah Council; grandson Willis Council; granddaughter Sarah
   Lawrence; son Hardy. Exs., sons, Charles and Joshua Council. D. April
   19, 1756. R. October 6, 1757.
   Wit: William Murphree, Robert Johnson.                 Page 294

WRIGHT, John: Leg. son John; daughter Ann Green; daughter Sarah Butler;
   daughter Elizabeth West; daughter Juliana Driver; granddaughter Juliana
   Green; to Sarah Alderson. Ex., son John Wright. D. September 1, 1753.
   R. November 3, 1757.
   Wit: Richard Reynolds, Martha Wright, William Brantley.
                                                          Page 297

ROBINSON, Richard: Leg. loving wife my whole estate, at her death to be
   divided beteen Edward Miller, son of Thomas Miller, and my God-daughter
   Betty Wilson. Ex., son-in-law Thomas Miller. D. September 20, 1757.
   R. November 3, 1757.
   Wit: George Wilson, Rebecca Miller.                    Page 299

GIBBS, Ralph: Leg. sister Sarah Gibbs; wife Mary; son John. Exs., wife
   and Giles West. D. July 8, 1757. R. November 3, 1757.
   Wit: Richard Reynolds, William Richard, Micajah Wills. Page 300

EVERITT, Joseph: Estate appraised by Samuel Mathews, Thomas Pinner, Samuel
   Everitt. R. December 1, 1757.                          Page 301

JOHNSON, Robert: Leg. daughter Sarah Britt; son Robert; daughter Mary
   Williford; son James; daughter Amelia. Exs., wife Ann and son Robert
   Johnson. D. November 3, 1757. R. December 1, 1757.
   Wit: Anthony Fulgham, Barnaby Little.                  Page 304

WRIGHT, John: Estate appraised by James Benn, George Benn, Giles West. R. December 7, 1757. Page 305

ALMAND, James: Leg. son Moses; son Lewis; son Aaron, land in Nansemond County; granddaughter Mary Fleming; grandson James Fossith; grandson Perrin Almand; grandson Thomas Almand; granddaughter Peggy Almand; daughter Sofia Rand; daughter Millison Fleming; wife. Exs., sons, Moses, Lewis and Aaron Almand. D. April 6, 1757. R. December 2, 1757. Wit: Edward Goodrich, Benjamin Bidgood, Mary Humphry. Page 306

WRENN, John: Estate appraised by Edward Goodrich, George Wilson, John Miller. R. December 2, 1757. Page 308

JONES, Abraham: Leg. son Mathew; son John; son Abraham; daughter Ann Pitman; daughter Martha Delk. Exs., sons Mathew and John Jones. D. March 28, 1757. R. January 5, 1758. Wit: Thomas Pretlow, Benjamin Gwaltney, James Gwaltney. Page 310

APPLEWHAITE, Ann: Of Newport Parish. Leg. Thomas Wills, the son of ------ Wills; sister Mary Wills; to Thomas Applewhaite, Jr.; brother Josiah Applewhaite. Ex., Miles Wills. D. October 16, 1757. R. January 5, 1758. Wit: James Fulgham, Sarah Tuell. Page 312

LAWRENCE, John: Leg. grandson Elisha Lawrence Ballard, land in Southampton County; to John Lawrence, my brother's son, land in Southampton County; granddaughter Honour Ballard; granddaughter Ann Ballard; daughter Ann Ballard. Ex., son-in-law Elisha Ballard. D. March 2, 1757. R. January 5, 1758. Wit: Hardy Lawrence, Joseph Lawrence, William Moore. Page 313

WRENN, John: Account estate, examined by John Mallory and William Glover. Signed John Wrenn. R. January 5, 1758. Page 315

NORSWORTHY, Joseph: Leg. granddaughter Carziah Godwin; son-in-law Robert Kinder; wife Rachel; son Joseph; daughter Mary Gross; daughter Elizabeth Reynolds. Ex., son Joseph Norsworthy. D. May 3, 1757. R. February 2, 1758. Wit: Thomas Gale, Jethro Gale, Thomas Gale, Jr. Page 316

DODGSON, Christopher: Estate appraised by James Easson, Robert Johnson, Miles Wiles. Ordered January 6, 1758. R. February 2, 1758. Page 317

BRIDGER, Joseph, Jr.: Additional appraisal by Richard Reynolds, Samson West, Thomas Miller. R. February 2, 1758. Page 325

SCOTT, William: Estate appraised by James Hough, Michael Eley, Daniel Herring. Estate appraised in Southampton County by Miles Cary, Henry Blunt, William Taylor. R. February 3, 1758. Page 326

HAIL, Elizabeth: Estate appraised by John Morris, Philip Moody, Thomas Turner. R. March 2, 1758. Page 364

POWELL, William: Estate appraised by John Bowden, Henry Johnson, William Gay. Ordered December 1, 1757. R. March 2, 1758. Page 366

MINIARD, Barnaby: Estate appraised by Samuel Whitfield, John Whitfield, Nicholas Parker. Ordered August 6, 1757. R. March 2, 1758. Page 368

JOHNSON, Robert: Estate appraised by Moses Almand, Arthur Turner, Barnaby Little. Signed Robert Johnson, Jr. R. March 2, 1758. Page 370

TOMLIN, Benjamin: Estate appraised by John Moore, Adam Brown, Arthur Turner. Ordered November 3, 1757. R. March 2, 1758. Page 374

HOUSE, George: Estate appraised by James Watson, Arthur Applewhaite, Bartholomew Lightfoot. R. March 2, 1758. Page 375

GIBBS, Ralph: Estate appraised by Joshua Hunter, John Wright, William Richards. R. November 3, 1758. Page 377

PARKER, Wilkinson: Leg. Thomas Parker. Ex., brother Thomas Parker. D. March 19, 1758. R. April 6, 1758.
    Wit: Tristram Norsworthy, Henry King. Page 378

WILSON, George: Leg. daughter Mary Wilson, bonds in the hands of Jordan Thomas and Richard Baker; daughter Betty; daughter Honour; daughter Ann; son Solomon; daughter Ridley; wife Judith; my mother to live where she now does, paying no rent. Exs., wife and brother Samuel Wilson. D. February 20, 1758. R. April 6, 1758.
    Wit: Richard Jordan, Thomas Miller, Thomas Goodson, Rebecca Miller. Page 379

CASEY, Thomas: Of Newport Parish. Leg. granddaughter Sarah Miller; William Miller; to Samuel Morgan; to William Richards; to Martha, daughter of John Miller; nephew Thomas Casey. Ex., friend Nicholas Miller. D. March 23, 1758. R. April 6, 1758.
    Wit: William Hodsden, Samuel Morgan. Page 282

WEST, Elizabeth: Estate appraised by Bartholomew Lightfoot, William Allmand, Christopher Reynolds. Ordered March 21, 1758. R. April 6, 1758.
    Page 383

WEST, Everitt: Account estate, examined by Bartholomew Lightfoot, Christopher Reynolds, William Allmand. Among items, to widow and three children. R. April 6, 1758. Page 384

BUTLER, John: Estate appraised by Bartholomew Lightfoot, Christopher Reynolds, William Allmand. Ordered March 2, 1758. R. April 6, 1758.
    Page 385

SMITH, Jesse: Estate appraised by Robert Tyens, Thomas Brock, Christopher Reynolds, James Watson. Ordered March 2, 1758. R. April 6, 1758.
    Page 387

PYLAND, Elizabeth: Estate appraised by John Carrell, Richard Hardy, Peter Fiveash. R. May 4, 1758. Page 388

APPLEWHAITE, John: Leg. son Benjamin; son John; wife Mary; daughter Mary. Exs., wife, Mr. Richard Baker, Mr. Charles Fulgham and brother Arthur Applewhaite. D. March 1, 1758. R. May 4, 1759.
    Wit: Charles Driver, Joseph Cutchins, Anthony Holladay.
    Page 390

CASEY, Thomas: Estate appraised by William Hodsden, Thomas Whitfield, John Bidgood. R. May 4, 1758. Page 391

WILSON, George: Estate appraised by William Harrison, William Carrell, James Dering. R. May 4, 1758. Page 395

WRIGHT, John: Leg. sister Sarah Butler; to Charles, John and Ann Butler; to Juliana Bailey; to William, Ann, Juliana, George and Sarah Green; to Olive Driver; to Selia West; to Ann and Randall West; debts to be paid John Butler. Ex., Augustine King. D. June 9, 1758. R. August 3, 1758.

Wit: John Conner, Hannah King. Page 400

WHITFIELD, Samuel: Leg. wife Elizabeth; son George; daughter Jemima; son Mathais land in Nansemond County adjoining that of Thomas Witfield; daughter Elizabeth; daughter Margaret Lad. Exs., wife and son George Whitfield. D. March 27, 1758. R. August 3, 1758.
Wit: John Sawyer, Arthur Benn. Page 401

ALLMAND, James: Estate appraised by John Hodges, John Gray, Henry Harrison. R. August 3, 1758. Page 403

HOLLIWOOD, Christopher: Estate appraised by Samuel Whitfield, Richard Bagnall, Nicholas Parker. Signed Joseph Copeland. Ordered April 7, 1757. R. August 3, 1758. Page 406

PENNY, John: Estate appraised by James Channell, George Whitfield, Joseph Copeland. Signed Robert Lawrence. Ordered May 4, 1758. R. August 3, 1758. Page 407

NORSWORTHY, Joseph: Estate appraised by Richard Reynolds, Samuel Holladay, Jonathan Godwin. R. August 3, 1758. Page 409

SMITH, Mary: Estate appraised by Bartholomew Lightfoot, Robert Tynes, Charles Driver. Ordered March 2, 1758. R. August 3, 1758. Page 411

HAIL, Edward: Estate appraised by William Jordan, Andrew Sykes, Anthony Crocker. R. August 3, 1758. Page 412

APPLEWHAITE, John: Estate appraised by Richard Reynolds, Giles Driver, Charles Driver. Signed Mary Applewhaite. Page 414

HOLLADAY, Jonas: Estate appraised by James Benn, George Benn, John Morris. Ordered May 12, 1758. R. August 3, 1758. Page 418

HODSDEN, William: Leg. son Henry, all my estate in Great Britain, he paying the balance due Robert Irvin; son William all my estate in Virginia. Exs., son Henry Hodsden in Great Britain and son William Hodsden in Virginia, with friend James Ridley. D. June 13, 1758. R. August 3, 1758.
Wit: Andrew Mackie, Robert Johnston. Page 419

BRIGGS, Charles: Leg. son Inglish; son Charles; son Elias; daughter Sarah; daughter Priscilla; son James; wife Ann. Extx., wife Ann Briggs. D. April 24, 1758. R. August 3, 1758.
Wit: Ann Smith, James Dering. Page 420

GLOVER, William: Leg. son William; son John land in Nansemond County; son Richard; son Benjamin; wife Ann; daughter Sally. Exs., wife and son William Glover. D. May 27, 1750. R. September 7, 1758.
Wit: James Baker, R. Baker. Page 422

JONES, Abraham: Estate appraised by Benjamin Gwaltney, Peter Woodward, Jr., James Gwaltney. R. September 7, 1758. Page 423

WIGGS, Luke: Estate appraised by Robert Tynes, John Woodley, Mathew Jones. R. September 7, 1758. Page 426

BRIGGS, Charles: Estate appraised by William Harrison, Henry Harrison, John Barlow. R. September 7, 1758. Page 427

LAWRENCE, William: Estate appraised by Daniel Herring, Michael Eley, Joshua Council. R. September 7, 1758. Page 429

MINIARD, Barnaby: Account estate, examined by James Jordan Scott and William Haynes. R. October 5, 1758. Page 432

WHITFIELD, William: Account estate, examined by Miles Wills and Nicholas Parker. R. November 2, 1758. Page 434

DAUGHTRY, Elizabeth: Leg. son William; son Richard, legacy which formerly belonged to my brother Elisha Williams; daughter Sarah Holland; son John; son Joshua; son Moses; son Benjamin. Ex., son Richard Daughtry. D. July 26, 1758. R. November 2, 1758.
    Wit: Benjamin Whitfield, Robert Whitfield, Louisa Hedgepeth.
Page 435

WHEADON, James: Estate appraised by Richard Hardy, Peter Fiveash, Samuel Wilson. R. November 2, 1758. Page 437

BROCK, Benjamin: Of Johnston County (N. C. ?). Leg. wife Elizabeth who is to maintain my children. Extx., wife. D.-----------. R. November 2, 1758.
    Wit: Robert Reynolds, Dorothy Brock, Richard Braswell. Page 440

FONES, Robert: Leg. wife Elizabeth; son John. Ex., son John Fones. D. March 1, 1753. R. November 2, 1758.
    Wit: James Shelly, George Wainwright. Page 442

SHELLEY, Jane: Leg. son Thomas; daughter Ann White; granddaughter Sylvia Carrell; grandson Thomas Phillips; grandson John Shelley; son James. Ex., son James Shelley. D. March 17, 1758. R. November 2, 1758.
    Wit: Benjamin Phillips, Benjamin Carrell, Ann White. Page 443

DAUGHTRY, John and Elizabeth: Estate appraised by Joshua Council, James Council, Peter Butler. R. December 7, 1758. Page 444

WHITFIELD, Samuel: Estate appraised by Joseph Copeland, John Norsworthy, Anthony Fulgham. R. December 7, 1758. Page 446

PARNALL, Thomas: Estate appraised by Adam Brown, William Jordan, Anthony Crocker. Ordered January 10, 1758. R. December 7, 1758. Page 448

JORDAN, John: Leg. son John, money in the hands of Richard Jordan, Jordan Thomas and James Jones; grandson Edmund Jordan; daughter Mourning; daughter Elizabeth Thorpe; daughter Margaret Sebrell; son Joseph; son Billingsley; son Joseph. Exs., sons Joseph and Billingsley Jordan. Overseers to will, James Jordan and James Pitt. D. October 28, 1757. R. December 7, 1758.
    Wit: James Jordan, James Pitt. Page 449

WHITLEY, George: Estate appraised by Jonathan Godwin, John Godwin, Nicholas Fulgham. Ordered November 18, 1758. R. December 7, 1758. Page 451

ASKEW, Thomas: Account of sale, returned by John Eley, Jr. R. December 7, 1758. Page 453

BROCK, Benjamin: Estate appraised by James Watson, Bartholomew Lightfoot, Arthur Applewhaite. R. December 7, 1758. Page 455

WIGGS, Luke: Account estate, examined by Robert Tynes, Bartholomew Lightfoot. R. December 8, 1758. Page 456

TEASLEY, Richard: Leg. brother John. Ex., brother John Teasley. D. January 8, 1752. R. January 4, 1759.
    Wit: John Sellaway, Sampson Underwood, John Powell. Page 457

CLAYTON, John: Of Newport Parish. Leg. son George and his wife; son
William and his wife; daughter Elizabeth Miller; granddaughter Elizabeth Miller; grandson John Pinhorn; grandson Robert Pinhorn; grandson
Benjamin Miller; daughter Mary Vellines; daughter Susannah Williamson;
daughter Rebecca and her husband Thomas Miller; son John Clayton and
his wife. Exs., son John Clayton and Twait Vellines. D. ------------,
1756. R. January 4, 1759.
     Wit: Thomas Williamson, Charles Cosby.       Page 458

WRIGHT, John: Estate appraised by James Benn, Giles West, William Richards,
John Morris. R. January 4, 1759.       Page 460

TOMLIN, John: Estate appraised by Adam Brown, John Harris, Thwait Vellines.
Ordered November 2, 1758. R. February 1, 1759.       Page 462

BROCK, Susannah: Leg. son John; grandson Peter Best; grandson Robert
-------; to James Brock, the son of Benjamin Brock; to James, the son
of Robert Brock; to Jacob, the son of William Mandling (?); son
Thomas Brock. Ex., son Thomas Brock. D. October 18, 1757. R. February 1, 1759.
     Wit: Benn Willett, Elizabeth Parrie (?), Sarah Hawks.     Page 463

BRANTLEY, Benjamin: Estate appraised by Benjamin Harrison, William Harrison, William Wrenn. Ordered January 5, 1759. R. February 1, 1759.
       Page 465

HOUSE, James: Estate appraised by John Pitt, Samuel Godwin, Joshua Godwin,
William Weston. Ordered December 1, 1757. R. February 1, 1759.
       Page 465

SMITH, Joseph: Estate appraised by Nicholas Smith, William Hawkins, Thomas
Murry. Ordered February 1, 1759.       Page 468

JORDAN, John: Estate appraised by John Marshall, Robert Driver, John Newman. Signed Joseph and Billingsley Jordan. R. March 1, 1759.
       Page 470

BARLOW, Benjamin: Of Newport Parish. Leg. estate to be divided between
my four brothers, viz.: John, James, Thomas and William Barlow and
sister Priscilla Barlow's son Nathaniel Barlow. Ex., brother Thomas
Barlow. D. December 26, 1757. R. April 5, 1759.
     Wit: James Dering, Samuel Bowden, Martha Dering.     Page 474

POWELL, William: Account estate, examined by John Eley and John Darden.
Signed Elizabeth Powell. R. April 5, 1759.       Page 475

BARLOW, Benjamin: Estate appraised by James Dering, Francis Wrenn, Samuel
Wilson. R. May 3, 1759.       Page 476

FONES, Robert: Estate appraised by James Dering, James Shelley, Samuel
Wilson. R. May 3, 1759.       Page 478

SHELLEY, Jane: Estate appraised by James Dering, Henry Harrison, Samuel
Wilson. R. May 3, 1759.       Page 480

GIBBS, Ralph: Account estate, examined by Richard Reynolds and Augustine
King. R. May 3, 1759.       Page 481

DAVIS, William: Of Newport Parish. Leg. son William, land bought of
Theophilus Williams; son John, land bought of Joseph Jones; son James;
wife Deborah. Exs., son John Davis and wife Deborah Davis. D. August
28, 1757. R. May 3, 1759.

Wit: Benjamin Pynes, Elizabeth Britt, Amey Britt, Susannah
Smith. Page 482

JONES, Britain: Estate appraised by Richard Jones, Benjamin Atkinson,
Joseph Mangum. Ordered April 5, 1759. R. May 3, 1759. Page 484

CLARK, Joseph: Of Newport Parish. Leg. wife Johanna; son Henry, among all
my children. D. September 17, 1758. R. May 3, 1759.
Wit: Henry Mitchell, Caspar Mintz. Page 485

FRIZZELL, James: Estate appraised by Joseph Driver, Anthony Fulgham,
Thomas Channell. Ordered February 1, 1759. R. June 7, 1759.
Page 486

MITCHELL, Henry: Of Newport Parish. Leg. wife Rebecca, land purchased of
Richard Bray. Extx., wife. D. July 4, 1758. R. June 7, 1759.
Wit: Joseph Clark, Jesse Atkinson, Thomas Crocker. Page 487

SMITH, Mary: Account estate, examined by Augustine King and Giles West.
R. June 7, 1759. Page 489

DAVIS, William: Estate appraised by William Blunt, William Crocker, John
Morris. R. June 7, 1759. Page 489

WEST, Elizabeth: Account estate, examined by John Wills and Bartholomew
Lightfoot. Paid estate to three children. R. July 5, 1759. Page 491

BEST, Peter: Estate appraised by George Norsworthy, George Whitfield,
Richard Bagnall, Samson West. Signed Cornelius Ratcliff. Ordered
June 7, 1759. R. July 5, 1759. Page 492

CLARK, Joseph: Estate appraised by Joseph Atkinson, Moses Exum, John
Thomas. R. July 5, 1759. Page 494

CUTCHINS, Joshua: Estate appraised by William Richards, Nicholas Wail,
Samuel Weston. Signed Elizabeth Cutchins. Ordered March 1, 1759.
R. July 5, 1759. Page 495

WILLIAMS, Joseph: Estate appraised by John Baldwin, John Marshall, John
Richards. Signed Jethro Gale. Ordered June 3, 1756. R. July 6, 1759.
Page 497

JONES, Elizabeth: Estate appraised by John Jordan, John Newman, John
Wright. Signed John Wrench. Ordered May 3, 1759. R. July 5, 1759.
Page 500

BENN, George: Leg. daughter Nancy; wife Mary, my children; unborn child.
Extx., wife Mary Benn. D. February 25, 1759. R. August 2, 1759.
Wit: Nicholas Parker, James Benn. Page 502

CASEY, Thomas: Account estate, examined by Joseph Bridger and Robert Tynes.
R. August 2, 1759. Page 503

GLOVER, William: Estate appraised by John Mallory, William Carrell, Edward
Goodrich. R. August 2, 1759. Page 504

BROCK, Susannah: Estate appraised at the house of Thomas Brock by Robert
Tynes, Bartholomew Lightfoot, Charles Driver. R. September 6, 1759.
Page 507

GOODRICH, Edward: Leg. son John, land purchased of Thomas Hill and the
right to a deed of gift made my wife in 1754 by her father; son Edward;

unborn child; daughter Elizabeth, a plantation purchased of Col. John Ruffin; sister Ann Gray; to John Miller; legacy to the widow Davis (in the Bay), the widow Bell, the widow Bell (relict of Charles Briggs), the widow Rosser and the widow Pollard; wife Juliana; to Simpkins Dorman. Exs., William Davis and Richard Hardy. Trustees, John Goodrich and Thomas Day. D. July 17, 1759. R. September 6, 1759.
    Wit: John Hodges, Moses Allmand, William Bidgood.    Page 508

HUNTER, Seth: Of Newport Parish. Leg. wife Mary; daughter Frances; daughter Rodith Hunter, the child which I had by Priscilla Braswell; son Seth; son Emanuel. D. May 2, 1759. R. September 6, 1759.
    Wit: Richard Baker, Benjamin Pynes, John Day.    Page 511

BENN, George: Estate appraised by Giles West, Anthony Fulgham, Augustine King. R. September 6, 1759.    Page 514

DAVIS, Edward: Leg. son John; son Thomas; son Edward; to all my children. Exs., Robert Tynes and daughter Ann Davis. D. March 14, 1759. R. October 4, 1759.
    Wit: Benjamin Davis, Edward Davis, Easter O'Neal.    Page 515

HUNTER, Seth: Estate appraised by Richard Jones, Samuel Jones, Francis Wrenn. R. October 4, 1759.    Page 517

CLARK, John: Leg. Mary Ingram; grandsons, Yarret and John Lucks; son William; friend Elizabeth Carrell to live with my daughter Mary Ingram. If my heirs should die without issue, my estate to the widows and orphans in this county. D. October 6, 1759. R. December --, 1759.
    Wit: Mary Broadfield, Wm. Morgan, Lewis Conner, Elizabeth Carrell.    Page 518

BARLOW, Benjamin: Account estate, examined by Robert Fry and James Dering. Signed Thomas Barlow. R. December 6, 1759.    Page 520

TEASLEY, Richard: Estate appraised by Jacob Jones, William Raiford, Jr., William Segrave. R. December 7, 1759.    Page 521

WHEADON, James: Account estate, examined by John Mallory, Richard Hardy. Among items, to a legacy received of the executors of Joyce Wheadon to Mary and John Wheadon, the children of James Wheadon, decd. R. December 7, 1759.    Page 522

GLOVER, William: Account estate, examined by Dolphin Drew and William Davis. Signed Ann Glover. Among items, paid Rosamond Wilson and Richard Jordan for schooling children. R. January 3, 1760.    Page 525

SMITH, Arthur: Account estate, examined by John Wills and Charles Fulgham. Signed Elizabeth Smith. R. January 3, 1760.    Page 526

STUCKEY, Simon: Estate appraised by Joseph Norsworthy, Jonathan Godwin. Ordered November 1, 1759. R. January 4, 1760.    Page 529

GALE, Thomas: Leg. son Jethro; son Thomas; daughter Ann; younger daughters, Tabitha and Alice; daughter Elizabeth if she does not marry Joshua Jenkins; daughter Mary Spencer; friend John Marshall, Jr. to have the care of Thomas, Tabitha and Alice Gale. Ex., friend John Marshall, Jr. D. January 1, 1760. R. February 7, 1760.
    Wit: John Baldwin, Lewis Baldwin, Ann Marshall.    Page 530

FULGHAM, Mary: Leg. cousin John, the son of my brother John Fulgham; cousin Anthony Fulgham, Jr. Ex., cousin John Fulgham. D. April 6, 1759. R. February 7, 1760.

Wit: Daniel Herring, Edmund Fulgham, Ann Harris.     Page 534

PITT, Captain Henry: Account estate, examined by Giles Driver and Joseph
    Copeland. R. February 7, 1760.                    Page 535

MITCHEL, Henry: Estate appraised by Thomas Crocker, William Crocker,
    William Blunt. R. February 7, 1760.               Page 537

JONES, Abraham: Account estate, examined by Arthur Williamson, Philip
    Moody and Adam Brown. R. March 6, 1760.           Page 538

SANDERS, Solomon: Estate appraised by George Whitley, Richard Reynolds,
    Jonathan Godwin. D. April 3, 1755. R. October 2, 1758.    Page 198

    Account of his estate examined by Charles Fulgham and Richard Reynolds.
    R. November 7, 1755.                              Page 204

READ, William: Account estate, examined by H. Edmunds and John Person.
    R. November 6, 1755.                              Page 199

HOLLEMAN, Susanna: Estate appraised by Edward Portis, Britain Jones,
    Peter Woodward. R. November 6, 1755.              Page 200

WHITFIELD, John: Estate appraised by Tristram Norsworthy, Thomas Parker,
    Henry King. D. October 5, 1758. R. November 2, 1758.    Page 434

———————————————

*VOLUME III*

BOOK III

## WILL BOOK SEVEN

JOHNSON, Robert: Appraised by John Eley, John Eley, Jr., Daniel Herring.
Signed by Robert Johnson. D. December 7, 1759. R. March 6, 1760.
Page 1

WESTRAY, Edward: Appraised by Robert Johnson, John Morris, Arthur Turner.
Signed, John Westray. R. March 6, 1760. Page 2

WRENCH, John: Appraised by James Jordan, Willis Wilkinson, Horatio Durley.
Signed, Elizabeth Wrench. R. March 6, 1760. Page 4

JONES, James: Account estate, to balance paid the heirs of the estate of
John Wrench; widow's dower; paid, James, Thomas and Jonathan Jones;
cash paid John Wrench; cash paid Samuel Farmer Wrench. Signed,
Elizabeth Jones. Examined by James Jordan, Willis Wilkinson, Horatio
Durley. R. March 6, 1760. Page 4

JONES, Elizabeth: Account estate, paid John Wrench, his father's estate.
Signed, John Wrench. Examined by James Jordan, Willis Wilkinson,
Horatio Durley. R. March 6, 1760. Page 5

GALE, Thomas: Appraised by William Pass, John Murphy, Jr., George Hall.
Signed, John Marshall. D. February 7, 1760. R. April 3, 1760.
Page 6

WESTRAY, Hardy: Leg. Aunt Patience Westray; brother Fulgham Westray; Sarah
Fulgham and Mary Westray. Extx., Patience Westray. D. February 5,
1760. R. April 3, 1760.
Wit: Edmund Westray, Benjamin Westray, Alice Westray. Page 9

BAKER, Lawrence, of the Parish of Newport: Leg. daughter Katherine; son
Richard, land in Isle of Wight and Surry Counties; daughter Ann Nelson;
son James Baker (if he should be alive) my land in North Carolina; wife
Ann; to all my children. Ex., son Richard Baker. D. December 25,
1758. R. April 3, 1760.
Wit: Robert Johnston, James Shelley, John Fones. Page 10

TOMLIN, Benjamin: Account estate, examined by Daniel Herring and John
Marshall. R. May 1, 1760. Page 12

HOUGH, James: Appraised by John Baldwin, John Marshall, William Pass.
Signed, Mary Hough. Ordered, October 4, 1759. R. May 1, 1760.
Page 13

HOUGH, James: Account estate, paid Hezekiah Hough; negro boy to Joseph
Sykes, which he claims. Examined by John Marshall, John Baldwin,
Michael Eley. R. May 1, 1760. Page 17

JONES, Mathew: Inventory returned by Abraham Jones. R. May 1, 1760.
Page 18

197

NORSWORTHY, John, of Newport Parish: Leg. wife Isabel; son Tristram; son John; son-in-law John Peal, after his mother's death a negro already given her. Exs., son Tristram and wife Isabel Norsworthy. D. March 5, 1760. R. May 1, 1760.
Wit: Tristram Norsworthy, Jr., John Whitfield, Samuel Bagnall.
Page 18

NORSWORTHY, John: Appraised by Nicholas Parker, Henry King, Anthony Fulgham. Signed, Tristram Norsworthy. R. July 3, 1760.                     Page 20

MOORE, Lucy: Inventory returned by Thomas Moore. D. 1759. R. July 3, 1760.                                                                Page 21

MONRO, John: Gentleman. Leg. daughter Mary Bryant; granddaughter Sarah Bryant; grandson John Monro Bryant; daughter Lydia; daughter Urania. Exs., son-in-law John Bryant and John Woodley. D. June 20, 1760. R. July 3, 1760.
Wit: Joshua Godwin, Thomas Cutchins, Martha Lillow (?). Page 22

ATKINSON, Mary: Single woman. Leg. to John, the son of William Davis; to William, son of William Davis; to James, son of William Davis. Ex., William Davis. D. May 5, 1749. R. August 7, 1760.
Wit: Celia Tynes, Josiah Hart, Thomas Tynes.                     Page 24

BAKER, Lawrence: Appraised by James Derring, Samuel Wilson, James Shelley. R. August 7, 1760.                                                Page 25

WAINWRIGHT, William: Account estate, to cash paid his brothers and sisters on account of his father's estate. Signed, Robert Campbell. Ordered, April 5, 1759. Examined by Nicholas Parker and Henry King.
R. August 7, 1760.                                              Page 29

BROWNE, Captain Samuel: Appraised by Richard Baker, James Sheddon, George Purdie. Ordered, July 3, 1760. R. August 7, 1760.              Page 30

TOMLIN, John: Account estate, examined by James Bridger and John Eley, Jr. Signed, Martha Tomlin. R. August 7, 1760.                       Page 32

GOODRICH, Edward: Appraised by William Harrison, Henry Harrison, John Mallory. Ordered, September 6, 1759. R. August 7, 1760.           Page 33

MILLER, Thomas: Appraised by Henry Harrison, John Hodges, John Gray. Ordered, April 6, 1758. R. November 6, 1760.                       Page 37

BUTLER, John: Account estate, examined by John Wills and Bartholomew Lightfoot. D. June 16, 1759. R. November 7, 1760.                 Page 39

WILSON, Rosamond: Appraised by Henry Harrison, William Davis, Joseph Cutchins. Ordered, March 6, 1760. R. November 7, 1760.            Page 40

ATKINSON, Mary: Appraised by Arthur Davis, William Blunt, John Woodley. R. December 4, 1760.                                             Page 41

BARLOW, Martha: Leg. daughter Ann Harrison; granddaughters, Molly and Martha Harrison; son Jesse Barlow. Exs., William Carrell and son Jesse Barlow. D. March 5, 1760. R. December 4, 1760.
Wit: Dolphin Drew, John Welch.                                  Page 41

JONES, Mathew: Account estate, divided into four equal parts. Examined by Adam Brown, Benjamin Gwaltney, James Gwaltney. R. December 4, 1760.
Page 43

STUCKEY, Simon: Account estate, examined by Charles Fulgham and Jonathan Godwin. R. December 4, 1760.                                  Page 44

MONRO, John: Appraised by John Pitt, Joshua Godwin, Samuel Godwin. Signed, John Bryant. R. December 4, 1760.                          Page 45

DAVIS, Edward: Appraised by Bartholomew Lightfoot, Charles Chapman, Joseph Hill. Ordered, October 4, 1759. R. January 1, 1761.        Page 47

NORSWORTHY, Joseph: Leg. wife Mary, my whole estate. Wife, Extx.
     D. December 14, 1760. R. January 1, 1761.
          Wit: Thomas Norsworthy, Wm. (or W. N.) Norsworthy, Thomas
               Miller.                                               Page 49

GODWIN, Joseph: Leg. grandsons, Joseph and James, the sons of my son Mathew Godwin; grandson James, the son of my son James Godwin; grandson Joseph, the son of my son James; grandson Joseph Pitt; grandsons Jonathan and Samuel, sons of my son Jonathan Godwin; daughter Patience Pitt; daughter Martha Milner; son Thomas; son Samuel; daughter Elizabeth Smith. Ex., son-in-law James Pitt. D. November 17, 1757. R. January 1, 1761.
          Wit: Thomas Godwin, James Godwin, Samuel Bridger.         Page 50

BRIDGER, Joseph: Account estate, to cash paid Andrew Mackie on account of Martha Wright. D. 1758. Examined by John Wills and Charles Fulgham.
     R. January 1, 1761.                                            Page 52

WHEADON, James: Additional account estate, to boarding three children. Signed John Carrell. Examined by Richard Hardy, William Davis.
     R. January 1, 1761.                                            Page 53

CROCKER, Joseph: Leg. son Samuel; son Robert; my father-in-law, Robert Lancaster to have the use of my son Robert's land until he is twenty-one; daughter Martha; daughter Mary; William Williford is to have my son Samuel; Robert Lancaster my son Robert; Elizabeth Jones, my daughter Martha; Martha Lancaster, Jr., my daughter Mary. Ex., William Williford. D. December 13, 1760. R. February 5, 1761.
          Wit: Thomas Pretlow, Elizabeth Crocker, Olive Crocker, Arthur
               Crocker. William Williford refused the Executorship,
               Thomas Pretlow qualified.                           Page 53

MILLER, Thomas: Estate account, examined by John Mallory and Moses Allmand.
     R. February 5, 1761.                                          Page 55

CROCKER, Joseph: Appraised by Thomas Holleman, James Gwaltney, Benjamin Gwaltney. March 5, 1761.                                       Page 56

BARLOW, Martha: Appraised by Richard Hardy, John Carrell, Jeremiah Peirce.
     R. March 5, 1761.                                             Page 57

MORRISON, William: Appraised by George Purdie and James Watson. Signed, James Sheddon. Ordered, September 8, 1758. R. March 5, 1761.
                                                                   Page 59

PITT, John: Leg. a suit now depending for 500 acres, that Captain John Monro died in possession of, to be continued for my son; wife Priscilla; son John; daughter Elizabeth; daughter Priscilla; son William Pitt.
     D. December 6, 1760. R. March 5, 1761.
          Wit: William Casey, Elizabeth Cutchins, Samuel Cutchins, Jr.
                                                                   Page 61

MORRISON, William: Estate account, to James Sheddon, paid for necessities for the children. Examined by Andrew Mackie, George Purdie, Will Robertson.
     R. April 2, 1761.                                            Page 62

MARSHALL, James: Leg. wife Mary; daughter Martha; daughter Mary; daughter
Ann Edwards; grandson James Edwards; daughter Patience Jordan. Ex.,
John Marshall, Jr. D. July 7, 1759. R. April 2, 1761.
  Wit: John Baldwin, William Lankford, Ann Marshall.     Page 64

PONSONBY, William: Merchant. Leg. my natural son, William Ponsonby, alias
Lewis; my natural daughter Mary Ponsonby, alias Lewis; to Sophia Lewis.
Exs., Mrs. Sophia Lewis and Joseph Scott. D. September 18, 1760.
R. April 2, 1761.
  Wit: William Ponsonby, Jr., Mary Ponsonby, Joseph Fulgham.
                                                          Page 66

SMITH, Elizabeth: Leg. granddaughter Silvia Jordan; daughter Mary Holladay;
granddaughter Charity Holladay; daughter Elizabeth Godwin; son Thomas
Smith. Ex., son Thomas Smith. D. April 15, 1760. R. April 2, 1761.
  Wit: James Pitt, Patience Pitt, Elizabeth Godwin.      Page 70

DAVIS, Edward: Account estate, examined by Bartholomew Lightfoot and Charles
Chapman. R. April 2, 1761.                               Page 72

HAWKINS, John, Sr.: Of Newport Parish. Leg. cousin Mary Norsworthy, the
wife of George Norsworthy. Exs., Mary and George Norsworthy.
D. August 12, 1754. R. May 8, 1761.
  Wit: Thomas Gale, Jethro Gale, Thomas Norsworthy, Joseph
  Lawrence.                                              Page 75

MONTGOMERY, Robert: Appraised by Tristram Norsworthy, Jr., Tristram Norsworthy, Sr., Henry King. Signed John Fulgham. Ordered March 5, 1761.
R. May 7, 1761.                                          Page 76

LILE, Thomas: Appraised by John Godwin, Joseph Fulgham, Jonathan Godwin.
R. May 7, 1761.                                          Page 77

CLARK, John: Appraised by Jonathan Godwin, George Reynolds, Augustine King.
R. March 7, 1761.                                        Page 79

NORSWORTHY, Joseph: Appraised by Brewer Godwin, Jonathan Godwin, Richard
Reynolds. R. May 7, 1761.                                Page 81

CHAPMAN, John: Appraised by William Harrison, William Davis, Benjamin
Harrison. Ordered, April 2, 1761. R. May 7, 1761.        Page 83

BRANTLEY, John: Appraised. Signed, Silvia Brantley. Ordered, January 1,
1761. R. June 4, 1761.                                   Page 84

JACKSON, Mary: Of the Town of Smithfield. Leg. Hannah Miller, for want of
heirs to my friend Richard Baker; to Lawrence, the son of Richard Baker;
to friend Bartholomew Lightfoot. Guardian to Hannah Miller and Exs.,
friends, Bartholomew Lightfoot and Richard Baker. D. September 22,
1760. R. June 4, 1761.
  Wit: Robert Crocker, John Day.                         Page 85

PEIRCE, Honour: Leg. son Jeremiah; grandson John Lightfoot; grandson Josiah
Wilson, the son of Samuel; granddaughter Honour Wilson, the daughter of
son George; son Samuel; daughter Honour Sims. Exs., Samuel Wilson and
Jeremiah Peirce. D. November 6, 1760. R. June 4, 1761.
  Wit: William Wrenn, William Webb, Elizabeth Miller.    Page 86

MARSHALL, James: Appraised by John Baldwin, William Pass, George Hall.
Signed, John Marshall. Ordered, April 2, 1761. R. June 4, 1761.
                                                          Page 87

NORSWORTHY, Rachel:  Of Newport Parish.  Leg. son Thomas Parker; son Elias Parker; grandson Joseph Bridger; to John Parker, son of Elizabeth Pilkington; granddaughter Siller Parker.  Ex., son Thomas Parker. D.  June 1, 1759.  R.  June 4, 1761.
    Wit:  Joseph Chapman, Joseph Hawkins.        Page 89

DELK, Roger:  Appraised by Richard Hardy, Henry Harrison, Peter Fiveash. Ordered, March 5, 1761.  R.  June 4, 1761.      Page 90

FLOYD, Thomas:  Appraised by Tristram Norsworthy, George Norsworthy, Thomas Parker.  Signed, Richard Jordan.  Ordered, December 4, 1760.  R. June 4, 1761.      Page 90

POPE, Robert:  Leg. son William; son John; wife Elizabeth.  Exs., wife Elizabeth and Moses Powell.  D.  --------- R.  June 4, 1761.
    Wit:  Theophilus Joyner, Thomas Edwards.      Page 92

PITT, ------ (Indexed as John Pitt):  Appraised by John Bryant, William Weston, Joshua Godwin.  Ordered, March 5, 1761.  R.  July 2, 1761.
        Page 93

RICHARDS, William:  Appraised by James Benn, Giles West, Joshua Hunter. Ordered, March 21, 1761.  R.  July 2, 1761.      Page 95

GODWIN, John:  Leg. wife Mary; daughter Martha; son John; son William; daughter Elizabeth Green Godwin; daughter Mary; daughter Ann Eley, items now in the hands of Capt. John Eley, Jr.; grandson Mills Eley. Exs., wife Mary and Jonathan Godwin.  D.  May 23, 1761.  R.  July 2, 1761.
    Wit:  Mary Hawkins, Jacoby West.      Page 97

PONSONBY, William:  Appraised by John Woodley, John Joyner, Arthur Apple-whaite.  R.  July 2, 1761.      Page 98

WHITLEY, John:  Of Newport Parish.  Leg. son Nathan; son William; wife Mary; daughter Mary; daughter Susanna; son John; son George; son Thomas; grandson William Whitley.  Ex., son Nathan Whitley.  D.  March 22, 1750.  R.  July 2, 1761.
    Wit:  Robert Edwards, William Edwards.      Page 102

SAUNDERS, Henry:  Appraised by John Baldwin, William Pass, Andrew Sykes. Ordered April 2, 1761.  R.  August 5, 1761.      Page 103

NOLLEY, Needham:  Appraised.  (No signatures)  Ordered May 7, 1761. R.  August 5, 1761.      Page 105

PEIRCE, Honour:  Appraised by Joseph Cutchins, John Pinhorn, Valentine Jenkins.  R.  August 5, 1761.      Page 107

TURNER, Martha:  Of the Parish of Newport.  Leg. grandson Thomas Turner; granddaughter Elizabeth Turner; granddaughter Martha Turner; daughter Elizabeth.  Ex., daughter Elizabeth Turner.  D.  March 2, 1752. R.  August 5, 1761.
    Wit:  James Bridger, Arthur Turner, Martha Turner.    Page 108

GODWIN, John:  Appraised by Joseph Fulgham, Nicholas Fulgham, George Reynolds. R.  September 3, 1761.      Page 109

HAWKINS, John:  Appraised by Joseph Copeland, Tristram Norsworthy, Thomas Parker.  Ordered, March 7, 1760.  R.  September 3, 1761.    Page 112

TOMLIN, Martha:  Leg. daughter Martha Evans; granddaughter Mary Tomlin;

granddaughter Celia Evans; to Hester Bracey; to daughter-in-law Ann Tomlin; daughter Ann Harris; daughter Mary Britt; to son-in-law ------; son James. Ex., son James. D. May 2, 1761. R. September 3, 1761.
Wit: Thomas Bracey, Hester Bracey. Page 112

HATTON, Thomas: Appraised by William Rand, Signe Parish, Bartholomew Lightfoot. R. September 3, 1761. Page 114

EATON, Thomas: Appraised by William Rand, Signe Parish, Bartholomew Lightfoot. R. September 3, 1761. Page 115

GODWIN, Joseph: Appraised by John Bryant, William Weston, Joshua Godwin. Signed, James Pitt. Ordered, January 1, 1761. R. October 1, 1761.
Page 115

COUNCIL, Peter: Appraised by Jacob Butler, John Daughtrey, Richard Bradshaw. Ordered, September 25, 1761. R. October 1, 1761. Page 117

POPE, Robert: Appraised by George Hall, Will Woodward, John Marshall. R. December 3, 1761. Page 119

WILSON, George: Account estate, examined by Dolphin Drew and Richard Hardy. R. December 3, 1761. Page 121

WHITLEY, John: Appraised by George Hall, John Morris, John Joiner. R. December 3, 1761. Page 122

TURNER, John: Leg. son William; son John; son James; son Thomas; daughter Penelope Whitley; daughter Elizabeth Whitley; daughter Patience Garner; son George. Ex., son George Turner. D. July 16, 1757. R. December 3, 1761.
Wit: Robert Tynes, Christopher Reynolds, John Joiner. Page 123

SMITH, Elizabeth: Appraised by Nicholas Smith, Joseph Hawkins, William Hawkins. Signed, Thomas Smith. 'R. January 7, 1762. Page 125

CLARKE, John: Account estate, examined by George Reynolds, Augustine King. R. January 7, 1762. Page 125

BRACEY, Hugh: Leg. son-in-law William Blunt; daughter Elizabeth Blunt; daughter Sarah Bracey. Extx., daughter Amey Bracey. D. March 26, 1749/50. R. February 4, 1762.
Wit: George Goodrich, Caspar Mintz, William Jordan. Page 126

RATCLIFFE, Cornelius: Leg. John Outland; Cornelius Moore; Martha Winslow; John Jordan, over the Nansemond River; to Richard Jordan and his wife Elizabeth and to his brothers and sisters; John Newman; Rachel Outland's heirs; Thomas Outland, my plantation on the Western Branch; to Cornelius Outland, son of Thomas Outland; to Giddion Moore. Exs., Thomas Outland and Giddion Moore. D. December 8, 1762. R. February 4, 1762.
Wit: Charles Driver, Henry Pitt, Samuel Cutchins. Page 128

HOLLADAY, Samuel: Appraised by Charles Driver, George Reynolds, Jonathan Godwin. Ordered, February 6, 1761. R. February 4, 1762. Page 129

BENN, Arthur: Of Newport Parish. Leg. three eldest sons, Tristram, Arthur and Thomas Benn; daughter Ann; to three youngest sons, Thomas, James and Wi----- (?); to cousin Tristram Norsworthy, Jr.; to George Whitfield. D. January 23, 1762. R. February 4, 1762.
Wit: Christopher Benn, Joseph Lawrence. Page 130

THOMAS, Richard: Of Newport Parish. Leg. loving wife ------ Thomas; son John; to Moses Exum; son William; daughter ------ Haile; to Mary Gale; to Sarah Haywood. Exs., son John Thomas and Moses Exum. D. October 30, 1761. R. February 4, 1762.
    Wit: Caspar Mintz, William Crocker.        Page 132

MILLER, Nicholas: Leg. daughter Lucie, wife Lucie; daughter Sarah. Extx., wife Lucie Miller. D. August 13, 1761. R. February 4, 1762.
    Wit: Thomas Miller, John Smith, John Bidgood.        Page 133

EXUM, Elizabeth: Appraised by John Baldwin, Robert Babb, Joshua Gay. Ordered, January 7, 1762. R. March 5, 1762.        Page 134

TOMLIN, Martha: Appraised by Adam Brown, Twaits Vellines, John Fulgham. Ordered, September 3, 1761. R. March 5, 1762.        Page 135

PARKER, Nathaniel: Appraised by Joseph Coupland, Henry King, Thomas Parker. Signed, Nicholas Parker. Ordered, February 4, 1762. R. March 5, 1762.
        Page 137

APPLEWHITE, John: Account estate, to dower; to Benjamin's share; John's share; Mary's share. Examined by Richard Reynolds and Charles Driver. R. March 5, 1762.        Page 138

PATTASON, Charles: Leg. daughter Hannah; son Sandford; daughter Elizabeth; son Benjamin Pattason. Ex., John Mallory. D. January 13, 1762. R. ----------
    Wit: William Webb, John Bidgood.        Page 139

WILSON, Henry: Appraised by Francis Ward, James Pitman, Thomas Womble. Ordered, March 4, 1762. R. April 1, 1762.        Page 139

POWELL, John: Leg. daughter Mourning Deloach; daughter Mary Riggins; daughter Elizabeth Pilkington; daughter Christian Garner; wife Alice; sister Sarah Powell; daughter Sarah Powell; daughter Lydia; son Moses Powell. Ex., son Moses Powell. D. June 14, 1760. R. April 1, 1762.
    Wit: John Marshall, Ann Marshall, Elizabeth Gale.    Page 140

PERSON, Samuel: Leg. wife Sarah; daughter Rebecah, with reversion to brothers, Joseph, Jacob and Jesse Person and sister Lucy Person. D. October 10, 1761. R. April 1, 1762.
    Wit: Caspar Mintz, Joseph Mangum, Henry Mangum, Michael Deloach, Mourning Deloach.        Page 141

MILLER, Nicholas: Appraised by Thomas Whitfield, William Harrison, Charles Chapman. R. April 1, 1762.        Page 142

COOK, Joel: Leg. son Rueben; daughter Sarah; son Josiah; all my children to be placed under the care of their grandfather, William Eley. Ex., William Eley, the Elder. D. October 12, 1761. R. April 2, 1762.
    Wit: William Eley, Jr., John Cathon, Thomas Draper.    Page 144

DAVIS, John: Leg. daughter Elizabeth; wife Jane; son William. Exs., son William Davis and Richard Hardy. D. February 1, 1762. R. April 2, 1762.
    Wit: William Carrell, William Chapman, Nicholas Bourden.
        Page 145

BRACEY, Hugh: Appraised by William Crocker, John Thomas, John Chapman. R. April 1, 1762.        Page 145

BENN, Arthur: Appraised by Christopher Benn, George Norsworthy, Thomas Parker. R. April 1, 1762.        Page 146

TURNER, John: Appraised by Theophilus Joyner, John Joyner, Nathan Bracey.
R. April 1, 1762. Page 147

ROBERTS, John, Sr.: Leg. son John; son Thomas; son William; daughter Martha;
grandson Jacob Roberts; grandson Thomas Roberts; granddaughter Christian
Roberts; granddaughter ----- Roberts. Ex., son John Roberts. D. March 22,
1758. R. April 1, 1762.
Wit: Mich'l Eley, Henry Wright, Robert Eley, Benjamin Eley.
Page 148

JACKSON, Mary: Appraised by William Rand, Andrew Mackie, Samuel Wentworth.
R. April 1, 1762. Page 149

WESTON, Mary: Appraised by Thomas Parker, John Williams, Thomas Murrey.
Signed, Samuel Hawkins. Ordered, March 4, 1762. R. May 6, 1762.
Page 152

JONES, Thomas: Appraised by John Bryant, Joshua Godwin, George Green.
Ordered, May 7, 1761. R. April 1, 1762. Page 153

DODGSON, Christopher: Estate account, with Sparling and Bolden, Administrators. D. January 1, 1762. R. April 1, 1762. Page 155

MANGUM, Joseph: Leg. eldest son Micajah; son Elisha; son Josiah; wife Lucy.
Exs., wife Lucy Mangum and son Micajah Mangum. D. February 28, 1762.
R. May 6, 1762.
Wit: Jacob Person, Henry Mangum, Samuel Person, William Davis.
Page 157

WRIGHT, John: Account current of estate. (No signatures) R. May 6, 1762.
Page 158

CHAPMAN, John: Account estate, examined by William Harrison and William
Davis. R. May 6, 1762. Page 159

DELK, Roger: Account estate, examined by Dolphin Drew and Richard Hardy.
Signed, Benjamin Edwards. R. May 6, 1762. Page 160

WILSON, Henry: Account estate, examined by Charles Chapman, Sr. and John
Woodley. Signed, Thomas Coffer. R. May 6, 1762. Page 161

GWALTNEY, Benjamin: Appraised by Peter Woodward, Solomon Delk, John
Stephenson. R. June 3, 1762. Page 161

JORDAN, James: Appraised by Robert Driver, Nicholas Wale, John Newman.
Ordered, September 25, 1761. R. June 3, 1762. Page 163

GREEN, George: Appraised by Augustine King, Giles West, Miles Wills.
Ordered, April 1, 1762. R. June 3, 1762. Page 164

POWELL, John: Appraised by John Marshall, John Smelly, John Joyner.
Signed, Moses Powell. R. June 3, 1762. Page 165

ROBERTS, John: Inventory of estate, presented by John Roberts, Jr.
R. June 3, 1762. Page 167

PERSON, Samuel: Appraised by Francis Ward, Thomas Cofer, James Pitman.
R. June 3, 1762. Page 167

SELLAWAY, Richard: Leg. wife Mary, all the land left me by my father; to
Jane Sellaway, the negro given me by John Sellaway, at the death of my
wife. Wife, Extx. D. March 19, 1762. R. June 3, 1762.
Wit: John Pinner, Sarah Pinner, John Pinner, Jr. Page 169

DAVIS, Major John: Appraised by Thomas Day, William Carrell, Moses Allmand. Ordered, April 5, 1762. R. July 1, 1762.                                    Page 170

MATHEWS, Joseph: Appraised by Samuel Everett, John Everett. Ordered, May 7, 1761. R. July 1, 1762.                                                       Page 172

SMELLY, John and Mary his wife, Plts. against Lydia Richards, for the division of the land and slaves, which the father of the Plt. and Deft. died siezed of. Divided by Giles Driver, James Benn, Charles Driver. Ordered, March 5, 1762. R. July 2, 1762.                                  Page 173

EDWARDS, Robert: Of Newport Parish. Leg. cousin William Edwards part of an escheat patent granted to my cousin Henry Edwards and the testator, with the proviso that he deeds 100 acres adjoining to my son Solomon; son Robert; daughter Martha Norsworthy; daughter Temperance Bracey. Ex., son Solomon Edwards. D. March 30, 1762. R. July 1, 1762.
      Wit: William Whitley, Joshua Edwards, William Edwards,
             Philip Moody.                                               Page 174

GODWIN, Edmund: Leg. to my wife, the plantation on which Martha Pitt now lives, with reversion to my son Edmund; son Jeremiah, with reversion to my three children, Edmund, Elizabeth and Millicent; daughter Priscilla; son Brewer; granddaughter Julia Pitt. Exs., wife and Mr. Arthur Applewhaite. D. January 31, 1762. R. July 1, 1762.
      Wit: Thomas Applewhaite, Nicholas Parker.                          Page 176

CROCKER, Joseph: Account estate, presented by Thomas Pretlow. R. July 1, 1762.                                                                        Page 176

JOHNSON, Ann: Appraised by Henry Lancaster, Edward Portis, Thomas Holleman. Ordered, June 5, 1762. R. July 1, 1762.                                       Page 177

COOK, Joel: Appraised by Adam Brown, Peter Woodward, William Woodward. R. July 1, 1762.                                                               Page 178

BATTEN, John: Leg. wife Martha; son John; son Joshua; to Moses Jordan; to Frances Jordan; equal division of my estate, between son Joshua, daughter Sarah and Frances Jordan and her daughter Mary. Wife, Extx. D. February 13, 1762. R. ----------
      Wit: Daniel Batten, John Stroud, William Batten.                   Page 180

JONES, Richard: Leg. son Benjamin, land bought of John Meacom; son Solomon, land bought of Major Richard Baker; son Jacob; son Richard; son Jesse. Extx., wife Mary Jones. D. March 7, 1757. R. ----------
      Wit: Caspar Mintz, Sarah Mintz, Benjamin Jones.                    Page 181

JACKSON, John, Sr.: Leg. son Elijah; son Elisha; son-in-law John Little; son-in-law John Edwards; son-in-law Thomas Childs; son John; son Jacob; son William; daughter Elizabeth; daughter Rachel; daughter Silvia; daughter Edney; wife Ann. Wife, Ann Jackson, Extx. D. October 4, 1761. R. May 6, 1762.
      Wit: James Bridger, Robert Coggan, William Webb.                   Page 181

RATCLIFF, Cornelius: Appraised by Joseph Coupland, Thomas Parker, Mathew Jordan. R. August 5, 1762.                                                      Page 182

GARNER, John: Leg. daughter Sarah Mathews; daughter Mourning Dixon; daughter Mary Everett; daughter Elizabeth Gale; daughter Garnes Neavill; daughter Penelope Bullock; wife Elizabeth; son John; granddaughter Margaret Bullock; son-in-law Jethro Gale; son-in-law Samuel Mathews. D. September 30, 1761. R. August 5, 1762.
      Wit: Samuel Everett, Sarah Everett, John Bullock, William
             Bullock.                                                    Page 184

GREEN, John: Appraised by John Brown, Joseph Cutchins, Samuel Cutchins. Signed, Sarah Covatan (Covington) Green. R. August 5, 1762. Page 186

SELLAWAY, Richard: Appraised by John Baldwin, Andrew Sikes, Gale Eley. R. August 5, 1762. Page 187

HALE, William: Appraised by William Jordan, Twaits Vellines, Adam Brown. Signed Tabitha Hale. Ordered May 6, 1762. R. August 5, 1762. Page 188

PATTASON, Charles: Appraised by John Mallory, Samuel Wilson, Henry Harrison. R. August 5, 1762. Page 190

JOYCE, Thomas: Appraised by Pitt Reynolds, Jonathan Godwin, Joseph Brantley. Ordered, April 1, 1762. R. August 5, 1762. Page 190

GROSS, Jonathan: Appraised by Richard Reynolds, Pitt Reynolds, Jonathan Godwin. Ordered, July 1, 1762. R. August 5, 1762. Page 191

REYNOLDS, George: Appraised by Charles Driver, John Smelley, Jr., John Brown. Ordered, May 6, 1762. R. August 5, 1762. Page 192

GARLAND, Samuel: Account estate, examined by Tristram Norsworthy, Joseph Coupland. R. August 5, 1762. Page 193

BULLOCK, Joseph: Appraised by Samuel Everett, William Everett, Thomas Sheavers. Signed, Penelope Bullock. Ordered, December --, 1761. R. August 5, 1762. Page 194

BULLOCK, John: Appraised by John Marshall, John Murfree, Jr., Thomas Smelley. Ordered, March --, 1762. R. August 5, 1762. Page 195

BULLOCK, John: Account estate, examined by Richard Hardy, Thomas Miller, John Marshall, Jonathan Godwin. Signed, Joseph Scott. R. August 5, 1762. Page 196

GODWIN, Sarah: Appraised by William Edwards, Joshua Edwards, Joshua Edwards, Jr. Signed, Robert Edwards. Ordered, July 1, 1762. R. September 2, 1762. Page 197

BRIGGS, Ann: Leg. daughter Ann Smith; daughter Elizabeth Smith; daughter Mary Harris; son James Briggs; daughter Priscilla; son James to be apprenticed to James Miller; daughter Priscilla to be bound to my sister Margaret Wilson, if she will take her, if not to James Shelley and his wife. Ex., Samuel Wilson. D. June 9, 1762. R. October 7, 1762.
    Wit: William Webb, Sarah Barmer. Page 198

GIBBS, John: Appraised by John Scammell, John Murry, John Barlow. Ordered, August 5, R. October 7, 1762. Page 199

HARRISON, William: Leg. son Benjamin; son William, tract bought of William Davis and one bought of John Chapman; son John, my house in Smithfield, occupied by Seth Pointer; son Henry; daughter Sarah Driver; daughter Ann Allmand; daughter Mildred; daughter Elizabeth; daughter Lucy; granddaughter Martha Fiveash; wife Elizabeth Harrison. Ex., brother Henry Harrison. D. October 11, 1762. R. November 4, 1762.
    Wit: Richard Hardy, Robert Johnston, Thomas Whitfield. Page 200

GODWIN, Edmond: Appraised by John Bryant, Joseph Coupland, Joseph Cutchins, Anthony Fulgham. R. November 4, 1762. Page 202

CAMPBELL, Robert:  Appraised by Nathaniel Smith, William Hawkins, Joseph
    Hawkins.  Signed, Richard Campbell.  Ordered, September 2, 1762.
    R.  November 4, 1762.                                    Page 203

BRIGGS, Ann:  Appraised by James Derring, John Barlow, John Bidgood.
    R.  November 4, 1762.                                    Page 205

COUNCIL, Peter:  Account estate, examined by James Bridger, John Eley, Jr.
    Signed, James Council.  R.  November 4, 1762.           Page 206

BATTEN, John:  Appraised by William Whitley, John Morris, Joseph Edwards.
    R.  November 4, 1762.                                    Page 207

THOMAS, Richard:  Appraised by William Jordan, William Crocker, Arthur Davis.
    Signed, John Thomas and Moses Exum.  R.  November 4, 1762.    Page 208

LAWRENCE, Sarah:  of Newport Parish.  Leg. son John; son Mills; daughter
    Mary; daughter Ann; to Thomas Lankford, Sr.  Ex., brother Arthur Apple-
    whaite.  D.  October 6, 1762.  R.  December 2, 1762.
        Wit:  Thomas Lankford, Hardy Lawrence, Jr., Sarah Lawrence.
                                                            Page 209

JOHNSON, Ann:  Account estate, examined by James Bridger, Daniel Herring.
    Signed, James Gwaltney.  R.  December 2, 1762.          Page 210

RICHARDSON, William:  Appraised by Jethro Gale, John Marshall, John Morris.
    Ordered, August 5, 1762.  R.  December 2, 1762.         Page 212

SMELLEY, Thomas:  Of Newport Parish.  Leg. son Thomas, land adjoining John
    Lawrence; son Robert, land adjoining Thomas Outland, Jacob Powell and
    Joseph Jordan; son William; wife Martha; daughter Mary.  Exs., sons,
    Thomas and Robert Smelley.  D.  October 12, 1762.  R.  December 2, 1762.
        Wit:  John Baldwin, Jesse Hutchens, Thomas Strickland.    Page 213

NORSWORTHY, Rachel:  Account of sales, returned by Thomas Parker.
    R.  December 2, 1762.                                    Page 215

MURRY, William:  Appraised by John Scammell, Wilson Brantley, Benjamin
    Harrison.  Ordered, June 3, 1762.  R.  July 1, 1762.    Page 215

WESTRAY, John:  Leg. son Exum; wife Sarah; daughter Martha; son Daniel; son
    James Westray.  Ex., Edmond Westray.  D.  November 29, 1762.
    R.  January 6, 1763.
        Wit:  Benjamin Westray, Benjamin Westray, Jr., Richard Pearce.
                                                            Page 216

MARSHALL, James:  Account estate, examined by Michael Eley, William Pass,
    John Baldwin.  R.  January 6, 1763.                     Page 217

BENN, James:  Appraised by Jonathan Godwin, John Clark, Augustine King.
    R.  January 6, 1763.                                    Page 218

GALE, Thomas:  Account estate, examined by Michael Eley, William Pass,
    John Baldwin.  R.  January 6, 1763.                     Page 220

JACKSON, John:  Appraised by John Bourden, William Raiford, William Peirce.
    Signed, Mary Jackson.  R.  January 6, 1763.             Page 221

EDWARDS, Robert:  Appraised by George Hall, Thomas Turner, Daniel Batten.
    R.  February 3, 1763.                                   Page 222

WESTRAY, Hardy:  Appraised by Robert Johnson, Daniel Batten, John Stroud.
    Ordered, April 6, 1760.  R.  February 3, 1763.          Page 223

WESTRAY, Edward:  Account estate examined by James Bridger and Daniel Herring.
R.  February 3, 1763.                                            Page 224

INGRAM, Jennings:  Leg. daughter Caty; wife Sarah; daughter Jane.  Ex.,
Valentine Jenkins.  D.  March 6, 1762.  R.  February 3, 1763.
Wit:  John Hodges, Jr., Simkins Dorman.                       Page 225

OGLESBY, Peggy:  Appraised by William Rand, Andrew Mackie, John Taylor.
Ordered, February 4, 1762.  R.  April 7, 1763.                  Page 225

GODWIN, John:  Account estate, examined by Richard Reynolds, Brewer Godwin.
R.  April 7, 1763.                                              Page 226

COUNCIL, James:  Appraised by Joshua Council, James Tallaugh, Edward Batten.
R.  April 7, 1763.                                              Page 227

DUCK, William:  Of Newport Parish.  Leg. son William land bought of William
Parker; daughter Sarah Owen; daughter Mary Johnson; son John; daughter
Elizabeth; son Robert; wife Ellinor; daughter Selah.  Ex., son William
Duck.  D.  February 7, 1763.  R.  April 7, 1763.
Wit:  Abraham Carr, Timothy Duck, John Gwin.                  Page 228

JONES, Richard:  Appraised by Mason Braddy, Henry Mangum, Joseph Atkinson.
R.  April 7, 1763.                                              Page 229

BROWN, John:  Appraised by Joshua Godwin, Joseph Cutchins, William Weston.
Signed, Mary Brown.  Ordered, October 7, 1762.  R.  April 7, 1763.
                                                                Page 232

GREEN, George:  Account estate, examined by Richard Reynolds, Giles West,
Augustine King.  R.  April 7, 1763.                             Page 232

HOUSE, Martha:  Appraised by Nicholas Wale, John Newman, John Wrench.
R.  April 7, 1763.                                              Page 233

WESTRAY, John:  Appraised by Daniel Batten, John Morris, Robert Johnson.
R.  April 7, 1763.                                              Page 233

HARRISON, William:  Appraised by John Mallory, Samuel Wilson, William Davis,
Thomas Whitfield.  R.  April 7, 1763.                          Page 235

MILNER, Betty:  Leg. brother Pate Wills Milner; brother John Milner, one-half
the money, which is in the possession of my uncle Benjamin Wills, the
other half to my aunt Martha Richards.  Extx., aunt Martha Richards.
D.  February 12, 1763.  R.  April 7, 1763.
Wit:  James Bidgood, Mary Wills.                              Page 238

WRIGHT, Henry:  Appraised by Andrew Sikes, Gale Eley, John Watkins.
Ordered, February 3, 1763.  R.  May 5, 1763.                   Page 238

BRIAND, James:  Leg. to John Briand's son John; grandson Peter Council;
son-in-law James Council; wife Joanna.  Ex., James Council.  D. May 2,
1761.  R.  May 5, 1763.
Wit:  Thomas Lankford, Jr., Andrew Griffin, Solomon Edmonds.
                                                                Page 240

BASLOR, Francis:  Appraised by William Blunt, William Crocker, Arthur Davis.
Ordered, April 7, 1763.  R.  May 5, 1763.                      Page 241

REYNOLDS, Christopher:  Leg. son Sharpe, the plantation I bought of my cousin
Christopher Reynolds; son Saunders; daughter Sweeting.  Ex., John Joyner.
D.  March 22, 1763.  R.  May 5, 1763.
Wit:  Robert Tynes, Bartholomew Lightfoot, Charles Driver.
                                                                Page 242

MURRY, John: Leg. son Thomas; son William (deceased); grandson John Scott; daughter Elizabeth; daughter Sarah; to my wife. D. May 28, 1762. R. May 5, 1763.
      Wit: Benjamin Harrison, Sally Glover.              Page 242

CASEY, Nicholas: Leg. son William, the plantation left me by my father; son Henry; daughter Jane Chapman; daughter Constant Barlow; daughter Harty Womble; wife Constant; son Thomas; daughter Selah. Exs., wife and son William. Overseer, friend Henry Harrison. D. March 14, 1763. R. May 5, 1763.
      Wit: John Bidgood, William Webb.             Page 244

GROSS, Jonathan: Account estate, among items-to Thomas Davis Gross' account. Examined by Richard Reynolds, Jonathan Godwin. R. May 5, 1763.
                                           Page 244

INGRAM, Jennings: Appraised by Thomas Whitfield, William Harrison, John Mallory. R. May 5, 1763.                  Page 245

BENN, James: Leg. Thomas Driver, son Giles Driver; sister Mary Haines; sister Julian Frizzell; to Elizabeth Reid; to my brother's children, George, Nancy and Thomas Driver. Ex., Giles Driver. D. April 6, 1762. R. May 6, 1763.
      Wit: John Clark, Robert Pitt, William Booker.      Page 246

BENN, James: Will presented by Giles Driver, thereupon Mary Benn, mother and next friend to George Benn, an infant and heir at law of the said James Benn, by Richard Kello her attorney, opposed the proof of same. Depositions taken of John Clark, Robert Pitt, William Booker, aged 18 years, Hannah King, aged 45 years, West Gross, Jonathan Godwin and William Green ----- the Court of the opinion that the said writing is the true last will and testament of the said James Benn, etc. Page 246

DARDEN, Jacob: Account estate, examined by John Baldwin, John Marshall, William Pass. R. June 2, 1763.                 Page 249

CARY, John: Appraised by Thomas Day, William Carrell, William Glover. Ordered, May 18, 1762. R. June 2, 1763.         Page 250

PEIRCE, Honour: Account estate, examined by Richard Hardy and Benjamin Harrison. R. June 2, 1763.                Page 252

JONES, Thomas: Account estate, examined by John Wills and John Scarsbrook Wills. R. June 2, 1763.                  Page 253

BASLOR, Francis: Account estate, examined by Robert Tynes, Arthur Applewhaite. Signed, John Chapman. R. June 2, 1763.    Page 254

DUCK, William: Appraised by Hardy Darden, John Darden, Timothy Duck. R. July 7, 1763.                        Page 254

CARR, Hardy: Appraised by Hardy Darden, Samuel Johnson, Timothy Duck. Ordered, June 24, 1763. R. July 7, 1763.        Page 256

HOLLADAY, Jonas: Account estate, examined by John S. Wills and Richard Reynolds. R. July 7, 1763.                Page 257

SMELLEY, Thomas: Inventory presented by Thomas and Robert Smelley. R. July 7, 1763.                      Page 258

SCOTT, William: Account estate, paid Elizabeth Scott, paid Elizabeth Bailey, paid William Scott, paid Mary Scott, paid Robert Scott and Sarah Scott.

Examined by James Bridger, Michael Eley and John Woddrop. (Covers 37 pages.) R. July 7, 1763. Page 260

HAILE, William: Account estate, examined by Daniel Herring, William Woodward. Signed, Tabitha Haile. R. August 4, 1763. Page 297

REYNOLDS, George: Account estate, examined by Richard Reynolds and Charles Driver. R. August 4, 1763. Page 298

HOUSE, James: Estate account. Signed Martha House. Paid dower to Martha House.
HOUSE, Martha: Account estate, examined by Willis Wilkinson and Samuel Godwin. Signed, Christopher Haynes. R. August 4, 1763. Page 299

RICHARDS, William: Account estate, to cash due John and Josiah Wills, orphans of Thomas Wills. Examined by John Scarsbrook Wills and Giles West. R. August 4, 1763. Page 300

JORDAN, Richard: Appraised by William Barlow, Thomas Cofer, Joseph Maddera. Ordered, April 7, 1763. R. August 4, 1763. Page 301

VAUGHAN, Samuel: Of Newport Parish. Leg. wife Rebeccah; daughter Elizabeth; daughter Sarah; son Thomas. Wife, Extx. D. March 29, 1763. R. September 1, 1763.
    Wit: Thomas Lankford, Jr., Robert Tallow, William Tallow. Rebecca Vaughan refused Extx., James Bridger qualified. Page 302

BATTEN, John: Account estate, examined by Bartholomew Lightfoot and Arthur Applewhaite. R. September 1, 1763. Page 303

APPLEWHAITE, John: Account estate, examined by Richard Reynolds and Charles Driver. R. September 1, 1763. Page 304

WILLS, Miles: Estate appraised by Richard Reynolds, John Smelley, Jr., Giles Driver. Ordered, July 7, 1763. R. September 1, 1763. Page 304

CASEY, Richard: Appraised by Bartholomew Lightfoot, James Watson, Anthony Holladay. Signed, John S. Wills. R. September 1, 1763. Page 305

WILLIS, Thomas: Examined by George Purdie, Richard Baker, James Easson. D. September 2, 1963. R. ---------- Page 306

LANE, Timothy: Appraised by Augustine King, Giles West, William Green. Signed, John Brown. D. October 7, 1762. R. ---------- Page 309

THOMAS, Richard: Account estate, paid legacies to Thomas Whitney Gale, Tabitha Haile, Sarah Westray. (?). Examined by Dolphin Drew and William Jordan. R. October 6, 1763. Page 310

MURRY, John: Appraised by James Derring, John Barlow, Wilson Brantley. R. October 6, 1763. Page 311

ATKINSON, Christopher: Leg. grandson Owen Atkinson; son Benjamin; daughter Elizabeth Manford; son Arthur; daughter Lucy; daughter Martha Arnall; wife Elizabeth. Exs., wife and son Benjamin Atkinson. D. July 17, 1763. R. October 6, 1763.
    Wit: John White, James Cofer, Edward Portis. Page 314

FONES, Elizabeth: Leg. son John, all my share of the estate of William Shelley, decd. D. February 12, 1763. R. October 6, 1763.
    Wit: Thomas White, James Shelley. Page 315

210

GRIFFIN, Katherine: Of Newport Parish. Leg. daughter Rebecca; son Lott; son Andrew. Exs., sons Lott and Andrew. D. March 14, 1763. R. November 3, 1763.
    Wit: Thomas Fowler, William Carr, Ann Griffin. Page 316

PARNALL, William: Leg. wife Sarah; son Benjamin, land on which Joseph Parnall now lives; son Frederick; daughter Olive; daughter Mary; daughter Elizabeth. D. February 2, 1763. R. November 3, 1763.
    Wit: William Jordan, Joseph Parnall, Mary Harris. Page 317

MILLER, Nicholas: Account estate, examined by Dolphin Drew and John Mallory. R. November 3, 1763. Page 317

BRYANT, James: Appraised by John Daughtrey, William Edmonds, Joshua Council. R. December 1, 1763. Page 319

GREEN, John: Account estate, examined by John S. Wills, Joseph Cutchins. R. December 1, 1763. Page 320

COOK, Joel: Account estate, examined by Michael Eley, John Eley, Jr. Signed, William Eley. R. February 2, 1764. Page 320

PARNALL, William: Appraised by William Jordan, George Goodrich, Benjamin Clark. R. February 2, 1764. Page 321

BRIDGER, Robert: Of Newport Parish. Leg. wife Mary; son James, in case he should marry Elizabeth Williams; son John; son William; son Samuel; son Joseph; son Lear; son Robert; granddaughter Sarah Jones; grandson Bridger Jones. Exs., sons Samuel and Joseph Bridger. D. November 17, 1763. R. February 2, 1764. Friends, Captain James Bridger and Colonel Joseph Bridger, Trustees.
    Wit: William Weston, James Pitt.
Joseph Bridger refused to serve as an Ex., Samuel Bridger qualified.
    Page 322

EXUM, Elizabeth: Account estate, examined by John Baldwin, John Marshall, William Eley. R. February 2, 1764. Page 324

CUTCHINS, Elizabeth: Leg. niece Sarah Scammell; sister Hanritten (?) Scammell; to Mary, Elizabeth and Ann Scammell; to William Mallory, the son of John Mallory; my money to be divided equally between my brothers and sisters. Ex., brother Joseph Cutchins. D. January 18, 1764. R. April 6, 1764.
    Wit: Wilson Brantley, Lucy Miller, John Mallory. Page 327

CUTCHINS, Joshua: Account estate, examined by John Bryant and William Weston. Signed, Elizabeth Cutchins. R. April 6, 1764. Page 328

VAUGHAN, Samuel: Appraised by Benjamin Darden, Thomas Lankford, Jr., John Daughtrey. Signed, James Bridger. Ordered, September 1, 1763. R. April 6, 1764. Page 329

DAVIS, Major John: Account estate, examined by Dolphin Drew, Richard Hardy, Thomas Day. Signed, Jane Davis and William Davis. R. April 7, 1764.
    Page 331

WASHINGTON, Sarah: Leg. cousin Timothy Tynes, the son of my brother Robert Tynes, the money I received from my husband's estate of Joseph Washington; sister Jane Tynes; my father's estate to be divided among the five children of my brother Robert, viz.-Robert, Henry, Mary, Jean and Sarah Tynes. Ex., cousin Timothy Tynes, the son of my brother Robert. D. March 6, 1764. R. April 6, 1764.

Wit: Robert Tynes, Sr., Robert Tynes, Jr., Mary Tynes.
Robert Tynes qualified, Timothy Tynes being under age.          Page 334

WILLS, John: Account estate, paid widow's dower, paid the orphans. Examined
    by James Pedin, John Bryant, Willis Wilkinson. Signed, Sarah Bryant.
    R.  April 6, 1764.                                          Page 335

REYNOLDS, Christopher: Appraised by Charles Driver, Jesse Atkinson, Thomas
    Uzzell.  Signed, John Joyner.  R.  April 6, 1764.           Page 337

WEBB, Samuel: Leg. son William; daughter Mary in care of son William; son
    Samuel; son Matthais; son James; daughter Martha; to Frances Merry; to
    John Berriman's first child by his last wife; wife Susanna.  Exs.,
    William and Samuel Webb, my sons.  D.  March 10, 1764.  R. ----------
        Wit:  William Glover, John Gray, John Glover.           Page 340

COUNCIL, James: Account estate examined by Daniel Herring and John Eley, Jr.
    Signed, Elizabeth Council.  R.  May 3, 1764.                Page 342

CUTCHIN, Elizabeth: Appraised by Benjamin Harrison, James Derring, John
    Barlow.  R.  May 3, 1764.                                   Page 343

HARRISON, Elizabeth: Her dower allotted in the estate of William Harrison
    by Dolphin Drew, William Davis and Richard Hardy.  R.  May 3, 1764.
                                                                Page 344

PITT, Joseph: Appraised by Joshua Godwin, Samuel Godwin, William Weston.
    Ordered, May 10, 1764.  Signed, Sarah Pitt.  R.  June 7, 1764.
                                                                Page 344

CARR, Hardy: Account estate, examined by Daniel Herring and John Eley, Jr.
    Signed, Robert Carr, Ex. of the estate of Robert Carr, Administrator of
    Hardy Carr.  R.  July 5, 1764.                              Page 347

HARRISON, William: Account estate, examined by Dolphin Drew and Richard
    Hardy.  Signed, Henry Harrison.  R.  July 5, 1764.          Page 348

DICKSON, Thomas: Inventory presented by Tristram Norsworthy.  R.  July 5,
    1764.                                                       Page 349

MURRY, Ann: Her dower allotted in the estate of John Murry, by Dolphin Drew
    and Richard Hardy.  R.  July 5, 1764.                       Page 350

GRIFFIN, Catherine: Appraised by John Gwin, James Council, Joseph Fowler.
    R.  August 2, 1764.                                         Page 351

BROWN, Robert: Leg. grandson John Weatherley; to Elizabeth Weatherley; to
    William Weatherley; to Elizabeth Jones; to son-in-law Jonathan Jones;
    to Robert, Thomas, James and Jonathan Jones; to Francis Brown; to Keziah
    Brown; daughter Margaret Snowden; cousin Mary Gray; cousin John Brown;
    to Peggy Snowden; to Mary Brown.  Ex., John Brown.  D.  October 31,
    1763.  R.  August 2, 1764.
        Wit:  Nathaniel Smith, George Brown.                    Page 351

WEBB, Samuel: Appraised by Moses Allmand, William Glover, William Carrell.
    R.  August 2, 1764.                                         Page 353

BIDGOOD, William: Appraised by Benjamin Harrison, William Carrell, John
    Wrenn.  Ordered, May 3, 1764.  R.  August 3, 1764.          Page 356

WESTRAY, John: Account estate, to Benjamin Westray, the guardian of Joseph
    Tomlin's orphans; to paid Edward Westray's orphans; to paid Edmund
    Westray for settling the estate of Edward Westray.  Examined by William

Eley and Daniel Derring.  R.  August 2, 1764.                    Page 358

GOODRICH, Edward:  Account estate, to cash paid for burying Joshua and
    George (Goodrich?).  Examined by Richard Baker and Dolphin Drew.
    R.  August 3, 1764.                                          Page 360

SELLAWAY, Richard:  Account estate, examined by James Bridger and Michael
    Eley.  Signed by Benjamin Stevens and Mary his wife, Extx.  R. August 3,
    1764.                                                        Page 363

SCOTT, James Tooke:  Appraised by Benjamin Harrison, Thomas Whitfield, John
    Barlow.  Ordered, November 3, 1763.  R.  June 7, 1765.       Page 365

BEALE, William:  Of Newport Parish.  Leg. wife Easter; son Jacob; son William;
    son Richard; grandchildren, Thomas and Elizabeth Vaughan; daughter Mary
    Joiner; daughter Priscilla Carr.  Ex., son Jacob Beale.  D.  October 13,
    1764.  R.  February 7, 1765.
        Wit: Edward Beaton, John Council, Thomas Inglish, Jr.   Page 368

SMELLEY, John:  Leg. son John; son James; daughter Jean Woodward; daughter
    Ann; wife Sarah; son Samuel.  Exs., wife and son John Smelley.
    D.  September 16, 1764.  R.  February 7, 1765.
        Wit: William Woodward, John Norsworthy, Mary Smelley.   Page 369

FULGHAM, Charles:  Of Newport Parish.  Leg. to brother Joseph Fulgham, now
    living in Plymouth, New England, with reversion of the bequest to his
    son Charles; to cousin Martha Reynolds, in case she dies, bequest to go
    to the use of a free school, to be kept in the town of Smithfield;
    Godson Brewer Godwin; Goddaughter Margaret Eason; to Priscilla Godwin;
    to Brewer Godwin's son Brewer; wife Ann.  Ex., wife Ann Fulgham, in
    case of her death, my friend James Eason.  I request Mrs. Eason to have
    the care of my darling Martha Reynolds.  D.  November 8, 1764.
    R.  February 7, 1765.
        Wit: James Ronaldson, Thomas Browne, Robert Sheddon.    Page 371

PERSON, Samuel:  Account estate, being guardian for Jesse Person, by cash
    due by the death of his two brothers James and Henry Person.  Examined
    by James Derring, Samuel Wilson and William Jordan.  R.  February 7,
    1765.                                                        Page 375

SMITH, Nicholas:  Appraised by Joseph Hawkins, Benjamin Hawkins and Thomas
    Murry.  Ordered, February 7, 1765.  R.  March 7, 1765.       Page 376

BROWN, Robert:  Appraised by Joseph Hawkins, Benjamin Hawkins, Samuel
    Hawkins.  R.  March 7, 1765.                                 Page 379

BRIGGS, Ann:  Account estate, examined by James Derring, Henry Harrison.
    R.  March 7, 1765.  Signed, Samuel Wilson.                   Page 380

GWALTNEY, Benjamin:  Account estate, examined by Dolphin Drew, R. Hardy,
    James Derring.  Signed, James Gwaltney.  R.  April 4, 1765.  Page 382

TEASLEY, John:  Leg. son John, the plantation on which George Teasley
    formerly lived; son Silas; wife Mary; to all my children.  Wife, Extx.
    D.  December 30, 1759.  R.  May 2, 1765.
        Wit: William Eley, Jacob Jones, Ann Peirce.             Page 383

GRAY, John:  Appraised by Twaits Vellines, Adam Brown, James Gwaltney.
    Ordered, March 7, 1765.  R.  May 2, 1765.                    Page 384

SMELLEY, John:  Appraised by Thomas Smelley, James Uzzle, John Daniel.
    R.  May 2, 1765.                                             Page 387

ATKINSON, Joseph: Leg. eldest son Jesse; son Joseph; son James; daughter
    Mary Person; daughter Celia; grandson Wilson Atkinson, son of Jesse
    Atkinson and Mary his wife; my wife Mary. Ex., son Joseph Atkinson.
    D. February 6, 1761. R. May 2, 1765.
        Wit: Jacob Person, James Jordan, John Smith, John Jordan.
                                                            Page 390

BEALE, William: Appraised by Joshua Council, Andrew Griffin, Thomas Lank-
    ford, Jr. R. June 6, 1765.                             Page 393

FIVEASH, Peter: Appraised by James Derring, Samuel Wilson, John Carrell,
    Henry Harrison. Ordered, March 14, 1765. R. June 6, 1765. Page 393

PITT, Sarah: Appraised by Samuel Godwin, Joseph Cutchins, Samuel Cutchins,
    Jr. R. June 7, 1765.                                   Page 394

TEASLEY, John: Appraised by Gale Eley, Robert Coggin, William Peirce.
    R. July 4, 1765.                                       Page 400

CROCKER, Joseph: Account estate, to cash paid William Williford as guardian.
    Examined by Bartholomew Lightfoot, Moses Allmand, Samuel Wilson.
    Signed, Thomas Pretlow. R. July 4, 1765.               Page 401

PATTERSON, Charles: Account estate, examined by Richard Hardy and Dolphin
    Drew. Signed, Robert Burwell. R. July 4, 1765.         Page 402

STAGG, Edward: Appraised by Adam Brown, Isaac Moody, Twaits Vellines.
    R. August 2, 1765.                                     Page 404

SCOTT, William: Account estate, among items, suit depending between Ben-
    jamin Bailey and wife Plts. against Elizabeth Scott and others.
    Examined by Richard Baker, Dolphin Drew, Richard Hardy. R. August 2,
    1765.                                                  Page 404

BENN, Arthur: Account estate, examined by Joseph Coupland, Thomas Parker.
    R. September 5, 1765.                                  Page 406

CAMPBELL, Robert: Account estate, to paid Wainwright's estate, paid the
    widow's share, paid Richard Campbell's share. Examined by Brewer God-
    win and Charles Driver. R. September 5, 1765.          Page 406

MONTGOMERY, Robert: Account estate, examined by Nicholas Parker and
    Tristram Norsworthy. R. September 5, 1765.             Page 407

PILAND, James: Account estate, to cash due the orphans. Examined by Richard
    Hardy and Dolphin Drew. R. September 5, 1765.          Page 408

DRIVER, Giles: Appraised by Tristram Norsworthy, Joseph Coupland, Thomas
    Parker. Ordered, April 4, 1765. R. September 5, 1765.  Page 409

PINNER, Thomas: Leg. wife Mary; son Thomas, land which was his mother's;
    daughter Hannah Right; grandson Joseph Right; grandson Henry Right;
    grandson Josiah Pinner; daughter Penelope Bullock; grandson Joseph
    Bullock; son John. Ex., son John Pinner. D. March 3, 1764.
    R. October 3, 1765.
        Wit: Christopher Reynolds, Thomas Dixon, Joseph Bullard.
                                                            Page 413

FLOYD, Francis: Appraised by Will Robertson, Thomas Miller, John Taylor.
    Ordered, April 4, 1765. R. October 3, 1765.            Page 415

MATHEWS, Joseph: Account estate, examined by Michael Eley and John Marshall.
    R. August 1, 1765.                                     Page 417

BEST, Martha: Appraised by Joseph Coupland, Mills (Miles) Wills, Richard Bagnall. Ordered, October 3, 1765. R. July 3, 1766. Page 417

PITT, Major Joseph: Account estate, examined by John S. Wills and William Weston. R. July 3, 1766. Page 418

PITT, John: Account estate, paid Lydia her part of her father's estate, paid Samuel Browne his part; paid Joseph Cutchin for expenses for a lawsuit in Williamsburg. Examined by John S. Wills and William Weston. R. July 3, 1766. Page 419

BRIDGER, Robert: Account estate, examined by John S. Wills, Samuel Godwin, Samuel Cutchins, Jr. R. July 3, 1766. Page 420

BRIDGER, Robert: Appraised by Samuel Godwin, Thomas Burk, William Weston. R. July 3, 1766. Page 421

SUMMERRELL, John: Account estate, by John Wills, administrator of the part of the estate which came into his hand after the death of Hugh Giles; paid Mary Wainwright's legacy; paid Mrs. Edward Goodson's legacy. Examined by Nicholas Parker, Robert Tynes and James Watson. R. September 5, 1765. Page 423

JOHNSON, Robert: Of the Upper Parish. Leg. son Robert; son Lazarus; son Jesse; wife Priscilla; son Mial; daughter Martha Coupland; daughter Mourning; daughter Priscilla. Exs., son-in-law James Coupland and son Mial. D. January 24, 1761. R. August 7, 1766.
    Wit: W. Baker, Hardy Darden, John Darden, Jr., Moses Johnson.
                                                              Page 424

APPLEWHAITE, Arthur: Leg. son Henry, the plantation at the Brick Church; son Josiah; son Arthur; son John; son Mills (Miles) land in Southampton County; son Thomas Land in Southampton County; daughter Ann; daughter Mary; wife Jane. Exs., wife, John Woodley and son Henry. D. June 23, 1766. R. August 7, 1766.
    Wit: Elizabeth Crofts, William White, Robert Tynes. Page 426

WARD, Joseph: Leg. son John; son Joseph; daughter Elizabeth Stallings; wife Elizabeth; bequest to be divided between son Joseph, daughter (s?) Ann Maddra, Unity Edwards, Sarah Berriman and Lucy Lee; at my wife's death her part of my estate to be divided among all my children. Exs., wife and son Joseph Ward. D. December 12, 1762. R. August 7, 1768.
    Wit: Richard Jordan, Francis Wrenn, Benjamin Jones. Page 428

RICHARDSON, William: Account estate, examined by Daniel Herring and John Eley, Jr. Signed, Ann Richardson. R. August 7, 1768. Page 430

ALLEN, Joseph: Leg. sister Sarah Allen. Ex., sister Sarah Allen. D. October 20, 1764. R. August 7, 1766.
    Wit: Thomas Street. Page 431

WHITLEY, Mary: Leg. grandson Thomas Whitley; son Nathan. Ex., son Nathan Whitley. D. July 1, 1766. R. August 7, 1766.
    Wit: William Ponsonby, George Hall. Page 432

SMITH, John: Leg. son John; daughter Faithy; to Elizabeth Miller. Exs., Henry Harrison and Samuel Wilson. D. October 29, 1765. R. September 4, 1766.
    Wit: William Webb, Samuel Webb. Page 433

MARSHALL, John: Leg. grandson Thomas Gale; granddaughter Ann Gale; granddaughter Elizabeth Gale; granddaughter Tabitha Gale; granddaughter Alice

Gale; son John. Ex., son John Marshall. D. April 11, 1760.
R. October 2, 1766.
        Wit: John Baldwin, Lewis Baldwin, Robert Eley, John Lawrence.
                                                            Page 433

WARD, Joseph: Appraised by James Derring, Samuel Wilson, William Barlow.
    R. October 2, 1766.                                      Page 435

BENN, George: Account estate, examined by Richard Reynolds and Giles West.
    R. September 4, 1766.                                     Page 437

WEBB, Samuel: Estate account examined by John Mallory and William Carrell.
    Signed, William Webb. R. October 2, 1766.               Page 438

CHANNELL, James: Of Newport Parish. Leg. daughter Pegga and Mary Sikes to
    have an equal share of my estate. Exs., Mary Sikes and Tristram Nors-
    worthy. D. February 10, 1765. R. October 3, 1766.
        Wit: Stephen Smith, Elizabeth Channell.             Page 439

RAMPHORN, Elizabeth: Appraised by John Pinner, Joseph Bullock, William
    Bullock. Ordered, August 7, 1766. R. November 6, 1766.   Page 440

JOHNSON, Robert: Appraised by Timothy Duck, John Daughtrey, Thomas Lankford,
    Jr. R. November 6, 1766.                                 Page 442

BURK, Thomas: Account estate, examined by John Scarsbrook Wills and Samuel
    Godwin. R. November 6, 1766.                             Page 443

HARRISON, John: Account estate, paid the widow; balance due the child.
    Examined by John S. Wills and Samuel Godwin. D. August 7, 1766.
    R. November 6, 1766.                                     Page 443

THOMAS, Jacob: Appraised by Jonathan Godwin, Charles Driver, John Smelley.
    R. December 4, 1766.                                     Page 444

STAGG, Edward: Account estate, among items, balance due the widow and orphan.
    Signed, Daniel Herring. Examined by James Bridger and John Eley, Jr.
                                                            Page 446

FULGHAM, Nicholas: Leg. son Nicholas; daughter Jemimah. Ex., brother
    Joseph Fulgham. D. January 18, 1766. R. December 4, 1766.
        Wit: Francis Murry, Elizabeth Fulgham, Chastity Godwin. Page 446

PARR, Thomas: Appraised by John Newman, Willis Bullock, Thomas Bullock.
    R. December 4, 1766.                                     Page 447

RAMPHORN, Elizabeth: Account estate, examined by John S. Wills and John
    Pinner. R. December 4, 1766.                            Page 449

PARR, Thomas: Account estate, examined by John S. Wills, John Newman and
    Willis Bullock. R. December 4, 1766.                    Page 450

FONES, John: Appraised by James Derring, Samuel Wilson, James Shelley.
    Ordered, November 8, 1766. R. December 4, 1766.         Page 451

HAYNES, William: Leg. wife Catherine; son William; if my son should die
    without heirs, my estate at my wife's death to be divided between
    Lawrence Baker, the son of Richard Baker and Mary Nelson, the daughter
    of William Nelson and wife Ann of Surry County; to John Drew, the son
    of John Drew of Nansemond County; to my nephew William Cole Haynes. Exs.,
    friend Richard Baker and wife. D. November 9, 1766. R. December 4,
    1766.

                                216

Wit: Dolphin Drew, Richard Hardy, William Piland, John
Carrell.                                                      Page 452

BROWNE, Samuel: Account estate, examined by George Purdie and John Mallory.
Signed, Samuel Wentworth. R. December 4, 1766.          Page 455

RICHARDSON, Ann: Her dower allotted in the estate of William Richardson, by
John Eley, Jr. and William Ponsonby. R. December 4, 1766.   Page 455

SMELLEY, John: Account estate, examined by John S. Wills and Bartholomew
Lightfoot. R. February 5, 1767.                          Page 457

CAMPBELL, Robert: Account estate, examined by Brewer Godwin and Charles
Driver. R. February 5, 1767.                             Page 457

BRIDGER, Joseph, Jr.: Account estate, examined by John S. Wills, John
Monro, Charles Fulgham. D. April 10, 1758. R. February 5, 1767.
                                                         Page 459

SMITH, John: Appraised by James Shelley, Samuel Wilson, William Clayton.
R. February 5, 1767.                                     Page 460

MURRY, John: Account estate, among items, due to orphans of William Glover;
estate in the hands of the widow, to be divided between the said Ann
and John Murry. Examined by James Derring and Benjamin Harrison.
R. February 5, 1767.                                     Page 461

MURRY, William: Account estate, to cash John Murry loaned his son William
Murry. Examined by James Derring and Samuel Wilson. R. February 5,
1767.                                                    Page 462

PINNER, Thomas: Appraised by William Bullock, Thomas Bullock, Joseph Bullock.
R. March 5, 1767.                                        Page 463

MILLER, John: Appraised by Benjamin Harrison, Joseph Cutchins, Valentine
Jenkins. R. April 2, 1767.                               Page 464

PORTLOCK, Charles: Account estate, to paid Thomas Walton's administrators
in trust for Robert Darwin and wife. Examined by R. Kello and D.
Fisher. Ordered, August 9, 1765. R. May 7, 1767.         Page 466

ELEY, William: Leg. daughter Sophia; wife Sarah; son William; to the
children of my daughter Priscilla Cook; to the children of my daughter
Martha Barrow; to the children of my daughter Doughtie Hall. Exs.,
son William and nephew John Eley, son of John Eley. D. December 21,
1766. R. May 7, 1767.
Wit: John Pretlow, Lazarus Johnson.                      Page 468

APPLEWHAITE, Arthur: Appraised in the County of Southampton, by Richard
Murfree, William Williams and William Edwards. R. May 7, 1767.
                                                         Page 469

CASEY, Nicholas: Appraised by William Davis, Benjamin Harrison and William
Hodsden. R. May 7, 1767.                                 Page 470

FLOYD, Thomas: Account estate, examined by Nicholas Parker and Thomas
Parker. Signed, Richard Jordan. R. May 7, 1767.          Page 472

EDWARDS, William: Appraised by John Marshall, Jethro Gale, Daniel Batten.
Ordered, May 7, 1767. R. June 4, 1767.                   Page 473

CASEY, Nicholas: Account estate, examined by William Davis and William
Hodsden. R. June 4, 1767.                                Page 475

DIXON, William:  Appraised by Jonas Shivers, Samuel Everett and Joseph
    Everett.  Ordered, May 6, 1762.  R.  July 2, 1767.          Page 476

SCOTT, James Tooke:  Account estate, examined by John Mallory and William
    Davis.  Signed, William Holowell.  R.  July 2, 1767.        Page 477

SHELLEY, James:  Leg. wife Mary; son James; son John; son William; daughter
    Ann; daughter Mary.  Exs., wife and brother Thomas Shelley.  D.  July 17,
    1766.  R.  September 3, 1767.
        Wit:  Thomas White, Shelton Delk.                       Page 479

GODWIN, Read:  Leg. wife and children; land in Nansemond County to be sold.
    Ex., brother Thomas Godwin.  D.  June 2, 1767.  R.  September 3, 1767.
        Wit:  James Pitt, Samuel Godwin, William Lawrence.      Page 479

FULGHAM, Nicholas:  Estate appraised by Jonathan Godwin, Augustine King,
    Thomas King, Jr.  R.  September 3, 1767.                    Page 480

JONES, John:  Leg. son James; grandson John Jones; wife Patience.  Extx.,
    wife Patience Jones.  D.  September 12, 1767.  R.  October 1, 1767.
        Wit:  Jethro Gale, John Coggan, Prudence Green.         Page 483

SHELLEY, James:  Appraised by James Derring, Henry Harrison and Samuel
    Wilson.  R.  October 1, 1767.                               Page 483

SWETT, Conny:  Appraised by James Gwaltney, Thomas Holleman, Benjamin
    Atkinson.  R.  November 5, 1767.                            Page 486

WOOTTEN, John:  Appraised by John Hodges, Jr., John Bidgood, William Hodsden.
    Ordered, September 15, 1767.  R.  December 3, 1767.         Page 487

DORMAN, Simpkins:  Appraised by William Carrell, Benjamin Harrison, Edward
    Dews.  Ordered, April 4, 1767.  R.  December 3, 1767.       Page 489

HODSDEN, William:  Account estate, examined by John Mallory and William
    Davis.  Signed, James Ridley.  R.  December 3, 1767.        Page 490

HODSDEN, William:  Appraised in Southampton County, by Thomas Moore, Timothy
    Thorpe, James Jones.  Ordered, May 31, 1759.  R.  December 3, 1767.
                                                                Page 492

APPLEWHAITE, Arthur:  Appraised by Robert Tynes, Jesse Atkinson, James
    Watson.  R.  May 7, 1767.                                   Page 492

HODSDEN, William:  Appraised by George Purdie.  Ordered, August 3, 1758.
    R.  December 3, 1767.                                       Page 494

GODWIN, Reade:  Appraised by William Weston, John Bridger, Nicholas Wail.
    R.  January 8, 1768.                                        Page 499

COLLINGS, William:  Leg. wife Sarah; son James; son Jesse; daughter Eliza-
    beth Keen; daughter Mary Keen; to Jethro Collings.  Wife Sarah, Extx.
    D.  August 14, 1767.  R.  February 4, 1768.
        Wit:  Thomas Lankford, Jr., Jonathan Robertson, Archelaus
            Robertson.                                          Page 500

BURT, John:  Account estate, examined by John Baldwin, Thomas Smelley, Robert
    Babb.  R.  March 3, 1768.                                   Page 501

COLLINGS, William:  Appraised by John Daughtrey, Jonathan Robinson, Joshua
    Council.  R.  March 3, 1768.                                Page 502

218

FULGHAM, Anthony: Of Newport Parish. Leg. wife; daughter Mary; son John; daughter Celia. Ex., son John Fulgham. D. January 3, 1768. R. March 3, 1768.
Wit: Edmund Godwin, Thomas Mackinnie, Stephen Smith.   Page 503

RICHARDS, Martha: Leg. son Miles Wills; son John Wills, Jr.; son Josiah Wills; daughter Mille Richards. Exs., sons Miles and John Wills, Jr. D. August 24, 1762. R. March 3, 1768.
Wit: Francis Milner, Samuel Morgan.   Page 504

MINYARD, Ezekiah: Appraised by Joseph Coupland and Thomas Parker. Signed, Richard Jordan. Ordered, March 5, 1767. R. March 3, 1768.   Page 505

GRAY, Aaron: Appraised by Tristram Norsworthy, Joseph Copeland, Henry King. Signed, Wm. Gray. R. May 5, 1768.   Page 506

SMITH, Stephen: Leg. daughter Martha; between all my children; son William Smith. D. April 16, 1765. R. May 5, 1768.
Wit: John S. Wills, Rachel Wills.   Page 507

RICHARDS, Martha: Appraised by John Butler, Giles West, Augustine King. R. May 5, 1768.   Page 508

SMITH, Stephen: Appraised by Bartholomew Lightfoot, Anthony Holladay, Charles Driver. R. June 2, 1768.   Page 509

PARKER, Martha: Leg. grandson Isham Coupland; granddaughter Ann Coupland; with reversion of bequest, first to Esther Holladay and then to Elizabeth Pinner, daughter of my brother John Pinner. Ex., friend Richard Parr. D. May 6, 1767. R. June 2, 1768.
Wit: John Wrench, Esther Holladay.   Page 510

WENTWORTH, Mary: Of Newport Parish. Leg. daughter Lois; grandson Thomas Peirce; grandson Davis Day; grandson Samuel Wentworth Browne; granddaughter Mary Peirce; granddaughter Frances Day; my deceased daughter Frances Purdie; daughter Ann Browne; daughter Mary Peirce; daughter Betty Day. Exs., sons-in-law Thomas Browne, Thomas Peirce, and John Day. D. May 31, 1768. R. July 7, 1768.
Wit: John Taylor, Luke Lewelling, Anna Hubard.   Page 511

WARD, Joseph: Account estate, paid legacy to John Stallings. Examined by Richard Hardy, Dolphin Drew, James Derring. Signed, Elizabeth and Joseph Ward. R. July 7, 1768.   Page 513

MANYARD, Hezekiah: Account estate, examined by Nicholas Parker and Joseph Coupland. R. August 4, 1768.   Page 514

SHELLEY, James: Account estate, examined by Richard Hardy, James Derring and Samuel Wilson. Signed, Mary and Thomas Shelley. R. August 4, 1768.   Page 515

RATCLIFFE, Cornelius: Account estate, examined by Nicholas Parker, Brewer Godwin, Joseph Coupland. R. September 1, 1786.   Page 516

INGRAM, Jennings: Account estate, examined by Richard Hardy and William Davis. R. September 2, 1768.   Page 517

PARKER, Martha: Appraised by William Bullock, Willis Bullock, Nicholas Wail, Thomas Howell. R. September 1, 1768.   Page 518

INGLISH, Thomas: Leg. wife Mary; son Nathan. D. September 21, 1768. R. December 1, 1768.
Wit: John Eley, Jr., Henry Johnson, Thomas Inglish, Jr. Page 520

WENTWORTH, Samuel: Appraised by Joseph Bridger, John Mallory, William Davis. R. December 1, 1768.                                                               Page 521

BENN, James: Account estate, examined by Nicholas Parker and John S. Wills. R. March 2, 1769.                                                                Page 528

COFFER, William: Leg. son Jesse; wife Mary; son William; daughter Elizabeth; daughter Lucy; daughter Rebecca; daughter Patty. D. October 23, 1768. R. March 2, 1769.
    Wit: Benjamin Gwaltney, William Jordan, Anthony Crocker, Thomas Betts, William Gay.                                                          Page 529

CORBELL, Benjamin: Appraised by Joseph Coupland, Mathew Jordan, Charles Herring. Ordered, February 2, 1769. R. March 2, 1769.                                 Page 530

SMITH, Stephen: Appraised by Henry Pitt, David Williams, John Williams. R. April 6, 1769.                                                                    Page 531

EVERITT, William: Appraised by John Newman, Joseph Everitt, William Bullock. Signed, Thomas Newman. R. April 6, 1769.                                         Page 532

GODWIN, Mrs. Elizabeth: Appraised by Augustine King, Giles West, Joseph Fulgham. Ordered, July 1768. R. April 6, 1769.                                        Page 533

JORDAN, Sarah: Leg. brother James; sister Ann; sister Elizabeth; to my mother, my part of my father's estate. D. June 7, 1768. R. ----------
    Wit: John Wrench, Nicholas Wail, William Parr.
Will presented by Patience Jordan.                                                                                                                           Page 534

BRITTAIN, John: Appraised by John Daughtrey, Job Holland, James Collins. R. May 4, 1769.                                                                      Page 535

ALLMAND, Tarlton: Leg. son Edward; grandson Solomon Allmand, son of John Allmand; son William; daughter Elizabeth Eaton; son Isaac. Ex., son Isaac Allmand. D. March 7, 1769. R. May 4, 1769.
    Wit: Jacob Person, James Pitman, James Stringfield.                                                                                    Page 537

BULLARD, Joseph: Appraised by Thomas Cowling, Jr., Henry Bullard, Thomas Dixon. Signed, John Pinner. Ordered, December 1, 1768. R. May 4, 1769.               Page 538

GRAY, William: Appraised by William Jordan, James Gwaltney, Benjamin Atkinson. Ordered, April 19, 1769. R. May 4, 1769.                                       Page 539

COPHER, William: Appraised by William Jordan, Moses Exum, William Harris. R. May 4,1769.                                                                      Page 540

FULGHAM, Anthony: Appraised by Joseph Copeland, Tristram Norsworthy, Frederick Parker. R. May 4, 1769.                                                        Page 541

GRAY, John: Account estate, examined by Thomas Day and William Webb. Signed, Sarah Gray. R. May 4, 1769.                                                      Page 543

ALLMAND, Tarlton: Appraised by James Pitman, James Stringfield, Benjamin Stringfield. R. June 2, 1769.                                                        Page 543

DELK, Shelton: Appraised by James Derring, Thomas Shelley, Francis Wrenn. R. June 2, 1769.                                                                    Page 544

ENGLISH, Thomas: Appraised by William Watkins, Aaron Spivey, Robert Coggan. R. July 6, 1769.                                                                 Page 546

220

SAUNDERS, Henry: Account estate, examined by John Eley, Jr., Thomas Smelley, Andrew Smelley, Andrew Sikes, Robert Babb. Signed, Mary Saunders. R. July 6, 1769. Page 546

PILAND, William: Leg. son James; son William; daughter Elizabeth; son John; wife Mary Piland. Exs., wife Mary and friend Richard Hardy. D. January 7, 1769. R. August 3, 1769.
        Wit: John Carrell, William Wills, George Goodrich, John Welch.
Page 547

---

## WILL BOOK EIGHT

---

JOHNSON, Rebecca: Leg. son James; daughter Elizabeth Simmons; daughter Rebecca Fulgham; son Henry; son Stephen; daughter Mary Coggan; daughter Ann Barnes; son Barnaby; son Joshua. Exs., sons Barnaby and Joshua Johnson. D. June 25, 1763. R. September 7, 1769.
        Wit: Hardy Darden, John Darden, Timothy Duck. Page 1

POPE, Priscilla: Of Newport Parish. Leg. daughter Sarah Daniel, to her son Miles Daniel; cousin John Pope; cousin Joseph Pope. Exs., son-in-law James Daniel and his wife Sarah. D. May -, 1768. R. September 7, 1769.
        Wit: Andrew Griffen, Joseph Pope, Sarah Daniel. Page 2

CHAPMAN, Jordan: Leg. son Charles; daughter Chloe Webb; granddaughter Fanny Casey; daughter Jordan Smelley. Ex., son-in-law Thomas Smelley. D. August 8, 1769. R. September 7, 1769.
        Wit: William Davis, Francis Murry. Page 3

PARNALL, William: Account estate, to paid John Parnall for keeping his brother's orphans; to funeral expenses for Frederick Parnall, orphan of William; paid John Parnall for keeping Mary and Benjamin Parnall; paid Thomas Pitman for keeping Elizabeth Parnall; paid Major Dolphin Drew for keeping Olive Parnall. Examined by James Derring and William Jordan. Signed, John Parnall. R. September 7, 1769. Page 4

JENKINS, Benjamin: Appraised by James Tomerlin (?), Arthur Williamson, Adam Brown. Ordered, May 21, 1761. R. October 5, 1769. Page 5

WESTON, Samuel: Appraised ----- "this appraisal was unfortunately burnt in Colonel Baker's time by the negligence of Mr. Sampson Willson, who was then recording it." Page 8

SMITH, John: Account estate, paid for Faithy Smith; paid John Rosser for board for two orphans in 1766, paid Henry Harrison for board for John Smith. Examined by James Derring and Samuel Wilson. R. October 5, 1769. Paid James Kea for schooling orphans. Page 9

GODWIN, Jonathan: Appraised by William Morrison, Thomas King, Giles West. Ordered, October 8, 1769. R. November 2, 1769. Page 10

COOPER, Mark: Account estate, examined by Thomas Day and John Day. Signed, Dolphin Drew. D. July 13, 1769. R. ---------- Page 12

PYLAND, William: Appraised by James Derring, Henry Harrison, John Welch, John Carrell. R. January 4, 1770. Page 15

221

WARD, Joseph: Appraised by James Derring, Samuel Wilson, Francis Wrenn, Sr. R. January 4, 1770. Page 15

PARNALL, James: Leg. daughter Mary Goodson; son James; daughter Charity Garner; son Jeremiah; daughter Sweeting Pope; wife Charity; son Henry; son Joshua. Exs., wife Charity and son Henry Parnall. D. October 11, 1769. R. January 4, 1770.
Wit: Joseph Neville, James Hall, Sarah Powell. Page 17

MERRY, Francis: Leg. sister Mary Berriman and her son Benjamin Berriman; cousin Martha Webb; to sister Mary Berriman's children. Ex., William Davis. D. Janaury 25, 1770. R. February 1, 1770.
Wit: William Hodsden, Sarah Hodsden. Page 18

PINNER, Thomas: Appraised by John Pinner, Henry Bullard, Thomas Dixon. R. February 1, 1770. Signed, Joseph Scott. Examined by John Taylor and Henry Applewhaite. Page 20

GIBBS, John: Estate appraised by James Derring, Samuel Wilson, Thomas Whitfield and Henry Harrison. Ordered, September 16, 1769. R. February 1, 1770. Page 21

HARRISON, William: Leg. my mother, brother Thomas Burk and sister Sally Burk. Mother, Extx. D. August 11, 1769. R. March 1, 1770.
Wit: William Casey, Godard Debruckle. Page 22

CUTCHINS, Samuel: Leg. son Samuel; son Joshua; son Thomas; son Joseph; daughter Mary; daughter Easter; son Jeremiah, the land bought of Christopher Reynolds and now rented to George Goodson. Ex., son Josiah Cutchins. D. October 12, 1769. R. March 1, 1770.
Wit: William Casey, Thomas Parker, Belingsle Jordan. Page 23

MERRY, Francis: Appraised by William Carrell, William Hodsden, Howell Edmunds. R. March 1, 1770. Page 24

JOHNSON, Rebecca: Appraised by Henry Johnson, Timothy Duck, Joshua Council. R. April 5, 1770. Page 25

WESTON, Samuel: Account estate, examined by Nicholas Parker and Joseph Coupland. R. April 6, 1770. Page 26

JORDAN, Mathew: Leg. wife and unborn child; to my mother. Wife, Extx. D. March 23, 1770. R. May 3, 1770.
Wit: Brewer Godwin, Mary Sikes, Thomas Parker. Page 27

CUTCHINS, Samuel: Appraised by Nicholas Wale, Belingsle Jordan, Thomas Waile, Thomas Hall. R. May 3, 1770. Page 28

MILLER, John: Appraised by William Davis, William Hodsden, William Casey. R. May 3, 1770. Page 29

HODGES, John, Sr.: Of Newport Parish. Leg. daughter Patty; son James; son Benjamin; granddaughter Rebecca Hodges, daughter of son John; daughter-in-law Comfort Hodges, wife of son John and her children by my said son. Ex., son John Hodges. D. April 3, 1770. R. May 3, 1770.
Wit: William Carrell, William Harrison, Jesse Bidgood. Page 30

JONES, Richard, Sr.: Account estate, examined by James Derring, Henry Harrison, Sr., Samuel Wilson. D. 1761. R. July 5, 1770. Page 31

GIBBS, John, Sr.: Account estate, examined by James Derring and Samuel Wilson. R. July 5, 1770. Page 32

222

ELEY, Michael: Appraised by John Baldwin, Andrew Sikes, Robert Babb, Gale Eley. Ordered, April 6, 1769. R. July 5, 1770. Page 33

SMITH, Stephen: Account estate, to Joseph Channel, as per agreement among the children; to paid Joseph Spruel account against William and Mary Smith; to Nathaniel Smith in account against Mary, the relict of William Smith, said Stephen Smith being the executor of William Smith; paid Joseph Smith his proportion of the dower of Mary Smith, same paid to Nathaniel Smith. Examined by Thomas Pearce and James Watson. July 6, 1770. Page 36

JONES, John: Leg. daughter Easter; son John; daughter Mary; son Frederick; wife Sarah; son William; son Allen Jones. Ex., Benjamin Bailey, Jr. of Surry County. D. May 19, 1770. R. August 2, 1770.
Wit: Thomas Betts, Mathew Harris, Robert Wall. Page 38

SCOTT, Elizabeth: Appraised by Andrew Sikes, Robert Babb, Thomas Smelley. Signed by William Scott and Benjamin Bailey. Ordered, February 2, 1770. R. August 2, 1770. Page 39

HODGES, John: Appraised by William Carrell, William Harrison, William Hodsden. R. August 2, 1770. Page 42

EVERITT, William: Account estate, paid widow's dower, rest of estate paid William, Mary and Samuel Everitt and Thomas Newman. Examined by John Scarsbrook Wills, John Pinner, John Newman. R. August 3, 1770.
Page 44

GODWIN, Edmund: Account estate, examined by Richard Hardy and Thomas Pearce. Signed, Ann Godwin. R. August 3, 1770. Page 45

JORDAN, Sarah: Account estate, examined by Robert Driver and John Jordan. Signed, Patience Jordan. R. August 3, 1770. Page 46

JORDAN, James: Account estate, examined by John Scarsbrook Wills, Robert Driver, John Jordan. R. August 3, 1770. Page 47

BRACEY, Elizabeth: Leg. grandson Armiger Bracey; granddaughter Ann Bailey; grandson Campion Bracey; daughter Mary Pretlow; son-in-law John Pretlow. Ex., John Pretlow and his wife Mary. D. October 13, 1765. R. October 6, 1770.
Wit: William Eley, Edmund Westray, Elias Westray, John Little.
Page 47

DELK, Shelton: Account estate, examined by Richard Baker and Samuel Wilson. Signed, James Barlow. September 6, 1770. Page 49

THOMAS, Jacob: Account estate, examined by Charles Driver and John Smelley. Signed by Tristram Norsworthy and Mary Thomas. R. September 6, 1779.
Page 50

WILLS, John: Leg. son Nathaniel, with reversion of bequest to my brother Josiah Wills; sister Milly Richards; to my brother's daughter, Martha Wills; to brother Miles Wills. Ex., brother Josiah Wills. D. April 23, 1770. R. October 4, 1770.
Wit: Richard West, Godheart Debruckle, Thomas Casey, William Casey. Page 52

WEST, Giles: Leg. to Giles Daniel, alias West; to Godson Giles Smelley; wife Sarah; to Richard West one half of the plantation on which I live, called the "Long Neck", at the death of my wife; to Ralph West; to Sarah Gibbs; to friend Richard Jordan. At the death of my wife the remainder of my

estate to be divided between Richard West, Ralph West, John Gibbs and Sarah Gibbs. Ex., friend Richard Jordan. D. May 12, 1766. R. October 4, 1770.
Wit: Elizabeth Jordan, Patience Jordan, John Jordan.     Page 52

DARDEN, Benjamin: Appraised by Joshua Council, Solomon Edwards, Richard Bradshaw. Ordered, September 26, and recorded October 4, 1770.
Page 54

BOON, James: Appraised by William Pearce, Henry Johnson, Robert Coggan. Ordered, December 9, 1769. R. November 1, 1770.     Page 55

GIBBS, John: In account current with Gabriel Gibbs, who files a suit against Ralph Gibbs. Examined by Richard Hardy and James Derring. R. November 1, 1770.     Page 56

APPLEWHAITE, Henry: Leg. sister Mary Robertson; to my brothers and sisters. Ex., William Robertson. D. October 24, 1770. R. November 1, 1770.
Wit: Elias Whitley, Coupland Whitfield.     Page 57

BRACEY, Elizabeth: Appraised by Daniel Batten, Benjamin Westray, Jr., Thomas Whitney Gale. R. December 6, 1770.     Page 57

JORDAN, Mathew: Appraised by George Norsworthy, John Williams, Henry Pitt. R. December 6, 1770.     Page 58

CASEY, Constant: Leg. son Henry; son Thomas. Ex., son Henry Casey. D. July 3, 1766. R. December 6, 1770.
Wit: William Webb, William Wrenn, John Jennings Wheadon.
Page 59

FULGHAM, Anthony: Account estate, examined by Nicholas Parker and Tristram Norsworthy. Signed, John Fulgham. R. December 6, 1770.     Page 60

BENNETT, John: Leg. eldest son John, land adjoining Sarah Marlowe; son William; wife Sarah; son James; son Jesse; son Thomas; son Edmund; daughter Martha; daughter Lucy Bennett. D. October 4, 1770. R. December 6, 1770.
Wit: Nicholas Cordall, Mathew Gray, George Goodrich.     Page 62

PITT, Sarah: Account estate, examined by Nicholas Parker, John Scarsbrook Wills. R. January 3, 1771.     Page 62

JENKINS, Benjamin: Account estate, examined by John Eley, Jr. and John Lawrence. Signed, Joshua Jenkins. R. January 1, 1771.     Page 63

APPLEWHAITE, Thomas: Leg. beloved wife; son Henry; son Josiah; daughter Sally; daughter Mary Robertson the money Mr. Robertson owes me; my son Thomas living in the Barbadoes. Exs., wife and son Henry Applewhaite. D. October 15, 1770. R. January 3, 1771.
Wit: Brewer Godwin, Mary Penny, Henry Pitt.     Page 64

JONES, Britain: Estate account, examined by Robert Tynes, John Woodley, Charles Chapman. R. January 3, 1771.     Page 65

CASEY, Constant: Appraised by Benjamin Harrison, William Carrell, William Harrison. R. January 3, 1771.     Page 66

HOUSE, Samuel: Leg. son Demise (Dempsey ?); son James; daughter Mary. Exs., friend John Wrench and son Demise. D. December 16, 1770. R. January 3, 1771.
Wit: John Wrench, Demise House.     Page 68

224

TYNES, Thomas: Leg. loving wife; daughter Mary; son West, land in Southampton; son Thomas; son Benjamin, the plantation I bought of George Benn; son-in-law John Lawrence; son-in-law Jeptha Mington; granddaughter Holland Lawrence. Exs., wife and son West Tynes. D. October 14, 1769. R. January 3, 1771.
    Wit: Nathan Tomlin, Robert Tomlin.            Page 69

EDMUNDS, William: Leg. wife Martha; son Solomon; daughter Mary Bracey; grandson William Beal; granddaughter Martha Beal; grandson Solomon Holland; grandson John Holland. Ex., son Solomon Edmunds. D. January 30, 1769. R. February 7, 1771.
    Wit: Thomas Lankford, Jr., William Lankford, Sr., William Lankford, Jr.            Page 70

BRITAIN, John: Examined by John Eley, Jr. and John Lawrence. Signed, Zelpah Britain, her security being Joshua Council and Thomas Lankford. R. March 7, 1771.            Page 72

WILLS, Prudence: The widow of John Wills, she renounces all benefits of the will of John Wills. R. March 7, 1771.            Page 72

EDWARDS, Robert: Appraised by George Hall, James Hall and Isaac Moody. R. March 7, 1771.            Page 73

JONES, Samuel, Sr.: Leg. son Samuel; son David; son Frederick; son Joseph; son Henry; son Mathew; granddaughter Lucy, daughter of my deceased son Britain Jones; daughter Prudence, wife of John Persons; daughter Sarah; wife Sarah; daughter Lucy Jones, daughter Ann, wife of Joseph Persons. Exs., Henry Mangum, son Samuel Jones. D. October 21, 1770. R. March 7, 1771.
    Wit: James Derring, Richard Jones, Nathan Ward, Benjamin Coapher.            Page 74

HAYSE, Robert: Leg. to Charles Harris, my land, the son of Elizabeth Harris; to Lucy, the daughter of Charles Harris; to Lowice Harris. Ex., Charles Harris. D. September 7, 1766. R. March 7, 1771.
    Wit: John Davis, John Thomas, John Darnal (Parnall ?). Page 76

BEATON, Edward: Appraised by Thomas Cutchins, James Tallow, John Council. Ordered, July 14, 1770. R. March 7, 1771.            Page 77

SANDERS, Martha: Her dower in the estate of Henry Sanders, allotted as the result of a suit brought by Sarah Sanders, by Martha Sanders, her next friend against Henry Sanders, Jr.: by John Eley, Jr. and Benjamin Eley. R. March 7, 1771.            Page 78

JOHNSON, William: Appraised by Hardy Darden, John Darden, Joshua Council. Ordered, December 13, 1770. R. March 8, 1771.            Page 78

JONES, Samuel, Sr.: Appraised by Henry Harrison, John Jordan, Francis Wrenn. R. May --, 1771.            Page 80

DRIVER, Thomas: Leg. Rhody Godwin, the wife of James Godwin; wife Judith and provision for unborn child. Exs., wife and Frederick Parker. D. January 24, 1771. R. May 2, 1771.
    Wit: Frederick Parker, Charles Herring, Richard Herring.
           Page 82

BENNETT, John: Appraised by James Derring, John Carrell, Jesse Glover. R. May 2, 1771.            Page 83

RICHARDS, Martha: Account estate, to cash paid Josiah Wills for his part of his father's estate. Examined by John Scarsbrook Wills and Bartholomew Lightfoot. R. June 6, 1771. Page 86

CHANNELL, James: Account estate, examined by Andrew Mackie and Bartholomew Lightfoot. R. June 6, 1771. Page 87

RICHARDSON, Ann: Account estate, to a balance in the hands of Mr. George Hall, Sr. Examined by Mr. John Day and Mr. Crocker. Estate appraised by Daniel Batten, John Marshall, Robert Johnson. Ordered, April 14, 1770. R. August 1, 1771. Page 88

ELEY, Michael: Appraised by John Eley, Jr., Jethro Gale, Josiah Jordan. Signed, Benjamin Eley. R. August 1, 1771. Page 90

JONES, John: Appraised by Jesse Holleman, John Stevenson, Henry Lancaster. Signed, B. Bailey. R. October 3, 1771. Page 91

SMITH, Nicholas: Examined by Nicholas Parker, Joseph Coupland. R. October 3, 1771. Page 94

WILLS, John: Appraised by Augustine King, James Wills, William Green. R. October 3, 1771. Page 95

DRIVER, Thomas: Appraised by Joseph Coupland, Tristram Norsworthy, David Williams. R. November 7, 1771. Page 96

WEBB, William: Appraised by John Wrenn, James Lupo, Philip Lupo. R. November 7, 1771. Page 98

VANCE, Lydia: Appraised by William Casey, William Hodsden, Henry Applewhaite. R. November 7, 1771. Page 99

BRIDGER, Col. Joseph: Appraised by Robert Tynes and William Davis. Ordered, January 4, 1770. R. November 7, 1771. Page 100

APPLEWHAITE, Captain Thomas: Appraised by Frederick Parker, David Williams, William Wesson. R. November 7, 1771. Page 105

NOLLEY, Needham: Account estate, examined by John Lawrence, John Marshall. R. November 7, 1771. Page 107

SHIELDS, Charles: Leg. son Robert, my land in Southampton County purchased of John Ingram; son John; son Charles; son Moss; son Thomas; daughter Mary; daughter Elizabeth. Exs., sons Robert and John Shields. D. September 25, 1771. R. November 7, 1771.
     Wit: Howell Edmunds, Mary Bidgood, Celia Jones, William
          Carrell. Page 108

ALLMAN, William: Leg. son William and his son John and daughter Anne; son John and his son William; son Augustine; son Thomas; son Elisha; daughter Margaret; son Hezekiah; wife nothing for she "hath absconded from me without any cause for several years." Exs., friend Jesse Atkinson and son William Allman. D. June 26, 1771. R. November 7, 1771.
     Wit: John Butler, Samuel Milner. Page 110

LITTLE, Barnaby: Leg. son William; wife Ann; daughter Mary; daughter Ann; daughter Damaris; daughter Keziah. Exs., wife and John Little. D. October 5, 1771. R. November 7, 1771.
     Wit: John Gay, Jr., Thomas Nelms, Anthony Fulgham. Page 111

ROSE, William: Leg. son John; wife Mary; sister Lucy Spyre, her husband

Benjamin Spyre (Speirs ?). Exs., Francis Rose and Thomas Lankford, Jr.
D. October 12, 1771. R. November 7, 1771.
Wit: Richard Bradshaw, Patience Bradshaw, Thomas Rose.  Page 113

RAND, William, Sr.: Leg. wife Sophia; son John; son William; son Walter;
daughter Catherine; daughter Mary; daughter Christian Rand. Exs.,
son John, James Forsyth and wife Sophia Rand. D. November 3, 1767.
New Exs., John Rand, wife and Lewis Almand. D. 1771.
Wit: William Rand, Jr., John Norsworthy, John Taylor, Jr.,
William Garton.  Page 116

BAKER, Richard: Leg. refers to lawsuit depending in Isle of Wight County
against the executors of Charles Fulgham, whereby I am endeavoring to
establish an agreement made with said Fulgham in his lifetime for lots
and houses in Smithfield, which I believe may be done by the testimony
of Andrew Mackie and Jeremiah Proctor; wife Ann; son Lawrence Baker.
Exs., wife Ann, friend Thomas Williamson and Lawrence Baker. D. July 12,
1771. R. January 2, 1772.
Wit:  Page 117

GROSS, Francis: Leg. son Thomas; son Willis; son Joshua; son William.
Exs., Josiah Cutchins and Thomas Gross. D. August 22, 1771.
R. January 2, 1772.
Wit: Thomas Hall, Ann West, Mary West.  Page 118

HUNTER, Joshua: Leg. wife Elizabeth; son James; daughter Elizabeth; to
John House. Extx., wife Elizabeth. Trustee, friend William Weston.
D. August 3, 1771. R. January 2, 1772.
Wit: John Day, Thomas Hall.  Page 119

GARNES, Elizabeth: Appraised by John Newman, Thomas Howell, Thomas Newman.
Ordered, June 6, 1771. R. January 2, 1772.  Page 120

BULLARD, Thomas: Appraised by John Pinner, Willis Bullock, Thomas Howell.
Ordered, November 7, 1771. R. January 2, 1772.  Page 121

GROSS, Francis: Appraised by John Butler, John Scarsbrook Wills, Richard
West. R. February 6, 1772.  Page 122

HUNTER, Joshua: Appraised by John Scarsbrook Wills, John Butler, Richard
West. R. February 6, 1772.  Page 123

BULLARD, Thomas: Account estate, to the widow, to Mary Bullard, to Elisha
Minton. (Each paid same.) Examined by John Scarsbrook Wills, John
Pinner. R. February 6, 1772.  Page 125

BEEL, William: Leg. wife Mary; daughter Priscilla; daughter Mary. Extx.,
wife Mary Beel. D. October 21, 1767. R. February 6, 1772.
Wit: Bridgeman Joyner, Edward Baton (?), James Jordan Scott.
Page 126

WELCH, John: Leg. wife Mary; at her death one-third to my friend Richard
Hardy; the balance between William, James, Jesse, Thomas and Edward
Bennett, the sons of my sister Sarah Bennatt. Ex., friend Richard
Hardy. D. February 1, 1769. R. February 9, 1772.
Wit: Marcella Hardy, Jesse Glover.  Page 127

MURPHEY, John: Leg. son John; son Charles; wife Sarah; son William; grandson Lemuel Murphey; daughter Frances Fathera; granddaughter Fanny
Fatheree; daughter Ann Murphey; son Michael; daughter Elizabeth Darden;
daughter Sarah Chestnutt; daughter Mary White; daughter Jane Butler;
daughter Elenorah Clenney, (McClenney ?). Exs., wife and son John

227

Murphey. D. December 6, 1769. R. March 5, 1772.
Wit: John Marshall, Mathew Jordan, Hannah Jordan.      Page 128

EDWARDS, Thomas: Leg. grandson Meredith Edwards and his son Thomas; daughter-in-law Elizabeth Stevens; daughter-in-law Susanna Davice (Davis) and her children; grandson Thomas Davice. Ex., daughter-in-law Elizabeth Stevens. D. December 6, 1769. R. March 5, 1772.
Wit: Robert Tynes, Sary Powell, John Garner.      Page 128

BENN, Tristram: Leg. brother Arthur; my wife; brother Thomas Benn; wife's daughter, Ann Browne. Ex., Tristram Norsworthy. D. February 16, 1772. R. March 5, 1772.
Wit: Tristram Norsworthy, Tristram King, Thomas Smith. Page 130

GOODRICH, George: Leg. wife Sarah; nephew Joseph, son of Samuel Goodrich; nephew Charles Goodrich; nephew William Goodrich. Wife, Extx.
D. September 7, 1771. R. March 5, 1772.
Wit: William Jordan, John Thomas, Joseph Womble, Jr.      Page 131

BELL, Patience: Leg. daughter Elizabeth Bell. Ex., William Davis.
D. May 20, 1771. R. April 2, 1772.
Wit: John Goodrich, Dorothy Davis.      Page 132

CROCKER, William: Leg. wife Martha; daughter Catherine; son Jesse; daughter Mary. Exs., wife and William Williford. D. March 2, 1772. R. April 2, 1772.
Wit: John Fiveash, Henry Lancaster, John Ezall (Ezell ?).
Page 133

ELEY, John Jr.: Leg. wife Ann; son John; daughter Sally; son Mills; daughter Molly; daughter Charlotte. Exs., wife, John Day and Thomas King. D. March 13, 1772. R. May 7, 1772.
Wit: Elias Herring, William Watkins, Jr., Hardy Darden. Page 134

SANDERS, John: Leg. son Thomas; son Joseph; son Jacob; son Henry; son John; daughter Sarah Dunston. Exs., wife Elizabeth and son John Sanders.
D. February 3, 1772. R. May 7, 1772.
Wit: Jethro Gale, Robert Sanders, Ann Sanders.      Page 136

DELK, Solomon: Appraised by James Gwaltney, John Stevenson, Jesse Holleman.
R. May 7, 1772.      Page 138

CROCKER, William: Appraised by James Gwaltney, John Stevenson, Henry Lancaster. R. May 7, 1772.      Page 140

WILLS, John: Of Newport Parish. Leg. wife Martha; son John Scarsbrook Wills; son James Wills; son Thomas; son Emanuel; son Benjamin; son Mills (Miles ?); son Micajah; son William. Captain Brewer Godwin to have the care of my sons, Emanuel, Benjamin and Mills Wills, to Hannah Godwin; to Lydia Pitt. Extx., wife Martha Wills. D. October 31, 1765. R. May 7, 1772. Security for Extx., Josiah Wills, James Wills, Pitt Reynolds, Brewer Godwin.
Wit: Macon Whitfield, Josiah Wills, Ann West.      Page 142

MURPHEY, John: Appraised by John Marshall, Samuel Everitt, Robert Smelley.
R. May 7, 1772.      Page 144

RAND, William: Appraised by Thomas Peirce, William Robertson, Thomas Smith.
R. May 7, 1772.      Page 146

CASEY, Constant: Account estate, examined by William Carrell, John Hodges, Benjamin Harrison. Signed, Henry Casey. R. May 7, 1772.      Page 148

PARNOLD (PARNALL ?), Joshua: Appraised by Robert Driver, Joseph Everitt, Mathew Pruden. Ordered, October 2, 1771. R. May 7, 1772. Page 148

CARRELL, Thomas: Nuncupative will, proven by Nathaniel Lee, Jesse Glover, James Barler (Barlow ?). Leg. wife Mary. Nathaniel Lee, Master of the schooner, America. D. April 6, 1772. R. May 7, 1772. Page 149

LAWRENCE, John: Leg. wife Martha, the plantation bought of Joseph and Joshua Tarleton, and land bought of John Bullock; son Ricks; daughter Elizabeth Pretlow; son John my land in Nansemond County; son Robert, the land bought of Frizzell; daughter Mary Newby my land bought of Jacob Darden and Nicholas Murphey. Exs., wife Martha and son John Lawrence. D. March 30, 1772. R. May 7, 1772.
Wit: Josiah Jordan, Thomas Jordan, Robert Abram. Page 150

SANDERS, John: Appraised by John Coggan, Benjamin Eley, George Norsworthy, Andrew Sykes. R. May 7, 1772. Page 152

DRIVER, Charles: Appraised by John Norsworthy, James Watson, William Robertson. R. May 7, 1772. Page 156

BENN, Tristram: Appraised by Joseph Coupland, George Norsworthy, Henry King. Signed, Tristram Norsworthy, Jr. R. May 7, 1772. Page 159

FOWLER, Arthur: Account estate, examined by John Lawrence, Joshua Council, Hardy Lawrence. Ordered, June 27, 1772. R. July 2, 1772. Page 160

EDWARDS, Thomas: Appraised by Robert Tynes, Jesse Atkins, Joseph Neville. Ordered, March 5, 1772. R. July 2, 1772. Page 161

ALLMAND, William: Appraised by Bartholomew Lightfoot, John Butler, James Wills. R. July 2, 1772. Page 163

MINTZ, Sarah: Appraised by Henry Mangum, William Barlow, Joseph Maddera. Signed, Edward Mintz. Ordered, May 7, 1772. R. July 2, 1772.
Page 165

CROCKER, Joseph: Appraised by William Jordan, Arthur Davis, Charles Chapman. Ordered, December 6, 1770. R. December 6, 1772. Page 166

APPLEWHAITE, Henry: Appraised by Joseph Fulgham, William Morrison, Jonathan Godwin. (No dates.) Page 167

PEIRCE, Peter: Leg. son William; son Peter; son Bennett; daughter Elizabeth, after the death of my wife. Ex., son Peter Peirce. D. May 3, 1771. R. August 6, 1772.
Wit: John Little, John Gay, Benjamin Westray. Page 168

JOHNSON, William: Account estate, amount due widow and children. Examined by Benjamin Eley and Jesse Watkins. Signed, Michael Johnson. R. August 8, 1772. Page 169

DAY, Thomas: Leg. wife Elizabeth; son James Bennett Day; daughter Mary; daughter Juliana. Exs., brother John Day and friend Richard Hardy. D. October 21, 1769. R. October 1, 1772.
Wit: Henry Harrison, George Thomas White, Thomas Brantley.
Page 170

HARRISON, Henry: Leg. son Henry; son John all the land in Surry County, which I purchased of John Driver; son Richard, the land in Surry County bought of Jesse Hargrave; daughter Constant; daughter Salley; daughter Christian; daughter Betsey; land bought of Benjamin Bell to be sold,

the land bought of Isaac Allmand to be sold to Joseph Goodrich. Exs.,
friends Richard Hardy, James Derring, nephew Henry Harrison and son
Henry Harrison. D. September 13, 1771. R. October 1, 1772.
Wit: George Thomas White, Etheldréd Edwards, James Derring.
Page 172

DARDEN, Benjamin: Account estate, examined by John Lawrence, Joshua Council.
Signed John Darden. R. October 1, 1772. Page 174

BURKS, Ann: Appraised by Horatio Durley, Samuel Godwin, Henry Pitt.
Ordered, February 6, 1772. (No recording date.) Page 175

SHIELDS, Charles: Appraised by Benjamin Harrison, William Hodsden, William
Casey. R. August 7, 1772. Page 177

ELEY, John, Jr.: Appraised by James Bridger, Daniel Herring, Jr., John
Lawrence. R. September 3, 1772. Page 180

JOYNER, John: Leg. daughter Mary; son John, land adjoining Hugh Provans and
Theophilus Joyner; son Thomas; daughter Catherine; daughter Elizabeth;
wife Sweeting. Exs., wife and son John Joyner. D. June 20, 1772.
R. September 3, 1772.
Wit: Jesse Atkins, John Crocker, John Daniel. Page 184

KING, Henry: Leg. son Tristram, the plantation purchased of Peter Best; son
Samuel, the plantation on which Elizabeth Harrison now lives; oldest son
Henry; son John; daughter Ann Godwin; daughter Martha; youngest daughter,
Sarah; wife Martha. Exs., brother-in-law Tristram Norsworthy and
Nicholas Parker. D. July 20, 1767. R. October 1, 1773.
Wit: Tristram Norsworthy, William Gray, Nathan Bagnall. Page 186

ROBINSON, Jonathan: Leg. wife Mary; son Jonathan; son Archelus. Trustees,
John Daughtrey, Thomas Lankford and Job Holland. Exs., sons, Jonathan
and Archelus. D. November 15, 1766. R. September 3, 1772.
Wit: Peter Butler, James Collins, John Fleming. Page 188

McKINNE, Thomas: Appraised by Joseph Coupland, Joseph Hawkins, Tristram
Norsworthy. Signed, Nicholas Parker. Ordered, July 2, 1772.
R. August 5, 1772. Page 190

GODWIN, Elizabeth: Account estate, to cash paid for legacies to the orphans
of James Godwin, decd. Examined by Nicholas Parker, Frederick Parker,
Brewer Godwin. R. October 1, 1772. Page 191

DUCK, Timothy: Leg. son Joseph; daughter Martha Johnson; wife Sarah; son
Jacob; son Nathan; son John, a pot at Isabel Johnson's house. Exs.,
wife and son Joseph Duck. D. October 3, 1772. R. January 7, 1773.
Security for Exs., Michael Johnson and Jesse Watkins.
Wit: Jesse Watkins, Obediah Jordan, Priscilla Johnson. Page 192

KING, Henry: Appraised by Thomas Parker, Frederick Parker, Tristram Norsworthy. R. January 7, 1773. Page 194

MORRIS, John: Leg. wife Mary; son Conyers; daughter Sarah Stroud; daughter
Hannah Haile; daughter Mary Harris; daughter Christian Hatchall;
daughter Elizabeth Haile; grandson Lawrence Haile; grandson Edy Haile.
Ex., son Conyers Morris. D. April 14, 1772. R. December 3, 1772.
Security for Ex., Jethro Gale and Daniel Batten.
Wit: Thomas Turner, John Day. Page 197

WILLS, John: Account estate, to cash paid Miles Wills, guardian to Milley
Richards. Examined by John Scarsbrook Wills and John Butler.
R. December 3, 1772. Page 198

LITTLE, Barneby: Appraised by Hezekiah Fulgham, Anthony Fulgham, Joshua
Powell. Signed, Ann and John Little. R. August 3, 1772. Page 200

BOON, Ratcliff, Jr.: Appraised by William ------, Henry Johnson, William
Gay, Jr. Ordered, October 1, 1772. R. February 4, 1773. Page 203

CAMPBELL, Elizabeth: Leg. son William; to my grandchildren, John Bridger's
two children, to John Williams' two children, to John Jordan's children,
also the one unborn. Son William, Ex. D. November 25, 1769.
R. April 1, 1773. Will presented by William Wainwright, security,
John Bridger.
Wit: Nicholas Parker, John Gray. Page 204

BROUGHTON, Adam: Appraised by John Reade and John Bridger. Ordered,
February 21, 1771. R. April 1, 1773. Page 206

TYNES, Timothy: Appraised by Charles Chapman, Jesse Atkins, Bartholomew
Lightfoot. R. April 1, 1773. Page 207

WOMBLE, John: Appraised by Thomas Copher, John Thomas, William Barlow.
Ordered, September 12, 1772. R. March 4, 1773. Page 208

DUCK, Timothy: Appraised by Hardy Darden, John Darden, John Owen.
R. March 4, 1773. Page 210

BAKER, Messr. Richard & Company: Inventory of goods. D. September 11,
1771. Page 214

BAKER, Richard: Appraised by Richard Hardy, Arthur Smith, James Derring.
R. May 6, 1773. Page 233

WEST, Giles: Appraised by Augustine King, William Green, James Wills.
R. May 6, 1773. Page 239

BAGNALL, Richard: Of Newport Parish. Leg. wife Elizabeth; daughter Elizabeth; son Joseph; daughter Ann; son William; daughter Mary; granddaughter Sally Pitt; daughter Judy Pitt. Exs., wife and brother
William Bagnall. D. February 13, 1773. R. May 6, 1773. Security
for Extx., Henry Pitt and William Bagnall.
Wit: Thomas Hall, William Weston, Samuel Whitfield. Page 241

BETTS, Thomas: Appraised by Henry Lancaster, Abraham Jones, William Harris.
R. May 6, 1773. Page 242

WILLIAMS, Joseph: Appraised by Thomas Durley, John Bridger, Randolph
Whitley. Signed, William Bagnall. R. June 3, 1773. Page 244

TURNER, Joshua: Leg. wife Sarah; son William, rest of my estate to be
divided among the rest of my children. Exs., son Joshua and William
Jordan. D. March 10, 1773. R. June 4, 1773. John Parnall, security
for Exs.
Wit: Joshua Jenkins, Michael Fulgham, Henry Fulgham. Page 245

CARRELL, Thomas: Appraised by Dolphin Drew, Goodrich Wilson; Henry Harrison,
Jr. Ordered, October 19, 1772. R. June 3, 1773. Page 247

HOLLADAY, Thomas: Appraised by Joseph Hawkins, William Godwin, Edmund
Outland. Signed, Ann Holladay. Ordered, July 1, 1773. R. August 5,
1773. Page 249

CAMPBELL, Elizabeth: Appraised by Elias Parker, David Williams, Richard
Williams. Signed, William Wainwright. R. August 5, 1773. Page 250

EDWARDS, Thomas: Appraised by Bartholomew Lightfoot, Henry Tynes, William Harrison. R. August 5, 1773.  Page 251

GALE, Ann: Appraised by (no signatures). Signed, Jethro Gale. Ordered, April 4, 1771. R. August 5, 1773.  Page 252

HARRISON, Henry: Appraised by William Davis, Timothy Tynes, Goodrich Wilson. Ordered, November 18, 1772. R. August 5, 1773.  Page 253

BURKS, Ann: Account estate, examined by Brewer Godwin and Hora Durley. Signed, Joseph Cutchins. R. August 5, 1773.  Page 257

DELK, Shelton: Account estate, examined by Samuel Wilson, Goodrich Wilson, Henry Harrison. Signed, James Barlow. R. August 5, 1773.  Page 258

TURNER, Joshua: Appraised by Charles Fletcher, John Harris, Robert Johnson. R. August 5, 1773.  Page 260

ROSE, William: Appraised by Richard Bradshaw, Joshua Council, Benjamin Holland. R. August 5, 1773.  Page 263

PYLAND, William: Account estate, paid John Salter for schooling three children, paid Jesse Glover for one half of all work, but that done at Mr. Haynes, as per agreement with William Pyland decd., to funeral expenses for John Pyland, orphan of William Pyland. Examined by Richard Hardy, Timothy Tynes. Signed, Mary Glover. R. September 2, 1773.  Page 265

ROSE, William: Account estate, examined by Joshua Council, Hardy Lawrence and John Lawrence. Signed, Francis Rose. R. September 3, 1773.
Page 266

TYNES, Robert, Jr.: Leg. sister Jean, my right in estate of my aunt Sarah Washington, from the estate of my grandfather, Timothy Tynes. Ex., father. D. November 13, 1772. R. October 7, 1773.
Wit: John Crocker, Rowland Reynolds.
Security, John Day.  Page 267

RAIFORD, William: Leg. daughter Mary Boon; daughter Ann Little; daughter Sarah Boon; daughter Rebecca; daughter Martha; daughter Damaris Gay. Exs., friends James Bridger and Lawrence Whitehead and daughter Rebecca Raiford. D. October 28, 1771. R. October 7, 1773.
Wit: James A. Bridger, William Bridger, John Lawrence.
Security, William Gay, Jr.  Page 269

WRENN, William: Leg. son Joseph; daughter Elizabeth; son John, money in the hands of cousin John Wrenn; wife Mary; to James and Richard Wrenn, the remainder of my estate. Ex., cousin John Wrenn. D. August 4, 1772. R. October 7, 1773.
Wit: Robert Tynes, Henry Tynes.
Security, John Day.  Page 271

HARRISON, Henry, Jr.: Appraised by James Jordan, Francis Wrenn, Joseph Atkins. Ordered, July 1, 1773. R. November 4, 1773.  Page 271

FULGHAM, Ann: Leg. estate to be divided between Brewer Godwin and Martha Reynolds. Ex., Brewer Godwin. D. February 15, 1770. R. November 4, 1773.
Wit: (None.)  Page 273

EDWARDS, William: Leg. son William; son James; son John; daughter Elizabeth Whitley; daughter Honour Nicols; wife Susanna. Ex., son James Edwards.

D. March 15, 1770. R. December 2, 1773.
    Wit: John Davis, George Whitley, Elisha Whitley.
    Security, Nathan Whitley.               Page 273

CHAPMAN, William: Appraised by William Hodsden, Nathaniel Smith, Charles
    Butler. Ordered, October 7, 1773. R. December 2, 1773.   Page 275

HARRISON, Henry: Account estate, examined by James Derring and Richard
    Hardy. Signed, Martha Harrison. R. December 2, 1773.   Page 277

SAUNDERS, Henry: Account estate examined by Benjamin Eley, Robert Babb,
    Andrew Sykes, Thomas Smelley. Signed, John Carstophen and wife Martha.
    R. January 6, 1774.               Page 278

REYNOLDS, Christopher: Account estate, examined by Bartholomew Lightfoot,
    Robert Tynes, John Scarsbrook Wills. Signed, John Joyner.
    R. January 6, 1774.               Page 279

WATSON, James: Of Newport Parish. Leg. son William; daughter Martha; son
    John; son James; wife Elizabeth. Exs., George Blair, wife Elizabeth
    and son William, when he becomes 21. D. November 23, 1773.
    R. January 6, 1774.
    Wit: Seth Hunter, John Vellines.
    Security, William Robertson, George Purdie.      Page 280

TYNES, Thomas: Appraised by James Tomlin, Mathew Tomlin, Nathan Tomlin.
    Ordered, January 11, 1771. R. January 6, 1774.     Page 284

RAIFORD, William: Appraised by Thomas Nelms, James Johnson, Joshua Powell.
    R. February 3, 1774.               Page 288

EDWARDS, Joshua: Leg. son Joshua; son Jacob; son Hezekiah; son Benjamin,
    land adjoining Philip Moody; son Mathew; daughter Ann Hale; daughter
    Mary Pope; grandson Nathan Pope; daughter Amey Smith; daughter Sary
    Whitley; wife Sary; at death of son Benjamin, bequest to granddaughter
    Frances Edwards; son Hezekiah, at his death to my grandson Etheldred
    Edwards, with reversion of bequest to his sister Mary Edwards. Ex.,
    son Jacob Edwards. D. January 1, 1774. R. February 3, 1774.
    Wit: Joshua Jenkins, Solomon Edwards, James Edwards.
    Security, James Edwards and George Hall, Jr.     Page 290

WILLIAMS, John: Leg. son Josiah; son John; daughter Charlotte; unborn child.
    Ex., brother David Williams. D. October 19, 1773. R. February 3,
    1774.
    Wit: Nicholas Parker, Richard Williams.        Page 292

POWELL, George: Leg. wife and my children. Exs., sons Thomas and Edmund
    Powell. D. December 14, 1773. R. February 3, 1774.
    Wit: Philip Moody, Charles Fletcher, Benjamin Edwards.
    Security, Conyons Morris, Valentine Jenkins.     Page 294

WRENN, Joseph: Account estate, examined by John Mallory and John Day.
    D. 1757. Signed, John Wrenn. R. February 3, 1774.   Page 296

REYNOLDS, Richard: Appraised by (no signatures). Ordered, April 2, 1772.
    Signed, Joseph Fulgham. R. February 3, 1774.     Page 298

DAY, Thomas: Appraised by Samuel Wilson, George Purdie, George Blair.
    Three negroes not appraised, title disputed by William Pulliam.
    Signed, John Day. R. February 3, 1774.       Page 301

NORSWORTHY, George: Leg. son John; son George; son Joseph; daughter Ann

Driver; granddaughters Rachel and Patty (or Betty) Driver.  Ex., son
George Norsworthy.  D.  January 13, 1774.  R.  February 3, 1774.
  Wit:  Jeremiah Outland, Josiah Outland.
  Security, Tristram Norsworthy, Sr., Tristram Norsworthy, Jr.
                                                              Page 306

INGRAM, Sarah:  Leg. grandson James Bidgood; grandson John Bidgood; daughter
Jean Bidgood.  Ex., friend William Carrell.  D.  October 20, 1773.
R.  March 3, 1774.
  Wit:  Jesse Bidgood, Edward Dews.
  Security, Richard Hardy.                                    Page 308

LITTLE, Barnaby:  Account estate, examined by Daniel Herring, Jr., John
Lawrence.  Signed, Thomas Nelms.  R.  March 3, 1774.          Page 309

HUTCHINS, Francis:  Leg. son Jesse; son Moses; grandson Jesse Hutchins;
daughter America Booth; wife Sarah.  Exs., sons Jesse and Moses Hutchins.
D.  September 3, 1773.  R.  April 7, 1774.
  Wit:  Robert Babb, Evans Murphrey, John Baldwin.
  Security, Jethro Gale, John Coggan.                         Page 310

KING, Augustine:  Leg. wife Sarah; son Thomas; son Augustine; daughter
Frances.  Exs., wife and son Thomas King.  D.  December 1, 1771.
R.  April 7, 1774.
  Wit:  John Scarsbrook Wills, John Hartwell, Jacob Dickenson.
  Security, William Morrison, Joseph Fulgham.                 Page 312

REID, John:  Appraised by James Wills, John Smelley, Joseph Fulgham.
Ordered, August 3, 1773.  R.  April 7, 1774.                 Page 314

SHIELD, Charles:  Account estate, examined by William Davis, William Carrell,
William Hodsden.  R.  April 7, 1774.                          Page 316

INGRAM, Sarah:  Appraised by Valentine Jenkins, Henry Applewhaite, William
Hodsden.  R.  April 7, 1774.                                  Page 318

CALL, Charles:  Appraised by William Woodward, Conyons Morris.  Ordered,
December, 1773.  R.  April 7, 1774.                           Page 320

SCAMMELL, John, Jr.:  Appraised by John Hodges, Gabriel Gibbs, Henry Harrison.  Ordered, December 20, 1773.  R.  May 5, 1774.          Page 321

BOON, Ratcliff, Jr.:  Account estate, examined by John Lawrence, Daniel
Herring.  Signed, Elizabeth Boon.  (No dates.)               Page 323

MERRY, Francis:  Examined by Thomas Whitfield, William Hodsden, Howell
Edmunds.  D.  November 7, 1771.  R.  July 7, 1774.            Page 324

CARRELL, Thomas:  Inventory of his estate, presented by Mary Carrell.
R.  August 4, 1774.                                          Page 326

EDWARDS, Hezekiah:  Leg. daughter Salley; wife Mary; son Etheldred; daughter
Mary Edwards.  Ex., brother-in-law Virgus Smith.  D.  July 28, 1774.
R.  November 3, 1774.
  Wit:  Joshua Jenkins, Jacob Edwards, Joshua Edwards.
  Security, Thomas Nelms and Jacob Edwards.                   Page 328

HUTCHINS, Francis:  Appraised by Robert Babb, John Deford, Robert Smelley.
R.  September 1, 1774.                                        Page 329

REYNOLDS, Pitt:  Appraised by Joseph Fulgham, Jonathan Godwin, James Wills,
James Peden.  R.  September 1, 1774.                          Page 331

234

HARRISON, Elizabeth: Leg. my oldest granddaughters, Ann Godwin, Ann Thomas, Elizabeth Pitt and Martha Norsworthy, in case Ann Thomas or Martha Norsworthy should die before they are twenty one, their legacies to go to Tabitha Thomas. Ex., son Tristram Norsworthy. D. November 16, 1773. R. August 4, 1774.
 Wit: Tristram Norsworthy, Elias Parker.
 Security, Bartholomew Lightfoot, Jr.     Page 332

POPE, Richard: Leg. son John; son Richard; wife Ann; daughter Isabella; daughter Ann; daughter Mary; daughter Winnefre; daughter Rebecca Pope. Exs., sons John and Richard Pope. D. February 11, 1774. R. October 6, 1774.
 Wit: John Norsworthy, John Gay, Rebecca Williams, John Baldwin.
 Security, John Norsworthy and John Pretlow.   Page 333

FRAISER, Frederick: Leg. son Solomon; unborn child; daughter Frese; wife Keziah; son Ab. (?) Exs., wife and John Winborne. D. September 17, 1773. R. May 5, 1774.
 Wit: Cuthbert Hedgepeth, Abram Johnson, Mason Johnson.
 John Dearden (Darden ?) qualified as Ex., Keziah Fraiser being dead and John Winborne refusing.
 Security, Jethro Gale.        Page 336

NELMS, Ann: Leg. to Benjamin Hampton's wife Mary Hampton; to John Everitt and his wife. Ex., John Everitt. D. February 21, 1764. R. November 3, 1774.
 Wit: Mathew Jordan, Samuel Everitt.
 Security, Samuel Everitt.       Page 339

ALLMAND, William: Account estate, examined by John Scarsbrook Wills and Bartholomew Lightfoot, Jr. R. December 1, 1774.  Page 340

CROCKER, William: Account estate, examined by William Jordan, James Gwaltney, Abraham Jones. Signed, William Williford. R. December 1, 1774.
              Page 341

JOHNSON, Isabel: Leg. William Duck; to John Duck; to Jacob Duck; to Nathan Duck; remainder of estate to be divided between Joseph Duck, Martha Johnson, John Duck and Sarah Duck. Ex., Joseph Duck. D. August 15, 1773. R. December 1, 1774.
 Wit: Joseph Holland, Obediah Johnson, Sarah Duck.
 Security, Jesse Watkins, Jethro Gale.    Page 342

WATSON, James: Appraised by Robert Tynes, John Taylor, John Woodley. R. January 5, 1775.        Page 344

CARRELL, Richard: Leg. wife Sarah; son James; son William; son Richard; son Gray. Extx., wife Sarah Carrell. Trustee, John J. Wheadon. D. ---------- R. January 5, 1775.
 Wit: Patrick Braddy, Mason Braddy, Mary Wheadon, John J. Wheadon.
 Security, John J. Wheadon.      Page 347

WOMBLE, John: Account estate, paid Britain Womble for looking after him, cash in the hands of Thomas Womble, Sr. Examined by William Hodsden and William Casey. R. January 5, 1775.  Page 348

GRAY, Mathew: Leg. friend Thomas Scott; brother Henry Gray. Ex., Thomas Scott. D. December --, 1774. R. January 5, 1775.
 Wit: William Hollowell, George N̲s̲. Scott.
 Security, William Hollowell.     Pagé 349

FRAISER, Frederick: Appraised by Henry Johnson, Sr., Aaron Johnson, Michael Johnson. R. February 2, 1775. Page 350

PITT, Thomas: Appraised by Joseph Fulgham, John Bridger, Roland Reynolds. Ordered, May 9, 1774. R. February 2, 1775. Page 353

JOHNSON, Isabel: Appraised by Aaron Johnson, Henry Johnson, Lazarus Johnson. R. March 2, 1775. Page 354

HARRISON, Elizabeth: Appraised by Thomas Parker, William Bagnall, George Norsworthy, Tristram Norsworthy. R. April 6, 1775. Page 355

PITT, Henry: Leg. wife; son Edmund; daughter Salley; daughter Esther. Exs., wife and brother Joseph Pitt. D. ---------- R. April 6, 1775.
Wit: Thomas Hall, Elias Whitley.
Will presented by Julia Pitt.
Security, Samuel Bridger. Page 357

GRAY, Mourning: Leg. nephew David Williams. Ex., nephew David Williams. D. April 2, 1774. R. May 4, 1775.
Wit: Nicholas Parker, Elias Parker.
Security, Nicholas Parker. Page 358

GIBSON, John: Appraised by John Syms, James Ronaldson. John Syms, Sr. departed this life since above appraisal. Signed, George Blair. R. June 1, 1775. Page 359

SMELLEY, Sarah: Leg. son John; son James; granddaughter Mary Woodward; grandson Thomas Smelley; granddaughter Sarah Smelley; grandson John Provins; grandson William Woodward; son-in-law William Woodward; son-in-law Hugh Provans, grandson John Smelley. Exs., sons John and James. D. May 31, 1775. R. July 6, 1775.
Wit: Robert Driver, Thomas Pitt, John Garnes.
Security, James Wills. Page 361

BAKER, Richard & Company: Goodrich Wilson a partner. Signed, Thomas Williamson and Ann Baker. R. August 3, 1775. Page 362

SMELLEY, Sarah: Appraised by Robert Driver, James Uzzell, Bartholomew Lightfoot, Jr. R. August 3, 1775. Page 387

TURNER, Thomas: Leg. son Thomas; son Nelson; wife Mary, at her death an equal division among her children. Exs., wife and Lazarus Holloway. D. April 26, 1775. R. August 3, 1775.
Wit: Joshua Jenkins, William Turner, Thomas Whitney Gale.
Security, Virgus Smith and Jacob Edwards. Page 388

BETTS, Thomas: Account estate, expense for burying his son Thomas Betts. Examined by William Jordan and Samuel Simmons. Signed, William Williford. R. August 3, 1775. Page 390

VANCE, Lydia: Account estate, examined by William Davis and William Hodsden. R. August 3, 1775. Page 391

KING, Augustine: Appraised by Richard West, John Clark, Miles Wills. R. October 5, 1775. Signed, Thomas King. Page 392

KING, Henry: Account estate, examined by Brewer Godwin and Thomas Parker. Signed Martha King. R. October 5, 1775. Page 394

CUTCHINS, Joseph: Of Newport Parish. Leg. wife Priscilla; son James; daughter Loice; son Joseph; daughter Jane. Wife, Extx.

D. August 8, 1775. R. October 5, 1775.
Wit: Mary Durley, Horatio Durley, John Pitt.
Security, Josiah Parker and Richard West.                Page 394

CLARK, John: Of Newport Parish. Leg. son John; sister Prudence Clark, the
land on which Adam McCoy now lives; to John Broadfield, alias Clark, if
he dies before he is 21, the bequest to be divided between John Dickinson and Mary Benn alias Clark, daughter of Prudence Clark; provision
for unborn child; reversion of bequests to wife and son to sister Mary's
son John Dickinson and sister Prudence Clark. Ex. and guardian to my
children, friend Jonathan Godwin. D. September 19, 1775. R. ---------
Wit: Joseph Fulgham, Jane Fearn, Adam McCoy.
Security, Thomas King and Joseph Fulgham.                Page 395

ROBERTS, Thomas: Leg. wife Becky and her heirs lawfully begotten of my body.
Exs., wife and Thomas Nelms. D. August 15, 1775. R. November 2, 1775.
Wit: Joshua Jenkins, John Nelms, Anthony Fulgham.
Security, Anthony Fulgham.                Page 397

WRENN, Francis: Leg. son Thomas; son Francis; son Richard, land adjoining
Henry Mangam; son Joseph, land adjoining Francis Ward; daughter Ann;
daughter Mary. Exs., sons, Thomas and Richard Wrenn. D. January 24,
1775. R. December 7, 1775.
Wit: Goodrich Wilson, Solomon Holmes, John J. Wheadon.
Security, Richard Hardy and William Gay.                Page 398

WATKINS, William: Appraised by William Watkins, John Roberts and Aaron
Spivey. Ordered, December 1, 1774. R. December 7, 1775.    Page 400

HILL, Joseph: Of Newport Parish. Leg. son Joseph; daughter Mary; daughter
Elizabeth; wife Frances. Ex., son Joseph Hill. D. October 9, 1775.
R. January 4, 1776.
Wit: Francis Young, Jesse Herring, John Woodley.
Security, John Woodley and Robert Tynes.                Page 403

WHITEHEAD, Lazarus: Leg. son Arthur, land adjoining Capt. John Eley; son
Jesse; daughter Molly; son John; daughter Salley; wife Elizabeth.
Exs., wife and neighbor, Jesse Watkins. D. June 7, 1775.
R. August 3, 1775.
Wit: Edmund Stevens, William Watkins, Alexander Saunders.
Security, Joshua Council, Robert Holland.                Page 404

ATKINSON, Joseph: Leg. son William; son James; wife Frances; daughter
Frances; daughter Mary; provision for unborn child; brother Jesse
Atkinson; brother James Atkinson; brother-in-law Jacob Person; brother-
in-law William Davis. Exs., wife and brother Jesse Atkinson.
D. November 28, 1775. R. February 1, 1776.
Wit: John Jordan, Jr., James Ward, William Barlow, Jesse Person.
Security, Jethro Gale, William Robertson.                Page 405

WHITE, John: Appraised by John Taylor, Thomas Smith, Micajah Wills.
Ordered, December 1775. R. March 7, 1776.                Page 406

POWELL, Sarah: Leg. daughter Honour Beal; daughter Patience Vaughan; grandson John Darden; daughter Sarah Darden; son Absalom Tallaugh. Ex.,
son Absalom Tallaugh. D. June 3, 1764. R. March 7, 1776.
Wit: Thomas Lankford, Jr., John Darden, George Lankford.
Security, John Darden.                Page 407

WRENN, William: Account estate, paid Mrs. Mary Wrenn for selling the estate.
Examined by William Blunt, John Woodley. R. March 7, 1776. Page 409

JOHNSON, Abraham: Leg. son Abraham; heir of my daughter Mourning Powell; son Nathan; son Thomas; heir of my daughter Ann Dunn. Extx., wife Ann Johnson. D. October 20, 1759. R. March 7, 1776.
Wit: William Moore, Henry Hedgepeth, Stephen Butler.
Security, Abraham and Eley Johnson. Page 410

WILLIAMS, John: Leg. wife Sarah; son John. Exs., wife and son John Williams. D. March 23, 1774. R. March 7, 1776.
Wit: Edmund Outland, William Hawkins.
Security, Samuel Holladay. Page 412

CROCKER, William: Leg. wife Sarah; granddaughter Sally Chapman; grandson Hardy Chapman; grandson Richard Chapman; grandson Neddy Chapman; son John. Exs., wife and son John Crocker. D. February 15, 1774. R. March 7, 1776.
Wit: William Goodson, John Thomas, Joseph Jordan.
Security, Jethro Gale. Page 412

PARR, Anthony: Leg. son Richard; son Anthony; wife. Exs., wife and brother, William Parr. D. February 7, 1776. R. April 4, 1776.
Wit: John Wrench, William Shivers, Richard Parr.
Security, John Scarsbrook Wills. Page 414

POWELL, Sarah: Appraised by Benjamin Holland, Richard Bradshaw, Cutchins Council. R. April 4, 1776. Page 416

CLARK, Benjamin: Leg. son William; son James, land adjoining Mr. Vellines; my land to be divided by John Thomas and Benjamin Harrison; son John; son Joseph; wife Mildred. Wife, Extx. D. January 22, 1776. R. April 4, 1776.
Wit: Benjamin Harrison, John Thomas, Mary Clark.
Security, Charles Fulgham and Samuel Simmons. Page 417

JOLLIFF, Thomas: Appraised by John Thomas, William Blunt, John Woodley. Ordered, November 9, 1775. R. May 2, 1776. Page 419

HILL, Capt. Joseph: Appraised by Samuel Webb, John Thomas, William Blunt, Jr. R. May 2, 1776. Page 420

GIBBS, Martha: Of Newport Parish. Leg. daughter Martha; grandson, John Harris Gibbs, son of Ralph Gibbs. Ex., son Ralph Gibbs. D. September 8, 1774. R. March 7, 1776.
Wit: Francis Young, Richard Bidgood, Martha Gibbs.
Security, Jeremiah Godwin. Page 424

JOHNSON, Abraham, Sr.: Appraised by Stephen Butler, Henry Hedgepeth, John Darden. R. May 2, 1776. Page 425

WAIL, Nicholas: Leg. wife Ann; daughter Mary Jordan's children, Anne, Nicholas and Rachel Jordan; grandson James Meacab Wail, the plantation I bought of Col. Anthony Holladay, with reversion to his brother John Wail; son Josiah; son John; son Nicholas; daughter Rachel; son Thomas; daughter Ann Green; granddaughter Rachel Green; grandson John Wail; granddaughter Barbary Wail. Exs., wife and son John Wail.
D. September 24, 1775. R. August 1, 1776.
Wit: John Wrench, Thomas Newman. Page 426

WARD, Francis: Leg. son Nathan, land adjoining Joseph Womble; son Britain; son John; son Francis; son Joseph; son James; daughter Lucy Walloo (?); wife Ann; daughter Ann; daughter Constant; daughter Mary. Exs., wife and son Nathan Ward. D. June 13, 1769. R. August 1, 1776.
Wit: Jacob Person, William Gay, David Strait, Thomas Copher.
Security, William Gay. Page 429

DAY, John: Leg. wife Betty and all my children. Friends, William Davis, Thomas Peirce and Richard Kelleo to have the care and education of my children. Exs., uncle, Mr. William Davis and friend Thomas Peirce. D. March 11, 1776. R. August 1, 1776.
Wit: Ann Brown, Elizabeth Davis, James Webb.
Security, Nathaniel Burwell and Goodrich Wilson.          Page 430

ROBERTS, Thomas: Appraised by William Woodward, Thomas Nelms, Virgus Smith. R. September 5, 1776.          Page 433

CUTCHINS, Joseph: Inventory, signed Priscilla Cutchins. September 5, 1776.
Page 435

EDWARDS, Hezekiah: Appraised by William Turner, Daniel Batten, Thomas W. Gale. R. September 5, 1776.          Page 442

HAYS, Arthur: Of Blackwater. Leg. to Sampson Pitman, the son of James Pitman; remainder of my estate, between William Flake, Faithy Flake and Mary the wife of James Pitman. Ex., James Pitman, Sr. D. June 27, 1767. R. October 3, 1776.
Wit: James Stringfield, William Flake, James Pitman.
Security, James Pitman, Jr. and William Flake.          Page 444

FRAISER, Frederick: Account estate, examined by Benjamin Eley and Joshua Cormide. Signed, John Darden. R. October 3, 1776.          Page 445

ELEY, John: Leg. grandson Mills Eley; son Robert; son William; daughter Elizabeth Boon; grandson John Eley Denson; daughter Martha Carr; daughter Sarah Darden; daughter Rebecca Denson. Exs., sons Robert and William Eley. D. September 18, 1775. R. November 7, 1776.
Wit: Jesse Watkins, Thomas English, Robert Watkins, Priscilla Watkins.
Security, John Darden.          Page 446

EXUM, Moses: Account estate, to orphan, Molly Exum. Signed, John Thomas. R. November 7, 1776.          Page 447

FUDGE, John: Appraised by John Lee, John Taylor, William Orr. Ordered, October 3, 1776. R. November 7, 1776.          Page 448

WALE, Nicholas, Sr.: Appraised by Thomas Cowling, John Pinner, Thomas Howell. R. January 2, 1777.          Page 448

MILLER, Benjamin: Leg. Captain Lewis Hatton to return to my Exs., the money paid him on land; wife Frankie; son William. Exs., wife and William Davis. D. August 31, 1772. R. December 7, 177-.
Wit: Robert Miller, Elizabeth Holmes, Elizabeth Wrenn.
Security, Josiah Jordan.          Page 450

FULGHAM, Edmund: Appraised by Thomas Nelms, Nathan Tomlin, Virgus Smith. Ordered, February 13, 1776. R. January 2, 1777.          Page 451

HAYS, Arthur: Appraised by William Gay, James Stringfield, Michl Deloach. R. January 2, 1777.          Page 453

ELEY, John, Sr.: Appraised by Joshua Council, Ratcliff Boon, William Peirce. R. February 6, 1777.          Page 454

HOWARD, Jane: son Henry, my dower in his father, John Howard's estate in the hands of the Sheriff of Brunswick County; daughter Elizabeth Davis; niece Elizabeth, the daughter of Richard Webb. Ex., friend Richard Hardy. D. June 20, 1774. R. February 6, 1777.

Richard Hardy refused to be Ex., Thomas Fearn qualified.
Wit: Ruth Bristor, William Carrell.                             Page 456

HOOKE, James: Appraised by Thomas Smelley, Robert Smelley, Andrew Sikes.
Ordered, February 18, 1775. R. February 6, 1777.                Page 456

COOK, John: Leg. nephew Demsey Cook; nephew Mathew Harris, son of Michael
and Sarah Harris. Ex., brother Nathan Cook. D. April 18, 1762.
R. January 2, 1777.
    Wit: Peter Woodward, Benjamin Lancaster, William Harris,
         Benjamin Bailey.
    Security, Jethro Gale.                                     Page 457

EDWARDS, Hezekiah: Account estate, examined by Daniel Herring, Jr. and
William Bridger. Signed, Virgus Smith. R. February 6, 1777.
                                                               Page 458

PARR, Anthony: Appraised by Thomas Howell, Thomas Newman. Signed, William
Parr. R. February 6, 1777.                                     Page 459

SHIVERS, Jonas: Appraised by Thomas Cowling and John Pinner. R. February 6,
1777.                                                          Page 460

PARKER, Frederick: son Earland; to Henry, Edmond, Jennie and Pollie Parker,
sons and daughters of my brother Richard Parker; brother William Parker;
sister Sary Hunt until my son is 21; to Richard, the son of Drury Parker.
Exs., brother Richard Parker and Rev. Mr. Henry John Burgess. Friend
Brewer Godwin to assist my Exs. D. March 7, 1777. R. April 3, 1777.
    Wit: Brewer Godwin, Mary Whitfield.
    Security, John Woodley.                                    Page 462

WESTON, William: Leg. wife and all my children; daughter Ann. Extx., wife
Ann Weston. D. February 3, 1777. R. April 3, 1777.
    Wit: William Orr, James Peden, Benjamin Applewhite, William
         Bagnall.
    Security, James Peden, William Bagnall.                    Page 462

PATTERSON, Sanford: Appraised by Francis Young, Jesse Barlow, Francis
Brantley. Ordered, March 7, 1776. R. April 4, 1777.            Page 464

COOK, John: Appraised by Samuel Simmons, James Hough, James Gwaltney.
R. May 1, 1777.                                                Page 465

GRAY, Mathew: Appraised by Wilson Brantley, Gabriel Gibbs, Thomas Whitfield.
R. May 1, 1777.                                                Page 465

SCOTT, James Tooke: Appraised by Gabriel Gibbs, Harrison Whitfield, Joseph
Hill. R. May 1, 1777.                                          Page 466

WRENN, Francis: Account estate, examined by John J. Wheadon and Mathais
Webb. Signed, Thomas Wrenn. R. May 1, 1777.                    Page 466

COLE, John: Appraised by Benjamin Hicks, Joseph Womble, William Jordan.
Ordered, January 16, 1777. R. May 1, 1777.                     Page 467

DAVIS, Arthur: Leg. son Nelson; son Isham; son William, land between here
and Charles Chapman's; son Thomas; wife Mary; daughter Sarah; daughter
Mary. Ex., son William Davis. D. October 29, 1776. R. June 5, 1777.
    Wit: John Davis, Benjamin Chapman, Henry Chapman.
    Security, John Davis and William Blunt, Jr.                Page 467

WAIL, Nicholas: Account estate, examined by Willis Wills, Thomas Hall, Thomas
Howell. Signed, John Wail. R. June 5, 1777.                    Page 468

CHAPMAN, Charles: Leg. son John; son William; son Henry, the use of my
plantation bought of Joseph Whitehead until my grandson John, his son,
is 21, reversion to my son Benjamin Chapman; son Joseph; daughter Mary
Milliken; daughter Frances Gale; son Charles; son Benjamin, the planta-
tion on which I now live. Exs., son Benjamin Chapman and Capt. Robert
Tynes. D. February 10, 1777. R. July 3, 1777.
　　　Wit: John Woodley, James Screws.
　　　Security, John Woodley and William Blunt.　　　　　　　Page 469

MANGUM, Joseph: Appraised by James Pitman and Thomas Copher. Ordered,
August 4, 1762. R. July 3, 1777.　　　　　　　　　　　　　Page 470

ELEY, John: Account estate, examined by James Allen Bridger and Joshua
Council. R. July 3, 1777.　　　　　　　　　　　　　　　　Page 471

COUPLAND, Joseph: Leg. my house and lot in Portsmouth to be sold; son
William; daughter Charlotte; one-half of my estate to Mary Burn, the
other half to daughter Charlotte. Exs., John Morris of Portsmouth
and Tristram Norsworthy of Isle of Wight County. D. November 20,
1775. R. September 5, 1776.
　　　Wit: Tristram Norsworthy, Ralph Frizzell.
Frederick Parker qualified as Ex., his security was Tristram Norsworthy.　　　　　　　　　　　　　　　　　　　　　　　　Page 472

CROCKER, William: Appraised by William Goodson, John Thomas, William Jordan.
R. September 4, 1777.　　　　　　　　　　　　　　　　　Page 472

WARD, Francis: Appraised by William Goodson, Thomas Wrenn, David Strait.
R. September 4, 1777.　　　　　　　　　　　　　　　　　Page 473

WARD, Thomas: Appraised by William Gay, Mathais Webb, John Stephenson.
Ordered, September 13, 1777. R. October 2, 1777.　　　　Page 473

DAVIS, Arthur: Appraised by William Goodson, John Thomas, John Jordan, Jr.
R. October 2, 1777.　　　　　　　　　　　　　　　　　　Page 474

ALMOND, Edward: Appraised by Joseph Chapman, Joseph Brantley, Samuel
Godrey. Ordered, November 1776. R. October 2, 1777.　　Page 474

HOLLAND, Samuell: Appraised by John Darden, John Daughtrey, Mills Lawrence.
Ordered, April 18, 1777. R. December 4, 1777.　　　　　Page 474

INGLISH, Mary: Leg. daughter Ann Carr; daughter Charity Edmonds, son-in-law
Demsey Carr; granddaughters, Patience, Keziah and Ann Carr; grandson
Thomas Carr; son-in-law Solomon Edmunds. Exs., sons-in-law Solomon
Edmunds and Nathan Carr. D. July 27, 1774. R. July 3, 1777.
　　　Wit: Robert Coggan, William Peirce, James Bridger.　　Page 475

LIGHTFOOT, Bartholomew: Leg. son Bartholomew; son Lemuel; daughter Ann;
daughter Mary; to Frances Willet, otherwise Lightfoot, daughter of
Mary Willet; to Patience Willet, otherwise Lightfoot; to Mary Willet.
Ex., son Bartholomew Lightfoot. D. February 26, 1775. R. October 5,
1775.
　　　Wit: Jesse Atkins, Joseph Brantley.
　　　Security, Jethro Gale, Willis Wills.　　　　　　　　Page 476

REYNOLDS, Isham: Leg. whole estate to grandmother Rachel Norsworthy. Ex.,
grandmother Rachel Norsworthy. D. August 12, 1776. R. January 1,
1778.
　　　Wit: Ranal (?) Reynolds, Christopher Dickinson.　　　Page 477

HOLLEMAN, Thomas: Leg. daughter Ann; daughter Patty; loving wife. Ex.,

William Holleman. D. April 5, 1775. R. January 1, 1778.
>    Wit: Jediah Holleman, Christopher Holleman, Robert Wall.
>    Security, Thomas Gwaltney, James Gwaltney.          Page 477

GODWIN, William: Leg. daughter Ann; daughter Easther; wife Margaret; son
>    William; son Joseph; son George; daughter Sarah; daughter Hannah.
>    Exs., wife, Col. Brewer Godwin, David Williams. D. January 13,1777.
>    R. January 1, 1778.
>>    Wit: Joseph Smith, Jr., Hezekiah Holladay, Mathew Whitfield.
>>    Security, Tristram Norsworthy, Anthony Holladay.          Page 478

TURNER, Joshua: Account estate, examined by Daniel Herring, Jr., Benjamin
>    Eley. Signed, Joshua Turner. R. January 1, 1778.          Page 479

ENGLISH, Sarah: Leg. brother Jacob English; cousin Ruth Spivey. Ex.,
>    brother Jacob English. D. December 19, 1775. R. February 5, 1778.
>>    Wit: Jesse Watkins, Isabel Whitehead, Catherine Lankford.
>>>                                                            Page 479

SMITH, Joseph: Appraised by Hezekiah Holladay, Joseph Godwin, Tristram
>    Norsworthy. Ordered, August, 1776. R. February 5, 1778.     Page 479

CHANNEL, Ann: Appraised by George Norsworthy, Ralph Gibbs, Joseph Lawrence.
>    R. February 5, 1778.                                        Page 480

WILLS, Micajah: Of Newport Parish. Leg. wife Mary not to give any part of
>    my estate to John, the son of Miles Taylor; nephew Miles son of brother
>    Miles Wills; to Peggy, daughter of Miles Taylor; to Richard, son of
>    Miles Taylor; to Peyton, son of Francis Young; to Frances daughter of
>    Francis Young; to John Scarsbrook, son of my brother John Scarsbrook
>    Wills; to Miles, son of Miles Taylor. Exs., friends Francis Young,
>    Goodrich Wilson and Jesse Atkinson. D. September 26, 1777. R. March 5,
>    1778.
>>    Wit: Francis Young, Henry Baker, Harrison Whitfield.
>>    Mary Wills qualified as Extx.
>>    Security, John Taylor and Francis Young.                    Page 481

HOLLEMAN, Thomas: Appraised by James Gwaltney, John Stevenson, Jesse Gray.
>    R. April 2, 1778.                                            Page 482

JOLLIFF, Thomas: Account estate, examined by John Thomas and William Blunt.
>    Signed, William Blunt, Jr. R. May 7, 1778.                   Page 482

BRYANT, Samuel: Of Newport Parish. Leg. Bryant kin, five shillings; wife
>    Joanna, reversion at her death to my neighbor Robert Johnson, Sr. and
>    his son Elijah Johnson. Ex., Elijah Johnson. D. April 19, 1776.
>    R. May 7, 1778.
>>    Wit: Jesse Watkins, Anna Rawls.
>>    Joanna Bryant qualified.
>>    Security, William Fleming, John Owen.                       Page 483

HOWELL, Thomas: Appraised by Thomas Cowling, Robert Driver, Thomas Newman.
>    Ordered, January, 1778. R. May 7, 1778.                      Page 484

SCAMMELL, John: Account estate, signed Richard Scammell. R. May 7, 1778.
>                                                                 Page 486

JONES, John: Appraised by Moreland Delk, James Copher, William Gay.
>    R. May 7, 1778.                                              Page 486

ROBERTS, Thomas: Account estate, examined by Daniel Herring, Jr. and
>    James Johnson. Signed, Rebecca Roberts. R. May 7, 1778.     Page 487

HUNT, Prudence: Appraised by George Norsworthy, Ralph Gibbs, Anthony Holladay. Ordered, April 26, 1777. R. May 7, 1778. Page 487

JOINER, Theophilus: Appraised by James Uzzell, Thomas Uzzell, William Morrison. Ordered, November 1, 1777. R. May 7, 1778. Page 488

WILLS, Micajah: Appraised by Thomas Peirce, Daniel Barraud, Robert Taylor. R. May 7, 1778. Page 489

WAIL, Ann: Of Newport Parish. Leg. son Josiah; daughter Rachel. Ex., son Josiah Wail. D. May 6, 1778. R. June 4, 1778.
  Wit: Thomas Hall, Mary Sikes.
  Security, Thomas Hall. Page 490

WILLS, William: Account estate, examined by Jesse Atkins and Josiah Wills. Signed, Mary Wills and Bartholomew Lightfoot. R. June 4, 1778.
Page 492

RAIFORD, William: Account estate, to cash paid Ann Little; to cash paid Ratcliff Boon as a legacy. Examined by James Bridger, Nathaniel Fleming, Daniel Herring, Jr. Signed, Thomas Holleman. R. June 4, 1778. Page 492

BENNETT, William: Letter recorded as his will, written from Portsmouth, September 28, 1776. -to embark that day for New York; states that his brother Jesse has enlisted for three years; if he fails to return his estate to be divided between his brothers and sisters, viz: James, Thomas and Edmund Bennett, Patty Dobbs and Lucy Stevens. States that he has sent John Lennard's note by Richard Hardy. R. June 4, 1778.
Page 492

LANKFORD, Thomas: Of Newport Parish. Leg. son Stephen, son Jesse, son Thomas, daughter Elizabeth Chappell; granddaughter Mary Watkins; grandson George, son of William Lankford decd.; grandson Ivey Lankford. Ex., son Thomas Lankford. D. May 24, 1778. R. June 4, 1778.
  Wit: Joseph Mountfort, Wade Mountfort, Thomas English,
    Patience Brittain.
  Security, John Lawrence. Page 492

WATKINS, Jesse: Leg. wife and my children; son Jesse. Exs., wife, Michael Johnson, Capt. John Darden. D. August 8, 1777. R. June 4, 1778.
  Wit: Thomas English, Sr., Thomas English, Jr., Ann English.
  Will presented by Priscilla Watkins.
  Security, John Darden, John Lawrence and Michael Johnson.
Page 494

BRYANT, Samuel: Appraised by Abraham Carr, William Duck, John Duck. R. August 6, 1778. Page 494

BURK, Mary: Appraised by John Wrench, Hora Durley. Ordered, February, 1777. R. September 3, 1778. Page 496

MILLER, Robert: Appraised by Robert Driver, John Butler, Jacob Dickinson. Ordered, February 5, 1778. R. September 3, 1778. Page 496

DOBBS, Josiah: Appraised by Luke Taylor, George Mallicoat, Abel James. Ordered, August 27, 1778. R. September 3, 1778. Page 496

RAND, William: Account estate, examined by Daniel Barraud, Goodrich Wilson, Thomas Smith. Signed, Sophia Hanson and Lewis Allmond. R. October 1, 1778. Page 499

BREWER, Michael: Leg. son Joshua; daughter Priscilla Fowler; son John; wife
Martha; son Joseph; son Benjamin; daughter Holland Brewer. Wife, Extx.
D. May 20, 1778. R. October 1, 1778.
    Wit: Thomas Lankford, William English, Joseph Fowler, Ann
    English, Peter Butler.
    Security, Peter Butler.                       Page 500

WRIGHT, Hannah: Leg. daughter Elizabeth; son Henry. Exs., son Henry Wright
and brother John Pinner. D. August 14, 1778. R. November 5, 1778.
    Wit: Mary Underwood, Jr., Mary Underwood, Sr.
    Security, Jethro Gale.                     Page 501

JORDAN, John, Jr.: Leg. father John Jordan; brother James Jordan; sister
Patience Jones; brother Thomas; brother William; sister Elizabeth
Jordan. D. September 15, 1778. R. November 5, 1778.
    Wit: Thomas Bland, Jr., William Barlow, Charity Jordan.
    Security, Francis Young.                   Page 502

TYNES, Martha: Leg. sister Mary Tynes; brother Robert Tynes; to Timothy
Tynes. Ex., cousin Benjamin Tynes. D. August 23, 1778. R. November 5, 1778.
    Wit: Henry Tynes, Benjamin Tynes.
Benjamin Tynes refused to be Ex., Sharp Reynolds qualified.    Page 503

CLAYTON, William: Leg. son William; daughter Catherine Clark; daughter Sally;
wife Priscilla and all my children. Wife, Extx. D. March 14, 1778.
R. November 5, 1778.
    Wit: William Jordan, Joseph Jordan.
    Security, Armistead Vellines, Joseph Wrenn.        Page 504

CARR, Spencer: Of Newport Parish. Leg. son John; brother John Carr; son
Amos; brother Hardy Carr; sister Amey Carr. Exs., brother John and
uncle Abraham Johnson, Sr. D. July 29, 1778. R. November 5, 1779.
    Wit: Elijah Johnson, William Carr, Andrew Carr.    Page 505

PINNER, Mary: Appraised by Thomas Cowling, Thomas Dixon, Thomas Bullock.
Signed, Thomas Pinner. R. November 5, 1778.        Page 506

LUPO, Philip: Leg. daughter Mildred; daughter Sally with reversion of bequest between the children of James Lupo and Mary Brantley; after
paying a sum of money to the children of John Hodges, which he had by
Comfort; his wife, daughter of John Cary. Brother James Lupo, the
guardian of my children and he is to see that my mother is provided
for. Ex., William Carrell. D. November 14, 1778. R. December 3,
1778.
    Wit: Mary Carrell, Comfort Carrell, John Wrenn.
    Security, John Wrenn.                    Page 507

BRANTLEY, Benjamin: Appraised by John Mallory, James Lupo, Willis Wilson.
Ordered October, 1778. R. December 3, 1778.        Page 508

GODWIN, James: Of Newport Parish. Leg. son Charles; son John; reversion
of bequests to my brother Lemuel, nephew Cary Godwin and Edward Driver;
brother-in-law John Driver. Exs., brother Lemuel Godwin and friend
Charles Driver. D. October 30, 1778. R. December 3, 1778.
    Wit: John Driver, Anne Driver, Betsey Driver, Keziah Driver.
    Security, Thomas King and John Driver.         Page 509

NORSWORTHY, Joseph: Leg. brother John; brother George; sister Ann Driver;
to Dolphin Driver. Ex., John Norsworthy. D. October 29, 1778.
R. December 3, 1778.
    Wit: John Deford, John Gay.
    Security, John Outland, Richard Pope.         Page 510

TYNES, Martha: Appraised by Josiah Wills, Charles Butler, Charles Driver.
R. December 3, 1778.                                                      Page 512

BREWER, Michael: Appraised by Mills Lawrence, Benjamin Bradshaw, Solomon
Edmonds. R. December 3, 1778.                                             Page 513

CUTCHINS, Joseph: Of Newport Parish. Leg. son William, land adjoining
William Davis and William Casey; son Mathew, the land I bought of John
Hodges and of the Ex., of Benjamin Miller; son Joseph; daughter Mary.
Exs., brother Thomas Cutchins and son-in-law Solomon Wilson.
D. December 14, 1778. R. January 7, 1779.
    Wit: Francis Young, Henry Applewhaite, Harrison Whitfield,
    Gabriel Gibbs.
    Security, Goodrich Wilson, Harrison Whitfield.                       Page 514

PRUDEN, Nathaniel: Leg. son Nathaniel; son Henry; daughter Sally; daughter
Betsey; daughter Polly. Ex., Thomas Cowling. D. December 10, 1774.
R. January 7, 1779.
    Wit: Thomas Everitt, John Everitt, Mathew Jordan.                    Page 515

GODWIN, James: Appraised by Josiah Wills, John Butler, Sharpe Reynolds.
R. January 7, 1779.                                                      Page 516

LUPO, Philip: Appraised by John Mallory, William Hodsden, Henry Applewhaite.
R. February 4, 1779.                                                     Page 517

WATKINS, Jesse: Appraised by Robert Coggan, Joshua Council, Robert Holland.
R. February 4, 1779.                                                     Page 518

CARR, Benjamin: Appraised by Eley Johnson, Abraham Johnson, Robert Duck.
Ordered November, 1778. R. February 4, 1779.                             Page 519

WOODLEY, John, Jr.: Appraised by John Mallory, John Wren, James Lupo.
Ordered October, 1778. R. January 7, 1779.                              Page 519

CARR, Spencer: Appraised by John Darden, Hardy Darden, Obediah Johnson.
R. February 4, 1779.                                                     Page 519

WRIGHT, Hannah: Appraised by Gale Eley, John Roberts, William Roberts.
R. March 4, 1779.                                                        Page 520

APPLEWHAITE, Arthur: Account estate, examined by Richard Hardy, William
Hodsden, William Casey. Signed, John Woodley and Henry Applewhaite.
R. March 4, 1779.                                                        Page 521

HARRISON, Henry, Sr.: In account with Henry Harrison, Jr., decd. Paid
legacy to John Harrison and Constant Harrison. Examined by Richard
Hardy and ------. R. March 4, 1779.                                     Page 523

HADLEY, Ambrose: Leg. son William; daughter Elizabeth Falconer; daughter
Sarah Davis; granddaughter Patience Blunt; granddaughter Elizabeth
Chapman; son-in-law James Davis and his wife Mary, a bond I hold of
Peter Bocock's; Jane Abigail Abbington and Joseph Abigail Abbington.
Ex., son-in-law James Davis. D. April 6, 1778. R. April 1, 1779.
    Wit: Robert Tynes, Richard Mathews.
    Security, Robert Tynes.                                              Page 526

HAWKINS, Samuel: Appraised by Hezekiah Holladay, Anthony Holladay, William
Bagnall, Joseph Smith. Ordered, February 1779. R. March 17, 1779.
                                                                         Page 527

PRUDEN, Nathaniel: Appraised by Jonas Shivers, Henry Parnall, Willis Bullock. Ordered January 7, 1779. R. April 1, 1779.       Page 1

HUNTER, Elizabeth: Of Newport Parish. Leg. son James; daughter Elizabeth; to Daniel Turner. Ex., William Bagnall. D. May 3, 1779. R. June 3, 1779.
       Wit: Thomas Hall, Giles Daniel.       Page 3

DAVIS, William: Nuncupative will, proven by Solomon Bracey, Hannah Haile, John Vellines and Peter Hatchell. Estate to his wife and mother. D. March 29, 1779. R. June 3, 1779.       Page 4

SMITH, Joseph, Jr.: Appraised by Hezekiah Holladay, Joseph Smith, Sr., Samuel Hawkins. Ordered January 6, 1778. R. June 3, 1779. Page 5

CLAYTON, William: Appraised by William Blunt, Jr., John Thomas, Josiah Wrenn. R. June 3, 1779.       Page 7

PRUDEN, Nathaniel: Account estate, examined by Robert Driver and John Pinner. Signed, Thomas Cowling. R. June 2, 1779.       Page 8

ELEY, Elizabeth: Appraised by Andrew Sikes, Robert Babb, Jethro Gale. Ordered November 6, 1777. R. July 1, 1779.       Page 9

BRANTLEY, Francis: Leg. wife Naney; daughter Sally; daughter Nancy Harrison. Ex., Benjamin Glover. D. May 24, 1779. R. July 1, 1779.
       Wit: John Hodges, Edward Dews, Patience Hodges.       Page 10

ORR, William: Of Smithfield. Leg. wife Mary; son John; son William. Exs., wife, James Peden, James Wills, John Applewhaite. D. April 1, 1779. R. July 1, 1779.
       Wit: John Orr, Jr., Jacob Ege.       Page 11

POWELL, Joshua: Appraised by John Bowden, Robert Eley, Robert Bowden. Ordered February 6, 1778. R. July 1, 1779.       Page 12

BRANTLEY, Francis: Appraised by Francis Young, Samuel Wilson, John Fones. R. August 5, 1779.       Page 14

HARVEY, John: Of Newport Parish. Leg. wife Prudence; daughter Mary. D. January 28, 1779. R. August 5, 1779.
       Wit: Josiah Parker, Mary Thomas, Abram Whitfield.       Page 15

EASON, James: Account estate, paid Mary Ronaldson her one-third, paid John Eason and Peggy Eason. Signed, Mary Ronaldson. R. August 5, 1779.
       Page 16

DAVIS, Arthur: Estate account, examined by John Thomas, William Blunt and William Goodson. R. August 5, 1779.       Page 17

HUNTER, Elizabeth: Appraised by Thomas Hall, Ralph West, Anthony Holladay. Ordered, June 3, 1779. R. August 5, 1779.       Page 18

BRIDGER, John: Appraised by William Hodsden, James Peden, James Wills. R. August 5, 1779.       Page 20

PINNER, Mary: Estate account, examined by Thomas Cowling, Robert Driver. Signed, Thomas Pinner. R. August 5, 1779. Page 22

ENGLISH, Jacob: Leg. Joseph Spivey; rest of estate between the children of Jacob Spivey and Joseph English. Ex., Joseph Spivey. D. December 19, 1772. R. September 2, 1779.
Wit: Jesse Watkins, Isabel Whitehead, Catey Lankford. Page 23

GWALTNEY, Benjamin: Leg. sister Elizabeth, my estate at the death of my mother; James Gwaltney. Ex., my uncle James Gwaltney. D. May 3, 1779. R. August 5, 1779.
Wit: Benjamin Hicks, Mathew Harris, Sarah Betts. Page 24

BAGNALL, Richard: Appraised by John Driver, John Williams, Edmund Godwin, Jr. R. February 7, 1779. Page 25

JONES, John: Account estate, examined by Robert Tynes, John Woodley. Signed, Jesse Cofer. R. October 7, 1779. Page 26

WHITFIELD, Harrison: Appraised by William Davis, William Hodsden, Gabriel Gibbs. D. June 25, 1779. R. October 7, 1779. Page 26

WEST, Giles: Account estate, paid legacy to Richard Jordan. Examined, Nicholas Parker, James Wills. D. October 4, 1779. Page 28

COLESTON, Samuel: Of Richmond County, North Farnham Parish. Leg. brother William; brother Rawleigh Coleston. D. March 3, 1779. R. December 2, 1779.
Wit: Nathaniel Parker, Pharoah Fitzpatrick, Nathaniel Norsworthy.
Page 29

BURK, Thomas: Leg. Rachel Wail, Richard West. Ex., Richard West. D. October 20, 1779. R. December 2, 1779.
Wit: John Jordan, Ralph West. Page 29

CARY, Patience: Leg. five granddaughters, Mary, Patience, Ann, Rebecca and Comfort Hodges; my three children, James Lupo, Philip Lupo and Mary Brantley. Ex., son James Lupo. D. December 7, 1772. R. December 2, 1779.
Wit: William Carrell, Jeremiah Proctor. Page 30

HEDGEPETH, Henry: Appraised by Stephen Butler, Robert Eley, Eley Johnson. Signed Mary Hedgepeth, Lemuel Hedgepeth. D. April, 1779. R. --------
Page 31

BUTLER, Jacob: Leg. son Jacob; daughter Isabel Boit; daughter Elizabeth Inman; son Peter; son James; son Stephen; son Jethro; daughter Zelpha Collins; son Ephraim; daughter Christian; grandson Jacob Butler; son Epaphroditus; son Eleazer. Exs., sons Epaphroditus, Eleazer Butler. D. June 25, 1778. R. February 3, 1780.
Wit: Nathan Carr, Jesse Johnson, John Duck. Page 34

SEAGRAVE, Francis: Leg. Ann Norsworthy; Elizabeth Norsworthy. Ex., Ann Norsworthy. D. October 9, 1779. R. February 3, 1780.
Wit: John Norsworthy, Dempsey Marshall. Page 36

CARY, Patience: Appraised by Benjamin Harrison, John Wrenn, Lewis Chapman. R. February 3, 1780. Page 37

WILLIAMS, John: Account estate, examined by Brewer Godwin and William Bagnall. Signed, David Williams. D. 1775. R. March 2, 1780. Page 38

INGLISH, Jacob: Appraised by Joshua Council, John Watkins, Nathan Carr.
R. March 2, 1780. Page 39

BULLOCK, Joseph: Leg. son Joseph, my whole estate, if he will take my place
as a soldier and redeem me from having to go to war, if he refuses whole
estate to my wife, Prudence; daughter Eleanor Goodson; daughter Mary
Pitt; son Joseph; daughter Peggy; son William; daughter Betsey; son
Thomas; son John; daughter Patsey; daughter Penelope and daughter Salley
Bullock. Exs., Robert Driver and son-in-law Thomas Pitt. D. October 16,
1777. R. May 4, 1780.
Wit: Richard Bowden, Samuel Bowden, Naney Bowden. Page 40

BARLOW, Jesse: Appraised by John Jordan, W. Goodson, and W. Davis.
R. May 4, 1780. Page 41

FULGHAM, Anthony: Leg. son Jesse; son Michael; son Ezekiah; wife Rebecca;
son Henry; daughter Celia; daughter Rebecca Bracy; son Rodwell Fulgham.
Ex., son Jesse. D. November 21, 1779. R. May 4, 1780.
Wit: Thomas Wills, James Johnson, James Bridger. Page 42

ALLMOND, Edward: Account estate, examined by Joseph Chapman, Charles Driver,
Thomas Smith. R. May 4, 1780. Page 43

BLUNT, William, Sr.: Appraised by Thomas Fearn, William Goodson, John
Thomas. Ordered May 15, 1780. R. July 6, 1780. Page 44

BLUNT, William, Sr.: Account estate, to balance due the widow, equal propor-
tion between, Isaac Moody, Willis Wilson and William Blunt, Jr.
Signed, William Blunt, Jr. Examined by Richard Hardy and Thomas Fearn.
R. July 6, 1780. Page 45

HARVEY, John: Appraised by Willis Wills, Ralph West, Richard West. Signed,
Prudence Harvey. Ordered May 4, 1780. R. July 6, 1780. Page 47

BRANTLEY, Benjamin: Account estate, examined by John Mallory and John
Wrenn. R. July 6, 1780. Page 49

BUTLER, Jacob: Appraised by John Darden, John Duck, William Duck.
R. August 3, 1780. Page 50

HOWELL, Thomas: Examined by Thomas Cowling and Robert Driver. Signed,
Mary Howell. R. August 3, 1780. Page 51

LIGHTFOOT, Bartholomew, Jr.: Appraised by Josiah Wills, Thomas Uzzell,
James Uzzell. R. August 3, 1780. Page 52

LIGHTFOOT, Bartholomew, Jr.: Account estate, to cash paid William Ward in
right of his wife, the admtx. of said Lightfoot. Examined by John
Butler, Sharpe Reynolds, Josiah Wills. R. August 3, 1780. Page 53

EDWARDS, Benjamin: Appraised by James Derring, William Heath, George
Malicote. Ordered, May 4, 1780. R. August 3, 1780. Page 54

SMITH, William: Of Newport Parish. Leg. wife Elizabeth; son Stephen house
in Smithfield bought of George Hall, formerly the property of William
Rand; daughter Ann; daughter Sarah. Exs., wife and Jonathan Godwin.
D. April 7, 1780. R. September 7, 1780.
Wit: Jethro Gale, Joseph Chapman, Thomas Smith. Page 56

MILLER, Robert: Account estate, returned by Frances Miller, now Frances
Whitfield. Examined by William Hodsden, John Goodrich, William Casey.
R. September 7, 1780. Page 57

SMITH, Nathaniel: Leg. wife Mary, reversion of bequest to the children of my sister Patience Inglish. Exs., wife Mary Smith and Joseph Inglish. D. May 6, 1780. R. September 7, 1780.
> Wit: Tristram Norsworthy, Lemuel Bowden, Stephen Gorton.

Page 58

HUNTER, Elizabeth: Account estate, to cash paid the estate of Joshua Hunter. Examined by Brewer Godwin, James Wills, James Peden, Joseph Fulgham. R. September 7, 1780. Page 58

GWALTNEY, James: Of Newport Parish. Leg. wife; son James; son Simmons; son John; son Josiah; son Jordan; son Henry; to son James, the land formerly belonging to Benjamin Gwaltney, decd.,; daughter Mary Gwaltney. D. September 20, 1780. R. December 7, 1780. Ex., son James Gwaltney.
> Wit: Mark Carrell, Samuel Simmons, Henry Cofer. Page 59

WESTRAY, Benjamin: Leg. wife Lucy; son Mathew, a tract of land formerly belonging to Benjamin Tomlin, decd.; daughter Chloe; son Mills the land on which William Westray now lives; daughter Sally; son John; to Margaret, the widow of Benjamin Tomlin. Ex., brother William Westray. D. January 10, 1780. R. February 1, 1781.
> Wit: Edmond Westray, Joseph Westray, Elias Westray. Page 60

GODWIN, George: Leg. sister-in-law Jemima Whitfield, the plantation bought of Henry White in Carolina; to my brother-in-law, Samuel Whitfield. Exs., Ralph Gibbs and George Norsworthy. D. June 13, 1778. R. March 1, 1781.
> Wit: George Norsworthy, Priscilla Norsworthy. Page 61

APPLEWHAITE, Jane: Of Newport Parish. Leg. son John; son Mills; son Thomas. Exs., son Henry Applewhaite and Joshua Carr. D. September 17, 1779. R. March 1, 1781.
> Wit: John Applewhaite, Arthur Applewhaite, Francis Young.
> Security, William Blunt. Page 62

SMELLEY, John: son John when 21; son Willis; to wife Mary and my four children, the land if recovered, for which I sued James Peden and Jeremiah Godwin. Exs., wife and William Ward. D. February 5, 1781. R. April 5, 1781.
> Wit: Charles Groce, Rachel Groce, Ann Weston.
> Security, Lemuel Lightfoot and Richard Williams. Page 63

MADDERA, Joseph: Leg. wife Sarah; son James; son Joseph; neighbor William Barlow. D. February 26, 1777. R. April 5, 1781.
> Wit: William Davis, James Barlow, William Barlow, William Davidson.
> Security, William Davis. Page 64

BARLOW, William: Leg. son James; son Sampson; son William; son John; son Nathaniel; daughter Ann Webb; daughter Martha. Exs., son James and Mathew Webb. D. August 1, 1780. R. April 5, 1781.
> Wit: William Davis, Thomas Coffield, Thomas Barlow, Joseph Maddera.
> Security, William Davis and Thomas Barlow. Page 64

NORSWORTHY, Patience: Leg. daughter Martha Somner; daughter Ann; daughter Elizabeth Norsworthy. Exs., daughters, Ann and Elizabeth Norsworthy. D. August 19, 1775. R. April 5, 1781.
> Wit: James Allen Bridger, William Gay, Milley Gay. Page 65

TYNES, Henry: Account estate, to paid John Whitley for keeping the child two years. Examined by William Blunt and William Morrison. Signed, Sarah Tynes. R. April 1, 1781. Page 66

TYNES, Henry:  Appraised by James Jordan, Thomas Goodson, William Davis.
R.  April 5, 1781.                                                    Page 67

ORR, Dr. William:  Appraised by Thomas Smith, Joseph Chapman, Charles Driver.
R.  May 3, 1781.                                                      Page 68

LANKFORD, William:  Appraised by Solomon Edmunds, John Daughtrey, Peter
Butler.  Ordered June 4, 1778.  R.  May 3, 1781.                     Page 68

DAUGHTRY, William:  Leg. son Mathew; son Ophilus; son Solomon; son Absolom;
daughter Lisbey Tallow; wife Elizabeth.  Exs., sons Mathew and Ophilus
Daughtry.  D.  March 5, 1781.  R.  May 3, 1781.
Wit:  James Vaughan, Henry Vaughan, Uriah Vaughan.
Security, John Cobb.                                                  Page 69

PITT, Jacob:  Leg. wife Tamar; son Parnall, when 21; to all my children.
Exs., wife, Brewer Godwin and Henry Pitt.  D.  September 4, 1778.
R.  May 3, 1781.
Wit:  John Scarsbrook Wills, Jeremiah Godwin, Martha King.
Security, George Norsworthy and Jeremiah Godwin.                     Page 70

WEST, Richard:  Leg. brother Ralph, horse which was taken into public service
by Capt. William Spiller; daughter Priscilla Pitt West; wife Elizabeth,
estate she inherited from her brother, John Pitt; son John Pitt West.
Ex., brother Ralph West, also the guardian of daughter, Priscilla Pitt
West.  D.  January 13, 1781.  R.  March 1, 1781.
Wit:  John Scarsbrook Wills, Josiah Cutchin, James Casey.
Security, Thomas King and James Wills.                               Page 71

POYTHRESS, Edward:  Leg. daughter Elizabeth; daughter Sarah; daughter Mary;
daughter Tabitha.  Richard Hardy, guardian of daughters Mary and Sarah.
Exs., Richard Hardy and James Davis.  D.  March 30, 1781.  R.  May 3,
1781.
Wit:  Samuel Hardy, Benjamin Atkins, William Hardy.
Security, Joseph Cornwell, James Peden, James Wills.                 Page 73

JONES, Frederick:  Leg. son Thomas; son James; wife Susannah, among all my
children.  Ex., brother David Jones.  D.  January 16, 1781.  R.  July 5,
1781.
Wit:  Mathias Webb, Jacob Jones.
Security, Jacob Jones and Thomas Barlow.                             Page 74

JORDAN, John:  Of Newport Parish.  Leg. son Thomas, the land left me by my
son John Jordan, decd.; son William; son James; daughter Patience Jones;
daughter Elizabeth; daughter Sarah; daughter Ann.  Ex., son James
Jordan.  D.  May 18, 1781.  R.  July 5, 1781.
Wit:  William Davis, Nancy Jordan, Thomas Barlow.
Security, Francis Wrenn, William Blunt.                              Page 74

FEARN, George:  Leg. wife Catherine; daughter Nancy Wills; granddaughter
Catherine Wills; granddaughter Sally Wills; daughter Catherine Fearn.
Ex., son John Fearn.  D.  February 10, 1781.  R.  July 5, 1781.
Wit:  Edmund Cosby, Benjamin Tynes, Drury Andrews.
Security, Benjamin Tynes and Thomas Fearn.                          Page 76

NORSWORTHY, Patience:  Appraised by William Peirce, Sr. and Dempsey Marshall.
R.  July 5, 1781.                                                    Page 77

DICKINSON, Christopher:  Leg. daughter Chasey; wife Mary; son John, to my
brother, Jacob Dickinson, daughter Martha Dickinson.  Extx., wife Mary
Dickinson.  D.  August 27, 1778.  R.  November 1, 1781.
Wit:  James Wills, John Whitfield, Rachel Norsworthy.
Security, James Wills.                                               Page 78

HEDGEPETH, Benjamin: Leg. wife Elizabeth and my children. Ex., John Worrell.
D. ---------- R. April 5, 1781.
Wit: Jonas Bradshaw, Robert Council, Peter Walkinson (?).
Security, Barnaby Drake. Page 79

WHITFIELD, Thomas: Of Newport Parish. Leg. granddaughters, Molly, Sally and
Jane Edmunds; grandson Thomas Whitfield; granddaughter Mary Whitfield;
grandson Harrison Whitfield; daughter Kernhappuch Edmunds; to Elizabeth
Goodrich; to son-in-law Howell Edmunds. Ex., Howell Edmunds.
D. July 9, 1781. R. January 3, 1782.
Wit: Wilson Whitfield, Mathew Whitfield, Robert Pully.
Security, William Goodson, John Crocker. Page 79

CARY, Patience: Account estate, examined by William Carrell and Benjamin
Harrison. R. January 3, 1782. Page 81

SMITH, Nathaniel: Appraised by William Hodsden, John Taylor, Mills (Miles)
Wills. R. January 3, 1782. Page 81

INGLISH, Joseph: Appraised by Jethro Powell, John Watkins, Nathan Carr.
Ordered March 21, 1781. R. January 3, 1782. Page 82

JENKINS, Valentine: Of Newport Parish. Leg. wife Mary; son William;
brother Edward Jenkins. Ex., William Davis. D. December 6, 1781.
R. January 3, 1782.
Wit: William Casey, John Hodges, Thomas Brantley, Elizabeth
Brantley.
Security, John Lawrence, John Mallory, Howell Edmunds, Francis
Young. Page 84

WESTRAY, William: Account estate, examined by Nathaniel Fleming and Daniel
Herring, Sr. Signed, Edmond Westray. R. January 3, 1782. Page 85

JORDAN, Richard: Of Newport Parish. Leg. son John, land that John Rat-
cliffe bought of William West and a tract which belonged to his grand-
father, Richard Jordan; son Robert; daughter Lydia; daughter Elizabeth
Outland; grandchildren, Edmund, Ann and Elizabeth Jordan. Exs., sons
John and Robert Jordan. D. February 3, 1781. R. January 3, 1782.
Wit: Brewer Godwin, Elias Parker, Patience Jordan. Page 85

JONES, Frederick: Appraised by Thomas Wrenn, Jacob Jones, Mathew Webb.
R. January 3, 1782. Page 86

SIKES, Andrew: Appraised by Jethro Gale, John Norsworthy. R. January 3,
1782. Page 88

COGGAN, John: Leg. daughter Mary Turner; son John; daughter Sarah Powell;
daughter Ann Mercer; daughter Catey Mercer; daughter Betsey; to my wife
and all my children. D. January 11, 1781. R. January 3, 1782.
Ex., son John Coggan.
Wit: John Norsworthy, John Gay. Page 90

SEGAR, Oliver: Appraised by Thomas Fearn, Thomas Wills. Ordered, December 5,
1781. R. January 3, 1782. Page 91

ROBERTSON, William: Of Newport Parish. Leg. son George; daughter Peggy; to
Catherine Penny. Exs., brother George Robertson, Rev. Henry John
Burgess, Mr. Richard Hardy and my son George, when he becomes 18.
D. December 24, 1781. R. January 3, 1782.
Wit: John Crocker, William Crocker, William Morrison. Page 92

FULGHAM, John: Leg. son Michael; son Edmund; son John; daughter Patience

Johnson; daughter Martha; daughter Ann; son Josiah Fulgham. Exs., wife Mary and son Edmund Fulgham. D. October 12, 1767. R. March 7, 1782. Wit: John Gay, Jr., Edmund Fulgham, Sr. Security, Ezekiah Fulgham. Page 94

EVERITT, Joseph: Appraised by Jacob Randolph, John Everitt, Thomas Smelley. Signed, Willis Everitt. Ordered January 8, 1781. R. January 7, 1782. Page 95

BULLOCK, Joseph: Appraised by Thomas Cowling, Thomas Newman, Thomas Bullock. R. February 7, 1782. Page 95

BABB, Robert: Appraised by Thomas Smelley, Jethro Gale, John Deford. Ordered May 7, 1781. R. February 7, 1782. Page 97

WRENN, Francis: Appraised by Richard Hardy, Goodrich Wilson, John Jennings Wheadon. R. February 7, 1782. Page 100

VAUGHAN, Henry: Appraised by John Daughtry, Job Holland, Miles Whitfield. Ordered May 12, 1781. R. February 7, 1782. Page 101

HOLLAND, Lemuel: Account estate, examined by John Darden and Mills Lawrence. Signed, Francis Vaughan. D. December, 1778. R. February 7, 1782. Page 104

HOLLOWELL, William: Leg. son Scott; son William; daughter Coutney; daughter Sarah; daughter Mary; son Thomas; wife Sarah Hollowell. Exs., wife and sons Scott and William Hollowell. D. May 2, 1781. R. February 7, 1782. Wit: Thomas Scott, William Outland. Security, Tho. Scott. Page 104

TYNES, Celia: Leg. son West; son Thomas; son Benjamin; daughter Mary; granddaughters, Holland and Celia Lawrence. Exs., sons West and Thomas Tynes. D. April 20, 1778. R. February 7, 1782. Wit: John Holladay, Nathaniel Vellines. Page 106

HOLLADAY, Anthony: Of Newport Parish. Leg. to Holland Holladay; son Anthony; wife Marah; son John; to my four youngest children. Wife, Extx. D. February 15, 1781. R. February 7, 1782. Wit: William Bagnall, Samuel Holladay. Security, William Bagnall, Samuel and Hezekiah Holladay. Page 107

GODWIN, Jeremiah: Leg. son Jeremiah; daughter Mary; daughter Elizabeth; wife Martha Godwin. Exs., wife, brothers, Brewer and Edmund Godwin and James Pedin. D. ------ 1782. R. February 7, 1782. Wit: Ralph Frizzell, Josiah Applewhaite, Jeremiah Outland. Page 107

LANGFORD (LANKFORD ?), Thomas: Appraised by Mills Lawrence, W. Mountford, Elisha L. Ballard. Ordered June 4, 1778. R. March 7, 1782. Page 108

MARSHALL, John: Appraised by Samuel Batten, Robert Johnson, David Briggs. Ordered December 17, 1781. R. May 2, 1782. Page 109

EVERITT, Joseph: Account estate, examined by Thomas Smelley, Jacob Randolph, James Jordan. R. March 7, 1782. Page 110

NEVILL, Joseph: Appraised by Robert Driver, Thomas Newman, Benjamin Beal. Ordered January 3, 1782. R. March 7, 1782. Page 111

HOLLOWELL, William: Appraised by Edward Dews, Wilson Brantley, John Pitman. R. March 7, 1782. Page 112

PLEDGER, Martha: Leg. daughter Nancy Pledger. Ex., friend William Allmond.
D. June 4, 1781. R. March 7, 1782.
Wit: Sweeting Pope, Charity Pope.                    Page 114

BARLOW, John: Leg. daughter Mary; daughter Sally; daughter Juliana Barlow;
friend, John Sinclair. Ex., daughter Mary Barlow. D. September 28,
1781. R. March 7, 1782.
Wit: Richard Hardy, William Brown, John Cawson.       Page 114

TURNER, Mathew: Appraised by Hezekiah Fulgham, James Johnson, Michael
Fulgham. R. April 4, 1782.                            Page 115

TOMLIN, James: Leg. wife Ann; to my children. D. December 23, 1776.
R. April 4, 1782.
Wit: Benjamin Fletcher, Edmund Fulgham, John Fearn.
Hezekiah Fulgham qualified as Ex., his security, Edmund Fulgham.
                                                     Page 115

TOMLIN, James: Appraised by William Bridger, James Johnson, Joshua Turner.
R. April 4, 1782.                                    Page 116

JORDAN, Richard: Appraised by Brewer Godwin, Ralph West, Josiah Cutchins.
R. April 4, 1782.                                    Page 117

NORSWORTHY, George: Leg. wife Christian; daughter Martha; son Thompson
and daughter Martha the plantation I bought of William Coupland.
Exs., wife and Nathaniel Norsworthy. D. February 18, 1781.
R. April 4, 1782.
Wit: Tristram Norsworthy, James West, Jeremiah Outland.
Security, Richard Williams.                          Page 118

MILLER, Lucy: Leg. daughter Lucy Hill; son Thomas; James Miller; negro
placed in charge of Joseph Hill. Ex., friends, Thomas Scott and
Joseph Hill. D. September 12, 1778. R. April 4, 1782.
Wit: Catherine Crocker, George N. Scott.
Security, John J. Wheadon.                           Page 118

HUGHES, Ephila: Leg. Whole estate to William Bagnall. D. -------- 1782.
R. May 2, 1782.
Wit: William Garton, James Bridger, Samuel Holladay.  Page 119

BARLOW, William: Appraised by John J. Wheadon, William Davis, Thomas Barlow.
R. May 2, 1782.                                      Page 119

COGGAN, John: Appraised by Benjamin Eley, Thomas Smelley, William Smelley.
R. May 2, 1782.                                      Page 121

ATKINS, Frances: Account estate, examined by Lemuel Lightfoot and John
Scarsbrook Wills. Signed, Jesse Atkins. R. June 6, 1782.  Page 122

ATKINS, Joseph: Account estate, examined by Lemuel Lightfoot and John
Scarsbrook Wills. Signed, Jesse Atkins. R. June 6, 1782.  Page 122

POPE, Edward: Leg. wife Mary; son Ephraim; daughter Sarah Bullock; son
William; son John; daughter Mary; daughter Anne. Ex., son John Pope.
D. March 12, 1782. R. June 6, 1782.
Wit: Tama Hall, Henry Parnall, Penelope Pope.
Security, Henry Parnall and James Hall.              Page 123

GRAY, William: Of Newport Parish. Leg. wife Ann; son Henry; son Joseph.
Extx., wife Ann Gray. D. March 26, 1782. R. June 6, 1782.
Wit: Thomas Hall, James Smelley.
Security, Richard Williams.                          Page 124

POPE, Richard: Appraised by Thomas Smelley, Jethro Gale, Andrew Sikes.
R. June 6, 1782. Page 125

GODWIN, George: Appraised by Joseph Lawrence and James Smelley. Signed,
Ralph Gibbs. R. June 6, 1782. Page 125

CHAPMAN, William: Examined by William Hodsden, Henry Applewhaite and William
Casey. Signed, Joseph Chapman. R. July 4, 1782. Page 126

MILLER, Lucy: Appraised by James Derring, Edward Dews, Samuel Wilson.
R. July 4, 1782. Page 126

LUPO, Philip: Account estate, to balance due the estate of Benjamin
Brantley. Examined by John Mallory and William Hodsden. R. August 1,
1782. Page 127

MATHEWS, Samuel: Of Newport Parish. Leg. wife Sarah; son John; son Richard;
to all my children. Exs., son Richard Mathews and Jethro Gale.
D. April 7, 1773. R. January 3, 1782.
Wit: Jethro Gale, John Garnes, John Murphry.
Security, John Gale. Page 128

BELL, William: Leg. son Elisha; son James; son William; daughter Nancy;
daughter Elizabeth Cole; to William, the son of Benjamin Smith. Exs.,
sons William and Elisha Bell. D. August 8, 1780. R. November 1, 1781.
Wit: William Blunt, John Bowne (?), Isaac Moody.
Security, Robert Edwards and George Hall. Page 129

BELL, William: Account estate, examined by William Blunt and John Thomas.
Signed, Elisha Bell. R. June 6, 1782. Page 130

GWALTNEY, James: Appraised by Samuel Simmons, James Copher, William Gray.
R. August 1, 1782. Page 131

TOMLIN, Mathew: Leg. son Mathew; son John; brother Nathan Tomlin; son
Nicholas; wife Mary; daughter Martha; daughter Edy; son Lewis. Exs.,
sons Mathew and Nicholas. D. March 12, 1782. R. August 1, 1782.
Wit: Robert Tomlin, Jacob Stevenson, John Hartwell.
Security, James Johnson. Page 132

WESTRAY, Benjamin: Appraised by John Benn, Conyons Morris, Samuel Batten.
R. August 1, 1782. Page 134

WESTRAY, Benjamin: Account estate, examined by Nathaniel Fleming and William
Bridger. Signed, James Johnson. R. August 1, 1782. Page 134

HEDGEPETH, Mary: Appraised by Eley Johnson, Stephen Butler, Nathan Carr.
Ordered January 15, 1782. R. September 5, 1782. Page 135

SHELLY, Thomas: Appraised by John J. Wheadon, William Davenport, David
Jones. Ordered September 17, 1782. R. October 3, 1782. Page 137

EDWARDS, James: Leg. wife Mary; son Mills (Miles ?); daughter Holland.
Ex., Francis Boykin. D. May 22, 1782. R. October 3, 1782.
Wit: Francis Boykin, Nathan Whitley, Elias Whitley. Page 139

BABB, Robert: Account estate, examined by Benjamin Eley, Thomas Smelly.
Signed, Ann Babb. R. November 7, 1782. Page 139

HEDGEPETH, Benjamin: Account estate, to maintaining the widow and two
children. Examined by David Chalmers and Francis Young. Signed, John
Worrell. R. November 7, 1782. Page 140

254

POWELL, Joshua, Jr.: Account estate, examined by Jesse Herring and James
Johnson. Signed, Thomas Bowden. R. November 7, 1782.    Page 141

BENN, Elizabeth: Leg. Leodicea Godwin; eldest son George; son Arthur.
Exs., brother Joseph Smith and Samuel Holladay. D. October 14, 1782.
R. November 7, 1782.
Wit: John Hawkins, Samuel Hawkins, Mills Holladay.
Security, John Hawkins.    Page 143

PARKER, William: Of the Parish of Newport. Leg. wife Mary. Ex., Benjamin
Beale, Sr. D. February 9, 1780. R. November 7, 1782.
Wit: John Green.    Page 143

BLUNT, Elizabeth: Leg. daughter Sarah Wilson; granddaughter Elizabeth Wilson; grandson William Wilson; grandson Joseph Moody; to all my children
and grandchildren; son-in-law Willis Wilson. Ex., William Jordan and
son-in-law Willis Wilson. D. February 9, 1781. R. November 7, 1782.
Wit: John Davis, John Chapman, Jr., John Chapman, Sr.
Security, William Gay.    Page 144

BRIDGER, James: The elder. Leg. wife Susanna; son Thomas Sinclair Bridger
at 21; son William; son James; to sons, William and James land on the
Chowan River in North Carolina; to son-in-law John Lawrence; daughter
Mary. Exs., wife and son William Bridger. D. August 13, 1782.
R. November 7, 1782.
Wit: R. Kello, Nathaniel Fleming, John Sinclair.
Security, John Sinclair.    Page 145

MANGUM, Britain: Appraised by John J. Wheadon, Benjamin Jones, Emanuel
Hunter. R. December 5, 1782.    Page 147

WARD, Willis: Appraised by Thomas Wrenn, Benjamin Jones, Thomas Copher.
R. December 5, 1782.    Page 148

INGLISH, Joseph: Account estate examined by Eley Johnson, Benjamin Eley
and Nathan Carr. Signed, John Darden. R. January 2, 1783. Page 149

HEDGEPETH, Henry: Account estate, examined by Eley Johnson, Benjamin Eley,
Nathan Carr. Signed, Lemuel and Mary Hedgepeth. R. January 2, 1783.
Page 149

BELL, James: Appraised by John Thomas, William Blunt, Isaac Moody.
R. February 6, 1783.    Page 150

SCOTT, Thomas: Leg. brother John; sister Ann Outland's children, the land
adjoining Joseph Ellis. Exs., brother John Scott and Scott Hollowell.
D. October 2, 1780. R. February 6, 1783.
Wit: William Hollowell, Ann Coffield.
Security, Joseph Ellis.    Page 152

DAUGHTRY, William: Appraised by Miles Whitfield, Job Holland, John Daughtry.
R. February 6, 1783.    Page 153

FRY, Robert: Leg. son Thomas; son William; grandchildren, Ann and John
Wright; wife Mary. Wife, Extx. D. June 28, 1782. R. March 6, 1783.
Wit: John Woodley.
Security, William Hubard, Gabriel Gibbs.    Page 155

SMITH, William: Appraised by Josiah Wills, Charles Butler, Sharpe Reynolds.
R. March 7, 1783.    Page 156

WHITFIELD, Miles: Leg. son Adkeson, land adjoining James Council, Cutchin

Council, Thomas Daughtry and Ivey Whitfield; provision for unborn child; wife Milla; daughter Tamar; daughter Milla; friend David Eley, brother Ivey Whitfield. Exs., David Eley and Ivey Whitfield. D. November 14, 1782. R. March 6, 1783.
    Wit: David Howell, William Tallow, Jesse Gardner.
    Security, Thomas Fearn.                           Page 158

BULLOCK, Willis: Appraised by Thomas Pitt, Thomas Bullock, Joseph Shivers. Ordered May, 1782. R. March 6, 1783.           Page 160

SCOTT, Thomas: Appraised by William Goodson, Thomas Goodson, Robert Glover. R. May 2, 1783.                        Page 161

JORDAN, James: Appraised by Josiah Wilson, John J. Wheadon, William Goodson. Ordered June 26, 1782. R. May 2, 1783.         Page 162

McCOY, Jesse: Leg. wife Elizabeth; son Asay; daughter Nancy McCoy; between all my children. Ex., Thomas Parker. D. April 22, 1783. R. May 1, 1783.
    Wit: John Butler, Thomas Uzzell.
    Security, Edmund Godwin.                         Page 166

MARSHALL, John: Estate account, examined by Daniel Herring, Jr. and John Powell, Jr. Signed, Conyons Morris. R. June 6, 1783.     Page 167

BELL, James: Account estate, examined by William Blunt and John Thomas. Signed, Elisha Bell. R. June 6, 1783.             Page 168

PYLAND, William: Leg. brother James; sister Elizabeth, if she pays a bequest to Jesse Glover. D. April 20, 1782. R. June 6, 1783.
    Wit: William Hardy.
    Security, Richard Hardy.                        Page 169

WARD, Willis: Account estate, examined by John J. Wheadon, William Gay and Thomas Wrenn. Signed, Emanuel Hunter. R. July 3, 1783.   Page 169

LIGHTFOOT, Bartholomew, Jr.: Account estate, examined by John Scarsbrook Wills, Jesse Atkins and James Wills. Signed, William Ward. R. July 3, 1783.                                  Page 170

TOMLIN, James: Account estate, examined by Daniel Herring, Jr., and John Fearn. Signed, Hezekiah Fulgham. R. August 7, 1783.     Page 171

NEWMAN, John: Leg. wife Elizabeth; grandson John Newman; granddaughter Polly Newman; granddaughter Gennet Newman; son Josiah one half of the land I bought of Henry Baker in Nansemond County; daughter Elizabeth; daughter Chloe; grandson Thomas Newman; grandson James Newman; daughter Gennett; son Thomas if he pays certain bequest to Mary Bullock, Tabitha Parr, Elizabeth Newman and Chloe Newman; to my six children and James Newman's children; wife Elizabeth. Exs., wife and son Thomas Newman. D. January 9, 1782. R. August 7, 1783.
    Wit: Robert Driver, Richard Parr, Edmund Jordan.
    Security, Thomas Pitt, Jacob Dickinson.           Page 172

PYLAND, William: Appraised by Richard Hardy, John Smelley, Joseph Carrell. R. August 7, 1783.                       Page 174

GODWIN, George: Account estate, examined by Tristram Norsworthy, William Bagnall, Josiah Applewhaite. Signed, Ralph Gibbs. R. August 7, 1783.                                Page 175

GAY, William: Leg. son James; son Willis; wife. Exs., William Peirce, Jr.

and Kinchen Crumpler. D. December 24, 1782. R. August 7, 1783.
Wit: James Johnson, John Powell, Thomas Bowden.
Security, John Powell. Page 176

PITT, Thomas: Account estate, examined by John S. Wills and James Pedin.
D. 1776. R. August 7, 1783. Signed, John Smelley. Page 177

MATTHEWS, William: Appraised by William Jordan, Robert Driver, Jethro Gale.
Ordered March 4, 1783. R. September 4, 1783. Page 178

EDWARDS, Benjamin: Account estate, examined by John J. Wheadon, Samuel
Wilson, James Derring. Signed, Richard Edwards. R. September 4, 1784.
Page 180

BRIDGER, James, Gent.: Appraised by Nathaniel Fleming, Daniel Herring, Jr.,
Francis Young, James Johnson. R. October 2, 1783. Page 181

KING, Henry: Appraised by Joseph Smith, Richard Williams, William Bagnall.
Ordered March 21, 1782. R. October 2, 1783. Page 184

COGGAN, John: Account estate, examined by Nathaniel Fleming and John
Lawrence. Signed, John Coggan. R. October 2, 1783. Page 185

LAWRENCE, Robert: Appraised by Dempsey Hunt, Joseph Lawrence, Arthur
Channell. R. October 2, 1783. Page 186

GODWIN, Jeremiah: Appraised by Richard Williams, William Bagnall, Ralph
Frizzell. Signed, Edmond Godwin. R. October 2, 1783. Page 187

HOLLADAY, Anthony: Appraised by Richard Williams, William Bagnall and
Edmond Godwin. R. October 2, 1783. Signed, Mary Holladay. Page 189

BROWN, Robert: Appraised by Dempsey Hunt, Giles Daniel, Arthur Channell.
R. October 2, 1783. Page 190

FULGHAM, John: Appraised by Michael Fulgham, Jesse Fulgham, Hezekiah
Fulgham. R. October 2, 1783. Page 192

BLUNT, Elizabeth: Appraised by John Thomas, Josiah Wrenn, John Chapman.
Signed, Willis Wilson. R. November 6, 1783. Page 194

MARSHALL, John: New account estate, examined by Daniel Herring, Jr.
Signed, Conyons Morris. R. November 6, 1783. Page 196

CARTER, Mary: Leg. Nancy Holladay, reversion to Thomas and Nathaniel Smith.
Exs., Samuel Holladay and Samuel Hawkins. D. ----------
R. November 7, 1783.
Wit: Samuel Holladay, Joseph Smith.
Security, Samuel Holladay, Sr. Page 197

HEDGEPETH, Mary: (Mary Hedgepeth, Admtx. of Henry Hedgepeth.) Account
estate, examined by Benjamin Eley and Nathan Carr. Signed, John
Darden. R. November 6, 1783. Page 198

WARD, Francis: Account estate, examined by William Goodson and Thomas Wrenn.
Signed, William Gay. R. November 6, 1783. Page 199

MURRY, Thomas: Appraised by Samuel Holladay, Jr., Joseph Smith, Samuel
Hawkins. Ordered, November 12, 1783. R. December 4, 1783. Page 200

CUTCHIN, Jeremiah: Appraised by Thomas Hall, Miles Wills, James Morrison.
Ordered February 11, 1783. R. December 4, 1783. Page 201

WATKINS, Honour: Leg. daughter Sally; to Mary Watkins; my brother James
Morris' children; to Josiah Winbourn. Exs., John Lawrence and James
Moore. D. May 12, 1779. R. December 4, 1783.
    Wit: Stephen Wright, William King.
    Security, Robert Watkins.                                    Page 203

GOODRICH, Sarah: Leg. to Elizabeth Harris; to Elizabeth Pernal (Parnall).
Extx., Elizabeth Harris. D. September 18, 1782. R. December 4, 1783.
    Wit: William Blunt, John Thomas, Josiah Wrenn.
    Security, Samuel Simmons.                                    Page 204

BROWN, Adam: Leg. Sarah Stagg; Fanny Hough; Ann Ingraham; Silvia Jackson;
William Urquhart; Martha Simpson; rest of estate to be sold and divided
among the following or their representatives: John Sikes, Andrew
Sikes, Mary Chapman and Elizabeth Busby. Exs., Thomas Fearn and
William Urquhart. D. November 11, 1783. R. December 4, 1783.
    Wit: John Thomas, Josiah Stagg, Elisha Bell.
    Security, Drury Andrews, Benjamin Tynes.                     Page 205

WOMBLE, Joseph: Leg. son Britain; son Thomas; son Henry; son Joseph; son
Mathew; daughter Elizabeth Cofer; daughter Tabitha Stringfield; daughter
Keziah. D. April 27, 1775. R. January 4, 1784. Ex., son Henry Womble.
    Wit: Jacob Person, Thomas Womble, William Womble.
    Security, John Womble.                                       Page 206

APPLEWHAITE, Henry: Leg. daughter Martha; daughter Sarah, refers to deceased father, Arthur Applewhaite; brother Arthur; brother John;
brother Mills; brother Thomas; wife Sarah Applewhaite. Exs., Richard
Hardy and brothers, Arthur and John. D. November 18, 1783.
R. January 1, 1784.
    Wit: John Pasteur, Samuel Webb, William Outland.
    Security, John Lawrence.                                     Page 207

JOHNSON, Henry, Sr.: Leg. son Aaron; son William; son Henry, land adjoining
Mason Johnson and Joseph Holland; granddaughter Mary Johnson, grandson
Britain Johnson. Exs., William Duck and sons Aaron and Henry.
D. February 26, 1782. R. January 1, 1784.
    Wit: John Darden, Barnaby Holland, Benjamin Holland.
    Security, Benjamin and Barnaby Holland.                      Page 209

BATTEN, Daniel: Leg. son William; wife Ann, the estate she held when I
married her; son Samuel Batten. Exs., sons William and Samuel Batten.
D. December 26, 1783. R. February 5, 1784.
    Wit: Joseph Westray, Britain Edwards, Elias Edwards.
    Security, Jesse Herring and James Johnson.                   Page 212

COPHER, Thomas: Leg. wife Oliff; son Jacob; grandson James Cofer; daughter
Olive Griffin; daughter Charity Holleman; son James; son Thomas;
daughter Mary Stevenson; daughter Ann Pitman; daughter Sarah Hunter;
daughter Jane Daniel; grandson Emanuel Powers; grandson John Holleman;
grandson Moody Cofer. Exs., Jesse Holleman and son Thomas Copher.
D. November 3, 1783. R. February 4, 1784.
    Wit: John Holleman, Christopher Holleman, Robert Wall.
    Security, John J. Wheadon, William Womble.                   Page 213

PEDIN, James: Of Newport Parish. Leg. wife Mary; daughters, Mary, Ann,
Elizabeth, Peggy, Fanny and Easter; son Edmund, land I bought of Thomas
and Elizabeth Pitt; son Jeremiah, the land I bought of Elias Herring
and his Keziah; my executors to deed to Brewer Godwin, the land which
I bought of Pitt Reynolds. Exs., Brewer and Robert Godwin.
D. February 15, 1784. R. March 4, 1784.
    Wit: Thomas Wills, George Benn, Charles Gross.
    Security, James Wills and Richard Hardy.                     Page 214

NELSON, Thomas: Appraised by Benjamin Barlow, William Casey, John Hodges.
Ordered October, 1779. R. March 4, 1784. Page 217

FLETCHER, Charles: Leg. wife Grace; daughter Nancy; daughter Sally; son
James; daughter Patsey. Extx., wife Grace Fletcher. D. August 9,
1783. R. March 4, 1784.
Wit: Joseph Westray, Peter Hatchell, Jeremiah Westray.
Security, James Johnson and William Woodward. Page 218

TURNER, Joshua: Appraised by William Woodward, Nicholas Fulgham, Champion
Bracey. Ordered December 29, 1783. R. March 4, 1784. Page 220

SIKES, Adam: Leg. Drury Andrews of Southampton County. Ex., Drury Andrews.
D. October 13, 1781. R. December 4, 1783.
Wit: John Archer, Edward Niblett.
Security, William Hardy. Page 221

SAUNDERS, Thomas: Leg. wife Elizabeth; son John; son Thomas; daughter Mary;
land inherited from my brother Jacob Saunders to son John. Exs.,
friend Henry Saunders, son of Henry Saunders and son John Saunders.
D. October 4, 1783. R. March 4, 1784.
Wit: Ezekiel Spencer, Henry Saunders, Sr.
Security, James Hough. Page 222

POWELL, Benjamin: Leg. son William; daughter Mary Jones; daughter Rebeckah
Watkins; son Joseph; son Arnold; daughter Elizabeth; son John; son
Mathew; daughter Alice; daughter Mourning; son Jethro; son Joshua;
wife Sary. Exs., sons William and Jethro Powell. D. August 11, 1783.
R. April 1, 1784.
Wit: Michael Johnston, John Watkins, John Darden.
Security, Michael Johnson. Page 223

ENGLISH, Joseph: Account estate, examined by Eley Johnson and Benjamin Eley.
Signed, John Darden. R. April 1, 1784. Page 225

NORSWORTHY, Tristram: Leg. son Nathaniel; son Joseph land on Ragged Island
Creek, on which Nathan Bagnall and Willis Pitt now live, also a tract
adjoining cousin Tristram Norsworthy and the land on which Thomas
Parker now lives; to son-in-law Isaac Hall; daughter Charlotte; son-
in-law Willis Pitt; son-in-law Ralph Frizzell. Exs., son Nathaniel
and cousin Tristram Norsworthy. D. January 5, 1784. R. May 6,
1784.
Wit: Roland Reynolds, William Walden, John King.
Security, James Wills and Roland Reynolds. Page 226

JOHNSON, Henry: Appraised by Michael Johnson, Robert Johnson, Joseph
Johnson. Ordered February 11, 1784. R. May 6, 1784. Page 228

HAWKINS, John: Nuncupative will, proven by Thomas Smith and Anthony Holladay.
Leg. son William; daughter Nansey; wife Easter. Exs., wife and Samuel
Hawkins. D. ---------- R. January 1, 1784.
Security, Samuel Holladay, Jr. Page 230

REYNOLDS, Sharpe: Leg. wife Sophis, the plantation on which John Garner
lives; son Henry; daughter Betsey; daughter Patsey. Exs., wife and
friend Mills Wills. D. February 13, 1784. R. May 6, 1784.
Wit: John S. Wills, Joseph Brantley, Samuel Atkins.
Security, John S. Wills, James Wills. Page 230

MARSHALL, John: Leg. daughter Ann Boykin; grandson Pleasants Jordan; grandson Thomas Jordan; grandson Robert Jordan; grandson John Boykin; grandson Francis M. Boykin; to Elizabeth Gale; son Robert; wife Ann Marshall.

Ex., son Robert Marshall. D. June 24, 1783. R. May 6, 1784.
Wit: William Baldwin, Thomas Powell, James Cowling, William
Everett.
Security, Francis Boykin.                                            Page 232

WOMBLE, Joseph: Appraised by Thomas Wrenn, William Gay, Emanuel Hunter.
R. May 6, 1784.                                                      Page 235

COPHER, Thomas: Appraised by Thomas Wrenn, William Gay, John Davis.
R. May 6, 1784.                                                      Page 235

NEWMAN, John: Appraised by George Goodson, James Jordan, Robert Driver.
Signed, Elizabeth and Thomas Newman. R. June 3, 1784.               Page 236

WESTRAY, William: Account estate, examined by Daniel Herring, Jr. and
Nathaniel Fleming. Signed, Edmond Westray. R. July 1, 1784.
                                                                    Page 238

WRENCH, John: Leg. son John; son Simon; daughter Elizabeth; daughter Elinor
Newman's heirs; to grandsons Thomas and James Newman; to wife. Exs.,
sons, John and Simon Wrench. D. March 10, 1782. R. June 3, 1784.
Wit: John S. Wills, Brewer Godwin.
Security, James Wills, Thomas Hall.                                  Page 239

GAY, Joshua: Leg. son Jesse; daughter Martha Lawrence; son Joshua; son
Robert; son Henry; daughter Ann Archer; daughter Keziah; son John Gay's
daughter. Ex., son Henry Gay. D. January 8, 1784. R. July 1, 1784.
Wit: William Babb, Fanny Babb, William Baldwin.
Security, William Baldwin.                                          Page 241

JONES, Jesse: Appraised by Thomas Wrenn, Benjamin Jones, Britain Ward.
Ordered May 14, 1784. R. July 1, 1784.                             Page 242

NELSON, William: Appraised by William Davis, William Casey, Benjamin Barlow.
Ordered June 25, 1784. R. July 1, 1784.                            Page 242

NELSON, Thomas: Account estate, examined by William Davis, William Casey,
Benjamin Barlow. Signed, Sophia Nelson. R. July 1, 1784.    Page 243

STEVENS, John: Leg. wife Elizabeth; son Robert; son Edmond; son John; son
Elisha; son Nathan; daughter Elizabeth; to Everaud Norsworthy, son of
my daughter Elizabeth. Exs., Robert and Nathan Stevens. D. Novem-
ber 4, 1783. R. July 1, 1784.
Wit: William Peirce, John Coggan, Jr., James Coggan.
Security, James Johnson.                                            Page 244

BURGESS, Charles: Account estate, examined by John S. Wills and Jesse
Atkins. R. July 1, 1784. Signed, John Godwin.                       Page 245

PARKENSON, John: Leg. wife Mary; son Henry; son John; son William; son
Jacob; daughter Ann Parkenson. Extx., wife Mary Parkenson.
D. January 3, 1784. R. August 7, 1784.
Wit: Ezekiel Spencer, Mathais Spencer, Mary Spencer.
Security, John Phillips.                                            Page 247

DAUGHTRY, John, Sr.: Of Newport Parish. Leg. wife Elizabeth; son John; son
Thomas; son Joshua; son Elisha; daughter Mary Holland; daughter Eliza-
beth; daughter Sally. Exs., wife and son John Daughtry. D. March 8,
1783. R. August 7, 1784.
Wit: Jonas Bradshaw, John Cobb, Uriah Vaughan.
Security, Joshua Council, Uriah Vaughan.                            Page 247

GAY, William: Appraised by Thomas Bowden, Robert Eley, John Powell.
  R. August 7, 1784.                                           Page 249

GODWIN, James: Account estate, examined by John S. Wills and James Wills.
  Signed by Lemuel Godwin and Charles Driver. R. September 2, 1784.
                                                                Page 250

BREWER, Michael: Account estate, signed by Mills Lawrence and Elisha
  Ballard. R. September 2, 1784.                                Page 251

BAGNALL, Nathan: Of Newport Parish. Leg. son Nathan; daughter Leah Grace
  (Groce ?). Exs., Willis Pitt and William Bagnall. D. April 2, 1784.
  R. September 2, 1784.
     Wit: James Hunter, Walter Stevenson.
     Security, Richard Williams.                                Page 252

BROWN, Adam: Appraised by Samuel Simmons, John Thomas, Charles Fulgham.
  R. November 4, 1784.                                          Page 253

POWELL, Benjamin: Appraised by Michael Johnson, John Watkins, Robert Watkins.
  R. November 4, 1784.                                          Page 256

BATTEN, Daniel: Appraised by David Briggs, Robert Johnson, Conyons Morris.
  R. November 4, 1784.                                          Page 257

FLEMYING, William: Appraised by Joshua Councill, Lemuel Councill, Joseph
  Duck. Ordered, February 26, 1784. R. November 4, 1784.        Page 259

POPE, Edward: Appraised by James Hall, Henry Parnall, Benjamin Beal.
  R. November 4, 1784.                                          Page 262

BRIDGER, John: Leg. wife Mary, provision for unborn child; daughter Betsey
  Quay; daughter Nancy. Exs., wife Mary and friend John S. Wills.
  D. June 30, 1784. R. January 6, 1785.
     Wit: Samuel Bridger, July Bridger, Thomas Hall.
     Security, James Wills.                                     Page 263

BUTLER, John: Appraised by Stephen Butler, Eley Johnson, Jethro Gale.
  R. January 6, 1785.                                           Page 264

WILSON, Willis: Of Newport Parish. Leg. Micajah Bidgood; Sarah Davis;
  Martha Bidgood; Benjamin Bidgood; Lewis Chapman; Andrew Woodley;
  Mildred Loopo; Margaret Roberts; brother John Wilson, at his death my
  estate to Joseph Hill and Micajah Bidgood if they see that good and
  due care is taken of my said brother. Exs., Joseph Hill and Micajah
  Bidgood. Trustee, Lawrence Baker. D. December 3, 1784. R. January 6,
  1785.
     Wit: Shadrack Ames, William Carrell.
     Security, Harwood Calcote.                                 Page 265

DRIVER, Charles: Of Newport Parish. Leg. wife Keziah; son William; son
  Edward; daughter Sarah Morrison; daughter Mary; daughter Jane; daughter
  Nancy. Exs., wife and James Morrison. D. October 8, 1784.
  R. January 6, 1785.
     Wit: Thomas Wills, John Broadfield, John Butler.
     Security, Thomas Wills and James Jordan.                   Page 266

WHITFIELD, Miles: Appraised by Joshua Councill, Sr. and Cutchings Councill.
  R. January 6, 1785.                                           Page 267

HEDGEPETH, Sarah: Leg. son Cuthbert; son Henry; son James; son Jesse; son
  Frizzell; daughter Efrica Whitfield; to heirs of my daughter Sarah

Bailey. Ex., son Benjamin Hedgepeth. D. September 14, 1773. R. September 7, 1780.
Wit: John Darden. Page 271

MURRY, Ann: Leg. son-in-law Lear Bridger; grandchildren, Ann and Hartwell Bridger; son Benjamin Glover; son Robert Glover; daughter Ann Glover. Ex., son Benjamin Glover. D. February 5, 1770. R. July 5, 1781.
Wit: Benjamin Harrison, Ann Harrison. Page 272

BULLOCK, Willis: Leg. wife Mary; son Willis; daughter Elizabeth; son Joseph. Exs., wife and Thomas Newman. D. August 6, 1782. R. May 2, 1782.
Wit: John Wrench, Joseph Shivers.
Security, Thomas Newman. Page 273

BUTLER, John, Sr.: Leg. son John; daughter Elizabeth Hedgepeth; daughter Sarah Powell; son Mason Butler's heirs; son Henry; grandson Allen Butler; wife Mourning. Extx., wife Mourning Butler. D. December 30, 1781. R. September 2, 1784.
Wit: Nathan Carr, Stephen Butler, Mial Macleny. Page 274

LANCASTER, Henry: Leg. wife Martha; daughter Lucy Barlow; daughter Nancy; daughter Jane; daughter Sally; daughter Patty Lancaster. Exs., wife and son William Barlow. D. February 6, 1784. R. March 3, 1785.
Wit: Jesse Holleman, John Holleman, Jesse Crocker, Belah Williford.
Security, James Deford. Page 276

FLETCHER, Charles: Appraised by Benjamin Tynes, John Powell, William Woodward. R. January 6, 1785. Page 277

WHITFIELD, Samuel: Of Newport Parish. Leg. daughter Mary; son Joshua; to Samuel Whitley. Ex., James Morrison. D. December 21, 1784. R. January 6, 1785.
Wit: John Williams, Thomas Hall.
Security, James Jordan. Page 278

BRIDGER, William: Leg. wife Amy. D. December 18, 1776. R. January 6, 1785.
Wit: Henry Pitt, Edmond Godwin, Robert Lawrence.
Security, Samuel Bridger. Page 279

GIBBS, Gabriel: Of Newport Parish. Leg. daughter Frances; son Ralph; son Henry John Gibbs; daughter Mary; wife Frances; son William; son Thomas; son Gabriel; son Robert. Exs., wife and son William Gibbs. D. October 8, 1784. R. January 6, 1785.
Wit: William Hubard, Francis Young, Robert Fry.
Security, William Hubard, Joseph Hill. Page 280

FRIZZELL, Ralph: Leg. wife Sally; sister Mary Outland's three daughters, Martha, Polly and Nancy. Exs., wife and Nathaniel Norsworthy. D. ---------- R. January 6, 1785.
Wit: Jeremiah Outland, Elizabeth Outland.
Security, Nathaniel Norsworthy. Page 281

JOHNSON, Robert: Leg. wife Martha; son Robert; daughter Rebecca Timlin; daughter Mary. Ex., brother James Johnson. D. November 27, 1784. R. January 6, 1785.
Wit: Joshua Jenkins, William Marshall, Mathew Tomlin.
Security, Mathew Tomlin. Page 282

HARRIS, John: Appraised by John Fearn, John Powell, Drury Andrews. Ordered January, 1784. R. January 6, 1785. Page 283

GARNER, John: Of Newport Parish. Leg. son Thomas; daughter Priscilla; daughter Rachel Saunders; son Richard; son James; daughter Sarah Daniel; daughter Ann. Ex., son Thomas Garner. D. January 20, 1784. R. January 6, 1785.
Wit: James Hall, Jesse Garner, John Garner.          Page 286

COX, Isaac: Account estate, examined by Goodrich Wilson, David Dick, John Cunningham. Signed, John Williamson. Ordered, June 10, 1781. R. January 7, 1785.          Page 288

BROWN, Adam: Account estate, to paid John Sykes, Andrew Sykes, William Chapman and Adam Busby. Examined by John Fearn, Joseph Jordan, Drury Andrews. Signed, William Urquhart. R. January 7, 1785.          Page 289

DAUGHTRY, John: Appraised by Michael Johnson, Richard Daughtry, Joshua Council. R. March 3, 1785.          Page 291

BAGNALL, William: Leg. wife Mary; son Charles; son William; daughter Charlotte. Wife, Extx. D. February 7, 1782. R. September 2, 1784.
Wit: James Pedin, Joseph Fulgham, Samuel Morgan, Mary Smelley.
Security, Joshua Council, William Casey.          Page 293

WOMBWELL, Thomas: Of Newport Parish. Leg. son William, bequest left him by the will of my father, Thomas Wombwell, decd.; brother John Wombwell, decd.; daughter Ann the wife of James Stringfield; grandson Joseph Stringfield; to James Pitman and his wife Sarah; daughter Christian; daughter Celia, wife of Simon Atkinson; daughter Mary, wife of James Maddery; daughter Margaret, wife of Joseph Maddery; to Elizabeth, wife of William Gwaltney; grandson Jacob Stringfield, the son of Benjamin and Mourning Stringfield; son Thomas Wombwell. Exs., sons William and Thomas Wombwell. D. November 11, 1784. R. March 3, 1785.
Wit: Francis Young, Sampson Flake, William Flake.
Security, Josiah Wrenn and James Pitman.          Page 294

PITT, Henry: Leg. son Isham; daughter Jule Brown; daughter-in-law Polly Fulgham; wife Penelope that which came from Fulgham's estate. Exs., wife and son Isham. D. December 1, 1781. R. March 3, 1785.
Wit: Ralph Frizzell, Jeremiah Outland, Mary Outland.
Security, Nathaniel Norsworthy.          Page 296

CARRELL, William: Leg. daughter Comfort Piland; daughter Molly; daughter Patience; wife Mary; son William; son Samuel; son Thomas; daughter Catherine; granddaughter Sarah Lupo, granddaughter Mildred Lupo. Exs., wife, John Wrenn, James Piland, William Gray. D. January 15, 1785. R. March 3, 1785.
Wit: William Perote (?), Benjamin Harrison, John Wrenn.
Security, John Mallory, Richard Hardy.          Page 298

TOMLIN, Nathan: Leg. brother Mathew; brother Robert; sister Martha Stevens; cousin Mathew Tomlin. D. August 28, 1777. R. March 3, 1785.
Wit: Joshua Jenkins, John Powell, Jancy Powell.
Security, James Johnson.          Page 300

FULGHAM, Edmund: Leg. wife and all my children. Exs., James and George Powell. D. January 28, 1785. R. March 3, 1785.
Wit: Henry Fulgham, Jesse Fulgham, William Marshall.
Security, John Powell.          Page 301

WEBB, Mathais: Leg. wife Nancy; daughter Patsy; daughter Fanny; daughter Betsey; son James Webb. Ex., wife, brother Samuel Webb and John J. Wheadon. D. January 23, 1785. R. March 3, 1785.
Wit: John Davis Carpenter, John Harrison, Benjamin Jones.
Security, Emelius Derring, Lawrence Baker.          Page 302

263

FULGHAM, Joseph: Leg. wife Mary; son Joseph; daughter Polly Cunningham; daughter Louisa; daughter Charlotte. Exs., wife, John Cunningham and Joseph Godwin. D. September 6, 1784. R. March 3, 1785.
Wit: Joseph Godwin, Jonathan Godwin.
Security, George Benn. Page 303

DERRING, James: Of Newport Parish. Leg. daughter Elizabeth; son Emelius; son William, my plantation in Surry, with reversion of bequest to his son James Derring; granddaughter Milley Harrison; daughter Ann Harrison. Ex., son Emelius Derring. D. January 14, 1784. R. March 3, 1785.
Wit: Goodrich Wilson, Josiah Bidgood, Thomas Williams.
Security, John J. Wheadon. Page 305

DAY, James Bennett: Leg. uncle William Mallory. Ex., uncle William Mallory. D. January 14, 1785. R. March 3, 1785.
Wit: William Perit, Nathaniel Mallory, Kizzy Harvey, Francis Day, Martha Todd.
Security, John Mallory. Page 307

BUTLER, John: Leg. son Charles; son John; all my children; daughter Ann; daughter Sarah Butler. Ex., friends Jacob Dickinson and Josiah Wills. D. January 17, 1785. R. March 3, 1785.
Wit: Joseph Brantley, George Dickinson.
Security, Jesse Atkinson, Emanuel Wills. Page 308

FONES, Shelley: Inventory, returned March 4, 1785. Page 309

CHALMERS, David: Leg. my natural son James Chalmers, by Avey Wright; my natural daughter Sarah Chalmers by Avey Wright. Exs., Col. Richard Kello and Elias Herring of Southampton County. D. May 7, 1782. R. January 6, 1785.
Wit: John Lawrence, Francis Young.
Security, James Wills. Page 309

SHELLEY, Thomas: Account estate, to cash paid Solomon Wilson for Mary Shelley. Signed, Lucy Goodrich. R. April 7, 1785. Page 310

WAILE, John: Leg. wife Sally; son Nicholas; daughter Nancy; daughter Sally. Ex., wife and brother Josiah. D. January 3, 1785. R. April 7, 1785.
Wit: Jesse Atkinson, James Morrison, James Taylor.
Security, Miles Wills. Page 311

SMITH, Thomas: Of Newport Parish. Leg. daughter Elizabeth; son William; daughter Martha Smith. Ex., Samuel Holladay, Jr. D. January 24, 1785. R. May 5, 1785.
Wit: Samuel Holladay, Sr., Edmund Holladay.
Security, Samuel Holladay. Page 314

TURNER, Mathew: Account estate, signed, Joshua Turner. R. May 5, 1785.
Page 315

CHANNELL, Jeremiah: Leg. cousin John Lawrence; cousin Josiah Lawrence; cousin Rachel Channell; sister Mary Lawrence; cousin Jeremiah Lawrence. Exs., Joshua Hunt and Demsy Hunt. D. February 14, 1785. R. May 5, 1785.
Wit: John Brown, Temperance Brown, Rhoda Lawrence.
Security, John Holladay. Page 316

TAYLOR, John: Leg. wife Esther, lots in Smithfield; to my nephews, the sons of my brother Miles Taylor. Extx., wife Esther Taylor. D. November 17, 1783. R. May 5, 1785.
Wit: Richard Kello, Thomas Peirce, Lemuel Bowden.
Security, Mills Wills, Charles Fulgham. Page 317

WOMBWELL, Thomas: Appraised by Thomas Wrenn, Will Gray, William Jordan.
R. May 5, 1785.                                                    Page 320

GAY, Joshua: Appraised by Thomas Smelley, John Norsworthy, John Deford.
. R. June 2, 1785.                                                 Page 323

SMITH, Joseph: Account estate, examined by John S. Wills, James Wills, Brewer
Godwin. R. July 7, 1785.                                           Page 325

HAWKINS, Benjamin: Leg. sister Mary Fife, chest at Samuel Hawkins; to
Malikey Fife. Ex., Malikey Fife. D. ---------- R. July 7, 1785.
Wit: James Pitt.
Security, James Pitt.                                              Page 326

SMELLEY, Robert: Appraised by Jesse Hutchings, Robert Babb, Jethro Gale.
Ordered September 5, 1776. R. July 7, 1785.                        Page 326

FULGHAM, Anthony: Appraised by Thomas Wills, Edmund Fulgham, Joshua Turner.
R. July 7, 1785.                                                   Page 330

MURPHRY, John: Account estate, examined by John S. Wills, Jethro Gale.
Signed, Sarah Murphry. R. July 7, 1785.                            Page 331

McCOY, Jesse: Appraised by John Butler, Lemuel Lightfoot, Joseph Brantley,
James Wills. R. July 7, 1785.                                      Page 332

GAY, Joshua: Account estate, examined by Thomas Smelley and William Babb.
R. July 7, 1785.                                                   Page 333

BRADDY, Mason: Leg. wife Priscilla; son Patrick; daughter Ann, wife of
Edward Mintz. Ex., son Patrick Braddy. D. April 15, 1785. R. July 7,
1785.
Wit: Patience Gwaltney, James Carrell, William Gay.               Page 334

GOODRICH, Elizabeth: Appraised by William Cary, Shadrack Ames, Benjamin
Barlow. R. August 4, 1785.                                         Page 335

WHITLEY, Randolph: Leg. John Saunders Whitley; brother Elisha; wife Tabitha;
son Randolph; son Elisha; daughter Polly; unborn child; daughter Betsey
Davis Whitley. Exs., wife and friend, William Eley. D. December 22,
1785. R. August 4, 1785.
Wit: Isham Whitley, Rachel Norsworthy.
Security, John S. Wills.                                           Page 335

MOODY, Isaac: Leg. my nine children. Ex., Joseph Moody and Samuel Simmons.
D. April 10, 1785. R. August 4, 1785.
Wit: Samuel Simmons, John Vellines, Isaac Vellines.
Security, William Blunt and John Thomas.                          Page 336

INGRAM, Sarah: Account estate, examined by William Mallory, John Goodrich,
William Hodsden. Signed, William Carrell. R. August 4, 1785.
                                                                   Page 337

JOHNSON, Aaron: Inventory, returned October 6, 1785.              Page 338

LAWRENCE, Joseph: Appraisal, dated July 24, 1780. R. May 5, 1785.
                                                                   Page 317

---

JORDAN, Mathew: Leg. son Richard; son Mathew; daughter Elizabeth Clary; daughter Mary; daughter Sarah; daughter Hannah; daughter Rebecca. Ex., sons Richard and Mathew Jordan. D. May 11, 1785. R. October 6, 1785.
  Wit: Thomas Newby, Robert Marshall, Thomas Gale, Jr.
  Security, Robert Marshall.                                    Page 1

BRADDY, Mason: Appraised by Patrick Gwaltney, James Carrell, Joseph Stallings. R. October 6, 1785.                          Page 2

FULGHAM, Joseph: Appraised by Ralph West, Charles Gross, Randolph Reynolds. R. October 6, 1785.                                Page 2

BAGNALL, Nathan: Appraised returned October 6, 1785. Not signed. Page 3

GIBBS, Sarah: Leg. daughter Elatch Cutchins; grandchildren, Louisa, Ralph, Polly, Nathaniel, Josiah, Sarah and Pitt Cutchins, with reversion to Ralph West. Exs., daughter Elatch Cutchins and Ralph West. D. March 7, 1785. R. June 3, 1785.
  Wit: Nancy Copeland, Isham Copeland, George Benn.
  Security, Ralph West.                                         Page 4

COGGIN, Robert: Leg. son Joshua; wife; son Lewis; son John; son James; son William; Nathaniel Fleming and William Bridger to divide my land assisted by James Allen Bridger, James Johnson, Thomas Bowden and Dempsey Marshall; son Robert; daughter Salley; daughter Betsey. Exs., son John, William Bridger, Nathaniel Fleming and Dempsey Marshall. D. June 7, 1785. R. November 3, 1785.
  Wit: Nathaniel Fleming, William Stevens, Randolph West.
  Security, John Coggin and Thomas Powell.                      Page 5

NELMS, John: Of Newport Parish. Leg. son-in-law Samuel Corbett; son-in-law Benjamin Johnson; son John; daughter Elizabeth; wife Elizabeth. Exs., son-in-law Shadrack Griffin and wife Elizabeth Nelms. D. April 18, 1785. R. November 3, 1785.
  Wit: Samuel Johnson, William Johnson, William English.
  Security, William English.                                    Page 6

PARNALL, John: Leg. Mary, the wife of Samuel Simmons; to Mary and Nancy, daughters of Thomas Parnall; to William Parnall; to Joseph Parnall; three-fourth of estate to John Hines. Ex., Samuel Simmons. D. October 2, 1785. R. November 3, 1785.
  Wit: Robert James, John Sykes, Bridget James.
  Security, Robert James.                                       Page 7

BRADSHAW, Richard: Of Newport Parish. Leg. daughter Patience Boon; grandson Jacob Corbett; son Benjamin; son Jonas; grandson Richard Bradshaw; wife Patience. Trustee, John Lawrence. Ex., son Benjamin Bradshaw. D. April 15, 1783. R. November 3, 1785.
  Wit: John Lawrence, Frankey Bradshaw, Martha Brewer.
  Security, William Kerr.                                       Page 8

PINNER, John: Leg. wife Mary; son Josiah, the bequest from his grandfather Thomas Pinner; son Thomas; son John; son William; son Jeremiah; daughter

Betsey Smelley; daughter Mary Pinner. Exs., wife Mary Pinner and son-in-law William Smelley. D. December 2, 1776. R. November 3, 1785.
Wit: Thomas Cowling, Thomas Johnson.
Security, Joseph Hill and Thomas Cowling.                                    Page 9

EVERETT, Samuel: Leg. son Joseph; son Thomas; daughter Cloe Jordan; daughter Charlotte; wife; son Joseph, Ex. D. April 8, 1784. R. December 1, 1785.
Wit: Thomas Smelly, John Everett, John Everett, Jr.
Security, Miles Wills.                                                       Page 10

HERRING, Daniel, Sr.: Leg. son Elias, land in Southampton County; son Daniel; son Jesse; son Mills; daughter Martha Batten. Exs., sons, Elias, Daniel, Jesse and Mills Herring. D. July 11, 1785. R. October 6, 1785.
Wit: William Woodward, Peter Woodward, John George Woodward.
Security, John Fearn and William Baldwin.                                    Page 11

BRADSHAW, Richard: Appraised by John Darden, James Fowler, William Carr. R. January 5, 1786.                                                           Page 12

BRIDGER, Samuel: Of Newport Parish. Leg. daughter Sally; daughter Mary. Exs., Thomas Hall, Josiah Wail. D. September 5, 1785. R. January 5, 1786.
Wit: William Green, Sarah Green, James Cutchins.
Security, William Green.                                                      Page 14

WRENN, John: Of Newport Parish. Leg. son John; daughter Martha; son James; son Joseph; wife Tabitha; to Martha Bidgood. Exs., wife, Davis Day and Micajah Bidgood. D. January 19, 1786. R. February 2, 1786.
Wit: Moses Shields, John Mallory.
Security, William Mallory.                                                    Page 15

WOMBLE, Thomas: Account estate, examined by John J. Wheadon, Thomas Wrenn, William Gay, John Thomas. Signed, William and Thomas Womble. R. February 2, 1786.                                                          Page 16

WAIL, John: Appraised by Thomas Hall, James Morrison, Josiah Cutchins. R. February 2, 1786.                                                          Page 17

GIBBS, Ralph: Leg. wife Polly; son John; sister Martha Gibbs; son Ralph; daughter Patsey Gibbs. Exs., wife and Robert Driver. D. May 2, 1785. R. April 7, 1786.
Wit: Samuel Whitfield, Jemima Whitfield.
Security, Samuel Whitfield.                                                   Page 18

DAUGHTRY, John: Account estate, examined by Elisha L. Ballard, Mills Lawrence, Solomon Edmonds. R. April 7, 1786.                                  Page 20

BUTLER, Peter: Appraised by Solomon Edmonds, John Carr, William Parker. R. April 7, 1786.                                                            Page 20

WELCH, Mary: Leg. Richard, son of Jesse Glover; Nancy, daughter of Jesse Glover, Mary, daughter of Jesse Glover. D. August 2, 1783. R. April 7, 1786. Ex., Jesse Glover.
Wit: William Hardy.
Security, Jesse Glover. Rodwell Delk qualified as Executor.
                                                                             Page 21

TAYLOR, John: Appraised by Edward Archer, John Sinclair, David Dick. Ordered June 18, 1785. R. April 7, 1786.                     Page 22

TOMLIN, Nathan: Appraised by John Powell, Jesse Fulgham, Lewis Harris.
R. July 7, 1786. Page 23

BATTEN, Samuel: Appraised by Francis Boykin, George Hall, Robert James.
R. July 6, 1786. Page 25

PARNALL, John: Appraised by William Jordan, John Thomas, James Cary.
R. July 6, 1786. Page 26

BRIDGER, Joseph: Leg. wife Ann. D. January, 1785. R. July 6, 1786.
Wit: Lemuel Bowden, John Murry. Page 27

WRENCH, John: Appraised by Joseph Shivers, Robert Driver, George Goodson.
Signed, John and Simon Wrench. R. July 6, 1786. Page 27

JORDAN, Mathew: Appraised by Thomas Smelly, Robert Driver, Thomas Newman.
R. July 6, 1786. Page 28

JORDAN, Josiah: Leg. wife; son Thomas; son Josiah; son Robert; grandson
Samuel Jordan if he pays Josiah, the son of Josiah Jordan a certain
sum; daughter Polly Brown; son-in-law John Pleasants; children of my
deceased son Hezekiah; to Hester Whitfield; daughter Peggy, decd.
Exs., wife, son-in-law William Brown and Jacob Randolph. D. March 25,
1786. R. July 6, 1786.
Wit: Jacob Wyatt, Joshua Wyatt, Peyton Randolph.
Security, Robert Jordan, Jr., Francis Boykin. Page 30

PITT, Henry: Appraised by Edmund Godwin, William Garton, Josiah Applewhaite.
R. July 6, 1786. Page 31

DEGGE, Anthony: Of Newport Parish. Leg. daughter Averilla Virginia Degge,
with reversion to my sisters, Elizabeth, Hannah, Averilla, Sarah, Ann
and Mary Degge and nephew Anthony Degge of Gloucester County. My
daughter to live with my sister Sally. Exs., John Goodrich, Josiah
Wilson, Thomas Hardy. D. April 19, 1786. R. July 6, 1786.
Wit: Thomas Smith, William Davidson, John Graham.
Security, Richard Hardy and John Goodrich. Page 33

HOLLIDAY, John: Appraised by Henry Lightfoot, Elias Parker, Copeland
Whitfield. R. December 7, 1786. Page 34

DARLEY, Mary: Appraised by William Shivers, Thomas Newman, Robert Driver.
D. September, 1786. R. December 7, 1786. Page 35

MOODY, Isaac: Appraised by John Fearn, Francis Boykin, William Downing.
R. December 7, 1786. Page 36

LANCASTER, Henry: Appraised by Jesse Holleman, James Gwaltney, Moreland
Delk. R. December 7, 1786. Page 38

BEAL, Benjamin: Leg. son Benjamin; daughter Mary Parker; daughter Honour
Jordan; son James Lawrence Beale; son Barney; wife Elizabeth; my
younger children, Barney, Lawrence, Sally, Rachel, Mary, Elizabeth
and Wilkinson Beal. Exs., wife and son James Beal. D. March 1, 1786.
R. December 7, 1786.
Wit: James Hall, Thomas Neville, Joseph Neville.
Security, Francis Boykin, Benjamin Harrison, Ephraim Pope.
Page 39

FULGHAM, Hezekiah: Leg. wife Patience; son Mathew; daughter Sally; son
Mills; son Willis; son Stephen; son James; daughter Nancy Fulgham.
Exs., brothers Michael and Jesse Fulgham. D. August 27, 1786.

R.  December 7, 1786.
    Wit:  James Johnson, Peter Marshall, Simon Haile, Isham Davis.
    Security, Francis Boykin, Mathew Tomlin.        Page 41

CARR, Abraham:  Of Newport Parish.  Leg. son Mills; son William; granddaughter
    Patience Carr; daughter Martha; granddaughter Sarah Carr; son Abraham;
    wife Susannah.  Ex., wife and son Mills Carr.  D.  January 10, 1786.
R.  September 7, 1786.
    Wit:  Elijah Johnson, William Carr, John Carr, Jr.
    Security, John Carr, Mills Carr.        Page 42

HANSFORD, Lewis:  Of Smithfield, Merchant.  Leg. wife Ann; son Cary Heslet
    Hansford; daughter Ann, wife of Philip Barraud of Williamsburg.  Exs.,
    son Cary, friends Robert Taylor and James Taylor.  D.  May 4, 1786.
R.  July 6, 1786.
    Wit:  Alexander Dick, Philemon Gatewood, Robert Woodside.
    Security, John Sinclair.        Page 43

DEGGE, Anthony:  Appraised by Charles Fulgham, William Whitfield, John
    Sinclair.  R.  September 7, 1786.        Page 44

BRIDGER, Joseph:  Appraised by William Hodsden, Charles Fulgham, Thomas King.
    R.  September 7, 1786.        Page 46

VAUGHAN, Henry:  Account estate, examined by Mills Lawrence and Elisha Bal-
    lard.  Among items, paid James Mills for a substitute to serve in the
    American Army.  Signed, John Cobb.  R.  September 7, 1786.    Page 47

NELMS, John:  Leg. son John; son Elias; son Thomas; son Mills; son Willis;
    son Josiah; son Jeremiah; son David; daughter Betsey Herring; wife
    Mary; negro to be sold at death of Ann Little and my one-fourth interest
    to son Elias.  Exs., wife Mary and friend Mathais Spencer.
D.  December 5, 1785.  R.  September 7, 1786.
    Wit:  Jesse Whitehead, Damaris Little.
    Security, Dempsey Marshall, Kinchen Crumpler.    Page 48

DURLEY, Mary:  Leg. grandson Horatio Durley; grandson Charles Durley;
    granddaughter Nancy Durley; daughter Charlotte Godwin.  Ex., son
    Horatio Durley.  D.  March 11, 1786.  R.  September 7, 1786.
    Wit:  William Eley, Joseph Godwin, Jr., Joseph Godwin, Sr.
        Page 49

GIBBS, Ralph:  Appraised by Edmund Godwin, Joshua Bunkley, Jeremiah Outland.
    R.  September 7, 1786.        Page 51

HAWKINS, Samuel and Tabitha:  Account estates, examined by John S. Wills,
    Brewer Godwin, Edmund Godwin.  Signed, George Norsworthy.
R.  September 7, 1786.        Page 52

HOLLAND, William, Sr.:  Leg. son Benjamin; son Miles; son Elisha; son
    Abraham; son William Holland.  Ex., son William Holland.  D.  February 5,
    1785.  R.  October 5, 1786.
    Wit:  Benjamin Holland, Barbary Holland, Jonathan Askey,
        John Darden.
    Security, Miles Holland.        Page 53

HUNT, Dempsey:  Leg. to Joshua Hunt; to my three children, when Willis Hunt
    becomes of age.  Ex., brother Joshua Hunt.  D.  May 18, 1786.
R.  October 5, 1786.
    Wit:  Samuel Whitfield, Mary Lawrence.
    Security, Samuel Whitfield.        Page 54

CHANNELL, Jeremiah: Appraised by Jeremiah Outland, Joseph Gray, John Brown.
R. October 5, 1786. Page 54

COOK, Nathan: Leg. sister Tamar Cole. D. August 19, 1786. R. October 5,
1786.
Wit: Nathaniel Fleming, Gardner Fleming, Nathan Stephens,
Amelia Halliford, Sally Duke, Bennett Peirce.
Mathew Harris qualified, security, Francis Young. Page 55

HOLLIDAY, John: Of Newport Parish. Leg. to wife after the death of my
mother; son Joseph; to my children. Exs., wife and Dempsey Hunt.
D. November 21, 1785. R. October 5, 1786. Presented by Elizabeth
Holliday.
Wit: Thomas Hall, Ralph Hunt, Samuel Holliday.
Security, Joshua Hunt. Page 56

ALLEN, Randall: Leg. son John; son Arthur; son James; to Joseph Riggan;
son William Allen. Ex., son William Allen. D. January 21, 1785.
R. October 5, 1786.
Wit: Benjamin Goodrich, Thomas Wrenn, Ann Wilson.
Security, Thomas Wrenn. Page 56

LANKFORD, Stephen: Of Newport Parish. Leg. wife; son Wiley; son-in-law
Mills Eley and his wife Catey; grandson Stephen Eley; daughter Mary;
daughter Isabel; daughter Patty Lankford. Exs., wife, Robert Watkins
and son-in-law Mills Eley. D. November 2, 1785. R. April 7, 1786.
Presented by Sarah Lankford.
Wit: Jesse Lankford, Thomas Inglish.
Security, Robert Watkins. Page 57

WRENN, John: Appraised by Shadrack Ames, James Lupo, John Mallory.
R. January 4, 1787. Page 58

MURPHRY, Sarah: Leg. George Murphry. Ex., George Murphry. D. December 13,
1785. R. January 4, 1787.
Wit: Mathew Jordan, Charles Murphry, William Murphry. Page 60

WATSON, William: Appraised by Thomas Smelley, Jethro Gale, Thomas Powell.
Ordered February 2, 1787. R. January 4, 1787. Page 60

SHIVERS, Jonas: Account estate, examined by Thomas Smelley and Robert
Driver. Signed, William Shivers. R. February 1, 1787. Page 62

MURPHRY, Sarah: Appraised by Thomas Newby, William Meer (?), Mathew Jordan.
R. February 1, 1787. Page 62

BRADSHAW, Richard: Account estate, examined by Mills Lawrence and Elisha
L. Ballard. R. February 1, 1787. Page 63

SAUNDERS, Thomas: Appraised by Thomas Smelley, John Deford, John Norsworthy.
Ordered March, 1784. R. February 1, 1787. Page 64

HANSFORD, Lewis: Appraisal of store by Francis Young, James Wills, George
Robertson. Signed, John Taylor, Esq. of the Islands of Antigua and
Robert Taylor, Attorney. R. February 1, 1787. Page 67

HANSFORD, Lewis: Appraisal of personal estate by Francis Young, James Wills,
George Robertson. R. February 1, 1787. Page 73

EVERETT, Samuel: Appraised by Thomas Smelley, John Everett and William
Shivers. D. December, 1785. R. February 1, 1787. Page 75

ALLMOND, Elizabeth: Account estate, examined by Thomas Wrenn, William Jordan, William Gay. R. April 6, 1787. Signed, William Womble.
Page 76

HOLLIDAY, Thomas: Account estate, to gold in the hands of Ann Holliday, Admtx. Examined by George Purdie, William Hodsden, Thomas Smith. Signed, Josiah Holliday. R. April 6, 1787.
Page 77

JONES, Jesse: Account estate, examined by Thomas Wrenn, John Thomas, Armistead Vellines. Signed, Josiah Wrenn. R. April 5, 1787.
Page 77

CARR, Abraham: Appraised by Robert Johnson, Elijah Johnson, John Carr, Jr. R. June 7, 1787.
Page 78

BULLOCK, William: Leg. granddaughter Ellenor Goodson; granddaughter Mary Goodson; grandson Joseph Bullock; to James Goodson; grandson William Bullock; wife Penelope. Exs., grandson Joseph Bullock and James Goodson. D. March 21, 1786. R. June 7, 1787.
Wit: Obediah Bullock, George Goodson.
Page 79

WAILE, Rachel: Of Newport Parish. Leg. brother Josiah Waile; sister Ann Green; to John Waile. Ex., Josiah Waile. D. October 31, 1781. R. June 7, 1787.
Wit: Thomas Hall, Elizabeth Gibbs.
Security, James Morrison.
Page 81

WHITFIELD, Abraham: Of Smithfield. Leg. son William; son Haynes a lot in Hampton; son John; daughter Elizabeth Peugh; to Ann Johnston. Ex., son William Whitfield. D. January 12, 1787. R. August 4, 1787.
Wit: Stephen Gorton, Thomas Peirce, William Groce.
Security, Lemuel Bowden.
Page 81

DAVIS, William: Account estate, examined by George Purdie, Thomas Smith, John Goodrich. Signed, Lawrence Baker, Sheriff. R. September 6, 1787.
Page 84

DUNSTON, Thomas: Leg. wife Sarah; daughter Elizabeth; son Josiah; son Hezekiah. Ex., wife Sarah Dunston. D. June 2, 1783. R. October 4, 1787.
Wit: Robert Eley, Jr., Robert Eley, Sr., Gale Eley.
Security, John Saunders.
Page 85

GOODWIN, Margaret: Widow of William Goodwin. Leg. son Joseph; son George; sister Elishe Williams. Ex., Walter Rand. D. February 13, 1786. R. January 3, 1788.
Wit: Joshua Bunkley, Amy Murry.
Security, James Morrison.
Page 86

DEFORD, John: Leg. son James; son William; wife; daughter Ann; daughter Fereby Deford. Exs., James Deford and friend Jesse Holleman. D. September 18, 1787. R. January 3, 1788.
Wit: Aaron Cornwell, James Lupo, Jane Deford.
Page 87

LAWRENCE, John: Leg. wife Mary; son William land in Southampton County; daughter Salley, one-half of the money due me from the estate of Benjamin Baker; son John; daughter Peggy; brother Mills Lawrence. Exs., wife Mary, brother Mills Lawrence and Elisha Lawrence Ballard. D. November --, 1787. R. January 3, 1788.
Wit: (None.)
Security, Joshua Council, Mills Eley.
Page 88

271

JOHNSON, Robert: Of Newport Parish. "Two acres of land for the use of our
    Meeting House, where it now stands to the Society of people called
    Quakers, as long as there are any of that name." Leg. daughter
    Christian Duck; daughter Jean Hare; wife Christian. Ex., son Elijah
    Duck. D. 12 mo. 8th day 1787. R. January 3, 1788.
        Wit: Joshua Councill, John Duck, Lazarus Johnson.
        Security, Joshua Councill.                                Page 89

MOODY, Philip, Sr.: Leg. wife Ruth; daughter Nancy; grandsons Samuel and
    West, the sons of Philip Moody; daughter Elizabeth Cofer; granddaughter
    Elizabeth Holleman; son John; son William; son Beverley; daughter
    Dianah; daughter Louhannah; daughter Mary Thomas; grandson Joseph
    Moody. Exs., wife Ruth, son-in-law Thomas Cofer, son John Moody.
    D. November 14, 1786. R. January 3, 1788.
        Wit: John Phillips, Sr., Solomon Bracey, William Whitley,
            John Parkerson.
        Security, John Moody.                                     Page 90

WOODLEY, John, Jr.: Account estate, examined by William Blunt, Arthur
    Applewhaite, Samuel Webb. Signed, John Woodley, Sr. R. January 3,
    1788.                                                         Page 91

JOHNSON, Robert: Appraised by John Duck, Willis Carr, Robert Watkins.
    R. February 7, 1788.                                         Page 92

STALLINGS, John: Leg. son Joseph; son William; daughter Nancy Whitley;
    daughter Elizabeth Turner; wife Elizabeth. Exs., wife and son Joseph
    Stallings. D. April 10, 1786. R. January 3, 1788.
        Wit: Benjamin Goodrich, James Pitman, Benjamin Pitman.
        Security, Thomas Womble.                                 Page 94

SIMMONS, Samuel: Of Newport Parish. Leg. wife Polly; daughter Elizabeth;
    daughter Polly; son James. Ex., James Cofer. D. February 11, 1788.
    R. April 3, 1788.
        Wit: Drury Andrews, John Sykes, Adam Busby.              Page 94

GODWIN, Read: Account estate, examined by James Wills and Thomas Hall.
    Signed, Col. Thomas Godwin. R. April 4, 1788.                Page 95

WILLS, Mary: Leg. Jenny, daughter of Mills Wills; Juley, daughter of
    Mills Wills; Davis, son of Mills Wills; David, son of David Dick;
    Dickey, son of Miles Taylor; James, son of Miles Taylor. Ex., Mills
    Wills. D. November 16, 1784. R. June 5, 1788.
        Wit: George Robertson, Ralph West.                       Page 96

CUTCHIN, Joseph: Account estate, examined by William Hodsden and William
    Davis. Signed, Solomon Wilson. R. June 5, 1788.              Page 96

POWELL, Joshua: Leg. daughter Patty; son John; daughter Grace Barnes;
    daughter Molly Barnes; granddaughter Milley Powell. Exs., daughter
    Catey Powell and grandson Samuel Powell. D. July 29, 1787.
    R. June 5, 1788.
        Wit: James Johnson, William Little, Thomas Bowden, Joshua
            Councill.
        Security, Thomas Bowden.                                 Page 98

CUTCHIN, Priscilla: Leg. son Joseph; grandson John West; son James Cutchin.
    Ex., son Joseph Cutchin. D. October 8, 1787. R. June 5, 1788.
        Wit: Willis Wilkinson, David Dick.
        Security, John S. Wills.                                 Page 99

CROCKER, Sarah: Leg. granddaughter Sally Tynes, widow of Henry Tynes, decd.;

272

grandson Richard Chapman; to children of my son John Crocker and
daughter Mary Chapman. Exs., son John and John Thomas. D. May 15,
1783. R. June 5, 1788. Codicil: to grandsons, Hardy and Richard
Chapman.
    Wit: Richard Hardy, Christian Womble, Philip Thomas, Jesse
        Thomas.
    Security, John S. Wills.                                    Page 99

FONES, John: Appraised by James Young, William Patterson, Jesse Atkins.
    D. October 13, 1787. R. June 5, 1788.                      Page 100

DEFORD, John: Appraised by Jesse Holleman, William Gay, William Gray.
    R. June 5, 1788.                                           Page 101

BULLOCK, Joel: Appraised by John Wrench, Thomas Pitt, George Goodson.
    Ordered January 7, 1786. R. June 5, 1788.                  Page 102

SMITH, Joseph: Account estate, paid Mary Carter her part. Examined by
    George Purdie. Signed, James Pitt. R. June 5, 1788.        Page 103

NEVILLE, Joseph: Account estate, examined by John S. Wills and Robert
    Marshall. Signed, William Jordan. R. June 5, 1788.         Page 104

COFER, Benjamin: Appraised by William Gay, Jacob Jones, Benjamin Jones.
    Ordered February 9, 1788. R. June 5, 1788.                 Page 105

WHITLEY, Randolph: Appraised by Jonathan Godwin and Roland Reynolds.
    Ordered October 5, 1785. R. June 5, 1788.                  Page 106

JORDAN, John: Account estate, examined by Lawrence Baker, John S. Wills,
    John J. Wheadon. Ex., James Jordan, decd.

JORDAN, John: Account estate, examined by Lawrence Baker, John S. Wills,
    John J. Wheadon. Signed, William Goodson, William Jordan and Thomas
    Goodson, Jr. Adms. R. June 5, 1788.                        Page 108

HARRIS, John: Account estate, examined by Daniel Herring, Drury Andrews,
    John Fearn, James Johnson. Signed, Lewis Harris. R. July 3, 1788.
                                                               Page 109

CARTER, Mary: Appraised by James Pitt, Samuel Hawkins, Joseph Godwin.
    Ordered December 7, 1783. R. July 3, 1788.                 Page 109

WHITFIELD, Samuel: Appraised by Thomas Hall, Henry Lightfoot, Samuel
    Bridger (died before signing). R. July 3, 1788.            Page 110

GOODWIN, William, Sr.: Account estate, examined by George Benn and James
    Pitt. R. July 3, 1788. Signed, Brewer Godwin.              Page 111

PARKER, Thomas: Leg. wife Mary; son Joseph; daughter Mary Houghlow; daughter
    Sally Hawkins; granddaughter Nancy McCoy; to all my grandchildren.
    Extx., wife Mary Parker. D. June 7, 1788. R. July 3, 1788.
        Wit: Brewer Godwin, John King, Samuel King.
    William Hoffler qualified as Ex.
        Security, Samuel Hawkins and Joseph Parker.            Page 112

MOODY, Philip: Appraised by John Phillips, William Whitley, Jr., Armistead
    Vellines. R. September 4, 1788.                            Page 112

HAWKINS, William: Leg. grandchildren, William and Nancy Hawkins; grand-
    children, Willis and Joseph Smith. Ex., daughter Agnes Hawkins.
    D. ---------- R. December 4, 1788.

Wit: Samuel Hawkins, Samuel Holladay.
Security, Samuel Hawkins.                                    Page 113

DUNSTON, Thomas: Appraised by Benjamin Gale, John Saunders, Robert Eley.
    R. September 2, 1788.                                    Page 114

PITT, Henry: Account estate, examined by John S. Wills, Emanuel Wills,
    Edmond Godwin. R. September 4, 1788.                     Page 115

LANKFORD, Stephen: Appraised by John English, Jesse Lankford, Jethro
    Powell. R. October 2, 1788.                              Page 115

LAWRENCE, Hardy: Of Newport Parish. Leg. son Robert; wife Patsey; daughter
    Polly Pope; son Ishmael, land in Southampton County; son Hardy, land
    in Southampton County; daughter Permely Lawrence. Exs., wife and son
    Robert. D. May 12, 1788. R. October 2, 1788.
        Wit: Mills Lawrence, George Lawrence, John Lawrence.
        Security, Elisha Lawrence Ballard.                   Page 116

MURPHRY, John: Leg. wife Patience; son Lemuel; daughter Sarah Pinner.
    Exs., wife and son Lemuel Murphry. D. January 3, 1788. R. June 5,
    1788.
        Wit: Thomas Newby, Thomas Jordan, Stephen Butler,
        -------- Chapman.
        Security, Jacob Darden.                              Page 118

VELLINES, Nathaniel: Of Newport Parish. Leg. brother Isaac, land bought
    of Mary Simmons and John Fearn; sister Caty's children; to my father
    and brothers. Ex., brother Isaac Vellines. D. ----------
    R. October 2, 1788.
        Wit: William Goodson, Thomas Goodson, James Barlow.
        Security, Joseph Moody.                              Page 118

PRETLOW, John: Leg. wife; Ann Bailey is to continue to live with my wife;
    to Mary, daughter of Samuel Pretlow; brother Samuel Pretlow; friend
    Thomas Newby; friend Armiger Bailey; to Mary Pretlow; to Ann, daughter
    of Trial Bailey; to Mary, daughter of Armiger Bailey. Exs., wife and
    brother Samuel Pretlow. D. ----------- R. December 4, 1788.
        Wit: Edmund Westray, Alice Westray.
        Security, Campion Bracey.                            Page 119

BOWDEN, John: Leg. son John; son Thomas; brother Richard Bowden; son Elias;
    son William; daughter Frances; daughter Mary; daughter Hannah; daughter
    Rhody; daughter Chley; to my grandchildren, Samuel, Lemuel, Catherine,
    Amey and Rhody Powell; wife Peggy Bowden. Exs., sons Thomas and
    Elias Bowden. D. September 11, 1786. R. December 4, 1788.
        Wit: William Bridger, James A. Bridger, Robert Eley.
        Security, William Bridger.                           Page 120

STALLINGS, John: Appraised by William Gay, William Gray, Jesse Holleman.
    R. January 1, 1789.                                      Page 121

PARKER, Thomas: Appraised by Samuel Whitfield, Edmond Godwin, Nathaniel
    Norsworthy, Samuel King. R. January 6, 1790.             Page 122

GODWIN, Margaret: Appraised by Samuel Holladay, Jr., James Pitt, Russell
    Godby. R. January --, 1789.                              Page 123

CORBITT, Samuel: Leg. son Johnson; son Richard; son John; son Samuel; son
    Shadrack; son Elias; daughter Mary; daughter Elizabeth; daughter Amey;
    daughter Cherry. Exs., Johnson and Elias Corbitt. D. May 6, 1788.
    R. February 5, 1789.

Wit: John Lucas, John Brewer, Edy Brewer, Francis Young,
John Lawrence, Will English.
Security, Will English.                                    Page 124

DARDEN, John: Leg. wife Charity; son John, plantation bought of Elisha
Darden; son Henry Goodman Darden; son Elijah; son Mills; son William;
daughter Salle; Henry and William Goodman to have charge of the estate
given sons Henry Goodman and Elijah Darden. Exs., Benjamin Eley,
William Goodman, Henry Goodman. D. May 11, 1788. R. February 5, 1789.
Wit: Michael Johnson, John Darden, son of Hardy Darden, John
Duck, Eley Johnson.
Security, Mills Lawrence.                                  Page 125

COPHER, Jesse: Leg. son John; son William; son Demsy; daughter Keziah;
daughter Hannah; daughter Dounder; daughter Martha; wife. Ex.,
Moreland Delk. D. October 20, 1788. R. February 5, 1789.
Wit: James Gwaltney, Thomas Hicks, Moreland Delk.
Security, Mathew Harris.                                   Page 127

MALLORY, John: Leg. wife Mary; son William; daughter Martha; daughter Mary;
daughter Frances; daughter Keziah; daughter Angelina's slaves to be
possessed by Captain Mallory Todd, with reversion at his death to my
grandchildren, Martha Van Wagnum and William Todd. Ex., wife Mary
Mallory, son William and son-in-law Samuel Davis. D. December 30,
1788. R. February 5, 1789.
Wit: Davis Day, James Lupo, Richard Todd.
Security, Davis Day and Mallory Todd.                     Page 128

BRIDGER, Martha: Widow of John Bridger. Leg. William son of Mallory Todd;
to William Mallory Harvey; to Mrs. Martha Van Wagenum; to Fanny
Robertson Todd; Godson Joseph Hodsden; to Mrs. Keziah Harvey; to
Frances and Elizabeth Day; to Sarah and Polly Degge; son Joseph;
sister, Mrs. Mary Davis; sister, Mrs. Keziah Harvey; sister Mrs.
Frances Brown; to the children of my sister Angelina Todd; brother
William Mallory. Exs., brother-in-law Capt. Mallory Todd and brother
William Mallory. D. January 15, 1789. R. February 5, 1789.
Wit: Richard Todd, John Day, Tabitha Wrenn.
Security, Davis Day.                                      Page 129

WILLIAM, John: Appraised by Richard Pope, John Coggan, Mial McClenny.
Ordered January 17, 1789. R. April 2, 1789.               Page 130

LAWRENCE, Hardy: Appraised by Mills Lawrence, Jesse Lankford, Joshua
Councill. R. April 2, 1789.                               Page 131

MURPHRY, William: Leg. wife Mary and the children I had by her; to son
Charles, the plantation on which my mother now lives; son Dempsey;
son Jesse. Exs., sons George and Charles Murphry. D. January 6,
1788. R. April 2, 1789.
Wit: Fairfax Fatherlie, Francis Fatherlie, John Phillips.
Security, Michael Murphry.                                Page 132

DARDEN, John: Appraised by Michael Johnson, Obadiah Johnson, Eley Johnson,
John Darden, son of Hardy Darden. R. April 2, 1789.      Page 133

DAVIS, William: Account estate, examined by Solomon Wilson and Sampson
Wilson. Accounts due from sales made by Celia Davis. Signed, James
Wills. R. April 2, 1789.                                  Page 136

COUNCIL, Jacob: Account estate, examined by Solomon Wilson and James Wills.
Signed, Daniel Herring, Sheriff. R. April 3, 1789.       Page 137

WILSON, Samuel: Leg. son Josiah; to children of son Goodrich Wilson decd., agreeable to his will in Norfolk Court; son Sampson; grandson John, son of Josiah Wilson; grandson Samuel, son of Josiah Wilson; grandson James, son of Josiah Wilson; grandson Samuel, son of Goodrich Wilson, decd.; grandson Goodrich, son of Goodrich Wilson, decd., land in Surry County, bought of Benjamin Carrell; grandson George, son of Goodrich Wilson, decd.; granddaughters, Nancy, Peggy and Harriet, daughters of Goodrich Wilson, decd.; granddaughter Peggy Wilson Watson, daughter of James Watson. Exs., sons Josiah and Sampson Wilson. D. January 24, 1789. R. April 3, 1789.
>> Wit: Hezekiah Dowty, Milby Dowty, Josiah Bidgood, John Nelson. Security, Francis Young. Page 137

CARY, James: Of Newport Parish. Leg. wife Mildred all she was possessed with when I married her, reversion to Thomas Cary's son William Cary of Warwick County. Ex., brother Thomas Cary. D. July 8, 1788. R. May 7, 1789.
>> Wit: Drury Andrews, Charles Fulgham, Josiah Davis. Security, William Cary and Richard Cary, Jr. Page 140

BUTLER, Peter: Account estate, audited by Elisha L. Ballard and Mills Lawrence. R. June 4, 1789. Signed, Joseph Duck. Page 140

WHITFIELD, Samuel: Appraised by Joseph Driver, John Brown, Samuel King. R. June 4, 1789. Page 141

PITT, Joseph: Appraised by Thomas Newman, James Cutchin, Willis Wilkinson. Signed, Elizabeth Pitt. R. June 4, 1789. Page 142

COPHER, Jesse: Appraised by James Gwaltney, William Brock, John Gray. R. June 4, 1789. Page 143

TURNER, William: Appraised by William Inglish, George Lawrence, John Watkins. Ordered February 20, 1789. R. June 4, 1790. Page 143

POWELL, Joshua: Appraised by James A. Bridger and Robert Eley. R. June 4, 1789. Page 145

GORDON, George: Of Smithfield. Leg. money to be remitted to William Duncan to discharge debts in Scotland; friend, Rev. Henry John Burgess, to pay account of John Hay & Co.; to Mrs. Gilson, formerly Mrs. Webb; as a token of esteem for Mr. Mallory Todd, to his daughter Mrs. Von Wagenum; to Dr. David Dick; my library and instruments to be divided between George Purdie and Dr. David Dick, to be kept for my two Godsons, David Dick and George Degge; to my friends, George Purdie, Mallory Todd, William Urquhart. Ex., George Purdie. D. May 19, 1789. R. June 4, 1790.
>> Wit: George Purdie, Jr., Seth Hunter. Security, David Dick. Page 146

JORDAN, William, Sr.: Leg. wife Mary, the whole estate, which came into my possession by my last marriage. Ex., son Joseph Jordan. D. May 13, 1789. R. June 4, 1789.
>> Wit: Drury Andrews, Armistead Vellines, Samuel Hicks. Security, Robert Marshall, Drury Andrews, Thomas Jordan. Page 147

CHAPMAN, Charles: Appraised by Samuel Webb, Arthur Applewhaite, Thomas Wooten. Ordered December 5, 1788. R. June 4, 1789. Page 148

BRIDGER, Martha: Appraised by Thomas King and Roland Reynolds. Ordered February 12, 1789. R. June 4, 1789. Page 148

JOHNSON, Thomas, Sr.: Appraised by Mills Eley, Eley Johnson, William Inglish.
R. July 2, 1789. Page 150

GODWIN, Jonathan: Appraised by Ralph West, Samuel Weston, Charles Groce.
Ordered March 11, 1789. R. July 2, 1789. Page 151

SCOTT, William: Appraised by Benjamin Eley, Thomas Smelly, Thomas Jordan.
Ordered April, 1786. R. July 2, 1789. Page 153

POPE, John: Account estate, examined by John S. Wills, Robert Marshall,
Thomas Newby. Signed, Jethro Gale. R. July 2, 1789. Page 155

MURPHRY, John: Account estate, examined by John S. Wills, Thomas Smelley,
Thomas Newby. Signed, Lemuel Murphry. R. July 2, 1789. Page 156

GIBBS, Martha: Leg. nephew William Gibbs; nephew John Gibbs, niece Patsey
Gibbs; to Nancy, daughter of Joseph Gray. Ex., William Gibbs.
D. December 1, 1788. R. July 2, 1789.
Wit: Lemuel Bowden, Josiah Applewhaite.
Security, Lemuel Bowden. Page 156

GAY, William: Account estate, examined by James Johnson, Benjamin Tynes,
Thomas Bowden. Signed, William Peirce. R. July 2, 1789. Page 157

GODWIN, Edmund: Appraised by Richard Williams, Lemuel Bowden, Hezekiah
Holladay. Ordered February 17, 1789. R. July 2, 1789. Page 158

MATHEWS, Richard: Of Newport Parish. Leg. to James Britt and Elizabeth
his wife, if they maintain my sister who lives with me; to Betsey
Britt, the daughter of aforesaid; to Thomas Harris. Ex., James Britt.
D. October 3, 1787. R. June 4, 1789.
Wit: Willis Wills, James Davis.
Security, Francis Young. Page 159

HOLLADAY, Thomas: Account estate, among items, gold in the hands of Ann
Holladay; estate in account with Jemima Holladay, the Admtx. of Josiah
Holladay, decd. Examined by J. Goodrich and W. Casey. R. August 6,
1789. Page 159

HUNTER, Joshua and Elizabeth: Estate in account with William Bagnall, decd.
Examined by John S. Wills, James Wills and Edmund Godwin. R. August 5,
1789. Page 160

ROBERTSON, William: Appraised by Thomas McWilliams, William Crocker, James
Johnston. R. September 3, 1789. Page 161

JOHNSON, Robert: Leg. son Abel, with the consent of my father Lazarus
Johnson; wife Patience; son Laban; daughter Martha Johnson. Exs.,
brother Joseph Johnson, brother-in-law Abraham Johnson and wife
Patience Johnson. D. January 1, 1789. R. September 3, 1789.
Wit: Elijah Johnson, Amos Johnson, Jesse Johnson, Elisha
Johnson. Page 162

WATKINS, William: (being very old). Leg. grandson Robert Watkins; grand-
daughter Isabell Bridger; daughter Mary Whitehead; daughter Ann Jenkins;
daughter Sarah Lankford; granddaughter Mary Lankford; grandson Robert
Saunders; to the children of my son Jesse Watkins, viz: Sarah, Martha,
Elizabeth, Rebecca, Penelope, Jesse and William Watkins. Ex., grand-
son Robert Watkins. D. June 28, 1786. R. December 3, 1789.
Wit: William Powell, Jethro Powell.
Security, Jethro Powell. Page 163

STEPHENS, Elizabeth: Leg. daughter Elizabeth; son William; son John; to
Nathan Stephens; to Mills Stephens, son of my daughter Elizabeth; to
Everett Stephens; to Sarah, daughter of James Mercer; to all my children.
D. September 21, 1791 (?). R. December 3, 1789.
Wit: John P. Heald, Dempsey Marshall.
William Stephens qualified, security, Dempsey Marshall.        Page 164

CUTCHINS, Joseph: Appraisal by William Casey and Henry Applewhaite.
Ordered January 9, 1779. R. December 4, 1789.                  Page 164

JONES, Frederick: Account estate, examined by Thomas Goodson and Thomas
Wrenn. Signed, David Jones. R. December 3, 1789.               Page 166

FISHER, Thomas: Leg. son Teakle; daughter Susannah; daughter Sarah; daughter
Rosey; son Fairfax John Throughgood Fisher; son Thomas George Washington
Fisher; grandson James Fisher; son William. Ex., Teackle Fisher.
D. September 14, 1789. R. January 7, 1790.
Wit: Moss Shields, Ezekiel Young, Robert Wilsom.
Security, William Hardy.                                       Page 167

CARRELL, William: Appraised by William Mallory, Shadrack Ames, James Lupo.
R. January 7, 1790.                                           Page 167

GODWIN, John: Leg. son John; son Barteley, the old warehouse, Joynes and
William Green's plantation; daughter Elizabeth; daughter Charlotte;
wife Silvia Godwin. Ex., son John Godwin. D. December 22, 1789.
R. January 7, 1790.
Wit: Samuel Weston, Copeland Whitfield, Jr., Tabitha Whitley.
Security, Thomas King.                                         Page 168

CARRELL, William: Account estate, examined by John J. Wheadon, Harwood
Calcote, John Harrison. Signed, Mary Carrell, William Gray, James
Piland. R. January 7, 1790.                                    Page 169

GODWIN, John: Appraised by John Cunningham, Samuel Weston, Charles Gross.
R. February 3, 1790.                                          Page 170

HOLLAND, Job: Of the Upper Parish. Leg. son Job; son Meredith; son Elijah;
daughter Bathsheba Watson; daughter Betsey; daughter Polly; wife Mary
Holland. Exs., wife and Job Holland. D. August 30, 1789.
R. February 3, 1790.
Wit: Thomas Daughtry, Uriah Vaughan, Aaron Holland.
Security, Thomas Daughtry and Uriah Vaughan.                  Page 172

HOLLAND, Job: Appraised by Joshua Councill, Richard Daughtry, John Saunders.
R. April 5, 1790.                                            Page 173

BOWDEN, John: Appraised by Robert Eley and Robert Holland. R. April 5,
1790.                                                        Page 174

JOHNSON, Aaron: Account estate, examined by Michael Johnson, Joseph Johnson,
John Johnson. Signed, Eley Johnson. R. April 5, 1790.        Page 175

CORBETT, Samuel: Appraised by William English, Francis Vaughan, Solomon
Edmunds. R. April 5, 1790.                                   Page 175

WRENN, Francis: Account estate, examined by ------ Young and Richard Yarbrough. Signed, Josiah Wilson, who married the Admtx. R. April 5,
1790.                                                        Page 176

STRICKLAND, Elizabeth: Account estate, examined by Emanuel Wills and Francis
Boykin. Money received of John Murphry, administrator of her father's
estate. Signed, John Phillips. R. April 6, 1790.             Page 178

WATKINS, William, Sr.: Appraised by John Watkins, William Powell, John English. R. June 7, 1790. Page 178

PEIRCE, Peter: Appraised by Michael Fulgham, Kinchen Turner, Campion Bracy. R. July 5, 1790. Page 179

ATKINSON, Owen: Appraised by William Gray, William Gay, Jesse Holleman. Ordered January 16, 1789. R. July 5, 1790. Page 180

STRINGFIELD, John: Appraised by Thomas Womble, William Gay, William Womble. Ordered June 13, 1789. R. July 5, 1790. Page 180

STEVENS, Elizabeth: Appraised by James Holland, John English, Kinchen Crumpler. D. December, 1789. R. July 5, 1790. Page 181

SMITH, Joseph: Appraised by Joshua Bunkley, Russel Godby, Isham Groce. Ordered May 16, 1789. R. July 5, 1790. Page 181

SMITH, Thomas, Sr.: Appraised by Isham Groce, Samuel Holladay, Sr., Anthony Holladay, Sr. D. May, 1785. R. July 5, 1790. Page 182

ROYALL, Thomas: Appraised by Thomas Newby, Joseph Everett, John Everett. Ordered March, 1790. R. September 6, 1790. Page 183

MINARD, Jesse: Appraised by Mills Lawrence, Francis Vaughan, Robert Lawrence. R. September 6, 1790. Page 183

BRITT, Jordan: Examined by William Bridger, Mills Eley, E. L. Ballard. Signed, Elizabeth Nelms. R. September 6, 1790. Page 184

JOHNSON, Nathan, Sr.: Leg. son Eley; son Nathan; son Stephen; daughter Tabitha; daughter Mourning; son Jordan; wife Amey. Exs., sons Eley and Jordan Johnson. D. August 31, 1785. R. September 6, 1790. Wit: Nathan Carr, Abraham Johnson, Jr., Amos Johnson. Page 184

LUPO, James: Leg. daughter Elizabeth Gray Lupo; daughter Mary; son William; son James; son Laban Lupo. Exs., sons James and Laban Lupo, Samuel Bidgood. D. January 15, 1789. R. September 6, 1790. Wit: John Woodley, Jr., Charity Brantley, Milly Lupo, John Hodges. Security, Benjamin Atkinson. Page 185

PEIRCE, Peter: Account estate, examined by Daniel Herring, William Bridger, Jas. (?) Johnson. R. September 6, 1790. Signed, William Woodward. Page 185

WHITFIELD, Samuel: Account estate, examined by John S. Wills and Godfrey Powell. R. September 6, 1790. Signed, James Morrison. Page 186

JORDAN, John: Leg. wife Elizabeth; son William; son John; son Robert, the plantation on which Nicholas Goodson lives; daughter Lidda; daughter Mary; daughter Nancy; daughter Rebecca; daughter Betsey Wainwright Jordan; brother Robert Jordan. D. February 15, 1790. R. September 7, 1790. Wit: Copeland Whitfield, Jr., John Reynolds, Permelia Whitfield. Security, George Benn. Page 187

WESTRAY, Robert: Leg. wife Polly; son Benjamin; daughter Sally; son Mathew; daughter Patsey Camp. Exs., wife and Elisha L. Ballard. D. August 27, 1790. R. October 4, 1790. Wit: Wade Mountfort, James Wilson, William English, Benjamin Wilson. Security, Mills Eley. Page 187

RAMPHON, Rhoda: Leg. daughter Mary Pinner Ramphon; cousin Obadiah Bullock; cousin John Bullock; Moses Hutching and his wife Mary to take my daughter. Ex., Thomas Newby. D. July 9, 1790. R. October 4, 1790. Wit: James Pinner, Lemuel Murphry, Sarah Powell. Security, Michael Murphry.                                    Page 188

JENKINS, Valentine: Account estate, examined by ---- Young, John Goodrich, William Casey. Signed, Capt. William Davis. Among items, paid Willis Brantley his part of estate; paid Benjamin Barlow for keeping the orphan. R. October 4, 1790.                                    Page 189

REYNOLDS, Pitt: Account estate, examined by John S. Wills, Mills Wills, Edmund Godwin. Signed, Brewer Godwin. Paid Benjamin Applewhaite and Charles Groce the same amount. R. November 2, 1790.          Page 190

CARY, James: Appraised by Drury Andrews, Thomas Fearn, Benjamin Tynes. R. December 6, 1790.                                             Page 191

FLEMING, Nathaniel: Leg. sister Helen of the city of Lincoln, in Great Britain; sister Mary Fleming of the city of York, my coat of arms; to Rev. Mr. Charlesworth, Ex. to the last will and testament of Edward Parker, Esq. of Glamford Briggs, Lincolnshire, to be applied to the uses of the said will. Ex., Mr. William Urquhart, Merchant of Southampton County. D. December 2, 1784. R. December 6, 1790. Wit. Security, Thomas Fearn.                                    Page 191

SMITH, William: Account estate, examined by Ralph West, Roland Reynolds, Randolph Reynolds. Signed, Jonathan Godwin. R. December 6, 1790. Page 192

JONES, Abraham: Leg. nephew William Jones; nephew Moreland Delk; father Abraham Jones; niece Esther Copher; niece Mary Stagg; friend Belah Williford; friend Jordan Williford. Ex., nephew Moreland Delk. D. September 4, 1787. R. December 6, 1790. Wit: Joseph Holleman, Mathew Harris, James Gwaltney, Simmons Gwaltney. Security, Joseph Holleman.                                    Page 193

COWLING, Thomas: Leg. wife; all my children. Exs., wife and brother-in-law Willis Cowling. D. January 18, 1783. R. December 6, 1790. Martha Cowling, Extx. Wit: Thomas Cowling, Sr., William Cowling, John Brown. Security, William Cowling and Josiah Pinner.          Page 194

DAUGHTRY, Joshua: Of Newport Parish. Leg. son John; daughter Sarah; daughter Charlotte; son Joshua; wife. Ex., brother Thomas Daughtry. D. October 10, 1790. R. February 7, 1791. Wit: John Daughtry, Jacob Beal, James Tallow, Jacob Johnson. Security, Joshua Daughtry.                                    Page 194

LANKFORD, Jesse: Of Newport Parish. Leg. cousin George Lankford. Ex., cousin Goerge Lankford. D. January 2, 1790. R. February 7, 1791. Wit: William English, John English, Josiah Duck. Security, Josiah Duck.                                    Page 195

HARRISON, John: Leg. wife Elizabeth; daughter Harriet; daughter Elizabeth Hill Harrison, land in Surry County, on which Samuel Bidgood now lives; daughter Moody (?) land in Surry County. Exs., wife Elizabeth, brother Richard Harrison and friend Sampson Wilson. D. April 1, 1790. R. February 7, 1791. Wit: Harwood Calcote, Betsey Harrison. Security, Willis Wills.                                    Page 195

JORDAN, Richard: Leg. daughter Peggy Drew, the plantation of my father
Mathew Jordan; son Belson; son Richard; wife Honour; to all my
daughters and my unborn child. Exs., wife, friend Robert Marshall,
Mathew Jordan. D. January 28, 1791. R. February 7, 1791.
    Wit: John S. Wills, Pleasant Jordan, Anselm Hargrave.
    Security, Robert Marshall, John S. Wills.          Page 196

FULGHAM, James: Leg. sister Elizabeth Applewhaite; nephew Josiah Applewhaite;
to Celia Casey. Ex., nephew Josiah Applewhaite. D. January 29, 1791.
R. February 7, 1791.
    Wit: John Williams.
    Security, Nathaniel Norsworthy, John King.          Page 197

BROWN, James: Leg. daughter Ann; daughter Martha; daughter Frances; daughter
Mary; daughter Elizabeth C.; daughter Catherine Brown. Exs., George
Mallicote and John J. Wheadon. D. January 1, 1791. R. February 7,
1791.
    Wit: Charles Hanson, John Shelley.
    Security, Lawrence Baker.          Page 198

WILLIAMS, David: Leg. wife and children. Exs., wife Prudence Williams and
Joseph Driver. D. December 15, 1790. R. February 7, 1791.
    Wit: Nathaniel Norsworthy, Josiah Williams.          Page 198

LUPO, Philip: Account estate, examined by Sampson Wilson, John J. Wheadon,
Harwood Calcote. Signed, William Carrell, decd. R. February 7, 1791.
                                                        Page 198

COWLING, Thomas: Appraised by John Everett, Joseph Everett, William Shivers.
R. February 7, 1791.                                    Page 199

HARDY, Thomas: Leg. wife Priscilla; daughter Elizabeth Crolby Hardy; son
Samuel; daughter Mary Chambers. Exs., Mr. Robert Hunnicutt, George
Hardy, William Hardy. D. March 11, 1790. R. October 4, 1790.
    Wit: Joseph Carrell, James Bennett.
    Security, Thomas King.          Page 200

PARKER, William: Leg. son John, land in Nansemond County; to the heirs of
my deceased son William Parker; daughter Nanney Holland; daughter
Elizabeth Beal; grandson Hardy Parker; wife Martha Parker. Ex.,
friend Joseph Duck. D. January 23, 1791. R. April 4, 1791.
    Wit: James Uzzell, Milly Carr, Robert Beal.
    Security, John Duck.          Page 201

STUCKEY, Edmund: Appraised by R. R. Read, Roland Reynolds, Joseph Driver.
Ordered April 22, 1790. R. April 4, 1791.          Page 201

KING, Martha: Of Newport Parish. Leg. grandson Henry King, with reversion
to son John; daughter Sally Bunkley and her husband, Joshua Bunkley;
son Samuel King. Ex., son John King. D. August 24, 1783.
R. October 4, 1790.
    Wit: Tristram Norsworthy, John Parker, Parmelia Smith.
    Security, Nathaniel Norsworthy.          Page 202

JONES, Abraham: Appraised by James Gwaltney, Mathew Harris, Jesse Holleman.
R. April 4, 1791.          Page 203

JONES, Mary: Leg. daughter Frances; to Nelson Jones. Ex., daughter Frances
Jones. D. November 4, 1790. R. April 5, 1791.
    Wit: James P. Bell, William Gay, Edward Gay, Robert Flake.
                                                        Page 204

ROYALL, Thomas: Account estate, examined by John S. Wills and Robert Marshall.
Signed, Mathew Jordan. R. June 6, 1791. Page 204

JAMES, Abel: Leg. son William; son Abel; daughter Peggy Applewhaite. Exs.,
son William and friend Sampson Wilson. D. January 15, 1789.
R. June 6, 1791.
Wit: Richard Hardy, William Hardy, James Coats.
Security, William Hardy, Harwood Calcote, Abel James. Page 205

GODWIN, Samuel, Sr.: Leg. daughter Lelia; daughter Silvia; daughter Sophia
Reynolds; son Samuel; to Mary Daniels; to Mary Hanes; to all my children.
Exs., son Samuel, Mills Godwin, George Robertson. D. February 10, 1791.
R. March 7, 1791.
Wit: Jonas Askew, Godfrey Powell, Hora. Durley.
Security, James Mitchell and Edmund Pitt. Page 205

STALLINGS, John: Account estate, examined by Moss Shields, Thomas Wrenn,
William Gay. R. June 6, 1791. Page 206

DAUGHTRY, Joshua: Appraised by David Eley, Cutchin Councill, Mathew
Daughtry. R. June 6, 1791. Page 207

PARKER, William: Appraised by Lott Griffin, Mills Carr, James Fowler.
R. September 5, 1791. Page 208

CROCKER, Sarah: Appraised by William Blunt, John Thomas, Philip Thomas.
R. September 5, 1791. Page 208

LANKFORD, Jesse: Appraised by Mills Lawrence, Wade Mountfort, Robert
Lawrence. R. September 5, 1791. Page 209

HILL, Frances: (Aged) Leg. son Joseph; daughter Elizabeth, the wife of John
Harrison. Ex., son-in-law John Harrison. D. June 4, 1788.
R. September 5, 1791.
Wit: Samuel Bidgood, Benjamin Tynes, Elizabeth Hill.
Security, David Bradley, Willis Wills. Page 210

HARDY, Richard: Leg. son Thomas; son George; son William, the lands located
by Capt. Johnston in the County of Bourbon; wife Marcella; daughter
Nancy; daughter Hannah; daughter Sarah; the property of Samuel Hardy
to be sold. Exs., sons Thomas and William Hardy. D. June 8, 1789.
R. September 3, 1789.
Wit: Josiah Wrenn, William Willis.
Security, William James. Page 211

HERRING, Mills: Leg. wife; daughter Martha, with reversion of bequest to my
brothers, Elias, Daniel and Jesse Herring. Ex., Daniel Herring.
D. January 22, 1791. R. February 7, 1791. Nancy Herring refused
terms of will.
Wit: William Woodward, Frederick Jones, John Woodward, Hardy
Chapman, William Woodward, Jr.
Security, Francis Young, William Bridger. Page 211

RONALDSON, Patrick: Of Smithfield. Leg. refers to late wife; Goddaughter
Fann, eldest daughter of Bridger Goodrich; to Margaret Easson, daughter
of my late wife; to John Easson the son of my late wife; my sister Ann
Handyside; to sister Jannett Ronaldson; my brother James Ronaldson;
nephew Peter (or Patrick) Handyside. Exs., John Easson, Robert Farmer
of Norfolk, Timothy Tynes. D. May 21, 1791.
Codicil, which revokes bequest to Margaret Easson "as she is now
married to Mr. William Patrick, to whom it would be no present."
R. October 3, 1791.

Wit: R. Yarbrough, Will Johnston.
Security, John Goodrich, William Patrick.　　　　　　　Page 212

WOODLEY, John, Sr.: Leg. wife Catherine; son Willis; son John, the profits
arising from the estate of John Wilson; son Andrew; son Samuel; daughter
Elizabeth; daughter Molly Blunt. Exs., Andrew Woodley and William
Blunt. D. February 3, 1791. R. October 3, 1791.
　　Wit: John J. Wheadon, Arthur Applewhaite, Joseph Crocker,
　　　　Charles Hanson.
　　Security, Francis Boykin.　　　　　　　　　　　　　　Page 214

BRADDY, Priscilla: Account estate, examined by John J. Wheadon, William
Gay and Thomas Wrenn. Signed, Mr. John Davis. R. October 3, 1791.
　　　　　　　　　　　　　　　　　　　　　　　　　　　Page 215

FOWLER, Elizabeth: Leg. daughter Ann Griffin; son James; daughter Tabitha;
son Arthur Fowler. D. September 9, 1773. R. December 5, 1791.
　　Wit: Samuel Corbett, William Carr, Lott Griffin.
　　Security, Lott Griffin.　　　　　　　　　　　　　　　Page 215

GALE, Thomas Whitney: Leg. son Thomas; granddaughter Polly Flood; daughter
Polly; daughter Sally; wife Sarah. Exs., son Thomas Gale and Edward
Davis. D. November 8, 1791. R. December 6, 1791.
　　Wit: Edward Davis, Everett Morris, Penelope Pope.
　　Security, Thomas Davis and Edward Davis.　　　　　　Page 216

PEIRCE, William, Sr.: Leg. son William; grandson Kinchen Crumpler; wife
Martha; grandson James Gay; grandson John Allen; grandson John Peirce.
Exs., son William Peirce and grandson Kinchen Crumpler. D. April 29,
1791. R. December 5, 1791.
　　Wit: Joshua Councill, William Coggan, John Coggan.
　　Security, William Coggan.　　　　　　　　　　　　　Page 217

TAYLOR, George: Of Newport Parish. Leg. daughter Mary Powell; grandson
David Carr; grandson Nathan Carr; to daughter Moore. Ex., Eley Johnson.
D. January 2, 1791. R. February 7, 1791.
　　Wit: John Johnson, Abraham Johnson, Jacob H. Johnson.
　　Security, Joseph Spivey.　　　　　　　　　　　　　Page 218

MUNFORD, Elizabeth: Leg. daughter Silvia Hicks; daughter Mary; daughter
Sarah; daughter Nancy; son Micajah; granddaughter Elizabeth Hicks;
granddaughter Sarah Hicks. Ex., son Micajah Munford. D. December 29,
1790. R. January 2, 1792.
　　Wit: Joseph Holleman, Zachariah Phillips, James Deford.
　　Security, Simon Atkins.　　　　　　　　　　　　　　Page 219

CHAPMAN, Joseph: Leg. wife Rhoda; daughter Mary; daughter Liddia; son
Joseph; son John; son Charles; granddaughter Liddia Reynolds, daughter
of Roland Reynolds. Exs., wife, James Smith, Joshua Bunkley.
D. February 22, 1791. R. December 5, 1791.
　　Wit: Josiah Wills, Anne Bowden, James Wallace.
　　Security, Thomas Hall.　　　　　　　　　　　　　　Page 220

WESTRAY, Mathew: Appraised by Joseph Westray and Hardy Chapman. Signed,
Jeremiah Westray and Sally Westray. Ordered February 17, 1791.
R. January 2, 1792.　　　　　　　　　　　　　　　　　Page 220

WILLIAMS, David: Appraised by Peter Cunningham, Henry Lightfoot, Richard
Williams. R. February 6, 1792.　　　　　　　　　　　　Page 221

JORDAN, Josiah: Account estate, examined by Robert Marshall and Thomas
Newby. Signed, Mourning Jordan. R. February 6, 1792.　　Page 222

JORDAN, Mourning: Leg. son Robert, land adjoining that of son Thomas; to
Sarah, wife of said son Robert, until my grandson Samuel Jordan is 21;
grandson Josiah, son of son Josiah Jordan; daughter Dolly Brown; grandson Robert Jordan, son of Hezekiah Jordan; to the representatives of
my son Josiah, Hezekiah and Peggy Pleasants. D. September 18, 1789.
R. January 2, 1792.
    Wit: Pleasants Jordan, Nathaniel Harrison, Mourning Eley.
    Security, Francis Boykin, Gent. and Robert Marshall.    Page 223

CHANNELL, Jeremiah: Account estate, cash paid Rachel Channell, cash paid
Jeremiah Channell. Examined by John Hutchinson and William Waltham.
R. April 2, 1792.                                          Page 225

CRUMPLER, Edmund: Leg. son Kinchen; son Mathew; son John; daughter Mary;
wife Mary; daughter Grace; son Samuel; daughter Meriam Crumpler.
Exs., wife and son Kinchen Crumpler. D. August 12, 1791. R. April 2,
1792.
    Wit: William Bridger.
    Security, William Bridger.                             Page 225

CUTCHIN, Mathew: Leg. sister Mary; refers to deceased father, Joseph Cutchin;
brother William; nephew Charles Pasteur, son of my sister Honour Pasteur;
nephew Solomon Wilson Pasteur; niece Mary Pasteur; niece Elizabeth
Pasteur; to Capt. John Pasteur; niece Margaret Sinclair; niece Mary
Sinclair; niece Honour Wilson Applewhaite; niece Mary Derring; brother-
in-law Capt. John Pasteur; sister Ann Sinclair; niece Nancy Sinclair.
Exs., Solomon Wilson of Richmond, John Sinclair of Smithfield and
Capt. John Pasteur. D. February 19, 1792. R. April 2, 1792.
    Wit: James Johston, Copeland Parker, Joseph Cutchin.
    Codicil: Capt. John Goodrich an additional Executor.
    Wit: William Derring, Merit M. Robinson.
    Security, John Goodrich.                               Page 226

WHITLEY, George: Account estate, cash allowed for the maintenance of Sarah,
orphan of Joseph Mintz. Examined by Emanuel Wills and Robert Marshall.
Signed, John Phillips. D. October 7, 1791. R. June 4, 1792.
                                                           Page 228

STOKELEY, William: Appraised by Rowland Reynolds, Randal Reynolds, Copeland
Whitfield, Sr. Ordered August 6, 1784. R. June 4, 1792.   Page 230

COPHER, Thomas: Account estate, paid legacies to Olive Griffin, Charity
Holleman, James Copher, Thomas Copher, Mary Stevenson, Ann Pitman,
Sarah Hunter, Jane Powell and Emanuel Powers. Examined by James
Gwaltney and William Gray. Signed, Jesse Holleman and Thomas Copher.
R. June 4, 1792.                                           Page 231

MOODY, Philip: Account estate, examined by Thomas Wrenn and William Gay.
Signed, Thomas Copher. R. June 4, 1792.                    Page 232

JORDAN, John: Appraised by Ralph West, Josiah Wail, Josiah Cutchin.
R. June 4, 1792.                                           Page 233

RONALDSON, Patrick: Appraised by Thomas King, Thomas Smith, Charles Fulgham.
R. July 2, 1792.                                           Page 234

FLEMING, Nathaniel: Appraised by William Bridger and Robert Holland.
R. July 2, 1792.                                           Page 236

CHAPMAN, Joseph: Appraised by Joseph Driver, Henry Lightfoot, John Brown.
R. September 3, 1792.                                      Page 237

LITTLE, Keziah: Appraised by James Johnson, Thomas Bowden. Ordered March 15, 1792. R. October 1, 1792. Page 239

OUTLAND, William: Leg. wife Rebecca; brother James; brother Elisha; sister Nancy Outland. Exs., wife and friend John Murry. D. August 5, 1790. R. December 3, 1792.
    Wit: John Murry, John Arnstrong, James Outland.
    Security, Joseph Stringfield. Page 239

DARDEN, Hardy: Leg. son Elisha; son John; daughter Alice Holland; son Dempsey; wife Alice Darden. Exs., wife and son John Darden. D. October 2, 1773. R. December 3, 1792.
    Wit: Jesse Watkins, Priscilla Watkins, Jethro Powell.
    Security, James Holland. Page 239

JOHNSON, Abraham: Appraised by Eley Johnson, Jordan Johnson, Stephen Bullock. R. December 3, 1792. Page 241

LITTLE, John: Of Newport Parish. Leg. wife; grandson John, son of Henry Parkerson; daughter Rebecca Parkerson and her children, Sally, John, Nancy and Polly Parkerson. Ex., Campion Bracey. D. -----------
R. December 3, 1792.
    Wit: John Woodward, Jane Blades, Armiger Bailey.
    Security, John Turner, John Saunders. Page 242

GROCE, William: Leg. wife Sally; brother Willis my lot in Smithfield; brother Joshua Groce. Extx., wife Sally Groce. D. September 14, 1792. R. December 3, 1792.
    Wit: Willis Wills, Josiah Wills, Joseph Driver.
    Security, Nathaniel Norsworthy. Page 242

GILES, Thomas: Leg. wife Rebecca; daughter Polly; daughter Elizabeth; son Thomas Giles. Exs., John Giles, Jr. and Rebecca Giles. D. October 13, 1792. R. January 7, 1793.
    Wit: Henry Howard, John Reynolds.
    Security, Mills Wills. Page 243

TOMLIN, Martha: Leg. to Martha Powell, daughter of Joshua Powell, Jr., decd.; to Rebecca, daughter of Joshua Powell, Jr.; daughter Holland Bowden; daughter Mary Powell; to Milly Barrett; to Thomas Bowden. Ex., Thomas Bowden. D. January 14, 1789. R. January 7, 1793.
    Wit: Elias Bowden, James Gay, Samuel Powell.
    Security, Samuel Powell. Page 243

WESTRAY, Robert: Appraised by William Eley, Sion Boon, Wade Mountfort. R. January 7, 1793. Page 244

WESTRAY, Robert: Account estate, examined by Mills Eley, Robert Watkins, Mills Lawrence. Signed, Elisha L. Ballard. R. January 7, 1793.
Page 245

ALMAND, Isaac: Leg. wife Mary; daughter Anne Vaniser; daughter Rebecca; daughter Mary Wombwell; daughter-in-law Susanna Smith. Ex., Peter Vaniser. D. January 27, 1786. R. January 7, 1793.
    Wit: Jesse Atkins, Sarah Atkins, Martha Applewhaite.
    Security, Joseph Stallings. Page 246

ELEY, Gale: Leg. wife Mary; son Robert; granddaughter Elizabeth Eley; grandson Gale Eley. Exs., wife and son Robert Eley. D. December 4, 1792. R. February 4, 1793.
    Wit: Benjamin Eley, Sally Johnson, Rebecca Butler.
    Security, John S. Wills. Page 247

BROWN, James: Appraised by Sampson Wilson, Wilson Brantley, Harwood Calcote, James Pyland. R. February 4, 1793. Page 248

BRIDGER, William: Leg. wife Patsey; son James; son William; daughter Patsey; son John; son Samuel; son Lawrence Bridger. Exs., Simon and Arthur Boykin. D. January 15, 1793. R. February 4, 1793.
    Wit: Benjamin Eley, William Eley, Henry Saunders, John Denson.
    Security, Francis Boykin. Page 249

CROCKER, William: Account estate, to paid the eight grandchildren. Examined by John Thomas, Andrew Woodley, William Blunt. Signed, William Crocker, the Younger. D. December 22, 1792. R. February 4, 1793. Page 250

CROCKER, William: Appraised by John Thomas, William Blunt, Andrew Woodley. Ordered December 30, 1791. R. February 4, 1793. Page 250

ALMOND, Augustine: Nuncupative will, presented by Mr. Thomas King. Leg. brother Hezekiah; sister Peggy Almond. D. April 17, 1787. R. February 4, 1793. Page 251

LITTLE, John: Appraised by Campion Bracy, John Saunders, John Woodward. R. February 4, 1793. Page 252

TAYLOR, George: Appraised by John Darden, son of John Darden, Jordan Johnson, Mills Darden. R. June 3, 1793. Page 252

BABB, Robert: Appraised by Thomas Smelley, William Baldwin, John Pope. R. June 3, 1793. Page 253

NORSWORTHY, John: Appraised by Benjamin Eley, John Pope, Richard Pope. R. June 3, 1793. Page 255

WOMBWELL, Joseph, Sr.: Account estate, examined by W. Goodson, Thomas Wrenn, William Gay. Signed, Henry Wombwell. R. January 3, 1793. Page 255

ELEY, Gale: Appraised by Benjamin Eley, Robert Eley, William Eley, Eley Johnson. R. June 3, 1793. Page 256

SAUNDERS, Henry: Appraised by Robert Eley, Jr., John Pope, son of Richard Pope, John Saunders, Sr. and John Coggan. Ordered April 2, 1792. R. June 3, 1793. Page 257

POWELL, Martha: Leg. to Martha, daughter of Joshua Powell, Jr. decd.; to Amy, daughter of John Powell, Sr.; to Lemuel Powell, son of John Powell, Sr.; to Mary Powell. Exs., Martha and Lemuel Powell. D. February 12, 1793. R. June 3, 1793.
    Wit: James Gay, Thaddeus Powell. Page 258

SMELLEY, Robert: Account estate, examined by Jethro Gale, William Baldwin, William Babb. R. January 3, 1793. Signed, Thomas Smelley. Page 258

COPHER, Benjamon: Account estate, examined by Thomas Wrenn and John S. Wills. Signed, Charles Goodrich. R. June 3, 1793. Page 259

CUTCHIN, Mary: Leg. brother Mathew Cutchin decd., mentioned; to the children of my four sisters, viz: to Charles, Solomon Wilson, Mary and Elizabeth Pasteur, the children of Honour Pasteur; to Margaret and Mary Sinclair, children of Ann Sinclair; to Ridley Honour Applewhaite, daughter of Ridley Applewhaite; to Mary Derring, daughter of Elizabeth Derring, decd., my father Joseph Cutchins. State that Margaret Sinclair is now dead.

Exs., brother Solomon Wilson and Capt. John Pasteur.  D.  March 27, 1793.  R.  June 3, 1793.
     Wit:  John Goodrich, Thomas Brantley, William Hardy.     Page 260

ALMAND, Isaac:  Appraised by Benjamin Stringfield, Benjamin Jones, Joseph Stringfield.  R.  July 1, 1793.                                Page 261

JOHNSON, Sarah:  Appraised by Eley Johnson, William Eley, Robert Eley.  R.  July 1, 1793.                                             Page 264

PEIRCE, John:  Appraised by Robert Eley and William Eley.  R.  July 1, 1793.
                                                                Page 264

CROCKER, Molly:  Leg. sister Sally; brother Milner; brother Henry Crocker.  Exs., William and Joseph Crocker.  D.  November 2, 1792.  R.  July 1, 1793.
     Wit:  William Blunt, Margaret Morrison.
     Security, Miles Wills.                                       Page 264

RONALDSON, Patrick:  Appraised by Thomas King, Charles Fulgham, ------ Young.  Signed, John Easson.  R.  July 1, 1793.                  Page 265

SYKES, Mary:  Let. to Sally Sykes, daughter of Mary Chapman; daughter Fanny Hough.  Extx., daughter Fanny Hough.  D.  November 9, 1791.  R.  September 2, 1793.
     Wit:  William Baldwin, Nancy Baldwin, Benjamin Eley,
            Benjamin Harrison.
     Security, Joseph Lawrence.                                   Page 267

BARLOW, Benjamin:  Appraised by John J. Wheadon, Charles Goodrich, William Goodrich.  Ordered December 18, 1792.  R.  September 2, 1793.  Page 268

COUNCIL, Joshua, the elder:  Leg. son Lemuel; son Joshua; son Miles; daughter Chasey Boon; son Godwin; daughter Betsey Council.  Ex., son Lemuel Council.  D.  May 27, 1793.  R.  September 2, 1793.
     Wit:  Elijah Johnson, Dempsey Johnson, Mathew Vaughan.
     Security, John S. Wills.                                     Page 268

KING, Samuel:  Of Newport Parish.  Leg. brother John; nephew Henry King; nephew Edmund Godwin.  Ex., brother John King.  D.  June 23, 1793.  R.  September 2, 1793.
     Wit:  J. Parker, Nathaniel Norsworthy, Mary Hall.
     Security, Nathaniel Norsworthy.                              Page 269

FOWLER, Thomas:  Leg. son Joseph; son Mills, daughter Charity; daughter Sarah; daughter Priscilla; grandson Silas Fowler.  Ex., son Joseph Fowler.  D.  April 30, 1793.  R.  October 7, 1793.
     Wit:  Samuel Fowler, John Stevens, John Rose, John Brewer.
     Security, John Rose.                                         Page 270

SAUNDERS, Robert:  Leg. daughter Ann Pope; daughter Catherine Pope; daughter Peggy Roberts; daughter Betty Carstaphen and her husband Perkins Carstaphen; to Robert Carstaphen, son of my daughter Betty; to Betty Pope, daughter of my daughter Ann; to Robert Roberts, son of my daughter Peggy; to Mills Pope, the land adjoining that of his father Richard Pope; to Lemuel Roberts, son of my daughter Peggy.  Ex., son-in-law Richard Pope.  D.  June 30, 1792.  R.  October 7, 1793.
     Wit:  Mills Eley, John Saunders, Jr., John Saunders, Sr.
     Security, Wright Roberts.                                    Page 270

STRINGFIELD, John:  Account estate, examined by William Outland, Thomas Wrenn, William Gay.  Signed, Joseph Stringfield.  R.  October 7, 1793.
                                                                 Page 271

BRIDGER, James Allen: Leg. wife Isabell; son Joseph Lawrence Bridger; daughter Molly; daughter Tempty; daughter Peggy; daughter Nancy Bridger. Estate to be divided by Drury Andrews, James Johnson, John Fearn and Daniel Herring. Exs., Mills Lawrence and Robert Eley. D. October 11, 1792. R. October 7, 1793.
    Wit: Mills Eley, Jesse Watkins, Thaddeus Powell.
    Security, Thomas Fearn.        Page 272

WILKINSON, Jane: Leg. sister Lois Wills and her son Henry D. Wills; to brother James Cutchins; brother Joseph Cutchins; sister Esther Cutchins. Exs., brother James Cutchins and George Benn. D. October 28, 1793. R. December 2, 1793.
    Wit: Henry Barradell, Rachel Godwin.
    Security, Mills Wills.        Page 273

POPE, Ephraim: Of Newport Parish. Leg. son William. D. June 15, 1793. R. December 2, 1793.
    Wit: James Hall, George Hall, Ann Hall.        Page 273

FOWLER, Elizabeth: Appraised by Joseph Duck, Lott Griffin, John Carr. R. January 6, 1794.        Page 273

MARSHALL, Dempsey: Appraised by Robert Holland, James Holland, James Johnson. Ordered March 26, 1792. R. January 6, 1794.    Page 275

CARR, John: Of Newport Parish. Leg. son Jacob, the land on which his grandfather lived; son Dempsey; son Elisha; daughter Honour; daughter Edey; daughter Priscilla; daughter Sally; wife. Ex., son Dempsey Carr. D. August 7, 1779. R. January 6, 1794.
    Wit: Joseph Duck, William Fleming, Dempsey Beal.
    Security, Joseph Duck.        Page 276

MICHAEL, John: Leg. daughter Rose, with reversion of bequest to my sisters, Patience and Esther Michael; my brother William Christian Michael; wife Mary, bill due from Joseph Jordan to my mother; brother Joachim Michael. Ex., Mr. Thomas Walke, Sr. D. October 26, 1793. R. December 2, 1793.
    Wit: Lawrence Baker, Henry Harrison, Ann Michael.
Thomas Walke, Sr., refused the executorship.        Page 276

TURNER, William: Account estate, examined by Mills Eley, William Eley, Eley Johnson. Signed, Joseph Spivey. R. February 3, 1794. Page 277

JORDAN, William: Leg. brother John after the death of my mother. D. August 31, 1793. R. February 3, 1794.
    Wit: John Pinhorn, Lydia Jordan, Robert Jordan.    Page 278

HANSON, Charles: Appraised by James Atkinson, James Barlow, William Atkinson, William Ward. Ordered February, 1794. R. April 7, 1794.
        Page 278

JAMES, William: Leg. daughter Elizabeth; daughter Nancy James. Exs., wife and brother Abel James. D. February 3, 1794. R. April 8, 1794.
    Wit: John Hutchinson, Josiah Bidgood, Richard Peirce.
    Security, William Hardy.        Page 279

JOHNSON, Robert: Account estate, examined by Joseph Duck and John Duck. Signed, Joseph Johnson. R. April 8, 1794.    Page 280

BAKER, Lawrence: Inventory of his personal estate. To negroes claimed by John Nelson of Surry County, to negroes claimed by Mary Baker. We, the subscribers, Justices of the Peace for the County of Isle of Wight, having examined the state of mind of Mr. Lawrence Baker of the said

County, do certify that it is our opinion that his insanity renders him incapable of transacting any kind of business whatsoever. Thomas Smith, ----- Young, Thomas Wrenn. R. May 7, 1794.  Page 280

DUCK, Jacob: Appraised by Jonathan Robertson, Thomas Carr, Willis Lankford. Ordered July 31, 1793. R. April 8, 1794.  Page 281

MATHEWS, William: Account estate, examined by John S. Wills and Emanuel Wills. Signed, John Jordan. R. April 7, 1794.  Page 283

DRUMMOND, Richard H.: Account estate, examined by William Casey, Charles Fulgham, ---- Young. Signed, William Drummond. R. May 6, 1794.
Page 284

SMITH, Joseph: Account estate, examined by George Purdie, James Wills, Thomas King. Signed, James Pitt. R. June 2, 1794.  Page 285

WOODLEY, John Sr.: Appraised by William Blunt, James Andrews, Samuel Webb, Arthur Applewhaite. Ordered November 15, 1791. R. June 2, 1794.
Page 285

FRIZZELL, Ralph: Account estate, examined by Brewer Godwin and Isham Pitt. R. June 2, 1794.  Page 287

WILLIAMS, John: Leg. brother Josiah Williams. Ex., brother Josiah Williams. R. June 2, 1794.
Wit: Nathaniel Gray, Joseph Driver, Richard Williams.
Security, Joseph Driver.  Page 287

ATKINSON, Amey: Account of sales. Ordered May 27, 1794. R. June 2, 1794.
Page 288

DARDEN, Hardy: Appraised by Michael Johnson, Obadiah Johnson, John Watkins. R. June 2, 1794.  Page 289

SIMMONS, Samuel: Account estate, examined by John S. Wills, Edmund Cosby, John Fearn and Benjamin Tynes. Signed, Drury Andrews. R. July 7, 1794.  Page 291

WILLS, John Scarsbrook: Of Newport Parish. Leg. son William Scarsbrook Wills; son Parker; son Willis, the tract I bought of Charles Butler of North Carolina, all but 50 acres, which I am going to convey to Capt. Edmund Godwin; daughter Nancy; daughter Hannah; daughter Lydia; son-in-law Thomas Darden; son-in-law Edmund Godwin; grandson Henry Wills Applewhaite, son of John Applewhaite; John Wills. I desire that my daughters, Nancy, Hannah and Lydia Wills and my sons Willis and Parker, my grandson Henry Wills Applewhaite and Nancy Milner, shall continue to live here, until my son William Scarsbrook Wills is married. Exs., Willis Wills, Emanuel Wills and Thomas Darden. D. June 11, 1794. R. July 7, 1794.
Wit: John Malcolm, Mills Wills, Elizabeth Ross.
Security, Francis Boykin, John Easson, John Godwin.  Page 291

WESTON, Charlotte: Appraised by Josiah Wail, Charles Groce, Henry Howard. R. July 7, 1794.  Page 293

WILLS, Miles: Appraised by Thomas King, Charles Fulgham, Richard Casey. Ordered October 15, 1792. R. July 7, 1794.  Page 293

NORSWORTHY, John: Account estate, examined by Thomas Smelley, Thomas Newby, William Baldwin. R. July 7, 1794.  Page 295

APPLEWHAITE, Josiah: Leg. daughter Mary; daughter Elizabeth; son Henry; daughter Patsey Gibbs; son Thomas; daughter Peggy Applewhaite. Ex., Nathaniel Gray. D. May 23, 1794. R. June 2, 1794.
    Wit: Charles Bagnall, Nathaniel Gray, William Bagnall, John Gibbs, Joseph Driver and James Wills deposed that the will was in the handwriting of the testator.
    Security, Joshua Bunkley and John Brown.    Page 295

GODWIN, Samuel, Sr.: Appraised by James Cutchins and James Mitchell. R. September 1, 1794.    Page 296

HAILE, John the elder: Leg. wife Hannah; son Simon; granddaughter Lavania Bracey; son Joseph; refers to son John, decd.; son-in-law Solomon Bracey; to Moses Hatchell; to William Hatchell; to Peter Hatchell; son Simon; to Diana Hatchell; after wife's death to Simon and Elizabeth Haile. Exs., wife and Simon Haile. D. January 1, 1792. R. September 1, 1794.
    Wit: Joseph Carpenter, William Segar, William Moody.
    Security, William Edwards.    Page 297

PARKER, Elias: Leg. son John; daughter Rachel Lawrence; grandson Nathaniel Wilkinson; granddaughter Elizabeth Wilkinson; daughter Mary Rand. Exs., friend Emanuel Wills and son John Parker. D. July 17, 1794. R. September 1, 1794.
    Wit: Richard Williams, James Pitt, Robert Jordan, Nathaniel Smith.
    Security, Robert Jordan and Nathaniel Gray.    Page 298

HAMPTON, Benjamin: Leg. son Francis; son Elijah; daughter Tabitha; daughter Martha; wife. Exs., sons Francis and Elijah Hampton. D. June 7, 1793. R. September 1, 1794.
    Wit: Thomas Smelley, Thomas Jordan, Thomas Gale.
    Security, Lemuel Murphry.    Page 298

WILLS, William Scarsbrook: Leg. sister Ann Wills; sister Hannah Wills. D. August 2, 1794. R. September 2, 1794.
    Wit: Willis Wills, Mills Wills.    Page 299

LAWRENCE, Hardy: Account estate, paid Patty, the widow; to Polly Roe, legacy from her father; paid Robert and Hardy Lawrence legacies; paid Mills Lawrence, guardian of Permelia and Ishmael, orphans. Examined by Elisha L. Ballard, Joseph Duck and Mills Lawrence. Signed, Robert Lawrence. R. October 6, 1794.    Page 299

CARR, John: Appraised by Willis Lankford, John Carr, Solomon Butler. Signed, Joseph Duck. R. October 6, 1794.    Page 301

PARKER, William: Account estate, to paid Martha Parker her part. Examined by Elisha L. Ballard and Solomon Edmunds. R. October 6, 1794.
    Page 301

SAUNDERS, Elizabeth, Sr.: Leg. son Thomas; son Henry; daughter Sarah Dunston; son John; son Joseph Saunders. Exs., son Henry and Robert Eley. D. March 17, 1779. R. October 6, 1794.
    Wit: Robert Eley, John Roberts, Elizabeth Roberts, Susannah Eley.
    Security, Henry Saunders.    Page 302

APPLEWHAITE, Elizabeth: granddaughter Mary Applewhaite; granddaughter Elizabeth Applewhaite; grandson Henry Applewhaite; grandson Thomas Garton; granddaughter Catherine Garton; grandson Thomas Applewhaite; granddaughter Peggy Applewhaite. Ex., Nathaniel Gray. D. ----------
R. October 6, 1794.
    Wit: Giles Daniels, John Giles.
    Security, Josiah Gray and Josiah Godwin.    Page 303

WEBB, Samuel: Leg. son Samuel; daughter Susannah Harrison Webb; daughter
     Nancy negroes left me by my brother James Webb. Exs., son Samuel and
     Willis Jones. D. January 28, 1792. R. October 6, 1794.
          Wit: David Bradley, William Outland.
          Security, Joseph McKinnell and Joseph Stallings.          Page 303

TYNES, Robert: Leg. son-in-law Charles Fulgham; son-in-law Thomas King; to
     Davis Day, who married my granddaughter Julianna Day; grandson Robert
     Tynes; wife Mary; son Timothy, my right in my father's estate. Ex.,
     friend Col. John S. Wills. D. September 21, 1790. R. December 1,
     1794.
          Wit: Lemuel Godfrey, William Goodrich, Robert Johnston,
          William Hubard.
          Security, Thomas King and John Easson.          Page 304

JOHNSON, Amos: Appraised by William Powell, Jethro Powell and John Watkins.
     Ordered October 30, 1793. R. December 2, 1794.          Page 305

PITT, Isham: Leg. to Henry Pitt son of Willis; to niece Polly Brown, daughter
     of John, with reversion of the bequest to the children of my cousin
     Charles Bagnall. Ex., Nathaniel Gray. D. ---------- R. December 2,
     1794.
          Wit: Joseph Driver, Jeremiah Lawrence, Giles Daniels.
          Security, John King.          Page 306

PINNER, Josiah: Leg. brother William Pinner, the plantation on which my
     mother now lives; the plantation on which Sweeting Pope lives to be
     sold; wife Tabitha; son John; provision for unborn child; to my three
     daughters. Exs., wife and William Powell of Nansemond County.
     D. September 15, 1794. R. December 1, 1794.
          Wit: Elizabeth Granberry, John Brown.
          Security, Willis Everett.          Page 307

JOHNSON, Henry: Leg. son John; daughter Honour Coggin; son Kinchen; grand-
     son Johnny Johnson of Kinchen; to grandson Robert Johnson, son of
     Kinchen; to grandson Joshua, son of John Coggin, Jr.; granddaughter
     Nancy Johnson, daughter of John; grandson Henry Coggin; grandson
     Jonathan Coggin. Exs., son John Johnson and Robert Eley, Sr.
     D. April 18, 1794. R. December 1, 1794.
          Wit: Thomas Holladay, Joseph Turner, John Eley, Jr.
          Security, Robert Holland and James Johnson.          Page 308

FRY, Mary: Leg. son Robert; daughter Ann Hubard; daughter Margaret; grand-
     son Andrew Reynolds; daughter Mary Ronald. Exs., son Robert and Mr.
     Andrew Ronald. D. May 26, 1783. R. October 6, 1794.
          Wit: Thomas Peirce, Mary Peirce.
          Security, William Hubard, William Patterson.          Page 309

HOLLAND, Job: Account estate, examined by Elijah Johnson, Mills Lawrence.
     Signed, Job Holland. R. December 2, 1794.          Page 309

LAWRENCE, Col. John: Appraised by Mills Eley, Wade Mountfort, James Johnson.
     Ordered January 21, 1788. R. December 2, 1794.          Page 310

LANKFORD, Isabella: Leg. mother Sarah Lankford. Extx., mother Sarah Lank-
     ford. D. September 3, 1794. R. December 2, 1794.
          Wit: Mills Eley, George Lankford.          Page 312

JONES, David: Leg. son Willis; daughter Frances; daughter Selah; daughter
     Constant; son Joseph; daughter Peggy; to wife with reversion to daughter
     Charlotte Jones. Extx., wife. D. May 17, 1793. R. January 5, 1795.
          Wit: William Barlow, Jesse Holleman, James Barlow.          Page 313

PHILLIPS, John, Sr.: Leg. son Mark; son Joel; son Benjamin; son John; wife
Selah; son Thomas; son Jesse; son Drury; daughter Elizabeth Murphry;
daughter Lucy Milner; daughter Sarah; daughter Selah; daughter Lucy
Phillips. D. November 29, 1794. R. January 5, 1795. Exs., wife and
son John Phillips.
    Wit: Emanuel Wills, Jacob Edwards, Elizabeth Edwards, Nancy
      Edwards.
    Security, Michael Murphry.            Page 313

JONES, Jacob: Leg. son Thomas; daughter Peggy; son John; daughter Lucy;
son Francis; son Riley; daughter Honour Jones. Exs., wife Frances
Jones, Charles Goodrich. D. October 25, 1794. R. January 5, 1795.
    Wit: Thomas Wrenn, Benjamin Shelley, Solomon Jones.
    Security, Philip Thomas, Solomon Jones.        Page 314

BEAL, Jacob: Leg. son Demcy; son Jacob; daughter Deliah; wife Elizabeth.
Exs., Absalom Beal and Joseph Duck. D. July 15, 1794. R. January 5,
1795.
    Wit: James Tallow, Robert Beal, Mills Beal, Jacob Johnson.
    Security, Robert Beal.             Page 315

LAWRENCE, Martha: Appraised by Joseph Duck, Francis Vaughan, Sion Boon.
Ordered, April 28, 1794. R. January 5, 1795.     Page 316

HAMPTON, Benjamin: Appraised by Thomas Smelley and Lemuel Murphry.
R. January 5, 1795.               Page 317

COUNCIL, John: Of Newport Parish. Leg. son Cutchins; daughter Sarah Gardner;
daughter Edy Tallow; granddaughter Peggy Council; son James Council.
Ex., son James Council. D. March 15, 1791. R. February 2, 1795.
    Wit: James Johnson, John Eley.
    Security, Jacob Johnson.            Page 317

POWELL, John: Leg. wife Sarah; daughter Catey; daughter Rhody; son Samuel;
son Lemuel; daughter Amy; son Howell; daughter Sally; daughter Tempy
Powell. Exs., sons Samuel and Lemuel Powell. D. July 28, 1793.
R. February 2, 1795.
    Wit: James Johnson, James Tomlin, Mills Fulgham, Mathew Fulgham.
    Security, James Johnson.           Page 318

GOODSON, Thomas: Leg. wife Priscilla; eldest son John; son James; son
Thomas; son William to be brought up by William Barlow and his wife,
said son to have the plantation on which they live at their deaths;
money to be divided between Josiah and Sampson Goodson; daughter Patsey;
daughter Rebeccah. Exs., wife Priscilla, William Barlow and Thomas
Wrenn, Sr. D. December 5, 1794. R. February 2, 1795.
    Wit: Thomas Wrenn, Sr., William Ward, William Goodson.
    Security, John Goodrich.           Page 320

PINNER, John: Account estate, examined by Robert Driver and William Jordan.
Signed, Josiah Pinner. R. April 7, 1795.       Page 321

PINNER, Josiah: Appraised by Robert Driver, William Jordan, William Shivers.
Ordered December 26, 1794. R. April 6, 1795.    Page 321

EDMUNDS, James: Leg. wife Jane Edmunds. Extx., wife. D. January 26, 1795.
R. April 6, 1795.
    Wit: James Taylor, John Coggin, Henry Coggin.
    Security, Robert Cooke.            Page 322

MANGAM, Henry, Sr.: Leg. son Henry; son Richard; son Samuel; son John; son
Goodrich; daughter Martha Carrell; refers to daughter Ann Jones, decd.;

daughter Hannah Chapman; son Britain. Exs., sons Henry and Richard.
D. November 17, 1790. R. April 7, 1795.
    Wit: William Person, Joseph Person, Josiah Mangam, Samuel Gray.
    Security, Lewis Chapman.        Page 323

BRIDGER, Joseph: Of Smithfield. Leg. guardian Mallory Todd; to Mary Degge
of Smithfield; to cousin William Harvey; to cousin Joseph Hodsden; to
Mallory Moore Todd; to Fanny the daughter of Mallory Todd; to aunt
Esther Bridger. Ex., Mallory Todd, the elder of Smithfield.
D. January 17, 1795. R. April 6, 1795.
    Wit: Merit Moore Robinson, John Casey, William Garton.
    Security, Merit M. Robinson, William Garton.    Page 323

JONES, Willis: Leg. wife; sister Sally; sister Peggy; worthy father. Ex.,
William Boyce. D. December 7, 1794. R. April 6, 1795.
    Wit: Thomas Wrenn, James Thomas.
    Security, Thomas Copher.       Page 324

FRY, Mary: Appraised by Scott Hollowell, William Hollowell, William Patteson.
R. April 7, 1795.        Page 325

YOUNG, Francis: Appraised by Thomas King, Charles Fulgham, Richard Taylor.
Ordered January 14, 1795. R. April 7, 1795.    Page 326

COPELAND, Sarah: Leg. son John Duck; daughter Salley Daughtry; daughter
Martha Johnson; son Joseph Duck. Ex., son John Duck. D. March 10,
1794. R. June 1, 1795.
    Wit: Elias Johnson, Juliet Holland.
    Security, Joseph Duck.      Page 327

LIGHTFOOT, Henry: Leg. estate to Mary Wills to maintain her children, Sharp
and Polly, at her death to my two children Sharp and Polly, with reversion of bequest to Sally Godwin Gray. Exs., Mary Wills and friend
James Gray. D. January 24, 1794. R. June 1, 1795.
    Wit: John House, John Handcock, Ann Hancock.
    Security, Josiah Gray.      Page 328

HARRIS, John: Leg. brother Lewis; sister Martha; sister Ann Harris. Ex.,
brother Lewis Harris. D. February 20, 1795. R. June 1, 1795.
    Wit: William Hatchell, Mills Stevens, Benjamin Tynes.
    Security, Benjamin Tynes.    Page 329

GOODRICH, Elizabeth: Leg. brother William; sister Sarah; to Thomas Goodrich,
son of William; estate between my two brothers and sister, Sarah,
Charles and William Goodrich. Ex., brother Charles Goodrich.
D. January 1, 1795. R. June 1, 1795.
    Wit: Thomas Wrenn, James Goodrich, Charles Goodrich.
    Security, James Carrell.     Page 330

HARRIS, Ann: Appraised by Benjamin Tynes, Mathew Tomlin, Joseph Moody.
Ordered January 12, 1795. R. June 1, 1795.    Page 331

BROWN, James: Account estate, examined by Sampson Wilson, William Hardy,
John J. Wheadon. Signed, George Mallicote. R. June 1, 1795.
        Page 331

MALECOTE, George: Appraised by John J. Wheadon, James Atkinson, Sampson
Wilson, John Shelley. R. June 1, 1795.    Page 333

THOMPSON, William: Appraised by John J. Wheadon, James Atkinson, John
Shelley. Ordered March 12, 1795. R. June 1, 1795.    Page 334

JORDAN, Josiah: Account estate, examined by John Barber and William Baldwin. R. June 1, 1795. Page 336

JONES, Jacob: Appraised by Charles Goodrich, Shadrack Goodrich, Benjamin Jones. R. June 1, 1795. Page 336

SCOTT, William: Account estate, to 1/3 paid Peggy Scott; to 1/3 paid Exum Scott by Jacob Randolph, Adm. of William Scott; Joseph Pretlow, 1/3 estate paid by Jacob Randolph. Examined by John Barber, Thomas Smelley, William Smelley. R. June 1, 1795. Page 338

LIGHTFOOT, Bartholomew: Account estate, cash furnished the children of Mary Willett; for Schooling Fanny Willett. Examined in front of Joshua Bunkley, Ex. of Joseph Chapman, decd. and Lemuel Lightfoot, surviving administrator of Bartholomew Lightfoot have settled the account between the said Joseph Chapman and estate of Bartholomew Lightfoot, Sr., by George Benn, Thomas King, James Johnston, Nathaniel Gray. R. June 7, 1795. Page 343

LIGHTFOOT, Bartholomew, Jr.: Account estate with John Scarsbrook Wills, to Lemuel Lightfoot, bought at his father's sale. Examined in the presence of Willis Wills, acting Ex. of John S. Wills and Lemuel Lightfoot, surviving Adm. of Bartholomew Lightfoot the elder, by George Benn, Thomas King, James Johnston. R. June 6, 1795. Page 345

MALCOLM, John: Leg. Molly Baker 1/4 of my estate; brother William Malcolm. Ex., attorney Merit Robinson, Esq. D. May 12, 1795. Codicil: If my brother Malcolm should die before he returns to America, then his part to go for the support and education of Frank's two children, Moses Moseley and Richard Moseley, which trust and confidence I place in the hands of my friend, Mr. David Bradley. D. May 12, 1795. R. June 6, 1795.
Wit: Elizabeth Bradley, Francis Young, Bennett Young.
Security, Emanuel Wills. Page 345

FRIZZELL, Joshua: Of Newport Parish. Leg. daughter Temperance Holladay; wife Julia; granddaughter Julia Holladay; grandson Thomas Holladay; grandson John Holladay. Exs., Thomas Hall and John Hall. D. ------- 1792. R. June 6, 1795.
Wit: Page 346

ATKINSON, Benjamin: Leg. daughter Jemima Gray; daughter Ann Lupo; son Benjamin; daughter Abigail; daughter Pheby; daughter Mary Fones Atkinson. Ex., son Benjamin Atkinson. D. June 13, 1794. R. July 6, 1795.
Wit: James Lancaster, Sarah Bell, Olive Gray.
Security, William White, William Gay. Page 347

EDWARDS, Jacob: Leg. son Jesse; daughter Nancy; daughter Rebecca; daughter Elizabeth; daughter Lucy; wife Rebecca. Exs., wife and Michael Murphry. D. March 31, 1795. R. July 6, 1795.
Wit: Willis Babb, Bolin Copeland, Elizabeth Murphry.
Security, William Brock. Page 347

MANGUM, Richard: Appraised by Benjamin Jones, Jacob Stringfield, Samuel Gray. Ordered April 11, 1795. R. July 6, 1795. Page 348

PARKER, Elias: Appraised by Nathaniel Gray, Robert Jordan, Richard Williams. R. July 6, 1795. Page 351

GODWIN, Jonathan: Account estate, examined in the presence of George Benn and Bennett Young, who intermarried with Polly Benn Godwin, heiress to said deceased; by Emanuel Wills, Thomas King and Thomas Hall. D. 1789.

R.  July 6, 1795.                                                     Page 353

ELEY, Benjamin:  Appraised by John Barber, William Smelley, Eley Johnson.
      Ordered October 22, 1794.  R.  September 7, 1795.           Page 355

ROBERTS, John, Sr.:  Leg. son John; son William; son-in-law William Watkins;
      daughter Sarah Maclenney; son Wright; daughter Charity.  Ex., son
      Wright Roberts.  D.  January 12, 1793.  R.  September 7, 1794.
            Wit:  Mills Eley, Robert Watkins, Jesse Bracey.
            Security, Richard Pope.                              Page 359

JONES, Frederick:  Account estate, examined by John Fearn, James Johnson,
      Benjamin Tynes.  R.  September 7, 1795.                    Page 360

SYKES, Mary:  Appraised by Thomas Smelley, William Smelley, William Eley.
      R.  September 7, 1795.                                     Page 360

SAUNDERS, Elizabeth:  Appraised by Henry Saunders, John Roberts, Wright
      Roberts.  R.  September 7, 1795.                           Page 361

FULGHAM, Hezekiah:  Account estate, examined by John Fearn, James Johnson,
      Thomas Bowden.  Signed, Jesse Fulgham.  R.  September 7, 1795.
                                                                 Page 362

SMITH, Nicholas:  Leg. Sarah Lane; brother Samuel Smith; wife Martha.  Extx.,
      wife Martha Smith.  D.  August 19, 1795.  R.  October 5, 1795.
            Wit:  Willis Wills, Thomas Carrell, Emanuel Wills.
            Security, Samuel Smith, Thomas Joyner.               Page 363

ELEY, Robert, Sr.:  Leg. daughter Elizabeth Council; son-in-law Robert
      Lawrence; granddaughters, Nancy, Betsey, Amey and Patience Lawrence;
      grandson Robert Lawrence; son Robert; son John Boykin Eley; wife
      Cherry; daughter Cherry; refers to deceased daughter Sarah Lawrence.
      Ex., son Robert Eley.  D.  August 30, 1795.  R.  October 5, 1795.
            Wit:  Mills Eley, Joseph L. Bridger, James Gay.
            Security, Mills Eley.                                Page 363

MINTZ, John:  Leg. wife Sarah.  Extx., wife Sarah.  D.  August 26, 1788.
      R.  October 5, 1795.
            Wit:  Benjamin Goodrich, Benjamin Shelley, Nancy Shelley.
            Security, James Morris.                              Page 365

WHITFIELD, Milley:  Appraised by Scutchins Council, Jacob Beal, David Eley.
      Ordered December 23, 1794.  R.  October 5, 1795.           Page 367

JONES, Richard:  Account estate, examined by Thomas Wrenn, William Gay,
      Benjamin Jones.  Signed, James Wills, Sheriff.  R.  October 5, 1795.
                                                                 Page 367

GIBBS, John:  Account estate, examined by George Benn and Thomas King.
      Signed, Elizabeth Gibbs.  R.  October 5, 1795.             Page 368

COOPER, Stephen:  Account estate, examined by John J. Wheadon and Sampson
      Wilson.  Signed, William Haynes.  R.  October 5, 1795.     Page 369

FLEMING, William:  Account estate, to cash paid John Fleming, decd., cash
      paid estate of Mary Fleming, cash paid John Weatherly.  Examined by
      Elisha L. Ballard and Joseph Duck.  R.  October 5, 1795.  Signed,
      Elijah Johnson.                                            Page 370

PARKER, Frederick:  Account estate, to paid Brewer Godwin.  Examined by
      Thomas King and William Patrich.  Signed, H. John Burgess and Richard
      Parker.  R.  October 5, 1795.                              Page 371

WESTRAY, Edmund: Leg. son Jeremiah; daughter Sophia Vick; son Samuel; son Joseph; son Elias; son Levy. Exs., sons, Jeremiah and Levi Westray. D. July 13, 1795. R. December 7, 1795.
    Wit: Nelson Westray, Jacob Parkerson, John Parnall.
    Security, Joseph Westray.                       Page 373

GOODRICH, William: Leg. son James; son Thomas the land adjoining that given him by his aunt Elizabeth Goodrich; to William Ward, son of Sally Ward; to Francis Ward, son of Sally Ward; to my wife; son Benjamin; son Bell; daughter Chloe; daughter Lucy; daughter Jane Goodrich. Ex., son James Goodrich. D. August 23, 1795. R. December 7, 1795.
    Wit: Lewis Jordan, William Bailey, Benjamin Ward.       Page 374

McCLENNY, Michael: Leg. wife Sarah; son Thomas; daughter Dicey; daughter Chacey; son John; son Thomas; son Jesse; son Zachariah. Ex., son Zachariah McClenny. D. May 10, 1795. R. December 7, 1795.
    Wit: Elizabeth Spencer, Samuel Peirce, John Darden.      Page 374

WHEELER, Jacob: Leg. wife Anne; daughter Elizabeth; daughter Miriam Wheeler. Ex., Benjamin Darden. D. January 11, 1794. R. December 7, 1795.
    Wit: Jacob Johnson, Jacob Beal, James Tallow, Jr.
    Security, James Tallough, James Johnson.         Page 375

MINTZ, John: Appraised by John J. Wheadon, Benjamin Jones, Jesse Gray. R. December 7, 1795.                        Page 375

STEVENS, John: Account estate, examined by William Baldwin, Eli Eley, Robert Eley. Signed, Robert Stevens. R. December 7, 1795. Page 376

STEVENS, John: Estate, signed James Holland.           Page 377

DRIVER, Charles: Account estate, examined by John Driver and Edmund Godwin. Signed, John Driver. D. 1771. R. December 7, 1795.    Page 377

MANGAM, Henry: Appraised by Jacob Stringfield, Benjamin Jones, Samuel Gray. R. December 7, 1795.                        Page 379

HOLLOWELL, William: Account estate, examined by Jesse Atkins, William Hardy, James Brantley. Exs., Scott and William Hollowell. R. December 7, 1795.                                  Page 380

CROCKER, John: Account estate, examined by Jesse Atkins, James Johnston, Charles Broadfield. Signed, Mary and William Crocker. Ordered September, 1787. R. December 7, 1795.           Page 380

CROCKER, Mary: Account estate, examined by William Blunt and Jesse Atkins. Signed, William Crocker. R. December 7, 1795.      Page 381

GODWIN, John: Account estate, examined by Joseph Fulgham and Ralph West. Signed, John Godwin. R. December 7, 1795.         Page 382

PASTEUR, John: Of Smithfield. Leg. wife Honour; daughter Polly; daughter Elizabeth; at the death of my mother-in-law Elizabeth Pasteur my house and lot in Hampton to be sold; son Charles; son Solomon W. Pasteur. Exs., Solomon Wilson and Arthur Applewhaite. D. August 21, 1794. R. December 2, 1794.
    Wit: Thomas Ashlock, Thomas Blow, James Young.      Page 383

JOHNSON, Robert: Account estate, examined by Drury Andrews, John Fearn and Thomas Bowden. Dated, 1785. R. January 4, 1796. Signed, James Johnson.                            Page 384

POWELL, Stephen: Account estate, examined by Drury Andrews, John Fearn, Thomas Bowden. Signed, Robert Johnson. R. January 4, 1796. Page 385

HAYES, Arthur: Account estate, examined by Thomas Wrenn, William Gay, Joseph Stallings. Signed, James Pitman. R. January 4, 1796.
Page 385

SAUNDERS, Elizabeth: Account estate, examined by Robert Eley and William Baldwin. Signed, Robert Eley, Sr. R. September 4, 1796. Page 386

GIBBS, Gabriel: Account estate, examined by Lawrence Baker, Richard Crump, Jesse Atkins, James Young. Signed, William Patterson. R. January 4, 1796. Page 386

BENN, Pompy: Leg. brother Minor Denson. Ex., brother Minor Denson. D. December 28, 1789. R. February 1, 1796.
Wit: Scott Hollowell, Robert Glover, James Outland. Page 387

WILLIAMS, David: Account estate, examined by Brewer Godwin, Nathaniel Gray, William Waltham. Signed, Joseph Driver. R. February 1, 1796.
Page 387

JOHNSON, Abraham, Sr.: Account estate, examined by Miles Darden and Eley Johnson. Signed, Abraham Johnson, Jr. R. April 5, 1796. Page 388

WOODLEY, John: Account estate, examined by James Wills, Francis Boykin, Arthur Applewhaite. Signed, Andrew Woodley. R. April 5, 1796.
Page 388

GOODRICH, Elizabeth: Appraised by Isham Jordan, Benjamin Ward, Samuel White. D. June 5, 1795. R. April 5, 1796. Page 389

GODWIN, Jonathan: Appraised by Ralph West, Charles Groce, Richard Williams. Ordered March 11, 1789. R. April 5, 1796. Page 390

WATKINS, Priscilla: Leg. son Jesse; son William; daughter Elizabeth, to all my children. Ex., son Jesse Watkins. D. October 9, 1795. R. April 4, 1796.
Wit: Jethro Powell, John Inglish.
Security, Robert Watkins. Page 391

BARLOW, Thomas: Leg. John Barlow, son of William Barlow, decd. Ex., John Barlow. D. January 22, 1796. R. April 5, 1796.
Wit: Benjamin Goodrich, William Ward, Nathaniel Barlow. Page 391

GOODSON, Thomas, Sr.: Leg. wife Sarah; son Jordan Thomas Goodson; to the children of my daughter Mary Jordan, deceased; to children of daughter Hardy Braswell; to children of daughter Sarah Mintz; daughter Sarah Jones; daughter Frances Jones; daughter Nancy Goodson. Extx., wife. D. September 24, 1793. R. April 4, 1796.
Wit: William Hardy, Jesse Gray, George Gray. Page 392

JORDAN, Joseph: Leg. wife Wilmoth; son James Williamson Jordan, land adjoining Armistead Vellines and Capt. Charles Fulgham; daughter Polly Jordan. Exs., wife and son James Williamson Jordan. D. June 5, 1795. R. June 6, 1796.
Wit: William Boyce, Charles B. Taylor, Will Bailey.
Security, William Boykin, John Urquhart, Thomas Fearn. Page 393

ELEY, Milly: Leg. son Michael, the land which belonged to his father, Benjamin Eley; daughter Lydia Ballard; daughter Holland Barkley Eley, land in Nansemond County; daughter Lydia, the plantation on which my father,

John Barkley lived; to Celia Peirce. Exs., friends, William Eley and Mills Eley. D. February 3, 1796. R. June 6, 1796.
    Wit: Thomas Smelley, Mourning Eley, Betsey Eley.
    Security, Rix Lawrence, Thomas Smelley.          Page 394

COPHER, James: Leg. wife Mary; daughter Olif Gray; daughter Joanna Cox; daughter Cloe Gray; son James; daughter Mary Edwards; to daughters, Ann, Sally, Rhodda, Jemima and Winifred Copher, the land on which Thomas Copher, decd., lived. Ex., son James Copher and James Gwaltney. D. December 20, 1794. R. June 6, 1796.
    Wit: John Wombwell, John Gwaltney, Benjamin Wombwell.
    Security, Joseph Stallings and Ishmael Moody.      Page 395

JORDAN, James: Leg. wife Mary; daughter Sally; son Robert; daughter Mary. Extx., wife Mary Jordan. D. January 31, 1796. R. June 6, 1796.
    Wit: Thomas Hall, George Murphry, Nicholas Goodson.
    Security, James Morris.            Page 396

WILLS, Thomas: Account estate, examined by Josiah Gray, Nathaniel Gray, Thomas Hall. Ex., John S. Wills, decd. R. June 6, 1796.    Page 398

JONES, Willis: Appraised by William Gay, Joseph Stallings, William Stallings. R. June 6, 1796.                Page 398

WATKINS, Priscilla: Account estate, examined by John Watkins, Robert Watkins, John English. Signed, Jesse Watkins. R. June 6, 1796.
                              Page 399

JOYNER, John: Account estate, examined by Emanuel Wills and Dolphin Driver. Signed, John Joyner. R. June 7, 1796.        Page 400

DERRING, Emelius: Account estate, examined by James Atkinson, Sampson Wilson, John J. Wheadon. Signed, William Hardy. R. June 6, 1796.
                              Page 401

ROUNDTREE, William: Of Newport Parish. Leg. Sally Garner, with reversion of bequest to her daughter Nancy Garner. D. ---------- R. July 5, 1796.
    Wit: James Martin, John Wacker (?), Mary Parsley.
    Administration granted Benjamin Wootten.
    Security, Thomas King.              Page 402

DAVIS, William: Of Newport Parish. Leg. wife Catey; son John, land inherited from my father John Davis; son William; daughter Sarah; daughter Catherine Matilda Davis; daughter Mary; daughter Holland a judgement which I hold against the estate of John Michael, decd.; William Christian. Exs., son-in-law Thomas Whitfield, friend Copeland Parker and Joseph Cutchin. D. July 9, 1796. R. September 5, 1796.
    Wit: Francis Young.                Page 402

BARLOW, Frances: Appraised by John J. Wheadon, William Gay, Joseph Stallings. R. September 5, 1796.           Page 404

STUCKY, Edmund: Account estate, examined by Brewer Godwin, Mills Wills, Peter Cunningham. Signed, Elizabeth Stucky. R. September 5, 1796.
                              Page 405

WILLS, John Scarsbrook:  Account estate, examined by George Benn, Ralph
West, Nathaniel Gray.  Signed, Willis Wills and Emanuel Wills.
R.  September 5, 1796.                                        Page 1

BRIDGER, John:  Account estate, paid John Williamson, legacy left him by
Mrs. Campbell; paid Josiah Waile, the legacy left his children; paid
Mrs. Quay, the legacy left by Mrs. Campbell; paid Mrs. Quay for the
support of Nancy Bridger.  Signed, John Scarsbrook Wills.

BRIDGER, John:  Account estate, paid Josiah and John Williams legacy left
them by Mrs. Campbell; paid William L. Campbell, the legacy left his
wife by Mrs. Campbell; paid Isaac Hall a legacy left him by Mrs.
Campbell; paid Elizabeth Bridger.  Examined by George Benn and Ralph
West.  Signed by Willis Wills and Emanuel Wills, Exs. of John Scarsbrook Wills.  R.  September 5, 1796.                          Page 5

COPHER, James:  Appraised by John Holleman, Simmons Gwaltney, John Wombwell.
R.  September 5, 1796.                                        Page 5

CROCKER, Anthony:  Leg. Rebecca Parnall; Dolly Addison; Anthony Addison;
Molly Pitman; Aron Pitman; John Pitman; Nancy Edwards; Bethreat
Lawler (?); Drue Crocker; Joseph Crocker; Hugh Montgomery; Thomas
Addison.  Ex., Thomas Addison.  D.  November 29, 1795.  R.  Septem-
ber 5, 1796.
          Wit:  Jacob Stringfield, James Pitman, Sampson Harrison.
          Security, William Addison.                         Page 8

COUNCIL, Lemuel:  Of Newport Parish.  Leg. wife Sarah; son James; son John;
daughter-in-law Elizabeth Jones; son-in-law William Jones.  Exs., wife
and brother Miles Council.  D.  December 23, 1796.  R.  September 5,
1796.
          Wit:  Elijah Johnson, Mathew Vaughan, Miles Council,
               Epaphroditus Butler.
          Security, William Faulk, Mathew Vaughan.           Page 9

POPE, John:  Account estate, examined by William Jordan, John Everett.
Signed, Josiah Pinner.  R.  September 5, 1796.               Page 10

OUTLAND, Sarah:  Nuncupative will, proven by Francis Jones, Justice of
Nansemond County, William Baldwin and John Outland, who calls her his
daughter-in-law.
          Affidavit of William Baldwin:  that he heard Sarah Outland his
daughter-in-law declare that her sister Nancy Babb should possess all
the land that they had purchased of their brother William Babb, the
said land being now in the occupation of the said William Baldwin.
D.  August 1, 1796.
          Affidavit of John Outland, that he heard his daughter-in-law say:
above statement.  D.  July 11, 1796.  R.  October 3, 1796.  Page 10

CHAPMAN, John, Sr.:  Appraised by Andrew Woodley, John Thomas, William
Crocker.  Ordered November 12, 1794.  R.  October 3, 1796.  Page 11

ELEY, Robert:  Appraised by James Johnson, Thomas Bowden, James Gay, James
Mercer.  R.  December 5, 1796.                               Page 12

WHEELER, Jacob: Appraised by Mathew Daughtry, John Darden, Kinchen Darden. R. December 5, 1796. Page 12

DAVIS, William: Appraised by John Goodrich, William Casey, Mathew Wills. Signed, J. Parker. R. December 6, 1796. Page 14

FULGHAM, Joseph: Account estate, paid George Benn, guardian of Joseph and Charlotte Fulgham, cash paid Peter Cunningham per spouse; cash paid myself for my wife's part. Signed, John Cunningham. Examined by John Godwin and Robert R. Read. R. December 6, 1796. Page 15

FATHERLY, Francis: Leg. daughter Ann Bowen; daughter Mealy; son Mexico; son Frederick; son Fairfax; daughter Lavisha; granddaughter Elizabeth Moody. Ex., son Fairfax Fatherly. D. December 10, 1796. R. January 2, 1797.
Wit: John Murphry, Charles Murphry.
Security, John Murphry. Page 17

JAMES, Abel: Leg. son John; daughter Betsey; daughter Tabitha. Extx., wife. D. October 20, 1796. R. January 2, 1797.
Wit: James Pitt, Polly Pitt.
Security, John J. Wheadon. Page 18

COPHER, Benjamin: Leg. sister Sealah; brothers John and Thomas Copher, the land formerly belonging to my father Benjamin Copher; sister's son Ridley Cofer; to mother Christian Copher. Ex., Abraham Jones. D. October 16, 1796. R. January 2, 1797.
Wit: Benjamin Goodrich, Solomon Jones, William Jones.
Security, Solomon Jones. Page 18

HODSDEN, William: Leg. sister Betsey Hodsden, the land which fell to me by the death of Joseph Bridger, whenever the said land is sold by the rest of the legatees; brother Joseph Bridger. Ex., Ralph West. D. November 26, 1795. R. January 2, 1797.
Wit: James Young, John Casey, Thomas Goodson, Jr. Page 19

FULGHAM, Michael: Of Newport Parish. Leg. daughter Holland Jones; son Allen; daughter Betsey; son Eley, the part of his grandfather Tomlin's estate, which falls to me; to my daughters all that part of my estate that comes from their grandmother's uncle and aunt. John Tomlin, guardian to my son Eley Fulgham. Exs., John Tomlin and John Woodward. D. January 26, 1794. R. January 2, 1797.
Wit: John Woodward, Jesse Fulgham, Mills Stevens.
Security, Jesse Fulgham. Page 19

CUTCHIN, Joseph: Account estate, paid John Sinclair for his wife's estate; paid John Pasteur for legacy due his wife; paid Arthur Applewhaite for legacy due his wife; paid William Derring for legacy due his wife. Signed, Solomon Wilson. R. January 2, 1797. Page 21

CUTCHIN, Joseph and estate of Mathew Cutchins: Examined by William Patrick, John Easson and Thomas King. Signed, Solomon Wilson. R. January 2, 1796. Page 22

WOODWARD, William: Leg. son John George Woodward; son William Hall Woodward; daughter Sally Woodward. Exs., sons, John George Woodward and William Hall Woodward. D. December 15, 1794. R. February 6, 1797.
Wit: Thomas Saunders, Joseph Westray, Bennett Peirce.
Security, Bennett Peirce, Henry Coggin. Page 27

DUCK, Joseph: Leg. wife Christian; son Joseph; daughter Pherba; daughter Millicent; son Jacob Holland Duck. Exs., wife and son Joseph Duck.

D. December 16, 1796. R. February 6, 1797.
  Wit: Dempsey Carr, Willis Lankford, Hardy Parker.
  Security, Willis Lankford, Godwin Councill.          Page 28

EDWARDS, J'Anson: Leg. eldest daughter Polly; daughter Leodicia; son John R.
  Edwards; wife Sarah and unborn child. Exs., wife, Newit Edwards and
  Benjamin Ward. D. November 4, 1796. R. February 6, 1797.
      Wit: Gray Carrell, Sampson White, John Mallicote.
      Security, Joseph Stallings.                      Page 29

WOMBWELL, Joseph: Appraised by James Gwaltney, William Gray, William White.
  R. April 3, 1797.                                    Page 30

REYNOLDS, Richard: Account estate, examined by George Benn, Willis Wills,
  Robert R. Read. Signed, Rowland Reynolds. R. April 3, 1797.
                                                       Page 32

PHILLIPS, John: Account estate, examined by William Jordan and Thomas Newby.
  Signed, John Phillips. R. February 6, 1797.          Page 34

SAUNDERS, John: Account estate, examined by John Pope, John Saunders,
  Richard Pope. Ordered September 6, 1796. R. February 6, 1797.
                                                       Page 35

MARSHALL, Dempsey: Account estate, examined by Sion Boon, Robert Eley, James
  Johnson. D. February 6, 1797. R. September 6, 1797. Signed, Mills
  Wills.                                               Page 35

JOHNSON, Amos: Account estate, which was received by the following: James
  McClenny, Abrahm Johnson, John Johnson and John Denson. Examined by
  Robert Eley, James Johnson, Thomas Bowden and Sion Boon. Signed,
  Mills Eley. D. 1792. R. February 6, 1797.            Page 38

CORBETT, Samuel: Account estate, examined by Mills Eley, Mills Lawrence.
  Signed, John Corbett. R. February 6, 1797.           Page 39

TOMLIN, Nicholas: Leg. wife Rebecca; brother Mathew; brother John; son
  Joseph; son Lewis; daughter Martha; daughter Lucresy Tomlin. Exs.,
  brothers Mathew and John Tomlin. D. August 22, 1795. R. June 5,
  1797.
      Wit: Joseph Westray, Humphrey Revell.
      Security, Joseph Westray.                        Page 40

JONES, Celia: Account estate, paid Gray Carrell legacy left Celia Jones;
  paid the guardians of Joseph and Peggy Jones; paid the orphans of
  Frances Barlow her proportion, by a legacy left in the will of Willis
  Jones. Examined by Nathaniel Gray and Bennett Young. Signed, William
  Boyce. R. June 5, 1797.                              Page 41

CROCKER, Anthony: Appraised by William Gay, Jacob Stringfield, James Pitman,
  Joseph Stringfield. R. June 5, 1797.                 Page 42

BUTLER, John: Account estate, examined by Nathaniel Gray and Thomas Hall.
  Signed, Josiah Wills. R. June 5, 1797.               Page 42

DAVIS, William: Account estate, examined by John Easson, George Purdie, M.
  Todd, William Patrick. Signed, Josiah Parker. R. June 5, 1797.
                                                       Page 44

BARLOW, Frances: Account estate, examined by John Parker and Nathaniel Gray.
  Paid Mildred Barlow, balance of an execution against Isham Jordan, as
  administrator of David Jones, decd., proportion of a legacy left Celia

Jones by the will of Willis Jones. William Boyce's bond signed by James and Henry Pitt. Signed, William Boyce. R. July 3, 1797.

Page 47

BARNES, John: Appraised by Michael Johnson, Elisha Johnson and Elias Johnson. Ordered May 27, 1797. R. July 3, 1797. Page 49

BARNES, John: Account estate, examined by Elijah Johnson and Michael Johnson. Signed, Abel Johnson. R. July 3, 1797. Page 49

CHAPMAN, Rhoda: Appraised by Robert R. Read, Josiah Wail, Charles Groce. Ordered November, 1796. R. July 3, 1797. Page 50

CALLECOTE, Harwood: Appraised by John J. Wheadon, James Atkinson. Ordered October 21, 1793. R. July 3, 1797. Page 50

CALLECOTE, Harwood: Account estate, examined by Thomas Wrenn, Sr., William Atkinson, James Barlow. Florentina Callecote was charged with many items, to Martha Jordan for boarding Ann, daughter of John Jordan, decd., Thomas Jordan, guardian of Ann Jordan. Signed, Lewis Jordan. R. July 3, 1797. Page 53

WOMBWELL, Britain: Appraised by Ishmael Moody, Thomas Wombwell, Jacob Stringfield, Joseph Stringfield. Ordered September 23, 1796. R. July 3, 1797. Page 53

ELEY, John: Account estate, examined by S. Wilson, John Easson and William Patrick. Signed, Thomas King. R. July 4, 1797. Page 54

WILLIAMS, Josiah: Leg. Josiah Hunter son of Frances Hunter with reversion of bequest to Polly Driver Whitfield; Martha Pitt; Sally Daniel; Betsey Daniel; Nancy Whitfield Driver, the balance due me from estate of John Williams to be divided among Martha Pitt, Sally Daniel, Betsey Daniel, Polly Driver Whitfield and Willis Driver. Ex., Joseph Driver.
D. June 13, 1797. R. July 3, 1797.
Wit: Nathaniel Gray, Henry Pitt, Julia Williams.
Security, Joshua Hunt. Page 57

CARRELL, William: Account estate, examined by John J. Wheadon, Sampson Wilson, Timothy Tynes. Signed, William Gray, James Pyland and Mary Carrell. R. July 3, 1797. Page 58

WATKINS, Priscilla: Account estate, examined by Robert Eley, Mills Eley and Robert Watkins. Signed, Jesse Watkins. R. September 4, 1797.
Page 59

BUTLER, Charles: Appraised by Josiah Wills, Lemuel Lightfoot. Ordered March, 1785. R. September 4, 1797. Page 60

HAWKINS, Samuel: Account estate, examined by William Goodwin, James G. Murrah and Thomas Hancock. Signed, William Rand Smith and Joseph Parker. R. September 4, 1797. Page 61

HOLLADAY, Samuel, Jr.: Appraised by Joshua Bunkley, William Smith, William Goodwin. Ordered October 8, 1796. R. September 4, 1797. Page 64

REYNOLDS, Richard: Account estate, examined by Willis Wills, Robert R. Read, George Benn. Signed, Rowland Reynolds. R. September 4, 1797.
Page 66

ELEY, Milley: Appraised by Eley Johnson, Jethro Powell, Wright Roberts, John Denson. Ordered February 18, 1796. R. September 4, 1797.
Page 67

WOODWARD, William: Appraised by Mathew Tomlin, James Johnson, Jesse Fulgham, John G. Woodward. R. September 4, 1797. Page 73

BARLOW, Benjamin: Account estate, examined by Davis Day and William Casey. Signed, John Goodrich. R. September 4, 1797. Page 74

BARLOW, Nathaniel: Appraised by W. Goodson, Lewis Jordan, William Atkinson. Ordered June 27, 1797. R. September 4, 1797. Page 76

DICKINSON, Chastity: Leg. brother Charles Groce; sister Martha Reynolds; to Janet Davis. Ex., brother Charles Groce. D. April 6, 1797. R. September 4, 1797.
  Wit: Richard Bidgood, Nancy Newman, George Baines. Page 76

MURRAY, Amey: Account estate, examined by Samuel Holladay, Jr., Joshua Bunkley and William Smith. Signed, James G. Murrah. R. September 4, 1797. Page 78

MURRAY, Amey: Appraised by William Smith, Joshua Bunkley and William Goodwin. Ordered November 20, 1794. R. September 4, 1797. Page 77

WHITFIELD, Milley: Account estate, examined by James Wills, Robert Eley, Jacob Johnson. Signed, Ivey Whitfield. R. September 4, 1797.
Page 79

WHITFIELD, Miles: Account estate, examined by James Wills, Robert Eley and Jacob Johnson. Signed, David Eley and Ivey Whitfield. R. September 4, 1797. Page 81

DAUGHTRY, Joshua: Account estate, examined by Abia Beal and Jacob Johnson. Signed, Jacob Beal. R. September 4, 1797. Signed by Absolom Beal, Ex. of Jacob Beal. Page 82

DAVIS, William: Account estate, to bonds delivered by John Goodrich, Esq. Examined by Solomon Wilson, Thomas King, William Patrick. Signed, James Barlow, guardian of Valentin Jenkins' orphans. Affidavit of John Goodrich that he paid to Capt. Davis the money due from Benjamin Barlow's estate to the Jenkins orphans. Signed, Francis Boykin. R. October 2, 1797. Page 85

PARNALL, Henry: Account estate, examined by George Benn, Robert R. Read, Ralph West, Nathaniel Gray. Signed, John Scarbrook Wills. R. November 10, 1797. Page 86

ANDREWS, Drury: Leg. son George; daughters Patsey and Belvidere the land I bought of John Sykes. Ex., friend John Urquhart. D. December 29, 1796. R. December 4, 1797.
  Wit: William Urquhart, Edmund Cosby, John Busby.
  Security, Edmund Cosby and Joseph Moody. Page 86

JORDAN, Lewis: Leg. wife Frances; daughter Polly; daughter Harriet; provision for unborn child. Ex., William Atkinson. D. August 29, 1796. R. December 4, 1797.
  Wit: William Atkinson, William Person.
  Security, James Atkinson. Page 87

EDWARDS, Jacob: Account estate, examined by Edward Davis, Elias Whitley, Elisha Whitley. R. December 4, 1797. Page 88

NEWMAN, Thomas: Appraised by William Mallory, John Woodley, William Proctor. Ordered September 22, 1797. R. January 3, 1798. Page 89

WATKINS, Sarah: Leg. daughter Mary Watkins. Ex., daughter Mary Watkins.
D. September 3, 1796. R. January 1, 1798.
Wit: Jesse Watkins, Wiley Lankford. Page 89

ELEY, Benjamin: Inventory of the personal estate of his infant, Holland B.
Eley. Signed, William Eley, guardian. Also personal estate of Michael
Eley, infant of Benjamin Eley. R. February 6, 1798. Page 90

NORSWORTHY, Elizabeth: Leg. cousin Betsey Crumpler; sister Ann Norsworthy.
Extx., sister Ann Norsworthy. D. February 27, 1791. R. December 4,
1797.
Wit: John Crumpler, Willis Gay.
Ann Norsworthy refused, Beasant Crumpler qualified.
Security, Mathew Johnson. Page 91

NEWBY, Thomas: Leg. wife Mary; daughter Anne; daughter Mary; son John
Newby. Extx., wife Mary Newby. D. 27th of 3rd mo. 1797.
R. February 5, 1798.
Wit: William Jordan, Sr., Richard Chapman, Simon Jordan,
Dixon Pinner. Page 91

LAWRENCE, Rix: Leg. daughter Marcia Rix Lawrence, my part of the Woddrop
Land, with reversion to my nephews, Robert and Thomas Lawrence, sons
of Robert Lawrence, Sr. of North Carolina; to Polly Strickland; niece
Nancy Newby. Ex., Thomas Smelly, Sr. D. July 18, 1797.
R. February 5, 1798.
Wit: Thomas Jordan, Sr., Hester Whitfield, Thomas Smelly.
Thomas Smelly refused, William Jordan qualified.
Security, Francis Boykin, Thomas Fanning. Page 92

EVERETT, Sarah: Leg. daughter Chloe Jordan; granddaughter Sarah Everett;
granddaughter Milly Everett. Ex., Nathaniel Jordan. D. September 4,
1795. R. February 5, 1798.
Wit: John Denson, John Everett, William Pruden.
Mathew Jordan refused, William Jordan qualified.
Security, Emanuel Wills. Page 93

JOHNSON, Henry, Sr.: Appraised by Sion Boon, John Eley, Wade Mountfort.
R. February 5, 1798. Page 94

WILLS, Mathews: Account estate. Among buyers, Joseph Garner, Thomas Hancock,
William Jordan, Langley C. Wills, Mills Holladay, etc. Signed,
Elizabeth Wills. R. February 5, 1798. Page 95

LAWRENCE, Martha: Account estate, paid Robert Lawrence his account as
surviving Ex. of Hardy Lawrence, paid Mills Lawrence as guardian.
Examined by Mills Eley and Sion Boon. Signed, Joseph Denson.
R. February 5, 1798. Page 96

BEAL, Jacob: Appraised by David Eley, Cutchin Council, James Tallow.
Ordered January, 1795. R. February 5, 1798. Page 97

BEAL, Jacob: Account estate, examined by Robert Eley and Jacob Johnson.
Signed, Absalom Beal. R. February 5, 1798. Page 98

GIBBS, Gabriel: Account estate, examined by ---- Young, F. Young and
Thomas King. Signed by William Patterson, who married Frances the
Extx. R. February 5, 1798. Page 99

COPHER, Benjamin: Appraised by John J. Wheadon, Solomon Jones, Richard
Thomas. Ordered January 11, 1797. R. February 5, 1798. Page 100

WATKINS, Sarah:  Account estate, examined by John Watkins and W. Lankford.
Signed, Jesse Watkins.  R.  April 2, 1798.                    Page 100

WATKINS, Mary:  Account estate, examined by John Watkins and W. Lankford.
Signed, Jesse Watkins.  R.  April 2, 1798.                    Page 101

LOWRY, Isaac:  Appraised by David Bradley, Samuel Woodley, William Davis.
Account of sales, among buyers, Peter Fagan, Randall Lowry, Jenny
Lowry.  Signed, Peter Fagen.  R.  April 2, 1798.
        Wit:  Andrew Woodley.                                 Page 102

BARLOW, William:  Leg. wife.  Exs., wife and James Deford.  D.  July 21,
1790.  R.  June 4, 1798.  Presented by Lucy Barlow, Security, Josiah
Holleman and James Deford.
        Wit:  David Jones, Francis Jones, Willis Jones, James
              Lancaster, John Gwaltney, Richard Crump, John Goodson,
              Thomas Wrenn, William Boyce.                    Page 103

WRENN, Thomas:  Leg. wife Mary; son Charles; son John, land on the James
River, bought of William Bidgood, Thomas Miller and John Goodrich;
reversion of bequests to my children . . . to the brothers and sisters
of my wife.  Exs., wife, Joseph Wrenn and Armistead Vellines.
D.  October 28, 1797.  R.  June 4, 1798.
        Wit:  Jesse Gray, Thomas Shelley.
        Security, Joseph Carrell.                             Page 103

OUTLAND, John:  Leg. daughter Betsey Jordan; daughter Jane Britt; grand-
daughter Polly Norsworthy; daughter Peggy Paine; grandson-in-law
Robert N. Cook and his wife Betsey Cook.  Ex., Robert Newton Cook.
D.  April 14, 1798.  R.  June 4, 1798.
        Wit:  John Barber, Edmond Peden, James Bullock.
        Security, Emanuel Wills, Dolphin Driver.              Page 104

VELLINES, Twait:  Leg. wife Mary; son Armistead; son John; to Caty Ponsonby;
son Isaac Vellines.  Ex., Isaac Vellines.  D.  May 16, 1796.  R.  June 4,
1798.
        Wit:  Drury Andrews, Edmund Cosby, John Sikes.
        Security, William Blunt.                             Page 106

WATKINS, Sarah:  Appraised by John English, John Watkins, W. Lankford.
R.  June 4, 1798.                                             Page 107

WATKINS, Mary:  Appraised by John English, John Watkins, W. Lankford.
R.  June 4, 1798.                                             Page 107

EDWARDS, Richard:  Appraised by John J. Wheadon, James Atkinson, John Shelley.
Ordered November 12, 1796.  R.  June 4, 1798.                 Page 108

DUCK, Jacob:  Account estate, examined by Elijah Johnson, Jacob Johnson.
Signed, Joseph Duck and John Duck.  R.  June 4, 1798.        Page 111

COUNCILL, Joshua, Jr.:  Appraised by Jacob Johnson, Joseph L. Bridger,
Thomas Bowden.  Ordered October 17, 1795.  R.  June 4, 1798.  Page 112

BARRETT, Hancock:  Account of sales.  D.  October 31, 1796.  R.  June 5,
1798.                                                        Page 114

SCOTT, Thomas:  Account estate, to loss in bringing suit against Charles
Chapman; paid John Scott, legacy left him by his grandfather, by his
uncle Thomas Murry and George Scott.  Examined by John Murry, William
Hollowell, James Barlow.  Signed, John Scott.  R.  June 5, 1798.
                                                             Page 115

SMITH, Joseph: Account estate, examined by Brewer Godwin, Nathaniel Gray, Joshua Bunkley. Signed, William Carter and wife. R. July 2, 1798.
Page 116

NORSWORTHY, Col. Tristram: Account estate, examined by Nathaniel Gray, Peter Cunningham and John King. Signed, Nathaniel Norsworthy. R. June 2, 1798.
Page 118

BARLOW, William: Appraised by William Patterson, John Murry, William Hollowell. R. July 2, 1798.
Page 119

GODWIN, Jeremiah: Account estate, examined by Joseph Driver, Nathaniel Gray and Peter Cunningham. Signed, Edmund Godwin. R. July 2, 1798.
Page 121

WAIL, John: Account estate, paid John Cook for a legacy left Rachel Green by her grandfather Nicholas Wail, whom the said Cook has married. Examined by Josiah Gray and Thomas Hall. Signed, Josiah Wail. R. July 2, 1798.
Page 122

FLINT, Thomas: Appraised. D. January 11, 1798. R. July 2, 1798.
Page 123

COPHER, Mary: Leg. daughter Rhody; daughter Gemimah; son Nathan. Ex., James Gwaltney. D. August 2, 1798. R. September 3, 1798.
Wit: Everett Gay, Samuel Jefferson, Lucy Person.
Security, James Deford.
Page 124

WOMBWELL, Mary: Leg. sister Tabitha Portis to keep my plantation and children; daughter Lucy; son Jordan; son Harrison; son Joel Wombwell. Exs., Henry Gray and John Gwaltney. D. February 12, 1798. R. September 3, 1798.
Wit: James Deford, Sarah Gwaltney, Tabitha Portis.
Security, James Gwaltney.
Page 125

HARRIS, Mathew: Leg. wife Mary; daughter Sarah Hair; son Samuel; son Michael; son John Harris. Extx., wife Mary Harris. D. 15th of 3rd mo. 1797. R. September 3, 1798.
Wit: Thomas Pretlow, John Pinner, Josiah Davis.
Security, Josiah Cook and James Gwaltney.
Page 126

WHITLEY, Nathan: Of Newport Parish. Leg. son Jesse; son Elias Whitley. Ex., Jesse Whitley. D. December 4, 1794. R. September 3, 1798.
Wit: David Edwards, Elias Edwards, Thomas Smith.
Security, David Edwards, Elias Edwards.
Page 128

PINNER, Josiah: Account estate, paid legacy to William Pinner, to Dixon Pinner, to Jeremiah Pinner, to Elizabeth Smelley, to Mary Powell, to John Pinner. Examined by William Jordan, Sr. and John Everett. D. November, 1795. R. September 3, 1798.
Page 129

EVERETT, Lemuel: Appraised by John R. Dixon, Nathaniel Pruden, William Dixon. D. January, 1796. R. September 3, 1798.
Page 130

JONES, Willis: Account estate, examined in the presence of Charles B. Taylor by William Eley and James Gwaltney. Signed, William Boyce and Charles B. Taylor, who married Lucy, the widow of Willis Jones. Signed, William Boyce. R. September 3, 1798.
Page 133

DIXON, Thomas: Leg. wife Penelope; son William; son Murphry; daughter Betsey; daughter Penelope; daughter Mary; daughter Martha Dixon. Ex., son William Dixon. D. December 31, 1791. R. February 3, 1794[?].
Wit: William Shivers, John Randle Dixon.
Page 133

WILLS, Miles: Leg. daughter Martha and her husband Josiah Gray; grandson
Miles Wills Gray; grandson Davis Gray; granddaughter Milley Everett;
granddaughter Sally Wills Everett; granddaughter Polly Godwin Gray,
the slave lent by me to my daughter Salley, wife of James Gray. Ex.,
Josiah Gray. D. February 25, 1796. R. October 1, 1798.
        Wit: Thomas West, John Casey.
        Security, Josiah Wills, Nathaniel Gray.                    Page 135

BARLOW, Thomas: Appraised by Thomas Wrenn, William Adkinson, James Barlow,
Sr. R. October 1, 1798.                                           Page 136

HARRIS, John: Appraised by John Powell, Mathew Tomlin, William Hatchell,
Benjamin Tynes. Ordered December 8, 1795. R. October 1, 1798.
                                                                  Page 137

WRENN, Thomas: Appraised by James Barlow, Moody Copher, Jesse Gray.
R. October 1, 1798.                                               Page 139

HARRISON, Elizabeth: Leg. sister Constant Wills, to her son Willis Wills;
to Henry Harrison, Jr.; sister Sally Lightfoot; sister Christian
Morris. Ex., brother Willis Wills. D. July 31, 1798. R. October 1,
1798.
        Wit: Ralph West, Lucy Wills, Sally West.
        Security, Robert R. Reade.                                Page 140

BALLARD, Sally: Leg. son Joseph W. Ballard; daughter Ellen; son Elisha L.
Ballard; son Robert M. Ballard; son Henry Augustus Ballard. Ex.,
friend Mills Eley. D. June 9, 1798. R. December 4, 1798.
        Wit: Anne English, Jesse Hampton.
        Security, John Eley.                                      Page 141

EVERETT, Sarah: Account estate, paid Simeon Jordan, a legatee; paid Mathew
Jordan for his five children. Examined by Emanuel Wills, Thomas
Smelley, John Barber. R. August 7, 1798. Signed, William Jordan.
                                                                  Page 143

BATTEN, Samuel: Account estate, examined by James Wills, Benjamin Tynes,
James Johnson, Francis Boykin. Signed, George Powell and Mathew
Powell. R. August 7, 1798.                                        Page 144

WOODWARD, John George: Of Newport Parish. Leg. wife Esther. Exs., wife
and her brother John King. D. April 17, 1797. R. December 3, 1798.
        Wit: John Gaskins, Sally Woodward, Josiah Nelms.
        Security, Jesse Fulgham.                                  Page 146

MOODY, Isaac: Account estate, paid by Elizabeth Blunt's Exs., the proportion
due to the eight youngest children. Examined by John Fearn, William
Blunt, Francis Boykin. Signed, Joseph Moody. R. December 3, 1798.
                                                                  Page 149

HARRISON, Richard: Appraised by Josiah Wills, Charles Broadfield, Henry
Howard. Ordered, September 30, 1797. R. December 3, 1798. Page 151

HARDY, William: Account estate, examined by Benjamin Goodrich, William Gay,
William Stallings. Signed, Joseph Stallings. R. September 3, 1798.
                                                                  Page 152

ATKINSON, Amey: Account estate, examined by Benjamin Goodrich, Moody
Copher, Jesse Gray. Paid funeral expenses for her son Timothy Atkinson.
R. December 3, 1798. Signed, Thomas Wrenn.                        Page 154

BUNKLEY, Joshua: Leg. wife Sarah; son Tristram; to my three children, Martha
King, John King and Samuel King. Exs., friends Nathaniel Gray and John

King. D. ---------- R. December 3, 1798.
    Wit: John Malcolm, Joseph Goodwin, George Goodwin.
    Security, Josiah Gray and John King.                    Page 155

COUNCIL, Joshua: Account estate, examined by Robert Eley, Solomon Butler,
    Mills Darden. Signed, Lemuel Council R. December 3, 1798.    Page 156

WHITLEY, Nathan: Appraised by Elisha Whitley, Robert Barradell. Ordered
    October 16, 1798. R. December 3, 1798.                   Page 158

LAWRENCE, John: Account estate, examined by James Wills, Mills Eley, Joseph
    Duck. Signed, Mills Lawrence and Elisha L. Ballard. R. December 3,
    1798.                                                    Page 161

OUTLAND, John: Appraised by Thomas Smelley, William Smelley, William Baldwin.
    R. December 3, 1798.                                     Page 164

WILSON, Solomon: Leg. daughter Emily Baker Wilson; son George; son James
    Riddick Wilson, all my land in Nansemond County. Exs. and Guardians
    for my children, William Patrick, John Goodrich and Robert Farmer.
    D. December 3, 1796. R. March 5, 1799.
        Wit: James Johnson, John Easson.
        Security, Emanuel Wills, Francis Boykin, Davis Day.   Page 167

GARTON, William: Appraised by William Mallory, Davis Day, Lewis Chapman.
    Ordered January 1, 1798. R. February 4, 1799.            Page 168

EDWARDS, Robert: Of Newport Parish. Leg. son Robert; wife; son Hardy, a
    bond in John Patterson's possession; son John; son Samuel; daughter
    Lydia; daughter Sally; daughter Saphire; son Permealy. Ex., David
    Edwards. D. August 21, 1798. R. February 4, 1799.
        Wit: Joseph Moody, John Goodrich, William Edwards.    Page 170

BLANEY, David: Leg. wife Helen; son Cadwallader; to my mother my estate in
    Isle of Wight called "Sprinfield"; my wife must not acknowledge or keep
    up the least connection with any of the family by the name of Maxwell
    or Read, Mr. Benjamin Payne, his wife and children excepted; to William
    Pennock, Jr.; copies of my will to be sent my brother Asa Blaney in
    New England, in the care of William Lee, Esq.; Colonel Godwin's son
    and Mr. Benjamin Payne to assist in selling my estate; refers to
    property in the hands of Dr. Foushee of Richmond, bond of General
    Lee's and the deed for "Chesterville", of which Col. Wm. Moore and
    his son are agents; to James Payne, son of Benjamin Payne. Exs.,
    William Pennock, Esq. and brother Asa Blaney. D. ----------
    R. February 4, 1799.
        Wit: Benjamin Payne, Brewer Godwin, Alexander Wilson.
        Security, John R. Read and James Maxwell.            Page 171

FOWLER, Joseph: Appraised by Lott Griffin, Shadrack Corbett, Shadrack
    Griffin. R. February 4, 1799.                            Page 171

FOWLER, Joseph: Account estate, examined by Mills Dearden, Elijah Johnson,
    Eley Johnson. D. January 30, 1796. R. February 4, 1799. Signed,
    Joseph Duck.                                             Page 172

BOON, Ratcliff: Leg. wife Patience; son William; son Jesse; son Sion;
    daughter Selah Bradshaw; grandson Willis English; grandson Ratcliff
    Boon; grandson Joshua Boon; the children of Mary Nelms to have her
    share of my estate; Elizabeth Webb has had her share of my estate.
    Exs., son Sion Ratcliff and Robert Eley. D. March 23, 1795.
    R. February 4, 1799.
        Wit: William Eley, Robert Eley, Jr., John Boykin Eley.
        Security, Daniel Simmons.                            Page 174

GOODRICH, Elizabeth: Account estate, paid Benjamin Ward, administrator of William Goodrich. Examined by Isham Jordan, Gray Carrell, William Atkinson. Signed, Charles Goodrich. R. February 4, 1799. Page 175

CUTCHIN, Polly: Of Newport Parish. Leg. sister Sally Pitt Cutchin. Exs., George Benn and Bennett Young. D. November 12, 1798. R. February 4, 1799.
      Wit: James A. Cunningham, Hannah West, Bennett Young, John Godwin. Page 177

COPHER, Mary: Appraised by Ishmael Moody, Moody Copher, Thomas Wombwell. Ordered October 23, 1798. R. February 4, 1799. Page 177

WESTRAY, Mathew: Account estate, examined by Daniel Herring and James Johnson. Signed, Jeremiah Westray. R. February 4, 1799. Page 178

FULGHAM, Edmund: Appraised by James Johnson, Michael Fulgham, Jesse Fulgham. Ordered March 14, 1785. R. February 5, 1799. Page 179

HOLLAND, Robert: Leg. wife Patience; son Everett; son James; daughter Sally Davis; daughter Betsey Randolph; daughter Milly Hancock; to Everett Holland, son of my son Everett; slaves given son Everett to be divided between Charles, Everett and Nancy Holland; grandson Robert Marshall. Ex., son James Holland. D. February 5, 1797. R. February 5, 1799.
      Wit: E. Herring (Hining), Elias Daniel, Joseph Pope. Page 183

WEBB, Anne: Leg. to John Shelly; daughter Frances; daughter Elizabeth; son James Webb; to my children by William Ward, viz. Virginia, Edward, Lucy and Polly Ward Webb; my interest in the estate of Thomas Barlow and of my brother Nathaniel Barlow. Ex., Benjamin Ward. D. June 9, 1798. R. February 5, 1799.
      Wit: Benjamin Goodrich, Priscilla Goodson, Juley Barlow.
William Ward qualified.
      Security, Benjamin Ward. Page 185

YOUNG, Elizabeth: Leg. daughter Anne, the money due from my son James Young; son Thomas; to Michael Young; son Francis; son Bennett Young. Ex., son Bennett Young. D. October 25, 1798. R. February 5, 1799.
      Wit: Rhoda Casey, William Bryant, Elizabeth Bryant.
      Security, George Baines. Page 186

HARRIS, Mathew: Appraised by Moreland Delk, John Gray, William Brock. Ordered March 25, 1799. R. April 1, 1799. Page 187

TOMLIN, Nicholas: Appraised by James Johnson, James Powell, Burwell Harris. Ordered March, 1797. R. April 1, 1799. Page 191

GODWIN, Joseph: Of Newport Parish. Leg. son Joseph; daughter Leodocia, with reversion of bequest to heirs of Joseph Godwin and Anne Godwin; grandson Elisha Godwin. Ex., son Joseph Godwin. D. November 18, 1797. R. April 1, 1799.
      Wit: Joseph Godwin, George Godwin.
      Security, George Godwin. Page 192

COGGIN, Catherine: Leg. son John; grandson Jonathan Coggin; daughter Mary Turner; among my other children. D. October 12, 1798. R. April 1, 1799.
      Wit: Daniel Sumner, Patsey Johnson Coggin, Robert Jordan.
      Security, John Turner. Page 193

BLANEY, David: Appraised by Joseph Chapman, Brewer Godwin. R. April 1, 1799. Page 194

BLANEY, David: Appraised at "Chesterville", in Elizabeth City County, by Miles King, William Moore and Augustine Moore. R. April 1, 1799.
Page 194

ELEY, William: Account estate, examined by Mills Eley, John Eley, Sion Boon. Signed, Mathew Johnson. Ordered March 12, 1799. R. April 1, 1799.
Page 196

HALL, Mary: (Widow of George Hall) Appraised by Jacob Darden, Pleasant Jordan, Robert Barradell, Elisha Whitley. Ordered January 14, 1794. R. April 1, 1799.
Page 197

HARRISON, John: Account estate, cash paid James Atkinson, on account Harrison's guardianship of Looper, by Mildred Looper's account. Examined by Francis Boykin, William Atkinson, James Johnston. Signed, David Bradley and Elizabeth his wife, Exs. D. 1790. R. May 6, 1799.
Page 199

MOODY, Philip: Account estate, examined by William Gay and William Gray. Signed, Thomas Copher. R. June 3, 1799.
Page 201

EDWARDS, Robert: Appraised by Joseph Moody, John Edwards, William Pinhorn. R. June 3, 1799.
Page 202

ATKINS, John: Leg. wife Elizabeth Atkins. Ex., Thomas Davis. D. October 10, 1798. R. June 3, 1799.
    Wit: Catherine Broadfield, Willis Martin.
    Security, Edward Davis.
Page 204

EDWARDS, Solomon: Leg. son-in-law and daughter, William and Martha Turner; son John; wife Martha, with reversion to my surviving children. Exs., Martha Edwards and Robert Edwards. D. February 4, 1795. R. June 5, 1799.
    Wit: William Blunt, William H. Blunt, Patsey Moody, Timothy Whitley, Randolph Whitley.
Page 205

HAILE, Hannah: Leg. son Simon and his daughter Olive Haile; niece Lavina Bracey; daughter Daisey Smith; son William Hatchel; stepdaughter Molly Harris. D. April 19, 1799. R. June 3, 1799.
    Wit: James Downing, Thomas Boldes.
    Security, James Johnson.
Page 205

WOMBWELL, Britain: Account estate, examined by Joseph Stringfield, Everett Gay, Ishmael Moody. Signed, Samuel Jefferson. R. July 1, 1799.
Page 206

COPHER, Christian: Leg. daughter Celia; son John; son Thomas. Ex., son John Copher. D. January 21, 1799. R. July 1, 1799.
    Wit: Gray Carrell, George Gray, Chloe Goodrich.
Page 208

GRAY, Nathaniel: Leg. daughter Jane Driver Gray, with reversion of bequest to my brothers and sisters. Ex., brother Josiah Gray. D. May 14, 1799. R. September 2, 1799.
    Wit: Josiah Wills, Ephraim Wheeler, William Pitt.
    Security, Thomas King.
Page 208

MITCHELL, James: Leg. wife Elizabeth; daughter Elizabeth and her unborn child; son Joseph; daughter Peggy; daughter Jane; son James. Exs., William Pinner and sister Ann Corbell. D. May 23, 1799. R. September 2, 1799.
    Wit: Ephraim Wheeler, Charity Mitchell, Joseph Brown.
    Security, Charity Mitchell and Emanuel Wills.
Page 209

EDWARDS, Britain: Appraised by Joseph Moody, Mathew Turner, Burwell Harris.
R. September 2, 1799.                                                    Page 210

SMITH, Thomas: Leg. daughter Elizabeth Johnston; daughter Sarah; daughter
Fanny; daughter Jenny; daughter Leliallas (?); wife Elizabeth, the
plantation my overseer, Edward Burt lives on, except that part which
is called Miller's plantation on Timothy Tynes Upper Quarter; son
Arthur and it is my wish that he shall study the art of surgery and
physics. Exs., wife Elizabeth Smith and son-in-law Major James Johnston.
D. April 17, 1799. R. September 2, 1799.
         Wit: J. Young, David Dick, Edward Burt.                        Page 211

APPLEWHAITE, Arthur: Leg. wife Ridley; son Henry; son George; daughter Ann
Wilson Applewhaite; daughter Ridley Honour Applewhaite. Exs., wife,
friends, Absalom Williams and Jesse Atkins. D. April 1, 1795.
R. September 2, 1799.
         Wit: Samuel Atkins, John Atkins, Edward Pitman.
         Security, Samuel Webb, Joseph Atkins, Andrew Woodley.      Page 214

PITT, James: Leg. wife Mary; son Thomas Walke Pitt; son James; son Edmund
Pitt. Exs., wife Mary Pitt and friend Thomas Walke. D. July 22,
1796. R. October 7, 1799.
         Wit: John Dobbs, Florea Calcote.
         Security, Henry Harrison.                                      Page 215

TYNES, Benjamin: Leg. son David; daughter Nancy; daughter Polly; daughter
Temperance; daughter Sally; refers to estate of his uncle Robert Tynes,
decd. Ex., friend John Urquhart. D. June 25, 1799. R. October 7,
1799.
         Wit: William Urquhart, Isaac Moody, William B. Moody,
              Edmund Stagg.
         Security, James Johnson.                                      Page 216

FLAKE, John: Account estate, examined by Everett Gay, Jacob Stringfield,
Ishmael Moody. Signed, Joseph Stringfield. R. October 7, 1799.
                                                                       Page 217

GODWIN, John, the elder: Account estate, examined by Bennett Young and
Mills Wills. Signed, John Godwin. R. October 7, 1799.       Page 218

PITT, Isham: Account estate, examined by Brewer Godwin and Josiah Godwin.
Signed, Nathaniel Gray. R. October 7, 1799.                 Page 218

YOUNG, Francis, the elder: Account estate, examined by John Godwin, Robert
R. Read, Willis Wills. R. October 7, 1799. Signed, Bennett Young.
                                                                       Page 220

NORSWORTHY, Nathaniel: Appraised by Josiah Godwin and Peter Cunningham.
Ordered October 12, 1797. R. October 7, 1799.               Page 221

FLEMING, Gardner: Account estate, examined by Thomas Smelley, William
Smelley, John Barber. Signed, Jacob Randolph. D. 1791. R. November 4, 1799.                                                           Page 222

EDWARDS, Richard: Account estate, examined by James Atkinson, Benjamin
Goodrich, John J. Wheadon. Signed, Martha Edwards. R. August 5, 1799.
                                                                       Page 223

UNDERWOOD, Sampson: Of Newport Parish. Leg. son Jesse; son Thomas; son
Joyner, with reversion of bequest to his son Thomas Underwood; son John;
son Josiah; daughter Mary; daughter Anne; son Theophilus; grandson
Joseph Underwood. Ex., son Josiah Underwood. D. August 28, 1797.

R. December 3, 1799.
> Wit: Juley Carrell, Elizabeth Clayton, Thomas Carrell, James
> Clayton.
> Security, James Clayton and Thomas Carrell.                    Page 225

BRIDGER, William: Account estate, examined by James Johnson, E. Herring,
Thomas Bowden. Signed, Simon Boykin. R. December 3, 1799. Page 226

PATRICK, Joseph: (Free negro) Appraised by Joseph Atkins, Joseph Crocker,
Charles Broadfield. R. January 6, 1800.                    Page 231

WOMBWELL, Mary: Appraised by James Gwaltney, William Gray, James Deford.
Ordered December 31, 1798. R. January 6, 1800.            Page 231

GODWIN, Brewer: Leg. wife Hannah; son Brewer; son Josiah; son John; daughter
Mary; daughter Dolly; daughter Priscilla Godwin. Exs., son Brewer, son
Josiah and friend Mills Godwin. D. January 25, 1799. R. January 6,
1800.
> Wit: John Barber, Edmund Pedin, John Clark.                Page 232

GIBSON, Richard: (Commonly called "Preaching Dick.") Nuncupative will.
Sister Judey; sister Rachel; to his wife and children. Exs., George
Benn and Randall Reynolds. D. January 12, 1800. R. February 4, 1800.
Page 234

GILES, John, Sr.: Leg. daughter Mary; son John; daughter Lucy Thompson;
daughter Elizabeth Pope; grandchildren, Elizabeth, Polly and Thomas
Giles. Ex., son John Giles. D. June 12, 1797. R. February 4, 1800.
> Wit: Joseph Carpenter, Elisha Minton, Jeremiah Gibbons.
> Security, Elisha Minton.                                 Page 235

HOUGH, Fanny: Nuncupative will, proven by Henry Gale, Mary Turner and Sarah
Gay. Estate to Sally, the wife of Joseph Lawrence. April 7, 1800.
Page 236

WEST, James: Leg. James West Daniel; Giles West Daniel; Henry Daniel; John
Daniel. Ex., Josiah Wills. D. January 9, 1800. R. April 7, 1800.
> Wit: Brewer Godwin, Willis Godwin, Giles Daniel.
> Security, John Lawrence.                                 Page 236

BARRETT, Hancock: Account estate, examined by James Johnson and Sion Boon.
Signed, Rawleigh Barrett. R. April 7, 1800.               Page 237

BRIDGER, Anne: Of Smithfield. Leg. nephew William Chapman. Ex., William
Chapman. D. October 13, 1793. R. April 7, 1800.
> Wit: Samuel Skinner, Nancy Harner, J. Young, Richard Brantley.
> Security, John Murray.                                   Page 238

WILLIAMS, David, the elder: Account estate, paid for schooling three
children. Examined by Peter Cunningham and Robert R. Reade. Signed,
Ann Williams and James Williams. R. April 7, 1800.       Page 239

BALDWIN, William: Leg. wife Ann, the land which my father, John Baldwin,
purchased of Thomas Bullock; sister Sary Chapman and her five children,
John and William Chapman, Silvia Babb, Elizabeth Chapman and Nancy
Chapman. Extx., wife Ann Baldwin. D. March 4, 1786. R. April 7,
1800.
> Wit: James Hough, William Bridger, Robert Babb, John Busby,
>      Rix Lawrence, John Babb, William Smelly, Wm. Chapman.
> Security, John Chapman and John Clark.                   Page 239

WRENN, Josiah: Leg. daughter Sarah Barlow; son Francis plantation called

"Fiveash"; son Josiah; daughter Patsey; daughter Betsey; Richard Peirce to keep all property that he is now in possession of. Exs., Richard Peirce and John Barlow. D. February 20, 1800. R. April 7, 1800.
 Wit: Joseph Carrell, Mary Carrell, Timothy Tynes, Martha Dobbs.
 Security, James Atkinson, James Pyland.    Page 240

DARDEN, John: Leg. wife Elizabeth; son Mills; son Ziza; daughter Chasey; daughter Sally Darden. D. January 23, 1800. R. April 7, 1800.
 Wit: John Darden, son of H. Darden, Jacob Spivey, Thomas Spivey.
 Security, Joseph W. Ballard.    Page 241

COOKE, Robert N.: Leg. wife Elizabeth, property in the Borough of Norfolk, which I claim from the death of my father, John N. Cooke and which Breasan Bourden now claims. D. December 30, 1799. R. April 5, 1800.
 Wit: Thomas Holladay, Richard Outland, James L. Beal,
 Jordan Williams.    Page 242

JOHNSON, Lazarus: Leg. son Robert's heirs; son Joseph; son Jesse; daughter Priscilla Butler; son Cornelius, land adjoining Joseph Butler and William Johnson; son Elisha; son Lemuel, land adjoining John Duck, Jr. and Godwin Council; son Lazarus; grandson Abel Johnson, the plantation on which his father lived; grandson Laban Johnson; granddaughter Martha Johnson; wife. Exs., sons Lazarus and Elisha Johnson. D. 5th of 8 mo. 1798. R. April 7, 1800.
 Wit: Abraham Johnson, John Johnson, Dempsey Johnson,
 Zachariah Johnson.
 Security, Abraham Johnson.    Page 243

POWELL, James: Leg. Sarah Edwards and her child; son Joseph Powell. Ex., Burwell Harris. D. February 5, 1800. R. April 7, 1800.
 Wit: Joseph Westray, Mathew Tomlin, Thomas Gaskins.
 Security, Mathew Tomlin.    Page 244

HOLLAND, Robert: Appraised by Mills Eley, Wiley Lankford, Thomas Bowden. Ordered January 14, 1799. R. April 7, 1800.    Page 246

AMES, Elizabeth: Account estate, administrator of Levy Amos, examined by John Brown, Joshua Hunt, George Lawrence. Signed, William Mease.
 R. June 2, 1800.    Page 249

AMES, Elizabeth: Appraised by John Brown, Joshua Hunt and Joshua Bunkley. Ordered February 24, 1790. R. June 2, 1800.    Page 251

TURNER, William: Leg. wife Elizabeth; son Mathew; son William; son Jesse; daughter Unity; daughter Elizabeth. Exs., William Turner and Jesse Turner. D. April 13, 1780. R. June 2, 1800.
 Wit: William Blunt, Isaac Moody, Joseph Moody.    Page 252

DRIVER, Lydia: Leg. sister Nancy Wills; sister Hannah Wills. Extx., Nancy Wills. D. January 16, 1800. R. July 7, 1800.
 Wit: Willis Wills, John Wills, Lucy Wills.    Page 254

BRYANT, William: Of Smithfield. Leg. wife Elizabeth, money left me by my uncle William Bryant of Trenton, New Jersey, to be drawn from the hands of Capt. Joseph Hardy of the City of New York; brother Charles, and his son William; to Polly Stucky; to Patsey Marshall Stucky; to Holland Stucky. Exs., wife Elizabeth Bryant and Josiah Gray. D. May 22, 1800. R. July 7, 1800.
 Wit: Thomas Grantham, John Reynolds, George Baynes.
 Security, Edward Davis.    Page 254

VANISER, Peter: Leg. to Chloe Womble; to Sukey Pitman the part of my planta- tion on which Mary Rebecca Allmond now lives, with reversion to John

and Isaac Pitman; Susanna Smith to live on my plantation her natural life. Exs., Joseph Stallings and Moody Cofer. D. June 27, 1800. R. July 7, 1800.
    Wit: Joseph Stallings, Samuel Jefferson, Moody Cofer.    Page 255

BRACEY, Selloway: Leg. wife Nancy, all her estate at marriage with me; brother Drury; brother John; brother Jesse; sister Sealah; sister Silvia; cousin Betsey Bracey. Exs., wife Nancy Bracey and brother Jesse Bracey. D. February 22, 1800. R. July 7, 1800.
    Wit: Mills Eley, Jesse Watkins, Willy Lankford.
    Security, Benjamin Westray and Thomas Camp.    Page 255

HOLLAND, Benjamin: Leg. daughter Ann Carr; daughter Elizabeth Darden; daughter Patience Johnson; son Jacob; to Eleanah Holland. Ex., son Benjamin Holland. D. December 16, 1799. R. July 7, 1800.
    Wit: Mills Butler, Mills Holland, Aron Holland.
    Security, Mills Darden.    Page 256

CLARK, Joseph: Leg. son Zachariah; daughter Nancy Reaves Clark. Exs., Armistead Vellines and John Barlow. D. March 24, 1800. R. April 7, 1800.
    Wit: John Stevens, James Clark, Elizabeth Coggin.
    Security, Machen Fearn.    Page 257

BOON, Ratcliff: Appraised by Wade Mountfort, Thomas Bowden, James Johnson. R. July 7, 1800.    Page 258

BALLARD, Sally: Appraised by Mills Darden, John Eley, Robert Watkins. Ordered December 8, 1798. R. July 7, 1800.    Page 259

SMITH, Thomas: Account estate, paid for schooling three children, examined by Thomas Hall and William Goodwin. Signed, Samuel Holladay. D. 1785. R. July 7, 1800.    Page 259

JORDAN, Robert: Account estate, examined by William Jordan, Francis Boykin, Thomas Smelley. Ordered February, 1795. R. July 7, 1800. Signed, Thomas Jordan.    Page 260

NORSWORTHY, George: Account estate, examined by George Benn, Josiah Gray, Joseph Fulgham. Signed, Nathaniel Norsworthy. R. July 7, 1800.
    Page 261

REYNOLDS, Rowland: Account estate, cash paid Randolph Reynolds and Lemuel Godfrey, distributees of the . . . Richard Reynolds, Sr. Examined by Thomas King, James Johnson, Charles Fulgham. Signed, Richard Reynolds. R. August 6, 1800.    Page 262

EDWARDS, James: Of Newport Parish. Leg. wife Susannah; son David; son James; daughter Jenny Wolles; daughter Rebecca; daughter Mary Edwards. Ex., son David Edwards. D. September 4, 1789. R. September 1, 1800.
    Wit: Lewis Turner, Henry Turner, William Edwards, Jr.,
       Elias Edwards.
    Security, Francis Boykin.    Page 263

ADKINS, Simon: Of Newport Parish. Leg. son Moses; son Axom; to Elizabeth Adkins; to Martha Adkins; to Cloe Adkins; wife Celia; daughter Lucy; daughter Rhoda; daughter Cherry; daughter Frances. Extx., wife Celia Adkins. D. April 2, 1800. R. September 1, 1800.
    Wit: Everett Gay, Henry Wombwell, Jordan Pitman.
    Security, Moody Cofer.    Page 264

GODWIN, Edmond: Account estate, examined by Henry Pitt, Joseph Chapman, Nathaniel Wills. Signed, Tristram Norsworthy. R. September 1, 1800.
    Page 265

WHITFIELD, Thomas: Appraised by John Woodley, William Casey, Davis Day. Ordered August 3, 1799. R. September 1, 1800. Page 267

CHAPMAN, Joseph: Account estate, examined by Willis Wills, James Morrison, Henry Pitt. Signed, Joshua Bunkley's executors. R. September 1, 1800. Page 268

ELEY, Robert, Sr.: Account estate, examined by Mills Eley and John Eley. Signed, Robert Eley, Jr. Robert Lawrence signed an acknowledgement as guardian for his five children. On bond, John B. Eley and Miles Council. R. September 1, 1800.
Wit: Mills Eley and John Eley. Page 270

MILLER, John: Appraised by William Casey, Joseph Wodsten, James Barlow. Ordered May 7, 1799. R. October 6, 1800. Page 271

McCAUL, John: Nuncupative will proven by Joseph Holmes and Thomas Hancock. A traveling merchant who died at Thomas Hancock's Tavern in Smithfield, leaving his whole estate to Michael Leonard. D. August 21, 1800. R. October 4, 1800. Page 272

COUNCIL, Joshua, Jr.: Account estate, examined by James Johnson, Thomas Bowden, Joseph Bridger. Signed, Sion Boon and Peggy Council. R. October 4, 1800. Page 273

BOON, Ratcliff: Account estate, receipt from William Bradshaw in right of his wife Selah, from Jesse Boon, Lucy Mountfort. Examined by Thomas Bowden, Wade Mountfort. R. October 6, 1800. Signed, Sion Boon. Page 275

CHAPMAN, John: Account estate, examined by James Morrison, Henry Pitt, William R. Smith. Signed, Joshua Bunkley. R. October 6, 1800. Page 276

DAUGHTRY, Mary: Leg. son Joshua; daughter Charlotte; daughter Salley Butler. Ex., friend Jacob Johnson. D. August 6, 1800. R. October 6, 1800. Wit: Francis Murfree, Mills Beal, William Powell.
Security, Francis Murphry. Page 277

WOODLEY, Elizabeth: Leg. brother John Woodley; brother Samuel Woodley; to Willis Woodley, Jr., son of Andrew Woodley; to Betsey and Polly Blunt, daughters of William Blunt. Ex., brother Andrew Woodley. D. June 1, 1799. R. October 6, 1800.
Wit: Abel Garrison, James Garrison, Margaret Garrison.
Security, John Gibbs. Page 277

UNDERWOOD, Anne: Leg. brother Josiah Underwood; sister Mary Underwood. Ex., brother Josiah Underwood. D. March 27, 1800. R. October 6, 1800. Wit: James Rhodes, Mary Rhodes, John Powell.
Security, James Rhodes. Page 279

TURNER, Mathew: Leg. son Josiah; wife; son Willis; daughter Patsey; provision for unborn child. Extx., wife. D. August 26, 1800. R. October 6, 1800.
Wit: Jordan Parr, Joseph Moody, William Turner.
Security, Joseph Moody. Page 279

TURNER, Jesse: Leg. wife Lucy; son Wiley; daughter Polly; son Jesse; daughter Lucy; to John Urquhart. Exs., wife, John Urquhart and Wiley Turner. D. May 8, 1800. R. October 6, 1800.
Wit: Joseph Moody, Josiah Stagg, William Turner.
Security, Joseph Moody and Isaac Vellines. Page 280

FOWLER, James: Leg. son John; son Edward; wife; daughter Mourning; son
    Abraham; daughter Anne Fowler; son Jobe. Exs., friend Joseph Duck
    and son Edmund Fowler. D. November 19, 1799. R. October 6, 1800.
        Wit: John Carr, Sr., Absalom Beal, Benjamin Bradshaw, Barden
        Turner.
        Security, Benjamin Bradshaw.                          Page 282

JOHNSON, Michael: Leg. son Jacob; daughter Memima Eley; son Elias; daughter
    Elizabeth Butler; daughter Sally; daughter Priscilla Johnson. Exs.,
    sons Jacob and Elias. D. February 19, 1800. R. October 5, 1800.
        Wit: Obadiah Johnson, Cornelius Johnson, Abel Johnson.  Page 283

BOWZER, James: Nuncupative will, proven by George Benn. Whole estate to
    wife Bridget Bowzer. D. September 5, 1800. R. December 1, 1800.
                                                              Page 284

PITT, Jacob: Account estate, examined by William Waltham, Joseph Driver,
    Willis Corbell. Signed by Ishmiah Pitt, administrator of Tamer Pitt,
    who was the administratrix of Jacob Pitt. R. December 1, 1800.
                                                              Page 284

TAYLOR, Richard: Leg. daughter Lucy Blow; son Richard; daughter Mildred D.
    Williams and her children, Meria A. Williams and Lucy G. Williams;
    daughter Mary Towns Taylor. Exs., wife and William H. Gregory.
    D. November 3, 1800. R. December 1, 1800.
        Wit: Joseph Holmes, Thomas Purdie, Francis Young.
        Security, James B. Southall and Thomas Blow.          Page 285

WHITFIELD, Samuel: Account estate, examined by Nathaniel Wills, Henry Pitt
    and Joseph Chapman. Signed, Tristram Norsworthy. R. December 1, 1800.
                                                              Page 286

SMELLY, Thomas: Leg. son Thomas; daughter Elizabeth; daughter Martha, the
    land left me by my brother Robert on which Levin Hudson now lives;
    son John land in Nansemond. Ex., son Thomas Smelly. D. September 3,
    1800. R. December 1, 1800.
        Wit: James L. Beal, William Eley.
        Security, William Jordan and William Eley.            Page 287

WOODWARD, William: Account estate, examined by Francis Boykin, Mills Eley,
    Robert Eley. R. December 1, 1800. Signed, Esther Woodward and John
    King.                                                     Page 288

DRIVER, Keziah: Account estate, examined by Thomas Hall, Nathaniel Wills,
    Edmond Godwin. Signed, James Morrison. D. November 21, 1800.
    R. December 1, 1800.                                      Page 289

WAILE, Josiah: Account estate, examined by Nathaniel Wills, John Waile,
    Thomas Hall. Signed, James Morrison. D. November 8, 1800.
    R. December 1, 1800.                                      Page 291

POWELL, Mordica: Leg. son Gideon; daughter Sally; son Micajah; son Hezekiah
    Powell. Ex., friend Thomas Smelly. D. November 19, 1800.
    R. December 1, 1800.
        Wit: Thomas Smelly, Everett Gay, Charles Powell.      Page 292

DRIVER, Charles: Account estate, examined by Thomas Hall, Nathaniel Wills,
    Edmund Godwin. Signed, James Morrison. D. November 8, 1800.
    R. December 1, 1800.                                      Page 294

FLEMING, Nathaniel: Account estate, examined by James Wills, Francis Boykin,
    Edmond Cosby. Signed, William Urquhart. R. December 1, 1800.
                                                              Page 296

HUNT, James:  Leg. cousin Samuel Hunt.  Ex., uncle Joshua Hunt.
      D.  December 17, 1800.  R.  February 3, 1801
            Wit:  William Bagnall, Easter Williams.
            Security, Joseph Godwin.                    Page 299

# INDEX *

322

324

325

Carr (cont.)
Ann 241, 314
Benjamin 245
David 283
Dempsey 288, 301
Demsey 241
Edey 288
Eleanor 119
Elisha 288
Elizabeth 119, 121
Grace 119
Hardy 119, 209, 212, 244
Honour 288
Jacob 288
John 103, 119, 120, 244,
  267, 269, 288, 290
John Jr. 269, 271
John Sr. 316
Joshua 249
Keziah 241
Martha 239, 269
Mary 119, 121
Mills 269, 282
Milly 281
Nathan 241, 247, 248, 251,
  254, 255, 257, 262, 279,
  283
Patience 241, 269
Priscilla 213, 288
Robert 119, 121, 133, 137,
  165, 212
Robert Jr. 114
Sally 288
Sarah 119, 269
Spencer 244, 245
Susannah 269
Thomas 241, 289
William 119, 211, 244, 267,
  269, 283
Willis 272
Carrell, (Mr.) 36
Benjamin 54, 118, 126, 189
Catherine 263
Comfort 244, 263
Elizabeth 54, 192
Gray 235, 301, 309, 310
James 57, 119, 120, 122,
  130-132, 134, 156, 162,
  169, 235, 265, 266, 293
John 5, 8, 10, 31, 32, 35,
  36, 38, 39, 54, 57, 81,
  137, 148, 149, 181-183,
  187, 199, 214, 217, 221,
  225
John Sr. 34
Joice 137
Joseph 54, 61, 118, 256,
  281, 305, 313
Joyce 133
Juley 312
Mark 249
Martha 292
Mary 54, 57, 59, 156, 162,
  163, 169, 181, 229, 234,
  244, 278, 302, 313
Molly 263
Richard 162, 235
Robert 118
Samuel 54, 118, 127, 131,
  132, 137, 148, 263
Sarah 107, 235
Sylvia 189
T. 163
Thomas 34, 54, 57, 118, 137,
  149, 162, 167, 169, 173,
  180, 182, 229, 231, 234,
  263, 295, 312

Carrell (cont.)
William 34, 54, 57, 115, 160,
  163, 174, 177, 181, 187,
  191, 198, 203, 205, 209,
  212, 216, 218, 222-224,
  226, 228, 234, 235, 240,
  244, 247, 251, 261, 263,
  265, 278, 281, 302
Carroll, Elizabeth 47, 48
Henrietta 48
John 24, 40, 48, 55, 96
Carstaphen, Betty 287
Perkins 287
Robert 287
Carstophen, John 233
Martha 233
Carter, Alexander 47
Ann 125
Benjamin 125
Elinor 64
Elizabeth 125
George 54, 89, 125
James 82, 125, 159
John 1, 82
Jonathan 113
Katherine 155
Keziah 155
Magdalen 36
Magdeline 54
Martha 47
Mary 257, 273
Ralph 178
Richard 162
Samuel 125
Sarah 125, 154
Thomas 4, 10, 12, 47, 54,
  64, 113, 125, 127
Thomas Jr. 38
William 125, 306
Cartwright, Charles 18
Carver, Daniel 42
Elizabeth 57
James 23
Patience 79
Cary, Charity 154
James 268, 276, 280
John 50, 173, 183, 209, 244
Joseph 154
Martha 154
Mildred 276
Miles 186
Patience 247, 251
Richard Jr. 276
Thomas 276
William 154, 174, 176, 183,
  265, 276
Casey, Ann 53, 156
Celia 281
Constant 209, 224, 228
Fanny 221
Harty 209
Henry 209, 224, 228
James 250
Jane 53, 116, 156, 209
John 293, 300, 307
Martha 53, 135, 152, 156
Mary 53
Nicholas 28, 47, 53, 115,
  136, 148, 161, 175, 182,
  209, 217
Patience 156
Rhoda 309
Richard 53, 55, 85, 92, 102,
  135, 156, 178, 210, 289
Richard Jr. 135
Ruth 53
Sarah 53, 156

Casey (cont.)
Selah 209
Thomas 53, 136, 175, 187,
  191, 209, 223, 224
W. 277
William 199, 209, 222, 223,
  226, 235, 245, 248, 251,
  254, 259, 260, 263, 278,
  280, 289, 300, 303, 315
Cashwell, Mary 184
Casse, Thomas 136
Casse (Casey), Thomas 136
Cathon, John 203
Caufield, Robert 22
Cawson, John 253
Chalmers, David 254, 264
James 264
Sarah 264
Chambers, Mary 281
William 37
Champion, Alice 36
Benjamin 36
Edward 7, 18, 30
Edward Sr. 36
John 23
Orlando 36
Priscilla 14, 36
Channel, Ann 242
James 185
Joseph 223
Channell, Arthur 257
Elizabeth 216
Grace 65
James 188, 216, 226
Jeremiah 264, 270, 284
Pegga 216
Rachel 264, 284
Ralph 8, 28, 65
Thomas 191
Chapman,_____ 40, 274
Alice 108
Ann 55, 143, 162
Anne 44
Benjamin 107, 240, 241
Charles 4, 36, 44, 49, 108,
  116, 130, 143, 157, 158,
  162, 163, 166, 169, 172,
  176, 199. 200, 203, 221,
  224, 229, 230, 240, 241,
  276, 283, 305
Charles Sr. 204
Chloe 221
Elizabeth 108, 130, 245, 312
Fanny 221
Frances 241
Hannah 293
Hardy 238, 273, 282, 283
Henry 240, 241
Jane 209
John 49, 54, 57, 80, 101,
  105, 107, 109, 112, 114,
  115, 117, 118, 123, 129,
  130, 143, 158, 200, 203,
  204, 206, 209, 241, 257,
  283, 312, 315
John Jr. 255
John Sr. 255, 299
Jordan 221
Joseph 49, 50, 55, 56, 58,
  82, 89, 95, 108, 109, 112,
  130, 162, 163, 165, 201,
  241, 248, 250, 254, 283,
  284, 294, 309, 314, 315,
  316
Lewis 247, 261, 293, 308
Liddia 283
Martha 108

330

331

Emson, Ann 17
  Elizabeth 17
  George 17
  Jane 17
  Martha 17
  Sarah 17
  Thomas 15, 16, 17
England, (Mr.) 7, 62, 63
  Ann 14
  Francis 14, 19, 61, 64
  (Capt.) Francis 7, 65
  Joyce 14
English (see also Inglish)
  Alice 17
  Ann 90, 243, 244
  Anne 307
  Elinor 99
  Elizabeth 17
  Francis 17
  George 5, 121
  Jacob 242, 247
  John 17, 274, 279, 280, 298,
    305
  Joseph 247, 259
  Martha 17
  Mary 17
  Sarah 17, 242
  Thomas 5, 82, 155, 158, 220,
    243
  Thomas Jr. 243
  Thomas Sr. 243
  Will 39, 275
  William 90, 115, 147, 244,
    266, 278, 279, 280
  Willis 308
Ennis, Walter 91
  Winifred 91
Enniss, Walker 117
Eppes, John 113
Ernest, William 10
Evans, Celia 202
  Dave 86
  David 126
  Elizabeth 126, 234
  Katherine 75
  Mary 94, 201
  Robert 30
  Thomas 30
  Will 19, 21-23, 29, 30
  William 21, 24, 28, 30, 37,
    71, 72, 75, 80, 89
Everett (see also Everitt)
  Anne 43
  Charlotte 267
  Chloe 267
  Elinor 154
  John 30, 205, 267, 270, 279,
    281, 299, 304, 306
  John Jr. 267
  Joseph 218, 267, 279, 281
  Lemuel 306
  Mary 205
  Milley 307
  Milly 304
  Sally Wills 307
  Samuel 111, 205, 206, 218,
    267, 270
  Sarah 205, 304, 307
  Simon 5, 30, 107, 108, 126
  Thomas 266
  William 206, 260
  Willis 291
Everitt (see also Everett)
  Elizabeth 185
  Jannett 95
  John 90, 95, 155, 180, 235,
    245, 252

Everitt (cont.)
  Joseph 95, 153, 185, 220,
    229, 252
  Mary 172, 223
  Samuel 90, 95, 180, 185,
    223, 228, 235
  Simon 95, 150, 153
  Thomas 90, 95, 245
  William 220, 223
  Willis 252
Exum, Ann 95, 96
  Anne 83
  Christian 80, 95
  Deborah 41
  Eliza 174
  Elizabeth 80, 95, 122, 124,
    203, 211
  Francis 41, 42, 83, 128,
    172, 182
  Jane 41, 80, 95
  Jeremiah 17, 25, 30, 44, 69,
    80
  John 83, 97, 104, 133, 174,
    176
  Joseph 83, 133, 174
  Mary 80, 172, 174
  Molly 239
  Moses 174, 191, 203, 207,
    220, 239
  Mourning 80, 95
  Patience 137, 150, 171
  Richard 44, 46
  Robert 83, 133, 137, 143
  Sarah 80, 83, 95, 174
  Susan 83
  William 31, 41, 42, 46, 83,
    87, 174
Ezall (Ezell ?), John 228
Ezell (Ezall), John 228


-F-


Fagan, Peter 305
Falconer, Elizabeth 245
Fanning, Thomas 304
Farecloth, Benjamin 101
  Elizabeth 101
  Hannah 101
  Martha 101
  Moses 101
  Samuel 101
  Sarah 101
  William 101
Farmer, Ann 41
  Robert 282, 308
Farnesfield/Farnsfield, Edward
  36, 38
Farnum, Joyce 27
Farrow (?), Elizabeth 86
Fathera, Frances 227
Fatheree, Fanny 227
Fatherlie, Fairfax 275
  Francis 275
Fatherly, Ann 300
  Fairfax 300
  Francis 300
  Frederick 300
  Lavisha 300
  Mealy 300
  Mexico 300
Faulk, William 299
Fearn, Catherine 250
  George 250

Fearn (cont.)
  Jane 237
  John 250, 253, 256, 262, 263,
    267, 268, 273, 274, 288,
    289, 295-297, 307
  Machen 314
  Nancy 250
  Thomas 240, 248, 250, 251,
    256, 258, 280, 288, 297
Fendry, John 6
Feneryear, Ann 7
  Edmund 7
Feneryeare, Ann 65
Feneryear(e), John 7, 65
Fenn, Elizabeth 29, 34
  Kae 34
  Martha 34, 48
  Mary 34
  Robert 30, 34, 35, 75
  Timothy 3, 10, 12, 24, 27,
    29, 30, 48, 67, 68, 75
Fern, Timothy 1
Ferrell, Silvester 125
Fields, John 59
Fife, Malikey 265
  Mary 265
Figg, Joseph 167
Filberd (?), Nicholas 34
Fisher, D. 217
  Fairfax John Throughgood 278
  James 278
  Rosey 278
  Sarah 278
  Susannah 278
  Teakle/Teackle 278
  Thomas 278
  Thomas George Washington 278
  William 278
Fitzpatrick, Pharoah 247
Fiveash, Alice 140, 144
  Francis 93
  John 48, 85, 93, 173, 178,
    228
  Martha 93, 173, 181, 206
  Mary 93
  Peter 30, 41, 93, 96, 97,
    104, 140, 144, 157, 160,
    173, 181, 182, 187, 189,
    201, 214
  Thomas 93
Flake, (Mr.) 6, 61, 62
  Faithy 239
  John 311
  Mary 239
  Robert 7, 8, 12, 14, 30, 65,
    68-70, 281
  Sampson 145, 263
  William 239, 263
Fleming, Gardner 270, 311
  Helen 280
  Isaac 165
  John 230, 295
  Mary 186, 280, 295
  Millison 186
  Nathaniel 243, 251, 254, 255,
    257, 260, 266, 270, 280,
    284, 316
  William 242, 288, 295
Flemying, William 261
Fletcher, Benjamin 253
  Charles 232, 233, 259, 262
  Grace 259
  James 259
  Nancy 259
  Patsey 259
  Sally 259
Fleuellen, Thomas 1

335

Fulgham (cont.)
Nancy 268
Nicholas 17, 24, 25, 31, 34, 37, 40-42, 48, 52, 55, 56, 71, 75, 92, 93, 127, 132, 189, 201, 216, 218, 259
Patience 157, 171, 252, 268
Polly 263, 264
Rebecca 221, 248
Rodwell 248
Ruth 31
Sally 268
Sarah 31, 81, 116, 197
Stephen 268
Susanna 31, 127
Susannah 92
Willis 268
Fuller, Ann 89
Arthur 89
Benjamin 89
Deborah 89
Ezekial 52
Ezekiell 89
Henry 89
John 89
Joseph 89
Martha 89
Mary 89
Onner 89
Solomon 89
Timothy 89
Fullgam, Michell 104

-G-

Gaine, John 3
Thomas 3
Gainer, Elizabeth 27, 40
Mary 47
Gainor, Samuel 36
William 80, 86
Gale, Alice 50, 115, 192, 216
Ann 192, 215, 232
Benjamin 274
Elizabeth 115, 192, 203, 205, 215, 259
Frances 241
Henry 312
Jethro 182, 186, 191, 192, 200, 205, 207, 217, 218, 226, 228, 230, 232, 234, 235, 237, 238, 240, 241, 244, 246, 248, 251, 252, 254, 257, 261, 265, 270, 277, 286
John 254
Mary 115, 155, 192, 203
Polly 283
Sally 283
Sarah 115, 283
Tabitha 192, 215
Thomas 5, 27, 44, 45, 50, 51, 55, 84, 86, 88, 112, 115, 118, 120, 123, 128, 132, 141, 142, 143, 148, 155, 162, 163, 167, 172, 173, 179, 182, 186, 192, 197, 200, 207, 215, 283, 290
Thomas Jr. 99, 101, 104, 106, 110-113, 186, 266
Thomas W. 239
Thomas Whitney 210, 224, 236, 283

Gandy, Elizabeth 16
Gany (?), Thomas 72
Gardner, James 39, 72
Jesse 256
John 23, 56, 71, 72, 149
Mary 72
Sarah 292
William 149, 151
Garell, Jone 81
Garland, Abigail 63
Ann 96, 147, 181, 183
Anna 39
Debora 39
Grace 39
Joan 2, 63
John 39, 49, 57, 58, 96, 97, 109, 117
Joseph 96
Martha 117
Mary 57, 63, 96
Patience 96
Peter 3, 6, 39, 62, 63, 96
Prudence 63, 96
Samuel 39, 49, 58, 96, 173, 181, 183, 206
Sarah 39, 96
Garner, Ann 263
Benjamin 158
Charity 222
Christian 203
Elizabeth 154, 205
Garnes 205
James 33, 107, 130, 157, 158, 162
Jesse 157, 263
John 101-105, 114, 124, 145, 148, 153, 157, 158, 170, 172, 173, 181, 205, 228, 259, 263
Joseph 124, 157, 158, 304
Mary 205
Mourning 205
Nancy 298
Olive 157
Patience 157, 202
Penelope 205
Priscilla 263
Rachel 263
Richard 263
Sally 298
Sarah 157, 158, 205, 263
Susannah 5
Thomas 263
Garnes, Elizabeth 227
John 236
Garnes (Garner), John 149
Garrell, Ann 89
Garrey, John 110
Garris, Amos 163
Garrison, Abel 315
James 315
Margaret 315
Garton, Catherine 290
Thomas 290
William 227, 253, 268, 293, 308
Gaskins, John 307
Thomas 313
Gatewood, Philemon 269
Gatlin, John 2, 25
William 25
Gawker, Thomas 114
Gay, _____ 84
Ann 260
Charles 165
Damaris 232
Edmond 165
Edward 281

Gay (cont.)
Everett 306, 310, 311, 314, 316
Foreby 176
Henry 84, 128, 260
James 256, 283, 285, 286, 295, 299
Jane 84
Jesse 260
Jethro 176
John 84, 128, 165, 176, 182, 184, 229, 235, 244, 251, 260
John Jr. 226, 252
Jonathan 165
Joshua 128, 184, 203, 260, 265
Keziah 260
Martha 184, 260
Mary 165, 176
Milley 249
Robert 260
Sarah 128, 184, 312
Thomas 128, 165, 166, 167, 176, 177, 179, 180
William 128, 165, 173, 176, 177, 186, 220, 237-239, 241, 242, 249, 255, 256, 257, 260, 261, 265, 267, 271, 273, 274, 277, 279, 281-284, 286, 287, 294, 295, 297, 298, 301, 307, 310
William Jr. 231, 232
Willis 256, 304
Gaymie, Thomas 9
Gayner, Elizabeth 47
Gaynie, Thomas 33, 38
Gemmell, (Rev.) John 143
Gemmill, John 134, 136, 153
(Rev.) John 149, 153
Gent, John 81, 99, 104, 117
Richard 52, 81
Thomas 99
George, Ann 17
Isack 17
John 3, 17, 43, 50, 51
(Lt. Col.) John 66
Rebecca 17
Sarah 17, 50
William 49, 50
Geruise, John 34
Gibbins, John 86
Gibbons, Jeremiah 312
Gibbs, Edward 7, 45, 61, 63, 64
Elizabeth 8, 64, 271, 295
Frances 262
Gabriel 224, 234, 240, 245, 247, 262, 297, 304
Henry John 262
John 80, 124, 125, 160, 162, 163, 166, 167, 177, 183, 185, 206, 222, 224, 267, 277, 290, 295, 315
John Sr. 222
John Harris 238
Martha 238, 267, 277
Mary 185, 262
Patsey 267, 277, 290
Polly 267
Ralph 152, 161, 185, 187, 190, 224, 238, 242, 243, 249, 254, 256, 262, 267, 269
Robert 262
Sarah 152, 170, 185, 223, 224, 266

337

341

342

343

345

349

350

354

363

365